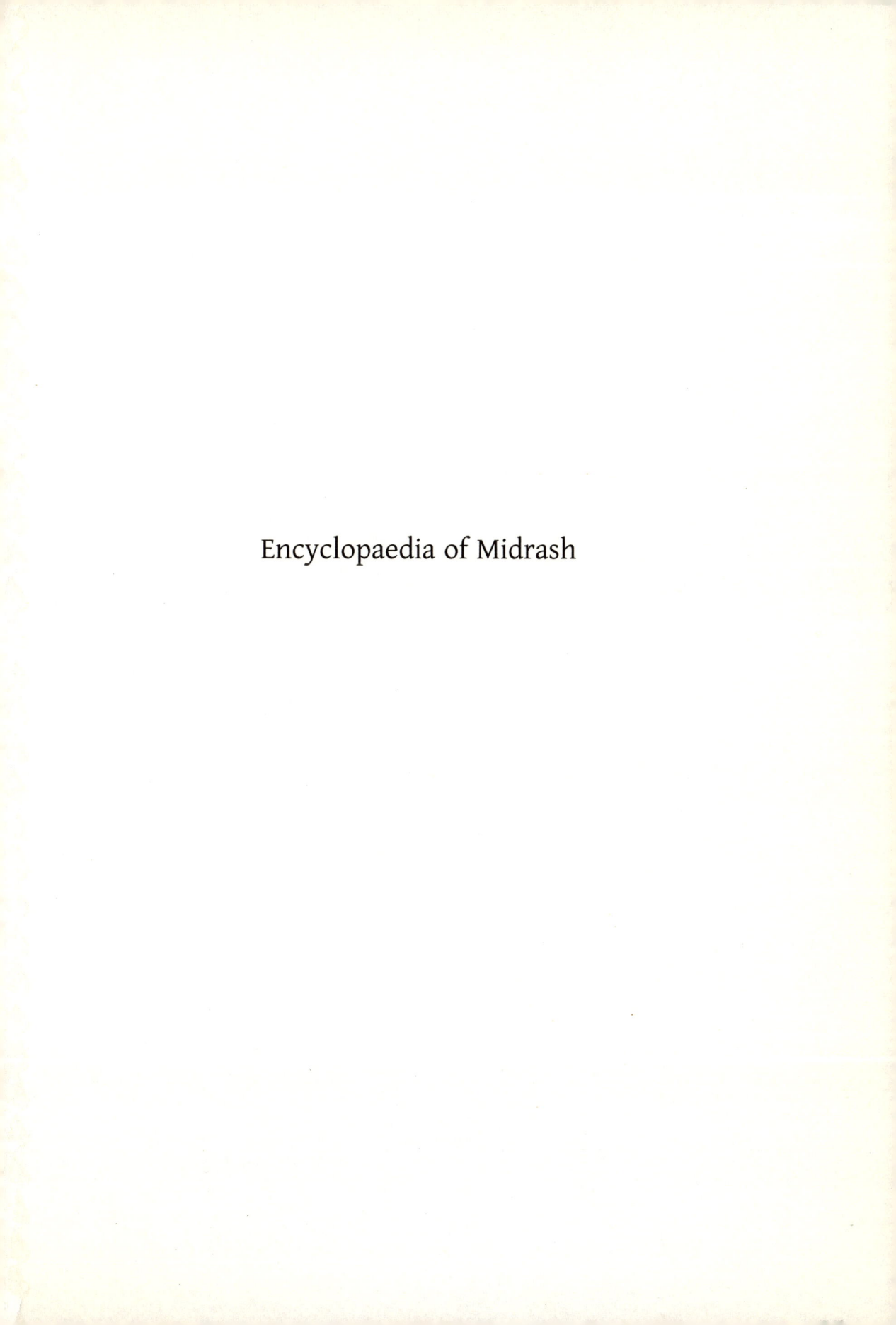

Encyclopaedia of Midrash

Encyclopaedia of Midrash

Biblical Interpretation in Formative Judaism
Volume II

Edited by
Jacob Neusner & Alan J. Avery-Peck

Consulting Editors
William Scott Green & Guenter Stemberger

BRILL
LEIDEN · BOSTON
2005

This book is printed on acid-free paper.

Library of Congress cataloging-in-publication data are available on the Library of Congress website: catalog.loc.gov.

LC control number: 2004058219

ISBN 90 04 14166 9

© Copyright 2005 by Koninklijke Brill NV, Leiden, The Netherlands

All rights reserved. No part of this publication may be reproduced, translated, stored in a retrieval system, or transmitted in any form or by any means, electronic, mechanical, photocopying, recording or otherwise, without prior written permission from the publisher.

Authorization to photocopy items for internal or personal use is granted by Brill provided that the appropriate fees are paid directly to The Copyright Clearance Center, 222 Rosewood Drive, Suite 910, Danvers, MA 01923, USA. Fees are subject to change.

PRINTED IN THE NETHERLANDS

Contents

Preface	ix
"Art" in Midrashic Literature	1
Steven Fine	
Church Fathers, Rabbinic Midrash and	20
Adam Kamesar	
Dead Sea Scrolls, Biblical Interpretation in	40
Lawrence H. Schiffman	
Deuteronomy in Sifre to Deuteronomy	54
Steven Fraade	
Esther in Esther Rabbah I	59
Jacob Neusner	
Exodus in Mekhilta Attributed to R. Ishmael	74
Jacob Neusner	
Genesis in Genesis Rabbah	88
Jacob Neusner	
Genesis Rabbah, Theology of	105
Jacob Neusner	
Genres, Midrash and	121
Dalia Hoshen	
Hagiographa, Targums to	148
Josep Ribera-Florit	
Halakhic Category Formations, Midrash and	173
Jacob Neusner	
Hellenistic Jewish Midrash, I: Beginnings	199
Folker Siegert	
Hellenistic Jewish Midrash II: Adopting the Allegoric Method. Aristobulus to Philo	220
Folker Siegert	
Hellenistic Jewish Midrash, III: Developed Non-Allegorical Forms. Josephus	232
Folker Siegert	
Hermeneutics, A Critical Approach	250
Gary G. Porton	
Hermeneutics, Techniques of Rabbinic Exegesis	268
Rivka B. Kern-Ulmer	
Hermeneutics, Theology of	292
David Instone-Brewer	
Josephus, Midrash in His Version of the Pentateuch	316
Louis Feldman	
Jubilees, Midrash in	333
Betsy Halpern-Amaru	
Karaite Conception of the Biblical Narrator	350
Meira Polliack	

Lamentations in Lamentations Rabbati	374
Jacob Neusner	
Lamentations Rabbati, Theology of	389
Jacob Neusner	
Language and Midrash	400
David Aaron	
Leviticus in Leviticus Rabbah	411
Jacob Neusner	
Leviticus in Sifra	429
Guenter Stemberger	
Leviticus Rabbah, Theology of	447
Jacob Neusner	
Liturgy, Midrash in	463
Richard S. Sarason	
Mekhilta deR. Simeon b. Yohai	493
W. David Nelson	
Midrash Tannaim	510
Herbert Basser	
Midrash, Definitions of	520
Gary G. Porton	
New Testament Narrative as Old Testament Midrash	534
Robert M. Price	
Numbers in Sifre to Numbers	574
Jacob Neusner	
Oral Torah, Midrash and	585
Jacob Neusner	
Origins and Emergence of Midrash in Relation to the Hebrew Bible	595
Timothy H. Lim	
Parable	612
Jacob Neusner	
Pentateuchal Targums as Midrash	630
Paul Flesher	
Pesiqta deRab Kahana, Synagogue Lections for Special Occasions in	646
Jacob Neusner	
Pesiqta deRab Kahana, Theology of	663
Jacob Neusner	
Pseudo-Philo's Biblical Antiquities	679
Daniel J. Harrington, S.J.	
Qabbalah, Midrash and	695
Ithamar Gruenwald	
Rabbinic Midrash in Historical Context, the Fourth and Fifth Century Compilations	709
Jacob Neusner	
Ruth in Ruth Rabbah	737
Jacob Neusner	
Ruth Rabbah, Theology of	752
Jacob Neusner	
Samaritan Midrash	762
Alan D. Crown	

Septuagint, Midrashic Traditions and	777
Giuseppe Veltri	
Sifra: Theology of	803
Jacob Neusner	
Sifre to Deuteronomy, Theology of	820
Jacob Neusner	
Sifre to Numbers, Theology of	833
Jacob Neusner	
Song of Songs in Song of Songs Rabbah	857
Luis F. Girón Blanc	
Song of Songs Rabbah, Theology of	871
Jacob Neusner	
Targum Jonathan of the Prophets I	889
Bruce D. Chilton	
Targum Jonathan to the Prophets II—The Former Prophets	908
Bruce D. Chilton	
Targum, Conceptual Categories of	927
Etan Levine	
Theological Foundations of Rabbinic Exegesis	944
Rivka B. Kern-Ulmer	
Theology of Rabbinic Midrash	964
Jacob Neusner	
Women, Midrashic Constructions of	979
Judith R. Baskin	
Index of Ancient Sources	999
Index of Subjects	1061

Origins and Emergence of Midrash in Relation to the Hebrew Bible

Most scholars probably would agree with a statement such as "The origins and emergence of midrash are to be found in the Hebrew Bible."[1] But ask them to elaborate what they mean by that phrase and they will disagree not only about what is midrash and when the authoritative texts became "the Bible," but also on other points implied in the summary statement, including the distinctiveness of midrashic exegesis and its affinities to late biblical texts and Jewish and Christian interpretations, old and new.

There is no consensus on the definition of midrash. One of the seminal publications in the last century comes from the French scholar Renée Bloch, who in 1957 described midrash as constituting "a reflection, a meditation on sacred texts, a 'study' of Scripture."[2] Contending against the view that takes midrash pejoratively in the sense of "a fable" or "fictitious legend," Bloch states that "[i]n reality, it designates an edifying and explicatory genre strictly related to Scripture, in which the portion of amplification is real but secondary and always remains subordinate to the essential, religious end, which is to place full value on the work of God, the utterance of God."[3]

Bloch believes that midrash is a genre, like prophecy, that is unique to Israel, outside of which there is no parallel, since it presupposes faith in revelation found only in Holy Scripture.[4] But this definition is not restrictive, since for Bloch "Israel" is understood in a broad sense that includes not only the Israelites of the biblical texts, the Jewish people from the post-exilic period onwards, but also the followers of Jesus and members of the early Church. Quite the contrary, Bloch is to be credited for enlarging the definition of midrash beyond the classical Rabbinic texts to include late biblical exegeses, translations, post-biblical Jewish interpretations of the late Second Temple Period and the New Testament Gospels and Epistles.[5] Subsequent scholarship can be divided along the lines of those who support her extension of the definition of midrash and those who advocate a stricter demarcation of the genre along the lines of the Rabbinic midrashim.

Bloch delineates five characteristics of Rabbinic midrash:

1) *It takes Scripture as the point of departure*—a fundamental characteristic of the genre.
2) *It is homiletic in character.* Those who scrutinize Scripture in this manner are not scholars who work in their rooms; nor is midrash a genre of the school. Its origins are to be found in the liturgical reading of the Torah on Sabbaths and during feasts.[6] The Palestinian targum, which is thoroughly midrashic, is

---

[1] See, for example, I.L. Seeligmann, "Voraussetzungen der Midraschexegese," in *Congress Volume, Cophenhagen, 1953. Vetus Testamentum Supplement 1* (Leiden, 1953), p. 151, who states that: "Es wird sich—um das vorweg zu nehmen—ergeben, dass sich die älteste Midraschexegese organisch aus der Eigenart der biblischen Literatur entwickelt hat."

[2] "Midrash" in H. Cazelles, ed., *Supplément au Dictionnaire de la Bible*. Volume 5 "Kalt-Mycènes" (Paris, 1957), col. 1265. English translations are by the present author.

[3] Ibid., col. 1263.

[4] Ibid., col. 1265: "Il y a donc là un genre propre à Israël, comme le prophétisme.... Le midrash ne peut en effet se rencontrer en dehors d'Israël, puisqu'il suppose la foi en la révélation consignée dans les Livres saints."

[5] See, e.g., Roger Le Déaut, "A propos d'une définition du midrash," in *Biblica* 50 (1969), p. 399, n. 3.

[6] This emphasis upon the interpretative community is taken up by James A. Sanders, *Torah and Canon* (Philadelphia, 1972). More

not to be conceived independently of the liturgical reading.

3) *It is a study that is attentive to the text.* Since the sacred text is read in the synagogue, it is necessary to comment on it, to preach it, and to try to understand it better. Obscurities are clarified and the sense of the text is grasped by scrutinizing it. Rare or difficult terms are explained by the use of synonyms from a cognate language. The principal process that permits the rabbis to explain Scripture is the recourse to parallel passages, since for them the Bible is a unity. They knew Scripture by heart; they constantly explained the Bible by the Bible.

4) *There is an adaptation to the present*, because the goal of midrashic exegesis is not purely theoretical, but practical. Its aim above all is to bring out the lessons of faith and of the religious life that are hidden in the biblical texts, and this practical preoccupation to reinterpret Scripture is to contemporize or "to actualize it" (*l'actualiser*). The tendency to make the message of the biblical texts relevant for contemporary life is not particularly evident in the biblical midrash, since the need for adaptation was not felt in the same way during that time. It is, however, already found in certain apocryphal writings like Jubilees, the Damascus Document and the Rule of the Community and also in the New Testament and the writings of the Church.

5) *Haggadah and Halakhah* are two types of midrashim that have their origins in the synagogue and schools respectively. The liturgical reading provides the material for the sermon that immediately follows it and comments on the text that is read. Whereas in the schools, which are often beside the synagogue, the same text serves the instruction by commentary and study in order to draw out the rule of life or halakhah. These two types of midrashim are distinguished by the kind of biblical material that they comment on. The legal portions of the Bible are interpreted by a midrash that can be designated "midrash halakhah" or the halakhic interpretation of the Torah. The midrash that uncovers the relevance of the narrative sections of the Torah and their historical events is called "midrash haggadah."

Having defined Rabbinic midrash thus, Bloch goes on to show how the birth of the midrashic process is to be found during the Persian period when the Hebrew Bible was canonized. Through the post-exilic period, the life of Israel was reorganized around the sacred texts that began to be codified into a canon of Holy Scripture. Between the rebuilding of the Temple during Cyrus's reign and the Maccabean revolt, many other writings were excluded from the canon of the Old Testament as the Pentateuch took its final form, the former prophets were definitively edited, the latter prophets reworked and put in order. Many of the writings date back to this time. She states: "The fixation of the Scripture is of the greatest importance for the genesis of the midrashic genre. Henceforth, there was a 'canonical' text on which one will reflect, with which one will pray, which will become the object of study, of transmission, instruction, and preaching."[7]

The closing of the canon will be discussed below, but it should be noticed at this point

---

recently, Sanders has emphasized the dialogical feature of the canonical process ("Canon as Dialogue," in Peter Flint, ed., *The Bible at Qumran. Text, Shape, and Interpretation* [Grand Rapids, 2001], pp. 7–26).

[7] Bloch, "Midrash," col. 1268.

that despite Bloch's own articulation of the process as "the fixation of the Scripture," her formulation, especially as regards the writings, shows that she does not hold the view of a closed, tripartite canon. She considers an open ended "writings" category with many of the texts dating back to this period. It should be noted that this is a very early dating of the closing of the canon, and while vital to her understanding of the origins of midrash it is not argued but merely asserted. Bloch concludes her synthesis of midrash by an illustrative examination of selected texts from Ezekiel, Isaiah, Proverbs, Song of Songs, Ben Sira, Qohelet, Psalms, the Habakkuk Pesher, Septuagint, and the New Testament.

In two lengthy articles published in the *Catholic Biblical Quarterly* nine years later, Addison G. Wright criticized Bloch for being imprecise before advancing his own definition of the literary genre.[8] His criticisms center on the way that Bloch's definition of midrash as "a homiletic reflection or meditation on the Bible" becomes very broad when she includes a wide variety of texts under the rubric, including historical works that gloss Scripture, meditation on history, reuse of sacred texts, anthological style, scriptural reminiscences based on a meditation of Scripture, and a development of Old Testament texts.[9] He notes that Bloch's article has influenced other scholars who now develop one or another aspect of her definition of midrash and apply it to other examples. "The result," states Wright, "is that the word midrash at present is an equivocal term and is being used to describe a mass of disparate material. Indeed, if some of the definitions are correct, large amounts, if not the whole of the Bible, would have to be called midrash. Hence, the word as used currently in biblical studies is approaching the point where it is no longer really meaningful and where some of the material designated as midrash resembles the later Rabbinic midrash only in a very superficial way."[10]

Wright advocates a definition of midrash as a literary genre rather than Bloch's "reflection."[11] Distinguishing between primary (literary structure) and secondary (exegetical techniques) features, he suggests that the midrashim are compilations that can be classified into three categories according to their artificial structures: 1) Exegetical Midrashim, expositions that intersperse comments between a series of biblical verses from different books (e.g., *Bereshit Rabbah* and *Midrash Tehillim*), prefaced with or without an introductory proem. 2) Homiletic Midrashim, sermonic treatises that interpret select passages more extensively. 3) Narrative Midrashim, or what Geza Vermes calls "rewritten Bible," a midrash that subsumes the biblical narrative under a well-neigh paraphrase, embellishing all the while extra-biblical material and legends (e.g., *Sefer ha-Yashar, Perqe de Eleazar*).[12]

In the second part of his article, Wright examines various examples of pre-Rabbinic midrash. He classifies as midrash several texts, including the Passover Haggadah, the Pesharim, Liber Antiquitatem Biblicarum, Genesis Apocryphon, some homilies of Philo, Wisdom 11–19, Damascus Document 4.12–19, and Hebrews 7:1–10.[13] But he rejects Bloch's suggestion that the Palestinian Targums are midrashim, since the former aim to provide translations with incidental material, while the latter are homiletic material that happens to have some connection to a biblical text.[14] Wright also discards the characterization of Chronicles as midrash, since

---

[8] "The Literary Genre Midrash" (Parts one and two), vol. 28 (1966), pp. 105–138 and 417–457, later republished as *The Literary Genre of Midrash* (Staten Island, 1967).

[9] "Literary Genre of Midrash," pp. 106–107.

[10] Ibid., pp. 107–108.
[11] Ibid., p. 138.
[12] Ibid., pp. 124–128.
[13] Ibid., pp. 417–438.
[14] Ibid., p. 423.

it is "a history and theology of history," independent of the Deuteronomic history.[15]

Wright defines midrash as follows:

> We may summarize the discussion to this point by saying that Rabbinic midrash is a literature concerned with the Bible; it is a literature about a literature. A midrash is a work that attempts to make a text of Scripture understandable, useful, and relevant for a later generation. It is the text of Scripture which is the point of departure, and it is for the sake of the text that the midrash exists. The treatment of any given text may be creative or non-creative, but the literature as a whole is predominantly creative in its handling of the biblical material. The interpretation is accomplished sometimes by rewriting the biblical material, sometimes by commenting upon it. In either case the midrash may go as far afield as it wishes, provided that at some stage at least there is to be found some connection, implicit or explicit, between the biblical text and the new midrashic composition.[16]

But this definition is similar to the one already offered by Bloch. As correctly pointed out by Le Déaut, the fundamental characteristics of midrash specified by Bloch are also to be found here, namely the use of Scripture as a point of departure and the adaptation of the biblical text to the contemporary situation by "actualization."[17]

In a review of his articles, Le Déaut correctly criticizes Wright's work for being reductive. According to him, Wright's attempt to define midrash strictly by its literary genre is like (adapting a famous saying of Gustave Flaubert) destroying a forest in order to make a box of matches.[18] He takes particular exception to Wright's view of the Palestinian targumim, stating that "[t]he Targum itself is *midrashic*, precisely in the measure where it proposes new imports (*significations nouvelles*) often very far from the texts from which they take the departure point."[19] Le Déaut himself does not propose a definition of midrash, observing with I.L. Seeligmann, that it is not easy to define the complex phenomenon that is called "midrash."[20] He suggests that for the period of the New Testament a good approach is to study the development of the traditions as Bloch had suggested.

Le Déaut's critique and refusal to define midrash are incongruous, for how can he know that a targum is midrashic when he finds it difficult to say what midrash is in the first place. He seems to be working with an implicit definition of midrash as a hermeneutical method and approach. His criticisms, however, are valuable in the way that they underscore how a discussion of midrash cannot be limited to a definition of its literary genre. To paraphrase him, midrash should not be restrained on a procrustean bed of literary genre.

Geza Vermes, in an influential article called "Bible and Midrash: Early Old Testament Exegesis,"[21] develops the work of Renée Bloch.[22] Like the latter, he dates the closing of the canon very early, to the third century B.C.E. Vermes states that at about that time the Palestinian religious authority decided to arrest the growth of sacred writings and establish a canon. With the exception of Daniel, their policy was carried through and from that point on the

---

[15] Ibid., p. 428.
[16] Ibid., p. 137.
[17] "A propos d'une définition du midrash," p. 397.
[18] Ibid., p. 402.
[19] Ibid., p. 407.
[20] Ibid., pp. 396 and 412 ("Nous ne proposerons d'ailleurs pas une autre définition du midrash").
[21] In P.R. Ackroyd and C.F. Evans, eds., *The Cambridge History of the Bible. From the Beginnings to Jerome* (Cambridge, 1970), pp. 199–231.
[22] Cf. *Scripture and Tradition in Judaism. Haggadic Studies* (Leiden, 1961), pp. 9–10.

nation's religious leadership was entrusted not to writers but interpreters. Similar to Bloch, Vermes describes the origin of midrash as found in the admonition of some of the Old Testament authors "to meditate on, recite, and rethink the Law."[23] This exegetical activity can be traced back to such passages as the Deuteronomic injunction for the king to copy, continually read, and observe the Mosaic code (Deut. 17:18–19) and the command for all Israelites to meditate and do the law (Josh. 1:7–8).

Vermes describes what he regards as two basic types of post-biblical interpretation, pure exegesis and applied exegesis. The former arises from four primary and technical causes: 1) there is uncertainty about the meaning of a word; 2) there are perceived gaps in the biblical passage; 3) apparently contradictory passages need to be harmonized and explained; and 4) the meaning is unacceptable.

As its name suggests, pure exegesis is that which the interpreter performs as he carefully reads and meditates on the word of God. Applied exegesis, on the other hand, occurs when the interpreter adapts the Bible to contemporary life: "The point of departure for exegesis was no longer the Torah itself, but contemporary customs and beliefs which the interpreter attempted to connect with Scripture and to justify."[24] This form of interpretation plays a role in the determination of halakhah, in doctrinal controversies and in the belief that the biblical prophecies have been fulfilled in the interpreter's day.

Vermes's division of all post-biblical interpretation into the categories of pure and applied exegeses has not been followed by many. What have been much more influential are the four causes that gave rise to pure exegeses: uncertainty about the meaning of words, perceived gaps in the scriptural narrative, the need to harmonize apparently contradictory passages, and unacceptability of the meaning. Repeatedly, these reasons are either re-iterated, expanded or adapted in subsequent scholarly discussions.

In an article completed in 1974, Gary Porton reviewed previous scholarship and defined midrash in the following manner: "midrash is a type of literature, oral or written, which has its starting point in a fixed, canonical text, considered the revealed word of God by the midrashist and his audience, and in which this original verse is explicitly cited or clearly alluded to."[25] His definition highlights the importance of canon. Midrash as a literary genre is "based upon a canonical text" and "canon designates those texts which were accepted as authoritative by the community."[26] This stress upon a canonical text echoes Bloch's own emphasis upon the fixation of Scripture, but important differences should be noticed in their conception and dating of the closing of the canon. Whereas Bloch assigns the closing of the bipartite canon to the period between the Persian period and the Maccabean revolt, thus defining late biblical texts and subsequent post-biblical exegeses as midrash, Porton holds to a first century C.E. date for the fixation of Scripture, in effect reserving the term midrash for post-70 writings.

Before the destruction of the Second Temple, according to Porton, Palestinian Jews did not consider the creation of midrash a central activity, since the Torah was not the sole source of authority nor was it "the constitution" in any meaningful sense.[27] Wisdom texts, like Ben Sira, used the Torah but also drew knowledge from experience, travel, and common sense. The priesthood also played a vital role, shaping

---

[23] Ibid., p. 199.
[24] Ibid., p. 221.
[25] "Midrash: The Palestinian Jews and the Hebrew Bible in the Greco-Roman Period," in H. Temporini and W. Haase, eds., *Aufstieg und Niedergang der römischen Welt* (Berlin, 1979), vol. II.19.2, p. 112.
[26] Ibid., p. 111.
[27] Ibid., pp. 112–118.

the legal systems of various Jewish communities (e.g., at Qumran). There is little evidence that midrashic activity accompanied the public reading of Torah in synagogues before 70. It was after the destruction of the Temple and its priestly cult that the Pharisees and rabbis focused on the Bible, stirred as they were by the competing Christian appropriation of the Hebrew Bible.

Porton defines midrash proper as a post-70 phenomenon but admits that midrashic activity may be found before that time. He believes that the superscriptions to certain psalms can be classified as midrashic but is less certain about other biblical texts, like Deuteronomy or Chronicles, as has been claimed by scholars. His hesitation is based on the difficulty of determining "whether or not the original passage had achieved canonical status and was considered part of God's revelation at the time it was reworked or commented upon."[28] He allows as midrashic, the targumim, rewritten biblical accounts (Genesis Apocryphon and Liber Antiquitatem Biblicarum) and the pesharim but observes that the flourish of midrashic activity occurs after 70.

Porton's cautious approach to the definition of midrash is laudable and while his stress upon the canonical text reflects a long standing recognition of its importance, Le Déaut[29] and Günther Stemberger[30] have pointed out that the events of biblical history are equally as important as the texts that furnish the stimulus for a midrashic creation. He also assumes that the Pesher is a well-defined genre when in fact there is much scholarly disagreement about the distinctiveness of its literary form and comparison to dream interpretations, revelatory exegesis, and, not least, midrash itself![31] Moreover, as will be discussed more fully below, it is important to distinguish between canon as a list of texts, the authority of individual books, and verses and the textual form of those biblical passages.

In 1987, Jacob Neusner articulated three different meanings that are commonly attributed to midrash. Midrash can refer to: 1) a concrete unit of scriptural exegesis; 2) a compilation of these exegeses; and 3) a process of interpreting a particular text.[32] In doing so, he has summarized the areas of previous disagreements and encapsulated the nub of the problem, since midrash as a term, both in its ancient and modern usage, has several signifiers—it can serve as the title of a literary genre; it can mean the specific exegesis of a particular verse; or it can connote an exegetical process.

Frederic Manns, in his 1990 study that traces the development of midrash from its biblical origins to the Rabbinic works, likewise distinguishes midrash as "an approach of Scripture" and the result of this method in the form of commentary or a literary work.[33] Recently, Philip Alexander too has noted that the term midrash is fundamentally ambiguous, even within its narrower Rabbinic usage, denoting a hermeneutical method, a concrete text that exemplifies that method, and its literary form of lemma plus comment.[34] He observes that midrash is now commonly applied to the whole of Second Temple Bible interpretation and this midrashic period is to be distinguished from the next phase of Jewish

---

[28] Ibid., p. 119.
[29] "A propos d'une définition du midrash," p. 406.
[30] *Introduction to the Talmud and Midrash* (Edinburgh, 1991), pp. 256–257.
[31] See my discussion of the genre in *Pesharim* (Sheffield, 2002), pp. 44–53.

[32] *What is Midrash?* (Philadelphia, 1987), pp. 9–12.
[33] *Le Midrash. Approche et Commentaire de l'Ecriture* (Jerusalem, 1990), pp. 1–2.
[34] "The Bible in Qumran and Early Judaism," in A.D.H. Mayes, ed., *Text in Context. Essays by Members of the Society for Old Testament Studies* (Oxford, 2000), p. 37.

bible commentary known as the *parshanut*. In this loose sense of the term, it means no more than "an example of early Jewish Biblical interpretation."[35]

Midrash and Literary Criticism

The phenomenon of midrash has also been discussed in the context of literary theory. Among the contributions to the important volume entitled *Midrash and Literature* is James Kugel's introduction to midrash,[36] in which he states that while the term has been used to designate both interpretative activity and result, "[a]t bottom midrash is not a genre of interpretation but an interpretative stance, a way of reading the sacred text."[37] This midrashic stance can manifest itself in diverse genres belonging to almost all of classical and much of medieval Jewish literature, from the Aramaic targumim and retellings of biblical passages to the exegetical portions of the Mishnah and Gemara to homilies, sermons, prayers, and poetry.

He refuses to define midrash, quipping sarcastically that since many recent studies "have already not defined midrash in ample detail, there is little purpose in our not defining it again here."[38] Kugel does, however, make two points about midrash: 1) The precise focus of this interpretative stance is the surface irregularities of the biblical text. This point is similar to Bloch's attentiveness to the text and Vermes's category of pure exegesis. 2) Basic to midrash is an exegesis of individual verses and not whole books. Each verse of the Bible is as connected to a verse sequential to it as to one far away from it. Thus, a midrashist may illuminate a verse from Genesis by another verse in the immediate context or by a line from the Psalms. This point is not unlike Bloch's articulation that the darshan's primary process of interpretation is to be found in drawing on parallel passages, since the Bible is considered a unity. But the emphasis upon individual verses over biblical books or the canonical list is important.

In a recent study of biblical motifs,[39] he reformulates and develops these points by suggesting that there are four assumptions shared by all ancient interpretations: 1) All ancient interpreters held that the Bible is a fundamentally cryptic document that requires interpretation. 2) Scripture is seen as one great book of instruction that is ethically relevant for its readers. 3) The biblical text is free of errors and is harmonious; therefore, no detail, however small, is insignificant. And 4) despite the questionable conduct of heroes or the content of its own teachings, at a later time it was assumed that all Scripture was divinely inspired.

Kugel's understanding of midrash and ancient biblical interpretation includes many of the elements already found in the writings of scholars. It is relatively conventional and many of the elements can be found in previous studies. It is not distinctive, even though it is frequently seen by others in the context of literary criticism. The strength of his work, especially of *Traditions of the Bible*, is in demonstrating in detail how various motifs can be traced through the diverse genres of ancient biblical interpretation.

A study that is more literary[40] in its approach to midrash is Daniel Boyarin's

---

[35] Ibid., p. 37, n. 3.
[36] "Two Introductions to Midrash" in Geoffrey H. Hartman and Sanford Budick, eds., *Midrash and Literature* (New Haven, 1986), pp. 77–103.
[37] Ibid., p. 91.
[38] Ibid., p. 91.

[39] *Traditions of the Bible. A Guide to the Bible as It Was at the Start of the Common Era* (Cambridge, MA, 1998), pp. 14–19.
[40] Literary critics too have taken up the term midrash. In a review of Kugel's book, Frank Kermode has suggested *en passant* that Milton's poem is in effect "an enormous

Intertextuality and the Reading of Midrash.[41] Following the desconstructionist agenda of Jacques Derrida, Boyarin articulates an eclectic theory of midrash. He advances an intertextual reading of midrash:

> Were I to attempt to define midrash at this point, it would perhaps be radical intertextual reading of the canon, in which potentially every part refers to and is interpretable by every other part. The Torah, owing to its own intertextuality, is a severely gapped text, and the gaps are there to be filled by strong readers, which in this case does not mean readers fighting for originality, but readers fighting to find what they must in the holy text. Their own intertext—that is, the cultural codes which enable them to make meaning and find meaning, constrain the rabbis to fill in the gaps of the Torah's discourse with narratives which are emplotted in accordance with certain ideological structures.[42]

Boyarin's analysis focuses on one document, the Mekhilta, whose exegeses he explores with categories and terms drawn from literary theory, including paradigmatic and syntagmatic structures, gap-filling, reading repetition, verbal ambiguity, dual sign, and double reading. He also attempts to demonstrate that while the midrashic process allows the darshan to cross over into the biblical world, he nevertheless remains in his own sphere.

Many of the features underscored by Boyarin have already been discussed by previous scholars. For example, the so-called "ungrammaticality"[43] of the biblical text of Exod. 15:22–26 and the Mekhilta's exegesis of its ambiguities is similar to Vermes's classification of pure exegesis that arises from textual ambiguities, perceived gaps and contradictions. In fact, most of the concepts, but perhaps not the terminology, have been anticipated by early studies. In an ironic, perhaps intended, sense, Boyarin's own study of midrash is an example of precisely the intertextuality that he has been advocating.

Boyarin underscores the importance of the intertextual nature of midrashic exegesis in which the supporting biblical verses are not simply to be understood as prooftexts, but as part of a distinctive strategy of "cocitation" that enriches the exegesis and creates new contexts and meanings in its intention to preserve the relevance of old texts.[44] Boyarin does not concern himself with pre-Rabbinic midrash, but he does sense an important distinction that needs to be made between midrash after the canon was established and pre-canonical inner biblical exegesis: "[I]t is misleading to speak of inner-biblical midrash. There is something else that is going on when the text being interpreted is canonized, than in the pre-canonical situation."[45]

Authoritative Texts and Midrashic Exegesis

As noted by several scholars, "the canon" is a vital element in the study of midrash. This, of course, is self-evident, since midrash is primarily an interpretation of the biblical text. But the concept of "canon" in the scholarly discussions is surprisingly unclear. For example, what Bloch defines by "canon" is not the same as what Porton means when

---

midrash" (*Pleasing Myself from Beowulf to Philip Roth* [London, 2001], p. 162). Cf. Golda Werman, *Milton and Midrash* (Washington, 1995), who argued that Milton knew a Latin midrash.
[41] Bloomington and Indianapolis, 1990.

[42] Ibid., p. 16.
[43] Ibid., pp. 57–70.
[44] Ibid., pp. 26–38.
[45] Ibid., p. 136, n. 12.

he uses the same term. As mentioned, by canon Bloch has in view the fixation (during the Persian and Hellenistic periods) of the torah and prophets and a large part, but not all, of the writings.[46] Porton's definition of midrash as a literature which has as its starting point a fixed, canonical text and his dating of the biblical text to the first century show that he has in mind the closed, tripartite, Hebrew Bible. He reserves the term "midrash" for those writings that interpret a canonical text, arguing that "if the prior text had not achieved canonical status, the later comment is not midrash."[47]

Part of the unclarity is due to the slipperiness of the concept of authoritative texts and the debates surrounding the fixing of the canon. Orthodox and conservative scholars, both Jewish[48] and Christian,[49] tend to date the closing of the Rabbinic canon early to approximately 160 B.C.E. More liberal scholars argue that the canon remained open well into the first centuries of the common era.[50] Between these polar positions lies a range of views. The majority of scholars continue to date the more or less closing of the canon to the first century C.E.[51]

Additionally, there has been insufficient attention paid to the variety of canons in the ancient period. The Samaritans, for example, recognized only the authority of their Pentateuch which, in light of the publication and study of 4QpaleoExod^M, appears to have been a version of the first five books of the Hebrew Bible.[52] The Qumranians regarded Jubilees, Enoch, and possibly the Temple Scroll as authoritative in addition to books that were eventually included in the Hebrew Bible. As is well known, Esther is not found in the Qumran corpus, and the recent claim by J.T. Milik that 4Q550 is a prototype of the book has found few supporters.[53] Alexandrian Jewry too had a longer list of books in the Septuagint, including Tobit, Judith, Esdras, 1–4 Maccabees, Baruch, Epistle of Jeremiah, Susanna, and Bel and the Dragon. These books are regarded by the Orthodox and Catholic Church as deuterocanonical books, meaning that they are authoritative. Or again, the New Testament quoted the book of Enoch (Enoch 1:9, quoted in Jude 14) in the same way as it did other books of the Old Testament.

Much has been made of the recently published Qumran scroll 4QMMT, "some precepts of the Torah," which reads in section C, line 10, "the book of Moses, [and] the book[s of the p]rophets and Davi[d]." This phrase has been seized on by scholars as evidence for the tripartite division of the canon, but its understanding is doubtful when interpreted by other Qumran scrolls and MMT in particular. I have argued that within the context of the Qumran community "and Davi[d]" does not refer to the psalms that were called "songs of David" (*shirey david* in 11QMelch) or "the book of

---

[46] "Une grande partie des 'Écrits' remontent à ce temps-là" ("Midrash," col. 1268).

[47] "Midrash: The Palestinian Jews and the Hebrew Bible," p. 111.

[48] Sid Z. Leiman, *The Canonization of Hebrew Scripture. The Talmudic and Midrashic Evidence* (New Haven, 1976), pp. 131–135.

[49] Roger Beckwith, *The Old Testament Canon of the New Testament Church and Its Background in Early Judaism* (Grand Rapids, 1985), pp. 434–437.

[50] Albert C. Sundberg, *The Old Testament of the Early Church* (Cambridge, 1964), John Barton, *Oracles of God: Perceptions of Ancient Prophecy in Israel after the Exile* (London, 1986), and "Canon" in R.J. Coggins and J.L. Houlden, eds., *Dictionary of Biblical Interpretation* (London, 1990), p. 102.

[51] See, e.g., James Barr, *Holy Scripture. Canon, Authority, Criticism* (Oxford, 1983).

[52] See Judith E. Sanderson, *An Exodus Scroll from Qumran. 4QpaleoExod^M and the Samaritan Tradition* (Atlanta, 1986).

[53] See now, Sidnie White Crawford, "4Qtales of the Persian Court (5Q550^{A-E}) and Its Relation to Biblical Royal Courtier Tales, Especially Esther, Daniel and Joseph," in E.D. Herbert and E. Tov, eds., *The Bible as Book. The Hebrew Bible and the Judaean Desert Discoveries* (London, 2002), p. 121.

the Psalms" (*sefer ha-tehilim* in a version of the War Scroll, 4Q491), but is probably an elliptical reference to "(the deeds of) David."[54]

Several of the studies mentioned above discuss midrash in relation to the biblical and post-biblical text as though all of the communities held the same view of authoritative texts. Manns, for instance, discusses midrash in the Greek Bible alongside the targumim, Ethiopic book of Enoch, Jubilees, Qumran sectarian biblical interpretations, Pseudo-Philo, Psalms of Solomon, Philo of Alexandria, and Josephus without the slightest hint that there may have been different understandings of the biblical text and canon.[55]

Midrash is an interpretation of the biblical texts. Some would prefer using the descriptor "scriptural texts,"[56] since for them the term "biblical" connotes the closing of the canon and is anachronistic. But the term "biblical" (in lower case) need not be so, if it is recognized that it describes those authoritative texts that eventually became part of the canon.

Another way of circumventing terminological impropriety is to say, as Kugel has done, that basic to the interpretative stance of midrash is the exegesis of individual verses and not whole books. While this observation is true, it does not entirely resolve the problem, since Kugel also holds that for the darshan each verse of Scripture is equally related to another sequential to it as it is to another one far removed from it. The concept of canon underpins this view, even if it is implied rather than explicit. The darshan could only draw on parallel biblical passages in the way that Kugel has described it, if he had already considered authoritative those books that were eventually included in the Hebrew Bible.

Is the solution, then, to distinguish, as Porton has done, between pre- and post-canonical exegeses, reserving the term "midrash" exclusively for exegesis after 100 C.E.? One difficulty is that the term "midrash" occurs before 100 C.E. As is well known, the root *drsh*, meaning "to seek, investigate, study," occurs several times in the Hebrew Bible. The masculine substantive *midrash* is found twice in 2 Chr. 13:22 ("in the *midrash* of the prophet Iddo") and 24:27 ("are written in the *midrash* of the book of kings"), referring respectively to the Chronicler's source for his account of Abijah and to a work containing the many oracles against Joash and the acts of his sons. Much scholarly attention has been trained on these two references and it is generally accepted that *midrash* here should be understood in the context of biblical Hebrew and means something like "story" or "commentary" in the non-Rabbinic sense of the term.[57]

The term "midrash" is also found in the apocryphal Psalm of the Wisdom of Ben Sira 51:23, in which the sage admonishes the unlearned to lodge "in my house of learning" (Masada MS B *be-beyt midrashi*),[58] and to the *yeshibah* (v. 29), in which his soul delights (*tismach naphshi bishybathi*). Ben Sira is dated to the second century B.C.E.

In the Qumran scrolls, the term "midrash" is used variously to designate communal study (1QS 8:14–16; 8:26), judicial inquiry (1QS 6:24), communal regulation (CD 20:6;

---

[54] "The Alleged Reference to the Tripartite Division of the Hebrew Bible," in *RevQ* 20.1 (2002), pp. 23–38.

[55] *Le Midrash. Approche et Commetaire*.

[56] Although he does not discuss terminology in connection with midrash, Eugene C. Ulrich argues for the descriptor "scriptural" over "biblical" in "The Qumran biblical Scrolls—the Scriptures of Late Second Temple Judaism," in Timothy H. Lim, et al., eds., *The Dead Sea Scrolls in Their Historical Context* (Edinburgh, 2000), pp. 69–72.

[57] Sara Japhet, *I & II Chronicle: A Commentary* (London, 1993), pp. 699–700 and 954.

[58] The Hebrew text is conveniently published in *The Book of Ben Sira: Text, Concordance and an Analysis of the Vocabulary* (in Hebrew) (Jerusalem, 1973).

4QD^a [4Q266], frag 18, col. 5:18–20), and the title for authoritative interpretation (4QS^d [4Q258] frag 1, col. 1:1 "midrash for the Maskil;" 4QS^b [4Q256] frag 5, col. 1:1; compare 1QS 5:1 where the variant title reads "this is the rule (*serekh*) for the men of the community").[59]

Stephen Pfann has suggested that 4Q249, "midrash sepher Moshe," is related to *midrash ha-torah* of 1QS 8:15 and that the latter may have referred to the writings issuing from the Qumran community's nightly deliberation of the way of the Torah.[60] On the verso or back of this text, written in cryptic script across the grain, is the first clear instance of the titular use of midrash for an extant text. Unfortunately, the scroll itself is badly mutilated and we have little idea of what this text is about or whether it is comparable to the Rabbinic midrash.

4Q174, frag 1, line 14, also attests to the term: "*midrash [of how] blessed is the man who does not walk in the counsel of the wicked* (Ps. 1:1). Interpreted (*pesher*), this saying [concerns] those who turn aside from the way [of the people]."[61] Though the double use of "midrash" and "pesher" is rather awkward, William Brownlee, the principal editor, has suggested that this line is the *incipit* for the entire section, and that it evidences a hybrid genre called "midrash pesher." The existence of the "midrash pesher" has been questioned, and line 14 may well refer to the interpretation (*pesher*) not just of Ps 1:1 but also the accompanying communal deliberations.[62] In my view, "midrash" is not used in its titular sense in 4Q174; it rather means "an explanation of" a communal tradition related to Ps 1:1.

Hitherto there is no decisive evidence to prove that the term "midrash" was used before 100 C.E. to designate a genre of biblical interpretation like that of the classical Rabbinic texts. But this does not mean that a similar kind of exegesis (both in structure and techniques) could not be found before the canonization of the Hebrew Bible. Continuity of exegetical traditions before and after 100 C.E. is evident.

The problems of delimiting midrash is analogous to the difficulties faced in defining the genre of pesher. Pesher is a distinctive genre of biblical interpretation of the Qumran community, but it also shares commonalities, both in structure and exegetical techniques, with dream interpretations, revelatory exegesis, and not least the Rabbinic midrashim. Likewise, midrash as a genre is properly attested among the Rabbinic midrashim after the canonization of holy Scripture. However, the structure of lemma plus comment is also found in pre-100 C.E. texts, above all among the pesharim, and its exegetical techniques are attested by writings that may or may not use the term "midrash."[63]

Intratextual Exegesis

It has long been recognized that the origins and emergence of midrash are to be traced to the Hebrew Bible. An important milestone in the history of scholarship is in the influential work of the French scholar André Robert, who wrote a series of articles on "the anthological method" (*le procédé anthologique*).[64] Robert's research, first

---

[59] For the evidence of the Qumran scrolls, see my "Midrash Pesher in the Pauline Letters," in *The Scrolls and the Scriptures. Qumran Fifty Years After* (Sheffield, 1997), pp. 280–292.

[60] See in *Qumran Cave 4. Halakhic Texts* (DJD 35 [Oxford, 1999]), pp. 1–3.

[61] Restorations after Michael Knibb, *The Qumran Community* (Cambridge, 1987), pp. 259 and 261.

[62] See my *Pesharim*, pp. 48–51.

[63] For a discussion of the pesharim in relation to midrash, ibid., chap. 3.

[64] "Littéraire (genres)," in H. Cazelles, ed., *Supplément au Dictionnaire de la Bible*, vol. 5, "Kalt-Mycènes" (Paris, 1957), cols. 411–412.

published in the 1930s,[65] preceded Bloch's seminal definition of midrash and Vermes's important study on the haggadic midrash.

He first turned his attention to the way that the literary links (*les attaches littéraires*) to both later and earlier material, especially the books of Deuteronomy, Jeremiah, and Isaiah, can be observed in the first nine chapters of Proverbs. Literary parallels can be found both in terminology (e.g., the religious and traditional sense of the terms *moreh* and *melamed* in Prov. 5:13 and 6:13) and moral teaching (e.g., exhortations against the seductive evils of money and adultery and the links with the Decalogue). Robert discusses the difficulties of establishing them as borrowings (*les emprunts*) as such rather than the common currency of terms and ideas that the redactor found in his environment. But according to him the extensive similarity of terminology and thought between Proverbs and its biblical sources is the justification for seeing them as direct borrowings.[66] The earlier material has been integrated in such a way as to give Proverbs the impression of being an entirely new work: the idea of the Torah has been transposed to that of Wisdom; Wisdom assumes the messianic role traditionally ascribed to the Davidic descendants; and the Temple of Jerusalem is transposed into the house of Wisdom study.

Robert extended his literary analysis to the Song of Songs[67] and Ezekiel 16.[68] He described the type of study that he is advocating as "intrabiblical comparativism" (*le comparatisme intrabiblique*), defining precisely the borrowing of earlier material by later biblical authors as the anthological method—"As the expression indicates, it consists of re-using, literarily or by equivalence, the words or formulas of earlier Scriptures."[69] The term midrash was not originally put to use by Robert until it became evident that what he was describing was a method of intrabiblical exegesis that was similar to haggadic midrash.[70] Only in Robert's later works and in the studies of his followers did the term midrash become prominent.

Bloch was influenced by Robert's pioneering research into intrabiblical exegesis. She felt, however, that insufficient attention had been paid by Robert to "the reflection of the new authors."[71] Exilic and post-exilic authors were not content simply to reproduce or re-use the thought of their predecessors; they also developed, enriched and transposed the primitive message. Believing in the unfolding nature of divine revelation, the authors often re-interpreted their source material and gave a sense to their writings different from the original.

For example, Ezekiel 16, dated to the beginning of the exile, concerns the disquiet of God over Israel, his unfaithful wife. It is manifestly an allegory based upon Hosea and Jeremiah and has several literary links to Deuteronomy. But the historical allusions in vv. 3, 27–29 to the Canaanites, Amorites, Hittites, daughters of Philistines, and Assyrians, show that the exilic author had reworked previous biblical sources into "an historical allegory," following the events of sacred history, such as it is recounted in Genesis to Kings (v. 3, the travels of the Patriarchs in Palestine; v. 6, the covenant with Abraham; vv. 7–8, the covenant with

---

[65] André Robert, "Les Attaches Littéraires Bibliques de Prov. I–IX," in *Revue Biblique* 43 (1934), pp. 42–68, 172–204, 374–384; 44 (1935), pp. 344–365.

[66] Ibid., 44 (1935), pp. 345–346.

[67] "Le Genre Littéraire du Cantique des Cantiques," in *Vivre et Penser* 1–3 (1941–1945 = *Revue Biblique* 50–52), pp. 192–213.

[68] "Ezéchiel XVI. Exemple parfait du procédé midrashique dans la Bible," in *Cahiers Sioniens* 9 (1955), pp. 193–194.

[69] "Littéraire (genres)," col. 411.

[70] Vermes, *Scripture and Tradition*, p. 4, observes that, "What Robert calls 'style anthologique' is, in fact, a process strangely similar to the midrash."

[71] "Midrash," cols. 1270–1272.

Moses, etc.). According to Bloch, this later writer, with consummate art, used earlier biblical material by "mixing constantly and intentionally the remembrance of the past, the problems of the present and poetic allegory."[72] The prophet sought to explain the cause of the catastrophe of the exile in the unfaithfulness of the people, at the same time deepening and developing the central notion of the covenant into a "matrimonial allegory."[73]

Michael Fishbane was more critical of Robert's method, arguing that "these proposed instances of *écrits midrashiques* are not so much citations of biblical texts as disjointed textual fragments, schematizations or résumés."[74] He notes that while there is ground for textual interdependence for certain sources, as say between Prov. 6:20–35 and Deut. 5:6–6:9, the references that Robert and others (M. Delcor, A. Feuillet, M. Löhr) adduce are "generally so vague and disconnected, with virtually no clusters of parallel terms or analogous contexts, that little is gained by calling them exegetical or 'midrashic.'"[75]

Careful to avoid the same methodologically questionable procedures as Robert,[76] in *Biblical Interpretation in Ancient Israel*, Fishbane has written the most comprehensive treatment of how the Bible interprets itself. He eschews the term "midrash," choosing instead to describe the phenomena with Nahum Sarna as "inner biblical exegesis."[77]

Sarna had previously published a study of Psalm 89 in which he argued that the oracle found between verses 20 and 38 is not a version or recension of Nathan's oracle to David (cf. 2 Sam. 7) but an interpretation of it.[78] Fishbane also steers clear of the terms "biblical" and "post-biblical interpretations," but rather distinguishes with Douglas Knight between *traditum*, the content of the tradition, and *traditio*, the process of transmission.[79]

This method circumvents some of the pitfalls related to the biblical canon, since the *traditum* "was not at all monolithic, but rather the complex result of a long and varied process of transmission, or *traditio*."[80] Conceptually Fishbane's method has much to be commended, but it has to be admitted that in the praxis of his exegesis—identifying the source texts, the variants from the versions (like the Samaritan Pentateuch, Septuagint, Targum or Peshitta) and the Qumran biblical scrolls and their interpretation in later biblical texts, Rabbinic literature and mediaeval commentaries—it is essentially the Masoretic Text that forms the basis of his intratextual comparisons. This method is sensible, given the high authority of the MT, but it is not necessary. It is equally defensible to conduct, say, an intratextual study on non-MT biblical texts found among the Qumran scrolls.[81]

Fishbane divides inner biblical exegeses into four broad overlapping categories

---

[72] Ibid., col. 1271.
[73] See further, her study, "Ezéchiel XVI: Exemple parfait du procédé midrashique dans la Bible," in *Cahier Sionien* 9 (1955), pp. 193–223.
[74] *Biblical Interpretation in Ancient Israel* (Oxford, 1985), pp. 286–289.
[75] Ibid., p. 287.
[76] Ibid., p. 12, n. 32.
[77] Ibid., pp. viii, 7, n. 21: "J. Sanders has frequently articulated the link between tradition-history and 'midrash' (by which is meant what is here called inner-biblical exegesis, as well as what post-biblical Judaism called 'midrash')."
[78] "Ps. 89: A Study of Inner Biblical Exegesis," in A. Altmann, *Biblical and Other Studies* (Cambridge, MA, 1963), pp. 29–46.
[79] *Biblical Interpretation*, p. 6 and n. 17.
[80] Ibid., p. 6.
[81] Intimations along this line of thinking are found in Alexander Rofé, "Moses' Mother and Her Slave-Girl According to 4QExod[b]," in *Dead Sea Discoveries* 9.1 (2002), pp. 38–43, who sees in the Qumran biblical text midrashic exegesis at work in the addition of a nursemaid to the well-known story of Moses's mother placing him in a basket among the bulrushes (Exod. 2:3).

(scribal, legal, aggadic, and mantological) and brings a wealth of examples under consideration. It is, of course, in the trench warfare of details that the battle of exegesis is won or lost. Not all of the examples that Fishbane adduces are equally convincing, but by common estimation he has advanced the frontline. A selection of examples includes:[82]

a) scribal updating of toponyms: "Luz: it is Bethel" (Joshua 18:13).
b) translation of foreign terms: "Pur: it is the lot" (Esther 3:7).
c) explanation of grammatical ambiguity: "this is the Temple" clarifies the pronoun in the phrase "when *it* was founded" (Ezra 3:12).
d) segmentation and identification of the divine oracle: "For YHWH has poured out over you a spirit of stupefaction: He has closed your eyes—*namely, the prophets*—and cloaked your heads—*the seers*" (Isaiah 29:10).
e) Deuteronomic revision of a priestly rule prohibiting different forms of mixtures: *kilayim* ("mixtures") in Lev. 19:19 is supplanted in favor of the pleonastic term *sha'atnez* ("mixed material") in Deut. 22:9–11.
f) exegetical extensions of sabbatical legislation: the rule on leaving agricultural land fallow after six years (Exod. 23:10–11) is extended ("you shall do likewise") to include vineyards and olive groves (Exod. 23:11b). The formula that introduces this innovation is then dropped and the addendum becomes normalized in Lev. 25:3–7.
g) legal clarification of the meaning of "work" in the sabbatical prohibition (Exod. 20:8–11; Deut. 5:12–15): the law applies even during plowing and harvest time (Exod. 34:21); starting fires is considered work (Exod. 35:1–3). Legal clarification is also evident in the narrative when work is defined as gathering food (Exod. 16:27–30) or wood (Num. 15:32–36). Prophetic oracles further define work to include the bearing of any burden from homes (original formulation) to the gates of Jerusalem (secondary addition) (Jer. 17:21–22). This innovation is made authoritative by the appeal to its apparent antiquity ("as I commanded your forefathers," v. 22).
h) strategic revisions of earlier traditions: Jeremiah reinterprets an obscure priestly legislation on consecrated offerings when it declares that Israel is consecrated (*kodesh*) to Yahweh, the first fruits of his (i.e., Yahweh's) produce; whoever destroys him (*okhelav*) will be judged guilty (*ye'eshamu*), and evil will befall them: oracle of Yahweh (Jer. 2:3).

Fishbane argues that this is dependent upon Lev. 22:14–16:

> And if a man eats consecrated (*qodesh*) donation by accident, he must add one-fifth to its value and give the consecrated item to the priest. And they [the priests] shall not allow the consecrated donation of the Israelites to be desecrated,[83] and thereby cause them [the Israelites] to bear [their] iniquity of guilt [*ashmah*] when they [the Israelites] eat [*okhelam*] their [own] consecrated donations....

He believes that the use of all three technical terms (*okhel, kodesh, 'asham*) shows

---

[82] As highlighted by Fishbane himself in "Inner Biblical Exegesis: Types and Strategies of Interpretation in Ancient Israel," in G.H. Hartman and S. Budick, eds., *Midrash and Literature* (New Haven, 1986), pp. 19–37.

[83] Not included in Fishbane's translation of "which they offer to YHWH."

that Jeremiah has metaphorically transformed this cultic law concerning the inadvertent eating of consecrated offering by the laity into a divine oracle about Israel's holiness and the punishment of her enemies. In the prophecy, Israel has become the consecrated offering and Yahweh's first fruits. The term *okhel*, which literally meant the eating of consecrated food, is understood figuratively as "to destroy." And the cultic sense of *'asham*, guilty, is transposed to historical accountability.

Such a revision, Fishbane avers, was probably drawn from the same Deuteronomic reinterpretation of the status of Israel as holy. In Exod. 19:5–6 it states: "if you heed my (i.e., Yahweh's) voice and observe my covenant then you will be my special possession among the nations ... and my ... holy [*qadosh*] nation." Israel's holy status is dependent upon her obedience to the commandments given through Moses. In Deut. 7:6, however, the requirement of obedience is dropped and Israel stands unconditionally as a holy nation: "For you are a holy [*qadosh*] people to Yahweh, your God ... [his] special people among the nations."

Moreover, in Deut. 14:1–2, the notion of Israel as a holy nation includes the prohibition against a man's cutting himself or pulling out the hair of his forehead during bereavement. This is the transformation of a law found in Lev. 21:5–6 that forbids the sons of Aaron from practicing bodily mutilation as part of the mourning rites. In its Deuteronomic recasting, the order is extended to apply to all Israelites and not just to the priests, since they are a people holy to the Yahweh.

Fishbane sees symmetry in the transformation of Lev. 22:14–16 to Jer. 2:3: both the cultic donations and Israel are the consecrated offerings to Yahweh; the retribution against Israel's enemies is analogous to the additional one-fifth a man must add to compensate for his inadvertent desecration of priestly food. But he also recognizes asymmetry: the accidental infringement of cultic law versus the intentional vengeance against Israel's enemies; the delict is committed on the one hand by the donor and on the other by a third party; and reparation is made by the lay donor in the case of ritual desecration and while punishment is exacted on the nations who destroy Israel, the figurative donation to Yahweh. These, Fishbane claims, do not subvert the analogical power of the prophetic application, since the tension gives greater rhetorical force to the Jer. 2:3 as it breathes new life into an old priestly legislation, providing an internal discourse between the divine voice that speaks through Moses and the same divine voice that proceeds from the mouth of Yahweh. But that is only one explanation. An alternative is that the passages are unrelated except for the coincidence of terminology.

i) anthological exegesis by the Chronicler: 2 Chr. 15:2–7 report an otherwise unknown oracle by a certain Azzariah ben Oded, admonishing the Judean King Asa to reform much like Hezekiah and Josiah before him:
²Yahweh will be with you when you are with him: for if you seek him (*tidreshuhu*), he will be present (*yimatse*) to you; but if you abandon him, he will abandon you. ³Now for a long time Israel was without a true God, without an instructing priest and without Torah. ⁴But when in distress (*bazar*) Israel turned (*vayashav*) to Yahweh, God of Israel, and sought him (*vayevakshuhu*), he was present (*vayimatse*) to them. ⁵On those times there was no peace for those who went out or came in [from battle], for tremendous disturbances (*mehumot rabot*) assailed the inhabitants of the lands. ⁶And nations and cities smashed each other to bits, for God confounded them with every distress. ⁷But now:

be you strong and do not slacken: for there is a recompense for your deeds.

According to Fishbane, this pseudepigraphic oracle, dated to the Persian period, draws upon several earlier sources (cf. "Yahweh will be with you;" "be strong"), but the core of the passage is v. 4, which is parallel to Deut. 4:29-30, in which the Israelites are admonished to seek Yahweh, who will be faithful to them: "[T]he Chronicler is actually alluding to the recent exile and reminding people that repentance may reverse the terror of divine abandonment."[84] The terminological similarity, according to him, is striking: beseeching (*uvikashtem*) and seeking (*tidreshenu*) Yahweh and repenting (*veshavta*) in distress (*batsar*) is the condition on which he will be present to you, the Israelites (*umetsa'ukha*). Framing the core are two verses that have been adapted from earlier prophetic oracles. V. 5 is drawn from Amos 3:17 (*mehumot rabot*) and v. 3 is based upon Hos. 3:4. In the latter case, the Chronicler has transposed the original oracle against the northern exiles (without king or prince, sacrifice or pillar, and image or household gods) in such a way as to emphasize the pedagogical, rather than the cultic, role of the priest. The mention of "Torah" is unparalleled in the Hosean text.

The dependence of 2 Chr. 15:3 on Hos. 3:4 has previously been noted with its parallel contexts of a state of confusion resulting from the absence of institutions.[85] Sara Japhet has argued that the source text is likely to have been Hos. 3:5, except that the tenses have been changed from the future to the past: "they turned" (*yashubu* of Hosea to *vayyshob*) and "they sought him (*ubiqshu* of Hosea to *vayyebaqshu*). Following a period of anarchy, the Israelites should turn to the Lord.[86]

It is difficult to say which source text was in the mind of the Chronicler. On the one side, Deut. 4:29-30 show a number of additional terminological parallels: "you will seek him" (*tidreshenu*), "in distress" (*batsar*) and "they [i.e., all these things] will find you" (*umetsa'ukha*). But the first and third parallels echo verse two of 2 Chr. 15: "you seek him" (*tidreshuhu*) and "he will be present" (*yimatse*). On the other side, Hos. 3:5 is the "natural sequel"[87] to the period of anarchy in v. 4 as Japhet has observed. Moreover, Jer. 2:2 "the devotion of her youth" is dependent upon Hos. 2:17.

In fact, it is unnecessary to choose one source over the other. The Chronicler may well have had in mind Hos. 3:4-5 as one of the prooftexts when he composed vv. 2-7 of chapter 15, but he was also familiar with Deut. 4:29-30, which says something similar. He either included "in distress" intentionally to underscore the period of disorder or he added it as a lexical reflex in his composition.

Fishbane's study is a worthy contribution to the phenomenon of intratextual exegesis. He, more than anyone else, has demonstrated how the Bible interprets itself. Though questions can be raised about particular examples, it is undeniable that he has with methodological care unpacked the complexities underlying the apparently straightforward thesis that from the beginning the biblical texts can be seen to interpret themselves.

---

[84] Ibid., p. 32.
[85] I.L. Seeligmann, "The Beginnings of Midrash in Chronicles," in *Tarbiz* 49 (1979-1980), pp. 20-21 (Heb).
[86] *I&II Chronicles*, p. 719.
[87] Ibid.

Conclusions

The Bible is its own first interpreter. By this is not to say that from the beginning there was already a fixed canon of Scriptures that fashioned its own hermeneutical and self-exegeting context. The original sources of the Bible are presumably to be traced back to the early history of Israel. One cannot be more precise than that. Many scholars view the Persian and Hellenistic periods as the time during which the various strands of the tradition were regularized into the first five books of the Bible by Ezra and other priestly scribes.[88] Several of the prophetic texts in part (e.g., Isaiah, Jeremiah, Nahum, Habakkuk, Amos) originate from the pre-exilic or exilic context, but the formation of the shorter of these texts (e.g., minor prophets) into a collection began in the centuries to follow. By the second century B.C.E., Ben Sira in his "Praise of the Fathers of Old" (49:10) mentions the shorter of these as "the twelve prophets." The third division of "writings," however, remained opened for much longer. By the first century C.E., most of the texts were considered authoritative, though debates continued about the holiness of Qohelet, Ben Sira, Song of Songs, Daniel, and Esther. To what extent this Rabbinic canon was considered normative for all Jews remains unclear and is the subject of another study.

The multifarious tradition, whether in oral or written forms, was from its inception interpreted by scribes, priests, prophets, and teachers. These interpretations themselves were committed to writing and in turn became authoritative. They were included in the list of writings regarded as holy books from the first century C.E. onwards. In this sense, the Bible is its own exegete.

Much has been written about whether this process should be described as "midrashic." The above survey of scholarship has shown that since the term was introduced by Bloch in the 1950s to describe intrabiblical exegeses, it has lost its potency and freshness. Mention "midrash" nowadays and a whole set of objections immediately come to mind. It has been overused to such an extent that it has come to mean little more than a sexy synonym for exegesis.

Midrash, properly speaking, is a distinct genre of Rabbinic exegesis. In this context, there was a fixed canon from which the darshan would draw his homiletic interpretation. However, both its hermeneutical stance towards Scripture and the exegetical techniques that it uses are paralleled elsewhere, including the intertextual comparisons between biblical texts. It is in this broader sense that the origins and emergence of midrash are to be found in the Hebrew Bible.*

Bibliography

Bloch, Renée, "Midrash" in Cazelles, H., ed., *Supplément au Dictionnaire de la Bible* (Paris, 1957), vol. V, cols. 1263–1281. An English translation appears in Green, William Scott, ed., *Approaches to Ancient Judaism: Theory and Practice* (Missoula, 1978), pp. 29–50.

Fishbane, Michael, *Biblical Interpretation in Ancient Israel* (Oxford, 1985).

---

[88] Another view is that of David Weiss Halperin, who sees the importance of Ezra in revision of the maculated Torah, *Revelation Restored* (Boulder, 1997).

* The research for this article was partly carried out at the Faculté de théologie protestante of the Université Marc Bloch, Strasbourg. Thanks to M. le Doyen André Birmelé and Professeur Marc Philonenko for making the library facilities available to me.

Kugel, James L., *Studies in Ancient Midrash* (Cambridge, Ma, 2001).
Lim, Timothy H., *Holy Scripture in the Qumran Commentaries and Pauline Letters* (Oxford, 1997).
———, "Midrash Pesher in the Pauline Letters," in *The Scrolls and the Scriptures. Qumran Fifty Years After* (Sheffield, 1997), pp. 280-292.
———, *Pesharim* (Sheffield, 2002).
Neusner, Jacob, *What is Midrash?* (Philadelphia, 1987).
Porton, Gary G., "Midrash: The Palestinian Jews and the Hebrew Bible in the Greco-Roman Period" in Temporini, H., and W. Haase, eds., *Aufstieg und Niedergang der römischen Welt* (Berlin, 1979), vol. II.19.2, pp. 103-138. Revised in "Defining Midrash" in Neusner, Jacob, ed., *The Study of Ancient Judaism* (New York, 1981), vol. 1, pp. 55-92. References are to the original article.

TIMOTHY H. LIM
University of Edinburgh

Parable (*Mashal*)

The marker *Mashal*, generally translated "parable," like the term *Ma'aseh*, "precedent," signals that certain distinctive rules of writing govern in a narrative composition. What defines the parable is the announcement contained in that marker that a case or proposition or transaction, Halakhic or exegetical-Aggadic, may be approached through a static simile or a dynamic metaphor. It is an account of a transaction the components of which are comparable in character or relationship to the case or proposition that requires explanation.

The marker *Mashal* travels from document to document but it gives diverse signals—lays down different rules of writing—as it moves. Even within a single document, the marker signals more than a single function. Sometimes—particularly in Halakhic contexts—the word *Mashal* signifies a static simile, indicating a comparison of one thing to something else, without a trace of narrative exposition: "sages have devised this as a simile for that" is the governing language. Other times it is dynamic, marking the narrative evocation of the presence of a transaction, not merely describing a situation, even an action with consequences. And that requires narrative, a sequence of actions and responses thereto, with an (at least) implicit outcome. Then the parable, comparing one thing to something else, shades over into the replication of a pattern formed by one set of actions deemed to correspond to another set of actions. The narrative of the *Mashal* recapitulates, in other terms, the transaction, whether Halakhic or exegetical or theological, that is subject to clarification. In that case the governing language is, "a parable: to what is the matter comparable?" The sign, *Mashal*, like *Ma'aseh*, may signify a composition that clarifies a Halakhic ruling or it may be one that embodies in concrete, social terms an otherwise abstract theological conception or an exegesis of a verse of Scripture.

The *Mashal* as narrative parable requires differentiation from the *Ma'aseh*, which also involves narrative, that is, description of something said and/or done, and which also clarifies both Halakhic and theological cases. Is there nothing that characterizes *every* composition bearing the marker, *Mashal*? In all documents these traits are routinely present where the signal *Mashal* occurs. The parabolic narrative is totally abstract, asking for an act of imagination, [1] not mentioning specific authorities, [2] not placing the action in concrete time and a determinate, locative setting, and [3] not invoking an authoritative text (e.g., a proof-text of Scripture or a citation of the Mishnah). The

Ma'aseh exhibits the opposite traits. It asks for an act of mimesis. For [1] it is concrete, involving determinate, named authorities, [2] it situates an event at a particular occasion, and [3] it takes for granted a Halakhic text and context, commonly but not invariably cited or at least supplied in the redactional placement of the *Ma'aseh* in the Mishnah or Tosefta. So the *Mashal* stands on its own, and the *Ma'aseh* is rarely autonomous of its redactional setting. This negative approach to definition both encompasses all compositions labeled *Mashal* and excludes most of those labeled *Ma'aseh*.

Documents make distinctive choices, and one may readily distinguish the *Mashal* as utilized in one from the same as utilized in another. The signal *Mashal* refers in the Mishnah to one kind of simile, in Song of Songs Rabbah to a different kind of narrative parable altogether. Documentary differentiation in the analysis of the *Mashal* is new.[1] Since, until now, studies of the *Mashal* have taken as their premise the uniformity of parables in canonical context[2] without regard to documentary programs and preferences, the eight documents yield jarring results for established approaches to the *Mashal*. The parable cannot in this context be viewed as a coherent corpus of data uniform throughout the Rabbinic canon without regard to venue. Sometimes a static simile, sometimes a dynamic narrative, sometimes abbreviated, sometimes protracted, the *Mashal* produces evidence that is formally and functionally to be differentiated and classified, then compared from one document to another in its classifications.

Some suppose the opposite: first comes the parable, a narrative about the king who did such and so with the prince, for example, then comes its utilization for—adaptation to—a particular Halakhic or more commonly exegetical task. The existence of a ready-made corpus of conventional parables, articulated stories that stand on their own and possess characteristics in common, is taken for granted. Thus we have catalogues of parables that, as in folklore indices, are organized by theme but indifferent to documentary origin or venue. So studies of *The* Parable log in types of *Meshalim*, as types of folklore-narratives are classified, e.g., "the story of the king who...," "the story of the prince and the pedagogue...," "the householder and the workers...," "the king and the queen who...," and other fixed thematic or topical taxa. These catalogues then yield knowledge of how the given type of parable could be adapted for specific exegetical tasks. Circulating hither and yon, these parabolic stories—so this theory holds—were ready-made, not bespoke but off the rack. Available parabolic narratives were merely adapted to the requirements of a particular task of exposition.

To explain: the parabolic narrative—the *Mashal* proper—is ordinarily seen as defined prior to the utilization of said parable to clarify a particular situation or transaction.

---

[1] See Clemens Thoma and Simon Lauer, *Die Gleichnisse der Rabbinen. I. Pesiqta deRav Kahana. Einleitung, Übersetzung, Parallelen, Kommentar, Texte* (Bern, Frankfurt am Main, New York, 1986); Clemens Thoma and Simon Lauer, *Die Gleichnisse der Rabbinen. II. Von der Erschaffung der Welt bis zum Tod Abrahams: Bereschit Rabba 1-63* (Bern, Frankfurt am Main, New York, 1991); Clemens Thoma and Hanspeter Ernst, *Die Gleichnisse der Rabbinen. III. Von Isaak bis Zum Schilfmeer. Ber R 63-100, ShemR 1-22* (Bern, Frankfurt am Main, New York, 1996). Clemens Thoma and Hanspeter Ernst, *Die Gleichnisse der Rabbinen. IV. Vom Lied des Mose bis zum Bundesbuch: ShemR 23-30* (Bern, Frankfurt am Main, New York, 2000). While he collects the parables of a specified document, he does not then characterize the lot of them or differentiate one document's parables from those of another. So he prepared the way for work he did not then do.

[2] That is, the *Mashal* is assumed to conform to a uniform program throughout the Rabbinic canon, or even throughout all Judaic ("Jewish") writings. And Gospels-scholarship has tended to take the *Mashal* as a fixed genre of writing even for Christian documents.

This may be expressed in the formal language of the matter, as between the *Mashal* (the parabolic narrative) and the *Nimshal* (the case subject to narrative exposition)—which comes first? To explain: the Hebrew word for parable, *Mashal*, yields a passive, [2] *Nimshal*, thus [1] the parable and [2] the base-pattern or situation or transaction or event or proposition that is replicated in the simile constructed by the parable, respectively. This is a bit abstract, so readers will be grateful for a concrete case. In the following composition, the exegetical task is defined at J-K, the *Mashal* is set forth at L, and the *Nimshal*—the explicit articulation of the point of the parable, at M.

> T. Ber. 1:11
> J. Similarly, "Remember not the former things, nor consider the things of old" (Is. 43:18). Remember not the former things—these are [God's mighty acts in saving Israel] from the [various] kingdoms; nor consider things of old—these are [God's mighty acts in saving Israel] from Egypt.
> K. "Behold, I am doing a new thing; now it springs forth" (Is. 43:19)—this refers to the war of God and Magog [at the end of time].
> L. *They drew a parable, to what may the matter be compared? To one who was walking in the way and a wolf attacked him, but he was saved from it. He would continually relate the incident of the wolf. Later a lion attacked him, but he was saved from it. He forgot the incident of the wolf and would relate the incident of the lion. Later still a serpent attacked him, but he was saved from it. He forgot the other two incidents and would continually relate the incident of the serpent.*
> M. *So, too is the case for Israel: the recent travails make them forget about the earlier ones.*

Here the *Nimshal*, M, briefly articulates the point of the *Mashal*, L, but in many instances the *Nimshal* is detailed and elaborate. This analytical provocation for the introduction of the *Mashal*, the *Nimshal*, meaning "that to which the parable forms a narrative simile," "that pattern of actions or events to which the comparison is drawn," is commonly deemed secondary, notional, and occasional. Hence, for example, catalogues of types of ready-at-hand parables, e.g., the king and the prince who . . ., such as Thoma compiles, may be gleaned from the particularities of writing marked *Mashal*.

But in most cases, first comes the exegetical task, J-K, M, above, then, in response, comes the parable, L, responding to the assignment detail by detail. It is the exact match of the *Mashal* to the *Nimshal* that tells the tale: the *Nimshal* is generative, the *Mashal*, responsive. And—so I claim, furthermore—the exegetical-theological assignment is documentary, in that the authorships of the several entire documents, respectively, define the task assigned to parabolic writing, as much as to any other kind of writing. For the specified occasion the *Mashal* is made up to carry out the work of exposition and clarification dictated by the document and its encompassing program, whether the Mishnah or the Tosefta or tractate Abot or Sifra. Consequently, the traits, other than those specified at the outset, of the received corpus of ready-made narratives to be adapted for particular purposes prove difficult to identify and describe in detail, though apart from the fixed marker, *Mashal*, a few generic traits of mind and rhetoric do surface, already specified. And the traits take on meaning only in the contrast with the Ma'aseh and its variations.

To summarize: the hypothesis emerging from the probe of eight documents is, then, readily stated. The primary task of the *Mashal* is defined by the *Nimshal*, meaning, the Halakhic or exegetical problem governs the formation and functioning of the parable. To state the matter in extreme but defensible form: numerous cases show that every single detail of the *Mashal* captures a component of the Halakhic or the exegetical situation subject to exposition. And the parable succeeds when it is evaluated by the criterion: has the simile left out even one detail of that which is subjected to comparison? Or has it added a detail not generated by that which is subjected to comparison? That exact match in detail of *Mashal* to *Nimshal* is the key. Seldom does the *Mashal* give evidence of constituting a free-standing story or situational simile, exhibiting marks of adaptation of a ready-made narrative. Commonly, though not always, the *Mashal* in its rich detail shows itself to be the formation of a narrative made up for the distinctive purpose at hand.

This ad hoc theory of the *Mashal*—seeing the *Mashal* as contextually-driven and made up for the occasion, not drawn upon from a ready-made corpus of conventional, available narratives—yields a clear result. The task assigned to the *Mashal* is primary and generative. Thus first comes the transaction or the situation to be illuminated, then comes the formation of the parable, first the *Nimshal*, then the *Mashal*. The exegetical or Halakhic task of exposition defines the character of the parabolic narrative, which only rarely has a free-standing existence and seldom transcends the limits of the exegetical or Halakhic case subject to illumination.

Mishnah

True to its Halakhic focus, the Mishnah is the natural homeland of the disciplined, *Halakhic Ma'aseh*. The *Mashal*, which in later documents was found quite serviceable even for Halakhic exposition, appears only three times in the entire document. All fall into the category of Halakhic similes. Static, none tells a story. Then in the Mishnah *Mashal* marks an inert simile that clarifies a normative law. These are the three instances in which the marker, *Mashal*, occurs in the Mishnah:

1. M. Suk. 2:9
   A. All seven days a person treats his Sukkah as his regular dwelling and his house as his sometime dwelling.
   B. [If] it began to rain, at what point is it permitted to empty out [the Sukkah]?
   C. From the point at which the porridge will spoil.
   D. They made a parable: To what is the matter comparable?
   E. To a slave who came to mix a cup of wine for his master, and his master threw the flagon into his face.

E on its own is curiously moot, making no point out of its Halakhic context, but slightly out of phase with that context. We do not know why the master threw the flagon in the slave's face, or what the slave did wrong. The Halakhic parable makes sense only in its context, B-C. Why choose as the moment at which it is permitted to empty out the Sukkah the point at which the porridge spoils? Because eating signifies dwelling in the Sukkah (in line with the conception of the Sabbath that where one eats his meal is what designates where he locates his domicile for the Sabbath). Then when the food is spoiling, it is a mark of rejection: the person for the dwelling. When the slave mixes the wine for the master, instead of drinking, the master throws the wine in his face. Now too, instead of eating, one is driven out. The Halakhic ruling to be clarified, C, then is more than closely tracked by the *Mashal*, D-E, it is required if D-E are not to be reduced to sheer gibberish.

2. M. Nid. 2:5
   A. The sages made a parable in connection with the woman:
   B. (1) the room, (2) the front hall, and (3) the room upstairs.
   C. Blood in the room is unclean.
   D. If it is found in the front hall, a matter of doubt concerning it is deemed

unclean, since it is assumed to come from the fountain [uterus].

C–D posit three spaces, to which the three areas, B, the downstairs room, the front hall, and the upstairs room, correspond. The Halakhic classification, C–D, then is clarified by the spatial relationships of the parable as not anecdote but simile. There is no pretense of a narrative here. It is self-evident that the simile is constructed in response to the data that the sages wish to clarify.

3. M. Nid. 5:7
A. Sages have made a parable in regard to the woman: (1) an unripe fig, (2) a ripening fig, and (3) a fully ripe fig.
B. An unripe fig—she is still a little girl.
C. And a ripening fig—these are the days of her girlhood.
D. In both periods her father is entitled to whatever she finds and to her wages and to annul her vows.
E. A fully ripe fig—once she has grown up, her father has no further right over her.

The same pattern recurs, the simile/parable, A, which clarifies the three stages of the Halakhah, B, C, and E. Absent the *Nimshal*, B-E, the *Mashal*, A, is pointless. Once more, the parable stands for a comparison of a Halakhic classification-system and its rules to a familiar natural phenomenon, the state of a fig at various points in its development. Without the Halakhic facts of B, C, and E, the parable—unripe fig, ripening fig, fully ripe fig—forms a set of facts bearing no meaning beyond themselves.

The initial canonical document beyond Scripture, with its static, inert simile, lacking all narrative articulation, refers to a comparison of a Halakhic category to an arrangement of rooms or to a growth-process of nature. Anyone who has examined the parables in other Rabbinic documents will be struck by what the Mishnah does not present, which is the parable as a story, a narrative of a particular kind. The marker scarcely hints at the development in the Tosefta and beyond of an anecdotal aspect of the *Mashal*, a more complex articulation of the simile as a narrative. Only when the marker, *Mashal*, referred to a dynamic narrative, not only a static simile, did the signal encompass a Halakhic transaction or event.

From the Mishnah to the Tosefta

Since that shift would surface in the Tosefta and not in the Mishnah we must wonder, why not? The answer is clear: it is a documentary choice deriving from the character of the compilation: the *Ma'aseh* yes, the *Mashal*, no! When the framers of the Mishnah wished to resort to narrative to clarify a Halakhic ruling, they invariably asked the *Ma'aseh*, precedent, to bear the burden of concretization. Indeed, most of the narratives of the Mishnah fall into the classification of Halakhic *Ma'aseh*. The framers of the Mishnah's compositions and composites think juridically, therefore seek precedents.

But the Tosefta served in part an exegetical purpose, the clarification of cited laws of the Mishnah, for example. It follows that exegetical thinking, focused not on the rule but on the case, would surface in the Tosefta alongside the other, the juridical mode of thought. In the exegetical-theological documents later on—self-evidently—exegetical thinking would predominate, to the near exclusion of the *Ma'aseh* as precedent and also, and concomitantly, of the *Mashal* as static simile. But it does not suffice to explain only, why not. Why does the writing of compositions for the Tosefta encompass exegetical, not only juridical writing, such as the Mishnah provoked? Within theory that the Tosefta contains not only free-standing writing, but also citation and gloss of Mishnah-rules the answer is clear. The Tosefta's compilers and authors and authorships undertook a subordinate, exegetical role, citing the Mishnah, not only setting forth Halakhic rulings in the manner of the Mishnah. So when they contemplated the *Mashal*, they asked of it service in the exegetical, not only in the juridical, labor, hence not only a simile to clarify a rule, but a narrative parable to make sense of a transaction, event, or activity.

The Tosefta

A striking contrast between the inert simile and the parabolic narrative marks the move from the Mishnah to the Tosefta. Now the *Mashal* occurs not only as a static declaration, "sages have compared this to that," thus, in the rhetorical pattern, "this is like that...." The dynamic, narrative *Mashal*, which we meet in the Tosefta—"They drew a parable, to what is the matter compared? To the case of a king who did such-and-such, and so-and-so resulted ... so when God/Israel does such-and-such, and so-and-so results ..."—had struck no one writing for the Mishnah as a promising medium of thought and argument. The simile was built on comparison and contrast of things in a static relationship, one in which nothing happens. The *Mashal* now makes its appearance, mostly, but not wholly, in the Aggadic discourse of the Tosefta. It comes to the fore as a dynamic, protracted narrative, involving a series of paradigmatic transactions.

Stated simply: things happen, with the result that actions or events or transactions form a pattern, and juxtaposed patterns sustain comparison and contrast between one transaction and the other. Throughout, the *Nimshal* then defines the pattern, and the *Mashal* replicates that pattern in other categories altogether. The task of the parabolic narrative then is to capture the base-pattern in other terms. So the Tosefta produces a dynamic simile, so to speak, or, more really, transforms the inert simile into an active metaphorical narrative.

Predictably, the innovation occurs in writing that serves for the Tosefta's speaking on its own, not citing and glossing the Mishnah or amplifying its Halakhic rulings. It concerns mainly, but not exclusively, theological or exegetical problems. Then some authorship conceived that the *Mashal* might render not only a comparable situation, a simile, but a comparable activity or transaction, a pattern shaped in one transaction set forth in a narrative of a comparable transaction. The Tosefta's *Meshalim* are far more elaborate and more diverse than those of the Mishnah. In the unfolding of the Rabbinic canon document by document, with the Mishnah followed by the Tosefta, yielding Sifra, and so onward, the Tosefta comes forth as the first canonical document after Scripture to conceive of not just an inert simile but a dynamic narrative as a medium for comparison and contrast. But the Tosefta both depends upon the Mishnah in passages, and also goes its own way in other passages. Consequently, the Tosefta's *Meshalim* are divided in two: [1] the familiar inert similes, containing no action, replicating the traits of the Mishnaic *Mashal*, and [2] the new model of exegetical or theological narratives, characterized by sequences of actions or events, two patterns of which are compared. So the Tosefta both continues the Mishnah's pattern for the *Mashal* and innovates—a documentary trait replicated in many aspects.

The source of the idea for exegetical and theological discourse is surely Scripture, which in Prophecy and in Wisdom affords models of parabolic writing. That is a plausible explanation for the Aggadic parable that surfaces in the Tosefta. But how about the Halakhic parables of the Tosefta, two of which, we shall see, concur in the value of narrative for illuminating a transaction, a possibility not explored in the Mishnah? To explain the appearance of a proportionately insignificant population of dynamic narrative parables in the Halakhic exposition, I appeal to the development of the narrative for Aggadic parabolic discourse. The model of the Aggadic narrative *Mashal* triggered the formation of at least two Halakhic ones, giving promise of future exploitation of the narrative *Mashal* for Halakhic purposes as much as for exegetical and theological ones.

The Tosefta's other-than-static (and other-than-Halakhic!) kind of *Mashal* is represented by the following, first in the conventional order of the document.

> T. Ber. 1:11
> J. Similarly, "Remember not the former things, nor consider the things of old" (Is. 43:18). Remember not the former things—these are [God's mighty acts in saving Israel] from the [various] kingdoms; nor consider things of old—these are [God's mighty acts in saving Israel] from Egypt.
> K. "Behold, I am doing a new thing; now it springs forth" (Is. 43:19)—this refers to the war of God and Magog [at the end of time].
> L. They drew a parable, to what may the matter be compared? To one who was walking in the way and a wolf attacked him, but he was saved from it. He would continually relate the incident of the wolf. Later a lion attacked him, but he was saved from it. He forgot the incident of the wolf and would relate the incident of the lion. Later still a serpent attacked him, but he was saved from it. He forgot the other two incidents and would continually relate the incident of the serpent.
> M. So, too is the case for Israel: the recent travails make them forget about the earlier ones.

Note the brevity of the *Nimshal*. M. But the narrative sequence, wolf/lion/serpent, is required to make the desired point that M expresses. So the narrative of the *Mashal*—the succession of travails—responds to its exegetical task, which is, to illustrate a case in which new travails obscure older ones.

What is important is two facts. First, the *Mashal* now portrays a series of events, happenings that form a pattern and bear meaning expressed in movement. Second, the *Mashal* produces a coherent composition out of relationship with the exegetical task defined by Is. 43:18. So it is only M, the *Nimshal*, that has—that can have—generated each detail of L, the *Mashal*. The completed *Mashal-Nimshal*, L-M, forms an awry comment on J-K, pointing out that not only are God's more current mighty acts likely to make Israel forget the former ones, but God's "new thing"—a travail, the opposite of saving Israel from the kingdoms—does the same. So the completed parable with its lesson form a comment on the exegesis of the cited verse, Is. 43:18, and the whole constitutes an exegetical parable.

To classify the data systematically: the *Mashal* in the Tosefta falls into these three categories:

[1] a simile in the model of the Mishnah's;
[2] Halakhic parables; always spun out in dialogue with the Halakhic case or transaction; and
[3] exegetical (including theological) parables.

The exegetical ones are divided into those that respond to the task of explaining theological or moral or ethical situation that provokes the formation of the parable, and those that are utilized to illuminate a transaction but do not respond to the details of the transaction. The Tosefta's indicative trait, its dual relationship to the Mishnah, recapitulates itself in the matter of the *Mashal*: half the time in the model of the Mishnah's, half the time not. The Mishnaic

Mashal, a static, inert simile serving Halakhic exposition, accounts for approximately half of the Tosefta's *Meshalim*. More to the point: when the Tosefta wishes to ask for a *Mashal* to help convey and clarify a Halakhic point, it ordinarily relies on the received definition of the matter. So the Mishnaic model persists in its original context: the resort to similes, lacking narrative initiatives, for Halakhic exposition. And no new model of Halakhic exposition complements the received one.

What is unexpected in the Tosefta therefore is the advent of the exegetical or theological parable, which (from the perspective of the Mishnah's record) is new both in its task and in its utilization of a kind of narrative (abstract, indeterminate in time, utopian in location) for carrying out that task. Where the task is exegetical or theological, the *Mashal* will take on a narrative quality, introducing sequences of actions with an indicated outcome. But the narrative *Mashal*, as distinct from the simile, also enters Halakhic discourse. So while the Halakhic *Meshalim* remain within the inert, Mishnaic model, still at some few points the exposition of Halakhic rules through the *Mashal* encompasses the utilization of narrative. These are precisely the results that the character of the Tosefta—recapitulating the Mishnah's Halakhic rules, also venturing to amplify and extend them, and furthermore setting forth compositions that do not intersect with the Mishnah at all—overall would lead us to anticipate.

So the program of the document's compilers has governed its repertoire of parables: types and functions. That is illustrated in a simple mental experiment. If we were given a random sample of *Meshalim* of the Tosefta together with a sample of those of the Mishnah, we should identify the Tosefta's items half of the time, and half of the time we should have no valid criterion for assigning an item to the Tosefta over the Mishnah. We shall now turn to a document, where none can mistake the *Mashal*—if it is a *Mashal*—that belongs there and no where else.

Abot

Tractate Abot is attached to, but topically, rhetorically, and logically distinct from, the Mishnah. The collection of wise sayings is put together in such a way as utterly to ignore the Mishnah's Halakhic topical program, its rhetorical plan, and the syllogistic logic of coherent discourse that govern in the Mishnah's other sixty-two tractates. I find in tractate Abot no compositions bearing the marker *Mashal*. But we have a number of similes, using the language of comparison ("to what is he/it to be likened?"). They all are inert similes, like the Halakhic similes of the Mishnah and the Tosefta, but they concern themselves with matters of wisdom, therefore representing the distinctive utilization of an established form for a new purpose. These are as follows:

Tractate Abot 3:17
I. He would say, "Anyone whose wisdom is greater than his deeds—to what is he to be likened? To a tree with abundant foliage, but few roots.
J. "When the winds come, they will uproot it and blow it down,
K. "as it is said, 'He shall be like a tamarisk in the desert and shall not see when good comes but shall inhabit the parched places in the wilderness' (Jer. 17:6).
L. "But anyone whose deeds are greater than his wisdom—to what is he to be likened? To a tree with little foliage but abundant roots.
M. "For even if all the winds in the world were to come and blast at it, they will not move it from its place,

N. "as it is said, 'He shall be as a tree planted by the waters, and that spreads out its roots by the river, and shall not fear when heat comes, and his leaf shall be green, and shall not be careful in the year of drought, neither shall cease from yielding fruit' (Jer. 17:8)."

The form varies from the familiar *Mashal* of the Mishnah and Tosefta in four ways, 1) the omission of the marker, *Mashal*; 2) the inclusion of proof-texts (K, N), which is unknown in the Mishnah's and the Tosefta's *Meshalim*; 3) the exposition of the point of the simile by J, M, as though conceding that the simile does not speak for itself. Finally, 4) the language is highly formalized and balanced, I matching L; the Mishnah's and Tosefta's parables rarely exhibit concern for the formalization of prose. The subject-matter—not Halakhic, not exegetical, not theological—conforms to that which defines the document, Torah-study, inclusive of fulfillment of the teachings thereof.

Tractate Abot 4:20
A. Elisha b. Abbuyah says, "He who learns when a child—what is he like? Ink put down on a clean piece of paper.
B. "And he who learns when an old man—what is he like? Ink put down on a paper full of erasures."
C. R. Yose b. R. Judah of Kefar Habbabli says, "He who learns from children—what is he like? One who eats sour grapes and drinks fresh wine.
D. "And he who learns from old men—what is he like? He who eats ripe grapes and drinks vintage wine."

The same distinguishing qualities noted above apply to these two *Meshalim* as well.

If we were given a collection of Meshalim without identification as to their sources, we should readily pick out those deriving from Abot. These obviously form a cogent set by reason of shared traits of rhetoric and topic, and clearly differ from those of the Mishnah and the Tosefta because of those same traits—beginning, after all, with the omission of the marker.

Sifra

What defines the parable in Sifra as in the Mishnah and the Tosefta is the announcement that a case or proposition may be approached through a simile, an account of a transaction the components of which are comparable in character or in relationship to the case or proposition at hand. That account, like the *Ma'aseh*, then may, but need not, report an anecdote, involving a transaction comparable to the one at hand but more readily accessible in its simplicity of detail than the one at hand.

Sifra's parable thus takes two forms. In the first, as with the Mishnah's similes, it simply sets up a situation comparable to the one under discussion, lacking all activity or movement. In the second, as in the Tosefta's exegetical and theological parables, it narrates a transaction or event deemed comparable to the one under discussion. In neither case does the logic of teleology, which characterizes authentic narratives, have to impart coherence to the composition. Rather, the context—the situation to be replicated in other, more accessible terms—does. In this document the parable serves two purposes, clarification of an exegesis of a verse of Sifra, or clarification of a Halakhic ruling set forth in Leviticus. Does the *Mashal* of either type stand on its own, or does it require the exegetical context to bear specific meaning? Ordinarily, but not always, the *Nimshal* governs the details of the *Mashal*, which, on their own, do not present a coherent statement.

The Halakhic Parable

Ordinarily, like that of the Mishnah, the Halakhic parable of Sifra is so closely tied to, generated by, the case at hand that it is incomprehensible beyond that context. That is to say, removed from the case that is clarified, the Halakhic parable yields no sense whatsoever; it is incoherent and gibberish. The Halakhic parables before us involve descriptions of situations, rather than unfolding transactions or singular events. They are inert, not dynamic, and they scarcely qualify even as anecdotal. The economical, stripped-down description of what is said and done recalls the Halakhic *Ma'aseh*. The difference is, the Halakhic *Ma'aseh* frames a transaction or a circumstance on which sages make a ruling, while the Halakhic *Mashal* establishes a counterpart situation in which the outcome is implicit and requires no articulated ruling. The power of the simile therefore lies in its self-evident implication.

> Sifra III:VI.2
> A. Might one suppose that one should not bring an offering of a wild beast, but if one has brought a wild beast as an offering, it is valid?
> B. The matter may be compared to the case of someone whose master said to him, "Go and bring me wheat," and he went and brought him both wheat and barley....
> C. Lo, to what may the matter be compared? To the case of someone whose master said to him, "Go and bring me only wheat."

The paired parables match the case and have no autonomous standing, since out of context they bear no point I can discern. Here there is no unpacking of a transaction, only the description of the case, lacking an outcome. This is simile in the form of a situation, not a transaction with secondary amplification.

We see two facts concerning Sifra's Halakhic *Meshalim*. First, it is a fixed trait of the Halakhic parables of Sifra that the case dictate the simile; only one of the Halakhic parables can stand outside of its Halakhic context. Second, the Halakhic parables tend not to entail the protracted description of an anecdotal transaction, e.g., actions and reactions. They tend to serve to replicate the relationships of a Halakhic problem in another, neutral situation not particular to the details of the Halakhic rule at hand.

The Exegetical Parable

The task of the exegetical or theological parable is to clarify not a law but a statement of Scripture or the theology implicit therein. The link to Scripture is intimate, and ordinarily the parable bears no self-evident meaning or message out of exegetical context, as we shall now see. It is necessary to articulate this connection point by point, e.g., in the first entry, "So with Aaron...." None of these parabolic compositions has the capacity to stand on its own. Most of them, however, involve protracted transactions, e.g., action and reaction. The *Nimshal* then governs the *Mashal*, the document, the detailed illustrative materials utilized by the document. In a commentary to the book of Leviticus, then, the task of expounding the verses of that book dictates where parables are required and the form that they are to take.

> Sifra XCVIII:VI.1
> A. "And Moses killed it and took the blood:" For all seven days of consecration, Moses served in the high priesthood. He would slaughter the beast, he would toss the blood, he would sprinkle the blood, he would

perform the rite of purification, he would pour oil, he would atone.

B. There is then a parable: to what may the matter be compared? To a princess who was married when she was a minor, and they made an agreement with her mother that the mother would serve until her daughter would learn [what was required of her].

C. So with Aaron, at first he was a Levite, as it is said, "And is not Aaron, your brother, the Levite" (Exod. 4:14). But when he was chosen to serve as High Priest, the Holy One, blessed be He, said to Moses, "You will serve me until Aaron will learn."

The parable, "A princess was married as a minor" matches the case point by point, as the articulation of matters makes explicit. I cannot think of what the parable as articulated here can mean outside of this particular context. What we see is how the exegetical parable constructs a situation, rather than tells a tale of what was said or done in sequences. There are no stages of activity, no initiative with its consequences, just the construction of a situation—a woman married under such-and-such stipulation—deemed to illuminate Aaron's situation in the priesthood.

Sifra is classified as a Halakhic Midrash-compilation, and with good reason. But when it comes to the principal classification of parables, the document favors the exegetical over the Halakhic. Of the twelve parables that I have identified, eight are exegetical, four Halakhic. Of that same population nine are particular to the exegetical setting. Those that on the surface can serve for some purpose other than the specific one at hand involve a more elaborate transaction than those that are particular to the terms of the verse that is amplified or the Halakhic ruling that is clarified.

As to the particularity of the parable, the result is congruent with the Tosefta and the Mishnah. Both the Halakhic and the exegetical types of parable in Sifra tend to emerge from the particular setting and to respond to an exegetical assignment. That is to clarify a distinctive case or problem or ruling. The parables, whether Halakhic or exegetical, that predominate emerge from the details of particular cases, translated into readily accessible similes. Some, to be sure, bear an autonomous, internally cogent, narrative; the free-standing parables then require and receive an explicit statement showing how the simile applies to the particular case at hand.

The upshot of Mishnah-Tosefta-Abot-Sifra may be simply expressed. Overall, parables appear more likely to commence within the exegetical process than outside its limits, to respond to a particular exegetical task, rather than to define one. To this point, therefore, the parable forms a minor component of documentary writing. That proposition proves coherent with the use of parables in the Mishnah, where, if only for three times in a vast document, the signal, *Mashal*, always promises an inert simile, meaning, this is like that, rather than an active narrative establishing a paradigm of conduct and consequence, "the matter may be compared to the case of a king who. . . ." In the Tosefta, the same kind of parable predominates, but the dynamic *Mashal*, bearing its own meaning out of exegetical/Halakhic context, does occur. That represents a step beyond the Mishnah's rather sparse and casual utilization of the genre. And Sifra follows suit. But if the Halakhic parable appears to have enjoyed a secure position within the repertoire of documentary authorships, that surmise proves false. We shall now address an exegetical document, covering matter of both Halakhah and theology, that nearly abandons the Halakhic parable and exacts from the parable principally exegetical service.

Sifre to Numbers

In Sifre to Numbers we find two Halakhic parables and twenty-nine exegetical parables. (We shall encounter the same remarkable disproportion in the companion, Sifre to Deuteronomy.) Since the book of Numbers is rich in Halakhic compositions, the disproportion is not to be predicted. And, by comparison to Sifra, Sifre to Numbers certainly finds more interest in parabolic writing than did the authorship of Sifra's compositions. But it is still an ancillary genre of writing, not principal to the documentary program.

In Sifre to Numbers nearly all of the parables take shape in close conversation with the verse subject to clarification, and the terms of the Halakhic simile too are particular to the context in which the simile serves. Rarely is a detail superfluous, a match other than exact between details of the parable and details of the verse clarified by the parable. Occasionally we find a component of a parable that is not commensurate, which marks the parable as not-particular to its exegetical task but adapted therefor.

The available, ready-made heritage of parables then consists of a literary convention available for articulation and particularization in response to the requirement of a distinctive context. Thus, while we commonly meet a king and a prince, a king and a queen, or a king and an ally, these take on meaning and significance only within the details modeled after the situation constructed by the base-verse, that is, God and Moses, or God and Israel. Allusion to "king/prince" or "king/ally" never leaves unclear the point of the parable in all its specificity—and most exegetical parables bear in their wake an explicit, wholly articulated message: so is it here, with God and Israel, or God and Moses, and so on throughout.

Sifre to Numbers' exegetical parables follow a simple form: citation of a verse and a comment on it, followed by a parable that embodies the relationships or terms, participants or transactions, of the base-verse. The parable sometimes involves action, other times requires only a static replication of the situation outlined by the base-verse. But that is now in other terms than Scripture's. The close correspondence comes to expression in many instances with an explicit exegesis of the parable, explaining how it is relevant to the base-verse and the situation portrayed therein. Consequently, the exegetical parable has no autonomous standing, being comprehensible only in exegetical context. And that is defined by the task of the document, as we have noted time and again. The relationships or terms, participants or transactions, of the parable originate in, and form obvious counterparts to, those of the base-verse. The parables are constructed to form similes of an abstract, but wholly conventional, character, meant to treat as general the particularities of the base-verse and its participants and transactions. In some instances the parable augments the proposition or adds to the message of the base-verse, in many it simply recapitulates that message.

Has the exegetical task provoked the parable, or did the parable take shape independent of the exegetical circumstance? The governing criterion is the question: is the parable in every last detail particular to the exegetical context, or is it necessary to adjust the parable to that context? We know that such a necessity comes into play when a detail of a parable proves superfluous, playing no role in the exposition of the base-verse or context. Overall, then, the answer to the question is this: in Sifre to Numbers, the exegetical task is primary, the construction of a pertinent, illuminating simile only secondary and derivative. What, then, can have circulated beyond the limits of Sifre to Numbers? The conception that similes involving the king and the prince, the king and the queen, the king and the ally, could be constructed: the generative force derives not from the fixed conventions of the abstract players, the king, the prince (not King Herod or King Ardavan, not Queen Shelomsiyyon/Salome). Like chess pieces, these nameless kings and princes and queens are available to be moved hither and yon, to reconstitute a relationship or a transaction in terms analogous to mathematical symbols: purely abstract, very precise.

Sifre to Deuteronomy

In Sifre to Deuteronomy we find no Halakhic parables and forty-five exegetical ones. On the one side, the character of the document, with its verse by verse exegesis, leads us to anticipate a bias in favor of the exegetical parable. On the other hand, given the Halakhic heart of Deuteronomy, formed by Chapters 12 through 26, and the systematic reading of those formidable chapters by Sifre to Deuteronomy's exegetes, the complete disinterest in the Halakhic parable is surprising. What we learn is that the *Mashal*, deemed illuminating for Halakhic as much as for Aggadic-theological discourse, in the purely-Halakhic documents, now loses its well-attested prior role, such as had been dominant in the Mishnah and important in the Tosefta.

Many, though not all, of the exegetical parables respond to the distinctive exegetical task at hand, and our friends, the king/queen/prince/ally on their own stand for nothing that transcends the limits of the case. Their persons, relationships, and transactions derive from the exegetical setting at hand. Only in the intersection with a particular verse of Deuteronomy do they take on specificity and become cogent as parables. It is a reciprocal process: the persons, relationships, and transactions depicted in the realized parables track those of the verse subject to clarification, and the parables reverse course and impart sense and meaning to their context as well. The formulaic quality of the parable now is such that given the problem, we can predict the course of the parabolic rendition of matters.

As before, I underscore the parabolic material, the simile itself, which affords perspective on the classification of the parable: particular to the exegetical task—or adapted thereto, as the case may be. It remains to note that there is, in addition, one parable that falls into neither classification.

We find nine parables not generated by the particular exegetical task at hand, not systematically replicating the situation or transaction predicated upon the base-verse and demanded by the exegesis thereof. And there are thirty-six instances (counting three ambiguous items) in which the parable is particular to its exegetical task, tracking the case that is generalized by the simile, commonly but not invariably narrative in execution. If we collect the nine parables that appear to enjoy an autonomous existence and to be adapted to the exegetical task, not invented for it, what we have is miscellaneous:

1. a king who, with his troops, went out into the field. His troops said to him, "Give us hot white bread."
2. A king had great wealth. He had a young son and had to go overseas. He said, "If I leave my wealth in the hands of my son, he will go and squander it. Lo, I shall appoint a guardian for him until he comes of age."
3. Someone who said to his fellow, "Sell me your ass." The other said, "All right." "Will you let me try it out?"
4. Someone sitting at a crossroads. Before him were two paths. One of them began in clear ground but ended in thorns. The other began

in thorns but ended in clear ground
5. A king had a field, which he handed over to tenant-farmers. The tenant-farmers began to steal the produce of the field that was owing to the king, so he took it from them and handed it over to their children
6. one said to his fellow, "I am going to sell you as a slave, to be delivered at some time in the future."
7. A man handed his son over to a teacher, who would take him about and show things to him and say to him, "All these trees are yours, all these vines are yours, all these olive trees are yours."
8. a reliable person was in a town, with whom everyone deposited their bailments for safe-keeping. When one of them would come to retrieve his property, the reliable man would produce and hand over the object, since he knew precisely where it was.
9. the king's butcher knows precisely how much the king is spending on his table

I see no traits that characterize the autonomous parables but not the tailor-made exegetical ones, nor even conventions to which they adhere. If there was a corpus of parables that circulated beyond documentary limits, I cannot point to the qualities that distinguish items in that corpus from the parables that are particular to documents.

To the compilers of Sifre to Deuteronomy, the exegetical parable presented a fine medium to advance the work of clarifying theological, but not Halakhic, messages of the book of Deuteronomy, and three-fourths of all the parables identified as such ("to what is the matter likened?") are devoted to that one task. That is so whether or not the *Nimshal* is articulated and matched to the *Mashal* in so many words. The parabolic conventions that transcend the particular exegetical cases before us generally involve the king/prince/ally/queen, in various commonplace relationships, but rarely can we reconstruct a considerable narrative account of those relationships. Once we have our king/prince/ally or king/queen, what happens to them or what they say or do generally proves fragmentary and not very illuminating. The lesson they embody turns out, even in the parables not particular to the exegetical setting, to emerge primarily within the exegetical setting for the purposes of which they have been adapted.

Song of Songs Rabbah

The whole of Song of Songs serves as a *Mashal* for God's and Israel's love for one another, which is why the Rabbinic sages adopted the Song in the canon. Given the task of the document—to articulate the parabolic character of the Torah's song, we cannot find surprising the compilers' systematic resort—fifty-six entries—to the exegetical parable as principal medium of their exposition. The question that once more engages us in the present context is, does the *Mashal* stand on its own, or does it require the exegetical context to bear specific meaning? At stake is the autonomy of the parable: does it represent writing distinct from documentary tasks but then adapted to the realization of those tasks? Or is the parable integral to the documentary writing of Song of Songs Rabbah in particular?[3]

---

[3] And along these same lines of Comparative Midrash, why does Lamentations Rabbah opt, among Rabbinic narrative types, for the authentic story rather than the parable. Its selection of parables is hardly comparable to that of Song of Songs Rabbah in volume or in documentary importance.

As in the Tannaite Midrash-compilations, so here too, the parable in Song of Songs Rabbah is more often an invention of the exegete of a particular passage than an adaptation by him of a ready-made narrative of exemplary quality. In three-fourths of the exegetical parables, the parabolic representations of relationships and transactions and even static similes respond to the exegetical tasks of a highly particular sort. Lest we doubt it, the *Nimshal* explicitly shows that they are linked to the accomplishment of those tasks. It follows from that persistent pattern that those items were written in the context of compiling this particular document. In one fourth of the whole, the matter is ambiguous, for reasons to be specified. These entries may or may not have responded to the tasks of compiling an exegetical exposition of Song of Songs Rabbah in particular.

In sum: 48 out of 59 parables, or 80%, assuredly originate within the framework of the documentary writing, and the other 20% may or may not undertake a comparable documentary task. Parabolic writing, like narrative writing, defined one of the media for the accomplishment of the tasks facing compilers of documents. If they drew upon a corpus of extra-documentary writing, e.g., broadly circulating parables, fully formed and available through a labor of adaptation, there is slight evidence in Song of Songs Rabbah to suggest so. Do the parables circulate independent of their documentary context? In approximately four-fifths of the instances, the parable is constructed in response to the case it is meant to clarify through a process of imaginative generalization. It is comprised therefore by the counterpart-players or counterpart-transactions set forth by the components of the verse subject to clarification and application. The parable then is integral to the exegetical process, applying the principle of the verse under discussion to exemplary cases. That is made explicit in the vast majority of instances.

Lamentations Rabbah

In Lamentations Rabbah the parable provides a subordinated medium of exegesis and exposition, eighteen in all against the document's forty-nine authentic stories, many of them elaborate and protracted. We find fourteen exegetical parables, a pair in the Halakhic realm occurs, and an unfamiliar utilization of the parable makes its appearance as well. When we recall that Song of Songs Rabbah required no fewer than fifty-six exegetical parables, but yielded only seven authentic narratives, none of them comparable to the massive constructions of Lamentations Rabbah, the picture is clear. The compilers of each document knew precisely what types of narratives they required to accomplish their purpose and deliver their message, and they accordingly subordinated the narrative to their documentary purposes.

A Diachronic View of the Parable: Three Propositions

The following generalizations emerge from the eight documents surveyed in this account of the parable.

1. The Parable Serves the Document and Responds to its Program: If we know the purpose of the document, we also can come to a fairly reliable prospect of how an authorship will find the parable useful and if so, how—in what form, for what purpose—it will serve. Halakhic documents choose the Halakhic parable, exegetical documents, the exegetical kind.

The Mishnah is principally a Halakhic statement, and the Mishnah's parables are similes that re-present Halakhic situations; they are not exegetical and they are not narrative. The Tosefta is a complex of types of writing and takes over but augments the Mishnah's repertoire. Tractate Abot uses parabolic materials to embody lessons of wisdom, and these ignore the marker, *Mashal*, but employ their own signal, "to what is he to be likened" without "A parable." The comparison then is to contrasting situations, If A, then X, if B, then Y. The Mishnah's similes meet their match in tractate Abot. Sifra finds use for both the Halakhic and the exegetical parable; Sifre to Numbers and its companion for Deuteronomy practically ignore the former and concentrate on the latter. Sifre to Deuteronomy in particular asks the exegetical parable to address broad, theological questions, with special reference to the Song of Moses at the end. Song of Songs Rabbah builds its many parables on Scripture's own generative parable, and Lamentations Rabbah assigns to parables a modest part of its burden, preferring another kind of narrative altogether.

The documents then present no uniformity in the type or use of parables. In each case we may correlate the type and use of parables with the documentary program in general. What about form-history, the diachronic perspective promised in the title of this book? So far as a form-history of the parable can be constructed, it forms a detail of the encompassing documentary history of forms; the parable has little autonomous standing beyond the boundaries of the documents that utilize the form for their distinctive purposes, signified, commonly, not only by topic but also by a particular choice of rhetoric, e.g., the Halakhic in one context, the exegetical in another.

2. The Parable Ordinarily, Though Not Always, Finds the Details of the *Mashal* in the Requirements of the *Nimshal*: That result is reinforced when we ask whence the parable to begin with: does it begin in the *Mashal*—the parable viewed autonomous of all particularity—or in the *Nimshal*—the point of contact between the parabolic narrative and its documentary occasion. Has the exegetical task provoked the formation of the simile and thus the parable, or did the parable take shape independent of the exegetical or Halakhic or theological or even biographical circumstance? The governing criterion is the question: is the parable in every last detail particular to the exegetical context, or is it necessary to adjust the parable to that context? We know that such a necessity comes into play when a detail of a parable proves superfluous, playing no role in the exposition of the base-verse or context. Overall, then, the answer to the question for our documents is, the expository task, defined by the *Nimshal*, whether Halakhic or exegetical, most of the time—75–80% of the sample—defines the program and traits of the parable. In constructing parables the exegetical task is primary, the construction of a pertinent, illuminating simile only secondary and derivative. We find little evidence that permits us to describe an autonomous corpus of narratives awaiting the parabolic vocation: stories of general motif awaiting case-by-case particularization.

3. Not "the Parable," an Autonomous Literary Genre, but Parabolic Writing, Part of, and Just Another Option in, the Composition of the Document: On its own, then, the *Mashal* has no form-history autonomous of the canonical documents. The diachronic approach yields evidence for testing a null hypothesis. What should we have anticipated were the *Mashal* to form an independent genre of writing? It is writing that we do not find in abundance in any of our documents: writing adapted for the particular setting but not a comfortable fit in that setting. For the opposite, the governing hypothesis, what we should have expected if the *Mashal* is defined by its documentary context is what has turned up, both in general and in detail: ample evidence that most of the time, if not always, the *Mashal* forms the outcome of the *Nimshal*.

There is no evidence of a vast, free-floating corpus of similes and exemplary narratives, snatched from on high and adapted to local purposes. Rather, we find the evidence of a mode of thought and expression, involving similes and metaphors of transactions. In the formation of most, though not all, exegetical parables in our documents, the generative force derives not from the fixed conventions of the abstract players, the king, the prince but from the transactions they embody, and these transactions are particular to the verse under study as set forth by the Rabbinic exegetes. Like chess pieces, the nameless kings and princes and queens are moved hither and yon, to reconstitute a relationship or a transaction in terms analogous to mathematical symbols: purely abstract, very precise.

The marker, *Mashal* on its own, outside of particular documentary settings, bears no fixed, universal traits of substance, only of form: the signal stands for itself, the context—the task defined by the composition of which the *Mashal* forms a principal part— defines all else, and the documents determine the context for most of their various compositions. Then is there no fixed corpus of stories, traveling here and there and serving diverse tasks? What collections of parables prove is that in detail, where it matters, there is none. What we see here is that, transcending documentary lines, more often than not, is simply the pattern, "There was a king who. . . ." The rest of the differentiated *Mashal*, e.g., ". . . had such and so," "who said such and such," "who did so and so"—with the result that such and such happened—all that realizes the *Mashal* in its specificity and context in most though not all instances proves particular to the specific context, not characteristic of the *Mashal* wherever it surfaces. The conception that a corpus of stories (parables) or fixed, conventional comparisons (similes, metaphors) surfaced promiscuously to be adapted for the use of a particular piece of writing finds little support but much contrary evidence in the repertoire of cases we have examined in documentary sequence.

So we cannot speak of the Parable, a fixed corpus of narratives that make their way hither and yon through the far reaches of a single, unitary "Rabbinic tradition," ignoring the lines of documentary boundaries. We can only differentiate by documents and consequently speak of how diverse documentary authorships in realizing their program and its tasks resorted, where they did, to the signal, *Mashal*. What then does the marker, *Mashal*, signal? The advent of some sort of static simile or dynamic metaphorical narrative, which will be brief, anecdotal, and abstract.

That signal never alludes to particular transactions or events, that is, invoking a specific moment in Israel's history to clarify another such moment. It homogenizes, humanizes, through concretization and particularization. When a king or other principal player is named, the signal, *Ma'aseh*, is invoked, and *Mashal* is not, even though the narrative that follows is indistinguishable in its indicative qualities from a *Mashal*. Common to all *Meshalim* in the Rabbinic corpus then are only some few rules of writing. These include one that is fixed: the signal, *Mashal*, never deals with determinate actors, e.g., named kings, queens, and princes and princesses, only with shadowy "there was a king" and his wife, the queen, his son or daughter.

The Precedent and the Parable in Diachronic View and the Documentary Hypothesis

The fulcrum of interpretation and analysis, for narrative as much as for all other kinds of canonical writing in formative Judaism, is the document. Narratives no less than expository, exegetical, and analytical writing, form part of the documentary self-definition of the Rabbinic canonical writings. The fulcrum of interpretation and analysis, for narrative as much as for all other kinds of canonical writing in formative Judaism, therefore is the document. It is analytically meaningless to talk about "the Rabbinic story" or "the Rabbinic narrative" or "the Rabbinic parable" or "the Aggadah" or "the Rabbinic folk-tale" or any comparable, generic category that ignores documentary boundaries. The principal, and prim-ary, analytical initiative commences with the document—the traits of its corpus of narratives.[4]

So the *Ma'aseh* and the *Mashal*, the precedent and the parable, change places in the unfolding in ordinal sequence of the eight documents probed here. The precedent begins subject to precise definition of form and function but loses particularity later on, and the proverb starts off serving a variety of purposes but later on comes to focus on some few, well-differentiated ones, which it serves with great effect. But that shift corresponds not only, or not mainly, to the ordinal sequence of the documents—first the Mishnah, then the Tosefta, then Sifra and the two Sifres, finally the Rabbah-Midrash-compilations. Rather, it corresponds to the character of the documentary assignments, the Mishnah and the Tosefta requiring a Halakhic form, the precedent, with its clearly defined, Sitz-im-Leben, for a Halakhic function, and the Midrash-exegetical compilations seeking an Aggadic form, the parable, with its power of universalization and concretization at the same time, for a Midrash-exegetical function. The curious insistence of the framers of Sifre to Deuteronomy that the parable serve only Aggadic-exegetical purposes and never intervene in the Halakhic expositions covering Deuteronomy 12–26, makes sense in this context.

The diachronic view of the precedent and the parable is readily stated. The precedent, well-defined and used with precision in the earlier, Halakhic documents of our probe, loses its particular functional definition in the later, Aggadic ones, and ultimately, the marker, *Ma'aseh*, comes to signal everything and its opposite. It also loses importance and becomes random and haphazard. The parable, rare and not fully articulated in the earlier, Halakhic documents, gains particularity and precise definition in the later, Aggadic-exegetical ones, and ultimately is differentiated and richly instantiated in precisely the document where parabolic thinking permeates. The two forms change places, the one deemed most useful in Halakhic discourse losing currency in the Aggadic compilations, and the one natural to Aggadic-exegetical purposes—how better explain a theological or ethical proposition than by appeal to a concrete, exemplary case conveyed as an abstract narrative to a universal audience?—gaining in prominence and utility, hence in precision and consistent differentiation.

Rabbinic narratives, represented by the precedent and the parable, respond to the documentary program and policy of the authorships that employ them. The result is easily summed up: the *Ma'aseh*, a Halakhic

---

[4] We may therefore speak of the narrative such as a parable (*Mashal*) or a case/precedent (*Ma'aseh*) in the Mishnah or the Tosefta or Sifra or one or another of the Midrash-compilations or of the Talmuds, and only then ask how the *Mashal* or *Ma'aseh* as represented by the one document compares or contrasts with that set forth in another. And that is the fact, even though a given narrative may serve the purposes of more than a single document. I discuss the fact that some few compositions move from document to document in *Extra- and Non-Documentary Writing in the Canon of Formative Judaism. I. The Pointless Parallel: Hans-Jürgen Becker and the Myth of the Autonomous Tradition in Rabbinic Documents* (Binghamton, 2001); *Extra- and Non-Documentary Writing in the Canon of Formative Judaism. II. Paltry Parallels. The Negligible Proportion and Peripheral Role of Free-Standing Compositions in Rabbinic Documents* (Binghamton 2001); *Extra- and Non-Documentary Writing in the Canon of Formative Judaism. III. Peripatetic Parallels* (Binghamton, 2001; second edition, revised, of *The Peripatetic Saying: The Problem of the Thrice-Told Tale in Talmudic Literature* [Chico, 1985].

form, is the form of choice of Halakhic documents, and the *Mashal*, an Aggadic-exegetical form, is the narrative form of choice of Midrash-exegetical ones. Within the documentary hypothesis for the analysis of the canonical documents of formative Rabbinic Judaism, that result stands to reason. But it contradicts the hypothesis that documentary lines do not make a difference, and documentary boundaries bear no significance.[5]

JACOB NEUSNER
Bard College

Pentateuchal Targums as Midrash

The most popular biblical books for translating into Aramaic, those of the Pentateuch, were translated in at least three different types of targums. The first is Targum Onqelos, probably composed in the land of Israel in the first or second century C.E. It became widely known among the Babylonian rabbis in later centuries and is cited as authoritative in the Babylonian Talmud, where it is referred to as "our targum."

The second type is known as the Palestinian Targum, of which several versions are known. The original was probably composed between the second and fourth centuries, although scholars have given both earlier and later dates. The most important versions of the Palestinian Targum are: 1) Targum Neofiti, discovered in the 1950s, which constitutes the only remaining Palestinian Targum with a complete translation of all five biblical books; 2) the targum fragments from the Cairo Geniza, which provide evidence of seven further manuscripts of the Palestinian Targum, probably complete when written, but now extant in only a few fragments; 3) several known types of Fragment Targum, the most well known of which are the manuscripts in Paris and the Vatican that contain verses, partial verses, and *lemmata* taken from complete versions of the Palestinian Targum. While not always exactly the same, these representatives of the Palestinian Targum are closely related.

The third type of Pentateuchal Targum is known as Targum Pseudo-Jonathan or the Targum attributed to Jonathan b. Uzziel. Providing an essentially complete rendering of the five Pentateuchal books, Pseudo-Jonathan is a mixed targum; it clearly borrows from both Targum Onqelos and the Palestinian Targum, but it also contains a large amount of distinctive material.

All three types of Pentateuchal Targums are related to each other, with shared features and content. Since all three seem to have been composed in the land of Israel, they can be called the "Targums of Israel."

---

[5] In the following I respond to critics in a systematic fashion: *The Documentary Foundation of Rabbinic Culture. Mopping Up after Debates with Gerald L. Bruns, S.J.D. Cohen, Arnold Maria Goldberg, Susan Handelman, Christine Hayes, James Kugel, Peter Schaefer, Eliezer Segal, E.P. Sanders, and Lawrence H. Schiffman* (Atlanta, 1995); *Are the Talmuds Interchangeable? Christine Hayes's Blunder* (Atlanta, 1996); *Judaic Law from Jesus to the Mishnah. A Systematic Reply to Professor E.P. Sanders* (Atlanta, 1993); *Are There Really Tannaitic Parallels to the Gospels? A Refutation of Morton Smith* (Atlanta, 1993); *Why There Never Was a "Talmud of Caesarea." Saul Lieberman's Mistakes* (Atlanta, 1994); *James Kugel in Canon and Connection: Intertextuality in Judaism* (Lanham, 1986); *Midrash as Literature: The Primacy of Documentary Discourse* (Lanham, 1987).

Targum as Midrash

The midrashic form found in the Pentateuchal Targums can be termed "hidden midrash," insofar as the targums' composers hid their exegesis within a literal translation of the biblical text. The result was to create an interpretation that is read as Scripture itself and so has the sacred standing of Scripture rather than the lower standing of a human creation. How did the Targums of Israel achieve this? They did it in the way they developed and then combined two separate midrashic components, literal translation and added interpretation.

The Pentateuchal Targums' translations are literal. As A. Samely observed, "In principle, all wording elements of Scripture are *also* in Targum, in translational or non-translational transformation."[1] Thus, as I have put it elsewhere, "The most persistent of Neofiti's modes [of literal translation] is its careful replication into Aramaic of the morphological, grammatical and syntactic elements of the Hebrew in the same order as the Hebrew text. Neofiti persistently places verbs, nouns, adjectives, adverbs, conjunctions, etc. into its translation in the location corresponding to their place in the Hebrew text."[2] This one-to-one formal correspondence takes place not only at the level of the word, but within the word as well, namely, in the constituent parts that make up Hebrew words, such as prefixes, suffixes, and even roots.

Sometimes the word-for-word correspondence keeps the Hebrew text's grammatical character but alters its semantics through substitution. For example, the Aramaic text occasionally replaces obscure Hebrew terms with current terminology, it sometimes replaces objectionable words with acceptable ones, and the like. But it is not an overstatement to claim that approximately 80% to 90% of the linguistic information found in the Hebrew text is replicated in the targum. This highly literal translation, with its substitutions, forms one component of the targum's hidden midrash.

A second component of the Pentateuchal Targums is expansions, that is, interpretations found within the translation. This interpretive material may be as small as a word or short phrase or as large as a sentence or sometimes even a paragraph or two. It appears in no regular order or placement. Several expansions may occur within the space of a few verses, or the translation may proceed for several chapters without any significant additions at all. These additions have sometimes enticed scholars to describe the targum as "paraphrastic." But this is inaccurate, since paraphrase intends to reproduce the sense or meaning of the original. Since the targumic expansions do not reflect any linguistic element in the Hebrew text, they do not fit the definition of paraphrase. The targumic approach thus cannot be described by the classic Aristotelian dichotomy of literal vs. paraphrastic translation. The targums' additional material, rather, is "midrash," and it is the link between it and the literal translation that yields a hidden form of midrash.

The final step in describing the targum's hidden midrash lies in the relationship between the two formal components of literal translation and additional material. The expansions are placed into the translation in a way that hides them within the text's flow. That is, the targumists provide no indication of when non-translational material is placed into the translation. Indeed, they place it into the translation with care so

---

[1] A. Samely, "Scripture's Segments and Topicality in Rabbinic Discourse and the Pentateuch Targum," in *Journal for the Aramaic Bible* 1:1 (1999), pp. 87–124, quote from p. 104. Italics are Samely's.

[2] P.V.M. Flesher, "Targum as Scripture," in P.V.M. Flesher, ed., *Targum and Scripture: Studies in Aramaic Translation and Interpretation in Memory of Ernest G. Clarke* (Leiden, 2002), pp. 61–78, quote from p. 65.

that its presence may go unnoticed. Sometimes expansions are interwoven with the translation so that the text moves back and forth from one to the other every few words. Other times, when a large insertion is placed into the text, the beginning and end are linked to the translation, so that the addition fits into the original story. The form of these larger expansions usually adheres to formats found in Scripture itself, as A. Samely has observed. Only a few have forms similar to those found in Rabbinic midrash (see below).[3]

Modern readers of the targums might easily overlook the "hidden" character of targumic midrash, for they regularly read the Targum against the Hebrew text of Scripture, which makes the existence of midrash elements obvious. Similarly, modern translations of a targum always point out the non-translational words and passages. But most Jews of the land of Israel in the Rabbinic period who heard the targum in the synagogue lacked ready access to the Hebrew text. Few could read at all, hand-copied texts were expensive and not readily available, and, since Aramaic was their native language, most lacked extensive knowledge of Hebrew or the Hebrew text. For them, the content of the Targums of Israel *was* the content of the Pentateuch. The interpretation hidden within the targum comprised Scripture as much as did the literal translation.

Comparative Midrash

To better understand how the hidden midrash of the Targums of Israel constitutes a distinctive approach to scriptural exegesis, it is helpful to compare them to two well-known categories of midrash from the Second-Temple and Rabbinic periods, specifically, Rabbinic midrash and the Rewritten Bible. We examine, first, the contrasts that emerge in an examination of each of the three aspects of Rabbinic midrash pointed out by J. Neusner, who notes that the term Midrash can refer to: 1) a written unit of scriptural exegesis—i.e., a write-up of exegesis of a biblical verse or verses; 2) a compilation or book of these written exegetical units; and 3) a process of interpretation or hermeneutic approach.[4]

1) G. Porton states: "Rabbinic midrash refers to a literary phenomenon—the juxtaposition of Rabbinic statements with the biblical text in a way that suggests that the latter is intimately related to the former."[5] This definition contains two important features. First, it notes that there are two distinct parts to the form: Scripture and the "Rabbinic statements" or interpretations. Second, these distinct components are related in an intimate manner. Midrashic form juxtaposes the two parts, both to enhance their separate character and to point to the relationship between them. Rabbinic midrash thus explicitly emphasizes that interpretation is interpretation and carefully links it to the Scriptural passage it interprets, thereby specifying the object of the interpretation.

Comparing this to what we find in the targums highlights targumic interpretation's hidden character. While Rabbinic midrash carefully distinguishes the interpretation from the biblical text, the targums do not. While Rabbinic midrash always joins an interpretation to the passage being interpreted, because the interpretation's separate character would otherwise be lost, the targum subsumes the interpretation

---

[3] Samely, "Scripture's Segments," p. 105.
[4] J. Neusner, *What is Midrash?* (Philadelphia, 1987), chapter one.

[5] G. Porton, *Understanding Rabbinic Midrash* (Hoboken, 1985), pp. 4–5.

within its scriptural translation in order to hide its separate nature. To further achieve this goal, targums normally cast their interpretations in forms of expression found in Scripture itself, quite different from the Rabbinic midrash's use of inherently non-biblical forms of expression.

2) Neusner notes that the term midrash refers to collections of written midrashic units that have been selected, collected, and organized by an editor into a book. Notably, while books of Rabbinic midrash are clearly collections of interpretations and cannot be mistaken for anything else, Pentateuchal Targums are outwardly translations, not interpretations at all. Their organization as continuous renderings of the biblical text helps hide the fact that they contain interpretation.

Along these same lines, other differences between targums and Rabbinic midrash stand out. First, a midrash's editor chooses the criterion by which to organize the book. While Scripture's order is often primary, works such as Pirqe d'Rabbi Eliezer show that, unlike in the case of a targum, it need not be. Furthermore, Neusner has shown that the Talmuds and midrashim share an organizational principle.[6] But the targumist had no such flexibility; a targum's organization must follow that of the biblical book being translated.

Second, the editor of a midrash compilation is free not to comment on sections of the biblical text. Even when the midrashist chooses to follow Scripture's order, he often leaves out verses. In some midrashim, such as Genesis Rabbah, the compilation only looks at a few selected verses, with most of the book being left out completely. The targumim, at least during the Rabbinic period, in principle leave out none of the book being translated. Their careful rendering moves word-by-word through the text. It is not until the medieval period that targums begin to be formed through a process of selection. Thus we find the Fragment Targums and Festival Collections extracted from earlier targums. As books, then, the targums and the midrashim of the Rabbinic period not only look different but are organized on the basis of completely different criteria. The targum, as a translation, hides the interpretive material within its overall form.

3) The third use of the term midrash identifies a distinctive process of interpretation, that is, a mode of analysis or hermeneutic procedure by which exegesis is undertaken. We find explicitly identified modes of interpretation, such as the *qal v'homer* or some other of the Middot, as well as other unidentified approaches. In Rabbinic midrash, such modes of analysis are often explicitly identified within the exegetical unit itself, so that the process of—indeed, the fact of—interpretation is made explicit. In the targums, by contrast, with only rare exceptions, the process of interpretation is not identified but is hidden by the targum's organization.

All three uses of the term midrash thus reveal the extent to which midrash is an overtly interpretative enterprise, a fact that stands in contrast to the interpretation found hidden within the Pentateuchal Targums. But there is more to this story. At issue is how these formal features also define the interpretation's status as authoritative within the community of believers.

In Rabbinic midrash, the relationship between Scripture and Rabbinic interpretation gives the latter a high status. By linking the interpretation to Scripture in a privileged position—that is, by having it say what the Scripture passage means—the Rabbinic comment becomes *like* Scripture. The formal distinction between the comment and Scripture itself prevents the comment from *becoming* Scripture, but the

---

[6] J. Neusner, *Midrash in Context: Exegesis in Formative Judaism* (Philadelphia, 1983), pp. 65–69 and 107–110.

relationship binding the two gives the interpretation a status *nearly* equal to that of the Holy text. In a midrash compilation, where this identification happens over and over again, even the form of the interpretation takes on this high status. Once the midrashic form becomes authoritative, whenever the form appears the interpretation automatically becomes authoritative as well.

The authoritative status of Rabbinic interpretation contains a further, social, dimension. Here, interpretative comments regularly are enhanced by the naming of the interpreter, nearly always a rabbi who is identified as such. This identification associates the interpretation with a person and a class. Thus, the Rabbinic movement gains status by creating or citing the interpretation and recording it in their names. The status Scripture gives to the interpretation is transferred to the interpreter and the interpreter's class, the rabbis. Rabbinic midrash thereby enhances the status of the Rabbinic movement. In Neusner's characterization, Scripture, as Torah, lends its true interpretation the status of Torah, which in turn is conferred upon the interpreters, identifying the rabbis as the embodiment of Torah.[7]

The hidden midrash of the Targums of Israel accomplishes both more and less than this. On the one hand, it achieves more because it gives the interpretation an even higher status than that attained by Rabbinic midrash; hidden midrash becomes Scripture itself. By incorporating the interpretation into its exacting rendering of the scriptural text and by formulating the interpretation's relationship to the translation so as to hide its character as interpretation, the targum defines the interpretation as Scripture. But it does so at a cost. By becoming Scripture, the interpretation loses its character as interpretation. It can no longer easily be recognized as such.

On the other hand, hidden midrash achieves less because, by losing its identification as interpretation, it cannot transfer its status to other interpretations. The category of hidden midrash cannot attain status, that is, since it is not even recognized. Thus, while Rabbinic midrash can attain an authoritative status, the hidden midrash of the targums cannot. It is only to the extent that it is seen as Scripture itself that it has status as Scripture. Furthermore, since hidden midrash is not recognized as interpretation, there can be no identified interpreters. While Rabbinic midrash confers a status onto its interpreters, the targums' hidden midrash does not. Hidden midrash's formal character has no social ramifications.

Rewritten Bible

We turn now to our comparison of the targums and the midrashic approach known as Rewritten Bible, a term coined by G. Vermes to identify a type of composition exemplified by Josephus' *Jewish Antiquities*, Pseudo-Philo's *Biblical Antiquities*, the Genesis Apocryphon from Qumran, Jubilees, and Sefer Ha-Yashar. While Vermes included the Palestinian Targums in this category, a comparison of the targums to the other texts makes clear that the targums' hidden midrash does not belong in this group.

Vermes described Rewritten Bible this way: "In order to anticipate questions, and to solve problems in advance, the midrashist inserts haggadic development into the biblical narrative."[8] On the one hand, the inserted "haggadic development" of the

---

[7] J. Neusner, *Torah: From Scroll to Symbol in Formative Judaism* (Philadelphia, 1985), pp. 140–144, and idem, *Midrash in Context*, pp. 136–137.

[8] G. Vermes, "Life of Abraham (1)—Haggadic Development: A Retrogressive Historical Study," in G. Vermes, *Scripture and Tradition in Judaism* (Leiden, 1973), p. 95.

Rewritten Bible sounds like the added interpretations found in the Palestinian Targum; this perhaps led Vermes to place the targums in this classification. On the other hand, Vermes states that the haggadic material is placed into the "biblical narrative." If we set aside the targums for a moment and examine the other texts of the Rewritten Bible, we find that "narrative" is a key term, for it is the biblical *story* rather than the biblical *text* into which these insertions are made. Neither Josephus' *Antiquities*, the Genesis Apocryphon, nor any other of these documents shows significant interest in the biblical text as a *text*. Their interest in Scripture is as the source of the stories, i.e., the narrative, they then retell and enhance. To be sure, Rewritten Bible texts occasionally use the wording of a passage of scripture, but never enough to suggest that it is the text *qua* text they are interested in. Usually, when the books of Rewritten Bible follow Scripture's story closely, they do so in their own words. So rather than using the biblical text as a place in which to hide interpretation, as the Pentateuchal Targums do, the Rewritten Bible follows Scripture's narrative—even while ignoring its text—and uses that scriptural narrative as the structure for its retelling or expanding on the biblical tale. Given Rewritten Bible's ignoring of the Hebrew text, the Pentateuchal Targums do not belong to that category.

The hidden midrash of the Pentateuchal Targums constitutes a distinctive form of midrash. Its key characteristics differentiate it from the midrashic forms of Rabbinic midrash and Rewritten Bible. It is the only type of midrash that brings Scripture and interpretation together in such a way as to conceal the interpretation within a representation of Scripture's texts.

Literary Character

The literary character of the targums and their hidden midrash reflects the key components of its form, literal translation and added interpretations. To fully understand how these two components comprise hidden midrash, we examine several examples drawn from the Balaam story (Num. 22–24) as found in Targum Neofiti.[9] Roman typeface indicates Aramaic renderings that directly translate the Hebrew text; italics indicates non-translational material.

Literal Translation

The key aspect of literal translation, as observed above, is the targum's ideal of providing an Aramaic equivalent to all grammatical, syntactical, and semantic information in the Hebrew text. This means that the targum essentially comprises a hyperliteral translation that may sometimes contain word-for-word substitutions (i.e., equivalent information). This provides the narrative and literary context in which the additional material can be hidden. Num. 22:14–17 provides a look at such translation over several verses:

> (14) And the princes of the *Moabites* rose and came to Balak and said: "Balaam refused to come with us." (15) And again, Balak sent *messengers*, more

---

[9] The translations of Targum Neofiti are based on M. McNamara, *Targum Neofiti 1: Numbers* (Collegeville, 1995), while those of the Hebrew text are based on the RSV and JPS translations.

numerous and honorable than they. (16) And they came to Balaam and said to him, "Thus says Balak, the son of Zippor: 'Let nothing withhold you, now, from coming to me; (17) for I will surely honor you greatly, and whatever you say to me I will do; and come, now, curse this people for me.'"

Of all the words in these four verses, only two do not follow an exactingly literal rendering of the Hebrew. The first is the word "Moabites," which the targumist has used in a plural, personalized form instead of singular form "Moab" found in the Hebrew. The second constitutes a substitution. In v. 15, instead of giving the Hebrew's "princes," as in v. 14, the translator substitutes the term "messengers." Apart from these two words, Neofiti provides a careful rendition that replicates the linguistic information in the original. Another example of straight translation comes from Num. 22:20–23:

(20) And the *Memra of the Lord was revealed* to Balaam at night and said to him, "If the men have come to call you, rise, go with them; but only the word which I speak with you, that shall you do." (21) And Balaam arose in the morning and *prepared* his donkey and went with the princes of the *Moabites*. (22) And the *Lord's* anger was kindled because he went; and the angel of the Lord placed himself in the way to impede him. And he was riding on his donkey and his two young men were with him. (23) And the donkey saw the angel of the Lord standing in the road with a sword unsheathed in his hand; and the donkey turned aside and went into the open field; and Balaam struck the donkey to direct it into the road.

These four verses provide another highly literal rendering of the Hebrew text. There are four substitutions. In v. 21, the specific Hebrew term "saddled" is replaced by a more general Aramaic one, "prepared;" and the Hebrew "Moab" is again replaced by "Moabites." In v. 22, instead of the Hebrew's "God" (*elohim*), the word "Lord" (represented by three *yods*) appears. In v. 20, anti-anthropomorphic substitutions occur, a common feature of the targums. First, "*memra*" ("word") appears as an intermediary for God. Thus it is the *memra*, not God himself, who appears to Balaam and talks to him. Second, the passive tense, "was revealed," is used. This way, neither God nor his *memra* are said to act in a physical way. Both approaches to translating anthropomorphism occur frequently in the targums and are considered standard translation techniques of the targumist, although they certainly have theological implications as well. Despite such minor changes, we see in these verses the character of the targum's straight translation. The targums painstakingly renders each piece of linguistic information, either directly or through one-for-one substitution.

Hiding the Additional Interpretation

Scholars have identified three main ways in which interpretations are added into the Pentateuchal Targums' literal translation: the interwoven expansion, the inserted expansion, and the free structured rendering. We illustrate each in turn.

The interwoven expansion weaves the additional material into the translation, alternating between translation of the Hebrew text and the added interpretation every few words. Often the interpretation's words are simply interspersed between the words of the translation, but sometimes they substitute for the translation. Num. 23:21 of Targum Neofiti contains both types of interweaving, interspersing and substituting. The Masoretic text is given first for comparison.

Num. 23:21 (MT)
1. He has not beheld wickedness in Jacob;
2. nor has he seen trouble in Israel.
3. The Lord their God is with them,
4. and the trumpeting of a king is among them.

Num. 23:21 (TN)
1. *I see no servants* of falsehood in *those of the house of* Jacob,
2. and no *servants of foreign worship* in *those of the house of* Israel;
3. *the Memra of* the Lord their God is with them,
4. and the trumpeting *of the splendor of the glory of their* king *is a shield above* them.

The opening parts of lines 1 and 2 are both substitutions, which replace the Hebrew text. This is also the case for the final words of line 4. But the remaining non-translational material is inserted into the translation. The targumist carefully alternates between the translation and the additions, weaving them together into a single sentence that flows unbrokenly and that carries a clear meaning. Another example of the interwoven expansion appear at Num. 24:1:

Num. 24:1 (MT)
1. When Balaam saw that it was good in the eyes of the Lord to bless Israel,
2. he did not go, as at other times, to read the omens,
3. but set his face toward the desert.

Num. 24:1 (TN)
1. And Balaam saw that it was good *before* the Lord to bless Israel,
2. and he did not go towards diviners as *he used to go on every occasion, to consult through ghosts*,
3. but *he went and* set his face towards the desert *and recalled for them the affair of the calf.*

The italics in the translation of Targum Neofiti indicates where the non-translational interpretation appears. In line 2, the Aramaic phrase "as he used to go on every occasion" replaces the Hebrew's "as at other times." The remaining additional material in lines two and three are placed there through interweaving. Again, it is evident how the targumist has skillfully woven the translation and expansion material into a single sentence, which flows without a break or interruption. It is easy to see how the interwoven expansion hides the midrash within the translation.

The second type of hidden midrash is the inserted interpretation. Insertions can be short, consisting of six or seven words or even fewer. Or they can be much longer, containing more than a hundred words. While the small insertions appear quite frequently, the larger ones are less common. Num. 24:14 provides a clear example of a short insertion:

Num. 24:14 (MT)
1. And now, behold, I am going to my people;
2. come, I will advise you
3. what this people will do to your people in the last days.

Num. 24:14 (TN)
1. And now, behold, I am going to my people;
2. come, I will give you advice;
2a. *cause them to sin, otherwise you will not be able to rule them;*
3. *however, in the future* these people *are to rule* over your people at *the end of* the last days.

Neofiti's third line (2a) clearly is an insertion. It translates no specific words in the Hebrew text. It is placed carefully, however, so that it fits into the narrative around it. In line 2, Balaam tells Balak to listen to his advice, and the targum's insertion in line 2a is simply part of that advice. The topic of that insertion, one people's ruling over another, is continued into the interwoven expansion of line 4. A second short insertion appears in the next verse, Num. 24:15:

Num. 24:15 (MT)
1. And he took up his discourse and said,
2. The utterance of Balaam the son of Beor,
3. the utterance of the man whose eye is opened.

Num. 24:15 (TN)
1. And he took up his *prophecy* in a discourse and said:
2. the speech of Balaam, the son of Beor,
3. the speech of the man *who is more honored than his father;*
4. *what was hidden from all the prophets has been revealed to him.*

In Num. 24:15, the insertion comes at the end of the verse; it consists of the end of line 3 and all of line 4. The insertion has been placed into the text so as not to interrupt the flow of the sentence, and indeed the insertion conforms well to the translation preceding it and seems naturally to be a continuation of it. Unlike the previous verse, where the insertion was simply placed into the text, here in Num. 24:15 its beginning eliminates several words of the Hebrew. So although it is composed to be hidden in the sentence's flow, it rides roughshod over the translational materials.

Long insertions usually follow the same formal guidelines as shorter ones. This passage is carefully placed in the translation without disturbing the rendering of the original text on either side:

Num. 22:30 (MT)
1. And the donkey said to Balaam
2. "Am I not your donkey, upon which you have ridden from your formation until this day? Was I ever accustomed to do so to you?" And he said, "no."

Num. 22:30 (TN)
1. And the donkey said to Balaam,
1a. *"Where are you going, wicked Balaam? You lack understanding! What! If you are not able to curse me who am an unclean beast, and die in this world and who do not enter the world to come, how much less are you able to curse the sons of Abraham, of Isaac and Jacob, on whose account the world was created from the beginning, and for whose merits it is remembered before them? And with regard to your having taken undue advantage of these men (saying): This is not my donkey; she is borrowed:*
2. "Am I not your donkey upon which you have ridden from your *youth* until this day? Have I ever *intended* to do so to you?" And he said, "no."

The long addition (1a) has the donkey make an important theological point and relate an instruction from God, telling Balaam that he cannot curse Israel. The end of the expansion then shifts into a comment that enables the expansion to segue into the translation of the biblical text. Indeed, the expansion sets up a biblical remark and thus links the expansion back into the translation. Thus the end of the expansion flows into the targum's rendering of the biblical text, again hiding the joint between the two types of material.

The third form of targumic addition is free structured rendering. This form follows the shape, or structure, of the biblical verse, using key words from it at specific points but taking a free approach to the verse's meaning and ignoring most of its wording. This form appears frequently in the rendering of Hebrew poetic texts. Rather than attempt to render the poetry outright—a difficult task—the targumist structures his rendering on the Hebrew text, using it as a touch-point for his own ideas. In the Targums of Israel, the resulting rendering is often prophetic, whether or not the Hebrew verse is. Here is an example from Num. 24:6.

Num. 24:6 (MT)
1. Like torrents that stretch afar,
2. like gardens beside a river,
3. like aloes that the Lord has planted,
4. like cedar trees beside the waters.

Num. 24:6 (TN)
1. Like *overflowing* torrents, *so shall Israel overflow on your enemies.*
2. Like gardens *planted* beside *sources of water, so shall their cities be producing sages and son of the Torah.*
3. Like *the heavens <which God has spread out> as the house of his Shekinah, so shall Israel live and endure forever beautiful and praised,*
4. and like the water cedars, *praised and exalted among his creatures.*

Each of the four lines of the Aramaic rendering begins like the Hebrew, with the word "like" followed by a noun. In lines 1, 2, and 4, the targum uses the same (first) noun as the Hebrew text. Only line 3 has a different noun altogether, "aloe" trees in the Hebrew and "the heavens" in the Aramaic. However, once the targum replicates that form, it follows its own interests, which have nothing to do with the original Hebrew. Only the Hebrew's repeated "like + noun" shapes the targum's structure, while its approach to the rest of the verse is free form. The first half of Num. 23:9 provides another example of this approach:

Num. 23:9a (MT)
1. For from the top of the mountain I see him,
2. From the hills I behold him.

Num. 23:9a (TN)
1. For I see *this people being led and coming in the merits of the just fathers who are comparable to the* mountains, *Abraham, Isaac and Jacob;*
2. and *for the merits of the just mothers who are comparable to the* hills, *Sarah, Rebecca, Rachel and Leah.*

In this verse, the targum identifies the words "mountains" and "hills" as the key terms. It keeps to the two-part, two-phrase structure of the Hebrew text and begins with the opening word "for." The targumist also take the verb "to see," which appears at the end of each phrase, and places it at the opening of the verse. Using the structure of the Hebrew text in this way, the targum freely brings in his point about the source of Israel's strength, the merit of the patriarchs and matriarchs.

Literary Artistry

Individual instances of hidden midrash frequently appear by themselves, inserted in a translation without any referent beyond their immediate location. But often the targumist uses a number of different expansions to reshape a story, to give it a different point, and/or to teach lessons not in the biblical narrative. By strategically hiding the interpretations at key locations in a story, the targumist can change important elements of the story while at the same time providing a highly literal rendering of its text.

The story of Balaam in Num. 22–24, from which we have illustrated individual types of hidden midrash, also exemplifies this more literary form of hidden midrash. First, Scripture's rather neutral depiction of Balaam's character is transformed in the Palestinian Targums into the picture of a truly wicked person. He personally desires to curse Israel rather than simply to act as Balak's hired man. When he is thwarted in his attempt to curse Israel and instead blesses them, Balaam advises Balak to "cause Israel to sin." Second, once Balaam is depicted as wishing to curse Israel, God's role and power in the story is emphasized. God does not merely overrule Balak's instructions but takes over Balaam's powers as a prophet and turns them to God's purpose. Third, specific interpretations refer to each other and help heighten narrative tension. In Num. 23:21, for example, God causes Balaam to prophesy that he sees no idolatry or foreign worship among the people Israel. But in Num. 24:1, Balaam himself brings up Israel's worship of the Golden Calf, thereby seeming to contradict the earlier declaration of their righteousness.

Even when a story is not extensively reshaped by hidden midrash, a key point may be added through the repetition of an interpretation within it. Targum Neofiti does this within the tale of Jacob's stay with Laban. In the early years of the twenty-one-year visit, Laban's sons observe that Jacob's presence has made the water in the wells remain consistently high (Gen. 29:22). At the end of the story, they know Jacob has left because the water level goes down (Gen. 31:22). Similarly, Targum Pseudo-Jonathan adds two related interpretations to the story of Jethro's visit to Moses. In Exod. 18:6, Jethro comes to Moses in order to become a proselyte. At the end of the story, Jethro leaves for his own people in order to make them proselytes (Exod. 18:27).

Repetition of interpretations even happens in different stories of the Pentateuchal Targums. In Gen. 3:25, for example, Targum Neofiti states that when the sons of Eve—implying the people Israel—study Torah and keep the commandments, they triumph over the adversary of the snake. This formula is repeated in Gen. 27:40, where it is explicitly applied to Jacob's descendants in terms of their adversary Esau: when the sons of Jacob study Torah, they triumph over Esau's descendants. The same formulaic promise appears in Deut. 32:14 and 33:29-30. In another instance of this characteristic of hidden midrash, Deut. 2:6 mentions a well of water that follows the people Israel while they journey towards the Promised Land. This same well appears in Deut. 32:10.

These are only the most obvious ways that the Targums of Israel use hidden midrash beyond the context of a single verse. Targumists repeatedly use hidden midrash in narrative artistry to reshape and even recreate many of the biblical tales and their emphases.

The Sources of the Targums of Israel

As a book, each Targum of Israel was treated differently from the others. In Babylonia, the *text* of Targum Onqelos became important, with much attention being paid to preserving its exact wording. Over the centuries, the rabbis even created a *masorah*, a set of textual notes, to maintain the accuracy of its transmission. In the land of Israel, by contrast, the targums were treated with more flexibility. While the various Palestinian Targums shared a common translation of the Hebrew text, the hidden midrash in those targums was treated less rigidly. Although they share the same added interpretations, the wording of those additions sometimes varies widely. In addition to the shared expansions, each targum added new expansions of its own. Targum Pseudo-Jonathan took this flexibility to a new extreme: although it drew from the shared body of hidden midrash in the Palestinian Targums, it used a different translation, and it added not just a *few* new expansions but more than twice the number of expansions of the Palestinian Targums.

Despite this diversity, it turns out that all three types of Pentateuchal Targums have more in common than simply being a translation of the same text. They were created from the same sources. First, the Targums of Israel all derive from a common targum, referred to as the Old Palestinian Targum, which is no longer extant. This targum provided the basis for the translations of these targums. Second, with the exception of Targum Onqelos, all the Targums of Israel share a source of hidden midrash called the Proto-Palestinian Targum. This source seems to have its initial impetus in the Old Palestinian Targum.

The explanation of the unity of these three targum types begins with the second type of Pentateuchal Targum, the Palestinian Targums. Each of these—the complete Targum Neofiti, the so-called Fragment Targums, and the targumic fragments from the Cairo Geniza—consists of three types of material: the translation, the hidden midrash shared with the other Palestinian Targums, and hidden midrash specific only to it. The first two of these constitute shared sources, while the third is distinctive to each targum.

The source of the shared expansions for the Palestinian Targums, the hidden midrash, is called the Proto-Palestinian Targum, or the Proto-PT source. It contains over five hundred different expansions shared among the Palestinian Targums. Or, to put it more precisely, when a targum is extant to the verse in which a hidden midrash appears, it shares that midrash. So for example, in the Fragment Targums, when the targumist selected a verse for inclusion, if that verse has a hidden midrash attached to it, the Fragment Targum contains that expansion. If a Fragment Targum lacks an expansion belonging to the Proto-PT source, it is because it lacks that verse entirely. (The same principle applies to the Cairo Geniza fragments.)

In this way, the hidden midrash of the Palestinian Targums is echoed from targum to targum. While the exact wording of these interpretations may vary, they clearly derive from the same source. This source, along with the shared translation, identifies the Palestinian Targums as a unified category. In addition, each targum adds its own distinctive hidden midrash as well. The number of these varies. The Paris version of the Fragment Targum adds only a couple of distinctive expansions, while Targum Neofiti brings in over a hundred.

The Palestinian Targums also share a common translation. This translation was created from the Hebrew text, but its translator seems to have consistently consulted the Old Palestinian Targum, borrowing from or improving upon the earlier translation at nearly every step. And although each of the Palestinian Targums treats its hidden midrash with some fluidity, they adhere to this single, shared translation.

Targum Pseudo-Jonathan, which is not a Palestinian Targum, has one important feature in common with them, namely, the hidden midrash of the Proto-PT source. It contains most of the over five hundred expansions of that source, more than any other targum except Neofiti. However, Pseudo-Jonathan lacks the translation used in the Palestinian Targums and instead uses a translation close to that found in Targum Onqelos. The most striking aspect of Pseudo-Jonathan, however, is its inclusion of a large number of expansions from outside the Proto-PT source. Beverly Mortensen has identified over 1500 expansions distinctive to Pseudo-Jonathan. She terms these expansions the PJ-unique source. These expansions take the form of hidden midrash, like those of the Proto-PT source. So the Palestinian Targums and Targum Pseudo-Jonathan are linked through their use of the hidden midrash of the Proto-PT source, but differ in their translations; the Palestinian Targums share a translation among them, while Pseudo-Jonathan has its own translation.

The interrelationship between these two targum types stands out further when Targum Onqelos enters the comparison. Scholars have long recognized that Pseudo-Jonathan's translation is quite close to that of Onqelos; indeed, it often seems to have copied it verbatim. But recent analysis suggests that the translation of the Palestinian Targums, at least in part, is also based on the translation found in Onqelos. So although the translations of the Palestinian Targums and Pseudo-Jonathan differ, they seem to have the same earlier translation as a source.

With regard to the hidden midrash, three

points bear upon Targum Onqelos. First, Onqelos lacks the extensive additions found in the other two types of targums. Onqelos' added interpretations are smaller. Most expansions are either interwoven or small insertions, often only two or three words, perhaps joined with a substituted word or two. In the poetic sections, especially Gen. 49, Deut. 32 and 33, there are a few expansions of free structured rendering. So although Onqelos contains hidden midrash, each unit tends to be shorter and less intrusive than in the later Pentateuchal Targums. Second, Onqelos has fewer of these added interpretations than the Palestinian Targums and certainly does not have all the expansions of the Proto-PT source. Third, however, much of Onqelos' hidden midrash provides the basis for the Proto-PT additions. Onqelos' short hidden midrash usually occurs at the same verse as a Proto-PT expansion, and its wording usually is either incorporated into the later expansion or provides the interpretive basis for the expansion. So Targum Onqelos is linked to both of the later types of Pentateuchal Targum by serving as the basis for their translations and by providing the basis for many expansions of the later Proto-PT source.

Given all the links among the Targums of Israel, why claim that they all descend from the Old Palestinian Targum rather than holding that the Palestinian Targums and Pseudo-Jonathan are based on Targum Onqelos? The answer is straightforward. Targum Onqelos contains a significant amount of hidden midrash that does not appear in the other targums. Thus Targum Onqelos, as we now have it, has been modified from the Onqelos known to the targumists of the Palestinian Targums and Targum Pseudo-Jonathan. It is this earlier form of Onqelos, often termed Proto-Onqelos, that constitutes the Old Palestinian Targum. It was this Old Palestinian Targum that was taken to Babylonia, where the rabbis recast it into the version we now know as Targum Onqelos.

To bring the pieces of this description together, let us rehearse these developments. First, sometime in the first or early second century C.E., the Old Palestinian Targum was composed. Second, sometime between the second and fourth century, the Old Palestinian Targum provided the basis for the new translation now found in the Palestinian Targum, and some of its hidden midrash gave impetus to the formation of the Proto-PT source of expansions. This targum became widely copied and used in the land of Israel, and today we possess remains of more than ten different versions. Third, after this, perhaps in the fourth century or later, Targum Pseudo-Jonathan was created by bringing together a new translation based on the Old Palestinian Targum, the hidden midrash of the Proto-PT source, and a large new collection of hidden midrash, now designated the PJ-unique source. Fourth, sometime after the first century, the Old Palestinian Targum was taken to Babylonia where it was recast into what we now know as Targum Onqelos. The diagram illustrates these developments.

Content of the Hidden Midrash of the Targums of Israel

The content of the added interpretations found in the Pentateuchal Targums has usually been studied in the context of Rabbinic writings and the texts of the Second Temple Period. The goal of scholarship was to see how the topics and exegesis of targumic literature fit with these writings. The targums have been compared to the texts of the Apocrypha and Pseudepigrapha, to midrashic works, to the Talmuds, and even to later medieval compilations. This has resulted in studies of comparative halakhah and aggadah as well as given rise to a genre of scholarly analyses listing parallel interpretations. In the end, most of these studies view the targums as secondary to, and

Targums of Israel

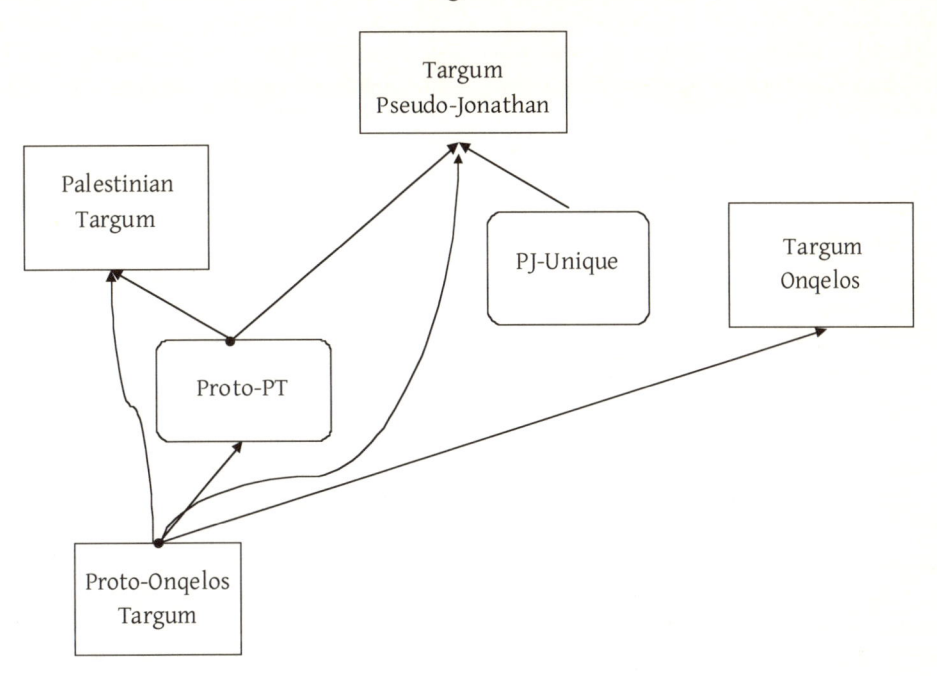

[Diagram showing relationships between: Palestinian Targum, Targum Pseudo-Jonathan, PJ-Unique, Targum Onqelos, Proto-PT, and Proto-Onqelos Targum]

dependent upon, Rabbinic material, with the exception of those that argue for the antiquity of the targums.

To be sure, many parallels exist between interpretations found in Rabbinic literature and in the Pentateuchal Targums. These can be of a general nature, such as "Balaam was wicked;" of a formal nature, such as the parallel structure of Judah's confession in Gen. 38:25–6; or of a minor detail, such as the requirement that the Red Heifer be taken from Temple resources, as found in Targum Pseudo-Jonathan to Num. 19:2. But the notion that these interpretations derive from the Rabbinic literature and hence are limited by it is overly simplistic. The situation is much more complex.

Careful study of a targumic passage usually shows that the targumists did not merely copy parallel traditions from Rabbinic material into their targum. As Robert Hayward has frequently demonstrated in his studies of Pseudo-Jonathan, even when Rabbinic texts and a targum show extensive interest in a subject, one does not appear to have copied the other, but rather each represents a voice in a debate.[10] Each of the two kinds of texts have interpretations distinctive or even unique to themselves, and even when they are in general agreement, they often differ in the details or in the interpretive basis. So the relationship between the Pentateuchal Targums and the Rabbinic literature is more complex than is usually acknowledged, and scholarly studies of it need to explicate those nuances.

It is difficult to characterize the hidden midrash in a text as large and as complex as the Pentateuch. It is not simply that the Pentateuch brings together five fairly long books, but that these books also contain a variety of material, from stories to genealogies, from laws to lists, from the design of clothing and buildings to lyrical poetry. It

---

[10] R. Hayward, "Red Heifer and Golden Calf: Dating Targum Pseudo-Jonathan," in P.V.M. Flesher, ed., *Targum Studies, vol. 1, Textual and Contextual Studies in the Pentateuchal Targums* (Atlanta, 1992), pp. 9–32.

turns out that identifying where a hidden midrash is located is as important as knowing what it talks about. To complicate matters further, each of the three different types of Targums of Israel approach this question differently, so three different characterizations of the content of the Pentateuchal Targums' hidden midrash must be given. Again, it is best to begin with the Palestinian Targums.

The Proto-PT source of the Palestinian Targums seems to recognize three different types of material in the Pentateuch and locates its expansions in light of them. The three areas are: narrative, legal/moral, and priestly.[11] Proto-PT heavily favors the areas of narrative and legal/moral, while ignoring almost totally the priestly sections. Targum Pseudo-Jonathan takes the opposite approach. It concentrates most of its PJ-unique expansions in the priestly sections, and, while it does not ignore the other two areas, it does not emphasize them either.

This difference in context is paralleled by a difference in the subject matter of the hidden midrash. The Palestinian Targums' Proto-PT source focuses on the general idea of Torah. It adds expansions that emphasize that one should practice Torah along with specific rules about what to do. It adds to the audience's knowledge of Israel's heroes and founders described in the Torah, as well as its villains—making some of them better, some worse, some more sympathetic, some less so. And finally it brings in specific theological beliefs of the Torah, such as life after death, reward and punishment, the justice of God, and the Tree of Life.

Although Pseudo-Jonathan's PJ-unique source does not ignore these aspects and certainly supports the idea of practicing Torah, it is far more interested in other matters. Indeed, it spends most of its time discussing priests, the Jerusalem Temple, and details of Temple worship. Even when it addresses topics it has in common with Proto-PT, it imposes its own views on them. When PJ-unique mentions judges, for instance, it adds the specific detail that they are priests, not just Israelites.

Most comments of the Proto-PT source and the PJ-unique source are rooted in the biblical material, whether to extend biblical mythology or to update biblically based moral expectations. And, although they occasionally mention synagogues and schools, they never refer to rabbis or to recognizable Rabbinic institutions.

The content of the hidden midrash found in Targum Onqelos is harder to characterize. Although individual interpretive passages have been studied and the entire text has been translated into a number of languages, there has never been an attempt to describe the overall character of all its hidden midrash. This is complicated by the fact, mentioned above, that most of its additions are small, and better hidden. Still, several observations can be made. First, Onqelos shares the other targums' dislike for anthropomorphism and takes many of the same steps to mitigate passages where it is found. Second, many of Onqelos' expansions occur where the later Palestinian Targums have a Proto-PT expansion and thus share an interest in the same kinds of alterations. Most prominent among these are an interest in clarifying aspects of biblical characters and heroes. But there is also an interest in updating rules as well as an occasional theological comment.

---

[11] These classifications basically conform to the Documentary Hypothesis. The three classes of material are as follows: Narrative—Gen. all; Exod. 1–11; 12:19–50; 13:17–22; 14–20; 24; 32:1–34:9; Lev. none; Num. 1–4; 7; 9:15–14:45; 16–17; 20–27; 31–34; 36; Deut. 1–11; 27–34. Legal/Moral–Exod. 21–23; Lev. 17–27; Deut. 12–26. Priestly—Gen. none; Exod. 12:1–18; 13:1–16; 25–31; 34:10–40:38; Lev. 1–16; Num. 5–6, 8:1–9:14; 15; 18–19; 28–30; 35; Deut. none.

Audience and Authors

For centuries, the same answers have been given to the questions of who composed the targums, who used them, and for what purpose(s). These answers assert that the targums were composed by rabbis and were used by common Jews in synagogues to make the biblical text clear and by students and teachers in schools for instruction in Scripture. These answers fit the evidence from Jewish society in Babylonia, at least at the time of the Babylonian Talmud. But for the Jewish community in the land of Israel, where the Pentateuchal Targums were composed, such explanations are more problematic.

First, the word *targum* can refer both to a translation and to the act of translating. In nearly all places in Palestinian Rabbinic literature where the word is used, it either refers to the act of translating or it is unclear whether the act or the result—the written targum—is meant. In only one passage, Y. Meg. 4:1, is the use of a written targum mentioned in the context of synagogue reading, and the point of that passage is to forbid its use.

Second, W. Smelik has recently shown that the picture of Aramaic targums given by the Palestinian Rabbinic literature is one of dislike and disapproval. Rabbis in the land of Israel prefer Greek translations and all but forbid Aramaic ones. Furthermore, the oft-cited dictum of T. Meg. 4:21 explicitly forbids targums with the key attributes of the Pentateuchal Targums: "He who translates a verse according to its form is a liar, and he who adds to it is a blasphemer." "According to its form" invalidates the straight translation of the Targums of Israel, while "adds to it" denies the validity of the hidden midrash. Given this attitude, the rabbis are unlikely to have composed the targums or promoted their use.

Where does this leave us? With regard to the question of audience, in essentially the same place. We can only say that in the land of Israel written targums must have been used in synagogue worship and/or schools. The act of translating must have presupposed preparation with a written text or the use of such a text, despite the Rabbinic dictum. Indeed, many of the Rabbinic comments indicating rabbis' dislike of Aramaic translation, as well as their guidelines for translation in the synagogue, center on the possibility that people might confuse the Aramaic translation with the Hebrew text of Scripture, especially in synagogue worship. This fear would have been aroused by the hidden midrash of the Targums of Israel, for the very goal of hidden midrash is to hide the interpretation and make it seem to be Scripture itself. That goal would be easiest to accomplish in the reading of Scripture and Targum in the synagogue.

The Rabbinic authorship of the targums seems to be on more solid ground, especially given the numerous parallels between targumic interpretations and those found in the midrashim and Talmudim. But the disapproval of Aramaic translations preserved in the Yerushalmi and other Palestinian Rabbinic texts, as well as the non-Rabbinic formal character of the targums, makes it seem unlikely that rabbis would have been responsible for creating the Pentateuchal Targums. Two possible alternative explanations exist. First, there may have been several Rabbinic groups or schools in the land of Israel with differing perspectives on this question. One group was responsible for the Yerushalmi and midrashim while another was responsible for the targums. Second, the targums may have come from a non-Rabbinic group. The most probable such group would be priests in association with lay people. After all, priestly association with synagogues remains well-known throughout the Rabbinic period. Roman legal sources and many early Christian writings refer to priests and synagogue officials as leaders of the Jewish community, but never to rabbis. Furthermore, priests are the only social group to have an assigned role in the synagogue liturgy, while the rabbis present themselves, at least in the Tannaitic texts, as uninterested in the synagogue, focusing most of their attention on the Temple, the *bet midrash*, and the *bet din*. These observations provide a picture not of a monolithic Jewish society in the land of Israel controlled by the Rabbinic class and its dictates but one in which different groups provide alternative, and perhaps rival, approaches to Jewish belief and practice. To the extent this is correct, the Targums of Israel provide evidence for the broader social and religious world in which the rabbis of the land of Israel lived and for which they ultimately defined Judaism.

Bibliography

Alexander, Philip S., "Jewish Aramaic Translations of Hebrew Scriptures," in Martin J. Mulder and Harry Sysling, eds. *Mikra* (Assen and Minneapolis, 1990), pp. 217-254.

Flesher, P.V.M., "Is *Targum Onkelos* a Palestinian Targum? The Evidence of Genesis 28-50," in *Journal for the Study of the Pseudepigrapha* 19 (1999), pp. 35-79.

Mortensen, B.P., *The Priesthood: A Modern Profession*, SAIS (Leiden, forthcoming).

Smelik, W.F., "Language, Locus, and Translation between the Talmudim," in *Journal for the Aramaic Bible* 3:1&2 (2001): 199-224.

PAUL V.M. FLESHER
University of Wyoming

Pesiqta deRab Kahana, Synagogue Lections for Special Occasions in

A compilation of twenty-eight propositional discourses, Pesiqta deRab Kahana (*pisqa* yields "chapter," so the plural can be rendered, "chapters attributed to R. Kahana"), innovates because it appeals for its themes and lections to the liturgical calendar rather than to a Pentateuchal book. The other midrash-compilations of Rabbinism's formative age are organized around books of Scripture, e.g., Leviticus Rabbah and Sifra both around passages of Leviticus. But that is not the case in Pesiqta deRab Kahana. It sets forth expositions of verses of Scripture chosen in accord with the requirements of the liturgical calendar, e.g., a verse important in the Passover lection or one pertinent to the Ninth of Ab. That is why we cannot present an account of how Pesiqta deRab Kahana treats the book of Leviticus, but only of how Pesiqta deRab Kahana treats the festival of Passover, and so throughout.

Pesiqta deRab Kahana marks a stunning innovation in midrash-compilation because it abandons the pretense that fixed associative connections derive solely from Scripture. Rather, the document follows the synagogal lections. A liturgical occasion of the synagogue, that is, a holy day, has told our authorship what topic it wishes to take up—and therefore also what verses of Scripture (if any) prove suitable to that topic and its exposition.

Adar-Nisan-Sivan
  Passover-Pentecost: *Pisqaot* 2-12
  [possible exception: *Pisqa* 6]

Tammuz-Ab-Elul
   The Ninth of Ab: *Pisqaot* 13–22
Tishré
   Tishré 1–22: *Pisqaot* 23–28

Only *Pisqa* 1 (possibly also *Pisqa* 6) falls out of synchronic relationship with a long sequence of special occasions in the synagogal lections. The twenty-eight parashiyyot of Pesiqta deRab Kahana in order follow the synagogal lections from early spring through fall, in the Western calendar, from late February or early March through late September or early October, approximately half of the solar year, twenty-seven weeks, and somewhat more than half of the lunar year. On the very surface, the basic building block is the theme of a given lectionary Sabbath—that is, a Sabbath distinguished by a particular lection—and not the theme dictated by a given passage of Scripture, let alone the exposition of the language or proposition of such a scriptural verse. The topical program of the document may be defined very simply: expositions of themes dictated by special Sabbaths or festivals and their lections.

PISQA (BASE-VERSE)	TOPIC OR OCCASION
1. *On the day Moses completed* (Num. 7:1)	Torah-lection for the Sabbath of Hanukkah
2. *When you take the census* (Exod. 30:12)	Torah-lection for the Sabbath of Sheqalim, first of the four Sabbaths prior to the advent of Nisan, in which Passover falls
3. *Remember Amalek* (Deut. 25:17–19)	Torah-lection for the Sabbath of Zakhor, second of the four Sabbaths prior to the advent of Nisan, in which Passover falls
4. *Red heifer* (Num. 19:1ff.)	Torah-lection for the Sabbath of Parah, third of the four Sabbaths prior to the advent of Nisan, in which Passover falls
5. *This month* (Exod. 12:1–2)	Torah-lection for the Sabbath of Hahodesh, fourth of the four Sabbaths prior to the advent of Nisan, in which Passover falls
6. *My offerings* (Num. 28:1–4)	Torah-lection for the New Moon that falls on a weekday
7. *It came to pass at midnight* (Exod. 12:29–32)	Torah-lection for the first day of Passover
8. *The first sheaf* (Lev. 23:11)	Torah-lection for the second day of Passover, on which the first sheaves of barley were harvested and waved as an offering
9. *When a bull or sheep or goat is born* (Lev. 22:26)	Lection for Passover
10. *You shall set aside a tithe* (Deut. 14:22)	Torah-lection for Sabbath during Passover in the land of Israel or for the eighth day of Passover outside of the land of Israel
11. *When Pharaoh let the people go* (Exod. 13:17–18)	Torah-lection for the seventh day of Passover
12. *In the third month* (Exod. 19:1ff.)	Torah-lection for Pentecost
13. *The words of Jeremiah* (Jer. 1:1–3)	Prophetic lection for the first of three Sabbaths prior to the Ninth of Ab
14. *Hear* (Jer. 2:4–6)	Prophetic lection for the second of three Sabbaths prior to the Ninth of Ab

15. *How lonely sits the city* (Lam. 1:1–2)	Prophetic lection for the third of three Sabbaths prior to the Ninth of Ab
16. *Comfort* (Is. 40:1–2)	Prophetic lection for the first of seven Sabbaths following the Ninth of Ab
17. *But Zion said* (Is. 49:14–16)	Prophetic lection for the second of seven Sabbaths following the Ninth of Ab
18. *O afflicted one, storm tossed* (Is. 54:11–14)	Prophetic lection for the third of seven Sabbaths following the Ninth of Ab
19. *I even I am he who comforts you* (Is. 51:12–15)	Prophetic lection for the fourth of seven Sabbaths following the Ninth of Ab
20. *Sing aloud, O barren woman* (Is. 54:1ff.)	Prophetic lection for the fifth of seven Sabbaths following the Ninth of Ab
21. *Arise, shine* (Is. 60:1–3)	Prophetic lection for the sixth of seven Sabbaths following the Ninth of Ab
22. *I will greatly rejoice in the Lord* (Is. 61:10–11)	Prophetic lection for the seventh of seven Sabbaths following the Ninth of Ab
23. The New Year	No base verse indicated. The theme is God's justice and judgment
24. *Return O Israel to the Lord your God* (Hos. 14:1–3)	Prophetic lection for the Sabbath of Repentance between New Year and the Day of Atonement
25. Selihot	No base verse indicated. The theme is God's forgiveness
26. *After the death of the two sons of Aaron* (Lev. 16:1ff.)	Torah-lection for the Day of Atonement
27. *And you shall take on the first day* (Lev. 23:39–43)	Torah-lection for the first day of the Festival of Tabernacles
28. *On the eighth day* (Num. 29:35–39)	Torah-lection for the Eighth Day of Solemn Assembly

This catalog draws our attention to three eccentric *pisqa'ot*, distinguished by their failure to build discourse upon the base verse. These are No. 4, which may fairly claim that its topic, the red cow, occurs in exact verbal formulation in the verses at hand; No. 23, the New Year, and No. 25, Selihot. The last-named may or may not take an integral place in the structure of the whole. But the middle item, the New Year, on the very surface is essential to a structure that clearly wishes to follow the line of holy days onward through the Sabbath of Repentance, the Day of Atonement, the Festival of Tabernacles, and the Eighth Day of Solemn Assembly.

It follows that, unlike Genesis Rabbah and Leviticus Rabbah, the document focuses upon the life of the synagogue. Its framers set forth propositions in the manner of the authorship of Leviticus Rabbah. But these are framed by appeal not only to the rules governing the holy society, as in Leviticus Rabbah, but also to the principal events of Israel's history, celebrated in the worship of the synagogue. What we do not find in this midrash-compilation is exposition of Pentateuchal or prophetic passages, verse by verse; the basis chosen by our authorship for organizing and setting forth its propositions is the character and theme of holy days and their special synagogue Torah-lections. That is, all of the selected base verses upon which the parashiyyot or chapters are built, Pentateuchal or prophetic, are identified with synagogal lections for specified holy days, special Sabbaths or festivals.

The contrast to the earlier compilations—this one is generally assigned to ca. 500—is striking. The framers of Sifra and Sifre to Numbers and Sifre to Deuteronomy follow the verses of Scripture and attach to them whatever messages they wish to deliver. The authorship of Genesis Rabbah follows suit, though less narrowly guided by verses and more clearly interested in their broader themes. The framers of Leviticus Rabbah attached rather broad, discursive and syllogistic statements to verses of the book of Leviticus, but these verses do not follow in close sequence, one, then the next, as in Sifra and documents like it. That program of exposition of verses of Scripture read in or out of sequence, of organization of discourse in line with biblical books, parallel to the Tosefta's and Talmuds' authorships' exposition of passages of the Mishnah, read in close sequence or otherwise, we see, defines what our authorship has not done. Pesiqta deRab Kahana has been assembled so as to exhibit a viewpoint, a purpose of its particular authorship, one quite distinctive, in its own context (if not in a single one of its propositions!) to its framers or collectors and arrangers.

Rhetoric

Following the model of Leviticus Rabbah, Pesiqta deRab Kahana consists of twenty-eight syllogisms, each presented in a cogent and systematic way by the twenty-eight *pisqa'ot*, respectively. Each *pisqa* or chapter (simply a different word for parashah, with the plural, *pesiqta*) contains an implicit proposition, and that proposition may be stated in a simple way. It emerges from the intersection of an external verse with the base verse that recurs through the *pisqa*, and then is restated by the systematic dissection of the components of the base verse, each of which is shown to say the same thing as all the others.

A *pisqa* in Pesiqta deRab Kahana systematically presents a single syllogism, which is expressed through the contrast of an external verse with the base verse—hence, the base verse/intersecting verse form. In this form the implicit syllogism is stated through the intervention of an contrastive verse into the basic proposition established by the base verse. The second type of material proceeds to the systematic exegesis of the components of the base verse on their own, hence through the Exegetical Form. There is a third form, a syllogistic list, familiar from the Mishnah and prior midrash-compilations as well. The first two forms occur in the same sequence, because the former of the two serves to declare the implicit syllogism, and the latter, to locate that implicit syllogism in the base verse itself. The third will then be tacked on at the end. Otherwise it would disrupt the exposition of the implicit syllogism. All of these forms are familiar and require no further explanation.

Topical Program

These synagogal discourses, read in their entirety, form a coherent statement of three propositions:

(1) God loves Israel, that love is unconditional, and Israel's response to God must be obedience to the religious duties that God has assigned, which will produce merit. Israel's obedience to God is what will save Israel. That means doing the religious duties as required by the Torah, which is the mark of God's love for—and regeneration of—Israel. The tabernacle symbolizes the union of Israel and God. When Israel does what God asks above, Israel will prosper down

below. If Israel remembers Amalek down below, God will remember Amalek up above and will wipe him out. A mark of Israel's loyalty to God is remembering Amalek. God does not require the animals that are sacrificed, since man could never match God's appetite, if that were the issue, but the savor pleases God (as a mark of Israel's loyalty and obedience). The first sheaf returns to God God's fair share of the gifts that God bestows on Israel, and those who give it benefit, while those who hold it back suffer. Observing religious duties, typified by the rites of The Festival, brings a great reward of that merit that ultimately leads to redemption. God's ways are just, righteous and merciful, as shown by God's concern that the offspring remain with the mother for seven days. God's love for Israel is so intense that he wants to hold them back for an extra day after The Festival in order to spend more time with them, because, unlike the nations of the world, Israel knows how to please God. This is a mark of God's love for Israel.

(2) God is reasonable and when Israel has been punished, it is in accord with God's rules. God forgives penitent Israel and is abundant in mercy. Laughter is vain because it is mixed with grief. A wise person will not expect too much joy. But when people suffer, there ordinarily is a good reason for it. That is only one sign that God is reasonable and that God never did anything lawless and wrong to Israel or made unreasonable demands, and there was, therefore, no reason for Israel to lose confidence in God or to abandon him. God punished Israel to be sure. But this was done with reason. Nothing happened to Israel of which God did not give fair warning in advance, and Israel's failure to heed the prophets brought about her fall. And God will forgive a faithful Israel. Even though the Israelites sinned by making the golden calf, God forgave them and raised them up. On the New Year, God executes justice, but the justice is tempered with mercy. The rites of the New Year bring about divine judgment and also forgiveness because of the merit of the fathers. Israel must repent and return to the Lord, who is merciful and will forgive them for their sins. The penitential season of the New Year and Day of Atonement is the right time for confession and penitence, and God is sure to accept penitence. By exercising his power of mercy, the already-merciful God grows still stronger in mercy.

(3) God will save Israel personally at a time and circumstance of his own choosing. Israel may know what the future redemption will be like, because of the redemption from Egypt. The paradox of the red cow, that what imparts uncleanness, namely touching the ashes of the red cow, produces cleanness, is part of God's ineffable wisdom, which man cannot fathom. Only God can know the precise moment of Israel's redemption. That is something man cannot find out on his own. But God will certainly fulfill the predictions of the prophets about Israel's coming redemption. The Exodus from Egypt is the paradigm of the coming redemption. Israel has lost Eden—but can come home, and, with God's help, will. God's unique power is shown through Israel's unique suffering. In God's own time, he will redeem Israel.

To develop this point, the authorship proceeds to further facts, worked out in its propositional discourses. The lunar calendar, particular to Israel, marks Israel as favored by God, for the new moon signals the coming of Israel's redemption, and the particular new moon that will mark the actual event is that of Nisan. When God chooses to redeem Israel, Israel's enemies will have no power to stop him, because God will force Israel's enemies to serve Israel, because of Israel's purity and loyalty to God. Israel's enemies are punished, and what they propose to do to Israel, God does to them. Both directly and through the prophets, God is the source of true comfort, which he will bring to Israel.

Israel thinks that God has forsaken them. But it is Israel who forsook God, God's love has never failed, and will never fail. Even though he has been angry, his mercy still is near and God has the power and will to save Israel. God has designated the godly for himself and has already promised to redeem them. He will assuredly do so. God personally is the one who will comfort Israel. While Israel says there is no comfort, in fact, God will comfort Israel. Zion/Israel is like a barren woman, but Zion will bring forth children, and Israel will be comforted. Both God and Israel will bring light to Zion, which will give light to the world. The rebuilding of Zion will be a source of joy for the entire world, not for Israel alone. God will rejoice in Israel, Israel in God, like bride and groom.

A Sample Passage

We consider the way in which this compilation treats Num. 7:1.

Pisqa One
On the day that Moses completed the setting up of the Tabernacle, he anointed and consecrated it (Num. 7:1)
I:I
1.A. I have come back to my garden, my sister, my bride (Song 5:1):
 B. R. Azariah in the name of R. Simon said, "[The matter may be compared to the case of] a king who became angry at a noble woman and drove her out and expelled her from his palace. After some time he wanted to bring her back. She said, 'Let him renew in my behalf the earlier state of affairs, and then he may bring me back.'
 C. "So in former times the Holy One, blessed be he, would receive offerings from on high, as it is said, And the Lord smelled the sweet odor (Gen. 8:21). But now he will accept them down below."
2.A. I have come back to my garden, my sister, my bride (Song 5:1):
 B. Said R. Hanina, "The Torah teaches you proper conduct,
 C. "specifically, a groom should not go into the marriage canopy until the bride gives him permission to do so: Let my beloved come into his garden (Song 4:16), after which, I have come back to my garden, my sister, my bride (Song 5:1)."
3.A. R. Tanhum, son-in-law of R. Eleazar b. Abina, in the name of R. Simeon b. Yosni: "What is written is not, 'I have come into the garden,' but rather, I have come back to my garden. That is, 'to my [Mandelbaum:] canopy.'
 B. "That is to say, to the place in which the principal [presence of God] had been located to begin with.
 C. "The principal locale of God's presence had been among the lower creatures, in line with this verse: And they heard the sound of the Lord God walking about (Gen. 3:8)."
4.A. [And they heard the sound of the Lord God walking about (Gen. 3:8):] Said R. Abba bar Kahana, "What is written is not merely 'going,' but 'walking about,' that is, 'walking away from.'"
 B. And man and his wife hid (Gen. 3:8):
 C. Said R. Aibu, "At that moment the first man's stature was cut down and diminished to one hundred cubits."
5.A. Said R. Isaac, "It is written, The righteous will inherit the earth (Ps. 47:29). Where will the wicked be? Will they fly in the air?
 B. "Rather, the sense of the clause, they shall dwell thereon in eternity is, 'they shall bring the presence of God to dwell on the earth.'"
6.A. [Reverting to 3.C], the principal locale of God's presence had been

among the lower creatures, but when the first man sinned, it went up to the first firmament.

B. The generation of Enosh came along and sinned, and it went up from the first to the second.

C. The generation of the flood [came along and sinned], and it went up from the second to the third.

D. The generation of the dispersion [came along] and sinned, and it went up from the third to the fourth.

E. The Egyptians in the time of Abraham our father [came along] and sinned, and it went up from the fourth to the fifth.

F. The Sodomites [came along], and sinned, ... from the fifth to the sixth.

G. The Egyptians in the time of Moses ... from the sixth to the seventh.

H. And, corresponding to them, seven righteous men came along and brought it back down to earth:

I. Abraham our father came along and acquired merit, and brought it down from the seventh to the sixth.

J. Isaac came along and acquired merit and brought it down from the sixth to the fifth.

K. Jacob came along and acquired merit and brought it down from the fifth to the fourth.

L. Levi came along and acquired merit and brought it down from the fourth to the third.

M. Kohath came along and acquired merit and brought it down from the third to the second.

N. Amram came along and acquired merit and brought it down from the second to the first.

O. Moses came along and acquired merit and brought it down to earth.

P. Therefore it is said, On the day that Moses completed the setting up of the Tabernacle, he anointed and consecrated it (Num. 7:1).

The selection of the intersecting verse, Song 5:1, rests on the appearance of the letters KLT, meaning, completed, but yielding also the word KLH, meaning, bride. The exegete wishes to make the point that in building the tabernacle, Moses has brought God down to earth, 6.P. This he accomplishes by bringing the theme of "garden, bride" together with the theme of the union of God and Israel. The parable at 1.B then is entirely apt, since it wishes to introduce the notion of God's having become angry with humanity but then reconciled through Israel in the sacrificial cult. 1.B then refers to the fall from grace, with Israel as the noble spouse who insists that the earlier state of affairs be restored. C then makes explicit precisely what is in mind, a very effective introduction to the whole. No. 2 pursues the exegesis of the intersecting verse, as does No. 3, the latter entirely apropos. Because of 3.C, Nos. 4 is tacked on; it continues the exegesis of the proof-text but has no bearing on the intersecting verse. But No. 5 does—at least in its proposition, if not in its selection of proof texts. No. 6 then brings us back to 3.C, citing the language of the prior component and then making the point of the whole quite explicit. Even with the obvious accretions at No. 4, 5, the whole hangs together and makes its point—the intersecting verse, Song 5:1, the base verse Num. 7:1—in a cogent way.

I:II.

1.A. King Solomon made a pavilion for himself (Song 3:9) [The New English Bible: The palanquin which King Solomon had made for himself was of wood from Lebanon. Its poles he made of silver, its head-rest of gold; its seat was of purple stuff, and its lining was of leather]:

B. Pavilion refers to the tent of meeting.
C. King Solomon made a . . . for himself: he is the king to whom peace [shalom/shelomoh] belongs.

2.A. Said R. Judah bar Ilai, "[The matter may be compared to the case of] a king who had a little girl. Before she grew up and reached puberty, he would see her in the market place and chat with her, or in alleyways and chat with her. But when she grew up and reached puberty, he said, 'It is not fitting for the dignity of my daughter that I should talk with her in public. Make a pavilion for her, so that I may chat with her in the pavilion.'

B. "So, to begin with: When Israel was a child in Egypt, then in my love of him, I used to cry out (Hos. 11:1). In Egypt they saw me: And I passed through the land of Israel (Exod. 12:12). At the sea they saw me: And Israel saw the great hand (Exod. 14:31). At Sinai they saw me: Face to face the Lord spoke with you (Deut. 5:4).

C. "But when they received the Torah, they became a fully-grown nation for me. So he said, 'It is not appropriate to the dignity of my children that I should speak with them in public. But make me a tabernacle, and I shall speak from the midst of the tabernacle.'

D. "That is in line with this verse: And when Moses entered the tent of the presence to speak with God, he heard the voice speaking from above the cover over the ark of the pact from between the two cherubim: the voice spoke to him (Num. 7:89)."

3.A. [The palanquin that King Solomon had made for himself was of wood from Lebanon. Its poles he made of silver, its head-rest of gold; its seat was of purple stuff, and its lining was of leather] . . . was of wood from Lebanon. Make for the tabernacle planks of acacia-wood as uprights (Exod. 26:15).

B. Its poles he made of silver: The hooks and bands on the posts shall be of silver (Exod. 27:10).

C. . . . its head-rest of gold: Overlay the planks with gold, make rings of gold on them to hold the bars (Exod. 26:29).

D. . . . its seat was of purple stuff: Make a veil of finely woven linen and violet, purple, and scarlet yarn (Exod. 26:31).

E. . . . and its lining was of leather:

F. R. Yudan says, "This refers to the merit accruing on account of the Torah and the righteous."

G. R. Azariah in the name of R. Judah bar Simon says, "This refers to the Presence of God."

4.A. Said R. Aha bar Kahana, "It is written, And there I shall meet with you (Exod. 25:22),

B. "to teach that even what is on the outside of the ark-cover is not empty of God's presence."

5.A. A gentile asked Rabban Gamaliel, saying to him, "On what account did the Holy One, blessed be he, reveal himself to Moses in a bush?"

B. He said to him, "If he had revealed himself to him in a carob tree or a fig tree, what might you have said?

C. "It is so as to indicate that there is no place in the earth that is empty of God's presence."

6.A. R. Joshua of Sikhnin in the name of R. Levi: "To what may the tent of meeting be compared?

B. "To an ocean-side cave. The sea tide flows and engulfs the cave, which is filled by the sea, but the sea is not diminished.

C. "So the tent of meeting is filled

with the splendor of the presence of God."

D. Therefore it is said, On the day that Moses completed the setting up of the Tabernacle, he anointed and consecrated it (Num. 7:1).

Seen by itself, No. 1 has no bearing upon the larger context, but it does provide a good exegesis of Song 3:9 in terms of the theme at hand, the tabernacle. The point of No. 2 is that the purpose of the tabernacle was to make possible appropriate communication between a mature Israel and God. Then the two items are simply distinct workings of the theme of the tabernacle, one appealing to Song 3:9, the other, Num. 7:89.

I:III

1.A. [Continuing the exegesis of the successive verses of Song 3:9ff.] Come out, daughters of Jerusalem, you daughters of Zion, come out and welcome King Solomon, wearing the crown with which his mother has crowned him, on his wedding day, on his day of joy (Song 3:11) [Braude and Kapstein: Go forth, O younglings whose name Zion indicates that you bear a sign]:

B. Sons who are marked [a play on the letters that stand for the word, come out] for me by the mark of circumcision, by not cutting the corners of the head [in line with Lev. 19:27], and by wearing show-fringes.

2.A. [... and welcome] King Solomon:
B. The king to whom peace belongs.

3.A. Another interpretation: and welcome King Solomon:
B. The King [meaning God] who brings peace through his deeds among his creatures.
C. He caused the fire to make peace with our father Abraham, the sword with our father Isaac, the angel with our father Jacob.

D. It is the king who brings peace among his creatures.
E. Said R. Yohanan, "Merciful dominion and fear are with him (Job 25:2) [that is, are at peace with him]."
F. Said R. Jacob of Kefar Hanan, "Merciful dominion refers to the angel Michael, and fear to the angel Gabriel.
G. "With him means that they make peace with him and do not do injury to one another."
H. Said R. Yohanan, "The sun has never laid eyes on the blemished part of the moon [the black side], nor does one star take precedence over another one, nor does a planet lay eyes on the one above it."
I. Said Rabbi, "All of them traverse as it were a spiral staircase."

4.A. It is written, Who lays the beams of your upper chambers in the waters, who makes the flaming fires your ministers (Ps. 104:2-3):
B. R. Simeon b. Yohai taught, "The firmament is of water, the stars of fire, and yet they dwell with one another and do not do injury to one another.
C. "The firmament is of water and the angel is of fire, and yet they dwell with one another and do not do injury to one another."
D. Said R. Abin, "It is not the end of the matter [that there is peace between] one angel and another. But even the angel himself is half fire and half water, and yet they make peace."
E. The angel has five faces—The angel's body was like beryl, his face as the appearance of lightning, his eyes as torches of fire, his arms and feet like in color to burnished brass, and the sound of his words like the sound of a roaring multitude (Dan. 10:6)—

[yet none does injury to the other].
5.A. So there was hail and fire flashing continually amid the hail (Exod. 9:24):
B. R. Judah says, "There was a flask of hail filled with fire."
C. R. Nehemiah said, "Fire and hail, mixed together."
D. R. Hanin said, "In support of the position of R. Judah is the case of the pomegranate in the pulp of which seeds can be discerned."
E. R. Hanin said, "As to R. Nehemiah's position, it is the case of a crystal lamp in which are equivalent volumes of water and oil, which together keep the flame of the wick burning above the water and the oil."
6.A. [So there was hail and fire flashing continually amid the hail (Exod. 9:24)]: What is the meaning of flashing continually?
B. Said R. Judah bar Simon, "Each one is eager in its [B&K, p. 10:] determination to carry out their mission."
C. Said R. Aha, "[The matter may be compared to the case of] a king, who had two tough legions, who competed with one another, but when the time to make war in behalf of the king came around, they made peace with one another.
D. "So is the case with the fire and hail, they compete with one another, but when the time came to carry out the war of the Holy One, blessed be he, against the Egyptians, then: So there was hail and fire flashing continually amid the hail (Exod. 9:24)—one miracle within the other [more familiar one, namely, that the hail and fire worked together]."
7.A. [Come out, daughters of Jerusalem, you daughters of Zion, come out and welcome King Solomon,] wearing the crown with which his mother has crowned him, on his wedding day, [on his day of joy] (Song 3:11):
B. Said R. Isaac, "We have reviewed the entire Scripture and have not found evidence that Bathsheba made a crown for her son, Solomon. This refers, rather, to the tent of meeting, which is crowned with blue and purple and scarlet."
8.A. Said R. Hunia, "R. Simeon b. Yohai asked R. Eleazar b. R. Yose, 'Is it possible that you have heard. from your father what was the crown with which his mother crowned him?'
B. "He said to him, 'The matter may be compared to the case of a king who had a daughter, whom he loved even too much. He even went so far, in expressing his affection for her, as to call her, 'my sister.' He even went so far, in expressing his affection for her, as to call her, 'my mother.'
C. "'So at the outset, the Holy One, blessed be he, expressed his affection for Israel by calling them, 'my daughter:' Hear, O daughter, and consider (Ps. 45:11). Then he went so far, in expressing his affection for them, as to call them, 'my sister:' My sister, my bride (Song 5:1). Then he went so far, in expressing his affection for them, as to call them, 'my mother:' Attend to me, O my people, and give ear to me, O my nation (Is. 51:4). The letters that are read as "my nation" may also be read as 'my mother.'" [The distinction between the *ayin*-sound, a rough breathing, and the *aleph*-sound, no rough breathing, is thus obscured for exegetical purposes, so that it is as if the one letter, yielding my nation, were interchangeable with the other, producing my mother.]

D. "R. Simeon b. Yohai stood and kissed him on his brow.
E. "He said to him, 'Had I come only to hear this teaching, it would have been enough for me.'"

9.A. R. Joshua of Sikhnin taught in the name of R. Levi: "When the Holy One, blessed be he, said to Moses, 'Make me a tabernacle,' Moses might have brought four poles and spread over them [skins to make] the tabernacle. This teaches, therefore, that the Holy One, blessed be he, showed Moses on high red fire, green fire, black fire, and white fire.
B. "He said to him, 'Make me a tabernacle.'
C. "Moses said to the Holy One, blessed be he, 'Lord of the ages, where am I going to get red fire, green fire, black fire, or white fire?'
D. "He said to him, 'After the pattern which is shown to you on the mountain (Exod. 25:40)."

10.A. R. Berekhiah in the name of R. Levi: "[The matter may be compared to the case of] a king who appeared to his household clothed in a garment [B&K, p. 11] covered entirely with precious stones.
B. "He said to him, 'Make me one like this.'
C. "He said to him, 'My lord, O king, where am I going to get myself a garment made entirely of precious stones?'
D. "He said to him, 'You in accord with your raw materials and I in accord with my glory.'
E. "So said the Holy One, blessed be he, to Moses, 'Moses, if you make what belongs above down below, I shall leave my council up here and go down and reduce my Presence so as to be among you down there.'
F. "Just as up there: seraphim are standing (Is. 6:2), so down below: boards of shittim-cedars are standing (Exod. 26:15).
G. "Just as up there are stars, so down below are the clasps."
H. Said R. Hiyya bar Abba, "This teaches that the golden clasps in the tabernacle looked like the fixed stars of the firmament."

11.A. [Come out, daughters of Jerusalem, you daughters of Zion, come out and welcome King Solomon, wearing the crown with which his mother has crowned him,] on his wedding day, [on his day of joy] (Song 3:11):
B. ... on his wedding day [B&K, p. 12:] the day he entered the tent of meeting.
C. ... on his day of joy:
D. this refers to the tent of meeting.
E. Another interpretation of the phrase, on his wedding day, on his day of joy (Song 3:11):
F. ... on his wedding day, refers to the tent of meeting.
G. ... on his day of joy refers to the building of the eternal house.
H. Therefore it is said, On the day that Moses completed the setting up of the Tabernacle, he anointed and consecrated it (Num. 7:1).

The exegesis of Song 3:11 now receives attention in its own terms, our point of departure having been forgotten. No. 1 simply provides a play on one of the words of the verse under study. Nos. 2–6 proceed to work on the problem of the name of the king, Solomon. We have a striking and fresh approach at Nos. 2–3: the reference is now to God as King, and the name, Solomon, then is interpreted as God's function as bringing peace both among his holy creatures, the patriarchs and the angels, and also among the elements of natural creation. Both topics are introduced and then, at Nos. 4–6, the latter is worked out. God keeps water and fire working together and to do his bidding, they do not injure one another. The prooftext, Exod. 9:24, then leads us in its own direction, but at No. 6 discourse returns to the main point. No. 7 moves us on to a fresh issue, namely, Solomon himself. And now we see the connection between the passage and our broader theme, the tabernacle. The Temple is now compared to a crown. No. 8 pursues the interpretation of the same clause. But the point of interest is the clause, not the theme under broader discussion, so what we have is simply a repertoire of exegeses of the cited verse. No. 9 carries forward the theme of making the tabernacle. It makes the point that Moses was to replicate the colors he had seen on high. I see no connection to the preceding. It is an essentially fresh initiative. No. 10 continues along that same line, now making yet another point, which is that the tabernacle on earth was comparable to the abode of God in heaven. No. 11 brings us back to our original verse. We take up a clause-by-clause interpretation of the matter. No. 11.H is an editorial subscript, with no connection to the foregoing except the rather general thematic one. But the original interest in working on the theme of the building of the tabernacle as Israel's wedding day to God is well expressed, beginning to end.

I:IV
1. A. Who has ever gone up to heaven and come down again? Who has cupped the wind in the hollow of his hands? Who has bound up the waters in the fold of his garment? Who has fixed the boundaries of the earth? What is his name or his son's name, if you know it? (Prov. 30:4):
   B. ... Who has ever gone up to heaven: this refers to the Holy One, blessed be he, as it is written, God has gone up to the sound of the trumpet (Ps. 37:6).
   C. ... and come down again: The Lord came down onto Mount Sinai (Exod. 19:20).
   D. ... Who has cupped the wind in the hollow of his hands: In whose hand is the soul of all the living (Job 12:10).
   E. ... Who has bound up the waters in the fold of his garment: He keeps the waters penned in dense cloud-masses (Job 26:8).
   F. ... Who has fixed the boundaries of the earth: ... who kills and brings to life (1 Sam. 2:6).
   G. ... What is his name: his name is the Rock, his name is The Almighty, his name is The Lord of Hosts.
   H. or his son's name, if you know it: My son, my firstborn is Israel (Exod. 4:22).
2. A. Another interpretation of the verse, Who has ever gone up to heaven: Who is the one whose prayer goes up to heaven and brings down rain?
   B. This is one who with his hands sets aside the tithes that he owes, who brings dew and rain into the world.
   C. Who has cupped the wind in the hollow of his hands? Who has bound up the waters in the fold of his garment? Who has fixed the boundaries of the earth? Who is the one whose prayer does not go up to heaven and bring down rain?
   D. This is one who with his hands does not set aside the tithes that he owes, who does not bring dew and rain into the world.
3. A. Another interpretation of the verse, Who has ever gone up to heaven:
   B. This refers to Elijah, concerning whom it is written, And Elijah went up in a whirlwind to heaven (2 Kgs. 2:11).
   C. ... and come down again: Go down with him, do not be afraid (2 Kgs. 1:16).

D. Who has cupped the wind in the hollow of his hands: Lord, God of Israel, before whom I stand (1 Kgs. 17:1).
E. Who has bound up the waters in the fold of his garment: And Elijah took his mantle and wrapped it together and smote the waters and they were divided (1 Kgs. 2:8).
F. Who has fixed the boundaries of the earth: And Elijah said, See your son lives (1 Kgs. 17:23).

4.A. Another interpretation of the verse, Who has ever gone up to heaven and come down again:
B. This refers to Moses, concerning whom it is written, And Moses went up to God (Exod. 19:3).
C. ... and come down again: And Moses came down from the mountain (Exod. 19:14).
D. Who has cupped the wind in the hollow of his hands: As soon as I have gone out of the city, I shall spread my hands out to the Lord (Exod. 9:29).
E. Who has bound up the waters in the fold of his garment: The floods stood upright as a heap (Exod. 15:8).
F. Who has fixed the boundaries of the earth: this refers to the tent of meeting, as it is said, On the day on which Moses completed setting up the tabernacle (Num. 7:1)—for the entire world was set up with it.

5.A. R. Joshua b. Levi in the name of R. Simeon b. Yohai: "What is stated is not 'setting up the tabernacle [without the accusative particle, et],' but 'setting up + the accusative particle + the tabernacle,' [and since the inclusion of the accusative particle is taken to mean that the object is duplicated, we understand the sense to be that he set up a second tabernacle along with the first].

B. "What was set up with it? It was the world that was set up with [the tabernacle, that is, the tabernacle represented the cosmos].
C. "For until the tabernacle was set up, the world trembled, but after the tabernacle was set up, the world rested on firm foundations."
D. Therefore it is said, On the day that Moses completed the setting up of the Tabernacle, he anointed and consecrated it (Num. 7:1).

The intersecting verse, Prov. 30:4, is systematically applied to God, to tithing, then Elijah, finally Moses, at which point the exposition comes to a fine editorial conclusion. I cannot imagine a more representative example of the intersecting verse-base verse exposition. No. 5 is tacked on because it provides a valuable complement to the point of No. 4.

I:V

1.A. Another interpretation of the verse: On the day that Moses completed the setting up of the Tabernacle, he anointed and consecrated it (Num. 7:1):
B. The letters translated as "completed" are so written that they be read "bridal," that is, on the day on which [Israel, the bride] entered the bridal canopy.

2.A. R. Eleazar and R. Samuel bar Nahmani:
B. R. Eleazar says, "On the day that Moses completed means on the day on which he left off setting up the tabernacle day by day."
C. It has been taught on Tannaite authority: Every day Moses would set up the tabernacle, and every morning he would make his offerings on it and then take it down. On the eighth day [to which reference is made in the verse, On the day that Moses completed the setting up of the Tabernacle, he

anointed and consecrated it] he set it up but did not take it down again.

D. Said R. Zeira, "On the basis of this verse we learn the fact that an altar set up on the preceding night is invalid for the offering of sacrifices on the next day."

E. R. Samuel bar Nahmani says, "Even on the eighth day he set it up and took it apart again."

F. And how do we know about these dismantlings?

G. It is in line with what R. Zeira said, "On the day that Moses completed means on the day on which he left off setting up the tabernacle day by day."

3.A. R. Eleazar and R. Yohanan:

B. R. Eleazar said, "On the day that Moses completed means on the day on which demons ended their spell in the world.

C. "What is the scriptural basis for that view?

D. "No evil thing will befall you, nor will any demon come near you [B&K, p. 15] by reason of your tent (Ps. 91:10)—on the day on which demons ended their spell in the world."

E. Said R. Yohanan, "What need do I have to derive the lesson from another passage? Let us learn it from the very passage in which the matter occurs: May the Lord bless you and keep you (Num. 6:24)—keep you from demons."

4.A. R. Yohanan and R. Simeon b. Laqish:

B. R. Yohanan said, "On the day that Moses completed means on the day on which hatred came to an end in the world. For before the tabernacle was set up, there was hatred and envy, competition, contention, and strife in the world. But once the tabernacle was set up, love, affection, comradeship, righteousness, and peace came into the world.

C. "What is the verse of scripture that so indicates?

D. "Let me hear the words of the Lord, are they not words of peace, peace to his people and his loyal servants and to all who turn and trust in him? Deliverance is near to those who worship him, so that glory may dwell in our land. Love and fidelity have come together, justice and peace join hands (Ps. 85:8–10).

E. Said R. Simeon b. Laqish, "What need do I have to derive the lesson from another passage? Let us learn it from the very passage in which the matter occurs: and give you peace.

5.A. [On the day that Moses completed] the setting up of the Tabernacle, [he anointed and consecrated it]:

B. R. Joshua b. Levi in the name of R. Simeon b. Yohai: "What is stated is not 'setting up the tabernacle [without the accusative particle, et],' but 'setting up + the accusative particle + the tabernacle,' [and since the inclusion of the accusative particle is taken to mean that the object is duplicated, we understand the sense to be that he set up a second tabernacle along with the first].

C. "What was set up with it? It was the world that was set up with [the tabernacle, that is, the tabernacle represented the cosmos].

D. "For until the tabernacle was set up, the world trembled, but after the tabernacle was set up, the world rested on firm foundations."

We work our way through the clause, on the day that Moses completed. No. 1 goes over familiar ground. It is a valuable review of the point of stress, the meaning of the word completed. No. 2 refers to the claim that from day to day Moses would set up and take down the tent, until on the day at hand, he left it standing; so the "completed" bears the sense of ceasing to go through a former procedure. The word under study bears the further sense of "coming to an end," and therefore at Nos. 3, 4, we ask what came to an end when the tabernacle was set up. The matched units point to demons, on the one side, and hatred, on the other. No. 5 moves us along from the word KLT to the following set, accusative + tabernacle.

I:VI.
1.A. [On the day that Moses completed the setting up of the Tabernacle], he anointed and consecrated it:
B. Since it is written, he anointed and consecrated it, why does it also say, he anointed them and consecrated them (Num. 7:1)?
C. R. Aibu said, "R. Tahalipa of Caesarea, and R. Simeon:
D. "One of them said, 'After he had anointed each one, he then anointed all of them simultaneously.'
E. "The other said, 'And he anointed them refers to an anointing in this world and another anointing in the world to come.'"
2.A. Along these same lines: You shall couple the tent together (Exod. 26:11), You shall couple the curtains (Exod. 26:6):
B. R. Judah and R. Levi, R. Tahalipa of Caesarea and R. Simeon b. Laqish:
C. One of them said, "Once he had coupled them all together, he went back and coupled them one by one."
D. The other said, "You shall couple the curtains and it shall be one meaning, one for measuring, one for anointing."

I:VII.
1.A. The chief men of Israel, heads of families—that is, the chiefs of the tribes, [who had assisted in preparing the detailed lists] came forward and brought their offering before the Lord (Num. 7:2):
B. [(Following B&K, p. 16:) The word for tribes can mean rods, so we understand the meaning to be, they had exercised authority through rods] in Egypt.
C. ... who had assisted in preparing the detailed lists: the standards.
2.A. ... came forward and brought their offering before the Lord, six covered wagons [and twelve oxen, one wagon from every two chiefs and from each one an ox] (Num. 7:2):
B. The six corresponded to the six days of creation.
C. The six corresponded to the six divisions of the Mishnah.
D. The six corresponded to the six matriarchs: Sarah, Rebecca, Rachel, Leah, Bilhah, and Zilpah.
E. Said R. Yohanan, "The six corresponded to the six religious duties that pertain to a king: [1] He shall not have too many wives (Deut. 17:17), [2] He shall not have too many horses (Deut. 17:16), [3] He shall not have too much silver and gold (Deut. 17:17), [4] He shall not pervert justice, [5] show favor, or [6] take bribes (Deut. 16:9)."
3.A. The six corresponded to the six steps of the throne. How so?
B. When he goes up to take his seat on the first step, the herald goes forth and proclaims, He shall not have too many wives (Deut. 17:17).
C. When he goes up to take his seat on the second step, the herald goes forth and proclaims, He shall not have too many horses (Deut. 17:16).
D. When he goes up to take his seat on the third step, the herald goes forth and proclaims, He shall not have too much silver and gold (Deut. 17:17).

E. When he goes up to take his seat on the fourth step, the herald goes forth and proclaims, He shall not pervert justice.

F. When he goes up to take his seat on the fifth step, the herald goes forth and proclaims, ... or show favor.

G. When he goes up to take his seat on the sixth, step, the herald goes forth and proclaims, ... or take bribes (Deut. 16:9).

H. When he comes to take his seat on the seventh step, he says, "Know before whom you take your seat."

4.A. And the top of the throne was round behind (1 Kgs. 10:19):

B. Said R. Aha, "It was like the throne of Moses."

C. And there were arms on either side of the throne by the place of the seat (1 Kgs. 10:19):

D. How so? There was a scepter of gold suspended from behind, with a dove on the top, and a crown of gold in the dove's mouth, and he [Moses] would sit under it on the Sabbath, and it would touch but not quite touch [I am not sure whether the "it" is the dove, scepter, crown, or what.]

5.A. The six corresponded to the six firmaments.

B. But are they not seven?

C. Said R. Abia, "The one where the King dwells is royal property [not counted with what belongs to the world at large].

We proceed with the detailed exposition of the verse at hand. The focus of interest, after No. 1, is on the reason for bringing six wagons. The explanations, Nos. 2 (+3-4), 5, relate to the creation of the world, the Torah, the life of Israel, the religious duties of the king, and the universe above. The underlying motif, the tabernacle as the point at which the supernatural world of Israel meets the supernatural world of creation, is carried forward.

I:VIII.

1.A. [... came forward and brought their offering before the Lord, six] covered [wagons and twelve oxen, one wagon from every two chiefs and from each one an ox] (Num. 7:2):

B. The word for covered wagons may be read to yield these meanings:

C. like a lizard-skin [B&K, p. 17: "it signifies that the outer surface of the wagons' frames was as delicately reticulated as the skin of a lizard"];

D. [and the same word may be read to indicate that the wagons were] decorated, or fully equipped.

E. It has been taught in the name of R. Nehemiah, "They were like a bent bow."

2.A. ... twelve oxen, one wagon from every two chiefs ...:

B. This indicates that two chiefs would together bring one wagon, while each tribe gave an ox.

3.A. These they brought forward before the tabernacle (Num. 7:3):

B. This teaches that they turned them into their monetary value and sold them to the congregation at large [so that everyone had a share in the donation].

4.A. And the Lord spoke to Moses and said, ["Accept these from them: they shall be used for the service of the tent of the presence"]: (Num. 7:45):

B. What is the meaning of the word, and said?

C. R. Hoshaia taught, "The Holy One, blessed be he, said to Moses, 'Go and say to Israel words of praise and consolation.'

D. "Moses was afraid, saying, 'But is it not possible that the holy spirit has abandoned me and come to rest on the chiefs?'

E. "The Holy One said to him, 'Moses, had I wanted them to bring their offering, I should have said to you to 'say to them,' [so instructing them to do so], but Take—it is from them [at their own volition, not by my inspiration] (Num. 7:5) is the language that means, they did it on their own volition [and have not received the holy spirit].'"

5.A. And who gave them the good ideas [of making the gift]?
B. It was the tribe of Issachar who gave them the good idea, in line with this verse: And of the children of Issachar came men who had understanding of the times (1 Chr. 12:33).
C. What is the sense of the times?
D. R. Tanhuma said, "The ripe hour [kairos]."
E. R. Yose bar Qisri said, "Intercalating the calendar."
F. They had two hundred heads (1 Chr. 12:33):
G. This refers to the two hundred heads of sanhedrins that were produced by the tribe of Issachar.
H. And all of their brethren were subject to their orders (1 Chr. 12:33):
I. This teaches that the law would accord with their rulings.
J. They said to the community, "Is this tent of meeting which you are making going to fly in the air? Make wagons for it, which will bear it."

6.A. Moses was concerned, saying, "Is it possible that one of the wagons might break, or one of the oxen die, so that the offering of the chiefs might be invalid?"
B. Said to Moses the Holy One, blessed be he, "They shall be used for the service of the tent of the presence (Num. 7:5).
C. "To them has been given a long-term existence."

7.A. How long did they live?
B. R. Yudan in the name of R. Samuel bar Nahman, R. Hunia in the name of Bar Qappara, "In Gilgal they sacrificed the oxen (Hos. 12:12)."
C. And where did they offer them up?
D. R. Abba bar Kahana said, "In Nob they offered them up."
E. R. Abbahu said, "In Gibeon they offered them up."
F. R. Hama bar Hanina said, "In the eternal house [of Jerusalem] they offered them up."
G. Said R. Levi, "A verse of Scripture supporting the view of R. Hama bar Hanina: Solomon offered a sacrifice of peace offerings, which he slaughtered for the Lord, twenty-two thousand oxen (1 Kgs. 8:63)."
H. It was taught in the name of R. Meir, "They endure even to now, and they never produced a stink, got old, or produced an invalidating blemish."
I. Now that produces an argument a fortiori:
J. If the oxen who cling to the work of the making of the tent of meeting were given an eternal existence, Israel, who cling to the Holy One, blessed be he, how much the more so!
K. And you who cling to the Lord your God are alive, all of you, this day (Deut. 4:4).

The exegesis of the verse in its own terms leads us through the several phrases, Nos. 1, 2, 3. No. 4, continuing at No. 6, with an important complement at No. 5, goes on to its own interesting question. No. 7 serves No. 6 as No. 6 serves No. 5.

JACOB NEUSNER
Bard College

Pesiqta deRab Kahana, Theology of

Pesiqta de Rab Kahana's compilers register standard points. The main lines of theological reflection and construction lead to such conventional propositions as this: the Temple is God's abode on earth, corresponding in nature to God's abode in heaven, at the seventh level of the fixed stars. And Israel meets God in God's house, the Temple, the fate of which therefore in nature's time and sequence embodies the condition of Israel's relationship with God. That proposition concerning the Temple as the critical component of Israel's covenanted relationship with God is unsurprising and unexceptional. What we have here is a new way of conveying a familiar theological proposition. But that makes all the difference.

Consider the unfolding message imposed by Pesiqta deRab Kahana upon the lectionary cycle and essentially distinct from it. From Hanukkah through Pentecost, Israel in nature's time celebrates its meeting with God in the Temple. Then follow the days of desiccation and death, three weeks of mourning, when Israel's rebellion against God brings about God's abandonment of the Temple. With Israel's rebellion fully requited in the disaster, there succeed the seven Sabbaths of consolation for the penitent, corporate Israel. Then, correspondingly, come the Days of Awe, the individual Israelite's time to recapitulate in his own being the main lines of corporate Israel's story of sin, punishment, suffering and atonement and the rest. The Days of Awe, the New Year and the Day of Atonement, marked by repentance for sin, atonement, and prayer for forgiveness, then correspond to the days from the seventeenth of Tammuz to the ninth of Ab and the weeks following. At the end follows the climactic moment, the Festival par excellence, Tabernacles, with the promise of renewal. That program, laid out in the lectionary cycle superimposed on the Pentateuchal one, presents the main points of Rabbinic theology in its doctrine that builds on the correspondence of Adam and Israel, Eden and the Land. And this rabbinization of the liturgical experience does not match the way in which the Pentateuchal lections, whether annual or triennial, organize the sacred calendar of synagogue worship. A curious disjuncture imposes itself on the two distinct sequences, the narrative-historical of the Pentateuch, the paradigmatic of the lunar cycle.

The Pentateuchal lectionary cycle recapitulates the narrative sequence from Adam to the border of the promised land. By extension through Joshua, Judges, Samuel, and Kings, the narrative (if not the lectionary) cycle ends where it began: loss of Eden, loss of Jerusalem. By contrast, the lectionary program of Pesiqta deRab Kahana hardly works through the same narrative in the same sequence at all. There is no beginning, middle, and end, constructed in a teleological sequence out of the narrative history of Israel. Now, the events of the natural year, signified in the movement of the lunar months correlated with the solar seasons, built around the first full moon after the vernal and autumnal equinoxes in particular, do match certain moments in Israel's life. But these are not in the temporal order so paramount in the lectionary narrative from Genesis through Numbers plus Deuteronomy. They follow their own order and sequence. The occasions of nature matched by moments in Israel's pattern of conduct and its consequence thus are removed from the narrative framework, e.g., of Genesis through Kings. Events are no longer unique, linear, sequential—teleological. They now are formed into moments of an exemplary character, out of time altogether, out of phase with the Pentateuchal-narrative setting. Thought is no longer teleological but rather paradigmatic.

No wonder, then, that Pesiqta deRab Kahana (as we now have it in Mandelbaum's edition) starts where it does, with the rededication of the Temple signified by Hanukkah. In the repertoire of events gathered in the document, that is the only logical starting point; the alternative, the end point, is impossible. That is then followed by the leap to the four Sabbaths preparatory to Passover, with the rest in sequence! With the preparations for the celebration of Israel's beginning in the Exodus and at Sinai marking the starting point, the rest of the natural year lays itself out against the main lines of the liturgical year. There is then this cycle:

[1] the preparation of the Temple, dedication, then purification;
[2] the beginnings at Passover-Pentecost;
[3] the catastrophe of Tammuz-Ab, the season of death, then the consolation quick to follow; and at the end,
[4] the recapitulation of the same cycle in Elul and Tishre—sin, punishment, atonement, consolation and renewal, as the life-cycle of nature and the rhythm of Israelite existence correspond and signify, each, the reliability and renewal of the other.

Change the order and the entire construction collapses into gibberish. Let me spell out in detail this theological reading of Pesiqta deRab Kahana.

The Unique Theological Perspective of Pesiqta deRab Kahana

What is unique in the document's theology emerges when we see the total message in lectionary context. It is the first, and, for the formative age, the only, midrash-compilation of Rabbinic Judaism that organizes its statement other than around, and in response to, a sequence of verses of Scripture, generally, but not invariably, a narrative. The other midrash-compilations follow the order and sequence of statements of a scriptural book, e.g., Genesis, Leviticus, Lamentations, Song of Songs, and the like. But that is not how the smallest whole units of thought (sentences) and intermediate units of thought (paragraphs) in Pesiqta deRab Kahana cohere. They form elements of an unfolding argument, a proposition that transcends the sentences or the paragraphs; their logic of coherent discourse is that of argument and exposition, not episodic comment on this that and the other thing, holding together only by adhering to a common, prior text. It is in its logic of coherent discourse that Pesiqta deRab Kahana lays claim to uniqueness among the Rabbinic documents of the formative age.

At issue is how one sentence links to another, fore and aft, to form a cogent statement. So far as individual units of thought form parts of a larger composition, in the other midrash-compilations, these hold together solely by reference to a common base-text, a book of Scripture. The sentences attain coherence in Scripture's verses, read in order. The comments hold together by reference to that common foundation in a sequence of verses. That is not the case with Pesiqta deRab Kahana. Its individual thoughts, the building blocks formed by pisqa'ot, hold together by reference to the course of the natural year. Within the pisqa'ot, the singleton-components, the individual thoughts, hold together because they contribute to the exposition of a common proposition, which we have identified for each of the pisqa'ot, respectively. So the theory of coherent discourse differs markedly from that of the Midrash-compilations built upon books of Scripture.

The upshot is, Pesiqta's "text" is the passage of the seasons, on the one side, and the sequence of lunar months, on the other, as these correlate and are correlated with exemplary occasions in Israel's existence—nature, not Scripture. The pisqa'ot follow the sequence of nature's year, as I have already stressed. Internally, the individual pisqa finds coherence in the unfolding of the message that pertains to that occasion. So Pesiqta deRab Kahana does not organize its discourse around Scripture at all. The base-verses all are selected out of the context of the books of Scripture in which they occur. And—what is amazing for Rabbinic Judaism but predictable in its own context—Pesiqta deRab Kahana in no way privileges the Pentateuch as the principal source of base-verses.

Rather, the authors of its compositions and framers of its composites have chosen as the source of coherent discourse the sacred calendar and its high points. They have selected for a focus those passages of Scripture that speak to liturgical occasions set by the passage of the moon and the solar seasons in the heavens. And the sequence and sense of coherence then derive from the lunar-solar calendar, that alone. Pesiqta deRab Kahana therefore forms an exercise in correlating Israel's affairs on earth with the movement of the heavenly bodies. Israel's history, linear and sequential, no longer governs. Now exemplary moments, chosen out of time and not arranged in temporal sequence, define matters. Hence—history set aside, its sequence no longer pertinent—the natural, seasonal passage of the moon in the heavens signals paradigmatic moments in Israel's life on earth. Israel on earth responds—and corresponds—to the heavenly bodies above. It would claim more than the document establishes to describe Pesiqta deRab Kahana as an exercise in astral religion—but not by much.

The parts count only as part of the whole; seen one by one, they find counterparts in other documents, if not verbatim then in proposition or implication. It is only as part of a whole possessing its own logic of coherent discourse that we grasp that logic and understand the documentary program and message. That is why, to grasp the theological statement made by Pesiqta deRab Kahana, we have to step back and see the document whole. When we look back over the theological compositions and composites, we discern the sequential unfolding of the document's themes. These form a continuous statement, with a beginning, middle, and end: beginning with the dedication of the Temple/tabernacle, ending with the climactic moments of Tabernacles (including the Eighth Day of Solemn Assembly). They therefore turn out to conform to a required, logical order. By that I mean, if we change the sequence of themes in any detail, situating one theme somewhere other than in its present location, and the entire document yields gibberish. Its logic and cogency then derive from the lunar calendar, which signals moments in Israel's encounter with God through the natural life of the Land and its seasons, rainy, then dry, then rainy, spring, summer, autumn. In their present sequence and only in that sequence, the purposeful ordering of the document's theological propositions emerge. And these represent a decision by the authorship of the document. They bring into relationship two cycles of time: historical-narrative and natural-paradigmatic, as I shall now explain.

1. The one—the historical-narrative built on teleology—recapitulates the cycle of synagogue lections of the Pentateuch, the one that sets into sequence the events of humanity's history from creation, through the fall, past the flood, to the formation of Israel as a family and its reformation as a kingdom of priests and a holy people. It is the story of Israel's recapitulation of Adam's experience, with its calamity but, in the case of Israel when repentant, also with the promise of a different ending.

2. The natural-paradigmatic, highlighted, among the Rabbinic midrash-compilations, only here, is the cycle of the seasons, as these flow in sequence from the dedication of the Temple through its rites on distinguished occasions defined by the movement of heavenly bodies, the moon correlated with the solar seasons. It is nature's logic, heaven's logic—a different mode of organizing time altogether, one in which the paradigm of Israel's existence is recast. It is transformed from a linear sequence of onetime historical events into a pattern of re-

current moments in nature. These heavenly occasions capture points of intersection between Israel and God, corresponding to the unfolding of the seasons—hence, in the language used earlier, "natural-paradigmatic."

The details correspond. And why not? For both cycles focus upon the same entity, Israel in relationship to God. But the one, the established lectionary cycle from Genesis through Deuteronomy, tells a story, and the other, the supererogatory lectionary cycle of particular Sabbaths and special occasions, celebrates events in the heavens and their corresponding moments in Israel's eternal existence. The narrative-teleological cycle conveys its messages through the story that it tells. By the natural-paradigmatic cycle these messages are abstracted from that story and set forth as propositions of a general character.

In the halakhic corpus, the relationship between the conventional midrash-compilations, built on sequences of verses of Scripture, and the unconventional one uniquely represented by Pesiqta deRab Kahana, with its logic of coherent discourse dictated by nature and corresponding earthly patterns, has a counterpart. It is the relationship between the Mishnah and the Tosefta, on the one side, and the two Talmuds, particularly the second one, on the other. As the Mishnah presents its system through cases that yield rules, so the Pentateuch relies on its stories to imply the governing rules: the covenant in detail. And in sequence, the midrash-compilations built on the Pentateuchal narrative and its order amplify stories to yield rules.

As the Talmud identifies the rules that are implicit in the Mishnah's cases, generalizes upon them, refines them, orders and regularizes them, so our document does the same in its appeal to the movement of the moon and the solar seasons to order and regularize Israelite existence. In the halakhic context we speak of the movement from case to rule to law to jurisprudence to social philosophy. In the aggadic context, the counterpart movement carries us from story to moral rule to free-standing theological system: the system provoked by sin and punishment, atonement and repentance, forgiveness and reconciliation, for both corporate Israel and the individual Israelite, represented by the movement from the seventeenth of Tammuz through the seventh Sabbath after the ninth of Ab, then its recapitulation in Elul through Tishre.

The upshot may be simply stated. In bypassing the Pentateuchal cycle altogether, the authorship of Pesiqta deRab Kahana has adopted an intellectual structure of its own. It is one that is different from the unfolding of Israel's life in time through a sequence of one-time, particular events: the day this happened, the time that remarkable, unique event took place. Sequence is everything, story nothing. The sequence invokes that logic to which I have already made reference: the logic of Israel's moral, covenanted existence, its life with God.

Highlighting this other cycle, the one of nature's recurrent and cyclical time endowed with meaning through Israel's recurrent and cyclical activities, serves to set forth a comment upon the alternative, and paramount lectionary cycle.[1] The distinct, contrasting cycle of special Sabbaths and their lections then recasts the encounter with God when the Torah is declaimed. The main point of Pesiqta deRab Kahana, implicit in every pisqa', then is clear. It is to highlight Israel as the counterpart, on earth, to the heavenly bodies. And, as I stress, the unfolding of Israelite existence on earth, the patterns of its relationship with God—these correspond down here to the move-

---

[1] While debates continue on the precise definition of the lectionary cycle, I know of no one who claims to have shown that, for the synagogue of Rabbinic Judaism, any other cycle but the sequence from Genesis through Deuteronomy prevailed. Whether it was an annual or a triennial cycle does not affect my argument.

ment of the moon and sun in the heavens above; but we should not miss the point: the stars in their courses respond to Israel's conduct. The cycle of time as told by Pesiqta deRab Kahana treats Israel not as a principal player in world history on earth alone, as does the Pentateuchal cycle as framed by the Rabbinic masters. Rather, Israel now represents a cosmic presence, a heavenly actor on the natural stage of the Temple, along with the moon in relationship to the sun and the passage of the natural seasons.

That is why Pesiqta deRab Kahana is unique among the midrash-compilations of the formative age of Rabbinic Judaism. No other Midrash-compilation organizes itself around that conception of Israel in relationship with heaven that governs here. No midrash-compilation viewed whole but Pesiqta deRab Kahana proposes that what happens to Israel on earth correlates with the movement of the heavenly bodies, the moon and the sun in particular. It is the midrash in the formative canon of Rabbinic Judaism that endows Israel with astral setting and dimensions, raising Israel from earth to heaven. Discerning in its activities the recurrent pattern of the skies, Pesiqta deRab Kahana substitutes theology for astrology. Then, along with the Bavli's famous composite, "Israel is not subject to planetary influences," it forms a kind of anti-astrology, one might say.[2] That is because the message throughout, normative for Rabbinic Judaism, is, Israel makes choices and bears responsibility for those choices. So it relates to the movement of the moon and the sun through the seven levels of heaven signified by the fixed stars. But this is not in the way in which others are subject to the same heavenly movements. Israel drives its own chariot through the skies, the nations are but passengers on a chariot of someone else's choosing, so to speak.

Pesiqta deRab Kahana builds upon its own, cosmic sense of world order. It makes its own judgment on the meaning of the cyclical sequence of the movement of the heavenly bodies. It defines in its own way the encounter of Israel and God, in earth and in heaven, always in correspondence. This is, then, a different way of framing Israel's and God's relationship from the established one that begins with Genesis and concludes with Deuteronomy, the familiar comparison of Adam and Israel, Eden and the Land.

The theology of astral Israel bears its consequences for the reading of Scripture. These we have already contemplated. Now the times and the seasons embody heaven's account of Israel on earth. Scripture is not the only voice of God, nature's time and sequence speaks for him as well. And, it follows, if Scripture is no longer the sole supernatural message, then Israel in time no longer follows a simple, linear sequence, this happened, then that; Israel did this, with that result. Rather we have a perspective on matters formed from Heaven's view: this season responds to Israel's conduct in that circumstance, this event in the heavens correlates with that activity of Israel on earth. And the account bears a cyclicality that the Pentateuchal narrative does not possess. Thus the document viewed whole imposes upon the cycle of narrative—the story of Israel in time—that other cycle, the cycle of nature. One may characterize the resulting cycle as a competing, or at least, as a correlative, mode of recapitulating Israel's record from its beginnings to now. Annually Israel dedicates the Temple, prepares it for the pilgrims, celebrates the advent of freedom and receives the Torah.

---

[2] The compilers of the composite, "Israel is not subject to planetary influences," at B. Shab. 156a–b, form the counterpart to those of Pesiqta deRab Kahana, with this difference. While the Bavli's elaborate composite states its point in so many words and repeats it throughout, the Midrash-compilation never articulates its proposition, only embodies it in its program and mode of organization.

Annually Israel rebels against the Torah and sins, is punished through the loss of the Temple. Annually Israel atones and repents, and God consoles and forgives. And annually Israelites recapitulate that same cycle of sin and atonement, consolation and forgiveness, so that, year by year, the rains follow the Festival, Tabernacles, in a renewal of nature's—and Israel's—cycle.

That brings us back to the main point. What has happened to the scriptural story, which is linear, sequential, and historical, not cyclical, episodic, and exemplary? Pesiqta deRab Kahana takes over and reshapes *the results* of Israel's continuous narrative from Creation to destruction and the hope of restoration and incorporates the linear into the paradigmatic structure. The narrative tells of Adam's loss of Eden, then— Genesis through Kings in hand—Israel's loss of the Land. The consequences to be drawn from that story—sin leads to punishment, but repentance leads to restoration and renewal—define the paradigm discerned in the very movement of the moon and the solar seasons by Pesiqta deRab Kahana. At issue then is how to break the cycle signified by the natural year. Israel has the power, any time, any year, to disrupt that cycle and inaugurate the end of history and nature as then known. So when I say that Pesiqta deRab Kahana has folded the results of Israel's narrative into a pattern yielded by the very givens of the natural world and its times and seasons, I refer to the recapitulation, in reference to the natural year, of the consequences to be drawn from the comparison of Israel and Adam, the Land and Eden, that the scriptural account, read continuously, has yielded.

Then the continuous, linear, one-directional narrative is folded into the cycle of nature's time, marked by seasons and events in heaven,[3] with their counterpart. That is the celebration of nature at the altar of the Temple through offerings that signify particular events in the unfolding of the natural year. These, further, are correlated with paradigmatic moments in Israel's year. So the story of the Temple on earth recapitulates in Israel's setting the story of the passage of the seasons. But that is with this proviso. The seasons follow the course that they do because they signal the unfolding existence of Israel, with special reference to its Temple altar, where God and Israel meet. Because Israel repeats its conduct, nature recapitulates its cycles. But there will come a new heaven and a new earth, when Israel completes the work badly begun by Adam.

Specifically, the twenty-eight pisqa'ot of Pesiqta deRab Kahana flow together in seasonal sequence, starting, of necessity, with Hanukkah (December), ending, inevitably, with Tabernacles (October). Why start with Hanukkah, the beginning of no new year known to the Mishnah (at M. R.H. 1:1, for example)? The liturgical year contemplated by the original minds of Pesiqta deRab Kahana begins with the Temple's point of origin, when it is dedicated. And that points, at Pisqa' One, to Hanukkah. Hanukkah invokes the dedication of the Temple, the point in the solar-lunar year at which the days begin to grow longer, light to increase (as in the kindling of the Hanukkah lights in accord with the position of the House of Hillel, from one to many). The annual cycle comes to its climax at the end of the Days of Awe with Tabernacles' invocation of the beginning of the rainy season. Then, the time judgment fulfilled, Israel's coming year is decided: rain and abundance, or drought and want. It is an open-ended ending.

Now we see the basis of the opening claim. It was that the tight logic of the document was such that changing the position

---

[3] I refer here to the results of my, *The Presence of the Past, the Pastness of the Present. History, Time, and Paradigm in Rabbinic Judaism* (Bethesda, 1996).

of a single exposition will have ruined the entire construction. A moment of reflection on the articulated plan of the whole shows that for a construction with its focus on the Temple, nexus of heaven and earth, the sole possible starting point was Hanukkah: today the Temple commences. Then what can have followed? The only logical continuation is with the four Sabbaths prior to the advent of Nisan, with Passover following two weeks later. These Sabbaths then prepare the way for the pilgrim festival, Passover-Pentecost. From the climactic season, Passover-Pentecost, with the end of the rains, follows the long dry season, marked by the Temple's destruction. Then comes Israel's repentance. That is in two correlated phases, corporate and individual. First is the corporate with the ninth of Ab, then the individual with the penitential season of Elul followed by the New Year, the day of remembrance, and the Day of Atonement. So is realized the time of renewal marked by judgment of the year gone by and renewal of life in the year to come. Once the natural year, celebrated in Temple rite, defines the heart of the matter, then the matter was set. That is why, within the logic of the natural year embodied in the Temple rites, there is no other sequence that can have served, no other starting point that can have realized the governing program of the document viewed whole.

Here—as mediated by the theology of Pesiqta deRab Kahana—is how Israel encounters that other reading of the Torah. That is the besides the one beginning with Creation and ending at the border of the Land of Israel in the lectionary cycle encompassing Genesis through Deuteronomy, week by week. The document's authorship has undertaken to expound the Torah in the sequence of the natural year in such a way as annually to tell the tale of Israel's conduct embodied in the passage of the seasons, celebrated in the realization of the Temple, where God and Israel meet. The plan is therefore to show how what happens to the Temple, then, now, and in time to come, signifies the relationship of God and corporate Israel and recapitulates the relationship of God and the individual Israelite. Then the liturgical lections of the synagogue's special occasions. It is the story encompassing the Festival cycle and related, special Sabbaths. Autonomous of the sequence of Sabbath lections that begins with Genesis and concludes with Deuteronomy, it makes its own selections of appropriate occasions and their inexorable themes. In its context, its statement is unique.

To conclude: through its lectionary cycle, Pesiqta deRab Kahana makes Israel's progress through the year of nature into an annual journey of renewal. So while Pesiqta deRab Kahana participates in the common theology of Rabbinic Judaism, it affords a rare theological moment within that same Judaism. That is the moment at which theology becomes natural, by which I mean, an interpretation, a realization, of nature. Here theology as intellectual proposition gives way to theology as the explanation of realized experience, both corporate and individual, of nature in all its majesty. No wonder, then, that the issue of the end of days, the resolution of linear time in its Messianic climax, plays so negligible a role in the document. Cyclicality in nature has taken over and assigned a marginal position to those critical components of the historical-messianic view of Israel's existence, the end of days and the advent of the messiah. Here, consolation means restoration, and the Temple is the focus. Then nature takes over and the movements of the heavenly bodies become determinative. And withal Israel makes all the difference. In the unfolding of the natural year within the theology of Pesiqta deRab Kahana, Israel lives out its theology of repentance and restoration in the inexorable passage of the times and the seasons. All that history can contribute is the unique event that can be transformed into a paradigmatic moment, part of a recurrent pattern.

The Theological Propositions of the Twenty-eight Pisqa'ot

So much for the document seen whole. What about the twenty-eight particular propositions of the pisqa'ot, read one by one? We shall now see that, viewed from the perspective of the individual components, the pisqa'ot and their parts, Pesiqta deRab Kahana occupies a place in the very center of the Rabbinic structure and system, containing much that is entirely familiar, and little that is new. And, to the logical next question: Does the shift in fundamental intellectual approach—from historical narrative to philosophical reading of nature—stimulate new theological proposals? A rapid survey of the twenty-eight pisqa'ot of Pesiqta deRab Kahana answers the question negatively. The substance of the correspondence between events in Israel's life on earth and events in the movement of the heavenly bodies, the conclusions to be drawn,—these go over familiar ground indeed.

Let us proceed systematically, through the principal parts of the Rabbinic theology that sustains the specificities of the aggadah. I epitomize the main points of the theological compositions and the composites they comprise. We focus on the most fundamental components: the principal actors in their relationships. These are, everyone must concur, God and Man (Adam), God and Israel, God, Israel, and the Nations. Then we turn to the role of the Torah in changing the course of creation, bringing into being a new moral entity, corporate Israel, and God's relationships with Israel, characterized by justice and mercy; and the restoration of Israel to the Land, thus Adam to Eden, in the end of days, when the cycle of rebellion, sin, punishment, atonement, repentance, forgiveness, is broken.

1. God and Man, God and Israel: In the beginning God and man to begin with lived together. But as the generations from Adam onward corrupted their way, God took his leave of man, moving upward in the seven firmaments signified by the fixed stars. With the advent of Abraham, Isaac, Jacob, Kohath, Amram, and Moses, God returned to live with man, descending through the seven firmaments to earth (I:I.4). God and Israel are lovers, united in the marriage canopy formed by the tabernacle in the wilderness and the Temple in Jerusalem (I:I.1). The tent of meeting provided an appropriate meeting place for God and Israel (I:II.1-2, 6). Israel forms the counterpart to Adam, living out the same paradigm of rebellion and sin, but with a different outcome. Israel sins but God forgives when Israel atones (II:I.1ff.). God forgave Israel even the sin of the golden calf, when Israel atoned (II:III).

God understood that Adam would enjoy free will and would therefore sin: In the first hour [the thought of creating him] entered [God's mind], in the second God consulted the ministering angels, in the third he collected dust, in the fourth, he kneaded it, in the fifth he wove together the parts, in the sixth he stood him on his feet as an unformed mass, in the seventh, he blew into it the breath of life, in the eighth, he put him into the Garden of Eden, in the ninth God gave him a commandment, in the tenth Adam violated his commandment, in the eleventh he was judged, in the twelfth God gave him a pardon (XXIII:I). The nations have many horns, only Israel has the shofar (XXIII:IV). The nations leave nothing over of their crops, so are judged by the principles of strict justice, while Israel leaves over something for the poor, so is judged mercifully (XXIII:VI).

The redemption at the Sea, the giving of the Torah, and the restoration of the Temple in the age to come, all represent covenantal moments (XIX:VI). Israel contrasts with Adam. Adam had scarcely a half-dozen commandments, but could not keep them. Israel received 613 commandments at Sinai, corresponding to the bones of the body and the days of the solar year, 248, 365, respectively, and keeps them all (XII:I). God rescued Israel from Pharaoh and the Egyptians, and lest the matter be deemed one-time only, also from the eternal Amalek. He gave Israel the Torah, and this he did because he trusted Israel and took delight in Israel's loyalty (XII:II). God's redemption of Israel from Egypt is comparable to Hosea's redemption of his straying wife; the fifty days from Passover to Pentecost compare with the fifty days of penance that Hosea's wife observed. The nations of the world fled before God when he gave the Torah. But Israel abided in his shadow. This was in Sivan, when the Torah was given (XII:X).

Just as Adam lost Eden, so Israel has lost the Land, and for the same reason, disobedience to God's commandments. Israel is compared to Adam, the land of Israel to Eden. Israel's loss of the Land is for the same reason that Adam lost Eden. Just as Adam disobeyed God's commandment, so Israel did the same. Just as God mourned for Adam, so he mourned for Israel. (XV:I). The specific sin that has brought on the gross punishment is forsaking the Torah: disobedience, just as in the case of Adam (XV:V). But Israel's relationship with God is unique and perpetual (XVI:III). God punishes Israel for its sins but forgives them when atoned for. In his mercy, he warns Israel through the prophets. But his capacity for forgiveness is without limit. The prophets provide the key to Israel's history. Their words endure, so what they said long ago continues to reveal the mystery of Israel's existence (XIII:III). God will redeem Israel and restore Israel to the Land (XIII:IX). So Israel from Sinai forward had the merit of hearing or obeying, until at last they lost that as well. Israel from Sinai forward had the merit of hearing or obeying, until at last they lost that as well (XIV:IV). Adam, Pharaoh, Moses found no wrong with God. What wrong has Israel found, that they have worshipped an idol, once more, an allusion to the golden calf (XIV:V).

Israel must acknowledge its complete dependence on God. That is for the crops, but still more important, it also is for the Land. The waving of the first sheaf of the barley crop is a mark of that right attitude, showing the Israelite acknowledge of God's complete mastery of Israel's destiny. The right way to express that attitude is through prayer and penitence, not through acts of violence and war (VIII:I). Israel depends on God for their sustenance. The advent of the crop embodied in the first sheaf of barley does not mean they do not need him any longer; the crop during the seven weeks between Passover and Pentecost, counted out in the sheaf of barley, also requires God's protection, now from hot wind. The sheaf of the first barley-crop is an offering meant to merit that protection. The broader proposition, however, links God's provision of Israel's sustenance to the state of Israel's merit. As is the way of the Midrash to find in Scripture examples of its paradigm of history, so here too, we find that Abraham, Moses and Aaron, Deborah and Barak, Isaiah and Hezekiah, Mordecai, Joshua and Caleb, all acquired the harvest of Israel's enemies without making war, but only through the merit of prayer, fasting and repentance. Then, in line with the same reasoning, the Israelites' merit of inheriting the Land from the Canaanites requires explanation. It is on account of a specific religious duty and the merit accruing thereby, which is, the duty of offering the first sheaf of barley. The actual performance of the rite—waving the sheaf forward and backward, upward and downward, points to God's ubiquity: "to him to whom the entire earth belongs, to him to whom the upper world and the lower world belong" (VIII:I.9, VIII:IV.1). Those that have merit provide for their needs without a sword or shield, but only with God's help. That is Abraham, taking over Nimrod's harvest; Moses and Aaron, taking over Pharaoh's; Moses and Aaron, taking over the harvest of Sihon and Og; Deborah and Barak, taking over Sisera's harvest; Isaiah and Hezekiah, taking over

Sennacherib's harvest; Mordecai, taking over Haman's, Joshua and Caleb, taking over the thirty-one kings of the Canaanites. All of that leads to No. 8: it is the merit of carrying out the religious duty of offering the sheaf of first barley that accorded to the Israelites possession of the Land (VIII:II).

Israel and God meet in the Temple, which realizes their relationship. Offerings on the altar represent a token; God does not depend on Israel for nourishment. The offerings represent God's grace: he accepts what is not commensurate to what is at stake. That is a mark of the righteous person, as against the wicked, who is never satisfied, thus Ruth by contrast to other gentiles, Eliezer of Damascus by contrast to Esau. Through the offerings Israel atones and attains forgiveness. Issues of sin and atonement yield the emphasis on the salvific power of Israel's atonement, on the one side, and the mercy that God will show in response to that atonement, on the other (VI:Iff.). God asks for only the scent of the offerings, which is intangible; that signals the on-going obedience of Israel to God's commandments in the Torah and suffices; even studying the Torah about the sacrifices suffices (VI:III). The offerings serve principally to atone for Israel's sin (VI:IV). God shrinks his presence to the dimensions of the Temple. He accepts the minimal offerings. And he accepts the half-shekel coin for the daily whole offerings of forgiveness, all incommensurate to what is vouchsafed in return: the Presence, atonement and forgiveness (VI:IV).

God asks Israel to tarry yet another day beyond the Festival (XXXVIII:I). Augmenting the festival presents the contrast between Israel and the gentiles. When God benefits the idolaters, they blaspheme, but when he benefits Israel, they bless him. On the extra day of the festival, gentiles carouse, on the extra day of the Israelite festival, the Israelites increase their praying and offerings (XXVIII:I). Once more the event in the sacred calendar is linked to this-worldly concerns about Israel among the gentiles. The Eighth Day of Solemn assembly marks the pleasure that God takes in Israel (XXVIII:V). It is an act of consideration on God's part for Israel's ease of making the pilgrimage, keeping contiguous two distinct holy days (XXVIII:VII), Tabernacles and the Eighth Day of Solemn Assembly. That day, further, provides an additional opportunity to pray for water in the coming rainy season (XXVIII:VIII). And while on the Festival, Israel offers atonement offerings for all of the seventy nations (CCVIII:IX).

The act of "taking" the instruction of the Torah instead of silver assures its just reward; because Israel does not sate itself with Torah, it suffers want. When Israel takes up what God commands, the bunch of hyssop in Egypt, it is rewarded manifold (XXVII:I).

2. God and the Nations, Israel and the Nations: The nations of the world had every opportunity to receive the Torah. It was given at the time of Esau and Jacob, so Esau, meaning Rome, had every opportunity to come and study the Torah, and God would accept him. He did not use the opportunity. The setting of Sinai, in the wilderness, which is free for all. That is regarded as a metaphor for the Torah: it is given only to those who surrender themselves to it, and it is without end and the reward for studying it is without end (XII:XX).

Israel's enemies are God's enemies as well. Israel preserves the name of Amalek/Rome down below, but God will blot it out in heaven. Second, God will ultimately punish Rome/Amalek for its treatment of Israel, then and now. But Amalek's treatment of Israel represents a just penalty exacted from Israel for its sin against God. God is just; Israel is on God's side; when Israel sins, by means of the nations God justly punishes Israel; but those that mistreat Israel ultimately are punished by God (Pisqa' Three).

Israel's history among the nations is replicated on the Temple altar itself, the various animals and rites embodying the various nations and their activities. Thus the red cow of Num. 19 stands for Babylonia, Media, Greece, but not Rome, and also stands for Israel (IV:IX-X). Israel is comparable to the great empires, having sinned in the time of Jeremiah. The nations rule by God's favor, and at their hands Israel suffers by God's decree. Israel is like Edom/Rome, in rejecting the yoke of God's dominion. God himself is represented in the eschatological resolution of the matter; he will collect the ashes of the cow, who are Israel's exiles, and bring them back to Jerusalem; and in the age to come, God himself will effect Israel's purification. Israel is compared to the moon, the nations of the world to the sun, Israel contrasted to Esau/Rome. Now Esau is great like the sun, Jacob small like the moon, but just as the sun rules by day, not by night, so Rome rules now but not in the world to come. Jacob rules day and night, and will rule in this world and the world to come (V:XIV). God exacts vengeance from the nations of the world (V:XVIII).

The redemption from Egypt could have been accomplished only by God, who alone can distinguish the first-born from the other sons, the midnight hour from the other hours of the darkness (VII:I, II). The message of Passover is the point at which Israel is differentiated for God's service, signified by the blood rite, whether at the altar or at circumcision—or at the lintel, which stands for the altar when Israel is preserved for life in Egypt (IX:Iff.) IX:II makes the point that if someone is devoted to God before receiving a benefit, God responds to such an act of faith with a generous reward. Observing the commandments gratuitously, and not in response to gifts already given, is then taken as an act of faith and loyalty. IX:IV compares Israel, pursued by Pharaoh at the Exodus, to the animals suitable for the altar, all of them hunted and not hunters; and in the course of the comparison, rings the changes on others of the same classification: Abel/Cain; Noah/his generation; Abraham/Nimrod; Isaac/Philistines; Jacob/Esau; Moses/Pharaoh; David/Saul; Israel/nations, and the like.

The distinction between righteous and wicked runs parallel to that between circumcised and not circumcised. Then the blood-rite of circumcision, which distinguishes Israel, is what marks Israel as righteous, and uncircumcision marks the gentiles as wicked. In the context of the Passover narrative, Exod. 12, with its stress on the blood placed on the lintel, which differentiates Israel from the Egyptians; the uncircumcised may not partake of the Paschal lamb on the fifteenth of Nisan. So the comparison of circumcision on the eighth day and readiness of a beast for the altar on the eighth day after birth links specifically to Passover. The deeper intent is to compare Israel, which is circumcised, to the righteous, and the gentiles, who are not, to the wicked (IX:I). The animals suitable for the altar represent Abraham, Isaac, and Jacob (IX:IX.1).

3. Israel's encounter with God through the Torah: At Sinai God appeared to the Israelites in many forms, XII:XXIV: Because the Holy One, blessed be he, had appeared to them at the sea like a heroic soldier, doing battle, appeared to them at Sinai like a teacher, teaching the repetition [of traditions], appeared to them in the time of Daniel like a sage, teaching Torah, appeared to them in the time of Solomon like a younger man, [it was necessary for] the Holy One, blessed be he, to say to them, "You see me in many forms. But I am the same one who was at the sea, I am the same one who was at Sinai." The Holy One appeared to them like an icon that has faces in all directions, so that if a thousand people look at it, it appears to look at them as well. So too when the Holy One, when he was speaking, each and every Israelite would say, "With me in particular the Word speaks." Words of the Torah are to appear as fresh and new, scarcely three days old. The Torah is to be received as though it were given that very day. The central encounter with God in the Torah, then, takes place in the acute present-tense: this very minute (XII:XII, also XII:XXI). The moment of the giving of the Torah is comparable to the moment of the raising of the dead. God renews Israel, so that they were made worthy of receiving the Torah. The marks of slavery in Egypt were allowed to dissipate, then, fifty days later, they were ready for redemption (XII:XIX).

4. Divine Justice and Mercy: The fate of the Egyptians represents an act of pure and perfect justice on God's part. The same principle of justice that consigns the Egyptian pursuers to the depths of the oceans saves Israel from the same fate (XI:Iff.) Precisely what Pharaoh said to Moses came back upon his own head, point by point (XI:I). Prosperity depends in the end on giving God's share of what God accords to the householder. Miserly behavior in the end impoverishes and does not enrich the miser. God is the model of generosity, asking that his sharecroppers deliver a mere ten per cent of the crop. If Israel tithes, it will prosper; if not, Esau will take over the crop anyhow.

5. God's Judgment, Israel's Repentance and atonement; God's Remorse, Israel's Consolation: God warned Israel to repent, because he does not want to punish sinners but wants them to repent, thus the realization of the theme of the Ten Days of Repentance (XXIV:I). If Israel repents, it will be forgiven on the Day of Atonement. Repentance is always possible, and God is always ready to forgive the penitent (XXIV:II). Atonement-rites through sacrifices are not possible, but Israel can offer appropriate offerings nonetheless: contrition and humility (XXIV:V). God teaches sinners to repent, because he does not want to punish them (XXIV:VI, VII). That is why he gives ample warning for what he is going to do. The response of repentance requires confession of sin (XXIV:VIII). Since God is not only just but merciful, that suffices to elicit forgiveness. The record of forgiveness of those who repent proves that point: Cain, Ahab, and others were forgiven (XXIV:X, XI). God has an infinite capacity to show mercy and forgive in the case of the repentant person (XXV:I). God's greatness is enhanced by his power of forgiveness, which he exercises like a weight-lifter. It is further augmented by the righteous who carry out God's will. Israel strengthens God when they do his will, and weaken him when not. Then comes the climax, No. 7: when Israel is redeemed, it will be through a fully-qualified person (XXV:I). How forgiveness works is clear in the record of the past. God forgives those who repent, not those who do not; he sweeps away sin in this world but not in the world to come. Generations that continue the tradition of their families are rewarded or punished, as the case may be, for that fact (XXV:IV). The death of the righteous, like the Day of Atonement, achieves atonement (XXVI:XII).

God participates in the mourning over Jerusalem, on a cosmic scale acting as does a mortal king (XV:III). God is comparable to man. So if Boaz could bring comfort to Ruth, or Joseph to his brothers (XVI:V), God can bring comfort to Jerusalem (XVI:I). The first Sabbath after the ninth of Ab brings the message that Israel is forgiven, and that God is the one who forgives. Job and Jerusalem suffered from the same punishments, Chaldeans for both, fire from heaven for both, the potsherd recurs, sitting on the ground in mourning, sackcloth, dust on the heads, enjoying no favor, punishment, but then as Job was restored, so will Jerusalem be restored (XVI:VI). So too the Ten Tribes went into exile but endured (XVI:VII).

Every part of the body of Israel was smitten, but through each part in sequence, God also brought comfort. When they sin with that part of the body, they are smitten too; but then when they repent, they are comforted through the same part of the body— but the comfort is in double measure (XVI:XI). Israel has been punished for its sin, but will be comforted when it atones. God is the comforter, acting in the model of Boaz with Ruth (XVI:I). God's messages to the prophets are contradictory. They were told to comfort Israel, but did not succeed in doing so. Thus Hosea, Joel, Amos, Micah, Nahum, Habakkuk, Zephaniah, Haggai, Zechariah, Malachi—all produced messages of both comfort and doom, thus "Which shall we believe?" But God then calls on the prophets to go together to comfort Jerusalem. Then all participate: living and dead, this world, world to come, Ten Tribes, Judah & Benjamin—all comforting "with me" (XVI:VIII). God shares, also, not only in Jerusalem's downfall but in the rejoicing of her restoration (XVI:IX). The comfort extends beyond the generation of the return to Zion; it is a comfort for all generations to come (XVI:X).

God remembers Israel, he remembers Israel's service (XVII:I). God cannot abandon Israel but his love endures through all time (XVII:I). God has been angry with Israel but there is hope, the anger is appeased (XVII:II). Adam, Jacob, Israel in the wilderness, and Zion are always complaining. But God has already written a good record for himself, having gotten rid of Babylonia, Media, and Greece, and can be relied upon to comfort Israel through the destruction of its ultimate foe, Rome (XVII:III). God, abandoning him and violating the covenant, and God has forsaken them. This is a familiar pattern: (Babylonia), Media, Greece, Edom. But the base-verse then makes its mark. God will ultimately save Israel and forgive her. That has happened before and it will happen again (XVII:IV). God will forget Israel's bad deeds, but not the good ones (XVII:VII). As David's enemies thought he had been abandoned, but God restored him to his throne, so Israel's enemies think the same, but God will restore Jerusalem (XVIII:I). Israel will have her comforter, the redeemer, just as Sarai ultimately had a son, and Hannah likewise (XVIII:III).

Sin is atoned for not only through the judgment and atonement of the New Year and the Day of Atonement, but through carrying out the religious duties of the Festival (XXVII:VII). The pertinence of the Festival to the Days of Awe, New Year and Day of Atonement, is made explicit. The nations indict Israel before God on the New Year. When Israel goes forth from the judgment bearing the palm branches and citrons in their hands, they mark themselves as the victors. So the Festival is the occasion for the celebration of the atonement season and its result (XXVII:II). The package of symbols of the Festival represented by the fruit of goodly trees, palm branches, and the like, which Israel is to take up on the Festival, represents God, Abraham, Sarah, the Great Sanhedrin, and Israel. Israel is saved by reason of those that are virtuous in Torah- learning and good deeds, and those that lack these are joined together with those that have them, the whole forming a single moral entity (XXVII:IX).

6. Consolation and Restoration: God personally comforts Israel (XIX:I). While Israel's loyalty to God separates her from the nations, God in the end will save Israel and do so on his own (XIX:II). God not only owes it to Israel to restore her fortune, but he is merciful and wants to do so. God has mercy on Israel like the merciful patriarchs: Abraham, or Jacob. God is compassionate with Israel the way a mother or a father is (XIX:III). Israel in exile is sustained by God's promises at Lev. 26:9, and it is the Torah that sustains Israel by preserving the hope for the future redemption (XIX:IV).

Since God drove Israel out of Jerusalem, when he brings her back, he doubles her reward. He, he alone restores her. Israel's acts of loyalty yield such certainty of the hoped-for response. Israel's uncertainty therefore is unwarranted (XIX:VI). Zion takes her place among the seven childless women of Scripture, whose ultimate joy outweighed their early sorrow (XX:I). Jerusalem is comparable to Rachel, who wept for the exiles and in response whose children, Joseph and Benjamin, bear the name of Israel (XX:II). The glory of restored

Zion will exceed that of the destroyed city, just as the deserted wife has more children than the wife in wedlock. The Temple when standing had a place for wicked kings, but in ruins has only righteous persons (XX:V, VI). Israel is partner in the restoration; God and Israel together bring light to Zion (XXI:I). Israel made a lamp for God, which was extinguished; from now on, Israel waits on God's light (XXI:III). At the beginning of the creation of the world the Holy One, blessed be he, foresaw that the Temple would be built, destroyed, and rebuilt (XXI:V). as in the redemption from Egypt, so in the redemption at the end of days, there will be darkness for the idolaters and light for those that worship God (XXI:VI).

7. The End of Days: Israel's merit is what brings about the return to Zion (XXII:III), and that derives from the heritage of the patriarchs. When God judges Israel, he does so bearing in mind the memory of those for whom, in the here and now of the judgment, Israel stands. The perfect obedience of Abraham and Isaac weighs in the balance against the imperfect obedience to the commandments on the part of their descendants (XXIII:I, XXIII:VIII, IX, XI). The shofar reminds God of the paradigm of Moriah (XXIII:II, VII).

Whatever God is going to do for the righteous in the world to come he has already done in this world (IX:IV.2). He will most certainly avenge the pursued and wreak vengeance among the pursuers (IX:IV.3). What will happen at the end of time has already happened at the beginning, and the advent of the end of time will mark the restoration of the condition of Eden. The redemption at the end of days will correspond in every detail to the redemption from Egypt (VII:XI). Just as God exacted vengeance from Egypt, so he will exact vengeance from Rome, and the end of days will be precisely a match for the end of Egyptian bondage (VII:XI, XII). Uncleanness represents death, cleanness, life. God's sayings are pure and he is the ultimate source of purity, thus of life (IV:Iff.) Only God can bring forth cleanness out of uncleanness, which stands for life out of the grave (IV:I).

When Israel has merit, it compares with the waxing moon, represented by the patriarchs, saints, and figures in the Messianic line; when Israel does not have merit, it is like the waning moon, represented by the kings whose line ultimately perished in the fall of Jerusalem. The coming redemption underlies the entire discourse: when Israel has merit, everything will follow (V:XII). What Israel had to its credit for the redemption from Egypt was the blood of the Passover-offering, prepared the night before and placed on the lintel of the house, and the blood of circumcision. That sufficed then—and will serve for the coming redemption, however, otherwise, Israel's condition may be degraded (VII:IV).

In Israel's joy the world rejoices. Thus, in the model of Sarah, when she produced a child, many other persons were remembered along with her: the deaf, the blind, the insane, all regained their senses. So too when Israel returns to Zion, the nations will rejoice alongside. Zion will rejoice only when God comes back to her (XXII:I).

We come to the final point: Are the theological propositions of Pesiqta deRab Kahana unique or at least particular to that document? At no point in detail do I find a conception that will have surprised the authors of compositions, and the authorships of composites, of any other Rabbinic compilation, whether of halakhah or of aggadah, from the Mishnah through the Bavli, from Sifra and the two Sifres through Song of Songs Rabbah. So while Pesiqta deRab Kahana takes a unique position in the theology of Rabbinic Judaism, that is not in detail, only in its fundamental claim. But that claim should not be missed; it concerns the conditions of Israel's direct and immediate encounter with God, which is when the Torah is declaimed in the synagogue.

Does Pesiqta deRab Kahana Form a Theological Statement?

Pesiqta deRab Kahana does form a theological statement. It is this: Israel on earth embodies the course of the moon and the solar seasons in heaven, and when Israel mends its way, all of astral nature will respond. All else—the particular theological statements I discern in the twenty-eight Pisqa'ot—forms a commentary and is made up of details. It is now my task to say what I think Pesiqta deRab Kahana says as its theological statement and to show that that statement in its own terms is cogent, if insufficient. Showing its cogency requires a measure of recapitulation. To locate the theological statement that I claim Pesiqta deRab Kahana sets forth, we have to double back and reconsider the document seen whole and in the larger lectionary context.

The synagogue through the paramount Torah-cycle (whether annual or triennial, and however divided) calls Israel to rehearse, week by week, the chapters of Israel's formative life: Genesis for the foundation of Israel, Exodus through Numbers, then Deuteronomy, for the definition of Israel. Then, on a given week, Israel once more recapitulates through its paradigmatic and definitive narrative the earthly story of itself. This week the world was made, that week recalls the Flood, the next, the call to Abraham, and so throughout. So through the lectionary cycle, annually or triennially, the past is made present, the present resituated in the past, historical time, marked by unique, one-time events, is recapitulated, the past both recognized and renewed. In that context, we recall, Pesiqta deRab Kahana has made a remarkable choice. It is to impose upon the story of Israel's formation and definition another dimension, another layer of being: the heavenly, as I said. It is now Israel in the context—indeed, in control—of natural time, marked by the stars and the seasons. The Sabbaths of Joseph's story, for example, that in the annual lectionary cycle come in Kislev in accord with the annual cycle of lections, embody also the occasion of the rededication of the Temple. But these do not intersect. While an exegetical initiative may link the one with the other (reading Scripture to underscore the Temple in the patrimony of Benjamin, for instance, joining the two distinct themes), that is a mere serendipity.

In fact, Pesiqta deRab Kahana invokes a distinct layer of Israelite being. Our review of the theological components of the document identifies that layer of being: it concerns Israel's celebration in the Temple, its loss of the Temple, and its hope for forgiveness and restoration of the Temple. It is no wonder that ten of the twenty-eight pisqa'ot concern the destruction and consequent consolation. Nor is it surprising that the following sequence of heavenly events—those of Elul and Tishre—recapitulates the pattern of Tammuz-Ab! The one concerns corporate Israel, the other Israel as Israelite, one by one, all before God but judged as individuals. So what Pesiqta deRab Kahana contributes to the Israel's encounter with God in the Torah is the matter of the coming consolation and redemption. That is now portrayed as heaven's promise. This survey shows that Pesiqta deRab Kahana makes a theological statement that is, in its own terms, entirely cogent.

On eschatological matters Pesiqta deRab Kahana has its own points of interest, even while concurring with the main propositions given here. The document wishes to underscore that what God is going to do he has already done; that what will happen in the ultimate redemption is already prefigured in this world's experience. What will happen at the end of time has already happened at the beginning, and the advent of the end of time will mark the restoration of the condition of Eden. These propositions do not fit tightly with the framing of matters in more general terms. For the correspondence of end to beginning, while part of the repertoire of the governing theology, hardly limits the eschatological doctrine of that theology. But it is the main point of Pesiqta deRab Kahana. So the theological structure of Pesiqta deRab Kahana is asymmetrical with that of the aggadic documents viewed systematically; but it coheres. Where Pesiqta deRab Kahana intersects, it conforms in conception with the encompassing system. But the proportions and the emphases are its own.

Pesiqta deRab Kahana takes an essential role in the larger theological program of Rabbinic Judaism. This it does by superimposing, upon the Pentateuchal story of Israel's beginning, the narrative of the ending—destruction but also atonement, forgiveness, renewal, for both corporate Israel and the Israelite. The reliable heavens then guarantee what is to come about, the seasons in their sequence embody the promise of the coming redemption: consolation and restoration following repentance, atonement, and forgiveness. The summer drought, the advent of the early rains—these now are made, in the very heart of synagogue liturgy, to signify the existential reality of Israel in its encounter with God.

What makes Pesiqta deRab Kahana's revision of the lectionary encounter powerful and persuasive ought not to be missed. It is its emphasis upon the correspondence of the cycle of nature with the exemplary moments of Israel's existence, the whole abstracted from linear history. The dedication and celebration in the Temple, loss of the Temple, atonement and renewal and restoration correspond to nature's cycle. Then, after the season of desiccation and death, the renewal signified by the winter rains, comes the climax of Passover-Pentecost. Then the sequence concludes with the advent of the summer's drought, followed by the renewal once more.

We should not miss the radical change represented by this reading of the cycle of nature that defines the rhythm of the Israelite year. While the lunar-solar calendar conventionally interpreted knows two climactic moments, the first full moon after the vernal equinox, then the same after the autumnal equinox, for Passover and Pentecost, respectively, Pesiqta deRab Kahana has constructed a single, continuous cyclical sequence, as I have explained. Events of nature, the unfolding of the lunar year, and events of history, the unfolding of Israel's life in historical time, are formed into a single, unitary construction. That is, furthermore, transformed into a paradigm of the life of not only corporate Israel but also the individual Israelite. Nature, Israel, the Israelite—all now are given their moment in the lectionary life of the synagogue.

In line with the intent of the whole, to augment the synagogue's weekly lections of the Torah into a coherent statement concerning the Temple and its embodiment of Israel's relationship with God, both collective and individual, the program therefore is clear. Seen start to finish, Pesiqta deRab Kahana could have commenced only where it does, with Hanukkah. That is, Kislev, corresponding to the winter solstice, marks the starting point: the Temple is dedicated anew. So, as we saw, the year begins with the building of the tabernacle and its reconsecration.[4] Then the four Sabbaths before the first pilgrim festival calls Israel to Jerusalem set the stage. The liturgical-cultic year reaches its first climax with Passover, continuing through Pentecost. Israel attains its freedom from slavery and receives the

---

[4] That is hardly a natural choice, since a long spell lacking noteworthy occasions follows, from Kislev to Adar. That is not to say the synagogue calendar lacks such occasions, e.g., the fifteenth of Shebat. But within the plan and program of Pesiqta deRab Kahana, those occasions are not noteworthy.

Torah: Israel is realized. Then follow the Sabbaths that recapitulate the sequence of destruction and consolation, three from the seventeenth of Tammuz to the ninth of Ab for the one, seven, until the eve of Tishre, for the other. Israel now engages with man's destiny, recapitulating Adam's fall. In Israel's case, that involves the Temple's being destroyed, Israel's being banished from the Land, all as it was with Adam before. It is at the end of this sequence of Tammuz-Ab sin, atonement, and forgiveness and restoration—that Elul-Tishre, the New Year, Day of Atonement, and Tabernacles, are situated. The condition of the Temple, Jerusalem, and corporate Israel then prefigures the situation of Israel, both individual and corporate, in the penitential season, reaching its climax with Tabernacles and its celebration of the renewal of life: the promise of life once more.

JACOB NEUSNER
Bard College

Pseudo-Philo's Biblical Antiquities

Pseudo-Philo's *Biblical Antiquities* (also known by its Latin title, *Liber Antiquitatum Biblicarum* = LAB) is a selective retelling of parts of the Bible from Genesis through 2 Samuel 1. It combines biblical quotations with exegetical and legendary developments of various texts. It is often described as an example of the "rewritten Bible." It now exists in eighteen complete and three fragmentary Latin manuscripts from the eleventh to the fifteenth centuries as well as a partial Hebrew retroversion in the *Chronicles of Jerahmeel*.

There is sufficient evidence in the Latin version to indicate that LAB is a translation of a Greek version, which was in turn based on a Hebrew original. Its composition in Hebrew, use of a non-Masoretic biblical text, knowledge of geography, and theology indicate that the work was written in the land of Israel. It may well have been written before the destruction of the Jerusalem Temple in 70 C.E. If not, then composition in the late first or very early second century C.E. seems likely.

In its genre, LAB is like Josephus' *Antiquities*, *Jubilees*, *Genesis Apocryphon*, and Qumran texts known as "Biblical Paraphrases." All these works take parts of the Bible as their lead text, omit some passages and expand others, and "solve" exegetical or theological problems in the process. In that sense they "rewrite" the Bible, though whether the "rewritten Bible" should be regarded as a literary activity or a literary genre is a matter of debate.

There is no indication that LAB was intended as a rival to or substitute for the Bible. The author assumes that readers know the Bible well, and so he can allude to various episodes without giving lengthy explanations. Because the book ends abruptly in 65:5 and gives the impression that the ending has been lost, we cannot be sure how far the author intended to take Israel's story. The major theological concerns—covenant, leadership, and eschatology—are so general and pervasive in Second Temple Judaisms that they provide little help in specifying a date for the work's composition. The lack of any clear reference to the destruction of the Second Temple (unless 19:7 is one) suggests a pre-70 C.E. origin. There is nothing like the sustained concern with the Temple's destruction that is found in the related but clearly post-70 C.E. apocalypses known as *4 Ezra* and *2 Baruch*.

LAB is a very large book. It is a sophisticated work of literature that responds well to narrative criticism. It is also a precious resource for understanding how some Jews in the first century C.E. read and interpreted Genesis through 2 Samuel 1. Taking LAB on its own terms, this essay traces its major religious concerns and analyzes some of its hermeneutical moves. The first part examines five themes that run through its retelling of the biblical story from Adam to David, with particular attention to LAB's unique or distinctive contributions to midrash. The second part provides translations and expositions of twelve short passages to illustrate concretely how ps.-Philo works with biblical texts and develops them in his own characteristic ways. All translations of LAB are taken from my "Pseudo-Philo" in J.H. Charlesworth, ed., *The Old Testament Pseudepigrapha. Volume 2* (New York, 1985), pp. 297–377.

PART ONE: FIVE MAJOR TOPICS: The main points in LAB are:

(1) The best leaders for Israel rely totally on God for guidance and success.

(2) God has chosen Israel and entered into a covenant relationship with Israel. If Israel observes its covenant obligations, all will go well. If not, Israel will be punished for its sins. God always remains faithful to Israel and is willing to forgive its sins and raise up new leaders.

(3) The Holy Land is a sign of God's special love for Israel.

(4) Marriage or sexual relations with gentile women leads to idolatry, and idolatry leads Israel to other sins.

(5) At the last judgment God will render "to each according to his works" (3:10). The criterion for judgment will be fidelity to God's will expressed in the Torah. Therefore sinners must confess and repent before they die because after death no one can repent.

God and Israel's Leaders

The best leaders for Israel rely totally on God for guidance and success.

Abraham. In the parts of LAB that correspond to Genesis (LAB 1–8) the first and most important leader is Abraham. The various genealogies and lists based on the early chapters of Genesis reach a kind of climax with the following prophecy about Abraham: "From him [Serug] there will be born in the fourth generation one who will set his dwelling on high and will be called perfect and blameless; and he will be the father of nations, and his covenant will not be broken, and his seed will be multiplied forever" (4:11).

Abraham's leadership style is illustrated in the retelling of the Tower of Babel episode in LAB 6, which links Genesis 11 and 12 and portrays Abraham's escape from the furnace of fire ('ûr/Ur) after the pattern of Daniel 3. According to LAB 6, Abraham was one of only twelve men who opposed the plan to build the tower on religious grounds: "We know the one Lord, and him we worship" (6:4). Ioktan, the chief of the leaders at Babel, devises a complicated plan to save the twelve resisters and presents it as God's will: "For the God in whom you trust is powerful" (6:9). All but Abraham accept Ioktan's plan. Reasoning that there would be no end to his flight, Abraham says: "I will not go forth, but I will stay here" (6:11). When Abraham alone is cast into the furnace, we are told that God caused a great earthquake, that the fire from the furnace burned all those in sight (83,500 persons), and that "there was not the least injury to Abram from the burning of the fire" (6:17). Ioktan's plan was well intentioned, clever, and even successful to a point. But it was not God's plan. And in LAB, following God's plan is the essence of good leadership.

LAB 6 presents a contrast between human plans and divine plans. It suggests that more is to be gained by following the faithful religious leadership of someone like Abraham than even the wise, benevolent, and pragmatic leadership of Ioktan. LAB's retelling of Genesis 11 marks Abraham as a true leader for God's people, one who acts consistently in accord with God's will.

Moses. The chapters of LAB (9–19) that correspond to the rest of the Pentateuch feature good leaders (Amram, Moses) and bad leaders (Korah, Balak). When the king of Egypt decrees that the male children of the Hebrews are to be thrown into the river, some of the people counsel sexual abstinence. Fearing that such a policy will destroy Israel, Amram refuses to participate in their plan and says: "Now therefore I will not abide by what you decree, but I will go in and take my wife and produce sons so that we may be made many on the earth" (9:4). Amram's resolve is approved by God on the grounds that "he has not put aside the covenant established between me and his fathers" (9:7).

Amram's son Moses is a very good leader. Indeed, when Miriam is granted a dream vision announcing Moses's birth, she is told that Moses "will exercise leadership always" (9:10). Moses is to be the servant of God (9:7) and the instrument of God in freeing the children of Israel (9:16). When Israel escapes from Egypt and finds itself caught between the Red Sea and the Egyptian army, God and Moses work together to produce a successful plan for crossing the sea (10:1–6). In his farewell speech (LAB 19), after many years of faithful leadership, Moses recognizes that at his death the people will lament and say: "Who will give us another shepherd like Moses or such a judge for the sons of Israel to pray always for our sins and to be heard for our iniquities?" (19:3). The ideal leader for Israel is perfectly attuned to God's will and serves as shepherd, judge, and mediator on behalf of God's people.

In LAB 16, Korah shows himself to be a bad leader. Ps.-Philo links the law about the tassels in Num. 15:37–41 with the Korah episode in Numbers 16, and makes this law into the occasion for Korah's rebellion against God and Moses. Korah complains: "Why is an unbearable law imposed upon us?" (16:1). Not only does Korah reject God's law but he fails to gain support even from his seven sons, who prefer to walk according to "the Law of the Most Powerful" (16:5). According to Balaam in LAB 18, what Balak fails to recognize in his effort at destroying Israel is that "the plan of God is not like the plan of man" (18:3) and whatever power he may exert over Israel is only temporary and is part of God's plan: "But our [= Balak and Balaam] ways are not straight unless God wishes it" (18:3).

Joshua. There is a smooth transition from Moses to Joshua as the leader of God's people. In fact, we are informed that Eldad and Medad had prophesied that the leadership of Moses would be given over to Joshua (20:5). And God tells Joshua directly to replace Moses: "Take his garments of wisdom and clothe yourself, and with his belt of knowledge gird your loins, and you will be changed and become another man" (20:2). In his prayer in LAB 21, Joshua asks that God supply a suitable successor as leader of the people: "And now let the fullness of your mercy sustain your people and choose for your heritage a man so that he and his offspring will rule over your people" (21:4). The quotation of Gen. 49:10 ("A ruler will not be lacking from Judah, nor a leader from his loins") indicates that the new leader will come from the tribe of Judah.

In settling the dispute about the altar across the Jordan (= Joshua 22), Joshua reminds the people that the Lord is "more powerful than a thousand sacrifices" (LAB 22:5) and that instead of offering sacrifices across the Jordan they should "teach your sons the Law and have them meditate on it day and night" (22:5). Of course, in the context of LAB, Joshua is not opposed to sacrifices and other cultic observances. But he insists that these be offered in accord with God's will as expressed in the Torah.

In Joshua's farewell speech in LAB 24, he says to the people: "Be mindful of me after my death and of Moses the friend of the Lord" (24:3). At Joshua's burial the people acknowledge that Joshua was the perfect fulfillment of Deut. 18:15, and so they ask: "And who will go and tell the just Moses that we have had a leader like him for forty years?" (24:6). Their question not only assumes that Moses lives on after his death but also celebrates Joshua's success as Israel's leader.

Kenaz. One of the most outstanding leaders in ps.-Philo's retelling of Israel's story is Kenaz (LAB 24–29). In the Bible, Kenaz is mentioned only in passing as the father of Othniel (Judg. 3:9, 11). Why ps.-Philo decided to make Kenaz an exemplary leader is unclear. But he is portrayed as embodying the best features of the Judges and as an ideal leader for Israel: open to God's will, the enemy of idolaters and other sinners, a warrior against Israel's rivals, and an honest and just ruler.

The choice of Kenaz as Israel's leader comes about by casting lots for the right tribe and for the right individual within that tribe (25:1–2). In this way God does the choosing. Before Kenaz can lead Israel in battle against its enemies, he must purify the people of their sinful members. He does this by isolating and examining those who are suspected of sin (25:3–13).

Then in a manner reminiscent of Gideon's defeat of the Midianites in Judges 7, Kenaz in LAB 27 singlehandedly kills 45,000 Amorites. In fact, while the sword of Kenaz does the killing, he is empowered by the angels Ingethel and Zeruel (27:10). The lesson of Kenaz's triumph is that "among men a great number prevails, but with God whatever he has decided" (27:12). The people grasp the lesson and say: "Now we know that the Lord has decided to save his people; he does not need a great number but only holiness" (27:14).

Before his death, Kenaz is told by Phinehas that the people will again "corrupt its ways and turn from my [God's] commands" (28:4). He is also granted an ecstatic experience (28:6–10), and his successor Zebul secures an inheritance for Kenaz's daughters "because their father during his lifetime refused to give anything to them lest he be called avaricious and greedy" (29:1).

Deborah. A good example of ps.-Philo's "feminism" is the section devoted to Deborah and Jael (30–33). In response to Israel's failure to keep the covenant, God declares: "And a woman will rule over them and enlighten them for forty years" (30:2). In retelling the story of Jael's decapitating of Sisera, LAB emphasizes the biblical motif of Judg. 4:9 (see also Judith) when Jael says to Sisera: "Go, boast before your father in hell and tell him that you have fallen into the hands of a woman" (31:7). At Deborah's death, the people mourn for seventy days and lament the passing of a great leader: "Behold there has perished a mother from Israel, and the holy one who exercised leadership in the house of Jacob. She firmed up the fence about her generation, and her generation will grieve over her" (33:6).

Other Judges. The period between Deborah and Samuel (LAB 34–48) features many bad leaders both within Israel and from outside Israel. A Midianite magician named Aod leads the people of Israel into idolatry by offering to show them "the sun by night" (34:1). While Gideon succeeds in defeating the Midianites (35), he ends up leading Israel into more idolatry (36:3). To foster his plan to become the "leader of the people" (37:1), Abimelech kills all his brothers and is compared to a bramble bush (37:4). When Jair builds a sanctuary to Baal, only seven men in Israel refuse to offer sacrifices to this god (38:1). While Jephthah has some military success, his foolish vow to sacrifice "whoever meets me first on the way" (39:10) results in the death of his own daughter Seila. The problem with all these leaders is that God does not stand behind them and they are not attuned to God's will.

While Abdon and Elon bring victory in battle to Israel (41:1–2), after their deaths "the sons of Israel forgot the Lord their God and served the gods of those inhabiting the land" (41:3). The result is forty years of servitude to the Philistines. Samson in LAB 42–43 carries out his God-given mission to "free Israel from the hand of the Philistines" (42:3). But because of his love for the foreign woman Delilah, he is led astray. In LAB 44 Micah and his mother Dedila make idolatry into a big business in Israel and lead Israelites into all the sins that God has forbidden. Ps.-Philo blames the victory of the Benjaminites over the rest of Israel (46) on the people's apathy regarding the idols of Micah and views as disproportionate their rage about the rape-murder of the Levite's concubine (who according to 45:3 and 47:8 was a sinner). In describing the time of the Judges, ps.-Philo makes his own the Bible's poignant summary of the period: "they had no leader in those days, and each one did what was pleasing in his own eyes" (48:4 = Judg. 21:25).

Samuel, Saul, and David. The rise of Samuel, Saul, and David to be leaders in Israel is described in LAB 49–65. Recognizing that "it is not appropriate for the people to be without a ruler" (49:1), the people cast lots (under divine guidance) and discover that Samuel is eventually to be their leader. It is precisely as a prophet that Samuel will exercise his leadership. In calling Samuel, God boasts that "he is like my servant Moses" (53:2).

When the people ask for a king, Samuel tells them that "it is not yet time for us to have an everlasting kingdom" (56:2). God tells Samuel that he "will send them a king [Saul] who will destroy them, and he himself will be destroyed afterward" (56:3). When Samuel presents Saul to the people as their king, they confess that "we have a king, because we are not worthy to be governed by a prophet" (57:4). Saul's refusal to kill Agag and his other failures in leadership are attributed to the people's premature desire for a king.

David is a legitimate king and leader. Samuel is told to anoint David "because the time in which his kingdom will come to pass has been fulfilled" (59:1). David emerges as the one who was protected by God and his angels (59:4). David drives out Saul's demons (60), defeats Goliath who is a descendant of Orpah (61), and pledges loyalty to Jonathan (62). The last words of Saul convey to David a message of reconciliation and recognition: "Be not mindful of my hatred or my injustice" (65:5).

God and Israel, or the Covenant

God has chosen and entered into a covenant relationship with Israel. If Israel observes its covenant obligations, all will go well. If not, Israel will be punished for its sins. God always remains faithful to Israel and is willing to forgive its sins and raise up new leaders.

In the Genesis sections (LAB 1–8) there are references (following the Bible) to God's covenants with Noah not to destroy the earth with a flood again (3:11) and with Abraham to provide "an everlasting seed" (8:3).

The revelation of the Torah through Moses on Sinai is presented as a new and decisive moment in the history of God's covenant with Israel: "I will show him my covenant that no one has seen. And I will reveal to him my Law and statutes and judgments, and I will burn an eternal light for him" (9:8). God's covenant and commandments are eternal (11:5). Ps.-Philo is a great proponent of moral causality: People get what they deserve, especially when they sin. So those who conspire in making and worshiping the golden calf have their tongues cut off (12:7). If Israel observes God's commandments, all will go well; if Israel grows corrupt, God will abandon Israel—but not forever since God will always remain faithful to his people (13:10; see 15:6).

The transfer of leadership from Moses to Joshua is described in terms of the covenant: "God established his covenant with Joshua the son of Nun" (20:1). Joshua's tenure of leadership is notable for Israel's entry into the promised land as the fulfillment of God's covenant promises to Israel. This fulfillment is publicly acknowledged by all the people: "Behold our Lord has fulfilled what he said to our fathers" (21:9). And Joshua's prayer for the people is this: "May the covenant of the Lord remain with you and not be broken" (21:10). God has been faithful to his covenant. But Israel is not.

In the Joshua chapters of LAB (20–24) there is an emphasis on the Torah given at Sinai as the expression par excellence of God's covenant with Israel. In LAB 22:3, the people acknowledge that God has "set up a light that they may see what is in darkness." And God reminds Israel that at Sinai he "gave them my Law and enlightened them in order that by doing these things they would live and have many years and not die" (23:10). At the covenant renewal ceremony based on Joshua 24, God reminds Israel that God has fulfilled his part of the covenant: "And I fulfilled my covenant that I promised your fathers" (23:11). But at his death Joshua foresees that Israel will fail to fulfill its covenant obligations: "Behold now I see with my own eyes the transgression of the people in which they are to stray" (24:4).

When Kenaz purifies the people of the sinners among them (LAB 25), the criteria for his investigation come from the Decalogue as symbolic of the covenant stipulations as a whole. The most frequent and heinous sin is idolatry, though there are other sins (child sacrifice, adultery, profanation of the Sabbath) as well as a curious sin from the tribe of Benjamin: "We desired in this time to investigate the book of the Law, whether God had really written in it or Moses had taught these things by himself" (25:13). Part of Kenaz's effort at purifying the people is to see to the destruction of whatever was associated with idolatrous worship (26). At his farewell (28) Kenaz is warned by Phinehas that despite all his success in purifying God's people and his military victories for them, they will once more depart from God's commands (28:4). While Kenaz recognizes the legitimacy of God's anger against Israel ("Will the Shepherd destroy his flock for any reason except that it has sinned against him?" 28:5), he also invokes the mercy of God and reminds God how much effort God has already put into the care of his people. In the face of Israel's infidelity, God remains faithful.

The occasion for Deborah's appointment as leader in Israel is the people's failure to observe the covenant. They admit: "We have transgressed the ways of God and of our fathers" (30:2). And yet the reason why God provides another leader is precisely God's loyalty to the covenant: "the Lord will take pity on you today, not because of you but because of the covenant he established with your fathers and the oath that he has sworn not to abandon you forever" (30:7). God's fidelity is further emphasized when he says: "even if my people have sinned, nevertheless I will have mercy on them" (31:2). However, Israel is still expected to live up to its obligations as God's people, and so Deborah challenges them in her farewell discourse: "while you have the time and the light of the Law, make straight your ways" (33:3).

Under the bad leaders from Deborah to Samuel (LAB 34–48), Israel repeatedly departs from the covenant, falls into idolatry and other sins, and is rescued by its faithful and merciful God. Aod the magician entices Israel by promising to them "something other than your Law" (34:1). The result is that the Midianites reduce Israel to slavery. An angel explains to Gideon that the reason for Israel's plight is its sinfulness: "as you have abandoned the promises that you have received from the Lord, these evils have found you out" (36:3). Nevertheless, God is willing to forgive the wickedness of his people: "I will forgive them and afterward I will rebuke them because they have acted wickedly" (36:4).

When Jair is to be burned for building a sanctuary to Baal, an angel communicates God's decree: "I have raised you up from the land and appointed you leader over my people, but you rose up and corrupted my covenant and deceived them . . ." (38:4). When Jephthah exhorts the people as they face battle with the Ammonites, he urges them to focus on the covenant ("set your hearts on the Law of the Lord your God," 39:6) and on the mercy of God ("even if our sins be overabundant, still his mercy will fill the earth," 39:6).

The effect of the idols of Micah is that "the sons of Israel were departing from the Lord" (44:6). LAB 44:6–10 presents a long speech purporting to say what God thought about Israel's sinfulness largely in terms of the precepts of the Decalogue (Exod. 20:2–17; Deut. 5:6–21). Here God reasserts the principle of moral causality that runs through LAB: "to every man there will be such a punishment that in whatever sin he shall have sinned, in this he will be judged" (44:10). The rape-murder of the Levite's concubine is explained in terms of her past transgression against her man (45:3; 47:8), thus tarnishing the claim that ps.-Philo is a "feminist."

In the material corresponding to 1 Samuel (LAB 49–65) the ark of the covenant becomes a major topic. God uses the ark to punish both Israel for its sins and Israel's enemies (54:2). God promises Samuel regarding the ark: "I will bring it back, and I will overturn those who have taken it away, and I will avenge my people from their enemies" (55:2). And the Philistines come to know that "they were being destroyed because of the ark" (55:8). In the chapter about David and Jonathan (62) the emphasis is on the covenant between them: "Come, and let us make a covenant before we are separated from one another" (62:3; see 62:11).

The Holy Land

The Holy Land is a sign of God's special love for Israel.

According to LAB 7:4, God preserved the Holy Land from the waters of the flood in the days of Noah: "I brought the water of the flood and I did not destroy it but preserved that land. For neither did the springs of my wrath burst forth in it, nor did my water of destruction descend on it." A rich source of references to the Holy Land is Moses' farewell in LAB 19. He warns that when the people abandon the commandments, "God will be angry and abandon you and depart from your land" (19:2). In Moses' tour of the Holy Land he is shown "the place where they will serve me for 740 years" (19:7)—the Jerusalem Temple. God also reveals to Moses the special water supply reserved for the Holy Land: "the place in the firmament from which only the holy land drinks" (19:10).

There are few references to Jerusalem and its Temple in LAB, since the narrative ends with Saul's death. But by way of foreshadowing or anticipation, there is in the golden calf episode (LAB 12) a preview of the First Temple and its destruction: "I will turn again and make peace with them so that a house may be built for me among them, a house that will be destroyed because they will sin against me" (12:4). Jerusalem itself is mentioned explicitly only in passing when the narrator explains that worship of God at Shiloh was acceptable "until the house of the Lord was built in Jerusalem and sacrifice offered on the new altar" (22:9).

Intermarriage and Idolatry

Marriage or sexual relations with gentile women leads to idolatry, and idolatry leads Israel to other sins.

An important aspect of ps.-Philo's worldview is his horror at Jews' marrying gentiles or having sex with them. A flashback associated with Moses' birth in LAB 9 defends Tamar's seduction of Judah in Genesis 38 as the lesser of two evils. Tamar says: "It is better for me to die for having intercourse with my father-in-law than to have intercourse with gentiles" (9:5). Balaam counsels Balak that Israel will be defeated only if they can be enticed into having sex with beautiful gentile women (18:13-14). And the unique claim is made that the rape and death of the Levite's concubine in Judges 19 were due to her "sin with the Amalekites, and on account of this the Lord delivered her into the hands of sinners" (45:3).

Several passages make a connection between sex with gentiles and idolatry. According to a tradition unique to LAB, the reason the Exodus generation was not allowed to enter the promised land was God's fear that they would see "the graven images with which this people will start to be deceived and led off the path" (19:7). God warns Joshua that when the Israelites become intermingled with those inhabiting the land of Canaan, they "will be seduced after strange gods" (21:1). Deborah recalls how Israelites "were led astray after the daughters of the Amorites and served their gods" (30:1). And the last (and climactic?) of the sins among those who worshiped Micah's idols (LAB 44; see Judges 17) is that "they lusted for foreign women" (44:7).

God and the Future, or Eschatology

At the last judgment, God will render "to each according to his works" (3:10). The criterion for judgment will be fidelity to God's will expressed in the Torah. Therefore sinners must confess and repent before they die because after death no one can repent.

While LAB is not an apocalypse, it does contain several substantial apocalyptic sections that show how apocalyptic thinking can be integrated into a non-apocalyptic work. After promising not to destroy the earth by a flood again, God in 3:10 launches into a apocalyptic scenario that includes the resurrection of the dead ("I will bring the dead to life"), the last judgment ("so that I may render to each according to his works"), and the existence of "another earth and another heaven, an everlasting dwelling place." In his farewell address in LAB 19 (= Deuteronomy 34), Moses recounts what God revealed to him about his own resurrection and the general resurrection (19:12-13). When Moses inquires about when this will happen, he is told enigmatically that "four and a half have passed, and two and a half remain" (19:15).

As Joshua ends his recital of the history of God's covenant with Israel (= Joshua 24) in LAB 23, he cites God's promise that if Israel listens to the fathers, "at the end the lot of each one of you will be life eternal for you and your seed, and I will take your souls and store them in peace until the time allotted the world be complete" (23:13). This passage is important for its references to eternal life, the continuing existence of souls after death, and the "treasury" or storehouse of souls awaiting the fullness of God's kingdom.

Kenaz's first task as Israel's leader is to discover the identity of the evildoers within Israel. As he tries to persuade them to confess their sins, he holds out to them the possibility of happiness with God at the last judgment: "And now declare to us your wicked deeds and schemes. And who knows that if you tell the truth to us, even if you die now, nevertheless God will have mercy on you when he will resurrect the dead?" (25:7).

Some of the most unusual eschatological teachings in LAB appear in Deborah's farewell discourse (33). She warns Israel that "after your death you cannot repent of those things in which you live" (33:2). She explains also that after death "the desire for sinning will cease and the evil impulse will lose its power" (33:3). The idea that the "evil impulse" ceases after death is unique to LAB. Furthermore, she insists that even the righteous dead like Deborah or the patriarchs cannot intercede for the living (but see 35:3), thus disputing the doctrine of the "merits of the fathers."

When Gideon falls into idolatry, God defers punishing him lest the people say "Baal has chastised him" (36:4). Rather, God warns that when Gideon is dead, "I will chastise him once and for all, because he has offended me" (36:4). Likewise, those who were led into sin by the idols of Micah are promised fitting punishments "when the soul is separated from the body" (44:10).

As Jonathan says farewell to David, he expresses his belief that they will meet again: "Even if death separates us, I know that our souls will know each other" (62:9). When Saul recognizes that he is about to die, he hopes that "perhaps my destruction will be an atonement for my wickedness" (64:9).

Twelve Sample Texts

These short passages give examples of how ps.-Philo worked with biblical texts and so illustrate the form, content, and technique of his work. The words in italics correspond to recognizable biblical texts and so are biblical quotations. Everything else represents ps.-Philo's wording. However, since he wrote in the "biblical style," practically everything can be traced to biblical models.

1. Expanded Genealogy—Adam's Sons and Daughters

> 1:1. In the beginning of the world Adam became the father of three sons and one daughter: Cain, Noaba, Abel, and Seth. 2. *And after he became the father of Seth, Adam lived seven hundred years; and he became the father of* twelve *sons* and eight *daughters*. 3. And these are the names of the males: Eliseel, Suris, Elamiel, Naat, Zarama, Zasam, Maathal, and Anath. 4. And these are his daughters: Fua, Iectas, Arebica, Sifa, Tetia, Saba, Asin.

The early chapters of LAB feature many expanded genealogies based on Genesis. The work begins by treating Genesis 5 before Genesis 4 (LAB 2), and refers to Genesis 1–3 only by means of flashbacks. However, the names of Adam's sons are taken from Genesis 4. Their sister (necessary for procreation and human survival?) is given the name Noaba. That Adam lived seven hundred years after Seth's birth (1:2) agrees with the Septuagint of Gen. 5:4 against the MT's eight hundred. In 1:3-4, only nine sons and seven daughters are named. Perhaps the numbers are meant to include the four children mentioned in 1:1. Or perhaps there has been textual corruption. Given the complicated linguistic transmission of the work (from Hebrew through Greek to Latin), it is often difficult to make sense out its names and numbers. The desired effect of supplying all these names and numbers, however, was presumably to inspire confidence on the reader's part that the author knew more than the Bible tells about the early history of humankind. Whether the author developed these lists from literary or oral sources, or he simply made them up, cannot be determined.

2. Exegesis—Moses Born Circumcised

9:15. Now Pharaoh's daughter came down to bathe in the river, as she had seen in dreams, *and* her maids *saw the ark. And she sent one, and she fetched and opened it. And when she saw the boy* and while she was looking upon the covenant (that is, the covenant of the flesh), *she said, "It is one of the Hebrew children."*

According to Exod. 2:5-6, Pharaoh's daughter came down to the river, discovered the infant Moses, and immediately recognized that the child was a Hebrew. LAB 9:15 answers two exegetical questions that might arise from a careful reading of the biblical text: Why did Pharaoh's daughter go to the river? How did she know that Moses was a Hebrew? That she went "as she had seen in dreams" fits with the earlier notice in 9:10 that the spirit of God revealed to Miriam in a dream that Moses would be a leader from his birth. The same spirit of God presumably used dreams to bring Pharaoh's daughter to the river. That she recognized Moses as a Hebrew child was due to his having been born circumcised: "Now that child was born in the covenant of God and the covenant of the flesh" (9:13). Pharaoh's daughter is said to have looked upon Moses' *zaticon* (a curious Latin form of the Greek *diatheke*), which is then explained parenthetically as *testamentum carnis*. This tradition probably arose from the exegetical problem posed by Exod. 2:6.

3. Reasons for Observing the Decalogue

11:10. You shall not commit adultery, because your enemies did not commit adultery against you, but *you came forth with a high hand.* 11. *You shall not kill,* because your enemies had power over you so as to kill you, but you saw their death. 12. *You shall not be a false witness against your neighbor,* speaking false testimony, lest your guardians speak false testimony against you. 13. *You shall not covet your neighbor's house or what he has,* lest others should covet your land.

The order of these commandments—adultery, murder, false witness, and coveting—in 11:10-13 fits with other ancient texts (LXX, Nash Papyrus, Philo, NT). The omission of the prohibition against stealing is probably due to textual corruption at some point. What is novel is that LAB supplies reasons for observing these commandments. The formal precedents for these additions appear in the biblical versions of the initial commandments and in LAB 11:6-9. In the cases of adultery and murder it appears that the motivations allude to God's protection of Israel during its sojourn in Egypt, so that their enemies did not get the opportunity to commit adultery against Israel or to kill them. In the commandments about false testimony and coveting, something like Jesus' Golden Rule (Matt. 7:12; Luke 6:31) or Hillel's Silver Rule (B. Shab. 31a) seems to be operative. The "guardians" who might bear false witness are presumably angels ("watchers" or guardian angels, see 15:5; 59:4), and so there is probably an eschatological dimension here.

4. Flashback—The Aqedah

18:5. And he [God] said to him [Balaam], "Is it not regarding this people that I spoke to Abraham in a vision, saying, '*Your seed will be like the stars of the heaven,*' when I lifted him above the firmament and showed him the arrangements of all the stars? And I demanded his son as a holocaust. And he brought him to be placed on the altar, but I gave him back to his father and, because he did not refuse, his offering was acceptable before me, and on account of his blood I chose them.

The binding of Isaac or the Aqedah described in Genesis 22 was a topic of great interest and much speculation in early Jewish and Rabbinic writings. Instead of treating it in the Genesis sequence of his work, ps.-Philo uses it as a prominent part in his extensive network of flashbacks and foreshadowings. This device enables the reader to see analogies between biblical episodes and to appreciate the divinely guided continuity present in Israel's history. The Aqedah motif appears as a flashback here in the Balaam episode (18:5) as well as in the hymn of Deborah (32:2-4) and the speech by Jephthah's daughter (40:2).

In his dialogue with Balaam, God introduces Genesis 22 with a quotation of 22:17 ("Your seed will be like the stars of the heavens") and suggests that God has given Abraham a tour of the heavenly realm (see *T. Abr.* 10). It is possible that the intertextual dynamics between the biblical versions of Genesis 22 and Numbers 22 led ps.-Philo to insert this flashback in LAB 18.[1]

What is curious in LAB 18:5 is the idea that Abraham's "sacrifice" of Isaac was acceptable to God "on account of his blood." But in Genesis 22 Isaac is spared from shedding blood! In LAB, even though Isaac's blood is not shed, it is still viewed as having some atoning value. In LAB 32:2-4, Isaac is depicted as willingly offering himself as a sacrifice, and he counts it as a great blessing and privilege to do so: "Yet have I not been born into the world to be offered as a sacrifice to him who made me?" In 40:2, both Abraham and Isaac are praised as willing parties to a sacrifice: "and he [Isaac] did not refuse him [Abraham] but gladly gave consent to him, and the one being offered was ready and the one who was offering was rejoicing."

5. Supplying Content—What Eldad and Medad Said

> 20:5. And the people said to him, "Behold we know today what Eldad and Medad prophesied in the days of Moses, saying, 'After Moses goes to rest, the leadership of Moses will be given over to Joshua the son of Nun.' And Moses was not jealous but rejoiced when he heard them. And from then on all the people believed that you would exercise leadership over them *and divide up the land* among them in peace. And now even if there is conflict, *be strong and act manfully*, because you alone are ruler in Israel."

According to Num. 11:26, the spirit of God rested upon Eldad and Medad, and "so they prophesied in the camp." But the Bible does not tell us what exactly they prophesied. Ps.-Philo uses the Eldad-Medad episode as a flashback in the context of Joshua's assuming the leadership of God's people in place of Moses (Joshua 1). And he supplies their prophecy with definite content by reporting that they said: "After Moses goes to rest, the leadership of Moses will be given over to Joshua the son of Nun." He ignores the fact that in the Bible it is Joshua who objects to their prophesying and urges Moses to stop them. Instead of Joshua's being jealous of the two irregular prophets for Moses' sake as in the Num. 11:29, in LAB one gets the impression that it was Moses who was not jealous of Joshua who was to replace him. Thus the episode reinforces the idea that Moses was a great leader. In LAB the people accept Joshua as Moses' divinely designated (through the prophets) replacement and as their only ruler ("you alone are ruler in Israel").

6. Nested Quotations—Phinehas' Advice to Kenaz

> 28:5. And then Phinehas said, "While my father was dying, he commanded me, saying, 'These words you will say to the sons of Israel, "When you were

---

[1] See B.N. Fisk, "Offering Isaac Again and Again: Pseudo-Philo's Use of the Aqedah as Intertext," in *Catholic Biblical Quarterly* 62 (2000), pp. 481–507.

gathered together in the assembly, the Lord appeared to me three days ago in a dream by night and said to me, 'Behold you have seen and also your father before you how much I have toiled among my people. But after your death this people will rise up and corrupt its ways and turn from my commands, and I will be very angry with them. But I will recall that time that was before the creation of the world, the time when man did not exist and there was no wickedness in it, when I said that the world would be created and those who would come into it would praise me. And I would plant a great vineyard, and from it I would choose a plant; and I would care for it and call it by my name, and it would be mine forever. When I did all the things that I said, nevertheless my plant that was called by my name did not recognize me as its planter, but it destroyed its own fruit and did not yield up its fruit to me.'"' And this is what my father commanded me to say to this people."

A frequent literary device in LAB is the quotation(s) within a quotation or "nested quotation." The most extreme example occurs in 28:4, where Phinehas tells Kenaz what Eleazar told Phinehas to tell the sons of Israel about what God told Eleazar in a dream. For good measure, God also recalls what he said at creation. Ps.-Philo often uses this device to convey his version of what God was thinking at certain decisive moments in the history of his relationship with Israel.

In the context of the leadership of Kenaz, God foresees that "this people will rise up and corrupt its ways and turn from my commands," thus bringing up the tensions between God's fidelity and Israel's infidelity that are so prominent in LAB. In reflecting on his love for Israel, God invokes the images of the vineyard and the plant on which he lavishes such care (see also 12:8; 18:10–11; 23:11–12; 30:4; 39:7). But Israel is so dense that it fails to recognize that God is its planter and so is destroying itself. In 28:5, Kenaz and the people acknowledge the sinfulness of Israel and throw themselves on the mercy of God: "And now he is the one who will spare us according to the abundance of his mercy because he has toiled so much among us."

7. Revealing God's Thoughts

30:2. And the Lord was angry at them and sent his angel and said, "Behold I have chosen one people from every tribe of the earth, and I said that my glory would reside in this world with it; and I sent to them Moses my servant, who would declare my laws and statutes; and they transgressed my ways. And behold now I will arouse *their enemies*, and they will rule over them. And then all the people will say, 'Because we have transgressed the ways of God and of our fathers, on account of this these things have come upon us.' And a woman will rule over them and enlighten them for forty years."

In 30:2, ps.-Philo purports to tell what God said about Israel's plight and his decision to appoint Deborah as Israel's leader. This is "insider information" made available only by ps.-Philo to his readers. The information, however, is quite familiar, since LAB 30:2 brings together the most prominent themes in the book.

At this point Israel needs a leader precisely because "they forgot the promise and transgressed the ways that Moses and Joshua the servants of the Lord had commanded them" (30:1). The reason for Israel's plight is the familiar combination of adultery and idolatry: "they were led astray after the daughters of the Amorites and served their gods" (30:1).

God's commentary on Israel's situation in LAB 30:2 consists of three elements: his choice of Israel, Israel's transgression, and Israel's punishment. God's election of Israel reaches a high point with Moses who was God's instrument in revealing the stipulations of the covenant: "I sent to them Moses my servant, who would declare my laws and statutes." The punishment for Israel's transgression of the covenant stipulations is that its enemies rule over them. And Israel's subjugation leads the people to recognize their sinfulness and to confess it.

God's willingness to send a new leader to Israel is another indication that God is faithful to Israel even if Israel is not faithful to God. In this case the leader is the woman Deborah. God's choice of a woman leader is another indication that true leadership resides in God and in being attuned to God's will. The choice of Deborah is also an example of ps.-Philo's "feminism" in the sense that he gives more prominence to the place of women in Israel's history than the Bible and most contemporary Jewish writings do.

8. Providing a Reason: Aod the Magician

34:1. And in that time there arose a certain Aod from the sanctuaries of Midian, and this man was a magician, and he said to Israel, "Why do you pay attention to your Law? Come, I will show you something other than your Law." And the people said, "What will you show us that our Law does not have?" And he said to the people, "Have you ever seen the sun by night?" And they said, "No." and he said, "Whenever you wish, I will show it to you in order that you may know that our gods have power and do not deceive those who serve them." And they said, "Show it." 2. And he went away and worked with his magic tricks and gave orders to the angels who were in charge of magicians, for he had been sacrificing to them for a long time. 3. Because in that time before they were condemned, magic was revealed by angels and they would have destroyed the age without measure, and because they had transgressed, it happened that the angels did not have the power, and when they were judged, then the power was not given over to others. And they do these things by means of those men, the magicians who minister to men, until the age without measure comes. 4. And then by the art of magic he showed to the people the sun by night. And the people were amazed and said, "Behold how much the gods of the Midianites can do, and we did not know it." 5. And God wished to test if Israel would remain in its wicked deeds, and he let them be, and their work was successful. And the people of Israel were deceived and began to serve the gods of the Midianites. And God said, "I will deliver them into the hands of the Midianites, because they have been deceived by them." And he *delivered them into* their *hands*, and the Midianites began to reduce Israel to slavery.

After the triumphant Song of Deborah in Judg. 5 (LAB 32), there is a rough transition to Judg. 6:1: "The Israelites did what was evil in the sight of the Lord, and the Lord gave them into the hand of Midian for seven years" (34:1). What evil did Israel do to merit such a severe punishment so soon? According to LAB 34, they allowed themselves to be seduced into idolatry by Aod the Midianite magician.

In an episode unique to LAB, Aod a magician from the sanctuary of Midian promises to show the Israelites "something other than your Law" (34:1). That something is the opportunity to see "the sun by night." Aod places the offer in the context of proving that the gods of Midian have greater power than the God of Israel has. In fact, according to LAB 34:2-3, Aod's magic tricks were made possible through the fallen angels (see *1 Enoch* 7-8).

When Aod succeeds in showing the sun

by night to the Israelites, they fall for his trickery and exclaim: "Behold how much the gods of the Midianites can do, and we did not know it" (34:4). In 34:5, the narrator explains that God intended this as a test for Israel, and so God allowed the people to be deceived and to serve the gods of the Midianites. Thus the reason why God gave Israel over to the Midianites was Israel's turn to idolatry and its failure to remain faithful to God and the Torah.

9. Moral Causality

> 43:5. Then Samson went down to Gerar, a city of the Philistines, *and he saw there a harlot whose name was Delilah*, and he was led astray after her and took her to himself for a wife. And God said, "Behold now Samson has been led astray through his eyes, and he has not remembered the mighty works that I did with him; and he has mingled with the daughters of the Philistines and has not paid attention to Joseph my servant who was in a foreign land and became a crown for his brothers because he was not willing to afflict his own seed. And now Samson's lust will be a stumbling block for him, and his mingling a ruin. And I will hand him over to his enemies, and they will blind him. But in hour of his death I will *remember* him, and *I will avenge him upon the Philistines once more.*"

In his introduction to the Samson and Delilah episode, ps.-Philo conflates the prostitute of Judg. 16:1 and Delilah of Judg. 16:4. The lesson is that Samson gets into trouble because he marries a notorious foreign woman. Since Samson was "led astray through his eyes," it is only right that his enemies should blind him. People get the punishment that they deserve and that fits their crimes. By way of a flashback to Genesis 39, ps.-Philo points to the good example of the patriarch Joseph who resisted the seductions of a foreign woman in Egypt. But even though Samson will be punished, God will show his fidelity and mercy even toward sinners. And so God promises to "remember" Samson and to avenge him upon the Philistines. This episode brings together some of LAB's most prominent themes: the evil of intermarriage with gentiles, moral causality and punishment in kind, and God's fidelity despite Israel's infidelity.

10. The Parable of the Lion

> 47:4. These words the Lord says: "There was a certain mighty lion in the midst of the forest to whose power all the beasts entrusted the forest that he might guard it lest perhaps other wild animals should come and destroy it. And while the lion was guarding these, some wild animals arrived from another forest and devoured all the young of the animals and destroyed the fruit of their wombs. And the lion looked on and was silent. And the animals were at peace, because they had entrusted the forest to the lion and did not realize that their own offspring had been destroyed. 5. And after a time there arose from those who had entrusted the forest to the lion a very small animal, and he ate up the small cub of another wicked animal. And behold the lion roared and disturbed all the animals of the forest, and they fought among themselves, and each attacked his neighbor....
> 47:7. "Micah arose and made you rich by these things that he and his mother made. And they were wicked and evil things that no one before them had discovered, but by his own craftiness he made them—graven images that had not been made until this day. And no one was provoked but all were led astray, and you saw the fruit of you womb destroyed and you were silent like that wicked lion. 8. And now on seeing how this man's concubine, who had done wicked deeds, died, you were

all disturbed and came to me, saying, 'Will you deliver the sons of Benjamin into our hands?' Therefore I have deceived you and said, 'I will deliver them to you.' And now I have destroyed you, who were silent then. And so I will take my revenge on all who have acted wickedly."

The parable of the lion (47:4–5) and its interpretation (47:7–8) link the episodes about the sin of Micah (Judges 17 = LAB 44), the rape and murder of the Levite's concubine (Judges 19 = LAB 45), and the Benjaminite war (Judges 20 = LAB 46). They emphasize that idolatry is the worst sin of all.

The parable (47:4–5) concerns a "mighty lion" (united Israel or Israel's leadership) who is supposed to protect all the beasts in the forest (the twelve tribes). But when "other wild animals" (Micah and Dedila) come to destroy all the young of the beasts (by seducing them into idolatry), neither the lion nor the other beasts pay much attention. However, when "a very small animal" (the Benjaminites) destroy the "small cub of another wicked animal" (the Levite's concubine), then the lion roars and all the animals of the forest set about fighting each other.

In the interpretation (47:7–8), God accuses the people of profiting from Micah's idols and of standing by silently while their children were being destroyed through idolatry and other sins. God plays down the significance of the rape and murder of the Levite's concubine on the grounds that she "had done wicked deeds" (see also 45:3). And God defends the bad advice that he gave to Israel in the war against the Benjaminites on the grounds that he was exacting vengeance from those who had acted wickedly.

11. David and Jonathan

> 62:11. *And they wept, one over the other, and they kissed one another.* But Jonathan was afraid, and he said to David, "Let us remember, my brother, the covenant begun between us and the oath set in our heart. And if I die before you and you are king as the Lord has said, do not remember the anger of my father but your covenant that has been established between me and you. Do not remember the hatred with which my father hates you in vain but my love with which I have loved you. Do not remember that my father was ungrateful toward you, but remember the table at which we ate together. Do not hold on to the jealousy with which he was jealous of you so evilly but the truth that you and I have. Do not care about the lie that Saul has lied but the oaths that we have sworn to one another." *And they kissed each other.* And after this *David went off* into the wilderness, and *Jonathan entered the city.*

In describing the farewell encounter between Jonathan and David (see 1 Sam. 20:41–42), ps.-Philo focuses on the oath between the two men and on their relationship with one another rather than with Saul. Jonathan says: "Let us remember, my brother, the covenant between us and the oath set in our heart." Five contrasts serve to sharpen the point: (1) Saul's anger at David versus the covenant between Jonathan and David, (2) Saul's hatred for David versus Jonathan's love for David, (3) Saul's ingratitude toward David versus the table fellowship shared by Jonathan and David, (4) Saul's jealousy of David versus the truth between Jonathan and David, and (5) Saul's lies about David versus the oaths that Jonathan and David swore to one another.

12. The Death of Saul—The End?

> 65:4. And he came to kill him. And Saul said to him, "Before you kill me, tell me who you are." And he said to him, "I am Edabus, son of Agag, king of the Amalekites." And Saul said, "Behold now the words of Samuel have come

to pass upon me, because he said, 'He who is born of Agag will be a stumbling block for you.' 5. Now go and tell David, 'I have killed your enemy.' And you will say to him, 'Be not mindful of my hatred or my injustice.'"

According to 1 Sam. 31:4, "Saul took his own sword and fell upon it." However, in 2 Sam. 1:10, a young Amalekite tells David that "I stood over him [Saul] and killed him." Many biblical interpreters regard the Amalekite's claim to be a lie (because he expected a reward from David for killing Saul). But ps.-Philo denies that Saul killed himself: "he fell upon his sword without being able to die" (65:3). Instead he identifies Saul's killer as Edabus, son of Agag, king of the Amalekites. He recalls Samuel's prophecy (not in the Bible) that Saul was to be killed by the child conceived by Agag and his wife: "He who will be born from her will become a stumbling block for Saul" (58:4).

According to 1 Samuel 15, Saul disobeyed God's order to kill Agag and to destroy their flocks. According to ps.-Philo, Saul's sin of disobedience made it possible for Edabus to be conceived the night before Agag was finally killed. And so in accord with the law of moral causality, it was fitting that Saul whose disobedience made it possible for Agag's son to be born should die by that son's hand.

According to LAB 65:5, Saul's final message to David is one of reconciliation: "Be not mindful of my hatred or my injustice." All the manuscripts end at this point. But did the book end here? Many interpreters find this ending too abrupt and suspect that the original ending has been lost. How much more of the book there might have been, of course, is impossible to determine. However, one can also make the case that the author deliberately and subtly broke off his story in order to end on a note of reconciliation between two rival leaders, Saul and David. In this perspective David is the goal toward which the whole narrative about the covenant and leadership in Israel has been moving and David emerges as the ideal ruler for Israel.

Bibliography

Fisk, Bruce N., *Do You Not Remember? Exegetical Appropriations of Biblical Narrative in Pseudo-Philo* (Sheffield, 2001).

Harrington, Daniel J., "Pseudo-Philo," in James H. Charlesworth, ed., *The Old Testament Pseudepigrapha* (Garden City, 1985) vol. 2, pp. 297-377.

———, and Jacques Cazeaux, *Pseudo Philon: Les Antiquités Bibliques*. Vol. 1, *Introduction et Texte Critiques* (Paris, 1976).

James, Montague Rhodes, *The Biblical Antiquities of Philo* (New York, 1971, with a new "Prolegomenon" by L.H. Feldman, pp. vii-clxix).

Jacobson, Howard, *A Commentary on Pseudo-Philo's* Liber Antiquitatum Biblicarum *with Latin Text and English Translation* (Leiden, 1996).

Murphy, Fredrick J., *Pseudo-Philo. Rewriting the Bible* (New York and Oxford, 1993).

Perrot, Charles, and Pierre-Maurice Bogaert, with Daniel J. Harrington, *Pseudo-Philon: Les Antiquités Bibliques*. Vol. 2, *Introduction Littéraire, Commentaire et Index* (Paris, 1976).

DANIEL J. HARRINGTON, S.J.
Weston Jesuit School of Theology

Qabbalah, Midrash and

Midrash is the operating system in the ritual of Torah study. Reading scriptural passages in the synagogue service and studying it in special study-houses characterize the two Judaic ways of relating to the Torah in a ritual mode. The fact that this ritual also enacts the covenant between God and his people and, complementarily, shapes the meaning of the scriptural Law into normative ruling(s) constitutes the theological framework in which the ritual of Torah study unfolds. We shall later on refer to this framework in terms of the midrashic condition. In Mishnaic and Talmudic times, reading the Torah in synagogues was accompanied by a translation (into Aramaic or Greek) and a homily. The translation always had a midrashic dimension, and the midrash incorporated elements that functioned as explicatory translations. In a more technical sense, midrash was the manner in which the Torah was studied in *scholae*, that is, among learned sages. In short, midrash developed as the referential language that took up in a creative manner subjects that appeared in earlier phases of these traditions.

In the main, Qabbalah, the Judaic forms of mysticism that evolved in theosophical circles in the late thirteenth and early fourteenth centuries C.E. appears, too, as midrashic explications of Scripture. In this respect, the discussion here, connecting Midrash and Qabbalah, creates an ideal opportunity to explore the kaleidoscopic configurations that characterize the almost endless diversification of the midrashic activity. We shall have a chance to see at some length what Midrash has to offer to Qabbalah, and, *mutatis mutandis*, how Qabbalah transformed Midrash. Furthermore, we shall have an opportunity to examine the manner in which its elastic qualities enabled Midrash to stretch and create dramatic distances and significant gaps between scripture and its explicatory oeuvre.

It should be noted, though, that as long as the scriptural text showed its qualities as the steadfast constant, the midrashic explications took on almost any form of multiplicity and variability that the words of Scripture could potentially tolerate. Whether midrash absorbed the status of the steadfast constant or roamed in evanescent territories is a question that has no universally applicable answer. However, one thing is certain. The stability of the scriptural text establishes the anchor-position from which the midrashic explications can take their departure without necessarily losing the connecting chains, which link them to their scriptural source. Complementarily, the map, which holds together the multiplicity of ways taken by midrash, even to the extent of maintaining opposite and polemical stances, owes its directional clarity to the anchor-position that the word of Scripture zealously maintains. Midrash shows up as a process with no boundaries; in fact, it turns scripture into a text with no boundaries. However, the scriptural text still has the power to hold matters together and safeguard the midrashic ruminations from disintegrating into utter redundancy.

M. Pe. 1:1 opens with a statement concerning "things the benefit of which a person enjoys in this world, while the principal remains for him in the world to come... But *Talmud Torah* (the study of the Law) is as important as all of them together." Midrash, though, was the technical term that gradually acquired a generic status in the explicatory activity of *Talmud Torah*. Originally, in its scriptural usage, the Hebrew verb *darash* indicated questions or supplications addressed to God or to a person who was divinely inspired. Thus, for instance, the helpless Rebecca went "*li-drosh 'et YHWH*," that is, to receive divine consultation, with regard to her troublesome pregnancy (Gen. 25:22). The word "midrash" occurs twice in the Hebrew Scripture, 2 Chron. 13: 22; 24: 27, but not in the sense it has acquired in the Rabbinic usage. In its Rabbinic usage, the word "midrash" assumes the existence of a spiritual milieu, or condition, in which almost everything said in relation to a specific scriptural text finds a linguistic or contextual logic, which is vital to giving the specific text an updated relevance.

Technically speaking, there are two complementary traditions, the one speaking of the thirteen and the other of the thirty-two *middot*, explicatory measures (alias, the method) applied in the creation of the midrashic sayings. However, the presence of these *middot* in the various forms of Mishnaic and Talmudic discourse is rarely noticeable. In short, midrash is the generic term that justifies the annexation of almost any saying to a Torah-text, or scriptural saying that is scrutinized for its relevant meaning. Since, as we have seen, the study of Torah ultimately received an absolute priority in the Rabbinic world, midrash became the universal qualifier of the hermeneutic activity connected with this study.

Before the rise of the Qabbalah, in the thirteenth century, the Torah was viewed as the word of God. It had an independent existence and deciding its meaning was largely in the hands of those who studied it. With the rise of Qabbalah, Torah received a new status. It now was viewed as the mirror reflection of the paradigmatic structure of the Ten Sefirot, the entities in which the supernal deity unfolds in meta-physical and meta-historical realms. In other words, those studying the Torah saw themselves as having a direct communion with a text that was not only divinely inspired but in a very concrete sense a projected manifestation of the divine essence.

According to the Qabbalistic belief, those immersing themselves intellectually in the divine text in reality immerse themselves in the deity whose essence is viewed as being incorporated in it. Thus, from whichever angle one views the Torah it positions itself as a multi-faceted existential realization of the metaphysical endlessness of the word of God. This endlessness is his ultimate all-being and, complementarily, his being everything to all. If a negative approach is adopted, one may speak here of the "fetishization" of the Torah. However, even at its most radical phases, the Qabbalistic oeuvre remains within the framework of Midrash. This means that the gap between the reader and the text is overcome by an inescapably existential experience. This experience exhausts itself in the hermeneutical stances, which the Qabbalistic midrash opens. In essence, it is a mystical experience.

There are various ways of approaching the subject of Qabbalah. Looking at Qabbalah from the angle of Midrash, as we do here, introduces a discourses that is both highly challenging and cross-thematically enriching. Let me start with a quote from the Book of the Zohar (the Book of the [Divine] Splendor). The *Zohar* is the major text of the Qabbalah. It was written as a mystical commentary to the Pentateuch, in the second half of the thirteenth century. The quote is the opening midrashic exposition on the first word in the Book of Genesis:

> "In the beginning"—At the beginning, the royal decree of the king engraved engravings in the supernal brightness. A light of blackness emerged in the enclosure-within-the-enclosure, from the head of *En Sof*, a mist within a shapeless mass, inserted in a ring, neither white, nor black, nor red, nor yellow—no color at all. When he was holding a measuring cord, he made colors to make that light shine. A stream came out from which the colors below received their variegation. And the innermost enclosure-within-the-enclosure in the mystery of *En Sof* (= "the One with No End," the uppermost God who reveals himself in the ten Sefirot; see blow) burst forth and did not burst forth its empty space. It was not at all known before the pressure of the bursting forth made one spot shine in the supernal enclosure. After that spot nothing at all was known. And for this reason it is called

Reshit (= beginning), the utterance that preceded everything.

By all standards, this is a unique interpretation of the first word in the Hebrew Scripture and a rather extraordinary description of the creation of the world. In the present context, we need not discuss the mystical ideas that the passage contains. However, if the passage has to be redeemed from the impression that it mere gibberish, a few words must be said on the intellectual milieu in which such a description needs contextualization.

I suggest viewing this passage in the larger context of Midrash. The reason for following this procedure is that the passage introduces itself in relation to a scriptural source. I view Midrash as the creative milieu as well as the methodological framework in which almost every kind of understandings, or readings, of scriptural texts is likely to evolve. We shall later see where certain constraints, or borderlines, limit the act of midrashic interpretation or else interfere with the thrust of its imaginative freedom. The Jewish mystics of the middle ages, the Qabbalists, introduced a mode of scriptural interpretation that is radically new and opens an unprecedented kind of reading Scripture. In every comparative respect, the Qabbalistic reading of Scripture looks like crossing such borderlines.

The history of the midrashic interpretation of Scripture offers a rich palette of examples in which all kinds of hermeneutic experiments found their way to the public eye and were accepted there as legitimate explorations of the extent to which one may stretch the word of Scripture. These explorations are all contained within a comfortable consensus, which facilitated stretching the creative thrust of the hermeneutic endeavor in almost every direction. Still, some modes of interpretation turned out to be more problematic. Readers certainly raised an eyebrow when confronted with Philo's ventures into the allegorical interpretation of Scripture. Philo of Alexandria established his hermeneutic technique trying to read the Pentateuch in a Platonic-Stoic context. One may even say that certain Rabbinic expositions of Scripture are rather far fetched and, for that reason, counter productive from an exegetical point of view.

However, as exemplified above, what the Qabbalists did is really ground breaking in every respect possible. The Qabbalists invented a code (often referred to as symbolic) in which every word in Scripture was shown to refer paradigmatically to one of the ten Sefirot. The Sefirot are spiritual entities, which unfold as the divine fullness, or Pleroma. The manner in which this code operates is quite extraordinary. No wonder, then, that soon after the *Zohar* was completed, Joseph Chicatella wrote the first dictionary of Qabbalistic terms, *Sha'arei Orah* (= The Gates of Light, or *Portae Lucis*, in the popular Latin translation published by the Christian Qabbalists of the Renaissance). The book is organized in ten chapters ("Gates"), each one of which is devoted to one of the Sefirot and the key scriptural words that refer to it. Furthermore, the book lucidly describes how these words operate in various contextual combinations. Originally, the ten Sefirot emanated, or radiated out, of God, who, as we have seen, is called *En Sof*. Although the Rabbinic sages advanced the idea that the world was created in "ten utterances" (in Hebrew, *ma'amarot*; M. Ab. 5:1), it is more likely that the ultimate model for the Qabbalists was the Aristotelian concept of the ten "cyclic heavens," or "spheres," as they could find it in the writings of Maimonides.

Since the Qabbalists believed that every word in Scripture corresponds to one of these Sefirot, when properly understood, every phrase or sentence in Scripture highlights one of the many aspects in which the internal modes of interaction between the Sefirot come into play. Furthermore, since the Sefirot are divine entities, their reflection in the scriptural text points to the divine essence that characterizes the scriptural text. The ten Sefirot have individual names: *Keter* (Crown), *Hokhmah* (Wisdom), *Binah* (Sagacity), *Hesed* (Grace or Compassion), *Gevurah* (Vigor), *Tiferet* (Glory), *Netsach* (Longevity), *Hod* (Majesty), *Yesod* (Foundation), *Malkhut* (Royal Sovereignty).

To make the reader realize what is at stake, I refer to two further examples taken from the Zohar. Gen. 1:1 reads: "In the beginning God created heaven and earth." We may not fully understand the manner in which this act of creation happened, but the Qabbalists had no second thoughts when they suggested reading these words as implying that "*Beginning* (subject) *created* (predicate) *Elohim* (object)." By all standards, this is a dramatic way of bypassing the innumerable commentaries that tried to say something coherent, from their point of view, on the act of creation. It is not for us to decide whether the *Zohar* succeeded in making matters clearer or more enigmatic. However, the idea behind the Qabbalistic reading of the opening verse of the Book of Genesis is, "In The Beginning" [that is, the second Sefirah, *Hokhmah*, also called *Reshit* (see the Hebrew text of Ps. 111: 10)] "created Elohim" [that is, the third *Sefirah*, *Binah*], and heaven [that is, the sixth Sefirah, *Tiferet*], and Earth [that is, the Tenth Sefirah, *Malkhut*]. This reading introduces a radical fragmentation of the verse as also a total eradication of its original grammar and meaning. Furthermore, it places Elohim, the Creator God, as the created third Sefirah. Finally, heaven and earth are the names of the sixth and the tenth Sefirot. Those familiar with the subject can easily make the comparison between the modern trend of deconstructionism and the Qabbalistic handling of the Scriptural text. Note, however, that all this happens in the framework of a midrashic move.

Another example is associated with the Qabbalistic reading of the verse "Lift up your eyes on high and see: *who created these*?" (Is. 40:26). In Hebrew, the italicized words read, "*mi bara eleh*." The Qabbalistic interpretation of these words turns the question into a statement, saying that "*Mi*" [a reference to the third Sefirah, *Binah*] created "*Eleh*" [that is, the rest of the Sefirot below *Binah*] (*Zohar* to Genesis, Introduction 1/b). The first thing to notice here is the metaphorical personification of the scriptural words. However, much more is involved than just an act of literary metaphorization. It entails a total deconstruction of everything that is based on accepted modes of understanding of what the text in Genesis can imply. In other words, the Qabbalistic type of Midrash creates a linguistic metamorphosis. However, this does not end our current story. If "*mi*" and "*eleh*" are read together—with the letters of "*mi*" in reverse order—the consonants are fused and become "*Elohim*." That is to say, the midrashic assumption behind this Qabbalistic reading is that the verse in Isaiah is in itself a latent midrashic elaboration on the word *Elohim*. However, a deconstructionist reading of the verse exposes the additional layer of meaning, as described above.

All this brings us to a point at which a more thoroughgoing discussion of the relationship between midrash and Qabbalah is needed. Hermeneutics is one of the major factors in creating the dynamics of development and change in Jewish thought and religious experience. Midrash is the generic term that covers a rich variety of hermeneutic stances in Judaism. Qabbalah ("received tradition"), the technical term for Jewish mysticism, is no exception to this rule, though, as we have just seen, its innovative and radical features require specific attention. In order to understand the unique position that midrash occupies in Qabbalah, a few preliminary observations have to be made about how I conceive of midrash in general. Midrash is more than a generic term indicating the explication of Scripture. Midrash is the intellectual forum in which people interacting with Scripture revive the ancient words and make them relevant to the situation in which this interaction takes place. More technically expressed, midrash creates "midrashic conditions," that is, hermeneutic frameworks, or territories, in which the scriptural words can receive and bring into effect new potentials of meaning. In this respect, I wish to argue, there is no essential difference between what to one reader looks as the plane and simple sense of the scriptural text (in Hebrew, *Peshat*) and to the other looks as its hyperbolic exposition (*Derash*). Qabbalah, in any event, bypasses this distinction, arguing that what it does is reaching to the divine secrets embedded in every word or utterance of Scripture. *Sod* and *Raz* ("secret" in Hebrew and Aramaic, respectively) are the terms used in this connection. Formally speaking, then, Qabbalah evolves in a midrashic context, which claims for itself the status of a revelation of divine secrets.

I believe that a connecting line can be drawn between the Qabbalistic approach to Scripture and the one that is applied in the Pesher literature of the Qumran library. In both cases, the attitude to the scriptural texts assumes the exposure of an esoteric layer of meaning. I understand the term Esotericism to indicate the existence of a supplementary revelation with regard to a scriptural text. This revelation exposes hidden layers of meaning in the text, which could not be discovered without this revelation. Whether God appears in the revelatory experience, an angel, or a more vague kind of inspiration does not make any substantial difference, in this respect.

A few additional comments on esotericism are in place, when a mystical book that addresses people who call themselves *Maskilim* is at the center of our discussion. Who are these *Maskilim* and what is their connection to the *Zohar*? To answer this question we have to refer to Dan. 12:3: "And those who are wise [*Maskilim*] shall shine [*yazhiru*] like the brightness [*zohar*] of the firmament." The anonymous writers of the Zohar call themselves *Maskilim*. There is no accident in the fact that a series of midrashic sections on this verse follows the opening passage of the Zohar, as quoted above. For lack of a better term (*Qabbalah, mequbalim, ba'alei-Qabbalah* were terms coined at a later stage), the people involved referred to themselves as *Maskilim*. The term *Maskilim* is loaded with philosophical and mystical meanings.

In its philosophical sense, the word derives from *sekhel*, the intellectual mind, or more technically expressed, the psychic intellect. According to Aristotle, Plato said that the cyclic movement of the stars is possible only because they have a psychic intellect (*On the Heavens*, Book II, 2). Humankind, too, has a psychic intellect. In medieval Islamic philosophy, and, in Maimonides, the acquired psychic intellect of the philosopher can merge with the active psychic intellect of the tenth heavenly sphere. This act of merging can happen during the philosopher's life, but then it is a temporary experience. When it happens after his death, this merging can last forever. In any event, the *sekhel* is an active agent, which facilitates knowledge and communion with the heavenly bodies. If the Sefirot, as the Qabbalists conceive of them, are heavenly spheres or entities, the psychic intellect of the Qabbalists is a major factor in what Qabbalah does and bring about. Thus, the word *Maskilim* makes perfect sense with regard to the self-identity of the early Qabbalists.

Like Maimonides, who in several discussions of this issue, argues that only few people can reach the stage of the true philosopher, the Qabbalists, too, said that only the *Maskilim* can have access to the secrets of the Torah. There is a paradigmatic relationship, or similarity, between the philosophical layers of the Torah as Maimonides conceives of them and the mystical reading of the secrets of the Torah as accomplished by the Qabbalists. In both cases, the midrashic condition is the same: It is the esoteric component in the reading and understanding of Torah. The human *sekhel* has access to these secrets, because it can communicate with the *sekhel* embodied in each of the upper spheres—the heavenly spheres and the Sefirot, alike.

Using more general terms, midrash can be viewed as anything that creates a live connection to something that happened or was written in the past. The live connection crystallizes in the form of an explicatory statement about that event or text. Structured actions, or rituals, various kinds of artistic expression (like liturgical music, icons and cultic artifacts), liturgical compositions (the Piyyut is a famous example), translations, and sermons—all potentially possess a similar function. More precisely expressed, rituals behavior is a form of midrashic attitude. Doing things in relation to events that happened in the past—rituals done as acts of memorization—possesses midrashic features. Passover and the Feast of Tabernacles are two elaborate examples to this effect. The words said in the Eucharist, "Do this in remembrance of me" (Luke 22:19), are a ritual extension, hence shaped in a specific "midrashic condition," of the Passover-night meal as conceived by the early Christians. In this respect, doing a ritual that is mentioned in the Mosaic Law in the manner in which it is described in later sources (the Mishnah, Talmud, New Testament) often entails a latent midrashic exposition. The notion of the "midrashic conditions" prevails, as long as previous "texts"—in the wide sense mentioned above—are discussed with an eye on their explication for theoretical and practical purposes. In other words, the moment a text or its interpretation is ignored it enters a state of cultural hibernation.

Living in a mystical mode the existential impact of Scripture, as we see in the case of the Qabbalists, is another way of recreating the midrashic conditions of Scripture, or creating for Scripture new midrashic conditions. The links created between what happened or was written in the past and that which is said about it in the mystical present always entails more than just an exegetical stance. Since the Torah tells a story that is paradigmatically embodied in the ten Sefirot, every time one reads the Scriptural text one participates in something divine. The *Maskilim* have the necessary mental capacity to exhaust the midrashic potentials created by the fusion of intellects—that of their own *sekhel* with that of the Sefirot. The midrashic potentials, in this case, create a spiritual cross-fertilization: Studying the Torah in the right way—that is, Qabbalistically—activates the inner life of the Sefirot. Consequently, the divine overflow reaches terrestrial domains and improves the learning capabilities of the Qabbalist. It is understood that this position is not explicitly stated in Scripture. However, it is the essential presupposition that enables the midrashic extension of Scripture in light of Qabbalistic premises. No wonder then that the Qabbalists argue that those who are unaware of the mystical dimensions implied by the scriptural text (the fools, *sekhalim*, as they are referred to by the early Qabbalists) are like people who read a text emptied of its basic meaning. The text has no life of its own, unless it is read with the hermeneutic premises that create the midrashic conditions of Qabbalah.

The true existence of the Torah, then, is in its being realized as the reflection of the paradigmatic existence of the Sefirot. More succinctly expressed, the Qabbalists argue that the whole Torah is full of the names of God. No word in Scripture is empty of its embedded divine presence. In Qabbalistic terms, the Torah creates woven textures composed of the names of God. Those who wish to find a clear and extensive explications of these notions may be referred to the opening pages in Chicatella's *Sha`arei Orah*, mentioned above. Consequently, the ultimate grammatical patterns of the language used in Scripture are not dictated by philological laws but the mystical message, which the words convey. In other words, what holds the words together and presents them as coherent sentences and cogent statements is the logic that permeates the inner structure of the Sefirot, with its unique dynamics and structure.

The discussion of midrash and Qabbalah as we present it here cannot but induce one conclusion. There are no, and there almost cannot be, any limitations on the directions and ways midrashic expositions can take. If we accept the complementary principle, namely, that any interpretive examination of a canonical text in Judaism potentially crystallizes as a normative statement with regard to the manner in which scriptural texts address those reflecting upon their meaning, then Qabbalah has a safe territory in which it can flourish and exert its limitless influence. In this respect, the Qabbalists would say, as indeed they do, that only their way of interpreting Scripture contains the ultimate and compelling truth Scripture wants people to realize. In short, then, in whatever format midrash presents itself, it is a creative kind of explanatory reference to any scriptural text that is examined for its potentially endless array of meanings and points of relevance. Qabbalah is a striking example of how far one can go with this assumption in mind.

Here a word is due on the semantic use of the terms "Scripture" and "canon." In the mind of many people, these terms are interchangeable. Indeed, in their common usage they often function as synonyms. I suggest viewing canon in a narrow technical sense, as the result of a formal decision taken by a group of authoritative people with regard to the question, which books are included in a certain literary corpus and which books are excluded. A canon means that, as a matter of principle, nothing can be either added or detracted from it. In most cases, a canonical corpus is the foundational text of a religion. The "Old Testament," the New Testament, and the Qur'an are famous examples of collections of books (in the case of the Qur'an, of Sura's) that have been given a canonical status. Scripture, however, is the word used for the divinely inspired nature of the writings at hand. Usually but not exclusively, though, canon and Scripture go together. I make the distinction between these terms to indicate that some books may be treated as scriptures, but in reality, they have no claim for divine inspiration. In this sense both the Mishnah and Zohar are scriptures, but they do not claim canonical status. In both cases, we know, additions and changes were introduced into the respective texts, and this long after they had been completed from an editorial point of view. Finally, it should be noted that the Hebrew term for both canon and Scripture does not make this kind of distinction. The term *kitvei ha-qodesh* applies to both. The term *kitvei ha-qodesh*, though, means "the writings of the Holy One." "Sacred writings" or "holy scriptures" would translate into Hebrew as *ketavim* (or *sefarim*) *qedoshim*.

In other words, the term scripture, in its non-canonical sense, should be understood in a more inclusive manner than is usually the case. In my understanding, "Scripture" indicates any text the explication of which creates a tradition of understandings or a normative stance within a certain cultural position. However, more complex is the idea, to which I want to draw attention, namely, that a scriptural status is attached to words uttered by political leaders, commentators, or academics, that is, to people who have or claim to have authority. To remind the reader, one of the major features in establishing the status of a Scripture is the awakening of interpretive attitudes. I would refer to this phenomenon as the "Scripture effect." This is generated in the process of elaborating upon the "text" in a hermeneutic environment. Examples of texts, which have the status of a scripture in the non-religious context, can be given *ad libitum*. Even news items and articles in newspapers sometimes receive this status in the eyes of the believing public. It should come as no surprise, then, that widening the scope of scripture makes it easy for us to include texts like the Mishnah and the Zohar in the framework of scriptural writings, whether they have canonical status or not.

Both, the Mishnah and Zohar create the needed midrashic conditions for their individual messages to receive and maintain their respective validity as advancing new modes of living the scriptural world. The

Mishnah refers to the Mosaic Law and expands it, making it rather widely applicable and organizing it in structured compositions. Whether the Mishnah includes explicit theological statements or not is debatable. However, the Mishnah makes an overall proclamation that is audibly theological. As indicated, the Mishnah is sometimes treated as a canon. The reason for this is that, in many essential and practical respects, the Mishnah replaces the Mosaic Law. In apposition to the somewhat loosely structured Pentateuch, the Mishnah makes its appearance as the well-organized Hexateuch. It builds its line of argumentation in uniquely structured category-formations. Consequently, every page in the Talmud, in its Jerusalem and Babylonian versions, shows how the Mishnah is the foundational text for the ensuing discussion.

One assumption, which certainly qualifies as a *sine qua non* in any understanding of midrash, in its non-biblical context, is that the word of God is no longer available in its audibly vocal immediacy. The word of God resonates through its midrashic interpretation. The essence of the midrashic condition is that the word of God depends on its human interpreters to receive its meaning. The objective status of the word of God is, paradoxically, its being in the hands of learned or inspired human beings. They establish the manner in which the word of God has its presence in any ritual, theological, or social setting. In other words, humans have to create the framework in which the words of God as preserved in Scripture make sense. These decisions are based on the erudition acquired in the Rabbinic *Beit* (= house of) *Midrash* or *Yeshivah* (literally, Place of Sitting), that is, in Rabbinic study houses.

God speaks neither in the Mishnah nor in any of the other writings reflecting the Rabbinic world. Even when a voice comes down from heaven in the form of a *Bat Qol* ("the daughter of a voice," that is, an indirect divine utterance) in support of a certain Halakhic opinion, it is declared to be ineffective. The famous example, in this respect, is the Halakhic debate between to Tannaim of the second generation (early decades of the first century C.E.), Eliezer and several Rabbinic sages. The issue was the susceptibility to impurity of a specially crafted clay oven. One of the things Eliezer did to show that he was right was to invoke a celestial decision. And, indeed, a *Bat Qol* came from heaven in support of Eliezer. However, Joshua, who was present on the scene, declared that decisions in Halakhic matters are not made on the basis of heavenly intervention (B. B.M. 59b).

The Qabbalists did the reverse of what Joshua wanted. They read the earthly Scripture, but argued that in doing so they are dealing with heavenly entities, the Sefirot. Explicating Song 2:2, "As a rose among the brambles," they say:

> What is a rose? It is the "Assembly (*Knesset*) of Israel" (a symbolic representation of the tenth Sefirah, which reflects the dialectic energies, or powers, of the upper Sefirot). Because there is a rose and there is a rose. As the rose that is among the brambles, which is red and white, so the "Assembly of Israel" incorporates stern judgment and compassion" (*Zohar* to Genesis [Introduction], 1/a).

Reading Scripture from the point of view of its multi-layered meaningfulness preserves the text. At the same time, it allows it to roam safely in a midrashic space, which is potentially infinite. In referring to the midrashic space as infinite, I mean that allegedly any scriptural word can have at least more than one meaning that the plane, lexical, one does not include. In this sense, one may argue that every midrash creates its own binary linguistic structures. Furthermore, with every midrash goes its own dictionary. Every midrashic system creates its own methodological categories, or midrashic conditions.

In short, existing midrashic expositions

of Scripture induce the impression that almost nothing can stop a midrashist from saying almost anything on a specific text. Almost everything passes as acceptable as long as it does not directly interfere with a rather flexible consensus, which regulates the coherence of the existing theological system. Mostly, this coherence is in no conflict with a non-compromising obligation to abide by the Torah Law. Pluralism is not necessarily the key word, in this case, though a considerable amount of positive flexibility in matters of belief and religious praxis must be assumed for the midrashic condition to take shape. There are always the borderlines between what passes as right and what shapes as heresy. Heresy, in this connection, means that the biblical text is taken to cultic and spiritual territories in which the text is made to convey the opposite of what the plane text says. For instance, this was the case in Gnosticism, in which the creator God, Elohim, was presented as the rebellious Demiurgos, an inferior god responsible for the creation of the material world.

Qabbalah, therefore, had to find ways of making itself acceptable and belonging into the wide consensus mentioned above. Thus, Qabbalah did not break its ties neither with the word of Scripture nor with world of Halakhah. However, essential modifications in the understanding of the word of Scripture and in the concept of the Halakhah established themselves as new norms in the literature of the Qabbalah. Obviously, they created antagonism, which did not stop before it succeeded to relegate Qabbalah in the minds of its opponents to the position of "idolatry." Idolatry is the technical term used to indicate beliefs in, and worship of, "other Gods." However, we often find that "idolatry" is a blanket that covers all kinds of relativistic usages. Religious authorities could use this term whenever they considered that a certain saying, a teachings, or a religious practice was contradicting what they held as the consensus representing the correct view and practice. The correct view or practice is the English equivalent to the (etymologically defined) Greek word "orthodoxy." Thus, for instance, those who opposed the kind of philosophical interpretation of Scripture as forwarded by Maimonides burned his books, while others declared the Qabbalah to be idolatry. In other words, deciding what is right or wrong in any midrashic undertaking depends on the point of view taken, by whom, and on the authority supporting the case at hand.

What must remain clear, however, is that cultures unfold and develop in the course of activities that revision their past and adapt it for present and future purposes. If the past is contained in texts, the cultural activity that links to them is their constant adaptation to areas of meaning in new modes of existence. One may argue that, in certain respects, the relationship of interpretation to the text reflected upon is like free associations to reality. In other words, I argue that interpretation is as vital to culture as dreaming is to the health of the psyche. If we need a direct and convincing proof of this fact, we may look at the first two chapters of Genesis. The book contains two parallel stories told by people who wanted to give themselves formalized accounts of the respective cosmos in which they lived. The people who preserved these accounts and then channeled them into a scriptural canon made their point: The two accounts can live together; in fact, they enrich one another, with, and because of, all the differences that they contain. The first story ends with the creation of humankind and the divine decree to procreate and multiply. The second story ends with a declaration that makes childbirth a painful, even, traumatic, event. The differences between the stories are the stimulants upon which interpreters thrive.

Any interpretation that is added takes a stand vis-à-vis these versions and the reality each of them wished to portray. In many of the traditional commentaries, Gen. 1 has the upper hand. The problematic aspects of the beginning, as presented in the second story, are simply ignored. People think that the purpose of the second story is to tell of important events that characterize the nature of humankind, disregarding the issue of the *Tselem Elohim*, mentioned in the first chapter.

If we include in our midrashic horizon the Gospel of John, we get an interpretation that establishes a new canon: "In the beginning (*en arche*, using the same word used by the Book of Genesis) there was the Word (*logos*)." When we look at these words, one conclusion suggests itself as obvious: Different versions of the same events do have an implied essence and purpose as polemical stances. If this is the case, then our perspectives have to change with regard to the two creation stories mentioned above. They do not complement each other but, in fact, pose rival positions right at the opening pages of the Hebrew Scripture. As indicated above, this sets the rules of the game: there is no explicit urge to create unanimity of opinion.

It is indeed tempting to say that two, or even three, voices are juxtaposed in these texts and that these voices reflect the views of different groups, or authors. However, what matters here is not the origin of these stories but the fact that they are placed side-by-side or one vis-à-vis the others. Evidently, this fact can easily lead to the conclusion that the same events cannot only be viewed from more than one angle but that in many cases the importance of the facts is established when they are preserved in more than one version. Plurality of views is not only indicative of the existence of rival interpretive stances with regard to what is true and what is false, but also with regard to what is and what is not.

Here hermeneutical processes do a good service. They alert the reader to watch his steps in the paths of the text. Hermeneutics points to the presence of certain obstacles in the text, to the significance of the diversity involved, to the danger of losing attention and letting the text snowball to the abyss marked by redundancy. Somebody enters the text and shows that it needs a comment, that it creates a conflict with another text, that there is significance in what may look trivial.

Not everyone will necessarily agree that a certain interpretation removes for him all the obstacles he meets. For instance, matters are quite complicated, when the two versions of the Decalogue, Exodus 20 and Deuteronomy 5, are juxtaposed and compared. The almost official stand that the Rabbinic authorities took over this issue is that the two versions were spoken simultaneously. In raising this issue, one shows that the people responsible for the editing of the text did not sweep their sensitivity to matters of textual and contextual diversity under the rug of indifference. On the contrary, they were aware of the exegetical difficulty, and the solution they offered shows the kind of mindset, which allowed diversity of opinions to finds modes of co-existence.

We can now have a closer look at the Qabbalistic modes of midrashic explication. In principle, the Zohar and other Qabbalistic text that use the midrashic technique do it as most Rabbinic midrashic compilations operate. A scriptural verse, or part of a verse, is quoted and is followed by a midrashic homily. As indicated above, the unique features of the Zohar are its claims to contain the revelation of divine secrets and the paradigmatic structure of the ten Sefirot that underlies, in a binary way, every utterance in Scripture. The literary environments that Zohar derive mostly from a fictitious representation of the land of Israel in Tannaitic times, that is in the second century C.E. Recent scholarship has shown that that a number of people took part in the composition of the Zohar, but it is still likely that the person whose name was associated with its composition, Moses de Leon, was the key figure in this respect. The Zohar comprises also several other tractates that were written later and do not belong in the main body of the book. Chief among them are the "New Zohar," *Zohar Hadash*, and the

Tiqqunei Zohar, the "Embellishments of the Zohar." These books and tractates make use of almost the same interpretive system as applied in the *Zohar*, though they bring forth new modes of Qabbalistic thinking.

To understand the manner in which the Qabbalists conceive of the Sefirot, two principles have to be taken into consideration. They concern the bi-directional dynamics in which the Sefirot operate one upon the other. Graphically they are arranged in three columns. The right column consists of *Hokhmah*, *Hesed*, and *Netsach*; the left column consists of *Binah*, *Gevurah*, and *Hod*; the middle column consists of *Keter*, *Tiferet*, *Yesod*, and *Malkhut*. The right column represents divine compassion, while the left column represents stern judgment. The tension between these two sides, or aspects, of the Sefirotic world rises from the opposite directions and inclinations that crystallize in them. Ideally, the side of divine compassion should prevail in the Sefirotic world. However, when the "left side" gains power, the balance is critically disturbed. Usually, the middle column creates the various balances between the right and the left extremes. However, when the horizontal balance is disturbed, the vertical dynamics marked by the divine affluence emanating from *En Sof* into *Keter*, from there into *Tiferet*, and from there, through *Yesod*, into *Malkhut*—is fatally disrupted.

The relationship between *Tiferet* and *Malkhut* is usually described in erotic terms. The Sefirah that plays a major role in this respect is *Yesod*. Quite commonly, it is described as having phallic functions. In other words, the orderly functioning of the vertical axis in the Sefirotic world depends on the balance contained in the horizontal axis. In this manner, the horizontal and the vertical dynamics in the Sefirotic world are made to interact. Once *Malkhut* is filled with the divine affluence, which comes from above, it streams forth acts of empathic grace the purpose of which is to revive and sustain the people of Israel. Any kind disturbance in the free flow of the divine affluence ends in disrupting this streaming forth of empathic grace from which the People of Israel draw their power to exist and withstand evil.

Evil, the "other side" (in Aramaic, *Sitra Achra*), is a predominant concern in Qabbalistic circles, both on the personal and the public-historical level. In many respects, the powers of evil are shaped in a dualistic mode. They entail a constant threat not only to people but also to the well-being of the lowest Sefirah, *Malkhut*. They feed on the powers of stern judgment and on misguided "lights" coming from the side of divine compassion. In a sense, when no stern judgment streams forth from the Sefirotic world or misguided acts (human sins) are avoided, they can be dried out.

In other words, empowering the right column of the Sefirot is in the interest of everyone wishing to maintain life and avoid death, physically and metaphysically speaking. The more misery the exilic existence brought upon the people of Israel, the more attention is given to the forces of the *Sitra Achra*. Every trouble and pain is attributed to its tribulations. Mystically speaking, redemption from the clasp of the Sitra Achra is conceived in processes generating, through the Torah Law, the positive energies of the divine compassion. However, there are cases in which messianic ideas, or even figures, are invoked, giving the whole structure a historical twist.

In a recently published study, Moshe Idel (*Absorbing Perfections: Kabbalah and Interpretation* [New Haven and London, 2002]) traced the various midrashic stages that finally crystallized in the worldview and cosmic/super-cosmic structure. Once Qabbalah established these matters, there was no limit to what it could do. The idealized patterns of the Sefirot serve like the harmonic rules in music. The Qabbalists will always argue that even when their music does not seem to obey the traditional harmonic rules, in its deep acoustic structure it *is* the real, and exclusive, harmony.

One of the major concepts that establish

the status of what may be called the non-scriptural text of Scripture is the notion of the Oral Torah. Allegedly this is the accompanying Word of God, explicates the Written Torah given to Moses on Mount Sinai. In the Qabbalistic interpretation, however, the notion of the Oral Torah corresponds to the tenth Sefirah, *Malkhut*. It houses, so to speak, the Written Torah, which is the sixth Sefirah, *Tiferet*. In other words, the dual aspects of the Torah in reality are dual gender-aspects in the divine world. It is customary to refer to the divine world, unfolding in the Sefirot, in the Neo-Platonic term, Pleroma ("Fullness"). The notion of Pleroma indicates that there are no breaches in the meta-cosmic and cosmic realities. However, in the theological thinking of the Qabbalists, such breaches are possible. They indicate the fact that the People of Israel have misused their theurgic potentials, that is, the powers that—magic-like—work upon the divine world. More specifically, the major and most devastating breach is between the sixth and the tenth Sefirah.

This breach concerns the gender duality in the Godhead and thus reflects a basic feature in the dynamics that characterizes the Sefirot. No wonder, then, that it engages an erotic language. The love affair, its activation and disruption, marks an inner relationship between the upper part of the Sefirot and their lower part. Union in the Sefirotic world means that the people of God live according to the decrees of the Torah (in its Qabbalistic understanding). Disruption and separation means the opposite.

In other words, the duty of the people of Israel is not only to keep the inner unity among the totality of the Sefirot, but also of the totality of the Torah as the mundane manifestation of the Sefirot, or the divine Word. Any change in what the text is has consequences in both the upper and the lower world. Thus, the duties vis-à-vis the Sefirot and the Torah are interlinked. *Qudsha Brich Hu*, "The Holy One, Blessed He Is," who is the Qabbalistic representation of *Tiferet*, and Knesset Yisrael, "The Assembly of Israel," which is a representation of *Malkhut*, have to be given their full chance to live a harmonious life together. The relationship between the Sefirotic configurations of God and Israel, respectively, mark the conjugal covenant between the People of Israel and their God. In the words of the prophets of ancient Israel, God and His People ideally live in a martial relationship (see, for instance, Hos. 2:21). In Qabbalistic terms, this covenant is has an additional phase in the Sefirotic world. The two phases are interlinked and interdependent. As indicated above, this unity is conceived as accomplishing a conjugal relationship within the Sefirot. The bridegroom is the sixth Sefirah, *Tiferet*, and the tenth Sefirah, *Malkhut*, is the bride.

In this respect, one may argue that the Qabbalistic concept of Torah guarantees not only the existential integrity of the text but also the wholeness of the Sefirotic world. Consequently, as the Qabbalists say, "all the worlds are in tact." On a completely different level, this conjugal union reflects the ideal complementarity between the Written and the Oral Torah. An inner splitting between the Written and Oral Torah is the theological trademark of the Qaraites. For them, the Rabbinic Oral Torah was anathema.

Reading Qabbalistic texts is always an interesting experience. On the one hand, fragments of scriptural verses are elaborated upon in a manner endlessly imaginative. The text is expanded to refer to almost everything that fits some structure, or cluster, of the Sefirot entity. On the other hand, there are not too many seminal-structure units that correspond to the central dynamics activating the ten Sefirot. The dialectic tension that is created, in this respect, manifests itself in various ways. One of them makes the reader realize the inner logic in the system. Almost every verse in Scripture can be taken to one of the few places that fit into the same structural horizon(s). Thus, there are endless quotes that serve to describe the special relationship mentioned above between *Tiferet* and *Malkhut*. Other are read as describing the numerical structures that specific clusters in the Sefirotic world. Any word, or subject, that relates to the numbers three, seven, ten, and fifty receives special attention. The gender factor plays a significant role, in this respect, too.

Any kind of contrast—between colors (black/white), directions (north/south), sides (right/left/centre), height (high/Low), time (this world/the world to come)—plays important roles in the way the Qabbalistic Midrash unfolds. As mentioned above, evil and sin receive not only factual attention, but also terminological fixation. A central motif in the Qabbalistic midrash is the likening of the Sefirotic to a tree. Various parts of the tree (the trunk, branches, roots) correspond to sections in the Sefirotic Pleroma. Thus, for instance, the trunk is the central column of the Sefirot, and is represented by *Tiferet*.

Divine names are one of the most secret doctrines of the Qabbalah. In fact, Qabbalists incline to see in every word of Scripture a divine name. Since almost every word in the Hebrew Scripture corresponds to one Sefirah or another (there are even words that "serve" two or more Sefirot), they can be equaled to the "divine" or "semi-divine" names of these Sefirot. An interesting domain of relating to these names is "wearing" them like garments. Furthermore, the order of the letters of each word can be changed according to special rules of permutation that were first laid down in *Sefer Yetsirah* (the Book of the Creation [of the World]). Events in the lives of the three patriarchs—Abraham, Isaac, and Jacob—and of other people in the history of ancient Israel are viewed as paradigmatically showing processes in the divine world. In fact, every single life story of these people is a live reflection of the dynamics of the Sefirot. In a sense, the lives of these people are pre-determined by divine pre-figurations that unfold in the Sefirot.

Scholars have suggested various explanations for this kind of scriptural interpretation. The most frequent terms of reference offered, in this respect, are symbolism and myth. It is argued that Qabbalah, and particularly the Book of Zohar, re-awakened in the Judaic world long forgotten, even eradicated, forms of myth and mythology. Furthermore, there is a consensus among scholars, namely, that the kind of midrashic interpretation applied in the Zohar enforces symbolic structures on the scriptural text. Both ways of looking at the materials at hand cannot be dismissed as wrong, though I would argue that these explanations are rather technical and do not exhaust the cognitive and psychological depth of the interpretative phenomenon in the Zohar.

I would like to suggest a new direction of looking at the midrashic process in general and of that of the midrash in Qabbalah in particular. In terms taken from the psychology of the psychoanalysis of the self, which was developed by the American psychoanalyst, Heinz Kohut, I suggest viewing the Qabbalistic attitude towards the scriptural text as an attempt to gain a mode of cognition in which the divine realms can be empathic self-objects. In many respects and cases, texts, and particularly religious texts of the past, present themselves as distant entities. People often find themselves distanced by the remote realities described in these texts. Midrash, as we saw above, is a way of appropriating old texts for new purposes. Midrash transplants the materials contained in the scriptural accounts into new realities, making those accounts relevant to every generation and group engaging in the midrashic activity. Exegesis works the other way around. It attempts to understand these texts in their own context. In a sense, midrash addresses issues, which activate the dynamics of decontextualizing the scriptural text. It finds for it a new context. Many a religious commentary works this way, and a word must is due on the benefits of this process and its price.

Since he positions the text in a completely different milieu from the original, a conscientious midrashist must ask himself, if by decontextualizing the text he does not destabilize its frame of references. Furthermore, when another midrashist, like the author(s) of the Zohar, adds another layer of meaning, what status does the ancient text preserve? Does the benefit of amplifying the contextual volume of the text not detract from the intrinsic value of the original text and its ability to offer a stable message or means of communication? Is not the scriptural text reduced to the position of a springboard which people use for making a high jump into new conceptual and contextual territories?

The answers to these questions seem to me to lie within the psychology of the self, and the psychoanalytic notions of the self/self-object relationship. Anything that comes across the life of a person has a potential of being a self-object. This includes people, objects, and, in our case, texts. Self-objects are there to transfer empathy, which is the principal factor in invigorating the self with the needed energy to sustain its health and ability to live a full life. Implied in the self/self-object relationship is a considerable degree of preparedness, technical as it may be, to be the self-object that is to fulfill its empathic functions towards the self.

To give an extreme example, one can view the comfort, which a chair is able to give to the person sitting on it, as constituting the necessary self-object quality for the self. Its empathy, in this case, is the fact that it facilitates the comfort of sitting. That this is not an altogether strange example may be seen from this quote from *Hekhalot Rabbati* ("the Great Book of the [Heavenly] Palaces," a major mystical treatise from Talmudic times. It refers to what the Throne of Glory says to God, inviting him to sit on it (Hebrew in: P. Schaefer, *Synopse zur Hekhalot-Literatur*, p. 99):

> Three times everyday your Throne of Glory prostrates itself and says to you, Zoharariel, Lord God of Israel, please be honored and take your seat on me, for your carriage is pleasant to me and I do not feel its weight.

This passage uses a poetic way of expression. Using imaginative language, it coveys a notion of throne-empathy.

A more familiar example will be the mother who is breastfeeding. Her breast is a self-object for the baby. The baby completely depends on the empathy that goes with the feeding. The mother's milk is a major factor here, but also the way she holds the baby, sings or talks. The mother must be there to take upon herself the function of being a self-object. If she is not there, if she is not available to the baby's needs in the manner the baby feels is conducive to his being what he is, then fatal consequences to the self can develop. Not having any self-object or denying the need to have a self-object may result in several things: fragmentation of the self, a serious harm to the self's ability to live its full and healthy life, an inclination to sexual perversion, and an utter deterioration of its ability to socialize.

In many cases, the self/self-object relationship crystallizes as a mirroring of the needs of the self. The self needs something and the self-object is there to satisfy this need. In other cases, the self is in need of an idealized figure, a grandiose being like God, to accomplish for him things, which the self cannot achieve unless this grandiose idealized being is there to give and transfer empathy. The interplay between the self and the self-object marks a state of fluctuation, in which the two interchange their respective roles, thus introducing changes and variations in their relationship.

Texts may have this capacity to be a self-object. The person who reads them finds in them the kind of empathy he needs. The same text can be different kinds of self-object to different people. In the case of texts, the self/self-object relationship often crystallizes in an act of interpretation. The more individual the interpretation, we are inclined to say, the more empathic are its midrashic characteristics. At a certain point, the midrash on the text becomes the idealized self-object. People using the midrash may find in it the needed directions to their daily, moral and theological wellbeing. In other words, the midrash is their empathy generating entity. Originally, this was the task of the text. However, after having undergone the process of replacing the original text, the midrash is there on its own merits. It is a metamorphosized text. The new metamorphosis may have a mythic or symbolic form of expression. We should note, though, that myth and symbolism are only instrumental entities, in this case, not the essence of the matter.

Finally, in maintaining that everything said in Scripture fits the pattern of the ten Sefirot, or may "collapse" into a fixed pattern in that realm, the Qabbalists created the notion of the absolute text. In other words, the Qabbalistic manner of reading Scripture is the epitome of midrash. On the one hand, it suggests a binary mode of reading Scripture; on the other, in essence it unfolds in a rather restricted realm of core meanings. This core has many variations. In essence, though, its patterned rigidity does not falter in the wake of the impact, which the endless variations have on a limited number of themes.

ITHAMAR GRUENWALD
Tel Aviv University

Rabbinic Midrash in Historical Context, the Fourth and Fifth Century Compilations

The fourth and fifth century midrash-compilations, represented by Genesis Rabbah, ca. 450 C.E., Leviticus Rabbah, ca. 500 C.E., and Pesiqta deRab Kahana, ca. 550 C.E., along with the Talmud of the Land of Israel, ca. 400 C.E., set forth the Rabbinic response to the triumph of Christianity in converting the Roman empire. First made a licit religion in 312 by Emperor Constantine, then, by the end of the fourth century, recognized as the official religion of the Roman empire, in that century Christianity gained unimagined political power. The triumphant Church briefly lost it, in the reign of Julian, 360–361, and, finally, regained the throne and assured its permanent domination of the state. Christians pointed to their triumph as evidence of God's favor. They further saw Israel as God's people that had been rejected by God for rejecting the Christ.

For their part, the Rabbinic sages could not ignore Christianity as they ignored paganism, because Christians shared the same Scriptures and regarded themselves as the continuators of the Israel of which those Scriptures spoke. These claims directly intersected with those of Judaism. To deal with the Christian problem, the Rabbinic sages conceded that Christianity cited Scriptures held in common but represented the wrong line out of ancient Israel. Thus contemporary Israel in the fourth and fifth century midrash-compilations saw Christians, now embodied in Rome, as Ishmael, Esau, Edom: the brother and the enemy.

The political revolution marked by Constantine's conversion thus forced the two parties to discuss a single agendum, the one set by Scripture, and defined the terms in which each would take up that agendum. The midrash-compilations of that period set forth systematic responses to some, though not all, of the issues in conflict between Christianity and Judaism by reason of the political changes of the time. Of special interest here are the midrashic response in Genesis Rabbah and Leviticus Rabbah and related Midrash-compilations to Christian challenges concerning [1] the identification of the true Israel, on the one side, and [2] the meaning of history, on the other.

Genesis Rabbah and Israel's History

The scriptural record of Israel, shared by both parties to the dispute, took as its premise a single fact. When God wished to lay down a judgment, God did so through the medium of events. History, composed of singular events, therefore spoke God's message. Prophets found vindication through their power to enunciate and even (in the case of Moses) to make, and change, history. Revealing God's will, history moreover consisted of a line of one-time events, all of them heading in a single direction, a line that began at creation and will end with redemption or salvation.

No stoic indifference, no policy of patient endurance could shelter Israel, the Jewish people, from the storm of doubt that swept over them in the fourth century. For if Constantine had become a Christian (312), if Julian's promise of rebuilding the Jerusalem Temple had produced nothing (360), if Christian emperors had through law secured control of the Empire for Christ and even abridged long-standing rights and immunities of Israel (387), as they did, then what hope could remain for Israel? Of greater consequence, did history vindicate the Christian claim that God had saved humanity through the suffering people of God, the Church? Christians believed that the conversion of Constantine and the Roman government proved beyond a doubt that Christ was the royal Messiah. For Israel the interpretation of the political happenings of the day required deep thought about the long-term history of humanity. Conceptions of history carried with them the most profound judgments on the character of the competing nations: the old people, Israel, and the Christians, a third race, a no-people—as some called themselves—now become the regnant nation, the Church. We do not know that the conversion of Constantine and events in its aftermath provoked sages to devote thought to the issues of history and its meaning. We know only that they compiled Midrash-documents rich in thought on the subject. What they said, moreover, bore remarkable pertinence to the issues generated by the history of the century at hand.

Christian theologians joined the issue with the claim that what had happened proved that Jesus demonstrated that fact. The empire that had persecuted Christians now had fallen into their hands. What better proof than that. Eusebius, for example, started his account of the age of Constantine with the simple statement: "Rejoicing in these things which have been clearly fulfilled in our day, let us proceed to the account. . . . And finally a bright and splendid day, overshadowed by no cloud, illuminated with beams of heavenly light the churches of Christ throughout the entire world."[1] Christians entered the new age, as Eusebius says, with the sense that they personally witnessed God's kingdom come, not "by hearsay merely or report, but observe . . . in very deed and with our own eyes that the declarations recorded long ago are faithful and true . . . 'as we have heard, so have we seen, in the city of the Lord of hosts, in the city of our God.' And in what city but in this newly built and god-constructed one, which is a 'church of the living God. . . .'" Then events that mattered are those that pointed toward the end-

---

[1] Eusebius, *Church History*, trans. Arthur Cushman McGiffert (repr. Grand Rapids, 1961), vol. I, p. 369.

result, the one at hand. The pattern of events, of course, presented a more complex exercise, since a great many matters had to fit into one large picture. The proposition, of course, posed no problem.

The Judaic sages, for their part, constructed their own position, which point by point denied the Christian one. They worked out a view of history consisting in a rereading of the book of Genesis in light of the entire history of Israel, read under the aspect of eternity, as realized in the fourth century. The book of Genesis then provided a complete, typological interpretation of everything that had happened as well as a reliable picture of what, following the rules of history laid down in Genesis, was going to happen in the future. The events of Genesis served as types, prefiguring what would happen to Israel in its future history. Just as the Christians read stories of the (to them) Old Testament as types of the life of Christ, so the sages understood the tales of Genesis in a similarly typological manner. For neither party can history have retained that singular and one-dimensional, linear quality that it had had in Scripture itself.

In looking to the past to explain the present, the Judaic sages turned to the story of the beginnings of creation, humanity, and Israel, that is, to the book of Genesis. In doing so, they addressed precisely that range of historical questions that occupied Eusebius: where did it all start? Both parties shared the supposition that if we can discern beginnings, we can understand the end. The Israelite sages took up the beginnings that, to Eusebius too, marked the original pattern for on-going history. Sages, of course, would not have added what to Eusebius was critical: "Where did it all start—now that we know where it was all heading all the time?" Sages could not imagine, after all, that what had happened in their own day marked the goal and climax of historical time. Rome formed an episode, not the end. But then, sages had to state what they thought constituted the real history of the world and of Israel.

The book of Genesis became the principal mode of historical reflection and response for the sages of the age. They chose that book to deal in precisely the same manner and setting with exactly the same questions that occupied Eusebius: to understand the (to Eusebius) end and realization of prophecy, or (to sages) critical turning in history, look back to the beginning. In fact, in the present context of debate, only Genesis could have served both parties so well. For Eusebius, the end would impart its judgment of the meaning of the beginning: this is where things all along had been heading. For the sages of Genesis Rabbah the beginning would tell where, in time to come, things will end up. That is the point on which the parties differed, making possible our reconstruction of their genuine argument, within agreed-upon limits.

Genesis Rabbah, a work that came to closure sometime after 400, forms a striking counterpart to the writing of Eusebius for one important reason. Its authors not only lived through that same period of radical political change, but also reconsidered the historical question—the theological meaning of political events—and they did so in the same way. That is, by reverting to the record of Creation, the beginnings of Israel in particular. That the Rabbinic sages found themselves impelled to do so by the triumph of Christianity we cannot show. But there is no inherent difference between the inquiry of Genesis Rabbah and the question of Eusebius: what patterns do we discern, now that (from Eusebius's perspective) we know where, all the time, things where heading? Since the method of the two parties proved identical, the issues the same, and the sources on which they drew the same, we may proceed to examine the arguments adduced by the parties. That is because they shared one and the same issue and also concurred upon the premises and the proofs for the propositions that, in the mind of each, would settle the issue.

In Genesis Rabbah, a commentary to the book of Genesis made up of episodic comments on verses and their themes, the Judaic sages presented a profound and cogent theory of the history of Israel, the Jewish people. But if the Christians began in the present and worked backward, the Rabbinic sages began in the past and worked forward. In contrast to the approach of Eusebius, the framers of Genesis Rabbah interpreted contemporary history in the light of the past, while Eusebius read the past in light of the present. So the Israelite sages invoked the recurring and therefore cyclical patterns of time, finding in their own day meaning imparted by patterns revealed long ago. Eusebius, for his part, stood squarely in the tradition that saw events not as cyclical but as one-time and remarkable, each on its own. So the one side looked for rules, somewhat like the social scientist-philosopher, asking how events form patterns and yield theories of a deeper social reality. The other side looked not for rules but for the meaningful exceptions: what does this event, unique and lacking all precedent, tell us about all that has happened in the past. But the two sides met with a single concern: what do the events of the day mean for tomorrow.

Accordingly the framers of Genesis Rabbah intended to find those principles of society and history that would permit them to make sense of the on-going history of Israel. That meant, to find the context, in God's plan, in which to make sense of the advent of Christianity to the imperial throne of Rome. They took for granted that Scripture speaks to the life and condition of Israel, the Jewish people. God repeatedly says exactly that to Abraham and to Jacob. The entire narrative of Genesis is so formed as to point toward the sacred history of Israel, the Jewish people: its slavery and redemption; its coming Temple in Jerusalem; its exile and salvation at the end of time. In the reading of the authors at hand, therefore, the powerful message of Genesis proclaims that the world's creation commenced a single, straight line of events, leading in the end to the salvation of Israel and through Israel all humanity. That message—that history heads toward Israel's salvation—sages derived from the book of Genesis and contributed to their own day. Therefore in their reading of Scripture a given story will bear a deeper truth about what it means to be Israel, on the one side, and what in the end of days will happen to Israel, on the other. But their reading makes no explicit reference to what, if anything, had changed in the age of Constantine. But we do find repeated references to the four kingdoms, Babylonia, Media, Greece, Rome—and beyond the fourth will come Israel, fifth and last. So sages' message, in their theology of history, was that the present anguish prefigured the coming vindication, of God's people.

Accordingly, sages read Genesis as the history of the world with emphasis on Israel. So the lives portrayed, the domestic quarrels and petty conflicts with the neighbors, all serve to yield insight into what was to be. Why so? Because the deeds of the patriarchs taught lessons on how the children were to act, and, it further followed, the lives of the patriarchs signaled the history of Israel. Israel constituted one extended family, and the metaphor of the family, serving the nation as it did, imparted to the stories of Genesis the character of a family record. History become genealogy conveyed the message of salvation. These propositions really laid down the same judgment, one for the individual and the family, the other for the community and the nation, since there was no differentiating. Every detail of the narrative therefore served to prefigure what was to be, and Israel found itself, time and again, in the revealed facts of the history of the creation of the world, the decline of humanity down to the time of Noah, and, finally, its ascent to Abraham, Isaac, and Israel.

So sages read Genesis as history, but history with a difference. It was literally and in every detail a book of facts. Genesis constituted an accurate and complete testimony to things that really happened just as the story is narrated. While, therefore, sages found in Genesis deeper levels of meaning, uncovering the figurative and typological sense underlying a literal statement, they always recognized the literal facticity of the statements of the document. In the fourth century the two heirs of ancient Israel's Scriptures, Judaism and Christianity, laid claim to the land of Israel/the Holy Land. Constantine and his mother dotted the country with shrines and churches, so imparting to the geography of the land a Christian character. Israel, for its part, was losing its hold on the Land of Israel, as the country gained a Christian majority. Here, in Genesis, sages found evidence for Israel's right to hold the land.

What are the laws of history, and, more important, how do they apply to the crisis at hand? The principal message of the story of the beginnings, as sages read Genesis, is that the world depends upon the merit of Abraham, Isaac, and Jacob; Israel, for its part, enjoys access to that merit, being today the family of the patriarchs and matriarchs. That sum and substance constitutes the sages' doctrine of history: the family forms the basic and irreducible historical unit. Israel is not so much a nation as a family, and the heritage of the patriarchs and matriarchs sustains that family from the beginning even to the end. So the sages' doctrine of history transforms history into genealogy, just as Eusebius's doctrine of history turns history into chronology. The consequence, for sages, will take the form of the symbolization through family relationships of the conflict between (Christian) Rome and eternal Israel. The rivalry of brothers, Esau and Jacob, then contains the history of the fourth century—from sages' viewpoint a perfectly logical mode of historical reflection. That, in detail, expresses the main point of the system of historical thought yielded by Genesis Rabbah.

Israel therefore endures, whatever happens. The relevance of that message to the time of the document is self-evident, but no one can maintain that the framers made up, or selected, the items at hand with the victory of Christianity in mind. The way in which the merit of the patriarchs and matriarchs protects their grandchildren finds abundant exemplification. Here is a brief instance (Genesis Rabbah XLIII:VIII):

2.A. "And Abram gave him a tenth of everything" (Gen. 14:20):
 B. R. Judah in the name of R. Nehorai: "On the strength of that blessing the three great pegs on which the world depends, Abraham, Isaac, and Jacob, derived sustenance.
 C. "Abraham: 'And the Lord blessed Abraham in all things' (Gen. 24:1) on account of the merit that 'he gave him a tenth of all things' (Gen. 14:20).
 D. "Isaac: 'And I have eaten of all' (Gen. 27:33), on account of the merit that 'he gave him a tenth of all things' (Gen. 14:20).
 E. "Jacob: 'Because God has dealt graciously with me and because I have all' (Gen. 33:11) on account of the merit that 'he gave him a tenth of all things' (Gen. 14:20).
3.A. Whence did Israel gain the merit of receiving the blessing of the priests?
 B. R. Judah said, "It was from Abraham: 'So shall your seed be' (Gen. 15:5), while it is written in connection with the priestly blessing: 'So shall you bless the children of Israel' (Num. 6:23)."
 C. R. Nehemiah said, "It was from Isaac: 'And I and the lad will go so far' (Gen. 22:5), therefore said the Holy One, blessed be he, 'So shall you bless the children of Israel' (Num. 6:23)."
 D. And rabbis say, "It was from Jacob: 'So shall you say to the house of Jacob' (Ex. 19:3) (in line with the statement, 'So shall you bless the children of Israel' (Num. 6:23)."

No. 2 links the blessing at hand with the history of Israel. Now the reference is to the word "all," which joins the tithe of Abram to the blessing of his descendants. Since the blessing of the priest is at hand, No. 3 treats the origins of the blessing.

Historical study commonly leads to the periodization of history, the division of time into a number of distinct epochs. That patterning of history, its division in eras each with its own definitive traits, indeed, constitutes one important exercise of historical thought of a social scientific order. Eusebius of course understood the importance of periodization. Reading Scripture, for example, Eusebius identified a number of distinct periods, each leading to the next and culminating in his own time. A principal mode of explaining the identification and status of Israel, the Jewish people, involved the periodization of history among four monarchies, as specified by Daniel, that is, for Leviticus Rabbah empires signified by various animals in Lev. 11 and other texts. Rome then stands as the penultimate epoch; Israel for the ultimate and the end. For the present topic, we consider how the patriarchs, for their part, contribute to the periodization of history—itself a source of comfort to doubting Israel even now. For if there is a well-defined sequence, then we can understand where we are and wait patiently until we reach the next, and better age. Time and again events in the lives of the patriarchs prefigure the four monarchies, among which, of course, the fourth, last (but for Israel), and most intolerable was Rome. Here is an exercise in the recurrent proof of that single proposition (Genesis Rabbah XLIV:XVII):

> 4.A. "[And it came to pass, as the sun was going down,] lo, a deep sleep fell on Abram, and lo, a dread and great darkness fell upon him" (Gen. 15:12):
> B. "... lo, a dread" refers to Babylonia, as it is written, "Then was Nebuchadnezzar filled with fury" (Gen. 3:19).
> C. "and darkness" refers to Media, which darkened the eyes of Israel by making it necessary for the Israelites to fast and conduct public mourning.
> D. "... great ..." refers to Greece.
> G. "... fell upon him" refers to Edom, as it is written, "The earth quakes at the noise of their fall" (Jer. 49:21).
> H. Some reverse matters:
> I. "... fell upon him" refers to Babylonia, since it is written, "Fallen, fallen is Babylonia" (Is. 21:9).
> J. "... great ..." refers to Media, in line with this verse: "King Ahasuerus did make great" (Est. 3:1).
> K. "and darkness" refers to Greece, which darkened the eyes of Israel by its harsh decrees.
> L. "... lo, a dread" refers to Edom, as it is written, "After this I saw ..., a fourth beast, dreadful and terrible" (Dan. 7:7).

The fourth kingdom is part of that plan, which we can discover by carefully studying Abraham's life and God's word to him. The inevitable and foreordained salvation follows this same pattern of historical epochs (Genesis Rabbah XLIV:XVIII):

> 1.A. "Then the Lord said to Abram, 'Know of a surety [that your descendants will be sojourners in a land that is not theirs, and they will be slaves there, and they will be oppressed for four hundred years; but I will bring judgment on the nation which they serve, and afterward they shall come out with great possessions']" (Gen. 15:13-14):
> B. "Know" that I shall scatter them.
> C. "Of a certainty" that I shall bring them back together again.
> D. "Know" that I shall put them out as a pledge [in expiation of their sins].

E. "Of a certainty" that I shall redeem them.
F. "Know" that I shall make them slaves.
G. "Of a certainty" that I shall free them.

Reading the verse as a paradigm for all time, we recognize its piquant relevance to the age of the document in which it occurs. There is oppression, but redemption is coming. The lives of the patriarchs bring reassurance. The proposition is that God has unconditionally promised to redeem Israel, but if Israel repents, then the redemption will come with greater glory. If Abraham, Isaac, and Jacob stand for Israel later on, then Ishmael, Edom, and Esau represent Rome. Hence whatever sages find out about those figures tells them something about Rome and its character, history, and destiny. So Genesis is read as both a literal statement and also as an effort to prefigure the history of Israel's suffering and redemption. Ishmael, standing now for Christian Rome, claims God's blessing, but Isaac gets it, as Jacob will take it from Esau. Details, as much as the main point, yielded laws of history. In the following passage, the sages take up the detail of Rebecca's provision of a bit of water, showing what that act had to do with the history of Israel later on. The passage at hand is somewhat protracted, but it contains in a whole and cogent way the mode of thought and the results: salvation is going to derive from the merit of the matriarchs and patriarchs (Genesis Rabbah XLVIII:X):

2.A. "Let a little water be brought" (Gen. 18:4):
B. Said to him the Holy One, blessed be he, "You have said, 'Let a little water be brought' (Gen. 18:4). By your life, I shall pay your descendants back for this: 'Then sang Israel this song," spring up O well, sing you to it'" (Num. 21:7).''
C. That recompense took place in the wilderness. Where do we find that it took place in the Land of Israel as well?
D. "A land of brooks of water" (Deut. 8:7).
E. And where do we find that it will take place in the age to come?
F. "And it shall come to pass in that day that living waters shall go out of Jerusalem" (Zech. 14:8).
G. ["And wash your feet" (Gen. 18:4)]: [Said to him the Holy One, blessed be he,] "You have said, 'And wash your feet.' By your life, I shall pay your descendants back for this: 'Then I washed you in water' (Ez. 16:9)."
H. That recompense took place in the wilderness. Where do we find that it took place in the land of Israel as well?
I. "Wash you, make you clean" (Is. 1:16).
J. And where do we find that it will take place in the age to come?
K. "When the Lord will have washed away the filth of the daughters of Zion" (Is. 4:4).
L. [Said to him the Holy One, blessed be he,] "You have said, 'And rest yourselves under the tree' (Gen. 18:4). By your life, I shall pay your descendants back for this: 'He spread a cloud for a screen' (Ps. 105:39)."
M. That recompense took place in the wilderness. Where do we find that it took place in the Land of Israel as well?
N. "You shall dwell in booths for seven days" (Lev. 23:42).
O. And where do we find that it will take place in the age to come?
P. "And there shall be a pavilion for a shadow in the day-time from the heat" (Is. 4:6).
Q. [Said to him the Holy One, blessed be he,] "You have said, 'While I fetch a morsel of bread that you may refresh yourself' (Gen. 18:5).

By your life, I shall pay your descendants back for this: 'Behold I will cause to rain bread from heaven for you' (Exod. 16:45)"

R. That recompense took place in the wilderness. Where do we find that it took place in the Land of Israel as well?

S. "A land of wheat and barley" (Deut. 8:8).

T. And where do we find that it will take place in the age to come?

U. "He will be as a rich cornfield in the land" (Ps. 82:16).

V. [Said to him the Holy One, blessed be he,] "You ran after the herd ['And Abraham ran to the herd' (Gen. 18:7)]. By your life, I shall pay your descendants back for this: 'And there went forth a wind from the Lord and brought across quails from the sea' (Num. 11:27)."

W. That recompense took place in the wilderness. Where do we find that it took place in the Land of Israel as well?

X. "Now the children of Reuben and the children of Gad had a very great multitude of cattle" (Num. 32:1).

Y. And where do we find that it will take place in the age to come?

Z. "And it will come to pass in that day that a man shall rear a young cow and two sheep" (Is. 7:21).

AA. [Said to him the Holy One, blessed be he,] "You stood by them: 'And he stood by them under the tree while they ate' (Gen. 18:8). By your life, I shall pay your descendants back for this: 'And the Lord went before them' (Ex. 13:21)."

BB. That recompense took place in the wilderness. Where do we find that it took place in the Land of Israel as well?

CC. "God stands in the congregation of God" (Ps. 82:1).

DD. And where do we find that it will take place in the age to come?

EE. "The breaker is gone up before them... and the Lord at the head of them" (Mic. 2:13).

The passage presents a sizable and beautifully disciplined construction, making one point again and again. Everything that the matriarchs and patriarchs did brought a reward to his descendants. The enormous emphasis on the way in which Abraham's deeds prefigured the history of Israel, both in the wilderness, and in the Land, and, finally, in the age to come, provokes us to wonder who held that there were children of Abraham beside Israel. The answer then is clear. We note that there are five statements of the same proposition, each drawing upon a clause in the base verse. The extended statement moreover serves as a sustained introduction to the treatment of the individual clauses that now follow, item by item. When we recall how Christian exegetes imparted to the Old Testament the lessons of the New, we realize that sages constructed an equally epochal and encompassing reading of Scripture. They now understood the meaning of what happened then, and, therefore, they also grasped from what had happened then the sense and direction of events of their own day. So history yielded patterns, and patterns proved points, and the points at hand indicated the direction of Israel. The substance of historical doctrine remains social in its focus. Sages present their theory of the meaning of history within a larger theory of the identification of Israel. Specifically, they see Israel as an extended family, children of one original ancestral couple, Abraham and Sarah. Whatever happens, then, constitutes family history, which is why the inheritance of merit from the ancestors protects their children even now, in the fourth century.

What, one asks, did sages find to validate their insistence that the biblical story, in Genesis, told the tale of Israel's coming salvation? Obviously, it is the merit of the ancestors that connects the living Israel to the lives of the patriarchs and matriarchs of old. The reciprocity of the process of interpreting Israel's history in light of the founders' lives and the founders lives through the later history of Israel infuses the explanation of the debate over Sodom. Never far from sages' minds is the entire sweep and scope of Israel's long history. Never distant from the lips of the patriarchs and matriarchs is the message of Israel's destiny. Israel's history takes place in eternity, so considerations of what comes first and what happens later—that is, priority and order—do not apply. The lives of the patriarchs and matriarchs therefore prefigure the life of Israel, as we have seen throughout. The entire history of Israel then takes place in each of the great events of the lives of the patriarchs, as in No. 2 of the following composition (Genesis Rabbah LIII.X):

2.A. "... and Abraham made a great feast on the day that Isaac was weaned" (Gen. 21:8):
B. R. Judah said, "The Great One of the ages was there."
C. R. Yudan in the name of R. Yose bar Haninah: "'The king made a great feast' (Est. 2:18). The Great One of the ages was there. That is in line with this verse: 'For the Lord will again rejoice over you for good' (Deut. 30:9), in the days of Mordecai and Esther, 'As he rejoiced over your fathers' (Deut. 30:9), in the days of Abraham, Isaac, and Jacob."

We see that in this typological reading Israel's history takes place under the aspect of eternity. Events do not take place one time only. Events, to make a difference and so to matter, constitute paradigms and generate patterns. Salvation is all the same; its particularization is all that history records.

So we can move in interrupted flow from Abraham to Esther to David. The lessons of history therefore do not derive from sequences of unique moments but from patterns that generate recurring and reliable rules. That is what I meant when I said that sages read the present in light of the past, rather than following the way of reading the past in light of the present. Given their present, they had little choice. In the passage at hand, No. 2 explicitly links Isaac's feast with the miracle in the time of Esther, and, should we miss the point, further links the two matters explicitly. The recurrent appeal to the events of the Book of Esther should not be missed. So the feast for Isaac prefigures the redemption of Israel. The reciprocal flow of merit found its counterpart in the two-way exchange of penalty as well. When Abraham erred, his descendants would pay the price. The merit of the patriarchs and matriarchs sustains, and the failures exact a cost, for the history of the nation and the on-going life of the family form a single entity in history.

An exemplary case derives from the binding of Isaac, the point from which the merit of Abraham flows. The aptness of the incident derives from its domestic character: relationship of mother, father, and only child. What Abraham and Isaac were prepared to sacrifice (and Sarah to lose) won for them and their descendants—as the story itself makes explicit—an on-going treasury of merit. So Abraham's and Isaac's children through history will derive salvation from the original act of binding Isaac to the altar. The reference to the third day at Gen. 22:2 then invokes the entire panoply of Israel's history. The relevance of the composition emerges at the end. Prior to the concluding segment, the passage forms a kind of litany and falls into the category of a liturgy. Still, the recurrent hermeneutic which teaches that the stories of the patriarchs prefigure the history of Israel certainly makes its appearance. Because of the importance of the treatment of the story at hand, we dwell on a protracted passage (Genesis Rabbah LVI:II):

> 2.A. Said R. Isaac, "Will this place [the Temple mount] ever be distant from its owner [God]? Never, for Scripture says, 'This is my resting place for ever; here I will dwell, for I have desired it' (Ps. 132:14).
>
> B. "It will be when the one comes concerning whom it is written, 'Lowly and riding upon an ass' (Zech. 1:9)."
>
> 3. A. "I and the lad will go thus far [and worship and come again to you]" (Gen. 22:5):
>
> B. Said R. Joshua b. Levi, "[He said,] 'We shall go and see what will be the end of "thus."'" [Freedman, p. 492, n. 5: God had said, "Thus shall your seed be" (Gen. 15:5). So the sense is, "We will see how that can be fulfilled, now that I am to lose my son."]
>
> 4. A. "... and we will worship [through an act of prostration] and come again to you" (Gen. 22:5):
>
> B. He thereby told him that he would come back from Mount Moriah whole and in peace [for he said that we shall come back].
>
> 5.A. Said R. Isaac, "And all was on account of the merit attained by the act of prostration.
>
> B. "Abraham returned in peace from Mount Moriah only on account of the merit owing to the act of prostration: '... and we will worship [through an act of prostration] and come [then, on that account] again to you' (Gen. 22:5).
>
> C. "The Israelites were redeemed only on account of the merit owing to the act of prostration: And the people believed... then they bowed their heads and prostrated themselves' (Exod. 4:31).
>
> D. "The Torah was given only on account of the merit owing to the act of prostration: 'And worship [prostrate themselves] you afar off' (Exod. 24:1).
>
> E. "Hannah was remembered only on account of the merit owing to the act of prostration: 'And they worshipped before the Lord' (1 Sam. 1:19).
>
> F. "The exiles will be brought back only on account of the merit owing to the act of prostration: 'And it shall come to pass in that day that a great horn shall be blown and they shall come that were lost... and that were dispersed... and they shall worship the Lord in the holy mountain at Jerusalem' (Is. 27:13).
>
> G. "The Temple was built only on account of the merit owing to the act of prostration: 'Exalt you the Lord our God and worship at his holy hill' (Ps. 99:9).
>
> H. "The dead will live only on account of the merit owing to the act of prostration: 'Come let us worship and bend the knee, let us kneel before the Lord our maker' (Ps. 95:6)."

No. 2 takes up the language of "seeing the place from afar," and by a play on the words, asks whether this place will ever be made far from its owner, that is, God. The answer is that it will not. No. 3 draws a lesson from the use of "thus" in the cited verses. The sizable construction at No. 4 makes a simple point, to which our base verse provides its modest contribution. But its polemic is hardly simple. The entire history of Israel flows from its acts of worship ("prostration") and is unified by a single law. Every sort of advantage Israel has ever gained came about through worship. Hence what is besought, in the elegant survey, is the law of history. The Scripture then supplies those facts from which the governing law is derived (Genesis Rabbah LVI:IX):

1.A. "And Abraham lifted up his eyes and looked, and behold, behind him was a ram, [caught in a thicket by his horns. And Abraham went and took the ram and offered it up as a burnt offering instead of his son]" (Gen. 22:13):

B. What is the meaning of the word for "behind"?

C. Said R. Yudan, "'Behind' in the sense of 'after,' that is, after all that happens, Israel nonetheless will be embroiled in transgressions and perplexed by sorrows. But in the end, they will be redeemed by the horns of a ram: 'And the Lord will blow the horn' (Zech. 9:14)."

D. Said R. Judah bar Simon, "'After' all generations Israel nonetheless will be embroiled in transgressions and perplexed by sorrows. But in the end, they will be redeemed by the horns of a ram: 'And the Lord God will blow the horn' (Zech. 9:14)."

E. Said R. Hinena bar Isaac, "All through the days of the year Israelites are embroiled in transgressions and perplexed by sorrows. But on the New Year they take the ram's horn and sound it, so in the end, they will be redeemed by the horns of a ram: 'And the Lord God will blow the horn' (Zech. 9:14)."

F. R. Abba bar R. Pappi, R. Joshua of Siknin in the name of R. Levi: "Since our father, Abraham, saw the ram get himself out of one thicket only to be trapped in another, the Holy One, blessed be he, said to him, 'So your descendants will entangled in one kingdom after another, struggling from Babylonia to Media, from Media to Greece, from Greece to Edom. But in the end, they will be redeemed by the horns of a ram: 'And the Lord God will blow the horn . . . the Lord of Hosts will defend them' (Zech. 9:14–5).

2.A. ". . . And Abraham went and took the ram and offered it up as a burnt offering instead of his son]" (Gen. 22:13):

B. R. Yudan in the name of R. Benaiah: "He said before him, 'Lord of all ages, regard the blood of this ram as though it were the blood of Isaac, my son, its innards as though they were the innards of Isaac my son.'"

C. R. Phineas in the name of R. Benaiah: "He said before him, 'Lord of all ages, regard it as though I had offered up my son, Isaac, first, and afterward had offered up the ram in his place.'"

For sages it is quite natural to link the life of the private person, affected by transgression, and the history of the nation, troubled by its wandering among the kingdoms. For the nation is a family. From the perspective of the Land of Israel, the issue is not Exile but the rule of foreigners. In both cases the power of the ram's horn to redeem the individual and the nation finds its origin in the Binding of Isaac. The exegetical thrust, linking the lives of the patriarchs to the life of the nation, thus brings the narrative back to the paradigm of individual being, so from patriarch to nation to person. The path leads in both directions, of course, in a fluid movement of meaning. No. 2 works on the language of "instead," a technical term in the cult, and so links the Binding of Isaac to the Temple cult.

While Abraham founded Israel, Isaac and Jacob carried forth the birthright and the blessing. This they did through the process of selection, ending in the assignment of the birthright to Jacob alone. The lives of all three patriarchs flowed together, each being identified with the other as a single long life. This immediately produces the proposition that the historical life of Israel, the nation, continued the individual lives of the patriarchs. Once more we see that the theory of who is Israel rested on genealogy: Israel is one extended family, all being children of the same fathers and mothers, the patriarchs and matriarchs of Genesis. This theory of Israelite society, and of the Jewish people in the time of the sages of Genesis Rabbah, we note once again, made of the people a family, and of genealogy, a kind of ecclesiology. The importance of that proposition in countering the Christian claim to be a new Israel cannot escape notice. Israel, sages maintained, is Israel after the flesh, and that in a most literal sense. But the basic claim, for its part, depended upon the facts of Scripture, not upon the logical requirements of theological dispute. And, we see abundantly, that claim constituted not merely a social theory of the classification of Israel—family, not nation like other nations,—but also the foundations of a historical theory of the past, present, and future of Israel.

Sages found a place for Rome in Israel's history only by assigning to Rome a place in the family. Their larger theory of the social identity of Israel left them no choice. But it also permitted them to assign to Rome an appropriately significant place in world history, while preserving for Israel the climactic role. Whatever future history finds adumbration in the life of Jacob derives from the struggle with Esau. Israel and Rome—these two contend for the world. Still, Isaac plays his part in the matter. Rome does have a legitimate claim, and that claim demands recognition—an amazing, if grudging—concession on the part of sages that Christian Rome at least is Esau (Genesis Rabbah LXVII:IV)

> 1.A. When Esau heard the words of his father, he cried out with an exceedingly great and bitter cry [and said to his father, 'Bless me, even me also, O my father!']" (Gen. 27:34):
> B. Said R. Hanina, "Whoever says that the Holy One, blessed be he, is lax, may his intestines become lax. While he is patient, he does collect what is coming to you.
> C. "Jacob made Esau cry out one cry, and where was he penalized? It was in the castle of Shushan: 'And he cried with a loud and bitter cry' (Est. 4:1)."
> 2.A. "But he said, 'Your brother came with guile and he has taken away your blessing'" (Gen. 33:35):
> B. R. Yohanan said, "[He came] with the wisdom of his knowledge of the Torah."

So Rome really is Israel's brother. No pagan empire ever enjoyed an equivalent place; no pagan era ever found identification with an event in Israel's family history. The passage presents a stunning concession and an astounding claim. The history of the two brothers forms a set of counterpoints, the rise of one standing for the decline of the other. I cannot imagine a more powerful claim for Israel: the ultimate end, Israel's final glory, will permanently mark the subjugation of Esau. Israel then will follow, the fifth and final monarchy. The point of No. 1 is to link the present passage to the history of Israel's redemption later on. In this case, however, the matter concerns Israel's paying recompense for causing anguish to Esau. No. 2 introduces Jacob's knowledge of Torah in place of Esau's view of Jacob as full of guile.

Apart from the struggle with Esau, Jacob still serves as a model and paradigm of Israel's history. For example, his dream of the ladder to heaven encompassed all of Israel's history, with stress not on Esau but on Sinai (Genesis Rabbah LXVIII:XII):

> 3.B. "'That there was a ladder:' refers to the ramp to the altar.
> C. "'... set up on the earth:' that is the altar, 'An altar of dirt you will make for me' (Exod. 20:24).
> D. "'... and the top of it reached to heaven:' these are the offerings,

for their fragrance goes up to heaven.

E. "'... and behold, the angels of God:' these are the high priests.
F. "'... were ascending and descending on it:' for they go up and go down on the ramp.
G. "'And behold, the Lord stood above it:' 'I saw the Lord standing by the altar' (Amos 9:1)."

4.A. Rabbis interpreted the matter to prefigure Sinai: "'And he dreamed:
B. "'... that there was a ladder:' this refers to Sinai.
C. "'... set up on the earth:' 'And they stood at the lower part of the mountain' (Exod. 19:17).
D. "'... and the top of it reached to heaven:' 'And the mountain burned with fire into the heart of heaven' (Deut. 4:11).
E. "'... and behold, the angels of God:' these are Moses and Aaron.
F. "'... were ascending:' 'And Moses went up to God' (Exod. 19:3).
G. "'... and descending on it:' "And Moses went down from the mount' (Exod. 19:14).
F. "'... And behold, the Lord stood above it:' 'And the Lord came down upon Mount Sinai' (Exod. 19:20)."

No. 3 reads the dream in terms of the Temple cult, and No. 4 in terms of the revelation of the Torah at Sinai, and No. 5 has the dream refer to the patriarchs.

None of these modes of reading the book of Genesis presents surprises. Since both Jacob and Moses explicitly spoke of the sons of Jacob as paradigms of history, the sages understood the text precisely as the Torah itself told them to understand it. That is, the sages simply took seriously and at face value the facts in hand, as any scientist or philosopher finds facts and reflects upon their meaning and the implications and laws deriving from them. So sages' mode of reading derived from an entirely inductive and scientific, philosophical mode of thought.

The laws of history begin with the principle that the merit of the founders sustains the children to come. The model for the transaction in merit—which underlines and explains the theory of genealogy as the foundation of Israel's social entity—comes to expression in the life of Joseph.

The typology proves a diverse, since Joseph, as much as Abraham, Isaac, and Jacob, provides a model for the future; reference to what Joseph did guides us to the later history of Israel. So the history of Israel here is compared to the life of Joseph (Genesis Rabbah LXXXVII:VI):

1.A. "And although she spoke to Joseph [day after day, he would not listen to her, to lie with her or to be with her. But one day, when he went into the house to do his work and none of the men of the house was there in the house, she caught him by his garment, saying, 'Lie with me.' But he left his garment in her hand and fled and got out of the house]" (Gen. 39:10–13):
B. R. Yudan in the name of R. Benjamin bar Levi: "As to the sons of Levi, the trials affecting them were the same, and the greatness that they achieved was the same.
C. "... the trials affecting them were the same: 'And although she spoke to Joseph [day after day.' 'Now it came to pass, when they spoke to him day by day' (Est. 3:4). [Mordecai, descended from Benjamin, was nagged every day.] 'He would not listen to her.' 'And he did not listen to them' (Est. 3:4).
D. "... and the greatness that they achieved was the same: 'And Pharaoh took off his signet ring from his hand and put it upon Joseph's hand' (Gen. 41:42). 'And the king took off his ring, which he had taken from Haman and gave it to Mordecai' (Est. 8:2).

E. "'And arrayed him in fine linen clothing and put a gold chain about his neck' (Gen. 41:42). 'And Mordecai went forth from the presence of the king in royal apparel of blue and white, and with a great crown of gold and with a robe of fine linen and purple' (Est. 8:15).

F. "'And he made Joseph ride in the second chariot which he had' (Gen. 41:43). 'And cause Mordecai to ride on horseback through the street of the city' (Est. 6:9).

G. "'And they cried before him, Abrech' (Gen. 41:43). 'And proclaimed before Mordecai, "Thus shall it be done to the man"' (Est. 6:11)."

The parallel drawn between Joseph and Benjamin, that is, Mordecai permits the exegete to draw a parallel between the life of Joseph and the history of Israel. No. 2 expands on the base verse, and No. 3 presents an argument in favor of its authenticity, at the same time linking the present story to the two that have preceded. God of course governed Joseph's destiny, detail by detail, and as this becomes clear, the Jewish reader concludes that God's providence and benevolence continues to dictate what is to happen to Israel, even though that fact does not always prove self-evident.

Sages had also to account for the present condition of Israel, not only make promises about future redemption. An established explanation held Israel responsible for its fate. When the nation did God's will, it enjoyed security, and when it violated God's will, it suffered. That basic theological conviction, familiar from ancient times, translated into quite specific statements on what sorts of sins had caused Israel to suffer in later times. The tribes would suffer punishment because of the misdeeds of their ancestors, a point we noted with reference to Abraham as well (Genesis Rabbah LXXXIV:XX):

1.A. "Then Jacob tore his garments and put sackcloth upon his loins and mourned for his son many days" (Gen. 37:34):

B. R. Phineas in the name of R. Hoshaiah: "The tribal fathers caused their father to tear his garments, and where were they paid back? In Egypt: 'And they tore their clothes' (Gen. 44:13).

C. "Joseph caused the tribal fathers to tear their clothes. He was paid back in the case of the son of his son: 'And Joshua tore his clothes' (Josh. 7:6).

D. "Benjamin caused the tribal fathers to tear their clothes. He was paid back in Shushan, the capital: 'Mordecai tore his clothes' (Est. 4:1).

E. "Manasseh caused the tribal fathers to tear their clothes. He was paid back by having his inheritance divided into half, half on the other side of the Jordan, and half in the land of Canaan."

2.A. "... and put sackcloth upon his loins:"

B. Said R. Aibu, "Because Jacob took hold of sackcloth, therefore sackcloth did not leave him or his children to the end of all generations:

C. "Ahab: 'And he put sackcloth on his flesh and fasted' (1 Kgs. 21:27).

D. "Joram: 'And the people looked, and behold, he had sackcloth within upon his flesh' (2 Kgs. 6:30).

E. "Mordecai: 'And he put sackcloth and ashes' (Est. 4:1).

Once more what the brothers did, their descendants had to pay for. The premise of this entire account comes to explicit statement in the treatment of Jacob's blessing of the tribal ancestors. Here he reviews the entire future history of Israel (Genesis Rabbah XCVIII:II):

7.A. "Then Jacob called his sons and said, 'Gather yourselves together, that I may tell you what shall befall you in days to come:'"

B. R. Simon said, "He showed them the fall of Gog, in line with this usage: 'It shall be in the end of days ... when I shall be sanctified through you, O Gog' (Ez. 38:15). 'Behold, it shall come upon Edom' (Is. 34:5)."

C. R. Judah said, "He showed them the building of the house of the sanctuary: 'And it shall come to pass in the end of days that the mountain of the Lord's house shall be established' (Is. 2:2)."

D. Rabbis say, "He came to reveal the time of the end to them, but it was hidden from him."

Genesis Rabbah XCIX:II.

1.A. "For the Lord God will do nothing unless he reveals his secret to his servants the prophets" (Amos 3:7).

B. Jacob linked two of his sons, corresponding to two of the monarchies, and Moses linked two of the tribes, corresponding to two of the monarchies.

C. Judah corresponds to the kingdom of Babylonia, for this is compared to a lion and that is compared to a lion. This is compared to a lion: "Judah is a lion's whelp" (Gen. 49:9), and so too Babylonia: "The first was like a lion" (Dan. 7:4).

D. Then by the hand of which of the tribes will the kingdom of Babylonia fall? It will be by the hand of Daniel, who comes from the tribe of Judah.

E. Benjamin corresponds to the kingdom of Media, for this is compared to a wolf and that is compared to a wolf. This is compared to a wolf: "Benjamin is a ravenous wolf, [in the morning devouring the prey, and at even dividing the spoil." And that is compared to a wolf: "And behold, another beast, a second, like a wolf" (Dan. 7:5).

F. R. Hanina said, "The word for 'wolf' in the latter verse is written as 'bear.' It had been called a bear."

G. That is the view of R. Yohanan, for R. Yohanan said, "'Wherefore a lion of the forest slays them' (Jer. 5:6) refers to Babylonia, and 'a wolf of the deserts spoils them' refers to Media."

H. [Reverting to E:] Then by the hand of which of the tribes will the kingdom of Media fall? It will be by the hand of Mordecai, who comes from the tribe of Benjamin.

I. Levi corresponds to the kingdom of Greece. This is the third tribe in order, and that is the third kingdom in order. This is written with a word that is made up of three letters, and that is written with a word which consists of three letters. This one sounds the horn and that one sounds the horn, this one wears turbans and that one wears helmets, this one wears pants and that one wears knee-cuts.

J. To be sure, this one is very populous, while that one is few in numbers. But the many came and fell into the hand of the few.

K. On account of merit deriving from what source did this take place? It is on account of the blessing that Moses bestowed: "Smiter through the loins of them that rise up against him" (Deut. 33:11).

L. Then by the hand of which of the tribes will the kingdom of Greece fall? It will be by the hand of sons of the Hasmoneans, who come from the tribe of Levi.'

M. Joseph corresponds to the kingdom of Edom [Rome], for this one has horns and that one has horns. This one has horns: "His firstling bullock, majesty is his, and his horns are the horns of the wild ox" (Deut. 33:17). And that one has horns: "And concerning the ten horns that were on its head" (Dan. 7:20). This one avoided kept away from fornication while that one cleaved to fornication. This one paid respect for the honor owing to his father, while that one despised the honor owing to his father. Concerning this one it is written, "For I fear God" (Gen. 42:18), while in regard to that one it is written, "And he did not fear God" (Deut. 25:18). [So the correspondence in part is one of opposites.]

N. Then by the hand of which of the tribes will the kingdom of Edom fall? It will be by the hand of the anointed for war, who comes from the tribe of Joseph.

O. R. Phineas in the name of R. Samuel b. Nahman: "There is a tradition that Esau will fall only by the hand of the sons of Rachel: 'Surely the least of the flock shall drag them away' (Jer. 49:20). Why the least? Because they are the youngest of the tribes."

We see the ultimate typology: each pagan empire finds representation among the brothers. This impressive theory of Israel's history finds a place here only because of E. Yet the larger relevance—Jacob's predictions of the future—justifies including the composition. What, then, tells sages how to identify the important and avoid the trivial? The answer derives from the fundamental theological conviction that gives life to their search of Scripture. It is that the task of Israel is to hope, and the message of Genesis—there for the sages to uncover and make explicit—is always to hope.

What sense, then, did sages in Genesis Rabbah make of the history of Israel? Israel is the extended family of Abraham, Isaac, and Jacob. Whatever happens now works out events in the life of the family long ago. The redemption in the past prefigures what is to come. The merit that protects Israel in the present derives from the heritage of the past. So history is one and seamless, as the life of a family goes on through time. Do people wonder, with the triumph of Christianity in politics, what is to become of Israel? In rereading the story of Israel's beginnings, sifting and resifting the events in the life of the patriarchs and matriarchs, sages found the answer to the question. What will happen is what has happened. History recapitulates the life of the family. And to a family, the politics of empire makes slight difference. Israel therefore will endure in hope.

Who Is the True Israel? Leviticus Rabbah, Genesis Rabbah, and the Identification of Israel

The legacy of ancient Israel consisted not only of Scriptures but also of the paramount social category, Israel, defined as a supernatural society. "Israel" refers to, is comprised by, those who accept the Torah and God's sovereignty, thus: God's people and first love. The Church from its origins in the first century confronted the task of situating itself in relationship to "Israel." For the society of the Church, like the society of Judaism, required a metaphor by which to account for itself. And revering the ancient Israelite Scriptures, each group found in "Israel" the metaphor to account for its existence as a distinct social entity. It follows that within the issue Who is Israel?

we discern how two competing groups framed theories, each both of itself and also of the other. We therefore confront issues of the identity of a given corporate society as these were spelled out in debates about salvation. The salvific framing of the issue of social definition—who is the true Israel today (for Judaism)?—served both parties.

We deal with a debate on a single issue. It finds its cogency in the common premise of the debate on who is Israel. The shared supposition concerned God's favor and choice of a given entity, one that was *sui generis* among the social groups of humanity. Specifically, both parties concurred that God did favor and therefore make use of one group and not another. So they could undertake a meaningful debate on the identity of that group. The debate gained intensity because of a further peculiarity of the discourse between these two groups but no others of the day. Both concurred that the group chosen by God will stand in covenanted relationship with him and will bear the name, "Israel." God's choice among human societies would settle the question, which nation does God love and favor? Jews saw themselves as the Israel today joined in the flesh to the Israel of the scriptural record. Christians explained themselves as the Israel formed just now, in the new covenant, those saved by faith in God's salvation afforded by the resurrection of Jesus Christ. In these statements on who is Israel, the parties to the debate chose to affirm each its own unique legitimacy and to deny the other's right to endure at all as a social and national entity.

But both parties shared common premises as to definitions of issues and facts to settle the question. They could mount a sustained argument between themselves because they talked about the same thing. They differed only as to the outcome. The issue of who is Israel, articulated in theological, not political, terms, covers several topics. First, was, and is, Jesus Christ? If so, then the Jews who rejected him enjoyed no share in the salvation at hand. If not, then they do. If Jesus was and is Christ, then Israel "after the flesh" no longer enjoys the status of the people who bear salvation. Salvation has come, and Israel "after the flesh" has denied it. If he is Christ, then what is the status of those—whether Jews or gentiles—who do accept him? They have received the promises of salvation and their fulfillment. The promises to Israel have been kept for them. Then there is a new Israel, one that is formed of the saved, as the prophets had said in ancient times that Israel would be saved.

A further issue that flowed from the first—the rejection of Jesus as Christ—concerns the status of Israel, the Jewish people, now and in time to come. Israel after the flesh, represented from the Gospels forward as the people that rejected Jesus as Christ and participated in his crucifixion, claims to be the family of Abraham, Isaac, Jacob. Then further questions arise. First, does Israel today continue the Israel of ancient times? Israel maintains that Israel now continues in a physical and spiritual way the life of Israel then. Second, will the promises of the prophets to Israel afford salvation for Israel in time to come? Israel "after the flesh" awaits the fulfillment of the prophetic promise of salvation. Clearly, a broad range of questions demanded sorting out. But the questions flow together into a single issue, faced in common. The Christian position on all these questions came to expression in a single negative: no, Israel today does not continue the Israel of old, no, the ancient promises will not again bear salvation, because they have already been kept, so, no, the Israel that declines to accept Jesus' claim to be the Christ is a no-people.

The response of Israel's sages in the fourth and fifth century midrash-compilations to these same questions proves equally unequivocal. Yes, the messiah will come in time to come, and yes, he will come to Israel of today, which indeed continues the Israel of old. So the issue is squarely and fairly joined. Who is Israel raises a question that stands second in line to the messianic one. And, it must follow, the further question of who are the Christians requires close attention to that same messianic question. The initial confrontation generated a genuine argument on the status and standing, before God, of Israel "after the flesh," the Jewish people. And that argument took on urgency because of the worldly, political triumph of Christianity in Rome, joined, as the fourth century wore on, by the worldly, political decline in the rights and standing of Israel, the Jewish people. Before Christianity had addressed the issue of who the Christians were, Paul had already asked what the Jews were not. Christians formed the true people of God.

Who and What Is Israel in Leviticus Rabbah

For Leviticus Rabbah, as for all Rabbinic writings, Israel remains Israel, the Jewish people, after the flesh, because Israel today continues the family begun by Abraham, Isaac, Jacob, Joseph and the other tribal founders, and bears the heritage bequeathed by them. That conviction of who is Israel never required articulation. The contrary possibility fell wholly outside of sages' (and all Jews') imagination. To state matters negatively, the people could no more conceive that they were not the daughters and sons of their fathers and mothers than that they were not one large family, that is, the family of Abraham, Isaac, and Jacob: Israel after the flesh. That is what "after the flesh" meant. The powerful stress on the enduring merit of the patriarchs and matriarchs, the social theory that treated Israel as one large, extended family, the actual children of Abraham, Isaac, and Jacob—these metaphors for the fleshly continuity surely met head on the contrary position framed by Paul and restated by Christian theologians from his time onward. In this respect, while Aphrahat did not deny the Israel-ness of Israel, the Jewish people, he did underline the futility of enduring as Israel. Maintaining that Israel would see no future salvation amounted to declaring that Israel, the Jewish people, pursued no worthwhile purpose in continuing to endure. Still, the argument is head-on and concrete: who is Israel? who enjoys salvation? To sages, as we shall see, the nations of the world serve God's purpose in ruling Israel, just as the prophets had said, and Israel, for its part, looks forward to a certain salvation.

The position of the framers of Leviticus Rabbah on the issues at hand emerges in both positive and negative formulation. On the positive side, Israel, the Jewish people, the people of whom Scriptures spoke and to whom, today, sages now speak, is God's first love. That position of course presents no surprises and can have been stated with equal relevance in any circumstances. We in no way can imagine that the authors of Leviticus Rabbah stress the points that they stress in particular because Christians have called them into question. I doubt that that was the case. While the argument on who is Israel did not take shape on the foundation of a shared program of verses, on which each party entered its position, the issue was one and the same. And the occasion—the political crisis of the fourth century—faced both parties.

Sages delivered a message particular to their system. The political context imparted to that message urgency for Israel beyond their small circle. As to confronting the other side, no sage would concede what to us is self-evident. This was the urgency of the issue. For the definition of what was at issue derived from the common argument of the age: Who is the messiah? Christ or someone else? Here too, while the argument between Christian theologians and Judaic sages on the present status of Israel, the Jewish people, went forward on the same basic issues, it ran along parallel lines.

The framers of Leviticus Rabbah laid forth thematic exercises, each one serving in a cumulative way to make a given point on a single theme. Therefore in order to describe sages' position, we do well to follow their ideas in their own chosen medium of expression. There is no more suitable way of recapitulating their reply to the question, Who is Israel? than by a brief survey of one of the sustained essays they present on the subject in Leviticus Rabbah. We proceed to the unfolding, in Leviticus Rabbah Parashah Two, of the theme: Israel is precious. At Lev. R. II:III.2.B, we find an invocation of the genealogical justification for the election of Israel: "He said to him, 'Ephraim, head of the tribe, head of the session, one who is beautiful and exalted above all of my sons will be called by your name: [Samuel, the son of Elkanah, the son of Jeroham,] the son of Tohu, the son of Zuph, an Ephraimite' [1 Sam. 1:1]; 'Jeroboam son of Nabat, an Ephraimite' [1 Sam. 11:26]. 'And David was an Ephraimite, of Bethlehem in Judah'" (1 Sam. 17:12). Since Ephraim, that is, Israel, had been exiled, the deeper message cannot escape our attention. Whatever happens, God loves Ephraim. However Israel suffers, God's love endures, and God cares. In context, that message brings powerful reassurance. Facing a Rome gone Christian, sages had to begin with to state the obvious—which no longer seemed self-evident at all. What follows spells out this very point: God is especially concerned with Israel (Leviticus Rabbah II:IV)

1.A. Returning to the matter: "Speak to the children of Israel" (Lev. 1:2).
  B. R. Yudan in the name of R. Samuel b. R. Nehemiah: "The matter may be compared to the case of a king who had an undergarment, concerning which he instructed his servant, saying to him, 'Fold it, shake it out, and be careful about it!'
  C. "He said to him, 'My lord, O king, among all the undergarments that you have, [why] do you give me such instructions only about this one?'
  D. "He said to him, 'It is because this is the one that I keep closest to my body.'
  E. "So too did Moses say before the Holy One, blessed be he, Lord of the Universe: 'Among the seventy distinct nations that you have in your world, [why] do you give me instructions only concerning Israel? [For instance,] "Command the children of Israel" [Num. 28:2], "Say to the children of Israel" [Exod. 33:5], "Speak to the children of Israel"' [Lev. 1:2].
  F. "He said to him, 'The reason is that they stick close to me, in line with the following verse of Scripture': 'For as the undergarment cleaves to the loins of a man, so have I caused to cleave unto me the whole house of Israel'" (Jer. 13:11).
  G. Said R. Abin, "[The matter may be compared] to a king who had a purple cloak, concerning which he instructed his servant, saying, 'Fold it, shake it out, and be careful about it!'
  H. "He said to him, 'My Lord, O king, among all the purple cloaks that you have, [why] do you give me such instructions only about this one?'
  I. "He said to him, 'That is the one that I wore on my coronation day.'
  J. "So too did Moses say before the Holy One, blessed be he, Lord of the Universe: 'Among the seventy distinct nations that you have in your world, [why] do you give instructions to me only concerning Israel? [For instance,] "Say to the children of Israel," "Command the children of Israel," "Speak to the children of Israel."'
  K. "He said to him, 'They are the

ones who at the [Red] Sea declared me to be king, saying, 'The Lord will be king'" (Exod. 15:18).

The point of the passage has to do with Israel's particular relationship to God: Israel cleaves to God, declares God to be king, and accepts God's dominion. Further evidence of God's love for Israel derives from the commandments themselves. God watches over every little thing that Jews do, even caring what they eat for breakfast. The familiar stress on the keeping of the laws of the Torah as a mark of hope finds fulfillment here: the laws testify to God's deep concern for Israel. So there is sound reason for high hope, expressed in particular in keeping the laws of the Torah.

We now come to the statement of how Israel wins and retains God's favor. The issue at hand concerns Israel's relationship to the nations before God, which is corollary to what has gone before. It is in two parts. First of all, Israel knows how to serve God in the right way. Second, the nations, though they do what Israel does, do things wrong. First, Israel does things right. Why then is Israel beloved? The following answers that question (Leviticus Rabbah V:VIII):

1.A. R. Simeon b. Yohai taught, "How masterful are the Israelites, for they know how to find favor with their creator."
 B. Said R. Yudan [in Aramaic:], "It is like the case of Samaritan [beggars]. The Samaritan [beggars] are clever at beginning. One of them goes to a housewife, saying to her, 'Do you have an onion? Give it to me.' After she gives it to him, he says to her, 'Is there such a thing as an onion without bread?' After she gives him [bread], he says to her, 'Is there such a thing as food without drink?' So, all in all, he gets to eat and drink."
 C. Said R. Aha [in Aramaic:], "There is a woman who knows how to borrow things, and there is a woman who does not. The one who knows how to borrow goes over to her neighbor. The door is open, but she knocks [anyhow]. Then she says to her neighbor, 'Greetings, good neighbor. How're you doing? How's your husband doing? How're your kids doing? Can I come in? [By the way], would you have such-and-such a utensil? Would you lend it to me?' [The neighboring housewife] says to her, 'Yes, of course.'
 D. "But the one who does not know how to borrow goes over to her neighbor. The door is closed, so she just opens it. She says [to the neighboring housewife], 'Do you have such-and-such a utensil? Would you lend it to me?' [The neighboring housewife] says to her, 'No.'"
 E. Said R. Hunia [in Aramaic:], "There is a tenant farmer who knows how to borrow things, and there is a tenant farmer who does not know how to borrow. The one who knows how to borrow combs his hair, brushes off his clothes, puts on a good face, and then goes over to the overseer of his work to borrow from him. [The overseer] says to him, 'How's the land doing?' He says to him, 'May you have the merit of being fully satisfied with its [wonderful] produce.' 'How are the oxen doing?' He says to him, 'May you have the merit of being fully satisfied with their fat.' 'How are the goats doing?' 'May you have the merit of being fully satisfied with their young.' 'And what would you like?' Then he says, 'Now if you might have an extra ten denars, would you give them to me?' The overseer replies, 'If you want, take twenty.'
 F. "But the one who does not know

how to borrow leaves his hair a mess, his clothes filthy, his face gloomy. He too goes over to the overseer to borrow from him. The overseer says to him, 'How's the land doing?' He replies, 'I hope it will produce at least what [in seed] we put into it.' 'How are the oxen doing?' 'They're scrawny.' 'How are the goats doing?' 'They're scrawny too.' 'And what do you want?' 'Now if you might have an extra ten denars, would you give them to me?' The overseer replies, 'Go, pay me back what you already owe me!'"

Church fathers claim Israel does nothing right. Sages counter, speaking in their own setting of course, that they do everything right. Sages then turn the tables on the position of Aphrahat—again addressing it head-on. While the nations may do everything Israel does, they do it wrong. The testimony of language itself proves that fact, for the same word, applied to Israel, brings credit, and applied to gentiles, brings derision:

2.A. Said R. Eleazar, "The nations of the world are called a congregation, and Israel is called a congregation.
B. "The nations of the world are called a congregation: 'For the congregation of the godless shall be desolate' [Job 15:34]. . . .
J. "The nations of the world are called sages, and Israel is called sages.
K. "The nations of the world are called sages: 'And I shall wipe out sages from Edom' [Ob. 1:8].
L. "And Israel is called sages: 'Sages store up knowledge' [Prov. 10:14].
M. "The nations of the world are called unblemished, and Israel is called unblemished.
N. "The nations of the world are called unblemished: 'Unblemished as are those that go down to the pit' [Prov. 1:12].
O. "And Israel is called unblemished: 'The unblemished will inherit goodness' [Prov. 28:10].
S. "The nations of the world are called righteous, and Israel is called righteous.
T. "The nations of the world are called righteous: 'And righteous men shall judge them' [Ez. 23:45].
U. "And Israel is called righteous: 'And your people—all of them are righteous' [Is. 60:21].
V. "The nations of the world are called mighty, and Israel is called mighty.
W. "The nations of the world are called mighty: 'Why do you boast of evil, O mighty man' [Ps. 52:3].
X. "And Israel is called mighty: 'Mighty in power, those who do his word' [Ps. 103:20].

The concluding element is the striking one. "Might" now takes on a meaning of its own, one that is comfortable for the subordinated party to the dispute. At each point Israel stands in the balance against the nations of the world, the one weighed against the other. We cannot identify the passage with the age at hand. "Rome" is hardly "the nations of the world." Even though the nations of the word are subject to the same language as is applied to Israel, they still do not fall into the same classification. For language is dual. When a word applies to Israel, it serves to praise, and when the same word applies to the nations, it underlines their negative character. Both are called congregation, but the nations' congregation is desolate, and so throughout, as the context of the passage cited concerning the nations repeatedly indicates. The nations' sages are wiped out; the unblemished nations go down to the pit; the nations, called men, only work iniquity. Now that is precisely the contrast drawn in Isaac's saying, so, as I said, the whole should be deemed a masterpiece of unitary composition. Then the two types of exegesis—direct, peripheral—turn out to complement one another, each making its own point.

Sages recognized in the world only one counterpart to Israel, and that was Rome. Rome's history formed the counterweight to Israel's. So Rome as a social entity weighed in the balance against Israel. That is why we return to the corollary question: who is Rome? For we can know who is Israel only if we can also explain who is Rome. And, I should maintain, explaining who is Rome takes on urgency at the moment at which Rome presents to Israel problems of an unprecedented character. The matter belongs in any picture of who is Israel. Sages' doctrine of Rome forms the counterpart to Christian theologians' theory on who is Israel. The Rabbinic sages in Leviticus Rabbah develop an important theory on who is Rome. They too propose to account for the way things are, and that means, they have to explain who is this counterpart to Israel. And sages' theory does respond directly to the question raised by the triumph of Christianity in the Roman Empire. For, as we shall see, the characterization of Rome in Leviticus Rabbah bears the burden of their judgment on the definition of the Christian people, as much as the sages' characterization of Rome in Genesis Rabbah expressed their judgment of the place of Rome in the history of Israel.

The polemic represented in Leviticus Rabbah by the symbolization of Christian Rome makes the simple point that, first, Christians are no different from, and no better than, pagans; they are essentially the same. Christians' claim to form part of Israel then requires no serious attention. Since Christians came to Jews with precisely that claim, the sages' response—they are another Babylonia—bears a powerful polemic charge. But that is not the whole story, as we see. Second, just as Israel had survived Babylonia, Media, Greece, so would they endure to see the end of Rome (whether pagan, whether Christian). But there is a third point. Rome really does differ from the earlier, pagan empires, and that polemic shifts the entire discourse, once we hear its symbolic vocabulary properly. For the new Rome really did differ from the old. Christianity was not merely part of a succession of undifferentiated modes of paganism. The symbols assigned to Rome attributed worse, more dangerous traits than those assigned to the earlier empires. The pig pretends to be clean, just as the Christians give the signs of adherence to the God of Abraham, Isaac, and Jacob. That much the passage concedes. For the pig is not clean, exhibiting some, but not all, of the required indications, and Rome is not Israel, even though it shares Israel's Scripture. That position, denying to Rome, in its Christian form, a place in the family of Israel, forms the counterpart to the view of Aphrahat that Israel today is no longer Israel—again, a confrontation on issues. Since the complete passage is given at the appendix to this chapter, I present only the critical passage at which the animals that are invoked include one that places Rome at the interstices, partly kosher, partly not, therefore more dangerous than anyone else (Leviticus Rabbah XIII:V):

> 9.A. Moses foresaw what the evil kingdoms would do [to Israel].
> B. "The camel, rock badger, and hare" (Deut. 14:7). [Compare: "Nevertheless, among those that chew the cud or part the hoof, you shall not eat these: the camel, because it chews the cud but does not part the hoof, is unclean to you. The rock badger, because it chews the cud but does not part the hoof, is unclean to you. And the hare, because it chews the cud but does not part the hoof, is unclean to you, and the pig, because it parts the hoof and is cloven-footed, but does not chew the cud, is unclean to you" (Lev. 11:4–8).]
> C. The camel (GML) refers to Babylonia, [in line with the following

verse of Scripture: "O daughter of Babylonia, you who are to be devastated!] Happy will be he who requites (GML) you, with what you have done to us" (Ps. 147:8).
D. "The rock badger" (Deut. 14:7)—this refers to Media.
E. Rabbis and R. Judah b. R. Simon.
F. Rabbis say, "Just as the rock badger exhibits traits of uncleanness and traits of cleanness, so the kingdom of Media produced both a righteous man and a wicked one."
G. Said R. Judah b. R. Simon, "The last Darius was Esther's son. He was clean on his mother's side and unclean on his father's side."
H. "The hare" (Deut 14:7)—this refers to Greece. The mother of King Ptolemy was named "Hare" [in Greek: lagos].
I. "The pig" (Deut. 14:7)—this refers to Edom [Rome].
J. Moses made mention of the first three in a single verse and the final one in a verse by itself [(Deut. 14:7, 8)]. Why so?
K. R. Yohanan and R. Simeon b. Laqish.
L. R. Yohanan said, "It is because [the pig] is equivalent to the other three."
M. And R. Simeon b. Laqish said, "It is because it outweighs them."
N. R. Yohanan objected to R. Simeon b. Laqish, "'Prophesy, therefore, son of man, clap your hands [and let the sword come down twice, yea thrice]' (Ez. 21:14)."
O. And how does R. Simeon b. Laqish interpret the same passage? He notes that [the threefold sword] is doubled (Ez. 21:14).
10.A. [Gen. R. 65:1:] R. Phineas and R. Hilqiah in the name of R. Simon: "Among all the prophets, only two of them revealed [the true evil of Rome], Assaf and Moses.

B. "Assaf said, 'The pig out of the wood ravages it' (Ps. 80:14).
C. "Moses said, 'And the pig, [because it parts the hoof and is cloven-footed but does not chew the cud]' (Lev. 11:7).
D. "Why is [Rome] compared to a pig?
E. "It is to teach you the following: Just as, when a pig crouches and produces its hooves, it is as if to say, 'See how I am clean [since I have a cloven hoof],' so this evil kingdom takes pride, seizes by violence, and steals, and then gives the appearance of establishing a tribunal for justice."
11.A. Another interpretation: "The camel" (Lev. 11:4).
B. This refers to Babylonia.
C. "Because it chews the cud [but does not part the hoof]" (Lev. 11:4).
D. For it brings forth praises [with its throat] of the Holy One, blessed be he. [The Hebrew words for "chew the cud"—bring up cud—are now understood to mean "give praise." GRH is connected with GRWN, throat, hence, "bring forth [sounds of praise through] the throat."
N. "The rock badger" (Lev. 11:5)—this refers to Media.
O. "For it chews the cud"—for it gives praise to the Holy One, blessed be he: "Thus says Cyrus, king of Persia, 'All the kingdoms of the earth has the Lord, the God of the heaven, given me" (Ezra 1:2).
P. "The hare"—this refers to Greece.
Q. "For it chews the cud"—for it gives praise to the Holy One, blessed be he.
S. "The pig" (Lev. 11:7)—this refers to Edom.
T. "For it does not chew the cud"—for it does not give praise to the Holy One, blessed be he.

U. And it is not enough that it does not give praise, but it blasphemes and swears violently, saying, "Whom do I have in heaven, and with you I want nothing on earth" (Ps. 73:25).

We first review the message of the construction as a whole, only part of which is before us. This comes in two parts, first, the explicit, then the implicit. As to the former, the first claim is that God had told the prophets what would happen to Israel at the hands of the pagan kingdoms, Babylonia, Media, Greece, Rome. These are further represented by Nebuchadnezzar, Haman, Alexander for Greece, Edom or Esau, interchangeably, for Rome. The same vision came from Adam, Abraham, Daniel and Moses. The same policy toward Israel—oppression, destruction, enslavement, alienation from the true God—emerged from all four. How does Rome stand out? First, it was made fruitful through the prayer of Isaac in behalf of Esau. Second, Edom is represented by the fourth and final beast. Rome is related through Esau, as Babylonia, Media, and Greece are not. The fourth beast was seen in a vision separate from the first three. It was worst of all and outweighed the rest. In the apocalypticizing of the animals of Lev. 11:4–8/Deut. 14:7, the camel, rock badger, hare, and pig, the pig, standing for Rome, again emerges as different from the others and more threatening than the rest. Just as the pig pretends to be a clean beast by showing the cloven hoof, but in fact is an unclean one, so Rome pretends to be just but in fact governs by thuggery. Edom does not pretend to praise God but only blasphemes. It does not exalt the righteous but kills them.

These symbols concede nothing to Christian monotheism and veneration of the Torah of Moses (in its written medium). Of greatest importance, while all the other beasts bring further ones in their wake, the pig does not: "It does not bring another kingdom after it." It will restore the crown to the one who will truly deserve it, Israel. Esau will be judged by Zion, so Ob. 1:21.

Now how has the symbolization delivered an implicit message? It is in the treatment of Rome as distinct, but essentially equivalent to the former kingdoms. This seems to me a stunning way of saying that the now-Christian empire in no way requires differentiation from its pagan predecessors. Nothing has changed, except matters have gotten worse. Beyond Rome, standing in a straight line with the others, lies the true shift in history, the rule of Israel and the cessation of the dominion of the (pagan) nations.

Jerome, great fourth century exegete of the Bible, dealt with the symbols of the animals of Leviticus 11, the apocalyptic reading of the humble matters of the beasts Israel may and may not eat:

> The Jew is single-hoofed and therefore he is unclean. The Manichean is single-hoofed and therefore he is unclean. And since he is single-hoofed he does not chew what he eats, and what has once gone into his stomach he does not bring up again and chew and make fine, so that what had been coarse would return to the stomach fine. This is indeed a matter of divine mystery. The Jew is single-hoofed, for he believes in only one Testament and does not ruminate; he only reads the letter and thinks over nothing, nor does he seek anything deeper. The Christian, however, is cloven-hoofed and ruminates. That is, he believes in both Testaments and he often ponders each Testament, and whatever lies hidden in the letter he brings forth in the spirit.

Rome is represented as only Christian Rome can have been represented: it looks kosher but it is unkosher. Pagan Rome cannot ever have looked kosher, but Christian Rome, with its appeal to ancient Israel, could and did and moreover claimed to. It bore some traits that validate, but lacked others that validate—just as Jerome said of Israel. It would be difficult to find a more direct confrontation between two parties to an argument. Now the issue is the same—who is the true Israel? and the proof-texts are the same, and, moreover, the proof-texts are read in precisely the same way. Only the conclusions differ!

Who Is the True Israel in Genesis Rabbah—The Conflicting Claims of Siblings

Sages' mode of thought required them to treat as personal matters of family relationships the history of Israel. That is how they could imagine relationships between Israel and other social entities: the treatment as persons and as parts of one family the social entities for which they sought an intelligible context. It followed from this policy of the Scripture's personalization of social entities—tribes as brothers, sons of one father—that if sages wished to absorb into their view of the world other components of the world community as they saw it, they would have to place into genealogical relationship with Israel these originally-alien elements. So it is quite natural that sages found a genealogical tie to Rome. In that way they fit Rome into the history of Israel. The biblical account of Israel's history in Genesis showed the way. The time and urgency of the enterprise—the genealogization of Rome—derived of course from the crisis of the fourth century. Prior to that time the documents of the canon that came to closure before Constantine reveal no such consideration. Afterward it became a commonplace in them.

Rome found representation in Genesis Rabbah mainly in Esau. The choice of Esau represents as powerful a judgment as the choice of the pig in Leviticus Rabbah. The message is the same. Rome is the brother—the genealogical connection—but the rejected brother. History thus has expanded to take account of what demanded explanation, what insisted upon categorization within the family-theory of history. But at what cost for the larger apologetic! For that symbolization of Rome as brother concedes much, specifically recognizing—if only for purpose of rejection—the claim of Christian Rome along with the family of Israel to inherit biblical Israel. Why Rome in the form it takes in Genesis Rabbah? And how come the obsessive character of sages' disposition of the theme of Rome? Were their picture merely of Rome as tyrant and destroyer of the Temple, we should have no reason to link the text to the problems of the age of redaction and closure, namely the late fourth or early fifth century.

But, as we have repeatedly observed, now it is Rome as Israel's brother, counterpart, and nemesis, Rome as the one thing standing in the way of Israel's, and the world's, ultimate salvation. So the stakes are different, and much higher. It is not a political Rome but a messianic Rome that is at issue: Rome as surrogate for Israel, Rome as obstacle to Israel. Why? It is because Rome now confronts Israel with a crisis, and Genesis Rabbah like Leviticus Rabbah responded to that crisis. Sages answered by saying, "Indeed, it is as you say, a kind of Israel, an heir of Abraham as your texts explicitly claim. But we remain the sole legitimate Israel, the bearer of the birthright—we and not you. So you are our brother: Esau, Ishmael, Edom." So in its Christian form, now Rome claimed to be Israel, and, indeed, sages conceded, Rome shared the patrimony of Israel. That claim took the form of the Christians' appropriation of the Torah as "the Old Testament," so sages acknowledged a simple fact in acceding to the notion that, in some way, Rome too formed part of Israel. But it was the rejected part, the Ishmael, the Esau, not the Isaac, not the Jacob. The advent of Christian Rome precipitated the sustained, polemical, rigorous and well-argued rereading of beginnings in light of the end. Rome then marked the conclusion of human history as Israel had known it. Beyond? The coming of the true Messiah, the redemption of Israel, the salvation of the world, the end of time. So the issues were not inconsiderable, and when the sages spoke of Esau/Rome, as they did so often, they confronted the life-or-death decision of the day. So, in all, the genealogical theory of Israel formed a whole and encompassing account of the social world at hand: who is Israel, then, also, who is Rome?

Here is a simple example of how ubiquitous is the shadow of Ishmael/Esau/Edom/Rome. Wherever in Genesis Rabbah sages reflect on future history, their minds turn to their own day. They found the hour difficult, because Rome, now Christian, claimed that very birthright and blessing that they understood to be theirs alone. Christian Rome posed a threat without precedent. Now another dominion, besides Israel's, claimed the rights and blessings that sustained Israel. Sages found comfort in the iteration that the birthright, the blessing, the Torah, and the hope—all belonged to them and to none other. As the several antagonists of Israel stand for Rome in particular, so the traits of Rome, as sages perceived them, characterized the biblical heroes. Esau provided a favorite target. From the womb Israel and Rome contended (Genesis Rabbah LXIII:VI):

11.A. "And the children struggled together [within her, and she said, 'If it is thus, why do I live?' So she went to inquire of the Lord. And the Lord said to her, 'Two nations are in your womb, and two peoples, born of you, shall be divided; the one shall be stronger than the other, and the elder shall serve the younger']" (Gen. 25:22–23):

3.A. "And the children struggled together within her:"

B. [Once more referring to the letters of the word "struggled," with special attention to the ones that mean, "run,"] they wanted to run within her.

C. When she went by houses of idolatry, Esau would kick, trying to get out: "The wicked are estranged from the womb" (Ps. 58:4).

D. When she went by synagogues and study-houses, Jacob would kick, trying to get out: "Before I formed you in the womb, I knew you" (Jer. 1:5)."

Genesis Rabbah LXIII:VII.

2.A. "Two nations are in your womb, [and two peoples, born of you, shall be divided; the one shall be stronger than the other, and the elder shall serve the younger]" (Gen. 25:23):

B. There are two proud nations in your womb, this one takes pride in his world, and that one takes pride in his world.

C. This one takes pride in his monarchy, and that one takes pride in his monarchy.

D. There are two proud nations in your womb.

E. Hadrian represents the nations, Solomon, Israel.

F. There are two who are hated by the nations in your womb. All the nations hate Esau, and all the nations hate Israel.

4.A. "... the one shall be stronger than the other, [and the elder shall serve the younger]" (Gen. 25:23):

B. R. Helbo in the name of the house of R. Shila: "Up to this point there were Sabteca and Raamah, but from you will come Jews and Romans." [Freedman, p. 561, n. 8: "Hitherto even the small nations such as Sabteca and Raamah counted; but henceforth all these will pale into insignificance before the two who will rise from you.]

5.A. "... and the elder shall serve the younger" (Gen. 25:23):

B. Said R. Huna, "If he has merit, he will be served, and if not, he will serve."

The verse underlines the point that there is natural enmity between Israel and Rome. Esau hated Israel even while he was still in the womb. Jacob, for his part, revealed from the womb those virtues that would characterize him later on, eager to serve God as Esau was eager to worship idols. The following is already familiar, but bears review because it links the two distinct symbolizations of Rome, the pig and Esau (Genesis Rabbah LXV:I):

1.C. R. Phineas and R. Hilqiah in the name of R. Simon: "Among all of the prophets, only two of them spelled out in public [the true character of Rome, represented by the swine], Asaf and Moses.
D. "Asaf: 'The swine out of the wood ravages it.'
E. "Moses: 'And the swine, because he parts the hoof' (Deut. 14:8).
F. "Why does Moses compare Rome to the swine? Just as the swine, when it crouches, puts forth its hoofs as if to say, 'I am clean,' so the wicked kingdom steals and grabs, while pretending to be setting up courts of justice.
G. "So Esau, for all forty years, hunted married women, ravished them, and when he reached the age of forty, he presented himself to his father, saying, 'Just as father got married at the age of forty, so I shall marry a wife at the age of forty.'
H. "'When Esau was forty years old, he took to wife Judith, the daughter of Beeri, the Hittite, and Basemath the daughter of Elon the Hittite.'"

The exegesis of course once more identifies Esau with Rome. The round-about route linking the fact at hand, Esau's taking a wife, passes through the territory of Roman duplicity. Whatever the government does, it claims to do in the general interest. But it really has no public interest at all. Esau for his part spent forty years pillaging women and then, at the age of forty, pretended, to his father, to be upright. That, at any rate, is the parallel clearly intended by this obviously unitary composition. The issue of the selection of the intersecting verse does not present an obvious solution to me; it seems to me only the identification of Rome with the swine accounts for the choice. The contrast between Israel and Esau produced the following anguished observation. But here the Rome is not yet Christian, so far as the clear reference is concerned. More compelling evidence that the radical change in the character of Rome lies behind the exegetical polemic at hand derives from the following.

The theories of the meaning of history and the identification of Israel, we see, cannot be sorted out. The one imparts its character on the other, and together, the two theories take up the pressing issue of the turning of the age, the meaning of the new era. That the whole bears a profoundly eschatological meaning emerges at the end. For, if we follow sages' thought to its logical conclusion, they express the expectation that after Rome will come Israel, so they have reframed history into an eschatological drama—in the here and now. The sequence of empires—Babylonia, Media, Greece, Rome, does not end the story. There then will come Israel, the conclusion and climax of human history. So Rome bears a close relationship to Israel in yet another respect, and the genealogical definition of who is Israel—and who is Rome—bears consequences in a world-historical framework. Here Roman rule comes prior to Israel's (Genesis Rabbah LXXV:IV):

2.A. "And Jacob sent messengers before him:"

B. To this one [Esau] whose time to take hold of sovereignty would come before him [namely, before Jacob, since Esau would rule, then Jacob would govern].

C. R. Joshua b. Levi said, "Jacob took off the purple robe and threw it before Esau, as if to say to him, 'Two flocks of starlings are not going to sleep on a single branch' [so we cannot rule at the same time].'"

3.A. "... to Esau his brother:"

B. Even though he was Esau, he was still his brother.

Nos. 2, 3 make a stunning point. It is that Esau remains Jacob's brother, and that Esau rules before Jacob will. The application to contemporary affairs cannot be missed, both in the recognition of the true character of Esau—a brother!—and in the interpretation of the future of history. Rome claims now to serve the Messiah. But Esau, meaning Rome, will fall by the hand of the Messiah. The polemic at that point is of course unmistakable. Not only is Rome not the messianic kingdom, but Rome will fall before the messianic kingdom that is coming (Genesis Rabbah LXXXIII:I):

1.A. "These are the kings who reigned in the land of Edom before any king reigned over the Israelites: Bela the son of Beor reigned in Edom, the name of his city being Dinhabah" (Gen. 36:31–32):

B. R. Isaac commenced discourse by citing this verse: "Of the oaks of Bashan they have made your oars" (Ez. 27:6).

C. Said R. Isaac, "The nations of the world are to be compared to a ship. Just as a ship has its mast made in one place and its anchor somewhere else, so their kings: 'Samlah of Masrekah' (Gen. 36:36), 'Shaul of Rehobot by the river' (Gen. 36:27), and: 'These are the kings who reigned in the land of Edom before any king reigned over the Israelites.'"

2.A. ["An estate may be gotten hastily at the beginning, but the end thereof shall not be blessed" (Prov. 20:21)]: "An estate may be gotten hastily at the beginning:" "These are the kings who reigned in the land of Edom before any king reigned over the Israelites."

B. "... but the end thereof shall not be blessed:" "And saviors shall come up on mount Zion to judge the mount of Esau" (Ob. 1:21).

No. 1 contrasts the diverse origin of Roman rulers with the uniform origin of Israel's king in the house of David. No. 2 makes the same point still more forcefully. How so? Freedman makes sense of No. 2 as follows: Though Esau was the first to have kings, his land will eventually be overthrown (Freedman, p. 766, n. 3). So the point is that Israel will have kings after Esau no longer does, and the verse at hand is made to point to the end of Rome, a striking revision to express the importance in Israel's history to events in the lives of the patriarchs. Rome's rule will extend only for a foreordained and limited time, at which point the messiah will come. Israel's saints even now make possible whatever wise decisions Rome's rulers make. That forms an appropriate conclusion to the matter. Ending in the everyday world of the here and the now, we note that sages attribute to Israel's influence anything good that happens to Israel's brother, Rome.

Sages framed their political ideas within the metaphor of genealogy, because to begin with they appealed to the fleshly connection, the family, as the rationale for Israel's social existence. A family beginning with Abraham, Isaac, and Jacob, Israel today could best sort out its relationships by drawing into the family other social entities with which it found it had to relate. So Rome became the brother. That affinity came to light only when Rome had turned Christian, and that point marked the need for the extension of the genealogical net. But the conversion to Christianity also justified sages' extending membership in the family to Rome, for Christian Rome shared with Israel the common patrimony of Scripture—and said so. The two facts, the one of the social and political metaphor by which sages interpreted events, the other of the very character of Christianity—account for the striking shift in the treatment of Rome that does appear to have taken place in the formative century represented by the principal midrash-compilations of the age, Genesis Rabbah and Leviticus Rabbah.

JACOB NEUSNER
Bard College

Ruth in Ruth Rabbah

Ruth Rabbah has only one message, expressed in a variety of components but single and cogent. It concerns the outsider who becomes the principal, the messiah out of Moab, and this miracle is accomplished through mastery of the Torah. The main points of the document are these:

[1] Israel's fate depends upon its proper conduct toward its leaders.

[2] The leaders must not be arrogant.

[3] The admission of the outsider depends upon the rules of the Torah. These differentiate among outsiders. Those who know the rules are able to apply them accurately and mercifully.

[4] The proselyte is accepted because the Torah makes it possible to do so, and the condition of acceptance is complete and total submission to the Torah. Boaz taught Ruth the rules of the Torah, and she obeyed them carefully.

[5] Those proselytes who are accepted are respected by God and are completely equal to all other Israelites. Those who marry them are masters of the Torah, and their descendants are masters of the Torah, typified by David. Boaz in his day and David in his day were the same in this regard.

[6] What the proselyte therefore accomplishes is to take shelter under the wings of God's presence, and the proselyte who does so stands in the royal line of David, Solomon, and the Messiah. Over and over again, we see the point is made that Ruth the Moabitess, perceived by the ignorant as an outsider, enjoyed complete equality with all other Israelites, because she had accepted the yoke of the Torah, married a great sage, and through her descendants produced the messiah-sage, David.

What changes a gentile into an Israelite is the Torah. That is the theological principle that animates the Rabbinic system throughout: the Torah is what makes Israel Israel. Here too sages impose upon the whole their distinctive message, which is the priority of the Torah, the extraordinary power of the Torah to join the opposites—Israelite/gentile, messiah/utter outsider—into a single figure, and to accomplish this union of opposites through a woman. The femininity of Ruth is critical to the whole as much as is the Moabite origin: the two modes of the (from the Israelite perspective) abnormal, outsider as against Israelite, woman as against man, therefore are invoked, and both for the same purpose, to show how, through the Torah, all things become one. That is the message of the document, and, seen whole, the principal message, to which all other messages prove peripheral.

In Rabbinic hands Ruth Rabbah proves nearly as much a commentary in the narrowest sense—verse by verse amplification, paraphrase, exposition—as it is a compilation. What holds the document together and gives it, if not coherence, then at least flow and movement, after all, are the successive passages of (mere) exposition. All the more stunning, therefore, is the simple fact that, when all has been set forth and completed, there really is that simple message that the Torah (as exemplified by the sage) makes the outsider into an insider, the Moabite into an Israelite, the offspring of the outsider into the Messiah: all on the condition, the only condition, that the Torah governs. This is a document about one thing, and it makes a single statement, and that statement is coherent.

The authorship decided to compose a document concerning the book of Ruth in order to make a single point. Everything else was subordinated to that definitive intention. Once the work got underway, the task was not one of exposition so much as repetition, not unpacking and exploring a complex conception, but restating the point, on the one side, and eliciting or evoking the proper attitude that was congruent with that point, on the other. The decision, viewed after the fact, was to make one statement in an enormous number of ways. It is that the Torah dictates Israel's fate, if you want to know what that fate will be, study the Torah, and if you want to control that fate, follow the model of the sage-Messiah. As usual, therefore, what we find is a recasting of the Deuteronomic-prophetic theology.

Three categories contain the topical and propositional messages of the document. These are as follows.

Israel and God

Israel's relationship with God encompasses the matter of the covenant, the Torah, and the land of Israel, all of which bring to concrete and material expression the nature and standing of that relationship. This is a topic treated only casually by our compilers. They make a perfectly standard point. It is that Israel suffers because of sin (I:i). The famine in the time of the judges was because of Israel's rebellion: "My children are rebellious. But as to exterminating them, that is not possible, and to bring them back to Egypt is not possible, and to trade them for some other nation is something I cannot do. But this shall I do for them: lo, I shall torment them with suffering and afflict them with famine in the days when the judges judge" (III:i). This was because they got overconfident (III:ii).

Sometimes God saves Israel on account of its merit, sometimes for his own name's sake (X:i). God's punishment of Israel is always proportionate and appropriate, so LXXIV:i: "Just as in the beginning, Israel gave praise for the redemption: 'This is my God and I will glorify him' (Exod. 15:2), now it is for the substitution [of false gods for God]: 'Thus they exchanged their glory for the likeness of an ox that eats grass' (Ps. 106:20). You have nothing so repulsive and disgusting and strange as an ox when it is eating grass. In the beginning they would effect acquisition through the removal of the sandal, as it is said, 'Now this was the custom in former times in Israel concerning redeeming and exchanging: to confirm a transaction, the one drew off his sandal and gave it to the other, and this was the manner of attesting in Israel.' But now it is by means of the rite of cutting off. "None of this forms a centerpiece of interest, and all of it complements the principal points of the writing.

Israel and the Nations

Israel's relationship with the nations is treated with interest in Israel's history, past, present, and future, and how that cyclical pattern is to be known. This topic is not addressed at all. Only one nation figures in a consequential way, and that is Moab. Under these circumstances we can hardly generalize and say that Moab stands for everybody outside of Israel. That is precisely the opposite of the fact. Moab stands for a problem within Israel, the Messiah from the periphery; and the solution to the problem lies within Israel and not in its relationships to the other, the nations.

Israel on Its Own

Israel on its own concerns the holy nation's understanding of itself: who is Israel, who is not? Within the same rubric we find consideration of Israel's capacity to naturalize the outsider, so to define itself as to extend its own limits, and other questions of self-definition. And, finally, when Israel considers itself, a principal concern is the nature of leadership, for the leader stands for and embodies the people. Therein lies the paradox of the base-document and the Midrash-compilation alike: how can the leader most wanted, the Messiah, come, as a matter of fact, from the excluded people and not from the holy people?

And, more to the point (for ours is not an accusatory document), how is the excluded included? And in what way do peripheral figures find their way to the center? Phrased in this way, the question yields the obvious answer: through the Torah as embodied by the sage, anybody can become Israel, and any Israelite can find his way to the center. Even more—since it is through Ruth that the Moabite becomes the Israelite and since (for sages) the mother's status dictates the child's, we may go so far as to say that it is through the Torah that the woman may become a man (at least, in theory). But in stating matters in this way, I have gone beyond my representation of the topical and propositional program. Let us review it from the beginning to the end.

The sin of Israel, which caused the famine, was that it was judging its own judges. "He further said to the Israelites, 'So God says to Israel, "I have given a share of glory to the judges and I have called them gods, and the Israelites nonetheless humiliate them. Woe to a generation that judges its judges" (I:i). The Israelites were slothful in burying Joshua, and that showed disrespect to their leader (II:i). They were slothful about repentance in the time of the judges, and that is what caused the famine; excess of commitment to one's own affairs leads to sin. The Israelites did not honor the prophets (III:iii). The old have to bear with the young, and the young with the old, or Israel will go into exile (IV:i). The generation that judges its leadership ("judges") will be penalized (V:i). Arrogance to the authority of the Torah is penalized (V:i). Elimelech was punished because he broke the peoples' heart; everyone depended upon him, and he proved undependable (V:iii); so bad leadership will destroy Israel. Why was Elimelech punished? It is because he broke the Israelites' heart. When the years of drought came, his maid went out into the market place, with her basket in her hand. So the people of the town said, "Is this the one on whom we depended, that he can provide for the whole town with ten years of food? Lo, his maid is standing in the marketplace with her basket in her hand!" So Elimelech was one of the great men of the town and one of those who sustained the generation. But when the years of famine came, he said, "Now all the Israelites are going to come knocking on my door, each with his basket." The leadership of a community is its glory: "The great man of a town—he is its splendor, he is its glory, he is its praise. When he has turned from there, so too have turned its splendor, glory, and praise" (XI:i.1C).

A distinct but fundamental component of the theory of Israel concerns who is Israel and how one becomes a part of Israel. That theme proves fundamental to our document, so much of which is preoccupied with how Ruth can be the progenitor of the Messiah, deriving as she does not only from gentile but from Moabite stock. Israel's history follows rules that are to be learned in Scripture; nothing is random and all things are connected (IV:ii). The fact that the king of Moab honored God explains why God raised up from Moab "a son who will sit on the throne of the Lord" (VIII:i.3). The proselyte is discouraged but then accepted. Thus XVI:i.2B: "People are to turn a proselyte away. But if he is insistent beyond that point, he is accepted. A person should always push away with the left hand while offering encouragement with the right." Orpah, who left Naomi, was rewarded for the little that she did for her, but she was raped when she left her (XVIII:i.1-3). When Orpah went back to her people, she went back to her gods (XIX:i).

Ruth's intention to convert was absolutely firm, and Naomi laid out all the problems for her, but she acceded to every condition (XX:i). Thus she said, "Under all circumstances I intend to convert, but it is better that it be through your action and not through that of another." When Naomi heard her say this, she began laying out for her the laws that govern proselytes. She said to her, "My daughter, it is not the way of Israelite women to go to theaters and circuses put on by idolators." She said to her, "Where you go I will go." She said to her, "My daughter, it is not the way of Israelite women to live in a house that lacks a mezuzah." She said to her, "Where you lodge I will lodge." "your people shall be my people:" This refers to the penalties and admonitions against sinning. "and your God my God:" This refers to the other religious duties. And so onward: "for where you go I will go:" to the tent of meeting, Gilgal, Shiloh, Nob, Gibeon, and the eternal house. "and where you lodge I will lodge:" "I shall spend the night concerned about the offerings." "your people shall be my people:" "so nullifying my idol." "and your God my God:" "to pay a full recompense for my action." I find here the centerpiece of the compilation and its principal purpose. The same message is at XXI:i.1-3.

Proselytes are respected by God, so XXII:i: "And when Naomi saw that she was determined to go with her, [she said no more]:" Said R. Judah b. R. Simon, "Notice how precious are proselytes before the Omnipresent. Once she had decided to convert, the Scripture treats her as equivalent to Naomi." Boaz, for his part, was equally virtuous and free of sins (XXVI:i). The law provided for the conversion of Ammonite and Moabite women, but not Ammonite and Moabite men, so the acceptance of Ruth the Moabite was fully in accord with the law, and anyone who did not know that fact was an ignoramus (XXVI:i.4, among many passages). An Israelite hero who came from Ruth and Boaz was David, who was a great master of the Torah, thus: he was "Skillful in playing, and a mighty man of war, prudent in affairs, good-looking, and the Lord is with him" (1 Sam. 16:18): "Skillful in playing:" in Scripture. "and a mighty man of valor:" in Mishnah. "A man of war:" who knows the give and take of the war of the Torah. "prudent in affairs:" in good deeds. "good-looking:" in Talmud. "prudent in affairs:" able to reason deductively. "good-looking:" enlightened in law. "and the Lord is with him:" the law accords with his opinions.

Ruth truly accepted Judaism upon the instruction, also, of Boaz (XXXIV:i), thus: "Then Boaz said to Ruth, 'Now listen, my daughter, do not go to glean in another field:'" This is on the strength of the verse, "You shall have no other gods before me" (Exod. 20:3). "'or leave this one:'" This is on the strength of the verse, "This is my God and I will glorify him" (Exod. 15:2). "But keep close to my maidens:" This speaks of the righteous, who are called maidens: "Will you play with him as with a bird, or will you bind him for your maidens" (Job 40:29). The glosses invest the statement with a vast tapestry of meaning. Boaz speaks to Ruth as a Jew by choice, and the entire exchange is now typological. Note also the typological meanings imputed at XXXV:i.1–5. Ruth had prophetic power (XXXVI:ii). Ruth was rewarded for her sincere conversion by Solomon (XXXVIII:i.1).

Taking shelter under the wings of the Presence of God, which is what the convert does, is the greatest merit accorded to all who do deeds of grace, thus: So notice the power of the righteous and the power of righteousness are the power of those who do deeds of grace. For they take shelter not in the shadow of the dawn, nor in the shadow of the wings of the earth, not in the shadow of the wings of the sun, nor in the shadow of the wings of the *hayyot*, nor in the shadow of the wings of the cherubim or the seraphim. But under whose wings do they take shelter? "They take shelter under the shadow of the One at whose word the world was created: 'How precious is your loving kindness O God, and the children of men take refuge in the shadow of your wings' (Ps. 36:8)."

The language that Boaz used to Ruth, "Come here," bore with it deeper reference to six: David, Solomon, the throne as held by the Davidic monarchy, and ultimately, the messiah, e.g., in the following instance: "The fifth interpretation refers to the messiah: 'Come here:' means, to the throne. "'and eat some bread:' this is the bread of the throne. "'and dip your morsel in vinegar:' this refers to suffering: 'But he was wounded because of our transgressions' (Is. 53:5). "'So she sat beside the reapers:' for the throne is destined to be taken from him for a time: For I will gather all nations against Jerusalem to battle and the city shall be taken' (Zech. 14:2). "'and he passed to her parched grain:' for he will be restored to the throne: 'And he shall smite the land with the rod of his mouth' (Is. 11:4)." R. Berekhiah in the name of R. Levi: "As was the first redeemer, so is the last redeemer: "Just as the first redeemer was revealed and then hidden from them, so the last redeemer will be revealed to them and then hidden from them" (XL:i.1ff.).

Boaz instructed Ruth on how to be a proper Israelite woman, so LIII:i: "Wash yourself:" from the filth of idolatry that is yours. "and anoint yourself:" this refers to the religious deeds and acts of righteousness [that are required of an Israelite]. and put on your best clothes:" this refers to her Sabbath clothing. So did Naomi encompass Ruth within Israel: "and go down to the threshing floor:" She said to her, "My merit will go down there with you." Moab, whence Ruth came, was conceived not for the sake of fornication but for the sake of Heaven (LV:i.1B). Boaz, for his part, was a master of the Torah and when he ate and drank, that formed a typology for his study of the torah (LVI:i). His was a life of grace, Torah study, and marriage for holy purposes. Whoever trusts in God is exalted, and that refers to Ruth and Boaz; God put it in his heart to bless her (LVII:i). David sang Psalms to thank God for his great-grandmother, Ruth, so LIX:i.5, "[At midnight I will rise to give thanks to you] because of your righteous judgments" (Ps. 119:62): [David speaks,] "The acts of judgment that you brought upon the Ammonites and Moabites. "And the righteous deeds that you carried out for my great-grandfather and my great-grandmother [Boaz, Ruth, of whom David speaks here]. "For had he hastily cursed her but once, where should I have come from? But you put in his heart the will to bless her: 'And he said, "May you be blessed by the Lord." Because of the merit of the six measures that Boaz gave Ruth, six righteous persons came forth from him, each with six virtues: David, Hezekiah, Josiah, Hananiah-Mishael-Azariah (counted as one), Daniel and the royal messiah.

God facilitated the union of Ruth and Boaz (LXVIII:i). Boaz's relative was ignorant for not knowing that while a male Moabite was excluded, a female one was acceptable for marriage. The blessing of Boaz was, "May all the children you have come from this righteous woman" (LXXIX:i), and that is precisely the blessing accorded to Isaac and to Elkanah. God made Ruth an ovary, which she had lacked (LXXX:i). Naomi was blessed with messianic blessings (LXXXI:i), thus: "Then the women said to Naomi, 'Blessed be the Lord, who has not left you this day without next of kin; and may his name be renowned in Israel:'" Just as "this day" has dominion in the firmament, so will your descendants rule and govern Israel forever. On account of the blessings of the women, the line of David was not wholly exterminated in the time of Athaliah.

David was ridiculed because he was descended from Ruth, the Moabitess, so LXXXV:i. But many other distinguished families derived from humble origins: "Said David before the Holy One, blessed be he, 'How long will they rage against me and say, 'Is his family not invalid [for marriage into Israel]? Is he not descended from Ruth the Moabitess?'" "'commune with your own heart upon your bed:' [David continues,] 'You too have you not descended from two sisters? You look at your own origins "and shut up." "'So Tamar who married your ancestor Judah—is she not of an invalid family? 'But she was only a descendant of Shem, son of Noah. So do you come from such impressive genealogy?'" David referred to and defended his Moabite origins, so LXXXIX:i: "Then I said, Lo, I have come [in the roll of the book it is written of me]' (Ps. 40:8). "[David says,] 'Then I had to recite a song when I came, for the word "then" refers to a song, as it is said, "Then sang Moses" (Exod. 15:1). "'I was covered by the verse, 'An Ammonite and a Moabite shall not come into the assembly of the Lord' (Deut. 23:4), but I have come "in the roll of the book it is written of me" (Ps. 40:8). "in the roll:" this refers to the verse, [David continues], "concerning whom you commanded that they should not enter into your congregation" (Lam. 1:10). "of the book it is written of me:" "An Ammonite and a Moabite shall not enter into the assembly of the Lord" (Deut. 23:4). "It is not enough that I have come, but in the roll and the book it is written concerning me:" "In the roll:" Perez, Hezron, Ram, Amminadab, Nahshon, Salmon, Boaz, Obed, Jesse, David. "in the book:" "And the Lord said, Arise, anoint him, for this is he" (1 Sam. 16:12)." Just as David's descent from Ruth was questioned, so his descent from Judah via Tamar could be questioned too, and that would compromise the whole tribe of Judah.

A Sample Passage

The document is comprised of two distinct types of compositions, first, the intersecting-verse/base-verse exposition; second, the verse-by-verse commentary. In the former, a verse of Ruth is juxtaposed with a verse selected from some other book of the Scriptures, and the latter imposes context and meaning on the verse of Ruth. In this way, Scripture is treated as unitary and not divided into books. In the latter, the verses of the book of Ruth are systematically cited and glossed, with the cumulative effect already epitomized above. Here is the first of the two types of compositions

RUTH RABBAH TO RUTH 1:1

I:i.1A. ["And it came to pass in the days when the judges ruled, there was a famine in the land, and a certain man of Bethlehem in Judah went to sojourn in the country of Moab, he and his wife and his two sons. The name of the man was Elimelech, and the name of his wife Naomi, and the names of his two sons were Mahlon and Chilion; they were Ephrathites from Bethlehem in Judah. They went into the country of Moab

and remained there:"] "And it came to pass in the days when the judges ruled [judged]:"
B. R. Yohanan commenced discourse by citing [the following verse of Scripture: "Hear, O my people, and I will speak; O Israel, and I will testify against you. [God, your God, I am.]" (Ps. 50:7).
C. Said R. Yohanan, "People give evidence only in the hearing [of the accused]."
2.A. R. Yudan b. R. Simon said, "In the past, Israel was called by a name just like every other nation, e.g., 'And Sabta and Raamah and Sabteca' (Gen. 10:7).
B. "But from now on, 'my people,' as in the verse, 'Hear, O my people, and I will speak; O Israel, and I will testify against you.'
C. "Whence did you gain the merit to be called 'my people'?
D. "It is from the time that 'I will speak.'
E. "That is, it is from what you said before me at Sinai: 'All that the Lord has spoken we will do and obey' (Exod. 24:7)."
3.A. Said R. Yohanan, "'Hear, O my people:' concerning the past.
B. "'and I will speak:' concerning the age to come.
C. "'Hear, O my people:' in this world.
D. "'and I will speak:' in the world to come.
E. "It is so that what to say before the angelic princes of the nations of the world, who are destined to complain before me, saying, "Lord of the ages, these worship idols and those worship idols, these practice fornication, and those practice fornication, these shed blood and those shed blood, these go down to the Garden of Eden, while those go down to Gehenna! [Unfair!]'

F. "At that moment the angelic defender of Israel [Michael] remains silent.
G. "That is the meaning of the verse, 'And at that time shall Michael stand up' (Dan. 12:1)."
4.A. And is there a session [of the court] that is held in heaven?
B. And did not R. Hanina said, "There is no sitting in heaven: 'I came near to one of the standing ones' (Dan. 7:16),
C. "and the meaning of the word for 'standing ones' is ones who stood by, as in this verse: 'Above him stood the seraphim' (Is. 6:2); 'And all the host of heaven standing on his right hand and on his left' (2 Chr. 18:18).
D. "And yet the verse at hand says, 'And at that time shall Michael stand up' (Dan. 12:1)!
E. "What is the meaning of 'And at that time shall Michael stand up' (Dan. 12:1)?
F. "He is silenced, as in this usage: 'And shall I wait because they speak not, because they stand still and do not answer any more' (Job 32:16)."
5.A. [Continuing 3.F:] "Said to him the Holy One, blessed be he, 'Do you stand silent and not defend my children? By your life, I shall speak in righteousness and save my children.'"
6.A. And in virtue of what righteousness?
B. R. Eleazar and R. Yohanan:
C. One said, "'In virtue of the righteousness that you did for my world by accepting my Torah. For had you not accepted my Torah, I should have turned the world back to formlessness and void.'"
D. For R. Huna in the name of R. Aha said, "'When the earth and all the inhabitants thereof are dissolved. [I myself establish the pillars of

it.]' (Ps. 75:4): the world should already have been dissolved were it not for the Israelites who stood before Mount Sinai. [Supply: For had you not accepted my Torah, I should have turned the world back to formlessness and void.]

E. "And who founded the world? 'I myself establish the pillars of it.'

F. "It is in virtue of the 'I' that 'I myself establish the pillars of it.'"

G. The other said, "It is in virtue of the righteousness that you did in your own behalf by accepting my Torah.

H. "For if you had not, I should have assimilated you among the nations."

7.A. "God, your God, I am:"

B. R. Yohanan said, "'It's enough for you that I am your patron.'"

C. R. Simeon b. Laqish said, "'Even though I am your patron, what good does my patronage do for you in judgment?'"

8.A. Taught R. Simeon b. Yohanan [concerning the verse, "God, your God, I am"], "I am God for everybody in the world, but I have assigned my name in particular only to my people, Israel.

B. "'I am called not 'the God of all nations' but 'the God of Israel.'"

9.A. "God, your God, I am:"

B. R. Yudan interpreted the verse to speak of Moses: "Said the Holy One, blessed be he, to Moses, 'Even though I called you 'God' as to Pharaoh, ' 'God, your God, I am' over you."

10.A. ["God, your God, I am:"]

B. R. Abba bar Yudan interpreted the verse to speak of Israel: "'Even though I called you 'gods,' as it is said, "I said, You are gods" (Ps. 82:6), nonetheless, "God, your God, I am 'over you.'"

11.A. ["God, your God, I am:"]

B. Rabbis interpreted the verse to speak of the judges: "''Even though I called you gods, "You shall not revile gods" [that is, judges] (Exod. 22:27), "God, your God, I am" over you.'"

C. "He further said to the Israelites, 'I have given a share of glory to the judges and I have called them gods, and the [Israelites] humiliate them.

D. "Woe to a generation that judges its judges."

E. [Supply: "And it came to pass in the days when the judges were judged."]

What joins Nos. 1, 2, 3? I see no shared proposition, but only a common reference-point, which is the intersecting verse. No. 4 is interpolated to enrich 3.G, No. 5 continues No. 3, and so does No. 6. From that point on, we have a sequence of discrete compositions, none of which acknowledges the presence of anything fore or aft. So, overall, the composite is a fine example of the working of fixed associative logic. The interest of the composition as a whole is achieved at No. 11, which (as I read it) wishes to explain why the famine came about. And the answer is that the people were judging the judges. The intersecting verse is beautifully attained in the concluding composition therefore, and it does lead to precisely what the framer of the whole has wanted to say. But the prior twists and turns are hardly required. No. 2, for example, has no bearing upon our issue, and No. 3 scarcely is relevant. Only if we assume that the purpose of Yohanan's exposition at No. 3 is to explain how the messiah comes about, which is at stake in the book of Ruth, can we suppose that there is any clear connection between Yohanan's exposition and the task at hand? But that is very farfetched, and, it follows, Nos. 3, with No. 4 tacked on, then 5–6, are simply parachuted down, serving the intersecting verse in its own terms, but the base verse in no way. Nos. 7–8 serve no more pertinently than the prior items. Nos. 9, 10, and 11 then form the bridge to our base-verse, and if my interpolation of 11.E is correct, then they do make the desired point.

Now we come to the second of the two types of compositions, the systematic citation and phrase by phrase gloss of a verse, the whole being purposeful and pointed. The passage is shared with another midrash-compilation and is not primary to Ruth Rabbah at all.

RUTH RABBAH TO RUTH 1:5

IX:i.1 A. ["and both Mahlon and Chilion died, so that the woman was bereft of her two sons and her husband:"] "and both Mahlon and Chilion died:"

B. [Leviticus Rabbah XVII:IV.1–4:] R. Huniah in the name of R. Joshua b. R. Abin and R. Zechariah son-in-law of R. Levi in the name of R. Levi: "The merciful Lord does not do injury to human beings first. [First he exacts a penalty from property, aiming at the sinner's repentance.]

C. From whom do you derive that lesson? From the case of Job: 'The oxen were plowing and the asses feeding beside them [and the Sabeans fell upon them and took them and slew the servants with the edge of the sword; and I alone have escaped to tell you' (Job 1:14). Afterward: 'Your sons and daughters were eating and drinking wine in their eldest brother's house, and behold, a great wind came across the wilderness and struck the four corners of the house, and it fell upon the young people, and they are dead' (Job 1:19)].

D. Now were the oxen plowing and the asses feeding beside them? Said R. Hama b. R. Hanina, "This teaches that the Holy One, blessed be he, showed him a paradigm of the world to come.

E. "That is in line with the following verse of Scripture: 'The plowman shall overtake the reaper'" (Amos 9:13).

F. "And the Sabeans fell upon them and took them and slew the servants with the edge of the sword" (Job 1:15).

G. Said R. Abba b. R. Kahana, "They left Kefar Qurenos and went through all of the Aelin towns and came to the Tower of the Dyers and died there."

H. "Only I alone have escaped to tell you" (Job 1:15).

I. Said R. Hanina "Whenever we find the world 'only' used, it serves to limit the sense of the passage, thus: even he survived only broken and beaten."

J. Said R. Yudan, "From the use of the word 'alone,' we derive the fact that he meant, 'I alone have the task of telling you.' And even here, once Job had heard his bitter news, the messenger forthwith perished."

K. "While he was yet speaking, there came another and said, 'The Chaldeans formed three companies and made a raid upon the camels and took them and slew the servants with the edge of the sword, and I alone have escaped to tell you' (Job 1:17).

L. R. Samuel b. R. Nahman said, "When Job heard this bitter news of his, he began to mobilize his forces for war. He thought, 'How many platoons can I enlist, how many companies can I collect.

M. [Lev. R. adds:] "That is in line with the following verse of Scripture: 'Because I stood in great fear of the multitude and the contempt of families terrified me' (Job 31:34).

N. "He said, 'This people is contemptible: "Behold the land of the Chaldeans, this people that was not" (Is. 23:13). Would that it were not! It has come only to put me in dread of it.'

O. "When they said to him, 'A fire of God fell from heaven and burned up the sheep and the servants and consumed them, and I alone have escaped to tell you' (Job 1:16).

P. "Job said, 'Now if this blow is from Heaven, when can I do about it?

Q. "'A voice from heaven has fallen, and what can I do?' 'So that I kept silence and did not go out of doors' (Job 31:34).

R. "So he took a potsherd with which to scrape himself, in line with the verse: 'He took a potsherd with which to scrape himself and sat among the ashes' (Job 2:8)."

2.A. So too it was in Egypt [that God punished the Egyptians' herds before he punished the people themselves: "He gave over their cattle to the hail and their flocks to thunderbolts" (Ps. 78:48).

B. And then: "He smote their vines and fig trees and shattered the trees of their country" (Ps. 105:33).

C. And finally: "He smote all the firstborn in their land, the first issue of all their strength" (Ps. 105:36).

3.A. [Lev. R. XVII:IV.3 gives what is here No. 4, and then gives the following:] So when leprous plagues afflict a person, first they afflict his house. If he repents the house requires only the dismantling of the affected stones. If not, the whole house requires demolishing.

B. Lo, when they hid his clothing, if he repents, the clothing has only to be torn. If he did not repent, the clothing has to be burned.

C. Lo, if one's body is affected, if he repents, he may be purified.

D. If the affliction comes back, and if he does not repent, "He shall dwell alone in a habitation outside the camp."

4.A. So too in the case of Mahlon and Chilion:

B. first their horses and asses and camels died, and then: Elimelech, and finally the two sons.

5.A. "so that the woman was bereft of her two sons and her husband:"

B. Said R. Hanina [son of R. Abbahu], "She was equivalent to the residue of meal-offerings."

Here is a fine example of how propositional logic holds together several well-crafted compositions. The proposition is this: The merciful Lord does not do injury to human beings first. First he exacts a penalty from property, aiming at the sinner's repentance. A sequence of demonstrations on the basis of probative cases follows. I cannot imagine a better set of well-joined paragraphs. Only No. 5 breaks ranks. Nos. 1–4 are given in the version of Lev. R., as indicated. I prefer Margoliot's text for the whole, because it is superior in clarity, but there are minor differences in Ruth Rabbah's version as now printed. The only material change comes at the end, No. 6, where the fresh material links the ready-made composition to the interests of our document; No. 5 proceeds to the next clause. So Nos. 1–4 have no close relationship to this document. They serve the interests of a document that wishes to set forth proofs for various theological propositions.

Finally, we take up an exposition of a verse of Ruth in its own terms. But here too we see that the documentary interest presides over the detailed and (formally) atomistic exegesis.

Ruth Rabbah to Ruth 1:17

XXI:i.1A. "where you die I will die:"
- B. this refers to the four modes of inflicting the death penalty that a court uses: stoning, burning, slaying, and strangulation.

2.A. "and there will I be buried:"
- B. this refers to the two burial grounds that are provided for the use of the court,
- C. one for those who are stoned and burned, the other for the use of those who are slain or strangled.

Nos. 1, 2, fit together as readings in a common way of related components of a verse. But I see no proposition here, rather a cogent exegetical composite.

3.A. "May the Lord do so to me and more also [if even death parts me from you]:"
- B. She said to her, "My daughter, whatever you can accomplish in the way of religious duties and acts of righteousness in this world, accomplish.
- C. "Truly in the age to come, 'death parts me from you.'"

No. 3 may be said to relate to Nos. 1, 2 through the shared base-verse, hence via fixed associative logic. I do not see anything that joins No. 4 to No. 3 or to No. 5.

4.A. This [proposition that after death one cannot repent (Rabinowitz, *Midrash Rabbah: Ruth* [London, 1948], p. 41, n. 1)] is in line with the following verse: "The small and great are there alike, and the servant is free from his master" (Job 3:19).
- B. Said R. Simon, "This is one of four scriptural verses that are alike [in presenting the same message]:
- C. "'The small and great are there alike:' In this world one who is small can become great, and one who is great can become small, but in the world to come, one who is small cannot become great, and one who is great cannot become small.
- D. "'and the servant is free from his master:' this is one who carries out the will of his creator and angers his evil impulse. When he dies, he goes forth into freedom: 'and the servant is free from his master.'"

No. 5 will now give us a story; it has no bearing on No. 4's message. The point of No. 4 is that in the world to come there is no way of improving one's standing, achieved in life. No. 5's story, we now see, is that people who are honored in this world are held in contempt in the world to come. But the appearance of Ez. 21:31 in No. 5 made it logical to the compiler to add No. 6, which deals with the same verse. How to explain the joining of two narratives that encompass the same proof-text? Clearly, the one who put them together thought that narratives on a common verse flow together, but to me the logic is still that of fixed association, pure and simple.

5.A. R. Miaha son of the son of R. Joshua fell unconscious from ill-ness from three days, and then three days later he regained consciousness.
- B. His father said to him, "What did you see?"
- C. He said to him, "In a world that was mixed up I found myself."
- D. He said to him, "And what did you see there?"
- E. He said to him, "Many people I saw who here are held in honor and there in contempt."

F. When R. Yohanan and R. Simeon b. Laqish heard, they came in to visit him. The father said to them, "Did you hear what this boy said?"

G. They said to him, "What?"

H. He told them the incident.

I. R. Simeon b. Laqish said, "And is this not an explicit verse of Scripture? 'Thus says the Lord God, the miter shall be removed, and the crown taken off; this shall be no more the same; that which is low shall be exalted, and that which is high abased' (Ez. 21:31)."

J. Said R. Yohanan, "Had I come here only to hear this matter, it would have sufficed."

6.A. R. Huna the exilarch asked R. Hisdai, "What is the meaning of this verse: 'Thus says the Lord God, the miter shall be removed, and the crown taken off; this shall be no more the same; that which is low shall be exalted, and that which is high abased' (Ez. 21:31)?"

B. He said to him, "The miter shall be taken away from our rabbis, and the crown shall be taken away from the gentile nations."

C. He said to him, "Your name is Hisdai [loving kindness[and what you say is full of hesed [grace]."

I see no way of accounting for the inclusion of the following item in just this position, that is, after Nos. 5–6. And what follows thereafter serves Qoh. 9:4, that is, Nos. 9, 10.

7.A. It is written, "For to him who is joined to all living there is hope; for a living dog is better than a dead lion" (Qoh. 9:4):

B. It has been taught on Tannaite authority there:

C. One who sees an idol—what should he say? Blessed is he who is patient with those who violate his will.

D. [One who sees a place in which miracles were performed for Israel says, "Blessed is he who performed miracles for our fathers in this place.] One who sees a place from which idolatry has been uprooted says, "Blessed is he who uprooted idolatry from our land" [M. Ber. 9:1A–B].

E. "And so may it be pleasing to you, Lord our God, that you uproot it from all places and restore the heart of those who worship idolatry to worship you with a whole heart."

F. But does he not then turn out to pray for wicked people?

G. Said R. Yohanan, "What is written [at Qoh. 9:4] is [not 'joined] but 'chosen.'

H. "Even those who laid hands on the Temple have hope.

I. "To resurrect them is not possible, for they have indeed laid hands on the Temple.

J. "But to exterminate them is not possible, for they have already repented.

K. "To them the following verse refers: 'They shall sleep a perpetual sleep and not awake' (Jer. 51:39)."

8.A. It has been taught on Tannaite authority:

B. Gentiles who die as minors and the armies of Nebuchadnezzar are not going to be either resurrected or punished.

C. To them the following verse refers: "They shall sleep a perpetual sleep and not awake" (Jer. 51:39).

9.A. "For to him who is joined to all living there is hope; for a living dog is better than a dead lion" (Qoh. 9:4):

B. In this world one who is a dog can be made into a lion, and he who is a lion can be made into a dog.

C. But in the world to come, a lion cannot become a dog, nor a dog a lion.

10.A. Hadrian—may his bones rot!—asked R. Joshua b. Hananiah, saying to him, "I am better off than your lord, Moses."

B. He said to him, "Why?"

C. "Because I am alive and he is dead, and it is written, 'For to him who is joined to all living there is hope; for a living dog is better than a dead lion' (Qoh. 9:4)."

D. He said to him, "Can you make a decree that no one kindle a fire for three days?"

E. He said to him, "Yes."

F. At evening the two of them went up to the roof of the palace. They saw smoke ascending from a distance.

G. He said to him, "What is this?"

H. He said to him, "It is a sick noble. The physician came to him and told him he will be healed only if he drinks hot water."

I. He said to him, "May your spirit go forth [drop dead]! While you are still alive, your decree is null.

J. "But from the time that our lord, Moses, made the decree for us, 'You shall not burn a fire in your dwelling place on the Sabbath day' (Exod. 35:3), no Jew has ever kindled a flame on the Sabbath, and even to the present day, the decree has not been nullified.

K. "And you say you are better off than he is?"

Nos. 11, 12, 13, 14, to the end go over the general theme that what you do not accomplish in this world you will not get to complete in the world to come. But I see no arrangement in such a way as to demonstrate that proposition; the sequence from the viewpoint of the theme is random and repetitious, rather than pointed and syllogistic. The mode of discourse is not argumentative but illustrative. So if there is a logic that joins one composition to the next, it is a logic that makes things seem cogent merely because they are on a single topic; and that is not propositional, or narrative, or fixed associative. I would call it "agglutinative." A given topic will hold together an agglutination of topically pertinent, but individually discrete, items. We shall now see how such a logic works.

11.A. "Tell me, O Lord, what my term is, what is the measure of my days; I would know how fleeting my life is. [You have made my life just handbreadths long; its span is as nothing in your sight; no man endures longer than a breath. Man walks about as a mere shadow; mere futility is his hustle and bustle, amassing and not knowing who will gather in]" (Ps. 39:5-7):

B. Said David before the Holy One, blessed be he, "Lord of the world, tell me when I shall die."

C. He said to him, "It is a secret that is not to be revealed to a mortal, and it is not possible for me to tell you."

D. He said to him, ". . . what is the measure of my days."

E. He said to him, "Seventy years."

F. He said to him, "'I would know how fleeting my life is.' Tell me on what day I am going to die."

G. He said to him, "On the Sabbath."

H. He said to him, "Take off one day [not on the Sabbath, since on that day the body cannot be tended].?

I. He said to him, "No."

J. He said to him, "Why?"

K. He said to him, "More precious to me is a single prayer that you stand and recite to me than a thousand whole-offerings that your son, Solomon, is going to offer before me: 'A thousand burnt offerings

did Solomon offer on that altar' (1 Kgs. 3:4)."
L. He said to him, "Add one day for me."
M. He said to him, "No."
N. He said to him, "Why?"
O. He said to him, "The term of your son is at hand."
P. For R. Simeon b. Abba said in the name of R. Yohanan, "Terms of office are defined in advance, and one does not overlap the other even to the extent of a hair's breadth."

12.A. He died on a Pentecost that coincided with the Sabbath.
B. The Sanhedrin went in to greet Solomon.
C. He said to them, "Move him from one place to another."
D. They said to him, "And is it not a statement of the Mishnah: **One may anoint and wash the corpse, so long as it is not moved [M. Shab. 23:5]**?"
E. He said to them, "The dogs of father's house are hungry."
F. They said to him, "And is it not a statement of the Mishnah: **They may cut up pumpkins on the Sabbath for an animal and a carcass for dogs [M. Shab. 24:4]**?"
G. What did he then do?
H. He took a spread and spread it over the body, so that the sun should not beat down on him.
I. Some say, he called the eagles and they spread their wings over him, so that the sun should not beat down on him.

13.A. It is said, "A twisted thing cannot be made straight, a lack cannot be made good" (Qoh. 1:15):
B. In this world one who is twisted can be straightened out, and one who is straight can become a crook.
C. But in the world to come, one who is twisted cannot be straightened out, and one who is straight cannot become a crook.

14.A. "a lack cannot be made good" (Qoh. 1:15):
B. There are among the wicked those who were partners with one another in this world.
C. But one of them repented before his death and the other did not.
D. It turns out that this one stands in the company of the righteous, while that one stands in the company of the wicked.
E. The one sees the other and says, "Woe! Is it possible that there is favoritism in this matter? Both of us stole, both of us murdered together. Yet this one stands in the company of the righteous, while I stand in the company of the wicked."
F. And they answer him, saying, "Fool! World-class idiot! You were despicable after you died and lay for three days, and did they not drag you to your grave with ropes? 'The maggot is spread under you, the worms cover you' (Is. 14:11).
G. "But your partner understood this and reverted from that path, while you had the chance to repent and did not do it."
H. He said to them, "Give me a chance to go and repent."
I. They reply to him, saying, "World-class idiot! Don't you know that this world is like the Sabbath, while the world from which you have come is like the eve of the Sabbath? If someone does not prepare on the eve of the Sabbath, what will one eat on the Sabbath?
J. "And furthermore, this world is like the sea, while the world from which you have come is like the dry land. If someone does not prepare on dry land, what is that person going to eat when out at sea?
K. "And furthermore, this world is

like the wilderness, while the world from which you have come is like the cultivated land. If someone does not prepare in the cultivated land, what is that person going to eat when out in the wilderness?"
L. So what does he do?
M. He folds his hands and chomps on his own flesh: "The fool folds his hands together and eats his own flesh" (Qoh. 4:5).
N. And he says, "Let me at least see my partner in all his glory!"
O. They answer and say to him, "World-class idiot! We have been commanded on the authority of the Almighty that the wicked will not stand beside the righteous, nor the righteous by the wicked, the clean with the unclean, nor the unclean with the unclean.
P. "And on what are we commanded? Concerning this gate: 'This is the gate of the Lord. The righteous [alone] shall enter into it' (Ps. 118:20)."
15.A. There is the following story.
B. On the eve of Passover (and some say it was on the eve of the Great Fast [of the day of atonement]), R. Hiyya the Elder and R. Simeon b. Halafta were in session and studying the Torah in the major school house of Tiberias.
C. They heard the noise of the crowd murmuring.
D. One said to the other, "As to these people, what are they doing?"
E. He said to him, "The one who has is buying, the one who doesn't have is going to his master to make him give to him."
F. He said to him, "If so, I too will go to my lord to make him give me."
G. He went out and prayed in the Isis of Tiberias [Rabinowitz p. 46, n. 1: the famous grotto], and he saw a hand holding out a pearl to him.
H. He went and brought it to our master [Judah the patriarch], who said to him, "Where did you get it? It is priceless. Take these three denars and go and do what you have to for the honor of the day, and after the festival, we shall announce the matter in the lost and found, and whatever price we get for it you will get."
I. He took the three denars and went and bought what he needed to buy and went home.
J. Said his wife to him, "Simeon, have you turned into a thief? Your whole estate is not a hundred manehs, and where did you have the money for all these purchases?"
K. He told her the story.
L. She said to him, "What do you want? That your canopy should be lacking by one pearl less than that of your fellow in the world to come?"
M. He said to her, "What shall we do?"
N. She said to him, "Go and return what you have purchased to the shopkeepers and the money to its owner and the pearl to its owner."
O. When our master heard about this, he was upset. He sent and summoned her.
P. He said to her, "All this suffering you have brought upon this righteous man!"
Q. She said to him, "Do you want his canopy should be lacking by one pearl less than yours in the world to come?"
R. He said to her, "And if it does lack, can't we make it up?"
S. She said to him, "My lord, in this world we have the merit of seeing your face. But has not R. Simeon b. Laqish said, 'Every righteous man has his own chamber'?"

T. And he conceded her point.
U. [Continuing S:] "'And not only so, but it is the way of the beings of the upper world to give, but it is not their way to take back.'"
V. [Reverting to T:] [Rabinowitz: "Nevertheless the pearl was returned"] and this latter miracle was greater than the former one.
W. When [Simeon] took it, his hand was below, but when he gave it back, his hand was on top,
X. like a man who lends to his fellow. [Rabinowitz, p. 47, n. 1: When R. Simeon took the pearl, it was as one receiving a gift, but when he returned it, it was as one giving a gift, in that the hand which received it was below his.]

Let us now review the whole. The theme that becoming an Israelite involves special obligations and liabilities is continued at Nos. 1, 2. No. 3 completes the exposition of what is involved at 3.B. I cannot quite grasp 3.C. Rabinowitz translates, "... acquire in this world, for in the world to come, 'death shall part you and me.'" This seems to bear the message that whatever good one can do must be done in this world. That point is then illustrated in the series of stories from No. 4 to the end. But the stories wander far from the point at hand, in no way respond unanimously to the concerns of that point, and in fact are worked out one by one for purposes that can be discerned wholly within the limits of the successive tales. But I cannot conceive of some other document, other than a biographical one, in which stories of this kind will have served a redactional purpose we can identify with the program of the canonical redaction now in hand. These are freestanding stories; they serve indifferently in any context, but have been worked out without a documentary stimulus.

JACOB NEUSNER
Bard College

Ruth Rabbah, Theology of

Ruth Rabbah sets forth a statement of Rabbinic theology that is necessary but insufficient to the theological structure of that Judaism viewed whole. It recapitulates familiar theological propositions, selecting among the encompassing, established repertoire only those relevant to the particular book of Scripture that defines the focus of the document. These category-formations are gentiles and Israel, on the one side, Israel in the here and now and at the end of days, on the other. These express the principal point the compilers wished to make in connection with the book of Ruth. There are three. First, to be, or to become, (an) Israel(ite), a person, whether of Israel by birth or by choice, situates himself under the wings of God's Presence. What defines Israel, hence also an Israelite by birth, is what defines an Israelite by choice, and that is, acceptance of the Torah and God's dominion through its commandments.

A corollary is, the nations are estranged from God by reason of their idolatry; they rejected the Torah. Because of its acceptance of the Torah, Israel alone realizes God's rule and purpose in creation. That is why Israel bears the burden of gentile contempt and hatred, e.g., for performing the rite of circumcision, separating itself from idolaters, and the like. On God's initiative, moreover, Israel is subjugated to gentile rule. That is by reason of its own sinfulness; in that way God uses the gentiles to punish Israel. But in the end of days, Israel, having suffered in this world, will get its portion in the world to come, and the gentiles, having prospered in this world, will suffer for their rebellion against God. Then the messiah will herald the end of days and the advent of the world to come. These are the principal propositions that animate the exposition of the narrative of the book of Ruth undertaken by Ruth Rabbah.

But not one of them is particular to that exegetical exercise. In fact, what we find before us is nothing more than a recapitulation of fundamental theological doctrines that originate in Scripture and are widely represented, in the Rabbinic recapitulation, in the entire range of the Rabbinic documents, particularly the midrash-compilations. The upshot is, the issues of Ruth Rabbah represent a selection among the larger, ubiquitous program of theology that animates all of the documents.

But then the question arises: why these particular items within the larger theological repertoire of Rabbinic Judaism in the midrash-compilations? The answer is, these are the questions—conversion from gentile to Israelite, the Moabite origins of the messiah, the power of the Torah to transform—that the sages quite reasonably find blatant in the book of Ruth itself. Ruth Rabbah simply retells in a dense, deep way, in the context of the Torah viewed whole, the story of Ruth the Moabite and her entry into Israel on terms defined by the Torah. That explains the theological foci of Ruth Rabbah. The issue of Israel and the nations is primary to the scriptural narrative, and the theme of the power of the Torah to naturalize people into God's dominion is natural to the Rabbinic reading of any story in which gentiles figure. The occasion is the figure of the convert, the outsider as not only gentile but a woman as well. But it is Scripture that defines the focus governing in Ruth Rabbah. For Scripture explicitly identifies the Moabite woman as the progenitor of the Messiah through the house of David. No wonder then that the issues of Israel and the gentiles, on the one side, and the end of days, on the other, predominate. These are the issues upon which the book of Ruth focuses. Why find surprising that Ruth Rabbah does the same? Ruth Rabbah then takes its assignment from the book of Ruth, and the book of Ruth as read by Ruth Rabbah situates itself within that larger theological structure yielded by Scripture to the Rabbinic sages.

That explains why the theological statements of Ruth Rabbah do not, on their own, constitute a complete and encompassing theological system. They deal with one important component of a system—the matter of Israel and the gentiles, the power of the Torah to transform a gentile into an Israelite, the provenience of the Messiah in that same context, as I just said. But they do not address other, equally important ones, e.g., theodicy, theology of history, or cosmology, to name three, the first urgent in Lamentations Rabbati, the second there and in Leviticus Rabbah, the third critical to Genesis Rabbah. These components of the Rabbinic theology, treated in other documents, surface here only marginally. So the Rabbinic theology seen whole takes up and systematically addresses all of these matters within a single cogent logic. Indeed, these chapters of theological thought and their companions represent necessary systemic components for the mythic monotheism set forth by Scripture. And, as a matter of fact, they are elaborately dealt with in other midrash-compilations. But they are given slight attention, or entirely ignored, here. It follows that, to Rabbinic theology as system and structure, Ruth Rabbah is necessary but not sufficient. Its critical contribution to the larger Rabbinic theology must find for itself its logical place within that sheltering system and structure.

Now we know why two facts characterize the theological corpus that is set forth in the document.

First, Ruth Rabbah does not form a complete systematic theological statement *on its own*.

Second, Ruth Rabbah does make a coherent statement *of its own*. What sages wished to say here they could say best, perhaps only, in response to the book of Ruth.

At issue is how the gentile becomes Israel, how the gentile woman enters the critical drama to be played out at the end of days. And the answer in both cases is, through the Torah, by acceptance of its disciplines and authority, the gentile becomes Israel. In the Torah, in her commendable realization of its requirements, the Moabite woman finds her place at the very height of Israelite aspiration. Indeed, a key point of emphasis, which my selection does not highlight, is on a very specific matter of Torah-learning. The key to the entire story—the possibility of a Moabite woman's marrying an Israelite man and producing legitimate offspring with him—is located in the Torah-learning required to know that while the Moabite male cannot enter the community of Israel, the Moabite female can do so. Boaz knew that, others did not. That is the point of the comment on the following verse: "And Boaz went up to the gate and sat down there; and behold, the next of kin, of whom Boaz had spoken, came by. So Boaz said, 'Turn aside, friend, sit down:'"

Ruth Rabbah LXVIII:i
3.A. [Supply: "So Boaz said, 'Turn aside, friend, sit down here.' And he turned aside and sat down":]
B. [As to the name Peloni-Almoni,] R. Samuel b. R. Nahman said, "He was dumb as to words of the Torah. [For the word for dumb and the name Almoni share the same consonants.]"
C. "[The reason I think so is as follows:] He thought, 'The ancients [Mahlon and Chilion] died only because they took them as wives. Shall I go and take her as a wife? God forbid that I take her for a wife! I am not going to disqualify my seed, I will not disqualify my children.'
D. "But he did not know that the law had been innovated: 'A male Ammonite' but not a female Ammonite,' 'a male Moabite' but not a female Moabite' [is subject to prohibition. Hence it was now legal to marry Ruth.]"

The important point is tangential in context but critical theologically: the next of kin, who had a prior claim on Ruth, did not know the law of the Torah as properly interpreted by the rabbis, so he lost out; but Boaz was a master of the Torah and did know the rule. So he had the honor of becoming the ancestor, along with Ruth, of the Davidic household and hence the Messiah. With the recognition of the centrality of the Torah, we come to our task. It is to identify the particular passages of Ruth Rabbah that set forth theological generalizations, articulating them and even amassing evidence in their behalf.

Propositions Shared among Pesiqta deRab Kahana, Genesis Rabbah, Song of Songs Rabbah, Leviticus Rabbah, Lamentations Rabbati, and Ruth Rabbah

Out of the repertoire of propositions common to the Midrash-compilations, Ruth Rabbah focuses, as we realize, on the two that the book of Ruth identifies as critical: the gentile in relationship to Israel (thus, also the nations and Israel, the nations and God), and the matter of the messiah. The point that the document repeatedly registers is, the Torah defines the perspective on all themes, explaining the relationship of the gentile to God, the fate of Israel in this world, and the standing of the messiah. Gentiles reject the Torah and so alienate themselves from God, Israel's fate is determined by its adherence to God's commandments, and the messiah will be a master of the Torah and embodiment of its teachings.

1. God and Man, God and Israel: The issue of the book of Ruth is how the gentile becomes an Israelite, meaning, how the gentile enters God's domain. That is a question that arises from the premise that Israel and gentiles are two distinct genera of humanity, not interchangeable. In the present context, it is further assumed that God intervenes in the relationships between the two genera, that he has a stake in the matter. God is estranged from gentiles and devoted to Israel, meaning, those who accept his dominion. That is what is encompassed in the category-formation, God and man, God and Israel, that is, the opposed, parallel relationships.

On the foundation of the stated premises, Ruth Rabbah constructs its doctrine, entirely familiar within the midrash-compilations of Rabbinic Judaism. Why should there be estrangement between God and the gentiles to begin with? It is not by reason of favoritism or prejudice, and it is not irrational or unfair or unjust. Indeed, the same rule of justice pertains to Israel and the nations. But there is a difference: Israel inherits the world to come, where it receives its reward, having suffered in this age for its sins. God treats the nations fairly and gives them their reward in this world, only to exact punishment in the world to come (III:i.2-3). So there is no understanding the fundamental theology of God and the nations, God and Israel, without invoking the principle of the resurrection of the dead, life after death, and the world to come.

But for theological reasons but in secular terms, Israel's condition in this world is unenviable; the gentiles rule, and they enjoy this world's benefits, while subjugating Israel. Ruth Rabbah accommodates these anomalies in a way that is quite familiar. It is, through the gentiles God afflicts Israel in this world, in that way exacting punishment from them now, while in the world to come, he will give them the full reward that is coming to them. That is why God torments the Israelites with famine in this world (III:i.4). That explains why the gentiles are able now to subjugate Israel. The nations fear Israel only by reason of God's paying attention to them. When Israel sinned and God ceased to take note of them in some small measure, the nations came and made war against Israel. To correct the situation, God could not exterminate them or bring them back to Egypt or trade them for some other nations. But God punished Israel by famine, leading them to repent (III:ii.1). The upshot is simple. By reason of idolatry, gentiles die for eternity; by reason of accepting God's dominion in the Torah, Israel enjoys the promise, the possibility, of triumph over the grave: resurrection, standing in judgment, the world to come, in sequence.

2. God and the Nations, Israel and the Nations: The issue repeats itself in a subset of the foregoing. It is readily framed. Do the gentiles then not have a share in the Creator of the world and all humanity? No, they have every right to a share, but they have lost their share. They have given up their share by their own deeds. God is God of all the nations but has assigned his name only to his people, Israel (I:i.8). This was because of Israel's accepting the Torah at Sinai. Esau/Rome estranged himself from God by not carrying out the rite of circumcision and other religious obligations. God gave him his reward in this world, but will exact punishment in the world to come. So too the nations of the world afflict Israel with harsh decrees. God treats them fairly and gives them their reward in this world, only to exact punishment in the world to come (III:i.2-3). The parallel relations between God and the nations, on the one side, and Israel and the nations on the other, recapitulate the relations between God and man, God and Israel.

3. Israel's encounter with God through the Torah: Then the centerpiece, the crux of matters, emerges in the Torah. Israel is Israel by reason of accepting the Torah, and the gentiles are what they are because they rejected, and reject, it. That conviction is critical to the exposition of the book of Ruth, since it represents the final solution to the gentile-problem: how the gentile overcomes his alienation from God and becomes Israel. His condition is not beyond remediation but readily corrected. And when the gentile becomes Israel, the book of Ruth underscores, then he or she joins Israel without differentiation as to origin or status, even becoming the ancestor of the messiah, that is, the figure who inaugurates the very resurrection of the dead that is Israel's coming glory.

Then what, specifically, is at stake in "being Israel"? The negative side is, restraint, avoidance of gentile ways: idolatry and its occasions. The positive aspect is, adherence to God's commandments, set forth in the Torah, God's self-manifestation. To be Israel therefore is to avoid theaters and circuses, to live in a house that bears a mezuzah, to be subject to penalties and admonitions against sinning and carry out other religious duties. It is also to go, instead of temples and circuses, to God's dwelling at the tent of meeting, Gilgal, Shilo, Nob, Gibeon, and Jerusalem, to make offerings and nullify idols, and to be responsible for one's actions (XX:I.3-4). The Israelite has no other Gods but God, glorifies God, and emulates the righteous (XXXIV:i.1). To be Israel is not an easy thing. Ruth is warned by Naomi of what is required and what is at stake. To be Israel means to be subject to the four modes of the death penalty for the specified sins, to carry out religious duties and acts of righteousness (XXI:i.1-3).

Then is Israel superior to gentiles? Not at all. Israel is no different from the nations in practicing idolatry, fornication, bloodshed, and being expelled from the Garden of Eden and sent down to Gehenna. But Israel became God's people when God spoke with Israel at Sinai. It was an act of righteousness that Israel performed in accepting the Torah. God speaks to Israel about this age and the world to come (I:i.2-3, 5). How does the Torah link God to man? It is the medium by which God's presence is brought to rest in the world. If there are no disciples of sages, there will be no sages, then no elders, then no prophets, then God will not bring his presence to rest in the world; if no Torah there are no synagogues and schools, and if no synagogues and schools, then God will not bring his presence to rest in the world (Gen. Rabbah XLII:III.1-6 = Lev. Rabbah XI:VII = Ruth Rabbah IV:ii.2). When Israel was to be redeemed from Egypt, they had in hand no religious deeds to carry out so that they would be saved, but God gave them the duties of the Passover offering and circumcision (LIX:i.4).

4. Divine Justice and Mercy: The book of Ruth, and its Rabbinic exposition, focus, then, on a theology of Israel and the gentiles. To that matter, some issues, integral to the system as a whole, prove tangential. And the matter of divine justice and mercy is one of these. The merciful Lord does not do injury to human beings first. First he exacts a penalty from property, aiming at the sinner's repentance (IX:I.1-2). The massive issues of divine justice and mercy hardly preoccupy the exegetes of the book of Ruth. They accept as their premise the framework defined by God's justice and mercy, as we see in their theory of Israel, God, and their respective relations with the gentiles. But they do not dwell on the matter.

5. God's Judgment, Israel's Repentance and Atonement; God's Remorse, Israel's Consolation: Divine justice leads to a pattern of punishment for sin, but reconciliation in response to repentance. This theme, paramount in Lamentations Rabbati, forms yet another subordinated topic in the present exposition of Rabbinic theology through exegesis of the selected scriptural narrative. An account of how the gentile accepts the Torah and becomes Israel is ill-served by stress on Israel's sin-fullness and suffering, repentance and atonement—themes that pertain but in context are incongruous, irrelevant, really. It is not surprising that the points that register are routine. Religious duties and acts of righteousness should be done in this world, in the world to come after death one cannot repent (XXI:i.4). When Israel worships idols, God deprives them of the Holy Spirit. When they do not repent, they suffer the consequences

(II:i.2, 3, 7). Famine comes about because Israel deceives God (I:ii.6). These data are routine and in the construction at hand systemically inert.

6. Restoration; God Will Bring the End through the Royal Messiah at a Time of His Own Choosing, and His Hand Is Not to Be Forced: By contrast with the routine presentation of the proposition that God is just and punishes sin, but Israel can repent and atone, the messiah-theme is critical. That is both because the book of Ruth focuses upon it at its climax, and because the logic of the Rabbinic theological system requires the remission and resolution that only eschatology accords to the dialectics of divine justice and omnipotence. The choice of the compilers of Ruth Rabbah to link the two themes is compelled by the scriptural book under study. For the book of Ruth is explicit in linking the exposition of the gentile become Israelite to the messiah-theme. Ruth, outsider both as woman and as Moabite, through her act of accepting the Torah becomes the ancestor of the messiah. Hence the messiah-theme is integral, and what is before us is the one Rabbinic document that systematically and explicitly links the great themes of Torah and messiah.

To the Rabbinic readers of the book of Ruth, the proposition that Israel is Israel by reason of the Torah, gentiles are gentiles by reason of their rejection thereof, is self-evident. They find it everywhere, as we already have seen, but in particular at the critical turning, "Your people shall be my people...." We recall the exposition of the verse, Ruth 1:16: "But Ruth said, 'Entreat me not to leave you or to return from following you; for where you go I will go, and where you lodge I will lodge; your people shall be my people, and your God my God...'"

Ruth Rabbah XX:i.3–4
3.A. When Naomi heard her say this, she began laying out for her the laws that govern proselytes.
B. She said to her, "My daughter, it is not the way of Israelite women to go to theaters and circuses put on by idolaters."
C. She said to her, "Where you go I will go."
D. She said to her, "My daughter, it is not the way of Israelite women to live in a house that lacks a *mezuzah*."
E. She said to her, "Where you lodge I will lodge."
F. "... your people shall be my people:"
G. This refers to the penalties and admonitions against sinning.
H. "... and your God my God:"
I. This refers to the other religious duties.
4.A. Another interpretation of the statement, "for where you go I will go:"
B. to the tent of meeting, Gilgal, Shiloh, Nob, Gibeon, and the eternal house.
C. "... and where you lodge I will lodge:"
D. "I shall spend the night concerned about the offerings."
E. "... your people shall be my people:"
F. "so nullifying my idol."
G. "... and your God my God:"
H. "to pay a full recompense for my action."

I find here the adumbration of the entire Rabbinic theology, with the proviso that the passage is read in the context of the centrality of the Torah stated elsewhere in Ruth Rabbah. Here the two themes—Israel is Israel by reason of the laws of the Torah, gentiles are what they are by reason of their rejecting those laws, and Israel is responsible for its deeds but therefore ends up in God's house—come together at the emotional climax of the narrative: the loyalty of the daughter-in-law to her mother-in-law, the pure love between the women then embodies the love of Israel for God, conveyed through its loyalty to the Torah, even acceptance of its penalties.

All the rest is comprised by details. But these bear heavy meaning. The messiah-doctrine of Rabbinic Judaism encompasses the pattern of the messiah's own suffering. The messiah lives out the fate of Israel. Israel got the Land, lost the Land, suffered, and was, and again would be, restored to the Land. So too the messiah, embodied by David, came to the throne, lost the throne, suffered, but was restored to the throne. The exposition of Ruth's coming to Boaz embodies the pattern. When Ruth came to Boaz, she came to the throne of David, his sufferings when he lost the throne, but his restoration to the throne, and would prosper in the days of the messiah and in the age to come. She came to Solomon, to the throne, to the loss of the throne, and to the restoration to the throne, so that he would prosper in the days of the messiah and in the age to come. She came to the throne of Hezekiah, who suffered but was restored to the throne, and who would prosper in this world, in the days of the messiah, and in the world to come, so too Manasseh, so too to the throne of the messiah, who would suffer and lose the throne but who would be restored to the throne, and who was comparable to Moses (XL:i.1–5).

The Torah figures as a matter of course. The messiah will be a master of the Torah and what he has to say will be measured against the criterion of the Torah. That is shown by the figure of David. David, the model of the messiah, was a master of Scripture, Mishnah, the give and take of Talmud-study, able to reason deductively, enlightened in the law, and the like; the Messiah then is measured by the criterion of the Torah (XXVII:i.2–4).

The Moabite woman who would be the ancestress of David, thence the messiah, exhibited exceptional modesty and discretion. So too did David, although he descended from a Moabite woman, exhibit distinguishing qualities of piety. It was the piety of Ruth that was carried forward (XXXI:i.2–3).

It is on the merit of "and he measured out six measures of barley and laid it upon her" that six righteous persons came forth from him, and each one of them had six virtues. These are David, Hezekiah, Josiah, Hananiah, Mishael, Azariah, Daniel, and the royal messiah (LXIV:i.4). A pattern governs moments of Israelite redemption, e.g., from Egypt, from Sihon and Og, from the thirty-one kings, and in connection with Ruth's meeting with her mother-in-law Naomi (LXVI:i.1). The redemption of Israel is subject to God's oversight at every detail. God is responsible for the coincidences in the story of Ruth and Boaz (LXVIII:i.1). In these ways, the Rabbinic exegetes of the book of Ruth transform the narrative into theological doctrine, while preserving the specificity and particularity of the narrative.

7. The End of Days: Paradoxically, while the messiah-theme proves central to our document, the compilation at no point offers any discussion of the character of the end of days, what happens when the messiah comes, the quality of the judgment, or the life in the world to come. On these themes, which would seem to be integral to the great theological affirmations of Torah and messiah, the compilation falls silent. So the eschatological principles are left without detailed, concrete exposition. The purpose of the compilation is to make its point about the link of Torah and status as Israel, extending to the link of Torah and messiah. By that point, an exposition of the details of the end of days is not required. The midrash-compilations work by a rule of intellectual economy. What is necessary to expound the proposition(s) they wish to register is going to be spelled out, what is not required will not be included.

8. Creation Contains within Itself Signals of What Would Happen in Future History: Here is another theme that is critical to the Rabbinic theological structure and system but not relevant to the program of Ruth Rabbah.

9. **The Merit that Accrues in One Generation to the Benefit of Another Generation:** The narrative of Ruth imputes to the house of David the merit attained by Ruth in her loyalty to Naomi and her finding shelter under the wings of God's presence, her joining Israel. So the conception that the generations are linked, that the virtue of the ancestors endows their descendants with unearned grace—that conception is central both in the book of Ruth and in the exposition thereof in Ruth Rabbah. The omission of the theme of *Zekhut* is only formal. The explicit linkage of Ruth to the house of David requires the conception of *Zekhut* as the currency of the heritage left by one generation to another. Why the language of accrued *Zekhut* does not occur I do not know.

10. **The Righteous Receive their Reward Later On:** God inflicts punishment in this world, but rewards the righteous in the world to come (XXV:i.5). This point is fully exposed in the theology of the gentiles and Israel, the one getting their reward in this world and punishment in the world to come, the other treated in the opposite way.

11. **Commandments are the Marks of Israel's Distinction before God:** Here, as with *Zekhut*, the conception that keeping the commandments marks Israel as God's friends, and not keeping them estranges the nations from God, is fully articulated in another setting. We recall that the fundamental theology of God, Israel, and the gentiles, in their parallel relationships, invokes the sanctifying power of the commandments. I find no composition in which on their own terms, not in relationship to other issues altogether, the commandments are expounded in a systematic way.

Why This, Not That: The Hermeneutics that Generates the Exegesis and Its Category-Formations

We have now identified five theological category-formations, fully exposed in other midrash-compilations, that play no critical role in the exposition of the book of Ruth by Ruth Rabbah: the end of days, creation and future history, the doctrine of *Zekhut*, the notion that the righteous receive their just reward in the world to come, and the conception that the commandments distinguish Israel from the nations before God. All of these notions are required by the system that is set forth in Ruth Rabbah, but none receives systematic exposition, as I said. They show in concrete terms why it is important to position Ruth Rabbah as I did at the outset. That is, I explained how Rabbinic theology plays its role in Ruth Rabbah, but how Ruth Rabbah does not set forth an autonomous theological system of its own. In all five instances we are amply justified in invoking as necessary to Ruth Rabbah theological principles that either do not occur in our document, or if they do occur, do not receive ample exposition. Not only so, but item by item, I have shown where and how Ruth Rabbah for its own purposes positions these necessary conceptions.

And that brings us to a clear view of what Ruth Rabbah contributes to the theology of Rabbinic Judaism. It has taken the narrative of the book of Ruth, on how a gentile becomes an Israelite, and infused that narrative with the theme of the Torah as the definition of what it means to be Israel. That is to say, the framers of Ruth Rabbah have read the book of Ruth as part of the Torah. That justifies their reading the whole of the Torah into the parts of the book of Ruth, as they do into the parts of all other components of that Torah. With the whole in hand, they conduct their engagement with each of the parts, finding the context for their selected text. They hermeneutical task—reading the parts in the context of the whole—then is carried out through the exegesis laid out before us. The result, in detail, is to tell in a coherent and consistent way the story of how the (whole) Torah accounts for the condition of Israel and the nations and explains the relationships of all things to the one, unique God self-revealed in the Torah.

Propositions Particular to Ruth Rabbah

The only proposition both important in, and particular to, Ruth Rabbah is that proselytes are precious to God. Once they decide to convert, they are equivalent to Israelites (XXII:i.1). Converting to Judaism is "to take shelter under the wings of the Presence of God," and marks a person as one who performs deeds of righteousness and grace. Those who do deeds of righteousness and grace take shelter not in the shadow of the dawn, nor in the shadow of the wings of the earth, not in the shadow of the wings of the sun, nor in the shadow of the wings of the hayyot, nor in the shadow of the wings of the cherubim or the seraphim, but only under the shadow of the one at whose word the world was created (XXXVIII:i.2). The convert to Israel is washed of the filth of idolatry and anointed in the religious deeds and acts of righteousness that are required of an Israelite (LII:i.1).

But are these propositions particular to Ruth Rabbah? The venue defined by the story before us requires an affirmative answer. But the logic of the theological system of Rabbinic Judaism demands a negative answer. If the Israelite is Israelite by reason of the Torah, then, simple logic insists, the Torah works its sanctification on any human being equally. It is what a person affirms and accepts and accomplishes that marks the person as Israel: affirming the Torah, accepting the dominion of God, accomplishing deeds that fulfill the law of the Torah—these signify that the individual is Israelite and belongs to that unique community, Israel. And since that is the fact, what basis is there for making distinctions within Israel or among Israelites? There is no such basis, the very definition of what is Israel and what are the nations of the world leaves no room for such a distinction. A person is either Israel or not, and within Israel are (from this perspective) no gradations or distinctions. True, the halakhah, in line with Scripture, recognizes Israel's castes, priests, Levites, Israelites, and the rest. But the same halakhic system recognizes the possibility that the convert's descendant may become High Priest—and the book of Ruth underscores the same conception in connection with the messiah. In that setting, the book of Ruth at its most particular turns out to form a generic work of Torah-exposition, pure and simple.

The inductively-framed category-formations cohere in an entirely familiar pattern. God relates to man through the Torah, which distinguishes humanity into two parts: Israel, accepting God's rule, and the nations, rejecting that rule. Israel meets God through the Torah. What Israel knows about God is that he is just and merciful. He is just, so he punishes sin, which is rebellion, and he is merciful, so he accepts the repentant sinner. In the end of days God will send a messiah. The particular statements, tied to specific verses, coalesce into the specified category-formations, which themselves cohere in a simple, systematic statement. And, for reasons amply spelled out in the opening unit of this chapter, that statement matches the encompassing structure and system that the Rabbinic documents yield when they are read within the logic of mythic monotheism.

What Does Ruth Rabbah Contribute?

Ruth Rabbah contributes the recapitulation of the message of the book of Ruth—its recapitulation and its "rabbinization." By "rabbinization" is meant, the introduction of the generative myths and symbols particular to Rabbinic Judaism. Working forward from the book of Ruth permits us to see how the Rabbinic compilers have imposed upon the narrative the givens of their structure and system. Take for example the symbolic centrality of Torah: its study and performance of its commandments. The book of Ruth knows nothing of the priority of the Torah as the formulation of Israel's being. For example, it is explicit in linking Ruth to her descendant, David, with a clear statement that she and Boaz are the ancestors of the Messiah through the house of David. But then David is not represented as the master of the Torah that, for Judaism, defines what matters about him and his Messianic descendant. Again, the book of Ruth does not articulate concern about the prohibition of marriage to a Moabite, though one may claim that the very siting of Ruth in Moab suffices to raise the issue. But for the Rabbinic sages, Ruth's Moabite affiliation forms one of the keys to the entire transaction, thus Boaz had to have mastered the Torah to know the correct exegesis of the prohibition of Moab (males, not females).

What the compilers of Ruth Rabbah have done is not impose the Torah—the perspective upon the written Torah read whole that defines the Rabbinic paradigm and its foci—upon the book of Ruth but discover the context, in the entirety of the Torah, for the book of Ruth. They read the book of Ruth in that broader context that is defined by the result of seeing Scripture whole and complete. Only when the entirety of the received Scripture is deemed a coherent whole does the concept of "the Torah" encompass all of the scriptural books. Only then does that whole, "the Torah," exceed the sum of the parts. Then the whole, the Torah, with its commandments and its power of regeneration and reconstruction, finds for each of the parts, the individual books, a distinctive task. Each of the biblical books is then assigned its particular place within the structure of that whole that the Torah read whole yields: the comprehensive theology. The exercise carried out in section I of this chapter in retrospect proves more critical than, at the outset, it appeared to have been.

So were we to limit our estimate of the contribution of Ruth Rabbah to the "rabbinization" of the narrative, we should miss the very heart and soul of the matter. The "Rabbinization" that the compilers of Ruth Rabbah have done takes on its own dimension. What is involved is finding in the book of Ruth those connections that link the book of Ruth to the other components of the Torah. The matrix then is the encompassing theology, the Torah read whole. The context is the theological system and structure that realize that theology, the particular assignment carried out, for the Torah, by the book of Ruth. And the contents are determined by finding in that book the answers to the questions precipitated for the Rabbinic compilers of the document by their theological task. The Rabbinic sages work from the Torah viewed whole to the hermeneutics required for each of its principal parts, and thence to the exegesis guided and shaped by the generative logic of that hermeneutics. "To rabbinize" is to see matters all together and all at once, complete, in proportion and in balance: systemically and systematically. It is to grasp the Torah, not just the components of the Torah one by one: to tell the story not bit by bit but whole and start to finish, as no one before them had done, and as no one after them would again have to do.

JACOB NEUSNER
Bard College

Samaritan Midrash

If midrash can be described as the "act and process of interpretation" of works in the halakhic and aggadic realms,[1] for the sake of dealing with cultural or religious tensions and discontinuity, the Samaritans have a very extensive body of midrash, including such substantial classical texts as the *Tibåt* or *Memar Marqe*[2] and the *Asatir* or legends of the birth of Moses.[3] They also have some later liturgical texts that are midrashic extensions and interpretations of the literature they hold to be truly sacred, the Torah. From the earliest setting down of their literature, successive generations of Samaritan scholars "have bent all their skills and learning to the development and enrichment of a textual exegesis which they think will give a firm basis to the Samaritan way of life."[4] The liturgical midrashim are centered in particular on the life of Moses as in, for example, the fourteenth century offerings of probably the second most important Samaritan writer, Abisha ba'al Hamemerim (d. 1376). In addition there are aggadic midrashim about magical events and pseudo-biblical characters that cross the boundary (if there is such a thing as a clear boundary) between folk-tale and midrash, such as the Samaritan parallel to the apocryphal story of Susannah that appears to have a moral didactic purpose[5] and may have been used in homilies in the synagogue. Further examples of the latter type may yet be found in such collections as the Cairo Geniza.[6] It is likely that because Samaritan theological doctrines and teachings originated in the Torah, they preserved similar traditions to those found in Jewish exegesis and, as parallels with numerous Jewish teachings and midrashim show, they have adopted ideas as their own, whether consciously or unconsciously, sometimes long after the rupture between Samaritans and Jews was finalized.

According to the Samaritan view of sacred history, the Holy Writ, which contains the five books of Moses alone, is not only the fundament of life but also the blueprint in congruence with which creation took place. The Pentateuch is seen to be the source of all inspiration, whether it be liturgical, historical, or halakhic. Given that the text of the Pentateuch does not reveal all its secrets at first glance, there is a need for some means of interpreting it so as to perceive every piece of information it contains to support every phase of Samaritan life and activity. The "tradition" plays a major role in the process of interpretation.[7]

---

[1] See Barry W. Holt, "Midrash," in his *Back to the Sources: Reading the Classic Jewish Texts* (New York, 1984), pp. 177–211.

[2] The best edition is that of Ze'ev Ben-Hayyim, *Tibåt Marqe: A Collection of Samaritan Midrashim* (Jerusalem, 1988). A translation and alternative but eclectic text is that of John Macdonald, *Memar Marqah (The Teaching of Marqah)* (Berlin, 1963).

[3] See M. Gaster, *The Asatir, the Samaritan Book of the Secrets of Moses Together with the Pitron or Samaritan Commentary and the Samaritan Story of the Death of Moses* (London, 1927).

[4] See Gladys Levine Rosen, "The Joseph Cycle (Genesis 37–45) in the Samaritan Arabic Commentary of Meshalma ibn Murjan," Columbia University Ph.D. (1951), p. vi.

[5] The story of the daughter of Amram, the equivalent to the story of Susannah, has been published several times. A convenient but truncated source is Micha Joseph bin Gorion, *Mimekor Yisrael, Classical Jewish Folktales* (Bloomington and London, 1976), vol. 1, pp. 205–206. The full story is to be found in M. Gaster, *Studies and Texts in Folklore, Magic, Medieval Romance, Hebrew Apocrypha and Samaritan Archaeology* (London, 1925–1928), 3 vols.

[6] See, for example, Friederich Niessen, "A Samaritan Discovery," in *Genizah Fragments: The Newsletter of Cambridge University's Taylor-Schechter Genizah Research Unit 40* (2000), p. 2. The item discusses T-S NS 188.20, which is a Samaritan folk tale in Judaeo-Arabic.

[7] See the study by Abraham Tal, "Hermeneutics" in A.D. Crown, R. Pummer, and A. Tal, eds. *A Companion to Samaritan Studies* (Tübingen, 1993).

Samaritan exegesis considers the text of the Pentateuch to be a unity, every word of which is indispensable. No repetition is redundant, and no expression is elliptic. Every word and every phrase has its *raison d'être*. What is not explicitly said is necessarily implied. This attitude to Scripture, which is not far from the basic Jewish approach, gave way to a multitude of midrashic interpretations of the text that never developed into a systematic collection of midrashim, arranged in conformity with the sequence of the books of the Pentateuch, as is the case with Jewish midrash. However, the same categories of interpretation and exegesis are found among the Samaritans as they are among the Jews. Midrash is there in abundance as well as P'shat, allegory is present with philosophical speculation. It is the midrashic element that receives preference, and so intense was the concentration on biblical exegesis that books that would not normally be considered as midrashic sources present important examples of the same.

From the internal evidence of the texts of the Samaritan Pentateuch (see below), it is apparent that the first writings of Samaritan exegetical midrash were in or before the period of the Qumran texts. However, there is some external evidence that the development of Samaritan homiletic midrash, of which there is internal evidence in the *Tibåt Marqe* by the fourth century, followed much the same course as among the Jews. In the text of the Samaritan chronicle, the fourteenth century *Kitab al Tarikh* of Abu'l Fath[8] the chronicler speaks of the work of the Samaritan hero, Baba Rabba, in restoring the study of the Torah and its public exposition to the populace. Baba is said to have reopened the Samaritan synagogues, where he and his followers publicly read the Torah to the people, in a manner reminiscent of Ezra.[9] According to the account, the people "multiplied their praises and glorified God with all their might."[10] Baba then searched for and found survivors of persecutions who were skilled in the torah and instructed them to "instruct all Israel—men, women and children—in the law," they were to "maintain the authentic reading of the law," i.e., the strictly Samaritan version, in the synagogue services and "the Blessing," by which is probably meant Deut. 27. The "Blessing" that is the subject of substantial homiletic midrash in the *Tibåt Marqe* is the title of one collection of homilies in book three, and that may be what is intended by Baba as recorded by Abu'l Fath.[11] However one must note the nature of the language of the third section (see below). Baba also chose seven sages whose special role was to interpret the law and guide the people in its reading. They are described as commentators and the choice of seven men in this role suggests some sort of liturgical cycle with a public exposition of Torah at a service.[12] Special notice is drawn to their teaching on the Sabbath. Another of Baba's acts is described as the construction of eight new synagogues, each of which was designed to incorporate a Beit Midrash for the interpretation of the Torah. At these synagogues, the sages were obliged to present themselves at the festivals and new moons. All of these traditions suggest a basis for the homiletic midrashim that are to be seen in the *Tibåt Marqe* of the following century and indicate that there may well have been a collection not unlike the *Pesiqta* cycle, possibly by the fourth century C.E. and certainly well before the thirteenth century C.E.

---

[8] Edited and translated by Paul Lester Stenhouse, *Kitab al-Tarikh of Abu'l Fath* (Sydney, 1985).

[9] It is interesting in this respect to note the introduction in W.G. Braude, *Pesikta Rabbati* (New Haven and London, 1968), p. 1.

[10] *Kitab al-Tarikh*, p. 177.

[11] See Ben Hayyim's edition, section 3, pp. 160ff., and Macdonald's edition pp. 97f.

[12] Idem, n. 795.

Three considerations indicate that the fourth century date is to be preferred for the beginning of the cycle and that the cycle was completed in one relatively early period of literary development, perhaps in the ninth century literary flowering. First, the reader of the *Tibåt Marqe* is vouchsafed no indication of previous authorities, and no names or opinions of earlier sages are offered, unlike the situation in Jewish midrashim. Second, chapter ten of book three, which deals with instructions by Moses to the leaders of the Israelites, is redolent of the appointment of Hukama by Baba Rabba as described by Abu'l Fath, as if the homily were purposely crafted to provide support for Baba Rabba's actions. Third, while the *Tibåt Marqe* enlarges on the traditions of the Pentateuch, giving new information about recorded events, there are no allusions to events outside the world of the Torah, with the possible exception quoted above in relation to Baba Rabba.

Samaritan midrash, like Jewish midrash, begins with the Torah, but whereas Jewish midrash is based on and extends the whole of the Tanakh, Samaritan midrash extends only Torah and, from time to time, the book of Joshua, despite that book's current lack of canonical status. For the Torah, Samaritan midrash begins with an attempt to fill in gaps and harmonize passages seen as being incomplete, whereas, for the Book of Joshua, midrash attempts to amplify his career, perhaps to turn him into a type of Moses, possibly for eschatological or sectarian reasons. Similarly, tales are told about sacred places such as Mount Gerizim (Argerizim/Argarizon)[13] and persons such as Abraham, not to fill in gaps but to justify Samaritan claims about themselves, their sacra, their traditions and religion, in contrast with Jewish traditions and belief.

Samaritan midrashic writing may be said to be found *inside* their Pentateuch version for it is held by contemporary scholars, on the basis of proto-Samaritan versions found among the Dead Sea Scrolls, to be a reworked or rewritten text, "which stands on the unclearly marked border between biblical text and biblical interpretation."[14] The Samaritan Pentateuch has evidently been edited for the purposes of resolving conflicts within the text, harmonizing accounts, and supporting distinctive Samaritan religious claims. The existence of differences between the Samaritan Pentateuch and the Jewish text is common knowledge. Scholars have listed, analyzed, and categorized some six thousand variations. A large number of these are of no material importance, since the Samaritan Pentateuch manuscripts lack scribal uniformity and the majority of the differences are cases of representing or non-representing of vowels. These may be left out of consideration for present purposes.

As Abraham Tal has demonstrated,[15] hermeneutic interpretation is incorporated even within the traditional reading of the Samaritan Pentateuch. For example, in Gen. 3:9 the word *'ayekh* is pronounced *'yka*, meaning *how are you* not *'ayyek* (like the Massoretic reading, *'ayyeka*, i.e., *Where are you*). This avoids the confusing image (which exercised Jewish commentators) of having the almighty God not knowing where Adam is hidden and having to ask him.

Differences other than the orthographic ones between the Samaritan Pentateuch and the Jewish text that reflects the textual status of the Samaritan Pentateuch may relate to religious-historical or literary factors and be of midrashic import.

To this group of variants belong many references to the holiness of Mt. Gerizim, where attempts are made not only to em-

---

[13] On the Samaritan name of the mountain, see Reinhard Pummer, *Early Christian Authors on Samaritans and Samaritanism* (Tübingen, 2002), pp. 423, 424, 429.

[14] See M. Bernstein, "Pentateuchal Interpretation at Qumran," in P. Flint and James VanderKam, eds., *The Dead Sea Scrolls after Fifty Years: A Comprehensive Assessment* (Leiden, 1998–1999), vol. 1, pp. 134–135.

[15] See Crown, et al., *Companion*.

phasize its sanctity, which is one of the main principles of Samaritan belief, as reiterated in their creed, but also to draw attention to Gerizim as the site of the *aqedah* and reduce the possibility of Shechem's being identified with Salem and hence with Jerusalem, and the *aqedah* on Mt. Zion. Since this matter is found both in Samaritan midrashic writing in the *Tibåt Marqe* and within the Pentateuch text itself,[16] the variants from the Jewish text of the Pentateuch must be seen as examples of rewriting having a midrashic purpose. Examples of the emphasis on Gerizim are Exod. 20:14 and Deut. 5:18, where a long passage (taken from Deut. 27:2-7, with slight stylistic alterations) creates a link between the Chosen Mountain and the Decalogue.[17] Thus:

> Deut. 27:4 And when you have passed over the Jordan, you shall set up these stones, concerning which I command you this day, on Mount Ebal, and you shall plaster them with plaster.
> Deut. 27:5 And there you shall build an altar to the Lord your God, an altar of stones; you shall lift up no iron tool upon them.
> Deut. 27:6 You shall build an altar to the Lord your God of unhewn stones; and you shall offer burnt offerings on it to the Lord your God;
> Deut. 27:7 and you shall sacrifice peace offerings, and shall eat there; and you shall rejoice before the Lord your God.

This is paralleled by the removal of any possible reference to Jerusalem, however remote. Thus, in Gen. 33:18 the Samaritan Pentateuch reads *shalom* for the Jewish text's place name, Salem, giving the word an adverbial function: "Jacob arrived safely in the city of Shechem," to avoid the possibility of Salem's being interpreted as a midrashic reference to Jerusalem in connection with Gen. 14:18, where Melchizedek, the king of Salem was a priest of God Most High. Ps 76:3 parallels Zion with Salem: "Salem became his abode; Zion, his den;" Zion is synonymous with both Jerusalem (Is. 2:3, Ps. 147:12) and the Temple Mount (Ps. 2:6, 74:2). That the *aqedah* and the stress on the identification of Mt. Moriah and Mt. Gerizim were issues is clarified by the alignment of Gen. 12:6 and 22:2 with Deut. 11:29-30, through the Samaritan readings (Gen. 22:2) *haMora'ah*, and *Elonei Mora'* (Deut. 11:29-30).[18]

Tal[19] has described other frequently found dissimilarities between the Samaritan and Jewish texts of the Pentateuch as "belonging to the literary realm ... attempts to reach a more complete narrative, that is, a smooth text, free of syntactical or logical failures." Yet, when we find similar statements in Jewish midrashim and in the collection within the *Tibåt Marqe* it is clear that these so-called harmonizations are exegetical midrashim preserved inside the Torah as part of the process of rewriting.

Perhaps the best known harmonization/midrashic comment is the addition in Gen. 4:8, which is defective in the Jewish text and the source of comment in Genesis Rabbah. The Jewish text states "Cain said to Abel his brother. And when they were in the field, Cain rose up against his brother and killed him." Obviously, what Cain said to his brother is missing. The Jewish midrash has much to say on the matter, because the

---

[16] Cf. Isaac Kalimi, "The Affiliation of Abraham and the *Aqedah* with Zion/Gerizim," in *Early Jewish Exegesis and Theological Controversy* (Assen, 2002), pp. 33-58.

[17] I am indebted to unpublished lecture notes of Abraham Tal for these examples.

[18] A.S. Halkin suggests that the change was derived from Jewish tradition as recorded in Gen. Rabbah 55, but there are obvious chronological problems with this suggestion, as there is early evidence of Samaritan usage here. See A.S. Halkin, "Samaritan Polemics against the Jews," in *PAAJR* 7 (1935-1936), pp. 13-59, n. 109.

[19] Unpublished lecture text delivered as scholar in residence, University of Sydney.

incomplete Jewish version leaves open the question of cause and responsibility for Abel's murder, with the possibility of implicating the Almighty. The Samaritan Pentateuch has an additional two words translated "let us go to the field" between the two clauses, which makes it clear that Cain was plotting Abel's death, avoiding the problems of divine implication in a murder that so exercised Simeon bar Yohai and his colleagues.[20]

It becomes clear as one looks for further examples of internal exegetical midrash in the Samaritan Pentateuch that a very important principle in the so-called harmonizing of the scriptures during the rewriting of the text is the creation of a theologically correct text. It is not simply that the Samaritans were anxious to reconcile matter that was presented differently in more than one place in the Pentateuch as is often suggested by scholars; the Samaritan Pentateuch, often, but not always, reconciles texts in a way that makes them ideologically or theologically acceptable to Samaritans. Such harmonizations are exegetical midrashim. A clear example of such an exegetical midrash is the linking of the two accounts of the spies who were sent to report on the land of Canaan, Num. 13 and Deut 1. Num. 13 relates that Moses sent the spies to Canaan in conformity with God's command, and Deut. 1:20ff. indicates that the spies were sent by Moses at the demand of the mutinous community. By copying the passage from Deuteronomy and placing it at the beginning of the narrative in Numbers, the Samaritan Pentateuch underlines the community's guilt and absolves God of any responsibility for the failure of the mission. As Tal observes[21] the Samaritan Pentateuch here clarifies that the spies were not sent at God's initiative: he simply conceded to the people's demand and Moses' consent, and helped them choose the spies to be sent.

Another very important series of harmonizations is the movement of Deut. 5:28–29, 18:18–22, and 5:30–31 to follow Exod. 20:21, apparently to enhance the status of Moses or of a prophet like Moses.[22] Examples of this sort of internal exegetical midrash can be multiplied.

Unlike the Jewish Targumim, the Samaritan Targum, the Aramaic translation of the Samaritan Pentateuch, composed in the third or fourth century C.E. in the Aramaic dialect of the land of Israel, has no midrashic *expansions*, even in its poetical parts. In this respect, the Samaritan Targum underwent very little changes throughout the ages. However, the Targum is an inexhaustible source of midrashic *interpretations*, most of them closely related to the particular Samaritan reading of the Torah. Tal notes the example[23] of the case of the unfaithful woman (Num. 5:12) introduced by the phrase *if any man's wife goes astray*. However, several manuscripts of the Targum utilized a phonetic shift characteristic of Samaritan Hebrew, in order to express disdain towards the sinful women and translated the word *tst^{a}y, will become foolish*. Because of the lack of midrashic expansions, the Targum can be ignored for our purposes.[24]

Another Targum, Abu Sa'id's Arabic translation of the Pentateuch, should also be briefly considered. In the second half of the thirteenth century, the Samaritan community in Egypt had in its possession the revised text of Abu Sa'id b. Abu'l-Hasan b. Abi Sa'id. The task of this thirteenth-century Egyptian scholar was two-fold-revision in order to eliminate Sa'adyanisms in the existing texts, called by him "pure heresy," and the addition of marginal notes. This

---

[20] Gen. Rabbah 22.
[21] Unpublished lecture notes, op. cit.
[22] Cf. Hans G. Kippenberg, *Garizim und Synagogue* (Berlin, 1971), chap. 12.
[23] Tal, "Hermeneutics," in the Crown, *Companion*.

[24] Quoted from Abraham Tal, "Targum," in ibid. Though Tal is undoubtedly correct, his assessment is at gross variance with that of Moses Gaster, *Samaritan Book*, pp. 80–120.

text manifests the Samaritan horror of anthropomorphisms that comes to color later exegesis and results in text changes as well as circumlocutory paraphrase. Physical actions or material attributes associated in the biblical text with God are transferred from the deity to men or angels. Thus the words *Vayered Hashem* in Gen. 11:5 are translated, "An angel of the Lord appeared," and in his comments on his translation, Abu Sa'id noted that the meaning of the expression "the Lord came from Sinai" is that God's glory wrought miracles, "for coming is an attribute of substances, whereas God is distinguished by his freedom from attributes."[25]

The nearest parallel that the Samaritans possess to the Jewish Midrash Rabbah is the *Tibât Marqe*, a collection of midrashim also known, from the eighteenth century onwards, as the *Memar Marqah*. It is generally considered to be the most important original composition of the Samaritans. However, unlike the Midrash Rabbah it does not parallel all the Pentateuch, since the book of Genesis is lacking and there is no evidence that a complete, Samaritan, exegetical midrashic collection on the first book of the Torah was ever extant, though there are traces of homiletic midrashim on Genesis especially relating to the *aqedah*.[26] The composition[27] is attributed to the foremost Samaritan scholar, philosopher, and poet, Marqe, who lived in the third or fourth century C.E., shortly after the Samaritan Pentateuch took its current, more or less fixed form and doubtless was inspired by Jewish midrashic writings. The composition consists of six separate books. The first five contain midrashim on portions of the Pentateuch, especially on Exod. 15 and Deut. 32, as well as expanded narratives of the main events related in the story of the Exodus and the subsequent wanderings in the desert, until Moses' death.

The first book, *The Book of Wonders*, is an enlarged version of the story of the deliverance from the Egyptian slavery, starting with God's revelation to Moses in the wilderness and ending with the crossing of the Red Sea. The prose is interrupted here and there by short rhythmic compositions, probably ancient poetic pieces incorporated into the text at a very early stage, without altering the uniformity of its literary structure. Its language is also uniform and belongs to the period when Aramaic was the Samaritan vernacular. The midrashic style is sometimes exegetical and sometimes homiletic. The exegetical midrashim are short and pithy expansions on verses in the text cited as lemma. Sometimes the same verse is cited repeatedly and each time given a different explanation. For example Exod. 12:1–2 appears in the following format,[28] which takes up some Samaritan eschatological ideas:

The Lord said to Moses and to Aaron, after these wonders that had gone before, *This month shall be for you the beginning of months*, the end of affliction and the beginning of relief.

This month shall be for you the beginning of months, the inauguration of favor and the conclusion of disfavor.

This month shall be for you the beginning of months, the end of punishment and the beginning of rest.

This month shall be for you the beginning of months, the entrance of good and the exit of evil.

This month shall be for you the beginning of months, the gateway to blessings and the end of cursing.

---

[25] Cf. A.S. Halkin, "The Scholia to Numbers and Deuteronomy in the Samaritan Arabic Pentateuch," in *JQR* 34, NS (1943–1944), pp. 41–59, and Rosen, "Joseph Cycle," p. xi.

[26] Cf. Ben-Hayyim, *Marqe*, p.145, Macdonald, *Marqah*, vol. 2, p. 95.

[27] The following note of the *Tibât Marqe* is based on the account in Crown, *Companion*.

[28] After Macdonald, *Marqah*, vol. 2, pp. 30–31.

The second book is less homogeneous than the first.[29] Several portions are written in Aramaic, like the first book, others in the late "Samaritan," i.e., in the hybrid language that developed from the twelfth century onwards, when Aramaic was no longer spoken. Obviously, more than one author was involved in its composition. The subjects treated and the methods of treating them are also very varied. Its main topic, and to some extent a unifying factor, is "The Song of the Sea," the book being a sequel of the preceding one. However, the multitude of inserted portions and their diversity have altered its original form considerably. Obviously, the ancient parts of this book originally formed a single unit with the first book. Later additions caused their separation into several sections. The later additions seem to be the homiletic midrashim of different types, which rarely, if ever, give a verse by verse commentary. One type, known to us from the style of the Passover haggadah, as are virtually all of the themes of book two, is a numerical exposition of events thus:[30]

> *Fourteen times water served all the hosts of the Lord through him (Moses).*
> *The first.* He took some water of the Nile and shed it on the dry land. . . .
> *The second.* He turned the water of the Nile into blood as . . . . . .
> *The third.* The water which became red blood . . . was undrinkable. . . .
> *The fourth.* The blood turned back into water . . . and was swarming with frogs . . .
> Etc.

The proems to some of the midrashim make it clear that these were homilies and the audience is addressed directly with such questions as, "What did God intend when he spoke to him (Abraham) and asked him to sacrifice Isaac?" or statements such as "We will expound now on what God . . .," "A question now arises," "Consider the beginning of the section."

The themes of book two are: 1) God's creation of man and all living creatures, the Torah being man's spirit and the reason why Moses redeemed the children of Jacob from Egypt; 2) The four foundations of the world, earth, air, fire and water take part in the Exodus from Egypt; 3) Moses' dialogues with Pharaoh at the Red Sea, the waters of which do not want to be contaminated by the death of the Egyptians; 4) A comparison between Moses, who leads the Israelites to freedom, and Pharaoh, who leads the Egyptians to annihilation. Then follows a detailed exegesis of the text of the Song of the Sea.

The third book is a midrash on Deut 27:9–27, containing teachings connected with the sins enumerated in that pericope. Its language, similar to that of the following books, is the late Samaritan. Ben-Hayyim draws attention to the fact that the third book is not so much aggadic midrash but halakhic, its purpose apparently being to teach what might and might not be possible within the law, but its style is homiletic. Part of the collection in book three apparently relates to some sort of formal teaching situation for it is almost unified by its introductory word "Question" = *shi'ala* (Samaritan orthography).[31] Other parts of the third book have a proem that suggests a weekly Torah reading leading to a halakhic homily.

The fourth book consists of a collection of homilies on "The Great Song" (Deut. 31:30ff.), which is considered by the learned Samaritans a compendium of the whole Torah and a key, via allusions, to matters that were transmitted orally. Ben Hayyim[32]

---

[29] Ben-Hayyim, *Marqe*, p. 108 (introductory notes).
[30] Cf. Macdonald, *Marqah*, vol. 2, pp. 50–52.
[31] For the spelling of the Samaritan form, see Abraham Tal, *A Dictionary of Samaritan Aramaic* (Leiden, 2000), vol. 2.
[32] *Marqe*, p. 228.

cites the example of the matter of resurrection, in which the Samaritans are said not to have believed but that is described in this section, which even includes a description of the resurrection of sinners as well as the righteous. The composition is a series of midrashim on Deut. 32 directed at arousing the fear of God in the community, encouraging its members to follow the example of ancestors who obeyed his commandments, by the promise of rewards. The midrashim are not presented in the order of verses but through an alphabetic and numeric exegesis. Similar midrashim are found in the halakhic compendium of Abu'l Hassan al-Suri in his *Kitab at-Tabbakh*, but in that case are in verse order.

The fifth book describes the events preceding Moses' death, from the time that he makes known his intention to ascend Mt. Nebo, where he is described as meeting ranks of angels, to the moment that a cave opened and allowed him access, where he died facing Mt. Gerizim. The Israelites delayed Moses' ascent, but God encourages him to hurry, and when he confronts the angelic hosts, all of them honor Moses seven times.

The story of a cave is not uncommon in Samaritan midrashim, and it reappears in several different contexts and is repeated in their chronicles. In the main it tends to be connected with the sacra and the tabernacle, which are swallowed up and hidden when the period of Divine Favor (see below) ends. It may well be that the story told by Josephus (*Antiquities* xviii, 85–89), of the uprising in the time of Pilate, with its background expectation that, in the future, the Mosaic tabernacle would be restored on Mt. Gerizim, is a reflex of the cave account in *Tibåt Marqe*, book five. The midrashim in the fifth book tend to be exegetical in that they are presented in a series of verse-by-verse analyses or section-by-section expositions.

Moses has a special place in Samaritan eschatology, and there are numerous midrashim about him. Though there are reasons to consider that the return of a prophet like Moses as some sort of messianic figure has considerable antiquity in Samaritanism, because of the nature of Pentateuchal references to Moses, the series of midrashim from the time of Marqah seems to be without the messianic overtones that appear in later midrashim. Moses explains to the Israelites that he had seen God face to face, twice on Mt. Sinai, and the third time he would see him on Mt. Nebo, but this time he would not come back. This series of midrashim perhaps lays the background for the Joshua-midrashim, as they conclude with praises of Joshua and the Torah.

The sixth book, "On the twenty two letters" of the alphabet, differs completely from the remainder of the collection of midrashim. It neither expands on the text of the Torah in verse-by-verse or passage-by-passage exegesis, nor is it a homiletical exposition of the Torah. Its purpose is to expound the secrets of the twenty-two letters of the alphabet that are the foundation of the words of the Torah. Ben Hayyim thus describes it as "letter midrash."[33] The book is in two sections: 1) a discourse on the Creation that takes up about one third of the book and has signs of oral teaching, and 2) a dialogue between Moses and the letters that has some traditional signs of preaching, such as the introductory comments "A question now," "Where is there . . . ?" "Why is . . . ?" As handed down to us, only twelve letters are preserved in the conversation, seven in one manuscript and five in another. It is highly probable that a part of this composition was lost since the end of the work indicates that all the letters were represented. Tal[34] indicates that the book deals with the role of the letters in the history and life of the Children of Israel, and with their spiritual meaning but there is an

---

[33] *Marqe*, p. 338.

[34] *Tibat Marqe*, in Crown, *Companion*.

emphasis throughout on the status of Moses: several of the rhetorical questions which mark the dialogue are aimed at a glorification of Moses and mark him out as different from all other men.

Two substantial works that focus principally on Moses are the *Molad Moshe* and the *Asatir*. Both are essentially works of aggadic midrash about Moses and other patriarchs. Just as many Jewish aggadic midrashim enhanced the moral greatness and wisdom of spiritual heroes,[35] so the Samaritan aggadic midrashim did the same: but of all the spiritual heroes, Moses was the greatest, with a very special place in Samaritan eschatology, as is reflected as early as the Gospels of John (John 4)[36] and Stephen in the New Testament.[37] Despite the debate about the antiquity of the belief that Moses was to return as a restorer, Taheb, the matter is surely settled by Origen's statement in *C. Celsum*, 1.57 that "Dositheos the Samaritan also wanted to persuade the Samaritans that he was the Christ prophesied by Moses,"[38] almost assuredly a reference to John 4:19, 25.

Moses is the prophet *par excellence*, in Samaritanism.[39] His position is expressed by the uniquely Samaritan formula "let us believe in him (God) and in Moses, his prophet," found in the ancient liturgical work, the *Defter*. This tenet of the creed has no parallel in Rabbinic Judaism. Moses is practically (except for references in Gen. 20:7 to Abraham and Exod. 7:1 to Aaron) the only acknowledged prophet. The picture of Moses as it appears in Samaritan literature is usually midrashic extension and exaggeration of what is related of Moses in the Pentateuch texts. Moses was the Standing One, who stood by God, and was exalted above the whole human race. Moses is seen to be the possessor of special powers and is capable of doing mighty works otherwise reserved for God. In this context, we are reminded that it was for Moses' sake that God appeared and brought forth wonders. The sayings about Moses presuppose the expectation of the coming of the one like Moses according to the eschatological interpretation of Deut. 18:15, 18, which had been widespread since the second century B.C.E.

The unique position of Moses in Samaritanism led to the embellishment of some episodes of his life, such as his birth and death, with aggadic elements. These may occur either on their own in such works as the *Molad Moshe* or in conjunction with other midrashim, such as are found in the *Asatir*.

Once claimed to be the oldest Samaritan chronicle known to us is the *Sefer haAsatir*, a name allegedly invented by Moses Gaster (but almost certainly the work was known by this name a century before his day)[40] for what is not really a chronicle. The name may well derive from the root *str*, (Deut. 31:18), implying that the collection was of hidden traditions about the heroes of the Pentateuch, or of Moses, though no secrets are treated, or even mentioned. In other words it is a collection of aggadic midrashim covering the whole of the Pentateuch, on the lives of the Patriarchs, including and especially Moses. It is not dissimilar in style

---

[35] See M. Gaster, *Ma'aseh Book* (Philadelphia, reprint: 1981), introduction.

[36] See M. de Jonge, "Jewish Expectations about the 'Messiah' according to the Fourth Gospel," in *New Testament Studies* 19 (1973), pp. 246–270.

[37] Cf., M.H. Scharlemann, *Stephen, A Singular Saint* (Rome, 1968).

[38] Pummer's translation, *Early Christian Authors*, p. 55.

[39] Excellent statements of Moses' position in Samaritanism are found in F. Dexinger, "Moses." in Crown, *Companion*, and John Macdonald, *Theology of the Samaritans* (London, 1964), chap. 5.

[40] Moses Gaster, *The Asatir*. J. Mills, *Three Months' Residence at Nablus* (London, 1864), p. 318, calls the work the *Kitab es Sateer*. In his introduction to the work, Gaster pointed to a collection of midrashim on Simeon b. Yohai with the parallel Hebrew name *Nistarot*, mysteries.

and content to parts of the *Tibåt Marqe*.[41] The work is attributed by the Samaritans to Moses, but it was written, almost certainly, according to Ben-Hayyim,[42] in the tenth century, during the second period of the Samaritan literary production, and not the third century, as Gaster claimed.[43] This judgment is made by Ben-Hayyim on the basis that its language displays a heavy Arabic influence, not only in lexicon and grammar, but also in phraseology and syntactic structure. The work incorporates an Arabic commentary (pitron) that has been compared with a Targum. It extends some of the midrashim by drawing on other Samaritan sources.

The *Book of Asatir* parallels and expands the Pentateuch narrative with legends and midrashic material and has no halakhic content. It deals mainly with the succession of personages from Adam to Moses. The succession is described as a string of generations supported by the four "foundations of the world," Adam, Noah, Abraham, and Moses. The whole book is written around the story of their lives and deeds, as handed down in oral traditions. In this it differs from Samaritan chronicles whose usual starting point is the end of the Pentateuch, i.e., the conquest of Canaan by the Israelites. The book is divided into twelve chapters, the first ten of which are devoted to the period between the Creation and the war against the Midianites (Num. 31). The eleventh chapter is partly a geographic account of Canaan according to Num. 34. The remainder deals with the days to come, until the coming of the *Taheb*, the Redeemer. Some of its midrashim are found in other Samaritan writings, and Gaster[44] argued that they are based in Jewish midrashim. Examples cited are those of the destruction of the Tower of Babel, which is recorded in a Samaritan commentary on Genesis and the Malef (see below) as well as the Asatir, and is found in almost identical form in the Sybilline literature, and the stories of the birth of Abraham, which have parallels in *PRE* and the Cairo geniza material. On the basis of these and other parallels, Gaster maintained[45] that the *Asatir* is "a product of an exegetical midrashic interpretation carried on for some time among the Samaritan inhabitants of Northern Palestine. Nor can their be any doubt that the Samaritans ... started their activity at a very early date." It is apparent from the internal exegesis in the Pentateuch and that of Marqah that this judgment cannot be gainsaid, despite the relatively late date of the compilation of the *Asatir*.

The *Pitron* to the *Asatir* seems to have drawn for some of its midrashic embellishments on the so-called *Molad Mosheh*.[46] This work is known in both Aramaic and Arabic. The Arabic text was composed in the sixteenth century by Ishmael ar Rumaihi, but he drew for his poetic series of midrashim on the theme of the birth of Moses on a number of antecedents. In the first place there are the accounts of Moses in *Tibåt Marqe*, which may also have once contained a poetical version of most of the midrashim now found the *Molad Mosheh*.[47] Then followed a series of liturgical compositions, praises and eulogies recited by the Samaritans whenever possible, which Dexinger has termed "Moseology.[48] Among

---

[41] The title of the work is also claimed to mean "The Book of the Ancestors," in keeping with its content. See József Szengellér, *Gerizim Als Israel* (Utrecht, 1998), p. 17.

[42] Z. Ben-Hayyim, "The Asatir with Translation and Commentary," in *Tarbiz* 14–15 (1943) (Hebrew).

[43] For the most recent assessment, see Abraham Tal's evaluation, which may have been based on the work of Ben-Hayyim, before him, in "Samaritan Literature," in A.D. Crown, ed., *The Samaritans* (Tübingen, 1989), pp. 465–467.

[44] See Gaster, *The Asatir*, p. 21.

[45] Op. cit., p. 39.

[46] S.J. Miller, ed., *The Molad Mosheh* (New York, 1949).

[47] Ibid., pp. 26–27.

[48] In Crown, *Companion*.

these were the elaborate treatise on the birth of Moses of Ghazal ad-Duwaik, written towards the end of the thirteenth century. These were followed by liturgical offerings of Joseph HaRabban and Abisha ba'al Hamemerim, whose work focused on Moses' ascent of Mt. Sinai.[49] In the fourteenth century, Abdallah ibn Salamah wrote a liturgical *Molad Mosheh*, all of which is quoted in the *Molad Mosheh* of Ishmael ar Rumaihi. Few decades pass without additional "Moseology" compositions. Among the more recent is that of Abraham b. Marhib Sedaqah Hasafari, *Songs in Praise of Moses b. Amram, the Prophet* (Holon, 1956).

Some of the midrashim have their counterparts in Jewish midrashim: the Samaritan belief that the world was created for the sake of Moses has its counterpart in Lev. Rabbah 36:4. The legend giving the reason for Moses' having killed the Egyptian, namely that the Egyptian violated and raped an Israelite woman, is found in Exod. Rabbah 1:28-29, which names the Hebrew officer, Dathan, and his wife, Shulamit.

The main theme of the Samaritan Aramaic version begins with an account of God's creating light, which in fact is really Moses. The light is placed in Adam to be transmitted by a series of meritorious men in each generation until the advent of Moses. The date of Moses' birth is given, after which the angels praise him. The Arabic and Aramaic versions differ in respect of Moses' birth date. The Arabic version says Moses' birthday is the seventh day of the seventh month, while the Aramaic version states that Moses was born on the fifth of Nisan. A commentary to the *Asatir* gives his birth date as the fifteenth of Nisan in accordance with the liturgical calendar. Then comes a series of legendary episodes. When Moses was conceived in his mother's womb, "the star of glory appeared in heaven" (13:26-27). When Moses was born "the house of Amram was filled with light and the angels arranged themselves around him (15:21-22). Moses then grew in wisdom, understanding, and knowledge (28:21-22).

The second section of the manuscript has signs of either careful editing or origins in a didactic situation, since there is a series of verses beginning with the words, "This is he who is. . . ."[50] The third section of the manuscript likewise begins with related rhetorical questions, "Where is the one like Moses?" and "Who is comparable with Moses?" etc. In fifty-three stanzas, Moses' biography is reviewed briefly, starting with the light and concluding with his death. The final section again holds signs of didacticism or homily, since there is a series of exhortations addressed to various groups and classes of people in the community emphasizing elements of the Samaritan creed.

The Samaritan Aramaic version has some additional matter not found in the Arabic version but fundamental to Samaritan theological beliefs, namely. the idea of periodicity in the world in which there is a period of divine favor, *Rahuta*, and a period of divine disfavor, *Fanuta* (God's turning away of his face). Samaritan religious philosophy to some extent turns on these periods. History begins with a period of grace, the birth of Adam and Adam's obedience ushers in the *Rahuta*. When Adam disobeyed the divine instruction in the Garden, the age of divine disfavor was brought upon the earth. The world was regenerated with the birth of Moses, and the revelation of Torah to Moses restored the *Rahuta*, which lasted until the Samaritan *bête noir*, when Eli moved the holy Tabernacle from the slopes of Mt. Gerizim to Shilo. At Shilo, a cave opened up and swallowed the Tabernacle, ushering in the long age of Fanuta that still prevails and will prevail until the

---

[49] A number of his works are reprinted in *Aleph Beth, Samaritan News* (1.6, 1979), issues 236-237, pp. 13-19.

[50] Miller, *Molad Mosheh*, p. 45.

prophet like Moses, the Taheb, comes.

The compiling of midrashim of the aggadic type has continued even to the twentieth century. The late compilation, the *Malef*,[51] has some similar midrashic material, as noted above. Variously described as a catechism for children, a systematic theology, and a theological exposition based in the Pentateuch, it is a sort of *fatawa* in the traditional format of question and answer. The text recapitulates the fortunes of man from Adam to Moses and incorporates both aggadic and halakhic material. The only publication in English has been by Bowman, who argues for the antiquity of the material despite the age of the manuscript.

The Samaritan chronicles are a rich source of aggadic midrash that may be found also in the *Tibåt Marqe, Asatir*, etc., sometimes extending the text of the Tanakh with additional material, despite the Samaritan claim that they have only one canonical book. It is evident that at some time they made extensive use Joshua, though the status they accorded it is difficult to ascertain,[52] and their chronicles also draw on Judges and 1 Samuel, Kings, and Chronicles. The fact that they knew the whole of the Tanakh is evident from discussions and exchanges recorded of and between Samaritan and Jewish sages and has been manifested more recently in the production of the chronicle known as *Samaritan Chronicle No II* by Macdonald,[53] though it probably owes its existence to the Samaritan possession of the Walton Polyglot Bible at the hands of James Ussher. Both the *Samaritan Arabic Book of Joshua*[54] and the *Kitab al Tarikh* of Abu'l Fath embellish the Joshua story with the account of Shaubakh, a Canaanite king who survived Joshua's onslaught and sought to destroy Joshua through magic. The account of their conflict includes a description of a letter sent by attaching the missive to the wings of a dove. The story seems to have originated in Islamic circles, though the place names mentioned were all extant sites in the first millennium C.E. in the valley of Jezreel. Both texts also carry the account of the end of the *Rahuta* and Eli's catastrophic loss of the ark. Such tales are clearly midrashim, and some, such as the Eli tale, are repeated in some of the Samaritan polemic literature or their equivalent of responsa literature with Jewish enquirers, such as the *Hillukh* or *Book of Questions and Answers*. This text was composed by the Samaritan High Priest, Jacob b. Aaron, in the nineteenth century and is a global exposition of Samaritan law in ten parts, probably written in response to questions from Moses Gaster.

Another example of Samaritan responsa that has both halakhic and midrashic import

---

[51] Samaritan name, *Malf ayyalidǝm*, the text is not known outside Nablus except for a copy in the Rylands Library, Manchester. The sole manuscript was transcribed into Hebrew in 1911, almost certainly for sale to Moses Gaster, and was probably composed by the scribe's father, Pinhas b. Jacob in the late nineteenth century.

[52] See the author's "Dositheans, Resurrection and a Messianic Joshua," in *Antichthon* 1:1 (1967), pp. 70–85, in which the possibility that Joshua was a canonical work for the Samaritan Dosithean sect is examined.

[53] Cf., John Macdonald, *The Samaritan Chronicle No II (or Sepher Hayamim)* (Berlin, 1969).

[54] See the author's "Was There a Samaritan Hebrew Book of Joshua," in R.A Kearsley, et al., eds., *Ancient History in a Modern University* (Grand Rapids, 1998), vol. 2, pp. 15–22. The older and original Book of Joshua occupies caps. 9–15 of the Leiden MS and which was copied in 764 H/1362–1363, by Ibn 'abd 'al Ghani, the Nablusi for 'Ali Rabbi ibn 'Amqa. The copyist transmits the compilers comments. The compiler tells us in the first paragraph that the original was in "Hebrew," which might in fact betoken Aramaic. Juynboll considered the origins of these chapters to be in the Hellenistic "Moses" literature that arose during the Alexandrian period and conjectured that there were three other sources for the rest of the book, all in Arabic: one source for the first eight chapters and the other two for chaps. 16–46 and chap. 47 to the end of the work.

is the composition of Jacob ben Aaron answering William Barton's questions and those most frequently asked of the High Priest by others. Barton published the English translation under the title given to him by the High Priest, the *Book of Enlightenment*.[55] It can be seen from the content that the questions and answers necessarily involve both commentary on and extension of the text of the Pentateuch and in one case the Book of Joshua, and some of the answers are seen to be halakhic midrash and others aggadic. The contents are:

1. Concerning the duration of the plagues of Egypt. (answer: two and a half months);
2. Concerning the number and classification of the miracles (eleven);
3. Concerning the origin and significance of the ceremonial year (at the Exodus, a new ceremonial calendar was instituted);
4. Concerning the time of the institution of the Passover (the Sabbath prohibition against using fire does not apply to Passover);
5. Concerning the Passover when the date falls on the Sabbath (the sacrifice must take place on Friday evening and only on Mt. Gerizim);
6. Concerning the forty years in the wilderness (ordinances of the Passover, circumcision, and the shekhita were faithfully observed);
7. Concerning the fasts of Moses (Moses fasted for three periods of forty days each and not two);
8. Concerning the writing of the commandments (they were written for verbal accuracy and permanent preservation);
9. Concerning the revelation of the Torah (the complete Torah was written in a single roll by the hand of God and came down to Moses complete);
10. Concerning the two stone tablets (God created the first set on the third day of creation);
11. Concerning the tablets of testimony (they testified to the will of God and the promise of his people);
12. Concerning the transcription of the Torah (it was copied by Moses and the priests. The original copy written by God was exhibited every seven years otherwise being kept in a tent under guard by Joshua);
13. Concerning the river Jordan (the Jordan is the river of Law for the manna ceased there and the Law became fully operative);
14. Concerning the shining of Moses' face (this was due to the effulgence of the angel Gabriel who lent Moses celestial brightness);
15. Concerning the water at Rephidim (the smiting of the rock was a rebuke to those who complained);
16. Concerning the battle with the Amalekites (this was a testimony to other nations of Yahweh's favor for his people);
17. Concerning the reasons for not destroying the Amalekites earlier (that Israel might know its strength was in Yahweh. The day stood still as the battle was on Friday and the Sabbath was to be preserved unbroken by battle);
18. Concerning the time of Jethro's visit (the second year of the Exodus);
19. Concerning the sons of Moses (the High Priest refutes the Jewish "slander" that Moses married a Negress);

---

[55] Jacob ben Aaron, *The Book of Enlightenment for the Instruction of the Inquirer*, translated by A. ben Kori and edited William Barton (Sublette, 1913).

20. Concerning the heir of an adulteress (the High priest who condemns her to death inherits her property);
21. Concerning the face of Laban (the face reveals the heart and Jacob read Laban's face).
22. Concerning oaths (there are permissible and prohibited oaths);
23. Concerning the inheritance of a woman who marries outside the tribe (her inheritance stays within the tribe but is forfeited by the woman);
24. Concerning the use of rennet (the use of the kid's stomach was not previously forbidden in the making of cheese, but Jacob ben Aaron ruled against it);
25. Concerning the abridgement by laymen of the authority of the priesthood (laymen have no authority to interfere in priestly concerns);

The book is especially illuminating because the circumstances of its composition are known precisely, yet it has many of the hallmarks of older midrashic works, including rhetorical and other questions, such as "What is meant by . . .? Should one ask . . . As to the question of . . ., I was asked by some . . .," and the author cites texts and explains its application to the current enquiry. He frequently alludes to midrash with words such as "It is said . . ., some say . . .," and introduces his own neologistic views with words such as, "I believe (and I pray God to shield me from mistakes)."

A considerable amount of Samaritan midrash is to be found in the halakhic and polemic writings as well as in commentaries. Though a canonical Samaritan halakhah resembling the Jewish compilations never existed, the Samaritans have a not inconsiderable body of such literature all composed after the language shift from Aramaic to Arabic took place in the period when Arabic was penetrating Samaritan religious writings.[56] They appear at the beginning of the Samaritan renaissance and continue to be written at intervals throughout the period. Rosen has argued that the Samaritan polemical writers, with the necessity for giving arguments a firm, textually supported base, resorted constantly to the interpretation of biblical verses in all possible nuances.[57] Many of the texts have been published in part or as a whole. The first of these to appear were the *Kitab al-Kafi* written by Yusuf ibn Salama b. Yusuf al-'Askari, in 1041/1042 C.E. and the *Kitab at-Tabbah* composed by Abu'l-Hasan as-Suri between 1030–1040. The two works are inter-related, and they may have been derived from a common source. They may have been written as part of the general Samaritan response to Karaism and Islam,[58] though Bóid[59] suggests that they draw not only on sources written in Arabic but on Hebrew and Aramaic materials composed well before the start of the Samaritan renaissance. The *Kitab al-Kafi* is a halakhic compendium, whereas the *Kitab at-Tabbah* (the Book of Insight)[60] is not only a halakhic work, since only the first part is devoted to halakhic problems, including dietary regulations, rules of purity,

---

[56] The following depends on chapter 1 of the author's, *Samaritan Scribes and Manuscripts* (Tübingen, 2001).

[57] Gladys Rosen, "The Joseph Cycle," p. vii.

[58] See Gerhard Wedel, "The Kitab at-Tabbah," in Crown, *The Samaritans*, pp. 468–480. The name *Kitab al-Kafi* is an abbreviated form of the longer title that makes it clear that the work was a response to Islam.

[59] I.R.M. Bóid, "The Samaritan Halachah," Crown, *The Samaritans*, pp. 624–649.

[60] Bóid's translation. The meaning usually allotted to this title is the *Book of Meats*, after the first chapter of the work, which deals with permitted meats. Some translate the title as *The Book of Cooking* (or slaughtering), following the reading *Tabbah* (after Gaster, in the supplement to his article in the *Encyclopaedia of Islam* (1925)).

marriage, observation of feasts, etc. All the evidence suggests that each part may have had a different name. The second part deals with philosophical problems, and the third part with Pentateuchal exegesis. It thus has a greater emphasis on matters of religious principle and may well have been in original form an unorganized collection of responses to Jewish polemics against the Samaritans. These works were followed by the *Kitab al-Khilaf* (the Book of Differences [between Samaritans and Jews]), written by Munajjah ibn Sedaqa in the mid-twelfth century, a treatise on the phases of the moon and the calendar, by the same author and the *Kitab al-Mirat* (Book of Inheritance—a juridical treatise dealing with the precepts of inheritance), written by Saladin's personal physician,[61] Abu Ibrahim ibn Faraj ibn Maruth. Bowman[62] has translated several parts of the *Kitab at-Tabbah* under the headings "Haggadic Midrash" and "Biblical Commentaries," and Halkin has also extensively commented on the exegesis of both the *Kitab at-Tabbah* and the *Kitab al-Khilaf*, especially in regard to its exegetical midrashim about Mt. Gerizim and the *aqedah*.[63]

Finally, one should note the exegetical works that were written in Arabic by the few Samaritan scholars who wrote commentaries on the Torah. As far as is known, a complete commentary on the Torah penned by one author is not available despite the fact that the Torah is the beginning and end of law and religion. Yet such works did exist, as is explicitly stated in some Samaritan and non-Samaritan sources. Thus, the eleventh-century scholar Yusuf b. Salama al-'Askari affirmed that he had written an exegetical commentary on the Torah. On the evidence of Ibn abi-Usaybya (1203–1269), a thirteenth-century physician, Sedaqa b. Munajja b. Sedaqa as-Samiri ad-Dimasqi, known as Sedaqa al-Hakhim, had written such a commentary, and this Sedaqa confirmed that his father, Munajja, composed a commentary on the Torah. Today only the commentary on Genesis, starting with 1:2 and ending with 50:5, is extant, but there are excerpts of other books, such as the commentary on the life of Moses, which survive in a single manuscript.[64] The fourteenth-century scholar Ghazal ad Doweik is said to have written a number of short treatises, among which was a *Dissertation on Balaam*, which is said to have been heavily midrashic.[65] Ghazal b. Abi as-Sarur (Ab Zehuta) al-Ma†ari al-Ghazzawi (1702–1759) wrote three commentaries, one on Exodus, one on Leviticus, and the other on Numbers. The first two of these were entitled *Kashaf al-Ghayahib*, "The Dissipater of Darkness," and were aggadic commentaries.

Rosen has published the Joseph Cycle narratives and midrashim from the commentaries by Muslim/Meshalma ibn Murjan (1699–1738). Muslim, a renowned liturgist and scribe, wrote the commentary on Genesis, and his nephew Ibrahim Ibn al-'Ayyah (1748–1787), a grammarian and liturgist, completed the text to the end of Numbers.[66] Rosen found the commentary to be an epitome of Samaritan exegesis, stemming from Samaritan belief and dogmatic

---

[61] See Leon Nemoy, "Abu Ishaq Ibrahim's Kitab al-Mirath," in *JQR*, 66 (1975), pp. 62–65.

[62] John Bowman, *Samaritan Documents Relating to the History, Religion and Life* (Pittsburgh, 1977).

[63] See A.S. Halkin, "Samaritan Polemics against the Jews," in *PAAJR* 7 (1935–1936), pp. 13–59; "From Samaritan Exegesis—The Commentary of Abu'l Hasan al Suri on Deuteronomy 31," in *Leshonenu* 32, nos. 1–2 (1968), pp. 208–246; "Controversies in the Samaritan Masa'il al Khilaf," in *PAAJR* 46/47, no 1 (1980), pp. 281–306.

[64] Ben-Zvi Institute 7072.

[65] The Balaam cycle is the source of many midrashim in the Sepher Hayamim. See the author's, "A Critical Re-Evaluation of the Samaritan Sepher Yehoshua," Doctoral dissertation, The University of Sydney (1967).

[66] Rosen, "The Joseph Cycle."

principle—a compound of commentary, and abundant midrashic, aggadic, and homiletical extensions to sacred writ. However, she noted that a comparison of the author's interpretations with those of the Jews brought out, in many cases, a close relationship between the author and at least one of the Jewish commentators. Sometimes the relationship was with an ancient midrash, and in other cases the parallel was with a medieval commentator. She concluded that despite the conscious Samaritan animosity to anything Jewish, the Samaritan midrashim were often influenced by Jewish sources.

ALAN D. CROWN
University of Sydney

Septuagint, Midrashic Traditions and[1]

The Septuagint is the old translation of the Torah into Greek, produced at the initiative of a Ptolemaic king, probably at the beginning of the third century B.C.E. The name Septuagint (often, "LXX") refers to the purported number of translators (in fact, the tradition vacillates between seventy, seventy-two, and seventy-five).[2] The Septuagint is one of the best attested texts of antiquity. For Jewish-Hellenistic communities, it represents the foundation document of their identity as a cultural minority within a pagan environment. The relatively voluminous production of Greek literary, philosophical, and religious works from the (mainly Alexandrian) diaspora can be explained as a corollary effect of the Septuagint, viewed as a publication reflecting Jewish wisdom and its heritage. For subsequent Christian writers, the Greek Torah and Jewish-Hellenistic literature constitutes the theological, philosophical, and even lexicological basis for their developments in the intellectual and religious tradition. The theory of the inspiration of the Septuagint, originated from the speculation of Philo of Alexandria and borne out in Christian sources, is nothing but a claim of canonicity that aims to confirm the importance of the translation for Christian identity. The Septuagint was transmitted almost only by the Christians who adopted it as their Bible, at least in the Eastern Church.

That the Septuagint translation contains elements of Jewish exegesis is obvious; it was, after all, a product of Jewish scribes or scholars in a tradition of continuity and dependence on the motherland—at least

---

[1] This article is part of a study on Jewish and Christian processes of (de)canonization: *Deconstructing Libraries, Texts, and Hermeneutics: Rabbinic and Patristic Decanonization of Oral and Written Traditions* (Leiden, forthcoming). The author thanks Mr. Bill Templer, Shumen University (Bulgaria) for his careful correction of the English. Biblical quotations are adapted from the New International Version—UK.

[2] For the sources of the "Legend of the Septuagint," see André Gallandi, ed., *Bibliotheca veterum Patrum antiquorumque scriptorum ecclesiasticorum* (Venice, 1767), vol. 2, pp. 805–824; Paul Wendland, ed., *Aristeae ad Philocratem epistula cum ceteris de origine versionis LXX interpretum testimoniis* (Leipzig, 1900), pp. 85–166 (only Greek and Latin texts); Henry St. John Thackeray, ed., *The Letter of Aristeas* (London, 1917), pp. 89–116; André Pelletier, ed., *Lettre d'Aristée à Philocrate* (Paris, 1962), pp. 78–98; Gilles Dorival, "Les origines de la Septante: la traduction en grec des cinq livre de la Tora," in Gilles Dorival, Margarethe Harl, and Olivier Munnich, eds., *La Bible grecque des Septante* (Paris, 1988), pp. 47–50 (enumeration and mostly doubtful dating of the texts); Giuseppe Veltri, "L'ispirazione della LXX tra leggenda e teologia. Dal racconto di Aristea alla *veritas hebraica* di Girolamo," in *Laurentianum* 27 (1986), pp. 3–71; idem, *Eine Tora für den König Talmai* (Tübingen, 1994), pp. 220–247; idem, *Gegenwart der Tradition* (Leiden, 2002), pp. 120–152.

according to the accounts of Aristeas, Philo of Alexandria, and Josephus. In analyzing the exegetical tradition in the transmitted Septuagint manuscripts, modern scholars face a crucial decision: whether to date midrash traditions in respect to their occurrence in the Greek Torah or to explain Septuagintal "changes" as textual variants and the midrash as commentary on earlier Hebrew texts other than the so-called Masoretic one, the *textus receptus* common in the Middle Ages onwards. Depending on whether we take as our starting point the Septuagint or the Rabbinic midrash, we have two different images or patterns of their mutual connections. In the first case, we have to postulate an influence of the Septuagint on Rabbinic midrash; in the second case we can date Rabbinic exegetical tradition as early as the first centuries B.C.E., as Zacharias Frankel in the nineteenth century hypothesized.[3]

A third question concerns the exegetical mirror of Rabbinic Judaism in relation to the Septuagint story and its text. According to the Rabbinic view, every translation is an authoritative interpretation, because it originated in the exegetical Rabbinic teaching. Seen from a Rabbinic perspective and speaking of the text of the Bible, there is no place for literary creation as an aesthetic paradigm. Accordingly, the biblical text is a multifarious hermeneutic grid, a map without territory, because it presupposes the rabbi/teacher or interpreter as draftsman of *his* landscape in accordance with precise hermeneutic rules. According to this view, the Septuagint crystallizes *one* moment of this eternal exegetical discourse. My interest here it not to draft the outlines of how translation—the original, its adaptation as well as transmission and history of transmitted variants—should be interpreted; I remain skeptical about the results of critical scientific research on the originality of some texts and their relationship to "later" adaptations of texts and traditions. Rather, my interest here is to introduce the perception of history in Rabbinic academies. My study seeks to explain the "canonization," or, better, decanonization, of the Septuagint in Rabbinic Judaism. The change in attitudes toward the Greek Torah was a prolonged process, considering the fact that different factors contributed to the dissociating of Judaism from its Greek heritage in which the Septuagint was included: the association of the Greek language with Greco-Roman imperial literature,[4] the discarding of Greek liturgy because of the increasing importance of the Hebrew language, the Christian attempt to control Jewish liturgy in the time of Justinian,[5] the debate on Greek wisdom, etc.[6]

The patristic thesis, still supported by scholars,[7] that Judaism before Constantine's seizure of power refused to use the Greek Torah because the Christians used it, is pure

---

[3] See *Vorstudien zu der Septuaginta* (Leipzig, 1841); idem, "Zur Frage über das Verhältnis des alexandrinischen und palästinischen Judenthums, namentlich in exegetischer Beziehung," in *Zeitschrift der deutschen Morgenländischen Gesellschaft* 4 (1850), pp. 102–109; idem, *Über den Einfluß der palästinischen Exegese auf die alexandrinische Hermeneutik* (Leipzig, 1851); *Über palestinische und alexandrinische Schriftforschun* (Breslau, 1854).

[4] To what extent the ban on Greek wisdom is an indirect product of Roman imperial politics is an unexplored and controversial aspect of ancient Judaism, if we call to mind that only Latin was defined as an "imperial language;" see Giuseppe Veltri, "Römische Religion an der Peripherie des Reiches: ein Kapitel rabbinischer Rhetorik," in Peter Schäfer and Cathrine Hezser, eds., *The Talmud Yerushalmi and Graeco-Roman Culture* (Tübingen, 2000), vol. 2, pp. 81–138, esp. 87–88.

[5] Giuseppe Veltri, *Gegenwart der Tradition*, pp. 104–119.

[6] Giuseppe Veltri, "On the Influence of 'Greek Wisdom:' Theoretical and Empirical Sciences in Rabbinic Judaism," in *Jewish Studies Quarterly* 5 (1998), pp. 300–317.

[7] See Veltri, *Eine Tora für den König Talmai*, pp. 15–21.

Christian propaganda. There is no Rabbinic source that we can date incontestably to this period that expressly attacks the Septuagint as being "Christian infected," as patristic authorities would have it. On the contrary: Greek language[8] and the Greek text of the Torah were highly honored in Palestinian and Babylonian academies insofar as they transmitted traditions about a Torah version written for King Ptolemy with no trace of blame or critical distance from it, except for the two texts to be discussed below.

Rabbinic literature offers two groups of traditions concerned with the Greek Torah:[9] quotations of verses or list of verses, "changed," or "written" for King Talmai,[10] and an account about the origin of this writing, mostly followed by a list of "changed" texts.[11] I present a synchronic analysis of the quotations of verses out of context and the contextual story that mentions biblical verses changed by the elders or sages for King Ptolemy. The stories or contexts in which the "changed verses" are transmitted belong to two patterns: parenthetic reference and the contextual story with an enumeration of examples.

Changed Verses as Midrashic Parenthetic Reference

In most instances, the parenthetic reference functions as an exegetical tool for introducing another explanation of a lexeme, a word, a preposition etc., especially a difficulty in a biblical verse that the elders or sages of Israel had to change for the King

---

[8] A turning point in the evaluation of Greek in Judaism is the sixth-seventh century in the inscription of Venosa, in which a revival of the Hebrew instead of Greek is present; see Vittore Colorni, "L'uso del greco nella liturgia del giudaismo ellenistico e la novella 146 di Giustiniano," in *Annali di Storia del Diritto* 8 (1964), pp. 33–42; Cesare Colafemmina, "Insediamenti e condizioni degli ebrei nell'Italia meridionale e insulare," in *Gli Ebrei nell'Alto Medioevo* (Spoleto, 1980), vol. 1, pp. 202ff.; idem, "Archeologia ed epigrafia ebraica nell'Italia meridionale," in *Italia Judaica. Atti del primo convegno internazionale* (Rome, 1983), pp. 199–210. On the first century, see Martin Hengel, *The 'Hellenization' of Judaea in the First Century after Christ* (London and Philadelphia, 1989), pp. 7ff.; and generally Heikki Solin, "Juden und Syrer im westlichen Teil der römischen Welt. Eine ethnisch-demographische Studie mit besonderer Berücksichtigung der sprachlichen Zustände," in *Aufstieg und Niedergang der römischen Welt* II.29/2 (1983), pp. 587–789; Shlomo Simonsohn, "The Hebrew Revival among Early Medieval European Jews," in *Salo Wittmayer Baron Jubilee Volume: On the Occasion of His Eightieth Birthday* (Jerusalem, 1974), vol. 2, pp. 838–840.

[9] On the modern evaluation of Rabbinic tradition concerning the Septuagint, see my *Eine Tora für den König Talmai*, pp. 15–18.

[10] On these "alterations," see Avigdor (Victor) Aptowitzer, "Die rabbinischen Berichte über die Entstehung der Septuaginta," in *Ha-Kedem* 2 (1908), pp. 11–27; 102–122; 3 (1909), pp. 4–17; Karl-Heinz Müller, "Die rabbinischen Nachrichten über die Entstehung der LXX," in Joseph Schreiner, ed., *Wort, Lied und Gottesspruch. Beiträge zur Septuaginta* (Würzburg, 1972), vol. 1, pp. 73–93; Emmanuel Tov, "The Rabbinic Tradition concerning the 'Alterations' Inserted into the Greek Pentateuch and Their Relation to the Original Text of the LXX," in Aharon Oppenheimer and David R. Schwartz, eds., *Isaac Leo Seeligmann Volume. Essays on the Bible and the Ancient World* (Jerusalem, 1983), vol. 2, pp. 371–393; Abraham Wasserstein, "On Donkeys, Wine and the Use of Textual Criticism: Septuagintal Variants in Jewish Palestine," in Isaiah M. Gafni, ed., *The Jews in the Hellenistic-Roman World. Studies in Memory of Menahem Stern* (Jerusalem, 1996), pp. 119–142.

[11] The Rabbinic source concerned with the "Torah for King Ptolemy" are Mekhilta de-R. Ishmael pisha 14; Genesis Rabbah 8:11; 10:9; 38:7; 48:17; 63:3; 96:6; Exod. Rabbah 5:5; Tanhuma Exod. 22; Tanhuma (ed. Buber) Exod. 19; Yalqut Gen. 3; wa-ethanan 825; Leqah Tov to Gen. 1:1 (1b); to Exod. 4:20 (12b); Sekhel Tov to Exod. 4:20; Midrash ha-Gadol to Exod. 4:20; to Deut. 4:19 and 17:3; Y. Meg. 1:11 (71d); B. Meg. 9a–b; Soferim 1:7; Soferim (version B)

Ptolemy. Before an explanation of such *figura rhetorica* can be offered, I present the corresponding changes that occur throughout Rabbinic literature as parenthetic references and enumeration of examples.[12]

Genesis 1:1—In the beginnings God created: All the midrashic material concerned with "verses changed for the King Ptolemy" agree that a change was been made in the order of the first three words of Gen. 1:1. Instead of "In the beginning God created" (*bereshit bar'a elohim*), they wrote: "God created in the beginning" (*elohim bara bereshit*). Midrash and Talmud did not transmit any explanation of this allegedly reordered verse, and neither the Greek translation nor the targum show peculiarities that could help us understand the change. Only in the Middle Ages do we find an explanation: the philosopher and historiographer Abraham Ibn Daud contended the change was made because of the nature of Greek language, "so that the King does not understand that *bereshit* is the creator and *elohim* the creation."[13] Ibn Daud's explanation results from his ignorance of Greek, as Azariah de' Rossi observed already in the sixteenth century.[14] For in Greek there is no difference in meaning between the two orderings of the words.

However, Ibn Daud is right in saying that the first three words of the Torah could lead to exegetical deviancy. Unfortunately, no Rabbinic text is eloquent enough about illustrating such difficulties so that we must suffice with only some very small hints and enigmatic allusions. Two attempts to explain the difficulty will be examined: the first, put forward by Ibn Daud, foresees a danger of polytheism; the second, followed by medieval exegetical discussion in Rashi and Ibn Ezra, avoids speaking of censorship because of deviant sects, preferring to see only a question of hierarchy in the creation.

a) *Polytheistic preoccupation.* Some worry about polytheism is surely not far-fetched if one thinks about the Gnostic adaptation and actualization of Gen. 1:1 in connection with creation myths and theory. The grammatical facts that God is named after two other words and that the consonant *beth* can also be interpreted as an instrumental preposition ("together with") could sustain the belief that *Elohim* created heavens and earth together with or by *Reshit*. This interpretation might be echoed by Prov. 8:22:[15] "The Lord created me beginning his ways," and is adopted by some targumim.[16] The danger of a polytheistic interpretation is echoed by some midrashim, as for example Genesis Rabbah 1:14, oft quoted as explanation of this "change" for King Ptolemy:

> "In the beginning, God created the heaven and the earth" (Gen. 1:1): R. Ishmael asked R. Aqiba, "You were a disciple of Nahum from Gam-Zu, according to whom [the words] *akh* ["only"] and *raq* ["only"] are limitation and *et* [accusative particle] and *gam* ["too," "also"] are inclusions. Tell me: what about the *et* here [in Gen. 1:1, before the words "heaven" and "earth"]?"
>
> He said to him, "If we had *Bereshit bara' elohim shammayim we-erets* [that is, without *et*], 'heaven' and 'earth' could be understood as godheads."

1:8; Sefer Torah 1:6; Avot de-R. Natan B 37. For a commentary on the manuscript material of these texts, see Veltri, *Tora*, pp. 220–242.

[12] I present the results of the Rabbinic discussion without lingering on the philological and text-critical analysis, treated in my *Eine Tora für den König Talmai*, pp. 22–112.

[13] Abraham Ibn Daud, *Divre Malkhe Yisrael* (Amsterdam, 1711), p. 50a.

[14] *Me'or 'Enayim, Imre Bina* chapter 7; see the English translation in Azariah de' Rossi, *The Light of the Eyes* (New Haven and London, 2001), p. 162.

[15] With Zacharias Frankel, *Vorstudien zu der Septuaginta* (Leipzig, 1841), pp. 30–31.

[16] Fragment Targum Paris Hébr. 110, Vatican Ebr. 440 (edition: Michael E. Klein, ed., *Fragment-Targum* (Rome, 1980)) and Neophyti 1.

He said to him, "'They are not just idle words for you' (Deut. 32:47). If the word is idle, it depends on yourself, because you are not able to search (further): *et shammayim* includes sun, moon, and constellations; *et ha-arets* includes trees, grass, and the Garden of Eden."

This well-known and often quoted midrash cannot explain the changed text for King Ptolemy, because the problem addressed is not heaven and earth (*shammayim we-eres*) but *bereshit*, the first word of the Torah. However, the reason for the popularity of this midrash among modern scholars hinges on its exegetical similarity to the translation of Aquila, who, slavishly faithful to the Hebrew text, as Jerome maintained,[17] tried to imitate Hebrew style, rendering *et* by the Greek *syn*.

b) *Hierarchy of creation*. Another midrash is directly concerned with the order of the first three words of the Torah. Tanhuma Genesis 4 states:

R. Azzai said: "Come and see the humility of the Holy, be he praised! If one mentions a king of flesh and blood, one names first his name and thereafter his work (Greek in text: *ktisma*). That is not the case of the Holy One, be He praised. For he (God) first mentions His work (*bereshit*) and afterwards his name (*elohim*), as it is said: *In the beginning God created* (Gen. 1:1).

Although this midrash focuses on the first word of the Torah, and therefore is quoted by some scholars in this context,[18] it nonetheless does not explain the difficulty of the "changed verse for King Ptolemy." What is the reason for an inversion of the first three words? Perhaps the intention is to treat Ptolemy with care, debasing God's humility to the pride of a king of flesh and blood? The explanation is still more inconsistent if the parallel tradition in Genesis Rabbah 1:12 is taken into account, a passage in which a *Roman prefect* and not a king is the subject of the parable!

My explanation of the changed verses goes back to the ancient and medieval discussion on *creatio ex nihilo*: the inversion of the first three words creates a modal sentence: "As God created the heaven and the earth ... and the earth was formless and empty ... God says: Let there be light." This translation presupposes a different vocalization, *bereshit bero' elohim*, instead of *bereshit bara' elohim*.[19] A changed order at the beginning prevents any other possibility. The Rabbinic Torah for Ptolemy focuses in this way on an old theological question we find in the Hellenistic book of Wisdom 11:17, according to which God created the world from a formless matter. Against this opinion, 2 Macc. 7:28 maintains: "God did not make them (heaven and earth) out of things that existed." This interpretation is also confirmed in a text cited by Jerome, who, quoting the Rabbinic understanding of some changes for Ptolemy in Gen. 1:1, reports that the seventy-two changed the text so that the *monotheistic* king would not be misled by a possible dualistic conception of reality in the Hebrew text.[20] He says "dualistic," meaning the Platonic distinction between matter and divine substance in the creative act.

---

[17] Hieronymus' *Liber de optimo genere interpretandi: (Epistula 57)*, pp. 19–20.

[18] See Barthélemy, "Eusèbe," pp. 61-62 (*Études*, pp. 189–190).

[19] For the modal sentence in Rabbinic and medieval exegesis, see Abraham Geiger, *Urschrift und Uebersetzungen der Bibel in ihrer Abhængigkeit von der innern Entwickelung des Judenthums* (Breslau, 1857), pp. 344ff. and 439; Peter Schäfer, "Bereshit bara 'Elohim. Zur Interpretation von Gen 1,1 in der rabbinischen Literatur," in *Journal for the Study of Judaism* 2 (1971), pp. 161–166.

[20] *Prologus in Pentateuchum, Patrologia Latina* 28:121 (see also *Biblia sacra iuxta Vulgatam versionem*, ed. Weber, 1975, pp. 3–4).

Genesis 1:26-27 and 5:1b-2a: Gnostic mythology in Rabbinic garb: According to the Rabbinic literature, two question are addressed by sages by changing Gen. 1:26-27 and 5:1b-2a for King Ptolemy: the plural form in "Let *us* make man in *our* image, in *our* likeness" (changed to singular) and the meaning of the creation of the human being in the image of God (see below). It would be erroneous to believe that the tradition of Septuagintal changes is concerned first and foremost with the problem of monotheism arising from "Let *us* make." For, in view of Gen. 1:27 ("God created *man* in his own image, in the image of God he created *him*; *male and female* he created *them*") Rabbinic exegesis also faces the question of how many and which human beings God created. Are they two or one, male or female? The *anthropologic* problem leads to the theological question of the uniqueness of the godhead.

The question of biblical monotheism is much discussed in Rabbinic literature. Some difficult verses were, of course, disputed in the Rabbinic school.[21] We read in B. San. 38b:[22]

> R. Yohanan says, "Every biblical verse the heretics take as a pretext [to found their criticism against monotheism] also has the correspondent answer nearby: "Let *us* make man in *our* image, etc." (Gen. 1:26), and "*he* created man in *his* own image" (Gen. 1:27); "Come, let *us* go down and confuse their language" (Gen. 11:5) and "The Lord *came* down to see the city and the tower etc." R. Yohanan said, "God does not undertake anything without getting advice from the celestial ministers [literally: family], etc.[23]

The plural is understood as the *pluralis maiestatis*, considering the advisory function of God's "family." But only God is indeed acting in creation, nobody else. A similar tradition is transmitted in the school of Simlai (Genesis Rabbah 8:9):

> R. Simlai said, "Every biblical verse the heretics (*minim*) take as pretext [to found their criticism against monotheism] has the healing nearby.[24] They [the *minim*] asked him further, "What is the meaning of the verse: 'Let us make man, etc.'?" He said to them," "Let us read further: It is not written 'and the gods created a man,' but 'and God created a man' (Gen. 1:27a)."
>
> When they [the heretics] left, his disciples said to him, "Your answer was too imprecise. [Perhaps it could satisfy them], but to us, what do you intend to answer?"
>
> He said to them, "One day Adam was created from the soil and Eve from Adam. From here on, 'in our image, in our likeness' [meaning]: neither man without woman, nor woman without man, neither of them without the divine presence [*shekinah*]."[25]

The disciples observe that, with his first answer, Simlai could convince the heretics but not them. The problem is that there are two other plurals in the sentence beyond, "Let us make." These are "in *our* image" and "after *our* likeness." Simlai explicitly responds to this problem. According to him, God first

---

[21] Our enumeration of scriptural examples as proposed by Wayne S. Towner, *The Rabbinic 'Enumeration of Scriptural Examples'* (Leiden, 1973).

[22] See Müller, "Nachrichten," p. 80, and Alan F. Segal, *Two Powers in Heaven. Early Rabbinic Reports about Christianity and Gnosticism* (Leiden, 1977), pp. 121-134.

[23] The midrash continues with Gen. 35:7; 35:3; Deut. 4:7; 2 Sam. 7:23 and Deut. 7:9; see Segal, *Two Powers*, p. 122.

[24] This translation follows my corrected text; see *Eine Tora für den König Talmai*, p. 39.

[25] See on this verse Arnold Goldberg, "Kain: Sohn des Menschen oder Sohn der Schlange," in *Judaica* 25 (1965), p. 218.

created Adam and Eva as prototypes, then, with the help of these prototypes, he created them as males and females.[26] The parallel text in Y. Ber. 9:1 (12d) confirms this interpretation, for it substitutes *mi-kan we-illakh* ("from here on") with *mi-adam we-illakh* ("from Adam and beyond"), supposing the double creation of man and reading *be-salmenu ki-dmotenu*, as related to male and female.

Simlai's interpretation is a careful consideration of all elements that contributed to the formation of a human being: the soil, *adamah*, as the *materia* of Adam, and Adam as the *materia* of Eve. These prototypes together with the divine Presence lie at the origin of the creation of male and female, expressed by *zakhar* and *neqevah*.

The " verses changed for Ptolemy" transmit another hermeneutical approach, because they reject the double creation of man in Gen. 1:26–27. For, according to the rabbis, the elders also changed *zakhar* and *neqevah* in the following ways:[27] 1) *zakhar u-nequvaw bra'o* ("he created him male with his holes); 2) *zakhar u-neqevah bra'o* ("he created him male and female"): i.e., creation of an androgynous type. These Rabbinic interpretations articulate the two most popular theories of creation of man in antiquity: the creation of an androgynous being and the creation of an male/or neutral being. Both theories have their origin in the Greco-Roman environment.

The creation of a male "with his holes" is the thesis of Genesis Rabbah 8:11:

"Male and female he created them" (Gen. 5:2). That is one of the verses they wrote for King Ptolemy: "Male *with his holes* he created him" (Gen. 5:2). R. Joshua b. R. Nehemiah in the name of R. Hanina b. Isaac and the rabbis in the name of R. Leazar: "He created in him four qualities from the higher and four from the lower hierarchy. From the higher hierarchy: 1) he stays erect like the ministering angels; 2) he is capable of understanding like the ministering angels; 3) he is capable of seeing like the ministering angels—but does a beast not see? Yes, but it sees like an animal![28] From the lower hierarchy: 1) he eats and drinks like an animal; 2) he is fruitful and increases in number like an animal; 3) he defecates like an animal; 4) he dies like an animal.

R. Tiflai in the name of R. Aha [said]: "The heavenly beings have been created with the image and the likeness. They are not fruitful and do not increase. The earthly beings are fruitful and increase. They have not been created with (his) image and (his) likeness. The Holy One, blessed be he, said: "Well, I will create him with the image and likeness from the higher beings. He has to be fruitful and to increase from the lower beings."

The changed verse concentrates in one sentence what the midrash seeks to explicate: the human being is a *synolon* of the higher and lower beings: "in God's image" from the ministering angels, and "male and female" from the animals, whence *neqevah*—female—is literally interpreted as "holes." The anthropologic statement of Joshua is clear: the human being has four holes: mouth, genitalia, anus, and nose.[29] A similar

---

[26] Against Arnold Goldberg, *Untersuchung über die Vorstellung der Schekhinah in der frühen rabbinischen Literatur* (Berlin, 1969), p. 353, who speaks of the contribution by God to the formation of the embryo.

[27] The manuscript's transmission shifts between plural and singular; see Veltri, *Eine Tora*, pp. 41f.

[28] On this translation, see ibid., pp. 42–43, n. 67.

[29] This "hole" is not directly understandable: through the nose God infuses the breath of light and according to Job 27:3 it will remain there as long we are alive.

conception of a male—or, better, neutral—creation is also supported by Philo of Alexandria, who, at *De Opificio Mundi* 134, discusses the creation of man—"without body, neither male nor female, naturally immortal"—as the prototype who, on the other hand, possesses the quality of male and female (see *De Opificio Mundi* 76).[30]

The second interpretation of the creation of man as echoed by the "verses changed for King Ptolemy" sees in the human being a hermaphrodite. Leviticus Rabbah 14:1 (see also Genesis Rabbah 8:1) reads:[31]

> R. Ishmael bar Nahman said, "As the Holy One, blessed be he, created the first human being, he created him androgynous. He cut him in two and formed two backs, one for one side and the other for the other side."
>
> R. Simeon b. Laqish said, "As the Holy One, blessed be he, created the first human being, he created him with two faces. He cut him in two and formed two backs, one for the man and the other for the wife."

It is very difficult to ascertain whether this exegetical tradition is influenced by the philosophy of Plato, *Symposium* 189–190a,[32] according to which the androgynous human being is the third gender besides male and female, a tradition we find in other Rabbinic texts, for example, M. Bik. 2:3: "and the androgyne has ways in common with males and females." Similarly, *Symposium* 189e reads:

> ... not merely the two sexes, male and female, as at present: there was a third kind as well, which had equal shares of the other two, and whose name survives though the thing itself has vanished. For "man-woman" was then a unity in form no less than name, composed of both sexes and sharing equally in male and female.[33]

The difference between Plato's text and M. Bikkurim lies in the fact that the androgyne no longer exists for Plato, while, for Rabbinic Judaism, hermaphroditism exists and presents a real halakhic question.

To my mind, the idea of the creation of an androgyne (not gender!) goes back to or at least is influenced by Gnostic mythology. According to the hermetic tractates *Poemendres*, the godhead is in its nature male-female, and his creation is also male-female. In specific reference to animals, the authors write: "The period being ended, the bond that bound them all was loosened by God's Will. For all the animals being male-female, at the same time with man were loosed apart; some became partly male, some in like fashion [partly] female...."[34] To be androgynous is highly positive, attributed also to the Son of Man, as "Eugnostos the Blessed" affirms: "Then Son of Man consented with Sophia, his consort, and revealed a great androgynous Light. His masculine name is designated 'Savior, Begetter of All things.' His feminine name is designated 'Sophia, All-Begettress.' Some call her 'Pistis.'"[35]

---

[30] On this question, see Richard A. Baer, *Philo's Use of the Categories Male and Female* (Leiden, 1961).

[31] On this text, see David H. Aaron, "Imagery of the Divine and the Human: On the Mythology of Genesis Rabba 8 §1," in *Journal of Jewish Thought and Philosophy* 5 (1995), pp. 1–62.

[32] On this aspect, see Ephraim Urbach, *The Sages. Their Concepts and Beliefs* (Jerusalem, 1975), p. 228.

[33] *Plato in Twelve Volumes* (Cambridge, MA, and London), vol. 3, p. 1967.

[34] *Poemandres* 18: English by G.R.S. Mead, http://www.hermetic.com/texts/hermetica/hermes1.html.

[35] *Eugnostos the Blessed*, translated by Douglas M. Parrott, available in http://www.gnosis.org/naghamm/eugn.html.

Genesis 2:2: The Sabbath of God or the eternal creation: A well known instance in which the Hebrew and Septuagint differ is Gen. 2:2: "On the seventh day, God finished the work he had been doing; and in the seventh day he rested from all his work." The Septuagint, the Peshitta, and the Samaritan tradition[36] state that God ceased work by the sixth, not the seventh, day. Rabbinic Judaism also sees in this verse a change for King Ptolemy, and this has been almost unanimously transmitted by all the midrashic texts related to this topic.[37]

My interest is not to search for exegetical or historical reasons why the Septuagint (and the Samaritan tradition) have a variant reading but to delve into the Jewish-Hellenistic and Rabbinic tradition to find any text that reveals the reason for this variant. The main problem of the traditional Hebrew text is that Gen. 2:2 clearly contradicts Exod. 20:11: "For in six days the Lord made the heavens and the earth, the sea, and all that is in them, but he rested on the seventh day." On the other hand, some modern scholars affirm that the Septuagint and the Samaritan text are "rigorist" in limiting the action of God.[38] Other scholars try to justify the Hebrew text by interpreting the first verb as *plusquamperfectum*: "he had finished by the seventh day," i.e., he brought to a close his work so that on the seventh day God ceased creating. Umberto Cassuto thus translated the verse: "Since God was on the seventh day in the position of one who had already finished. . . ."[39] Modern exegesis thus minimizes the tension between "he finished" and "he rested," a contrast acknowledged by the ancient hermeneutics. For the very fundamental question in this verse is whether the divine resting on the Sabbath also represents the completion and end of his creative act.

The Septuagint reading had little to do with Sabbath rest but, rather, concerns the act of creation and its interpretation beyond the Sabbath. In rendering Gen. 2:2, the translators had Exod. 20:11 in mind, because the creation of the world and everything in it had to be finished in six days, so that further creation ceased after the first six/seven-day week: "For in six days the Lord made the heavens and the earth, the sea, and all that is in them, but he rested on the seventh day. Therefore the Lord blessed the Sabbath day and made it holy." But is this creative act the image of the Sabbath? Can it in this meaning be repetitive of the divine act, or is it an act that *finishes* by or on the Sabbath? We read in Jubilees 2:16:

> And he finished all his work on the sixth day—all that is in the heavens and on the earth, and in the seas and in the abysses, and in the light and in the darkness, and in everything.

The emphasis is unambiguously on "all." The reason for this stress goes back to the opposite opinion, which contended that creation is continuous, as Aristobulos and Philo of Alexandria[40] argued. For Artistobulos, the Sabbath was the day of the creation of the light in which all things are contemplated; on the seventh day, he did not rest, but ordered all things.[41] A similar opinion was reflected in a gloss of the Septuagint minuscule manuscript 135: "The 'Hebrews' say: If God ceased in the seventh day, that

---

[36] On the Samaritan tradition, see Simeon Lowy, *The Principles of Samaritan Bible Exegesis* (Leiden, 1977), pp. 106–107.

[37] Veltri, *Tora*, p. 48, and n. 83.

[38] See Bernd Schaller's dissertation ("Gen 1,2 im antiken Judentum," Universität Göttingen, 1961), quoted by Werner H. Schmidt, *Die Schöpfungsgeschichte der Priesterschrift* (Neukirchen-Vluyn, 1964), p. 156.

[39] *A Commentary to the Book of Genesis* (Jerusalem, 1961), vol. 1, p. 62.

[40] See *Decalogus* 97–98.

[41] Text transmitted by Eusebius, *Praeparatio Evangelica* 13:12:9ff.; Denis, *Fragmenta*, p. 224. See Walter, *Der Thoraausleger Aristobulos*, p. 59.

means that he made something in this day!"

Speculation on the eternal creation of the world could be possible only following the Hebrew text. Rabbinic tradition does not particularly focus on the question (see Genesis Rabbah 10:10–11), but openly supports the idea of a continuous creation. According to Targum Pseudo-Jonathan to Gen. 2:3, "he rested from his whole works, which God created (and from them) he intended to created in future."

If a continuous creation was the common opinion of Jewish-Hellenistic and Rabbinic tradition, the question arises why the Elders proposed a change in Gen. 2:2. It is not important to ascertain whether the rabbis really had a Septuagint manuscript at hand, because the very reason for the change—according to Rashi and the Tosafists—was apologetic: Ptolemy could take Gen. 2:2 as evidence against the Sabbath rest. The same opinion is shared several centuries earlier by Jerome, who saw the change of Gen. 2:2 as inhibiting possible polemics against the Sabbath.

Genesis 11:7 and the Tower of Babel: Ancient mythologies pertaining to the origin of languages suggested that humanity at its beginnings spoke a single language, as Gen. 11:1 maintains. Still, the Tower of Babel story does not only explain human ambitions and pride and consequent divine punishment. Other problems and issues are involved, as we see in the attention of ancient hermeneutics to this story.

Gen. 11:7 presents three exegetical difficulties: the anthropomorphic appearance of God, the plural form, and the confusion of *one* language as the origin of the (seventy) languages of the world. The changes in the Torah for Ptolemy address the second and third difficulty by changing the plural to singular and interpreting the confusion of languages as the destruction of the generation of the Tower.

The preoccupation with the plural is not the main problem of Jewish-Hellenistic and Rabbinic literature; rather, interest centers on how to interpret the confusion and, related to this, the question of how languages and the destruction of the Tower are connected. The first question was emphasized by scholars concerned with Jewish and Christian relations. They hold that Rabbinic Judaism proposed a change in the plural of Gen. 11:7 to counter Christianity's Trinitarian use of the verse.[42] This interpretation presupposes that the rabbis' sole concern in their exegesis of Scripture was to defy Christian exegesis. But it should recalled that, in Christianity, too, the Trinitarian interpretation of this verse was not commonly accepted. Augustin of Hippo, for example, mentions in *Quaestiones in Genesim* the Trinitarian interpretation, adding the other one (*pluralis maiestatis* and the inclusion of angels) as possible.[43] It is striking that Targum Onkelos does not "correct" the plural of Gen. 11:7; rather, it is worried about the anthropomorphism, and, instead of "Come, we will go down," translates: "Come, we will reveal ourselves." Moses Aberbach and Bernard Grossfeld comment: "Jews had long ceased questioning the monotheistic basis of their faith."[44] I am not convinced that the disappearance of a particular textual and therefore exegetical difficulty in the targumim reveals a consensus of the Rabbinic academies; clearly, every exegete cannot delve into every difficulty of the biblical text. Thus we can only infer that Onkelos's particular concern was to avoid anthropomorphism.[45]

---

[42] Geiger, *Nachgelassene Schriften*, p. 51; Etan Levine, *The Aramaic Version of the Bible* (Berlin and New York, 1988), p. 190. Margherite Harle, *La Bible d'Alexandrie. La Genèse* (Paris, 1986), p. 149, mention as an unambiguous example only Basilius in the fourth century.

[43] *Corpus Christanorum Series Latina* 33:7.

[44] *Targum Onkelos to Genesis* (Denver, 1982), pp. 74–75. See also Andrew Chester, *Divine Revelation and Divine Titles in the Pentateuchal Targumim* (Tübingen, 1986), p. 100.

[45] Michael L. Klein, *Anthropomorphisms and Anthropopatisms in the Targumim of the Pentateuch* (Jerusalem, 1982), pp. VII-VIII.

The real problem of Gen. 11:7, rather, is the appearance of the divinity and the destruction of the common language. While the majority of Rabbinic sources for the changed verses do not comment, Genesis Rabbah 38:7 gives a reason for the "change:"

> "Come, let us go down" (Gen. 11:7): That is one of the verses they changed for King Ptolemy. [They wrote)] *Come, I go down and confuse their language.* R. Abba said: "I will make them cadavers by their languages. One said to the other: 'Hand me water' and the other handed him dust. The [first] beat him and split his skull. [One said to the other]: 'Hand me an ax,' and the other handed him a shovel. The [first] beat him and split his skull, as it is written: "I will make them cadavers (*nebelah*) by their languages.'"

"I will make them cadavers by their languages" is not biblical, only a typical Rabbinical example in which the Hebrew verse and the Rabbinic exegesis are summed up together. The redactor plays here with the meaning of the verb *bll* and the correspondent word *nevelah* (destruction, but also cadaver) and corrects the Hebrew text, because there the redactor speaks of a singular: *their language*, relating to Gen. 11:1: "Now the whole world had one language." For the Rabbinic mind, the action of the divinity cannot imply that he was teaching or creating new languages for the world. On the other hand, how can we reconcile the confusion with the origin of the languages? This question was put by Philo of Alexandria, who objects that instead of "confusion" we should write "division" (*De Confusione Linguarum* 181). Nevertheless, he explains the "confusion" as a chemical process of dissolution of the constructed unity into its original elements.[46]

The question of whether the origin of the languages is a result of the destruction/confusion has no satisfactory explanation in ancient sources. Josephus refers to the book of the *Sybillae* by suggesting that God sent winds to let the tower collapse and to teach each people their language.[47] The text of *Sibyllae* reports, however, that God sent winds (*pneumata*) to destroy the tower, but the languages were *already* present as God enacted the confusion.

The changed verse for Ptolemy is a reaction to the question of the origin of the languages that, according to ancient opinion, were spoken at the time of the building of the Tower of Babel. The action of the divinity consisted in confounding communication between the workers on the tower so that they were unable to complete their project. The origin of the languages of the world was too positive an element to have been generated by a punishment.

Genesis 18:12: Sarah's laughter: In Mamre, God promised Abraham that Sarah would give birth a year hence. She was eavesdropping at the entrance to the tent and laughed to herself, saying: "After I am worn out and my master is old, will I now have '*ednah*"? The difficulty of this verse is not primarily the meaning of '*ednah*, which remains today a subject of controversy, but rather its congruence with Gen. 18:13, where God says to Abraham: "Why did Sarah laugh and say, 'Will I really have a child, now that I am old?'" If Sarah was laughing to herself, why does God ask Abraham, who could not hear? Genesis Rabbah 48:17 states:

> "And Sarah laughed to herself and said:" That is one of the verses they changed for King Ptolemy in this way: *And Sarah laughed among her relatives saying: "After I am worn out and my master is old, will I now have 'ednah?"*

---

[46] *De Confusione Linguarum* 187. On Philo's position, see Giuseppe Scarpat, "La torre di Babele in Filone e nella Sapienza (Sap 10,5)," in *Rivista Biblica* 39 (1991), pp. 167–173.

[47] *Sybillae* 3:97–98 according to Josephus, *Antiquitates* 1:118.

The woman said: "As long as a woman can give birth to a child, she has pieces of jewelry and I, *after I am worn out, will I now have 'ednah?' 'Ednah* means "pieces of jewelry," as in the verse: "I adorned you with jewelry" (*wa-e'dekh 'edi*; Ezek. 16:11).

The woman [said]: As long as a woman can give birth to a child, she menstruates and I, *after I am worn out, will I now have 'ednah?* ['Ednah] means period.[48] But *my husband is old* (Gen. 18:12). R. Judah said: He grinds but does not produce anything![49]

R. Yudah in the name of R. Simeon [said], "You considered yourselves young and treat your friends as old. Am I perhaps too old to perform miracles?"

The change for King Ptolemy consists of the addition of the consonant *waw*: instead of *be-qirbeha*, (to herself), the sages read *be-qerovehah* (among or by her relatives). The change explains why God and Abraham hear of her skepticism about the promise of a child. In the perspective of the midrash, the situation is now clear enough. Sarah is skeptical of the fulfillment of the divine promise but not in reference to herself. For they will get menstruation and pieces of jewelry, meaning, she becomes or is considered a young woman. But what about her husband? He is old and cannot father a child.

The dictum of Judah introduces something new. He reads the text to state that Sarah and Abraham consider themselves young and the three men of Mamre ("the friends") old, as if the sentence "And my master is old" refers to God, not to Abraham.

How can this reading be explained? The primarily reference is of course Gen. 18:13: "Why did Sarah laugh and say, 'Will I really have a child, now that I am old'." The midrash asserts that God consciously misread the antecedent of the second "I" to be himself and supposes that *God* then felt insulted at Sarah's assertion. This "change" for Ptolemy is based on a further midrashic list of biblical verses according to which God is forced to lie for the sake of freedom. There Gen. 18:12 is also listed:[50] By saying that Sarah's statement about being too old to father offspring was understood by God to refer to God, the midrash removes the difficulty of the biblical verses and salvages the honor of the patriarch.

The variant reading *be-qerovehah* has nothing to do with the transmitted text of the Septuagint. However, the Greek text for Gen. 18:13 shows an addition: "to herself." The Septuagint tried in this way to solve the problem the rabbis solved by means of an aggadic innovation.

Genesis 49:6: Simeon and Levi: In Gen. 49:5–7, Jacob excludes Simeon and Levi from his benediction, because "they have killed men (*ish*) in their anger and hamstrung oxen as they pleased." The difficulty of this verse lies in the hamstringing of an ox (*shor*). Gen. 34 (to which Jacob alludes) reports of killing men (as revenge for the abominable deed against their sister Dinah) and plundering of the city but not of hamstringing an ox.[51] This verse was difficult to explain, as the history of the exegesis shows. The word *ish* was interpreted either as Hamor ("the father of Shechem" (Tanhuma, ed. Buber, *wa-yehi* 12) or as the whole city of Shechem (Tan-

---

[48] A popular etymology from *'iddan* ("period of time").

[49] A euphemism for coitus. To grind corresponds to Greek *myllein*; see Job 31:10.

[50] See Sifre Numbers 42; Leviticus Rabbah 9:9; Y. Pe. 1:1 (16a); see Gerard Wewers, *Pea. Ackerrecke* (Tübingen, 1986), p. 25, n. 191.

[51] On modern attempts to solve the question, see Bruce Vawter, "The Canaanite Background of Genesis 49," in *Catholic Biblical Quarterly* 17 (1955), pp. 1–17; Patrick D. Miller, "Animal Names as Designations in Ugaritic and Hebrew," in *Ugarit Forschungen* 2 (1970), pp. 177–186; Calum M. Carmichael, "Some Sayings in Genesis 49," in *Journal of Biblical Literature* 88 (1969), pp. 435–444; R. Peter, "Note de lexicographie hébraïque," in *Vetus Testamentum* 25 (1975), pp. 486–496.

huma *wa-yehi* 10). The targumim, Aquila, and Symmachus understood the *shur* as the wall of the city (*shor*).

The midrashic topic of the "verses changed for Talmai" transmits two different variant readings to solve the difficulty: according to some sources, the elders changed *shur* in *abus* or *ebus*, while other sources transmit a first alteration from *ish* to *shor* (in the first hemistich)[52] and from *shor* to *abus* (in the second hemistich).[53] The first interpretation relates the verse to the story of Shechem, as Genesis Rabbah 98:6 (fragment from the Cairo Genizah) states:

> "For they have killed men in their anger" (Gen. 49:6a). This refers to Hamor, the father of Shechem. "And hamstrung oxen as they pleased" (Gen. 49:6b). You have demolished the wall of the proselytes.
>
> R. Huna and R. Jeremiah in name of R. Hiyyah bar Abba [said], "For sake of satisfaction of your desire, your have demolished the wall of the proselytes."
>
> Another explanation: For they have killed men in their anger and hamstrung an '*bws* as they pleased (Gen. 49:6). That is one of the verses they changed for King Ptolemy.

The first exegetical explanation reads *shwr* as *shur* (wall) and calls to mind the episode of Gen. 34, where Simeon and Levi "looted the city where their sister had been defiled" (Gen. 34:27). The changed verse for Ptolemy introduces a change from *shwr* to *abus*. '*bs* can mean either "fattened" from *ebus*, "manger" (see Is. 1:3) or even Greek from *bous* (cattle) with article (female), and that is also the meaning of the Septuagint, which has *tauros* (ox, bull). This interpretation would of course satisfy the stream of Rabbinic tradition that transmitted only *one* variant reading in the second hemistich.

Yet there is reason to doubt a consonance of the Rabbinic tradition of the "verses changed for Ptolemy" with the Greek text. The alteration of the *first* hemistich (*ish* to *shor*) in some of the Rabbinic sources cannot be explained as an accident of transmission, with only the variant reading of the *second* hemistich deemed "original," as some scholars maintain.[54] I suspect that a new (or just another) tradition is expressed in these changes: the identification of Joseph in *shor* and *abus*, with reference to Deut. 33. We read in *Leqah Tov wa-yehi* to Gen. 49:6:

> "For they have killed men in their anger" (Gen. 49:6a): These are the inhabitants of Shechem. "And hamstrung a *shwr* as they pleased" (Gen. 49:6b). That is the wall of the city. For "wall" (*humah*) is in Aramaic *shur*.
>
> Another opinion: "And hamstrung a *shwr* as they pleased" (Gen. 49:6b). That is Joseph, because it is written in reference to him: "Here comes that dreamer! They said to each other (*ish el ahaw*)" (Gen. 37:19). These are Simeon and Levi, called here "brothers."

And in *Midrash ha-Gadol* to Gen. 49:6:

> "For they have killed men in their anger" (Gen. 49:6a): This is Hamor, the father of Shechem. "And hamstrung a *shwr* as they pleased" (Gen. 49:6b). That is the wall of the Goyim.
>
> Another opinion: "For they have killed men in their anger" (Gen. 49:6a):

---

[52] As, for example, Mekhilta de-R. Ishmael *Bo'* (in the printed versions); a fragment from the Cairo Genizah of Genesis Rabbah 98:6, published by da Sokoloff.

[53] As in the manuscripts of Mekhilta de-R. Ishmael Bo', Y. Meg. 1:11 (71d), and B. Meg. 1:8 (9a–b).

[54] On this variant, see Geiger, *Urschrift*, pp. 442–443; idem, *Nachgelassene Schriften*, vol. 4, p. 52; Müller, "Die rabbinischen Nachrichten," p. 78; Tov, "The Rabbinic Tradition," p. 88; and my critics in *Eine Tora für den König Talmai*, pp. 66–67.

That is Joseph, because it is written in reference to him: "In majesty he is like a firstborn bull (*bekhor shoro*)" (Deut. 33:17).

This midrash offers us the second way to interpret Gen. 49:6: Jacob does not refer to the episode of Shechem but to the collaboration of the two brother to kill Joseph (Gen. 37:19: "But they saw him in the distance, and before he reached them, they plotted to kill him"). The brothers of Joseph here means only the two brothers Simeon and Levi.

The Rabbinic tradition of the "changed verses" alludes to this interpretation in changing *ish* to *shor* in the first hemistich and *shor* to *abus* in the second. That *'bws* has something to do with Joseph was the opinion of Michael Sachs, a view seconded by Nehemias Brüll and Samuel Krauss.[55] In my opinion, Sachs rightly maintains that *'bws* is nothing but another transcription of *Apis* or *Sar Apis* (the bull god of Memphis), as we read in B. A.Z. 43a:

> It is taught: R. Judah added also the images of *Meniqah* and Sar Apis. *Meniqah*, because of Eve who suckles the entire world; Sar Apis, because of Joseph who rules the entire world (*sar*) and brings peace to it (*mapis*).[56]

The identification of Joseph with Serapis may be inferred from his identification with a bull (Deut. 33:17). The fact that that this second interpretation (*shur* = Joseph) against the former (*shur* = wall of Shechem) is transmitted as "another interpretation" testifies to a change in the exegetical mentality and hermeneutical school: The plain meaning refers to the episode of Shechem, the other interpretation tries to spare the other brothers of Joseph, with critics attributing the intention to kill their brother only to Simeon and Levi, who are indeed excluded from Jacob's benediction.

Exodus 4:20b: Moses and the Donkey: After the revelation on the Sinai, Moses traveled together with his wife and children to Egypt: "And Moses took his wife and sons, let them ride on a donkey (*hamor*) and started back to Egypt." The Septuagint translated its *Vorlage* "and Moses took his wife and his sons, put them on *ta hypozygia* ("beasts of draught/burden"). The rabbis held that the Torah for King Ptolemy contained a variant reading here, changing *'al ha-hamor* into *'al nos'e adam*, probably to be translated "draught animals/chariots, reserved for human beings." Some scholars hold that a variant reading is indeed present in the Septuagint, and that can explain the rabbi's concern with this verse.[57] Perhaps, they note, the donkey was not appropriate for Moses; he had to take an animal more suitable like a camel or horse.[58] On the other hand, there may be something to this, considering the contempt and simultaneous awe of the Egyptians for such an animal.[59]

---

[55] Michael Sachs, *Beitraege zur Sprach- und Alterthumsforschung: aus jüdischen Quellen* (Berlin, 1854), vol. 2, p. 99; Nehemias Brüll, Fremdsprachliche Wörter in den Talmuden und Midrashim," in *Jahrbuch für jüdische Geschichte und Literatur* 1 (1874), pp. 144–145; Samuel Kraus, "Ägyptische und syrische Götternamen im Talmud," in George Alexander Kohut, ed., *Semitic Studies in Memory of Rev. Dr. Alexander Kohut* (Berlin, 1897), pp. 341–342.

[56] On this text, see Saul Lieberman, *Hellenism in Jewish Palestine*, pp. 136–138; and Margarete Schlüter, *D^eraqon und Götzendienst. Studien zur antiken jüdischen Religionsgeschichte, ausgehend von einem griechischen Lehnwort in mAZ III 3* (Frankfurt a.M., 1982), pp. 65ff. and 95ff.

[57] See Carmel McCarthy, *The Tiqqune Sopherim and Other Theological Corrections in the Masoretic Text of the Old Testament* (Fribourg and Göttingen, 1981), p. 135.

[58] See Jakob Levy, *Neuhebräisches und chaldäisches Wörterbuch über die Talmudim und Midrashim* (Leipzig, 1876–1889): vol. 3, p. 447.

[59] Geiger, *Nachgelassene Schriften*, p. 53; idem, *Urschrift*, p. 360.

In the end, Jews were also confronted with the reproach of venerating a donkey, a reproach extended also to Christians.[60]

Although many elements of this discussion are very important for illustrating the history of the Jews in Egypt, they do not satisfactorily explain the Greek and Rabbinic variant reading attributed to the Septuagint. For *ta hypozygion* is synonymous with *onos*, the common Greek word in a later period for donkey,[61] as Emmanuel Tov correctly maintains.[62] Abraham Ibn Daud (*Divre Malkhe Isra'el*, 50b) construed the verse's difficulty as the improbability of what it depicts, although he also alludes to the ancient theory of honor: "[The Elders altered this verse] so that the kind did not despise our teacher, because he rode on a donkey and also did not have to object: How could *one* donkey transport *a* woman and *two* children?" This observation is surely not illogical and can explains the *plural* of the Greek Septuagint and of the Rabbinic Torah for King Ptolemy, regardless of whether the rabbis had *really* seen the text of the Septuagint and its variant reading.

Ibn Daud of course is not alone in his explanation of the difficulty. A relatively young collection of midrashim, *Sekhel Tov* to Exod. 4:20 (ed. Buber, 28) transmits the following meaningful exegesis of the verse:

> *And Moses took his wife and sons, let them ride on a donkey*. In [the word] *W-yrkbm* [Masoretic text: *wa-yarkivem*] the consonant *yud* is lacking. In *h-hmr* [Masoretic text: *ha-hamor*], a *waw* is lacking.

The verse teaches us that he had only a donkey. He only let his two sons ride on the donkey, but not his wife. That is one of the verses the elders of Israel changed for King Ptolemy. They wrote for him: *he let them ride on a draught animal for man*. [They did this] because of Moses' honor.

The absence of the consonants *waw* and *yud* refers to the *plene* and *defective* of the Masoretic text. The very peculiar interpretation that had only the two children ride on the donkey returns not only to the problem of "three persons on a donkey" but also to the violation of Moses' honor, since he was forced to walk. What justified such an interpretation? Simply: *And Moses took his wife; his sons he let ride on a donkey*. The grammar is damaged, but Moses' honor is saved!

Exodus 12:40: The sojourn of Israel in Egypt: A further verse from the Torah considered by the rabbis as having been changed for King Ptolemy is Exod. 12:40: "Now the length of time the Israelite people lived in Egypt was 430 years." The Masoretic text is not consistent in giving the length of the stay: unlike Exod. 12:40, Gen. 15:13 speaks of 400 years, while, according to Gen. 15:16, the fourth generation will come back to the land of Canaan.

The Samaritan Pentateuch and the Septuagint add to Exod. 12:40, "and in the land of Canaan." Modern scholars disagree on whether this is an addition of the scribes or simply another way of interpreting chronological data.[63] According to the Rabbinic

---

[60] Elias J. Bickermann, "Ritualmord und Eselkult. Ein Beitrag zur Geschichte antiker Publizistik," in *Monatsschrift für Geschichte und Wissenschaft des Judentums* 71 (1927), pp. 171–187; 255–264; see also Peter Schäfer, *Judeophobia* (Cambridge, MA, and London, 1997), pp. 55–62 and *passim*.

[61] See Xenophon, *Oeconomicus*, 18:4, and Liddell and Scott, *A Greek-English Lexicon*, p. 197.

[62] Tov, "Rabbinic Traditions," p. 88.

[63] Ludwig Couard, "Gen 15,12–16 und sein Verhältnis zu Ex 12,40," in *Zeitschrift für Alttestamentliche Wissenschaft* 3 (1893), pp. 156–159; Harold H. Rowley, *From Joseph to Joshua. Biblical Traditions in the Light of Archaeology* (London, 1950, reprint 1964), pp. 66–73; Naftali H. Tur-Sinai, "Auf wieviel Jahre berechnet die Bibel den Aufenthalt der Kinder Israels in Ägypten?," in *Biblia et Oriens* 18 (1961), pp. 16–17; Ben Zion Wacholder, "How Long Did Abram Stay in Egypt? A Study in Hellenistic, Qumran, and Rabbinic Chronography," in *Hebrew Union College Annual* 35 (1964), pp. 42–56; idem., *Eupolemos. A Study of Judeo-Greek*

literature,[64] the disagreement between Genesis and Exodus is settled by adding the thirty years from the promise to the birth of Isaac.[65] Indeed, a certain agreement exists this literature on the length of the Egyptian period, which should be distinguished from the actual period of slavery, 210 years. According to Rabbinic sources, this calculation is confirmed by Gematria, as the numerical value of the word *rdu* ("they oppressed") at Gen. 42:2 is 210 (see on this Genesis Rabbah 91:2).

By contrast to the tradition based on the Masoretic text, a Samaritan source, the Septuagint, Demetrius, and Josephus give a different figures for the period spent in Egypt. According to the Samaritan source, *Memar Marqa* 2:11, the actual period of slavery was 140 years, since the seventy-five years of Joseph must be subtracted. This results in 260 years of sojourn in Egypt and 140 years for the period spent in Canaan, adding up to the 400 years of Gen. 15:13. For the historiographer Demetrius, the period spent in Egypt amounted to 215 years, the same as the period in Canaan.[66] On the basis of this precise chronology of Eupolemos, Ben Zion Wacholder holds that the Septuagint variant was close to his if not created by him.[67] Josephus vacillates between the four hundred years of Gen. 15:13 in *Antiquities* 2:204 and the 430 years of Exod. 12:40 in *Antiquities* 2:318.

Some modern scholars maintain that the reading of the Samaritan and Septuagint text is original because of a simple calculation, taken from the Masoretic text:[68]

Gen. 12:4:	Abraham 75 years old	0
Gen. 16:3:	10 years in Canaan	10
Gen. 16:16:	Abraham 86 years old, birth of Ishmael	1
Gen. 17:24:	Abraham 99 years old	13
Gen. 21:5:	Abraham 100 years old, birth of Isaac	1
Gen. 21:26:	Isaac 60 years old; birth of Esau and Jacob	60
Gen. 47:9:	Jacob, 130 years old; Jacob arrival to Egypt	130
Total:		215

There is doubt that these figures, taken from the Hebrew text, support the reading of the Samaritan and Septuagint texts ("the length of time the Israelite people lived in Egypt and in the land of Canaan"). Nevertheless, there is no doubt that they are a later attempt to harmonize Gen. 15 and Exod. 12. Note the purely historiograpical disharmonic information: Egypt and Canaan,

---

Literature (Cincinnati, 1974), pp. 97–128; Pierre Grelot, "Quatre cent trente ans (Ex 12,40)," in L. Alvarez Verdes and E.J. Alonso Hernández, eds., *Homenaje a Juan Prado: Miscelánea de estudios bíblicos y hebráicos* (Madrid, 1975), pp. 559–570; Siegfried Kreuzer, "430 Jahre, 400 Jahre oder 4 Generationen. Zu den Zeitangaben über den Ägyptenaufenthalt der Israeliten," in *Zeitschrift für Alttestamentliche Wissenschaft* 98 (1986), pp. 199–210; Osvalda Andrei, "The 430 Years of Ex. 12:40, from Demetrius to Julius Africanus; A Study in Jewish and Christian Chronography," in *Henoch* 18 (1996), pp. 9–67.

[64] See Ginzberg, *The Legend of the Jews*, vol. 5, p. 420; Josef Heineman, "210 Years of Egyptian Exile. A Study in Midrashic Chronology," in *Journal of Jewish Studies* 22 (1971), pp. 19–30; Hartmut Hahn, ed., *Wallfahrt und Auferstehung zur messianischen Zeit. Eine rabbinische Homilie zum Neumond-Shabbat (PesR 1)* (Frankfurt, 1979), pp. 331–333.

[65] Mekhilta de-R. Ishmael, pisqa 14; Mekhilta de-R. Simeon b. Yohai Bo' to 12:40; Seder 'Olam Rabbah 3; Pirqe de-R. Eliezer 48; cf. Lieber Antiquitatum Iudaicarum 9:3.

[66] Apud Eusebius, *Praeparatio Evangelica* 9,21:18; see Carl R. Holladay, ed., *Fragments from Hellenistic Jewish Authors*, vol. 1: *Historians* (Chico, 1983), p. 72.

[67] Wacholder, *Eipolemos*, p. 102; but see Gooding, "On the Use," p. 4.

[68] Klaus Koch, "Sabbatstruktur der Geschichte," in *Zeitschrift für Alttestamentliche Wissenschaft* 95 (1983), p. 416; Dieter Lührmann, "Die 430 Jahre zwischen den Verheißungen und dem Gesetz (Gal 3,17)," in *Zeitschrift für Neutestamentliche Wissenschaft* 100 (1988), pp. 420–423.

where one should expect Canaan and Egypt. The Samaritan redactor noted this incongruity, adding "in the land of Canaan" before "in Egypt." The logic is apparently resolved, though not completely, because the Samaritan text adds "and their father" after "the Israelite people" or "the sons of Israel," inverting the historical order.

The Rabbinic topic of the verses changed for King Ptolemy, which include Exod. 12:40, is a different question, although bound up with the chronological difficulty. Only relatively late sources have the "right" Septuagint variant (Soferim 1:7, manuscript Adler 3861, which also added the variant *bi-she'ar 'artsot* ("in the other lands")). This variant reading, present in almost all the Rabbinic sources of the verses changed for Ptolemy, testifies that the redactors of Rabbinic traditions had no control over the Greek Septuagint and thus quoted what they assumed to have been in the Torah for Ptolemy. Perhaps a tradition of this change was known to the writers, though without a reference to a precise text, as confirmed by Genesis Rabbah 63:3, where the variant reading is quoted without reference to the Torah for Ptolemy as "a deep word/meaning."

Numbers 16:15: Moses' behavior: In the revolt of Dathan and Abiram, the authority and the competence of Moses is criticized and questioned, because they assert that he had not led them into the Promised Land. In his complaint before God, Moses says: "Do not accept their offering. I have not taken so much as a donkey from them, nor have I wronged any of them." Instead of the common *onos* ("donkey"), the Septuagint translated *epithymēma*, which corresponds to the Hebrew *himmud*. The Rabbinic "changes for king Ptolemy" show a variety of solutions: *hemed* ("beauty"); *himmud* ("desire") or *hamud* ("valuable object").

Some authors explain this variant reading as a change made because of Moses' honor: he should not be associated with a donkey.[69] A further approach is to justify the Masoretic reading "donkey." Emmanuel Tov refers in this context to 1 Sam. 12:3, where the prophet defends his behavior: "Here I stand. Testify against me in the presence of the Lord and his anointed. Whose ox have I taken? Whose donkey have I taken (*hamor mi laqahti*)?"[70] Similar to the case of Samuel, Moses is called to justify his conduct. That is a plausible parallel, also acknowledged by ancient sources such as Avot de-Rabbi Natan 37, where in addition to the variant reading *nasa'ti* (from Num. 16:15) we also have the reading *laqahti* (clearly taken from 1 Sam. 12:3). The Rabbinic tradition also considers both episodes very similar. According to Numbers Rabbah 18:10, Midrash Exodus 14:9, and Tanhuma Qorah 7, only Moses and Samuel have been guilty of theft. The Midrash Exodus thus testifies to a high political commitment: Moses had the right to demand help from the people to transport his belongings, because he acted in the general interest, even so, he did not demand help. According to this interpretation, the object of theft is not very important; rather, what is central is the deed itself. The explanation of the innocence of Moses is also supported by the Rabbinic Torah for Ptolemy, which says "I have not taken something *desirable* from them," because desire (*lahmod*) results in theft.

Yet the traditional explanation of the verse is not cogent. The context of Dathan and Abiram's confrontation with Moses speaks neither of theft nor of cartage but of the claim of the Levites to the same rights as the priests (see Num. 16:10). Therefore they contest the authority of Moses. There is no point of similarity with Samuel,

---

[69] So Geiger, *Urschrift*, p. 360; Müller, "Die rabbinischen Nachrichten," p. 84.

[70] See Emanuel Tov, *The Text-Critical Use of the Septuagint in Biblical Research. Revised and Enlarged Edition* (Jerusalem, 1981), pp. 157–158.

because in this episode the catchword is the charge of corruptibility, not the contesting of authority. The answer of Moses in his complaint to God is consistent: "Do not accept their offering." This has to do with their function and claim to have more competence in the cult and therefore greater influence in the community. The accusation of having stolen a donkey makes no sense in this context. The Septuagint's attempt to gain meaning also is marked by difficulties. For the Septuagint text can be translated in three ways: 1) "I have not desired something that belongs to them;" 2) "I had no sexual desire for them;"[71] 3) "I have not taken something they loved."[72] None of these renderings fits into the context if we consider the second part of the verse: "... nor have I wronged any of them." According to the context of Numbers 16, there was something that wronged them: the refusal of the high honor to be priest.

The variant reading of some manuscripts of the "verses changed for Ptolemy" *hamud* can perhaps help us to gain a new dimension in this discussion. *hmd* and all its derivatives has something to do with desire, passion,[73] and denotes above all the object of desire, the precious and valuable object. In Ps. 39:12, Ezra 8:27, Job 20:20, and Dan. 11:38, *hmd* signifies a cult object needed in the Temple or in idolatrous cults. Presumably such an object is meant here, for example, the Urim and Tummim for the sacerdotal class. This interpretation is confirmed by Num. 16:17, where the censer is the status symbol of the Levites. So the meaning of the verse can be: "I have not taken any precious object from them (belonging to their class)." That means: Moses behaved rightly and politely with them, without wronging them.

Deuteronomy 4:19 and 17:3: star worship: Star worship in Egypt was not unknown and that is the reason, according to ancient and modern scholars, the rabbis stress a change in the Torah for King Ptolemy, so that he might say after reading the Torah: "The Holy One, blessed be he, has apportioned them (the heavenly bodies) to all the nations and allowed to them to worship them!" (Ibn Daud, *Divre Malkhe Isra'el* 50b). We do not know whether Rabbinic Judaism worried about "pagan" criticism of monotheism resulting from a pagan cult's being "tolerated" by the Torah, as some scholars maintain.[74] Contrary to the fundamentalist position of Deuteronomy, Rabbinic tradition does not reject *a priori* the "power" of the stars and their influence on human destiny.[75] A form of star worship is also present at least in mystical-magical groups, as *Sefer ha-Razim* shows. There, a prayer to the sun and invocation of the moon appear.[76] The reason for a fundamental skepticism against the position of Deuteronomy lies in the fact that there was no clear distinction between astrology and astronomy or in the everyday experience of atmospheric phenomena, such as the sun and moon. Lucian of Samosata saw the peculiarity of the cult of Helios and Selene in the fact that neither are local deities.[77]

It is not surprising that the rabbis had

---

[71] On this meaning, see Josephus, *Liber Antiquitatum* 7:134.

[72] On this meaning, see Philo, *De Confusione Linguarum* 50.

[73] See Tov, *The Text-Critical Use*, pp. 157–158; Gerhart Wallis, "Hmd," in *Theologisches Wörterbuch zum Alten Testament* 2 (1977), p. 1024.

[74] See Etan Levine, *The Aramaic Version of the Bible: Contents and Context* (Berlin, 1988), p. 183.

[75] See Veltri, *Gegenwart der Tradition*, pp. 226–232.

[76] See Johann Maier, "Die Sonne im religiösen Denken des antiken Judentums," in *Aufstieg und Niedergang der römischen Welt* II/19.1 (1979), pp. 346–412; Günter Stemberger, "Biblische Darstellungen auf Mosaikfußböden spätantiker Synagogen," in *Jahrbuch für biblische Theologie* 13 (1998), pp. 145–170.

[77] *De Dea Syria* 34: "In the temple itself on the left side when entering one first sees a throne of Helios the Sun, but there is no image of him on it. For they display no statues of the Sun and Moon, and I learned why they

knowledge of astronomy. It was of vital importance both for the liturgical year and for everyday life. The determination of the calendar required "a sound knowledge of astronomy, since not only were Jewish festivals fixed on given days of the lunar month, but they also depended on the position of the sun."[78] The Babylonians collected portents of lunar and solar eclipses, of meteorological phenomena that were used for the calculation of the calendar as well as prognostications for kings or country, and the Rabbinic literature shows a similar use.[79] The influence of the stars starts with birth and ends with death. B. M.Q. 28a reads:

> Longevity, offspring, and sustenance depend not upon merit but upon the planets. Consider the experience of Rabba and R. Hisda, who were both righteous men. One used to pray for rain and it descended, whereas the prayer of the other was of no avail. R. Hisda reached the age of ninety-two, and Rabba died at the age of forty.

The same circumstances, the unpredictability of human fate, led other rabbis to critical statements against astrology and prognostics (B. Shab. 156a):

> R. Ashi said, "I and Dimi bar Qaquzita were born on Sunday. I became king [i.e., Head of the School], and he became leader of robbers. All things can lead to lucky or unlucky fate."

A preoccupation with monotheism was not the reason for the transmission of Deut. 4:19 and 17:3 in the list of verses changed for the royal Torah. Once more, an exegetical problem led the rabbis to resort to direct intervention in the text. In the first text, star worship by non-Jews is tolerated: "And when you look up to the sky and see the sun, the moon and the stars—all the heavenly array—do not be enticed into bowing down to them and worshipping things the Lord your God has apportioned to all the nations under heaven." In 17:3, however, it was forbidden, at least for "pagans" living in the land of Israel: "[man or woman living among you] has worshiped other gods, bowing down to them or to the sun or the moon or the stars of the sky which I have not allowed to them."

According to the "verses for Ptolemy," the solution to the difficulty required an addition to 4:19 "after has apportioned to all the nations *to illuminate (leha'ir)* under heaven" and in 17:3 at the end: "... which I have not allowed them to worship *(le'ovdam)*." Here too we deal with an exegetical problem of the Hebrew text without any relevance for the real Septuagint text. This is confirmed by Sifre Deut. 148, where the addition "to worship them" in Deut. 17:3 is considered canonical, and in *Aggadah wa-'ethannan* to 4:19:

> *And when you look up to the sky and see the sun, the moon and the stars-all the heavenly array* (Deut. 4:19): For they had still not seen the sun and the moon until now because of the cloud (of the Shekhina) which surrounded them. Moses said to them: "You will see the sun and the moon. Do not think that they are deities! For God created them so that they illuminate the earth, as it is written: ... *the Lord your God has apportioned to all the nations to illuminate (them) under heaven.*

---

follow this custom. They say it is lawful to make statues of other gods, because their shapes are not visible to all. But the Sun and Moon are completely visible and all behold them. So why make statues of things that appear in plain air?" (transl. by Harold W. Attridge & Robert A. Dolen (Missoule, MO: Scholar Press, 1976)).

[78] W.M. Feldman, *Rabbinical Mathematics*, p. 5.

[79] See Erica Reiner, *Astral Magic in Babylonia* (Philadelphia, 1995), p. 12ff.

The tradition of "verses changed for King Ptolemy" is nothing but an exegetical method to resolve difficulties in the Hebrew text by introducing emendations, usually without commentary on them.

Contextual Stories and Deconstructed Elements

Three elements in the Rabbinic interpretation of the Torah for the King prove a direct and indirect knowledge of Septuagint traditions: 1) the interpretation of Exod. 24:11, 2) Lev. 11:6, and 3) the contextual story of the origin of the Torah *le-Talmai ha-Melekh*.

The Seventy of Exodus 24 and the LXX of Alexandria: According to Daniel Heinsius (1580–1655), the story of the Septuagint is in its core a literary development of Exodus 24.[80] Exod. 24:11 tells about the establishment of a group around Moses, Nadab and Abihu, and seventy of the elders of Israel, a medium between God and the people with the aim of worship. They "went up and saw the God of Israel" (Exod. 24:9–10). The Hebrew adds: "But God did not raise his hand against these leaders of the Israelites; they saw God, and they ate and drank." They are thus privileged over against the masses of the people. The Septuagint reads: "And of the chosen ones of Israel none died" or "And of the chosen ones of Israel none disagreed." The second translation hints at the legend of the Septuagint.[81]

Heinsius reference to Exodus as a source of the legend was neither new nor original. The idea goes back at least to the Church fathers Epiphanis of Salami and Hilarius of Poitiers. The Babylonian Rabbinic tradition indirectly refer to this, quoting a "change" in Exod. 24:5 and 24:11 for King Ptolemy: "Then he sent young Israelite men (*na'ar bne isra'el*), and they offered burnt offerings and sacrificed young bulls as fellowship offerings," and "But God did not raise his hand against these leaders of the Israelites (*atsile bne Israel*); they saw God, and they ate and drank." Both *na'ar bne isra'el* and *atsile bne israel* have been changed into *za'atute bne isra'el*. However, the fact is that these "changes" go back to another tradition, called the "three scrolls of Torah found in the Temple court," which has another historical and literary background, different from the "changes for King Ptolemy." The Babylonian rabbis must have read Christian sources and combined both traditions. This is confirmed by the fact that only the Babylonian tradition of the "changes for king Ptolemy" also contain the peculiar element of the "cells" (see below), taken from Christian sources, probably from Epiphanius, who notably associated also the Septuagint of Alexandria with the Septuagint of Exod. 24:1ff.

The tradition of the "three scrolls of Torah found in the Temple court"—Sifre Deut. 356, Y. Ta. 4:2 (68a), Soferim 6:4, and Avot de-Rabbi Natan 46—has nothing to do with the Septuagint. However, it touches on our main topic, the decanonization of libraries, text, and hermeneutics, and so it is useful to sum up the main results.[82] According to

---

[80] Heinsius was professor at Leiden University and one of the most famous Dutch scholars of the late Renaissance. In his *Aristarchus sacer*, he attacked the textual validity of the Septuagint, considering its origin as a myth.

[81] See Henry St. J. Thackeray, *The Septuagint and Jewish Worship. A Study in Origins* (2nd edition: London, 1923), p. 12; see also Tramontano, *La lettera di Aristea*, p. 208.

[82] Azaria de' Rossi, *Meor Enayim*, chap. 7 (ed. Cassel, vol. 1, p. 131); Alexander Kohut, "Correction d'une erreur de copiste plusieurs fois séculaire," in *Revue des Études Juives* 22 (1891), pp. 210–212; Christian D. Ginsburg, *Introduction to the Massoretico-Critical Editions of the Hebrew Bible*, pp. 408–409; Ludwig Blau, *Studien zum althebräischen Buchwesen und zur biblischen Litteratur- und Textgeschichte* (Straßburg, 1902),

this tradition, three scrolls were found in the Temple court: one of the *me'onim*, the second of the *hi' hi'* and the third of the *za'atutim*.

> In one scroll the words *me'ona elohe qedem* (Deut. 32:27) were found, in two others the words *me'onah elohe qedem*; the sages declared the first invalid, the second valid. In one scroll nine *hi'* were found, in the other two, eleven; the sages declared the first invalid, the second one valid. In one scroll it was written: *wa-yishlah et za'atute bne isra'el* [Exod. 24:5] and *we-el z'atute bne Israel* [Exod. 24:11]. In the other two *wa-yishlah et na'are bne isra'el* and *we-el atsile bne Israel*. The sages declared the first invalid, the second one valid.[83]

As Saul Lieberman stated, the terminology here is very similar to the Alexandrian grammarians use of the locution: "it was found written."[84] According to Lieberman, an authoritative copy of the Torah was stored in the Temple, an idea he borrowed from the above quoted passage of Deuteronomy Rabbah. According to him, the aggadah does not deal with a correction of this original text of the Bible, stored in the Temple, but rather with the revision of the "common text," the *vulgata*. I think, on the contrary, that here the aggadah talks about a comprehensible correction of the stored manuscripts on the basis of a chosen *Vorlage*. The text declared valid is in each case identical with our Masoretic text, a testament to the accurate work of the "commission,"

regardless of whether this aggadah refers to a unique work or to continuous care to assure accurate copies of the Torah. We thus have precisely the text they wanted to hand down.

While the first two variant readings found in the Temple scroll concern the text as written and pronounced, the third is not a variant reading but a problem of exegesis that nonetheless denotes a change in understanding of the authority on the biblical texts. According to the Rabbinic literature, the young people who made burnt offerings and sacrificed young bulls as fellowship offerings have no precise identity as priests or Levites. According to M. Zeb. 14:4, they are the firstborn who practiced the sacerdotal service before the Levites. A sign of the radical change appears in Targum Onkelos, M. Kal. 1:17, and Seder Eliyahu Rabbah (ed. Friedman, 52), for they interpreted them purely as common Israelites ("Even Israel may offer offerings on the altar"). Targum Onkelos offers the same translation in Exod. 24:5 and. 24:11 in reference to the *atsile bne Israel*. However, the variant reading of the three scrolls or of the Babylonian version of the verses changed for King Ptolemy stresses the same matter, because *z'atute bne Israel* is Aramaic for "young Israelites."

Here was a radical change in leadership and a new shift in understanding. For the first time, as testified by Josephus, the storage of the biblical books was a sacerdotal task (*Contra Apionem* 1:35ff.). The priests were entrusted with the correction of the Torah for the king (Sifre Deut. 160), a task

---

pp. 102–106; Jacob Z. Lauterbach, "The Three Books Found in the Temple at Jerusalem," in *Jewish Quarterly Review* NS 8 (1917–1918), pp. 385–423; *Massekhet Soferim*, ed. Michael Higger (New York, 1937), pp. 169–170, n. 17; Elias J. Bickerman, "Some Notes on the Transmission of the Septuagint," in Saul Lieberman, ed., *Alexander Marx Jubilee Volume* (New York, 1950), pp. 167–168; idem, *Hellenism*, pp. 22–27; Shemaryahu Talmon, "The Three Scrolls of the Law that were Found in the Temple Court," in *Textus* 2 (1962), pp. 14–27; Veltri, *Eine Tora für den König Talmai*, pp. 82–86; Solomon Zeitlin, "Were There Three Torah-Scrolls in the Azarah?" in *Jewish Quarterly Review* 56 (1965–66), pp. 269–272

[83] Sifre Deuteronomy 356. For the other versions of this midrash, see Veltri, *Eine Tora für den König Talmai*, pp. 81–82.

[84] Lieberman, *Hellenism*, p. 21.

passed on to the Sanhedrin in Y. San. 2:4 (20c). The Babylonian list of verses changed for Ptolemy and the list of the three scrolls testify to this radical change in leadership, stressing that the people chosen to see God without suffering death are not priests or Levites but the young Israelites. This matter was of course only exegetical, and that is the reason the revisers of the texts corrected them in the now-authoritative Masoretic text.

Leviticus 11:6: the Lagides and the impurity of rabbit: The rabbit is listed among the impure animals at Lev. 11:6. The Septuagint translated *arnevet* with *dasypous*, not with *lagos*.[85] The rabbis noted this peculiarity, assuming a conscious change to avoid Ptolemy's anger, because the rabbis believed, wrongly, that his mother or wife was called "rabbit." Still, they were right in stressing that the term *lagos* could provoke Ptolemy's anger, because the whole dynasty was named the Lagides. There is no doubt that the rabbis acknowledged the problem, since they said that the elders or sages changed *arnevet* to *se'irat regalim*, the perfect re-translation of *dasypous dasys*, that is, hairy foot.

Contextual stories: The third example in which Babylonian Rabbinic authority shows some familiarity with the legend of the Septuagint is at B. Meg. 9a–b (see also Soferim 1:7):[86]

> The permission of our teachers to write in Greek is extended only to the Pentateuch, because of the events with King Ptolemy. It is taught there: It so came to pass that King Ptolemy summoned seventy-two elders and put them in seventy-two houses without communicating to them why he had summoned them. He went to everyone separately, saying to them: "Write out for me the Torah of Moses, our teacher." The Holy One, blessed be he, conceded knowledge in the hearth of everyone, and they agreed with each other in their judgment. They wrote for him: (here the changed verses follow).

The number and separation of the elders, the houses (or cells), the divine intervention either to inspire the "writing" or translating of the Pentateuch, and the royal attempt to avoid agreement among the elders/translators are all basic elements in the *Christian* version of the Septuagint legend. Although this tradition is transmitted as a *baraita*, there is no doubt that it is a product of the Babylonian academies. For no Palestinian source before the Babylonian Talmud is concerned with the story of the seventy-two or seventy. They speak only of "changes for the King Ptolemy/Talmai" in the form of lists or individual verses. But no mention is made of the circumstances of the translation. I suppose that Babylonian teachers read the legend of the Septuagint in the edition of Epiphanius of Salami, the only patristic source that collected all the elements the rabbis needed, with the notable exception of the number (Epiphanius speaks of 36, not of 72 cells). However, Epiphanius is of the opinion that divine "inspiration" produced the agreement among the translators in making *changes* in the text, precisely the changes of the Babylonian teachers. At any rate, a Christian influence on the Gemara is undeniable.

The sources examined so far are either positive or indifferent regarding the circumstances of the translation of the Torah into Greek. However, there are two other sources that are definitely negative in judging the process of translation and its aftermath. The first is *Soferim* 1:7:

---

[85] The first to note the consonance between the Septuagint and the Rabbinic "verses changed for Ptolemy" was Menasse ben Israel, *Vindiciae Iudaeorum* (Amsterdam, 1656), p. 33.

[86] Soferim is a later tractate that depends on Talmudic material existing at the time of the writer; see Veltri, *Eine Tora für den König Talmai*, pp. 236–239.

The text of the Torah must not be written either in (Old) Hebrew or in Aramaic, or in Median or Greek. Scripture (*ktav*), in every language and every writing, may only be recited if it was written in Assyrian script.

It came to pass that five elders wrote the Torah for King Ptolemy. This day was as ominous for Israel as the day on which the golden calf was made, for the Torah could not be adequately translated.

Once again it happened that King Ptolemy summoned seventy-two elders and put them in seventy-two houses without communicating to them why he had summoned them. He went to everyone separately, saying to them: write out for me the Torah of Moses, our teacher. The Holy One, blessed be he, conceded knowledge in the hearth of everyone and they agreed with each other in their judgment. Each person wrote a Torah for him in which they changed thirteen passages (here the changed verses follow).

To understand this text, we also have to quote Sefer Torah 1:6:

The text of the scroll of the Torah must not be written in (old) Hebrew, or in Elamitic, or in Median, or Greek. Seventy elders wrote the whole Torah in Greek for king Ptolemy and that day was as ominous for Israel as the day the Israelites made the golden calf, for the Torah could not be adequately translated. They changed thirteen passages (the changed verses follow).

In Megillat Ta'anit Batra, a geonic scroll of fasts, we read:[87]

On the eighth of Tevet, the Torah was translated into Greek at the time of King Ptolemy. For three days, darkness descended upon the world.[88]

There is no doubt that Soferim, Sefer Torah, and B. Meg. follow the same tradition; only the small details are different, although they seem to speak of two different translations. The negative aspects of translating are emphasized only by Soferim (first translation), Sefer Torah, and Megillat Ta'anit Batra, which refer only to the "execrable" deed without specifying a reason for it. The Babylonian Talmud is openly positive in following the halakhah of the Mishnah, which permits Greek letters (and language).

The story of the two translations reported by Soferim has occupied ancient and modern Jewish scholars since the Renaissance. According to the Italian humanist Azariah de' Rossi, the first negative report refers to the translation of Aquila, Symmachus, and Theodotion.[89] Geiger held that the editor of Soferim was confused and fused the positive report of the Bavli with the negative story of Sefer Torah.[90] Joel Müller, editor of Massekhet Soferim, considers both translations to refer to one, unique translation; however the negative report on the Torah of the five translators goes back in his opinion to a later period, under the negative influence of *Megillat Taanit Batra*.[91] Manuel Joël distinguishes between a first translation of the seventy-two and that of the five translators at the time of Traian or Hadrian, as

---

[87] On the scroll, see Sid Z. Leiman, "The Scroll of Fasts: The Ninth of Teveth," in *Jewish Quarterly Review* 74 (1983), pp. 174–195; on the fast of the eighth of Teveth, see Veltri, *Gegenwart der Tradition*, pp. 144–150.

[88] On the text of the scroll, see Hans Lichtenstein, "Die Fastenrolle: eine Untersuchung zur jüdisch-hellenistischen Geschichte," in *Hebrew Union College Annual* 8–9 (1931–1932), pp. 318–351.

[89] *Me'or 'Enayim*, chap. 8 (ed. Cassel), vol. 1, p. 136.

[90] Geiger, *Urschrift*, pp. 419–420 and 441. According to Frankel, the report of five translators is fictitious; see his *Vorstudien*, p. 61, n. k.

[91] Joel Müller, ed., *Masechet Sopherim. Der Tractat der Schreiber, eine Einleitung in das Studium der althebräischen Graphik, der Masora und der altjüdischen Liturgie, nach Handschriften*

the first was considered a danger for Israel.[92]

The idea of a translation worked out by five translators had no lasting influence in modern scholarship, because the number five can be explained on the basis of other considerations: a misprint in the manuscript (Berliner), an indirect or direct reference to the five books of the Torah (Frankel, Graetz, Aptowitzer, Hadas),[93] or as an allusion to the fifth column of the Hexapla of Origen (Joël).[94]

The number of translators[95] shifts in Jewish and Christian sources between seventy (Sefer Torah and Soferim, manuscript Halberstamm), seventy-two (B. Meg. 9a–b), and five (Sefer Torah, Soferim and Avot de-Rabbi Natan, ed. B 37). An explanation for Aristeas's report is surely the number of the tribe, while Josephus gives seventy beside the traditional seventy-two. Gematria may also have played a role, since the geographical name of Greece, Yewwan, yields 72. The number seventy refers to the elders of Exod. 24. The number five can also be explained through the influence of Avot de-Rabbi Natan (version B, 37), provided that this source does not depend on the same one, the allusion to the "five Elders" in M. Erub. 3:4, B. R.H. 15a and T. Sheb. 4:21,[96] and, finally, a reference to the tradition of the five sages, entrusted by Moses to restore the Bible after its destruction/fire (4 Ezra 14). The number five is, in my opinion, no proof or historical reference to a new translation different from the Torah for King Ptolemy, but only a literary clue to distinguish two different traditions, one negative and the other positive.

The only constant in every report on the "Septuagint" is the information about the aim of the translation: *for* Ptolemy according to Rabbinic sources, *for* the royal library of Alexandria according to Jewish-Hellenistic and Christian literature. The king plays a role in Jewish-Hellenistic tradition as a patron and lover of Jewish wisdom, while in the Christian tradition he emerges as an "unwilling" initiator of the Christian religion. In the Jewish tradition, in the main Palestinian in origin, Ptolemy is neither the initiator nor the mentor/patron, but the addressee of the Torah, and that is an intriguing peculiarity. For the tradition of a Torah for the king is not new in Rabbinic sources and refers to Deut. 17:18: "When he takes the throne of his kingdom, he is to write for himself on a scroll a copy of this law, taken from that of the priests, who are Levites." *Katav lo* (so the Masoretic text) can mean either that he should write it for himself or that someone else should write it for him.[97] That is also the explanation of Y. San. 2:4 (20c): "They wrote for him [means] in his name." According to Sifre Deut., the

---

herausgegeben und kommentiert (Leipzig, 1878), p. 12.

[92] Manuel Joël, *Blicke in die Religionsgeschichte zu Anfang des zweiten christlichen Jahrhunderts* (Breslau, 1880), vol. 1, p. 3.

[93] Frankel, *Über den Einfluß*, pp. 228–231; Graetz, *Geschichte*, vol. 3/2, p. 579; Aptowitzer, "Die rabbinischen Nachrichten," in *Ha-Kedem* 2 (1908), p. 120; Hadas, *Aristeas to Philocrates*, p. 81.

[94] *Blicke in die Religionsgeschichte*, vol. 1, p. 4.

[95] The number of translators was also discussed in Jewish-Hellenistic and Christian literature. On the number 70 and 72, see Moritz Steinschneider, "Die kanonische Zahl der muhammedanischen Secten und die Symbolik der Zahl 70–73, aus jüdischen und muhammedabisch-Quellen nachgewiesen," in *Zeitschrift der deutschen morgenländischen Gesellschaft* 4 (1850), pp. 145–170; idem, "Nachtrag," 57 (1903), pp. 474–507; Bruce M. Metzger, "Seventy or Seventy-two Disciples," in *New Testament Studies* 6 (1959–60), pp. 319–321; Gill Dorival, "La Bible dela Septante: 70 ou 72 traducteurs?" in G.J. Norton and S. Pisano, eds., *Tradition of the Text. Studies Offered to D. Barthélemy in Celebration of his Seventieth Birthday* (Freiberg and Göttingen, 1991), pp. 45–62.

[96] See Berliner, *Targum Onkelos*, vol. 2, p. 78, n. 2.

[97] See M.A. Friedman, "u-katevu lo, 'ose lo ktav," in *Sinai* 84 (1979), pp. 177–179.

priests correct the copy of the king, while the above quoted Y. San. 2:4 (20c) adds that the Sanhedrin should correct the copy on the basis of the scroll of the Temple court. In this context, it is obvious that the text of Deut. 17:18 is read in a different way: instead of *mishneh torah*, they understand *meshanneh torah* ("he changes the Torah") or even *meshunnah torah* ("an altered Torah"). And this tradition is also present in Rabbinic tradition as an expression of a change of the Torah (perhaps in the messianic era), a possible reference to the cyclic change of the Torah beginning in Ezra's time.[98]

If interpreted in terms of this logic, the Rabbinic interpretation of the Septuagint as Torah for King Ptolemy suggests a deconstruction of meaning in the history of hermeneutics: the high value of this translation lies in its nature as a *written* (*ketav*) alteration of the Torah of Moses, an alteration implemented by the Priests or by the Sanhedrin. This is only the copy for royal needs. Of course, this means the Septuagint cannot be a liturgical or didactic document: it is solely a Torah for the king's use, so that he may learn from it.

Returning to the relation of Sefer Torah and Soferim (first report) to the Mishnaic and Talmudic halakhah, we have to stress that both tractates should be dated *after* the Talmudic period, because they prohibit what the Talmud allowed. Both Soferim and Sefer Torah do not distinguish clearly between writing and language and confuse the halakhah they are quoting. The redactor of Soferim affirms that one is not permitted to write in Old Hebrew, Median, and Greek. If one has written in other languages, he could recite from them in the liturgy only if written in Assyrian script (*ashshurit*). What is the aim of this halakhah, to preserve the script or the language? The question is not pointless: from the time of the Mishnah until at least Maimonides, a very lively discussion took place on whether other alphabets were suitable for liturgy.[99] In the Middle Ages the opinion gained acceptance that in the time of the Mishnah, only the Greek alphabet (not the language) was allowed; later it was replaced by the Assyrian square characters.[100] The disharmony between the premise (no other *alphabet* is permitted) and the conclusion (reading in other *languages*) is also confirmed by the sentence "The Scripture (*ktav*) in every language and every form of writing may be recited only if it was written (*ketuvah!*) in Assyrian script." The feminine *ketuvah* is a small but precious reference to the fact that the redactor of Soferim is quoting from earlier texts: the expression "only if it was written in Assyrian writing" originates from the rule for the liturgical reading of the Scroll of Esther, which, according to the M. Meg. 2:1 (cf. B. Shab. 115a; B. Meg. 18a), has to be written in Assyrian characters and recited in Hebrew. The redactor of Soferim deconstructs the original context and applies and extends a ban on other scripts to the Torah, without specifying whether he opts for Assyrian characters or language. This confusion proves that he collects texts without much interest in really understanding them.

The distortion of earlier halakhot can also be observed in the case of Sefer Torah, where the redactors maintain: "Seventy elders wrote (*katevu*) the whole Torah in Greek for King Ptolemy and that day was as ominous for Israel as the day the Israelites made the golden calf. For the Torah could not be adequately translated (*tirgem*)." The final sentence quotes Y. Meg. 1:11 (71c), with the

---

[98] See Y. Meg. 11 (71b); T. San. 4:7–8; B. San. 21b–22a; see also Peter Schäfer, "Die Torah der messianischen Zeit," in idem, *Studien*, pp. 210ff.

[99] See Maimonides, *Mishneh Torah, Hilkot Tefillin* 1:19.

[100] See the fragment published by Etan N. Adler in *Jewish Quarterly Review* 9 (1897), pp. 669–716, and Meiri, *Beyt ha-behirah 'al masekhet megillah*, ed. M. Herschler (Jerusalem, 1962), pp. 35–36.

omission of "with the exception of Greek." The Yerushalmi states that only the Greek language is suitable for the translation (as targum), while the redactor of Sefer Torah omits the language and extrapolates from this sentence an absolute ban on all languages. The comparison with the golden calf is also a quotation from earlier Rabbinic traditions, namely Y. Shab. 1:4 (3c) and B. Shab. 17a. where the comparison to the execrable day refers to the (historical?) dispute between the schools of Hillel and Shammai, which ended in violence. The golden calf here symbolizes the division between two Rabbinic schools and the consequences of that division.

It is not clear what the redactor of Sefer Torah was aiming at when comparing the Septuagint translation to the golden calf. But if we think that according to Pesiqta Rabbati 5 the written Torah is an example of a discussion between the nations of the world—which translated the Torah and read it in Greek—and Israel, then we can perhaps conclude that what is important here is the claim to possess the written Torah. However, there too the texts are not clear enough to spell out the controversy: the written or the oral Torah, the text (*ketav*) or the liturgical, didactic translation (*targum*)? In any event, the negative stories and reports on the Septuagint should be placed in a later post-Talmudic period, when a revival of Hebrew took place accompanied by dangers to one's identity because of Christian or Gnostic adoption of the Jewish Torah. In the Talmudic period, the Septuagint was seen as a particular example of the Torah for the king, an altered text: "For he had too little knowledge to reflect on the midrash of the Torah" (*Leqah Tov* to Gen. 1:1).

Bibliography

Aejmeleus, Anneli, "What Can We Know about the Hebrew Vorlage of the Septuagint?," in *Zeitschrift für Alttestamentliche Wissenschaft* 99 (1987), pp. 58–89.

De Lange, Nicholas M.R., *Origen and the Jews. Studies in Jewish-Christian Relations in Third-Century Palestine*, Cambridge, 1976.

Jellicoe, Sidney, "Aristeas, Philo and the Septuagint "Vorlage," in *Journal of Theological Studies* 12 (1961), pp. 261–271.

———, *The Septuagint and Modern Studies* (Oxford, 1968).

Tov, Emmanuel, "The Rabbinic Tradition concerning the 'Alterations' Inserted into the Greek Pentateuch and Their Relation to the Original Text of the LXX," in Alexander Rofé, Yair Zakovitch, ed., *Isaac Leo Seeligmann Volume. Essays on the Bible and the Ancient World* (Jerusalem, 1983). vol. 2, pp. 371–393, and in *Journal for the Study of Judaism* 15 (1984), pp. 65–89

Wasserstein, Abraham, "On Donkeys, Wine and the Use of Textual Criticism: Septuagintal Variants in Jewish Palestine," in Gafni, Isaiah M., Aharon Oppenheimer, David Schwartz, eds., *The Jews in the Hellenistic-Roman World. Studies in Memory of Menahem Stern* (Jerusalem, 1996), pp. 119*–142.

GIUSEPPE VELTRI
University of Halle-Wittenberg, Germany

Sifra, Theology of

The book of Leviticus is mediated to Judaism by two Rabbinic readings of the Priests' Torah. The first, Sifra, ca. 300 C.E., asks about the relationship of the laws of the Mishnah and Tosefta to the teachings of Scripture. The second, Leviticus Rabbah, ca. 450-500 C.E., forms of selected passages of Leviticus, read in light of other passages of Scripture altogether, large propositional expositions.

Sifra, a compilation of midrash-exegeses on the book of Leviticus, forms a massive and systematic statement concerning the definition of the Mishnah in relationship to Scripture. The authorship of Sifra produced a document that coheres not only in its main formal and logical traits but also in its few governing demonstrations. Sifra is unitary, cogent, and purposive, start to finish, and in no way a random sample of we know not what. The authorship of Sifra composed the one document to accomplish the union of the two Torahs, Scripture, or the written Torah, and the Mishnah, or the oral Torah. This was achieved not merely formally by provision of proof texts from Scripture for statements of the Mishnah—as in the two Talmuds—but through a profound analysis of the interior structure of thought. It was by means of the critique of practical logic and the rehabilitation of the probative logic of hierarchical classification (accomplished through the form of *Listenwissenschaft*) in particular that the authorship of Sifra accomplished this remarkable feat of intellect. That authorship achieved the (re-)union of the two Torahs into a single cogent statement within the framework of the written Torah by penetrating into the deep composition of logic that underlay the creation of the world in its correct components, rightly classified, and in its right order, as portrayed by the Torah.

This theological exercise in the criticism of reason in the name of revelation was carried out in two ways. Specifically, it involved, first of all, systematically demolishing the logic that sustains an autonomous Mishnah, which appeals to the intrinsic traits of things to accomplish classification and hierarchization. Secondly, it was done by demonstrating the dependency, for the identification of the correct classification of things, not upon the traits of things viewed in the abstract, but upon the classification of things by Scripture in particular. The framers of Sifra recast the two parts of the Torah into a single coherent statement through unitary and cogent discourse. So in choosing, as to structure, a book of the Pentateuch, and, as to form, the exegetical form involving paraphrase and amplification of a phrase of a base-text of Scripture, the authorship of Sifra made its entire statement *in nuce.* Then by composing a document that for very long stretches simply cannot have been put together without the Mishnah and at the same time subjecting the generative logical principles of the Mishnah to devastating critique, that same authorship took up its position. The destruction of the Mishnah as an autonomous and freestanding statement, based upon its own logic, is followed by the reconstruction of large tracts of the Mishnah as a statement wholly within, and in accord with, the logic and program of the written Torah in Leviticus. That is what defines Sifra, the one genuinely cogent and sustained statement among the four Midrash-compilations that present exegetical discourse on the Pentateuch.

The dominant approach to uniting the two Torahs, oral and written, into a single cogent statement, involved reading the written Torah into the oral. In form, as we noted in the two Talmuds, this was done through inserting into the Mishnah (that is, the oral Torah) a long sequence of proof texts. The other solution required reading the oral Torah into the written one, by inserting into the written Torah citations and allusions to the oral one, and, as a matter of fact, also by demonstrating, on both philosophical and theological grounds, the utter subordination and dependency of the oral Torah, the Mishnah, to the written Torah—while at the same time defending and vindicating that same oral Torah. Sifra, followed unsystematically to be sure by the two Sifres, did just that. Sifra's authorship attempted to set forth the dual Torah as a single, cogent statement, doing so by reading the Mishnah into Scripture not merely for proposition but for expression of proposition. On the surface that decision represented a literary, not merely a theological, judgment. But within the deep structure of thought, it was far more than a mere matter of how to select and organize propositions.

That judgment upon the Mishnah forms part of the theological polemic of Sifra's authorship—but only part of it. Sifra's authorship conducts a sustained polemic against the failure of the Mishnah to cite Scripture very much or systematically to link its ideas to Scripture through the medium of formal demonstration by exegesis. Sifra's rhetorical exegesis follows a standard redactional form. Scripture will be cited. Then a statement will be made about its meaning, or a statement of law correlative to that Scripture will be given. That statement sometimes cites the Mishnah, often verbatim. Finally, the author of Sifra invariably states, "Now is that not (merely) logical?" And the point of that statement will be, Can this position not be gained through the working of mere logic, based upon facts supplied (to be sure) by Scripture?

The polemical power of Sifra lies in its repetitive demonstration that the stated position, citation of a Mishnah-pericope, is not only not the product of logic, but is, and only can be, the product of exegesis of Scripture. That is only part of the matter, as I shall explain, but that component of the larger judgment of Sifra's authorship does make the point that the Mishnah is subordinated to Scripture and validated only through Scripture. In that regard, the authorship of Sifra stands at one with the position of the authorships of the other successor-writings, even though Sifra's writers carried to a much more profound level of thought the critique of the Mishnah. They did so by rethinking the logical foundations of the entire Torah.

The framers of the Mishnah effect their taxonomy through the traits of things. The authorship of Sifra insists that the source of classification is Scripture. Sifra's authorship time and again demonstrates that classification without Scripture's data cannot be carried out without Scripture's taxonomic givens, and, it must follow, hierarchical arguments based on extra-scriptural taxa always fail. In the Mishnah we seek connection between fact and fact, sentence and sentence, by comparing and contrasting two things that are like and not alike. At the logical level the Mishnah falls into the category of familiar philosophical thought. Once we seek regularities, we propose rules. What is like another thing falls under its rule, and what is not like the other falls under the opposite rule. Accordingly, as to the species of the genus, so far as they are alike, they share the same rule. So far as they are not alike, each follows a rule contrary to that governing the other.

So the work of analysis is what produces connection, and therefore the drawing of conclusions derives from comparison and contrast in the syllogism, 1+1=2—the *and*, the *equal*. The proposition then that forms the conclusion concerns the essential likeness of the two offices, except where they are different, but the subterranean premise is that we can explain both likeness and difference by appeal to a principle of fundamental order and unity. To make these observations concrete, we turn to the case at hand. The important contrast comes at the outset. The high priest and king fall into a single genus, but speciation, based on traits particular to the king, then distinguishes the one from the other. All of this exercise is conducted essentially independently of

Scripture; the classifications derive from the system, are viewed as autonomous constructs; traits of things define classifications and dictate what is like and what is unlike.

In the text before us, we shall examine examples of how Sifra's authorship rejects the principles of the logic of hierarchical classification *as these are worked out by the framers of the Mishnah*. It is a critique of designating classifications of things without Scriptural warrant. The critique applies to the way in which a shared logic is worked out by the other authorship. For it is not the principle that like things follow the same rule, unlike things, the opposite rule, that is at stake. Nor is the principle of hierarchical classification embodied in the argument *a fortiori* at issue. What our authorship disputes is that we can classify things on our own by appeal to the traits or indicative characteristics, that is, utterly without reference to Scripture. The argument is simple. On our own, we cannot classify species into genera. Everything is different from everything else in some way. But Scripture tells us what things are like what other things for what purposes, hence Scripture imposes on things the definitive classifications, that and not traits we discern in the things themselves.

Three forms dictate the entire rhetorical repertoire of this document. The first, the dialectical, is the demonstration that if we wish to classify things, we must follow the taxa dictated by Scripture rather than relying solely upon the traits of the things we wish to classify. The second, the citation-form, invokes the citation of passages of the Mishnah or Tosefta in the setting of Scripture. The third is commentary form, in which a phrase of Scripture is followed by an amplificatory clause of some sort. The forms of the document admirably expressed the polemical purpose of the authorship at hand. What they wished to prove was that a taxonomy resting on the traits of things without reference to Scripture's classifications cannot serve. They further wished to restate the oral Torah in the setting of the written Torah. And, finally, they wished to accomplish the whole by rewriting the written Torah. The dialectical form accomplishes the first purpose, the citation-form the second, and the commentary form the third.

In the simple commentary form, a verse, or an element of a verse, is cited, and then a very few words explain the meaning of that verse. Second come the complex forms, in which a simple exegesis is augmented in some important way, commonly by questions and answers, so that we have more than simply a verse and a brief exposition of its elements or of its meaning as a whole. The authorship of the Sifra time and again wishes to show that prior documents, the Mishnah or Tosefta, cited verbatim (here given in italics), require the support of exegesis of Scripture for important propositions, presented in the Mishnah and the Tosefta not on the foundation of exegetical proof at all. In the main, moreover, the authorship of Sifra tends not to attribute its materials to specific authorities, and most of the pericopae containing attributions are shared with Mishnah and Tosefta. As we should expect, just as in Mekhilta Attributed to R. Ishmael, Sifra contains a fair sample of pericopae which do not make use of the forms common in the exegesis of specific Scriptural verses and, mostly do not pretend to explain the meaning of verses, but rather resort to forms typical of Mishnah and Tosefta. When Sifra uses forms other than those in which its exegeses are routinely phrased, it commonly, though not always, draws upon materials also found in Mishnah and Tosefta. It is uncommon for Sifra to make use of non-exegetical forms for materials peculiar to its compilation. To state matters simply, Sifra quotes the Mishnah or Tosefta, but its own materials follow its distinctive, exegetical forms.

Topical Program

As we realize, for its topical program the authorship of Sifra takes the book of Leviticus. For propositions Sifra's authorship presents episodic and ad hoc sentences. If we ask how these sentences form propositions other than amplifications of points made in the book of Leviticus itself, and how we may restate those propositions in a coherent way, nothing sustained and coherent emerges. Sifra does not constitute a propositional document transcending its precipitating text. But, as we have now seen in detail, that in no way bears the implication that the document's authorship merely collected and arranged this and that about the book of Leviticus. For three reasons, we must conclude that Sifra does not set forth propositions in the way in which the Rabbah-compilations and Sifre to Deuteronomy do.

First, in general there is no topical program distinct from that of Scripture. Sifra remains wholly within Scripture's orbit and range of discourse, proposing only to expand and clarify what it found within Scripture. Where the authorship moves beyond Scripture, it is not toward fresh theological or philosophical thought, but rather to a quite different set of issues altogether, concerning the Mishnah and Tosefta. When we describe the topical program of the document, the blatant and definitive trait of Sifra is simple: the topical program and order derive from Scripture. Just as the Mishnah defines the topical program and order for Tosefta, the Yerushalmi, and the Bavli, so Scripture does so for Sifra. It follows that Sifra takes as its structure the plan and program of the written Torah, by contrast to the decision of the framers or compilers of Tosefta and the two Talmuds.

Second, for sizable passages, the sole point of coherence for the discrete sentences or paragraphs of Sifra's authorship derives from the base-verse of Scripture that is subject to commentary. That fact corresponds to the results of form-analysis and the description of the logics of cogent discourse. While, as we have noted, the Mishnah holds thought together through propositions of various kinds, with special interest in demonstrating propositions through a well-crafted program of logic of a certain kind, Sifra's authorship appeals to a different logic altogether. It is one that I have set forth as fixed-associative discourse. That is not a propositional logic—by definition.

The third fundamental observation draws attention to the paramount position, within this restatement of the written Torah, of the oral Torah. We may say very simply that, in a purely formal and superficial sense, a sizable proportion of Sifra consists in the association of completed statements of the oral Torah with the exposition of the written Torah, the whole *re*-presenting as one whole Torah the dual Torah received by Moses at Sinai (speaking within the Torah-myth). Even at the very surface we observe a simple fact. Without the Mishnah or the Tosefta, our authorship will have had virtually nothing to say about one passage after another of the written Torah. Far more often than citing the Mishnah or the Tosefta verbatim, our authorship cites principles of law or theology fundamental to the Mishnah's treatment of a given topic, even when the particular passage of the Mishnah or the Tosefta that sets forth those principles is not cited verbatim.

It follows that the three basic and definitive topical traits of Sifra, are, first, its total adherence to the topical program of the written Torah for order and plan; second, its very common reliance upon the phrases or verses of the written Torah for the joining into coherent discourse of discrete thoughts, e.g., comments on, or amplifications of, words or phrases; and third, its equally profound dependence upon the oral Torah for its program of thought: the problematic that defines the issues the authorship wishes to explore and resolve.

That brings us to the positive side of the

picture. While Sifra in detail presents no paramount propositions, it demonstrates a highly-distinctive and vigorously-demonstrated proposition. We should drastically misunderstand the document if the miscellaneous character of the parts obscured the powerful statement made by the whole. For while in detail we cannot reconstruct a topical program other than that of Scripture, viewed in its indicative and definitive traits of rhetoric, logic, and implicit proposition, Sifra does take up a well-composed position on a fundamental issue, namely, the relationship between the written Torah, represented by the book of Leviticus, and the oral Torah, represented by the passages of the Mishnah deemed by the authorship of Sifra to be pertinent to the book of Leviticus. Sifra joins the two Torahs into a single statement, accomplishing a re-presentation of the written Torah in topic and in program and in the logic of cogent discourse, and within that rewriting of the written Torah, a re-presentation of the oral Torah in its paramount problematic and in many of its substantive propositions. What we now wish to find out is what parts of the document bear that burden, and in what proportion; and what the other parts of the document, besides those particular to the document itself, propose to contribute.

In Sifra no one denies the principle of hierarchical classification. That is an established fact, a self-evident trait of mind. The argument of Sifra's authorship is that, by themselves, things do not possess traits that permit us finally to classify species into a common genus. There always are traits distinctive to a classification. Accordingly, it is the argument of Sifra's authorship that without the revelation of the Torah, we are not able to effect any classification at all, are left, that is to say, only with species, no genus, only with cases, no rules. The thrust of Sifra's authorship's attack on the Mishnah's taxonomic logic is readily discerned. Time and again, we can easily demonstrate, things have so many and such diverse and contradictory indicative traits that, comparing one thing to something else, we can always distinguish one species from another. Even though we find something in common, we also can discern some other trait characteristic of one thing but not the other. Consequently, we also can show that the hierarchical logic on which we rely, the argument *a fortiori* or *qol vehomer*, will not serve. For if on the basis of one set of traits that yield a given classification, we place into hierarchical order two or more items, on the basis of a different set of traits, we have either a different classification altogether, or, much more commonly, simply a different hierarchy. So the attack on the way in which the Mishnah's authorship has done its work appeals not merely to the limitations of classification solely on the basis of traits of things. The more telling argument addresses what is, to *Listenwissenschaft*, the source of power and compelling proof: hierarchization. That is why, throughout, we must designate the Mishnah's mode of *Listenwissenschaft* a logic of hierarchical classification. Things are not merely like or unlike, therefore following one rule or its opposite. Things also are weightier or less weighty, and that particular point of likeness of difference generates the logical force of *Listenwissenschaft*.

Sifra's authorship repeatedly demonstrates that the formation of classifications based on monothetic taxonomy. What that means is this: traits that are not only common to both items but that are shared throughout both of the items subject to comparison and contrast, simply will not serve. These shared traits are supposed to prove that the items that are compared are alike, and therefore should be subjected to the same rule. But the allegation of comparability proves flawed. The proposition maintains that the two items are alike, because they share one trait in common (thus: "monothetic taxonomy"). But I shall show you that they also exhibit traits that are different for the respective items. Then we have both likeness and difference.

Then, the argument proceeds, at every

point at which someone alleges uniform, that is to say, monothetic likeness, Sifra's authorship will demonstrate difference. Then how to proceed? Appeal to some shared traits as a basis for classification: this is not like that, and that is not like this, but the indicative trait that both exhibit is such and so, that is to say, polythetic taxonomy. The self-evident problem in accepting differences among things and insisting, nonetheless, on their monomorphic character for purposes of comparison and contrast, cannot be set aside: who says? That is, if I can adduce in evidence for a shared classification of things only a few traits among many characteristic of each thing, then what stops me from treating all things alike? Polythetic taxonomy opens the way to an unlimited exercise in finding what diverse things have in common and imposing, for that reason, one rule on everything. Then the very working of *Listenwissenschaft* as a tool of analysis, differentiation, comparison, contrast, and the descriptive determination of rules yields the opposite of what is desired. Chaos, not order, a mass of exceptions, no rules, a world of examples, each subject to its own regulation, instead of a world of order and proportion, composition and stability, will result.

Sifra's authorship affirms taxonomic logic when applied to the right categories. It systematically demonstrates the affirmative case, that *Listenwissenschaft* is a self-evidently valid mode of demonstrating the truth of propositions. But *the* source of the correct classification of things is Scripture and only Scripture. Without Scripture's intervention into the taxonomy of the world, we should have no knowledge at all of which things fall into which classifications and therefore are governed by which rules. How then do we appeal to Scripture to designate the operative classifications?

Here is a simple example of the alternative mode of classification, one that does not appeal to the traits of things but to the utilization of names by Scripture. What we see is how by naming things in one way, rather than in another, Scripture orders all things, classifying and, in the nature of things, also hierarchizing them. Here is one example among many of how our authorship conceives the right way of logical thought to proceed:

7. PARASHAT VAYYIQRA DIBURA DENEDABAH PARASHAH 4
VII:V.1A. "... and Aaron's sons the priests shall present the blood and throw the blood [round about against the altar that is at the door of the tent of meeting]:"
B. Why does Scripture make use of the word "blood" twice [instead of using a pronoun]?
C. [It is for the following purpose:] How on the basis of Scripture do you know that if blood deriving from one burnt offering was confused with blood deriving from another burnt offering, blood deriving from one burnt offering with blood deriving from a beast that has been substituted therefor, blood deriving from a burnt offering with blood deriving from an unconsecrated beast, the mixture should nonetheless be presented?
D. It is because Scripture makes use of the word "blood" twice [instead of using a pronoun].
2.A. Is it possible to suppose that while if blood deriving from beasts in the specified classifications, [the blood of the sacrifice] is to be presented [on the altar, as a valid offering], for the simple reason that if the several beasts while alive had been confused with one another, they might be offered up,

B. but how do we know that even if the blood of a burnt offering were confused with that of a beast killed as a guilt offering [it is to be offered up]?
C. I shall concede the case of the mixture of the blood of a burnt offering confused with that of a beast killed as a guilt offering; it is to be presented, for both this one and that one fall into the classification of Most Holy Things.
D. But how do I know that if the blood of a burnt offering were confused with the blood of a beast slaughtered in the classification of peace-offerings or of a thanksgiving offering [the mixture is to be presented]?
E. I shall concede the case of the mixture of the blood of a burnt offering confused with that of a beast slaughtered in the classification of peace-offerings or of a thanksgiving offering [it is to be presented], because the beasts in both classifications produce blood that has to be sprinkled four times.
F. But how do I know that if the blood of a burnt offering were confused with the blood of a beast slaughtered in the classification of a firstling or a beast that was counted as the tenth [that is, it is to serve as the tithe of that herd or flock] or of a beast designated as a Passover [it is to be presented]?
G. I shall concede the case of the mixture of the blood of a burnt offering confused with that of a beast slaughtered in the classification of firstling or a beast that was counted as a tenth or of a beast designated as a Passover [it is to be presented], because Scripture uses the word "blood" two times.
H. Then while I may make that concession, might I also suppose that if the blood of a burnt offering was confused with the blood of beasts that had suffered an invalidation, it also may be offered up?
I. Scripture says, "... its blood" [thus excluding such a case].
J. Then I shall concede the case of a mixture of the blood of a valid burnt offering with the blood of beasts that had suffered an invalidation, which blood is not valid to be presented at all.
K. But how do I know that if such blood were mixed with the blood deriving from beasts set aside as sin-offerings to be offered on the inner altar [it is not to be offered up]?
L. I can concede that the blood of a burnt offering that has been mixed with the blood deriving from beasts set aside as sin-offerings to be offered on the inner altar is not to be offered up, for the one is offered on the inner altar, and the other on the outer altar [the burnt offering brought as a free will offering, under discussion here, is slaughtered at the altar "... that is at the door of the tent of meeting," not at the inner altar].
M. But how do I know that even if the blood of a burnt offering was confused with the blood of sin-offerings that are to be slaughtered at the outer altar, it is not to be offered up?
N. Scripture says, "... its blood" [thus excluding such a case].

In place of the rejecting of arguments resting on classifying species into a common genus, we now demonstrate how classification really is to be carried on. It is through the imposition upon data of the categories dictated by Scripture: Scripture's use of language. That is the force of this powerful exercise. No. 1 sets the stage, simply pointing out that the use of the word "blood" twice encompasses a case in which blood in two distinct classifications is somehow confused in the process of the conduct of the cult. In such a case it is quite proper to pour out the mixture of blood deriving from distinct sources, e.g., beasts that have served different, but comparable purposes. We then systemically work out the limits of that rule, showing how comparability works, then pointing to cases in which comparability is set aside. Throughout the exposition, at the crucial point we invoke the formulation of Scripture, subordinating logic or in our instance the process of classification of like species to the dictation of Scripture. I cannot imagine a more successful demonstration of what the framers wish to say.

The reason for Scripture's unique power of classification is the possibility of polythetic classification that only Scripture makes possible. Because of Scripture's provision of taxa, we are able to undertake the science of *Listenwissenschaft*, including hierarchical classification, in the right way. What can we do because we appeal to Scripture, which we cannot do if we do not rely on Scripture? It is to establish the possibility of polythetic classification. We can appeal to shared traits of otherwise distinct taxa and so transform species into a common genus for a given purpose. Only Scripture makes that initiative feasible, so our authorship maintains. What is at stake? It is the possibility of doing precisely what the framers of the Mishnah wish to do. That is to join together masses of diverse data into a single, encompassing statement, to show the rule that inheres in diverse cases. In what follows, we shall see an enormous, coherent, and beautifully articulated exercise in the comparison and contrast of many things of a single genus. The whole holds together, because Scripture makes possible the statement of all things within a single rule. That is, as we have noted, precisely what the framers of the Mishnah proposed to accomplish. Our authorship maintains that only by appeal to The Torah is this fete of learning possible. If, then, we wish to understand all things all together and all at once under a single encompassing rule, we had best revert to The Torah, with its account of the rightful names, positions, and order, imputed to all things.

22. Parashat Vayyiqra Dibura Denedabah Parashah 11

XXII:I.1A. [With reference to M. Men. 5:5:] There are those [offerings that require bringing near but do not require waving, waving but not bringing near, waving and bringing near, neither waving nor bringing near: These are offering that require bringing near but do not require waving: the meal offering of fine flour and the meal offering prepared in the baking pan and the meal offering prepared in the frying pan, and the meal offering of cakes and the meal offering of wafers, and the meal offering of priests, and the meal offering of an anointed priest, and the meal offering of gentiles, and the meal offering of women, and the meal offering of a sinner. R. Simeon says, "The meal offering of priests and of the anointed priest—bringing near does not apply to them, because the taking of a handful does not apply to them. And whatever is not subject to the taking of a handful is not subject to bringing near,"] [Scripture] says, "When you present to the Lord a meal offering that is made in any of these ways, it shall be brought [to the priest who shall take it up to the altar]:"

B. What requires bringing near is only the handful. How do I know that I should encompass under the rule of bringing near the meal offering?
C. Scripture says explicitly, "meal offering."
D. How do I know that I should encompass all meal offerings?
E. Scripture says, using the accusative particle, "the meal offering."

2.A. I might propose that what requires bringing near is solely the meal offering brought as a free will offering.
B. How do I know that the rule encompasses an obligatory meal offering?
C. It is a matter of logic.
D. Bringing a meal offering as a free will offering and bringing a meal offering as a matter of obligation form a single classification. Just as a meal offering presented as a free will offering requires bringing near, so the same rule applies to a meal offering of a sinner [brought as a matter of obligation], which should likewise require bringing near.
E. No, if you have stated that rule governing bringing near in the case of a free will offering, on which oil and frankincense have to be added. will you say the same of the meal offering of a sinner [Lev. 5:11], which does not require oil and frankincense?
F. The meal offering brought by a wife accused of adultery will prove to the contrary, for it does not require oil and frankincense, but it does require bringing near [as is stated explicitly at Num. 5:15].
G. No, if you have applied the requirement of bringing near to the meal offering brought by a wife accused of adultery, which also requires waving, will you say the same of the meal offering of a sinner, which do not have to be waved?
H. Lo, you must therefore reason by appeal to a polythetic analogy [in which not all traits pertain to all components of the category, but some traits apply to them all in common]:
I. the meal offering brought as a free will offering, which requires oil and frankincense, does not in all respects conform to the traits of the meal offering of a wife accused of adultery, which does not require oil and frankincense, and the meal offering of the wife accused of adultery, which requires waving, does not in all respects conform to the traits of a meal offering brought as a free will offering, which does not require waving.
J. But what they have in common is that they are alike in requiring the taking up of a handful and they are also alike in that they require bringing near.
K. I shall then introduce into the same classification the meal offering of a sinner, which is equivalent to them as to the matter of the taking up of a handful, and also should be equivalent to them as to the requirement of being drawn near.
L. But might one not argue that the trait that all have in common is that all of them may be brought equally by a rich and a poor person and require drawing near, which then excludes from the common classification the meal offering of a sinner, which does not conform to the rule that it may be brought equally by a rich and a poor person [but may be brought only by a poor person,] and such an offering also should not require being brought near.

M. [The fact that the polythetic classification yields indeterminate results means failure once more, and, accordingly,] Scripture states, "meal offering,"

N. with this meaning: all the same are the meal offering brought as a free will offering and the meal offering of a sinner, both this and that require being brought near.

The elegant exercise draws together the various types of meal offerings and shows that they cannot form a classification of either a monothetic or a polythetic character. Consequently, Scripture must be invoked to supply the proof for the classification of the discrete items. The important language is at H–J: these differ from those, and those from these, but what they have in common is.... Then we demonstrate, with our appeal to Scripture, the sole valid source of polythetic classification, M. And this is constant throughout Sifra.

While setting forth its critique of the Mishnah's utilization of the logic of comparison and contrast in hierarchical classification, the authorship of Sifra is careful not to criticize the Mishnah. Its position favors restating the Mishnah within the context of Scripture, not rejecting the conclusions of the Mishnah, let alone its authority. Consequently, when we find a critique of applied reason divorced from Scripture, we rarely uncover an explicit critique of the Mishnah, and when we find a citation of the Mishnah, we rarely uncover linkage to the ubiquitous principle that Scripture forms the source of all classification and hierarchy. When the Mishnah is cited by our authorship, it will be presented as part of the factual substrate of the Torah. When the logic operative throughout the Mishnah is subjected to criticism, the language of the Mishnah will rarely, if ever, be cited in context. The operative language in dealing with the critique of the applied logic of *Listenwissenschaft* as represented by the framers of the Mishnah ordinarily is, "is it not a matter of logic?" Then the sorts of arguments against taxonomy pursued outside of the framework of Scripture's classifications will follow. When, by contrast, the authorship of Sifra wishes to introduce into the context it has already established a verbatim passage of the Mishnah, it will ordinarily, though not always, use, *mikan amru*, which, in context, means, "in this connection [sages] have said." It is a simple fact that when the intent is to demolish improper reasoning, the Mishnah's rules in the Mishnah's language rarely, if ever, occur. When the authorship of Sifra wishes to incorporate paragraphs of the Mishnah into their re-presentation of The Torah, they will do so either without fanfare, as in the passage at hand, or by the neutral joining-language "in this connection [sages] have said."

The authorship of Sifra never called into question the self-evident validity of taxonomic logic. Its critique is addressed only to how the Mishnah's framers identify the origins of, and delineate, taxa. But that critique proves fundamental to the case that that authorship proposed to make. For, intending to demonstrate that *The Torah* was a proper noun, and that everything that was valid came to expression in the single, cogent statement of The Torah, the authorship at hand identified the fundamental issue. It is the debate over the way we know things. In insisting, in agreement with the framers of the Mishnah, that there are not only cases but also rules, not only species but also genera, the authorship of Sifra also made its case in behalf of the case for The Torah as a proper noun. This carries us to the theological foundation for Sifra's authorship's sustained critique of applied reason.

At stake is the character of The Torah. I may phrase the question in this way: exactly what do we want to learn from, or discern within The Torah? And the answer to that question requires theological, not merely literary and philosophical, reflection on our part. For in their delineation of correct hierarchical logic, our authorship uncovered within The Torah (hence by definition, written and oral components of The Torah alike) an adumbration of the working of the mind of God. That is because the premise of all discourse is that The Torah was written by God and dictated by God to Moses at Sinai. And that will in the end explain why our authorship for its part has entered into The Torah long passages of not merely clarification but active intrusion, making itself a component of the interlocutorial process. To what end we know: it was to unite the dual Torah. The authorship of Sifra proposed to regain access to the modes of thought that guided the formation of the Torah, oral and written alike: comparison and contrast in this way, not in that, identification of categories in one manner, not in another. Since those were the modes of thought that, in our authorship's conception, dictated the structure of intellect upon which the Torah, the united Torah, rested, a simple conclusion is the sole possible one.

In their analysis of the deepest structures of intellect of the Torah, the authorship of Sifra presumed to enter into the mind of God, showing how God's mind worked when God formed the Torah, written and oral alike. And there, in the intellect of God, in their judgment humanity gained access to the only means of uniting the Torah, because that is where the Torah originated. But in discerning how God's mind worked, the intellectuals who created Sifra claimed for themselves a place in that very process of thought that had given birth to The Torah. Our authorship could rewrite the Torah because, knowing how The Torah originally was written, they too could write (though not reveal) The Torah. Here is a sample passage.

SIFRA PARASHAT BEHUQOTAI PARASHAH 1
CCLX:I
1.A. ["If you walk in my statutes and observe my commandments and do them, then I will give you your rains in their season, and the land shall yield its increase, and the trees of the field shall yield their fruit. And your threshing shall last to the time of vintage, and the vintage shall last to the time for sowing; and you shall eat your bread to the full and dwell in your land securely. And I will give peace in the land, and you shall lie down and none shall make you afraid; and I will remove evil beasts from the land, and the sword shall not go through your land. And you shall chase your enemies, and they shall fall before you by the sword. Five of you shall chase a hundred, and a hundred of you shall chase ten thousand; and your enemies shall fall before you by the sword. And I will have regard for your and make you fruitful and multiply you, and will confirm my covenant with you. And you shall eat old store long kept, and you shall clear out the old to make way for the new. And I will make my abode among you, and my soul shall not abhor you. And I will walk among you and will be your God and you shall be my people. I am the Lord your God, who brought you forth out of the land of Egypt, that you should not be their slaves; and I have broken the bars of your yoke and made you walk erect" (Lev. 26:3-13).]
B. "If you walk in my statutes:"
C. This teaches that the Omnipresent desires the Israelites to work in the Torah.
D. And so Scripture says, "O that my people would listen to me, that Israel would walk in my ways! I would soon subdue their enemies and turn my hand against their foes" (Ps. 81:13-14).
E. O that you had hearkened to my commandments! Then your peace would have been like a river, and your righteousness like the waves

of the sea; your offspring would have been like the sand, and your descendants like its grains; their name would never be cut off or destroyed from before me" (Is. 48:18).

F. And so Scripture says, "Oh that they had such a mind as this always, to fear me and to keep all my commandments, that it might go well with them and with their children forever" (Deut. 5:29).

G. This teaches that the Omnipresent desires the Israelites to work in the Torah.

2.A. "If you walk in my statutes:"

B. Might this refer to the religious duties?

C. When Scripture says, "and observe my commandments and do them,"

D. lo, the religious duties are covered. Then how shall I interpret, "If you walk in my statutes"?

E. It is that they should work in the Torah.

F. And so it is said, "But if you will not hearken to me."

G. Might that refer to the religious duties?

H. When Scripture says, "and will not do all these commandments,"

I. lo, the religious duties are covered.

J. If so, why is it said, "But if you will not hearken to me"?

K. It is that they should be working in the Torah.

3.A. And so Scripture says, "Remember the Sabbath day to keep it holy" (Exod. 20:8).

B. Might one suppose that what is involved is only to do so in your heart?

C. When Scripture says, "Observe [the Sabbath day]" (Deut. 5:12), lo, keeping it in the heart is covered.

D. How then am I to interpret "remember"?

E. It means that you should repeat with your mouth [the teachings concerning the Sabbath day].

F. And so Scripture says, "Remember and do not forget how you provoked the Lord your God to wrath in the wilderness, from the day you came out of the land of Egypt until you came to this place" (Deut. 9:7).

G. Might one suppose that what is involved is only to do so in your heart?

H. Scripture says, "and do not forget."

I. Lo, forgetting in the heart is covered.

J. How then am I to interpret "remember"?

K. It means that you should repeat with your mouth [the record of your behavior in the wilderness].

L. And so Scripture says, "[Take heed, in an attack of leprosy, to be very careful to do according to all that the Levitical priests shall direct you; as I commanded them, so you shall be careful to do.] Remember what the Lord your God did to Miriam on the way as you came forth out of Egypt" (Deut. 24:9).

M. Might one suppose that what is involved is only to do so in your heart?

N. When Scripture says, "Take heed, in an attack of leprosy, to be very careful to do,"

O. lo, forgetting in the heart is covered.

P. How then am I to interpret "remember"?

Q. It means that you should repeat with your mouth [the lessons to be learned in respect to Miriam].

R. And so Scripture says, "Remember what Amalek did to you on the way as you came out of Egypt ... [you shall blot out the remembrance of Amalek from under heaven; you shall not forget]" (Deut. 25:17, 19).

S. Might one suppose that what is involved is only to do so in your heart?

T. When Scripture says, "you shall not forget,"

U. lo, forgetting in the heart is covered.

V. How then am I to interpret "remember"?

W. It means that you should repeat with your mouth [the record of Amalek].

4.A. And so Scripture says, "And I will lay your cities waste."

B. Might one suppose that that is of human settlement?

C. When Scripture says, "And I will devastate the land,"

D. lo, that covers human settlement.

E. Then how am I to interpret, "And I will lay your cities waste"?

F. It means there will be no wayfarers.

5.A. And so Scripture says, "and will make your sanctuaries desolate."

B. Might one suppose that that is desolate of offerings?

C. When Scripture says, "and I will not smell your pleasing odors,"

D. lo, that covers the offerings.

E. Then how am I to interpret, "and will make your sanctuaries desolate"?

F. They will be laid waste even of pilgrims.

6.A. "If you walk in my statutes and observe my commandments and do them:"

B. One who studies in order to do, not one who studies not in order to do.

C. For one who studies not in order to do—it would have been better for him had he not been created.

The proposition, No. 1, that the reference is to study of Torah is demonstrated at No. 2. The rhetoric, "might this refer... when Scripture says...," and so on, then generates a series of compositions that use the same rhetorical pattern. The pattern goes forward at Nos. 4, 5, and only at No. 6 do we revert to the point that No. 1 wished to introduce: study in order to observe.

PARASHAT BEHUQOTAI PEREQ 3
CCLXIII:I

1.A. "And you shall eat old store long kept, [and you shall clear out the old to make way for the new. And I will make my abode among you, and my soul shall not abhor you. And I will walk among you and I will be your God and you shall be my people. I am the Lord your God, who brought you forth out of the land of Egypt, that you should not be their slaves; and I have broken the bars of your yoke and made you walk erect:]"

B. This teaches that whatever is better aged tastes better than its fellow.

C. "...old:"

D. I know only that the rule applies to wine, which customarily is kept for aging. How do I know that the same rule applies to everything that is allowed to age?

E. Scripture says, "Old store long kept."

2.A. "...and you shall clear out the old to make way for the new:"

B. The granaries will be full of new grain, and the storage bins will be full of the old,

C. so you will wonder how we shall take out the old on account of the new harvest.

3.A. "And I will make my abode among you:"

B. this refers to the house of the sanctuary.

4.A. "...and my soul shall not abhor you:"

B. Once I shall redeem you, I shall never again reject you.

5.A. "And I will walk among you:"
  B. The matter may be compared to the case of a king who went out to stroll with his sharecropper in an orchard.
  C. But the sharecropper hid from him.
  D. Said the king to that sharecropper, "How come you're hiding from me? Lo, I am just like you."
  E. So the Holy One, blessed be He, said to the righteous, "Why are you trembling before me?"
  F. So the Holy One, blessed be He, is destined to walk with the righteous in the Garden of Eden in the coming future, and the righteous will see him and tremble before him,
  G. [and he will say to them,] "[How come you're trembling before me?] Lo, I am just like you."
6.A. Might one suppose that my fear will not be upon you?
  B. Scripture says, "and I will be your God and you shall be my people."
  C. "If you do not believe in me through all these things, nonetheless 'I am the Lord your God, who brought you forth out of the land of Egypt.'
  D. "I am the one who did wonders for you in Egypt. I am the one who is going to do for you all these wonders."
7.A. "... that you should not be their slaves:"
  B. What is the point of Scripture here?
  C. Since it is said, "And he redeemed you from the house of slavery" (Deut. 7:8), might one suppose that they were slaves to slaves?
  D. "... their slaves:"
  E. they were slaves to kings, not slaves to slaves.
8.A. "... and I have broken the bars of your yoke:"
  B. The matter may be compared to the case of a householder who had a cow for plowing, and he lent it to someone else to plow with it.
  C. That man had ten sons. This one came and ploughed with it and went his way, and that one came and plowed with it and went his way, so that the cow got tired and crouched down.
  D. All the other cows came back, but that cow did not enter the fold.
  E. The owner hardly agreed to accept consolation from that man, but he went and broke the yoke and cut off the carved ends of the yoke.
  F. So is Israel in this world.
  G. One ruler comes along and subjugates them and then goes his way, then another ruler comes along and subjugates them and goes his way, so that the furrow is very long.
  H. So it is said, "Plowmen plowed across my back; they made long furrows. [The Lord, the righteous one, has snapped the cords of the wicked]" (Ps. 129:3–4).
  I. Tomorrow, when the end comes, the Holy One, blessed be He, will not say to the nations, "Thus and so have you done to my children!"
  J. Rather, he will immediately come and break the yoke and cut off the ends of the yoke.
  K. For it is said, "and I have broken the bars of your yoke."
  L. And further, "The Lord has snapped the cords of the wicked."
9.A. "... and made you walk erect:"
  B. R. Simeon says, "Two hundred cubits in height."
  C. R. Judah says, "A hundred, like the first Adam."
  D. I know that that statement applies only to men. How do I know that it applies to women too?

E. Scripture says, "[For our sons are like saplings, well tended in their youth;] our daughters are like cornerstones, trimmed to give shape to a palace" (Ps. 144:12).

F. And how high was the cornerstone of the temple? A hundred cubits.

10.A. Another teaching concerning the clause, "and made you walk erect:"

B. Upright, not fearful of anyone.

The eschatological focus is made sharp at No. 4. The polemic throughout is now uniform: Israel is destined to be redeemed in the future, and when that happens, it will be for all time. Then the return to Zion and rebuilding of the temple did not fulfill the prophecies of redemption; Israel will have a future redemption, of which the prophets, including Moses, spoke. The text of No. 5 is somewhat flawed, but the sense is readily recovered. No. 6 reworks the materials at hand for the same purpose. No. 8 once more is explicit, with its parable of how God's redemption of Israel will take place: with impatience, when it comes.

PARASHAT BEHUQOTAI PEREQ 8
CCLXIX:I

1.A. "And you shall perish among the nations, [and the land of your enemies shall eat you up. And those of you that are left shall pine away in your enemies' lands because of their iniquity; and also because of the iniquities of their fathers they shall pine away like them]:"

B. R. Aqiba says, "This refers to the ten tribes who went into exile in Media."

C. Others say, "'And you shall perish among the nations:' The reference to 'perishing' speaks only of going into exile.

D. "Might one suppose that the sense is literal [that Israel really will perish among the nations]?

E. "When Scripture says, 'and the land of your enemies shall eat you up,' lo, we find a reference to literally perishing.

F. "Then how am I to interpret 'And you shall perish among the nations'?

G. "The reference to 'perishing' speaks only of going into exile."

2.A. "And those of you that are left shall pine away in your enemies' lands because of their iniquity:"

B. The sense of "pining away" is on account of their iniquity.

3.A. "... and also because of the iniquities of their fathers they shall pine away like them:"

B. Now has not the Omnipresent already assured Israel that he will not judge the fathers on account of the sons or the sons on account of the fathers?

C. For it is said, "The fathers shall not be put to death for the children, nor shall the children be put to death for the fathers; every man shall be put to death for his own sin" (Deut. 24:16).

D. If so, why is it said, "and also because of the iniquities of their fathers they shall pine away like them"?

E. When for generation after generation they are enthralled in the deeds of their fathers, then they are judged on their account.

"Exile" is taken to fulfill the curse of "perishing," and then comes the religious duty of "pining away." The important clarification comes at Nos. 2–3, which draws into alignment a variety of pertinent verses.

CCLXIX:II

1.A. "But if they confess their iniquity and the iniquity of their fathers [in their treachery which they committed against me, and also

in walking contrary to me, so that I walked contrary to them and brought them into the land of their enemies; if then their uncircumcised heart is humbled and they make amends for their iniquity; then I will remember my covenant with Jacob, and I will remember my covenant also with Isaac and my covenant also with Abraham, and I will remember the land. But the land shall be left by them and enjoy its Sabbaths while it lies desolate without them; and they shall make amends for their iniquity, because they spurned my ordinances, and their soul abhorred my statutes. Yet for all that, when they are in the land of their enemies, I will not spurn them, neither will I abhor them so as to destroy them utterly and break my covenant with them; for I am the Lord their God; but I will for their sake remember the covenant with their forefathers whom I brought forth out of the land of Egypt in the sight of the nations, that I might be their God: I am the Lord. These are the statutes and ordinances and laws which the Lord made between him and the people of Israel on Mount Sinai by Moses]" (Lev. 26:40–46):
   B. This is how things are as to repentance,
   C. for as soon as they confess their sins, I forthwith revert and have mercy on them,
   D. as it is said, "But if they confess their iniquity and the iniquity of their fathers in their treachery which they committed against me."
2.A. "... and also in walking contrary to me, so that I walked contrary to them:"
   B. In this world they treated my laws in a casual way, so I shall treat them in a casual way in this world."
3.A. "... and brought them into the land of their enemies:"
   B. This is a good deal for Israel.
   C. For the Israelites are not to say, "Since we have gone into exile among the gentiles, let us act like them."
   D. [God speaks:] "I shall not let them, but I shall call forth prophets against them, who will bring them back to the right way under my wings."
   E. And how do we know?
   F. "What is in your mind shall never happen, the thought, 'Let us be like the nations, like the tribes of the countries, and worship wood and stone.' 'As I live,' says the Lord God, 'surely with a might hand and an outstretched arm and with wrath poured out, I will be king over you. [I will bring you out from the peoples and gather you out of the countries where you are scattered, with a mighty hand and an outstretched arm and with wrath poured out'" (Ez. 20:33–3).
   G. "Whether you like it or not, with or without your consent, I shall establish my dominion over you."
4.A. "... if then their uncircumcised heart is humbled and they make amends for their iniquity:"
   B. This is how things are as to repentance,
   C. for as soon as they humble their heart in repentance, I forthwith revert and have mercy on them,
   D. as it is said, "if then their uncircumcised heart is humbled and they make amends for their iniquity."
5.A. "... then I will remember my covenant with Jacob, [and I will remember my covenant also with Isaac and my covenant also with Abraham]:"
   B. Why are the patriarchs listed in reverse order?

C. It is to indicate, if the deeds of Abraham are not sufficient, then the deeds of Isaac, and if the deeds of Isaac are not worthy, then the deeds of Jacob.

D. Each one of them is worthy that the world should depend upon his intervention.

6.A. And why with reference to Abraham and Jacob are remembrance mentioned, but not with respect to Isaac?

B. His ashes are regarded as though he were scooped up on the altar.

C. And why with respect to Abraham and Isaac, but not with respect to Jacob, is there mention of "also"?

D. This teaches that the bier of Jacob our father was without flaw [since he did not produce an evil son, unlike Abraham with Ishmael and Isaac with Esau].

7.A. I know only that the patriarchs are covered. How about the matriarchs?

B. Scripture uses the accusative particle, and the accusative particle encompasses only the matriarchs,

C. as it is said, "There they buried Abraham and [the accusative particle] Sarah his wife" (Gen. 49:31).

8.A. And how do we know that the covenant is made with the land?

B. Scripture says, "and I will remember the land."

9.A. "But the land shall be left by them and enjoy its Sabbaths [while it lies desolate without them]:"

B. "I said to them to sow for me for six years and release the year for me for one year, so that they might know that the land is mine.

C. "But that is not what they did, get up and go into exile from it, so that it may enjoy release on its own for all the years of release that it owes to me."

D. For it is said, "But the land shall be left by them and enjoy its Sabbaths while it lies desolate without them, and they shall make amends for their iniquity."

10.A. "... because [Hebrew: because] and because, [that is, for this item and for that item, exactly] [they spurned my ordinances, and their soul abhorred my statutes]:"

B. "Now did I collect item by item from Israel? And did I not exact punishment for them only for one out of a hundred sins that they committed before me?

C. "Why then is it said, 'because' [as though the penalty were exact]?

D. "It is because 'they spurned my ordinances'—this refers to the laws;

E. "and because 'their soul abhorred my statutes'—this refers to the exegeses of Scripture.

11.A. "[Yet for all] that"—this refers to the sin committed in the Wilderness.

B. "... yet for"—this refers to the sin of Baal Peor.

C. "... yet for all that"—this refers to the sin involving the kings of the Amorites.

12.A. "[Yet for all that, when they are in the land of their enemies,] I will not spurn them, neither will I abhor them so as to destroy them utterly:"

B. Now what is left for them, but that they not be spurned nor abhorred? For is it not the fact that all the good gifts that had been given to them were now taken away from them?

C. And were it not for the Scroll of the Torah that was left for them, they were in no way be different from the nations of the world!

D. But "I will not spurn them:" in the time of Vespasian.

E. "... neither will I abhor them:" in the time of Greece.

F. "... so as to destroy them utterly and break my covenant with them:" in the time of Haman.

G. "... for I am the Lord their God:" in the time of Gog.

13.A. And how do we know that the covenant is made with the tribal fathers?

B. As it is said, "but I will for their sake remember the covenant with their forefathers whom I brought forth out of the land of Egypt:"

B. This teaches that the covenant is made with the tribal fathers.

14.A. "These are the statutes and ordinances and Torahs:"

B. "... the statutes:" this refers to the exegeses of Scripture.

C. "... and ordinances:" this refers to the laws.

D. "... and Torahs:" this teaches that two Torahs were given to Israel, one in writing, the other oral.

E. Said R. Aqiba, "Now did Israel have only two Torahs? And did they not have many Torahs given to them? 'This is the Torah of burnt-offering' (Lev. 6:2), 'This is the Torah of the meal-offering' (Lev. 6:27), 'This is the Torah of the guilt-offering' (Lev. 7:1), 'This is the Torah of the sacrifice of peace-offerings' (Lev. 7:11), 'This is the Torah: when a man dies in a tent' (Num. 19:1)."

15.A. "... which the Lord made between him and the people of Israel [on Mount Sinai by Moses]:"

B. Moses had the merit of being made the intermediary between Israel and their father in heaven.

C. "... on Mount Sinai by Moses:"

D. This teaches that the Torah was given, encompassing all its laws, all its details, and all their amplifications, through Moses at Sinai.

Some of the items begin to reveal a protocol or pattern, e.g., Nos. 2, 3, 4, 9, 14. But overall, the impression I gain is one of a miscellany, since I see no polemical and well-focused proposition. The exegesis of the verse involving the patriarchs is full and rich, Nos. 5, 6, 7. The *heilsgeschichtliche* exercises, e.g., No. 11, 12, are not sustained and lack conviction; the order is wrong, and no point is drawn from them. The upshot is that the methodical and rigorous discourse established with reference to the legal passages finds no counterpart here.

JACOB NEUSNER
Bard College

Sifre to Deuteronomy, Theology of

The book of Deuteronomy reaches Judaism through Sifre to Deuteronomy, attributed to Tannaite authors, a commentary to Deuteronomy that reached closure at ca. 300 C.E. Out of cases and examples, the Rabbinic sages seek generalizations and governing principles. Since, in the book of Deuteronomy, Moses explicitly sets forth a vision of Israel's future history, sages in Sifre to Deuteronomy examined that vision to uncover the rules that explain what happens to Israel. That issue drew attention from cases to rules, with the result that, in the book of Deuteronomy, they set forth a systematic account of Israel's future history, the key to Israel's recovery of command of its destiny. Like Sifra, Sifre to Deuteronomy pursues a diverse topical program in order to demonstrate a few fundamental propositions. The survey of the topical and propositional program of Sifre to Deuteronomy dictates what is truly particular to that authorship. It is its systematic mode of methodical analysis, in which it does two things. First, the document's compilers take the details of cases and carefully re-frame them into rules pertaining to all cases. The authorship therefore asks those questions of susceptibility to generalization ("generalizability") that first-class philosophical minds raise. And it answers those questions by showing what details restrict the prevailing law to the conditions of the case, and what details exemplify the encompassing traits of the law overall. These are, after all, the two possibilities. The law is either limited to the case and to all cases that replicate this one. Or the law derives from the principles exemplified, in detail, in the case at hand. Essentially, as a matter of both logic and topical program, our authorship has reread the legal portions of the book of Deuteronomy and turned Scripture into what we now know is the orderly and encompassing code supplied by the Mishnah. To state matters simply, this authorship "mishna-izes" Scripture. We find in Sifre to Numbers no parallel to this dominant and systematic program of Sifre to Deuteronomy.

But in other aspects, the document presents no surprises. In the two Sifres and Sifra we find a recurrent motif, intense here, episodic there, of how the written component of the Torah, that is, revelation in written form, serves as the sole source of final truth. Logic or reason untested against Scripture produces flawed or unreliable results. The Torah, read as rabbis read it, and that alone proves paramount. Reason on its own is subordinate. For their search for the social rules of Israel's society, the priority of the covenant as a reliable account of the workings of reality, and the prevailing laws of Israel's history decreed by the terms of the covenant, their fundamental claim is the same. There are rules and regularities, but reason alone will not show us what they are. A systematic and reasoned reading of the Torah—the written Torah—joined to a sifting of the cases of the Torah in search of the regularities and points of law and order—these are what will tell the prevailing rule. A rule of the Mishnah and its account of the here and now of everyday life rests upon the Torah, not upon (mere) logic. A rule of Israel's history, past, present, and future, likewise derives from a search for regularities and points of order identified not by logic alone, but by logic addressed to the Torah. So there are these modes of gaining truth that apply equally to Mishnah and Scripture. There is logic, applied reason and practical wisdom, such as sages exhibit; there is the corpus of facts supplied by Scripture, read as sages read it. These two together form God's statement upon the world today.

The topical program of the document intersects at its fundamental propositions with programs of other authorships—beginning, after all, with those of Scripture itself. The writers and compilers and compositors of Deuteronomy itself will have found entirely familiar such notions as the conditional character of Israel's possession of the land of Israel, the centrality of the covenant in Israel's relationship with God and with the other nations of the world, and the decisive role of the covenant in determining its own destiny, and the covenantal responsibilities and standing of Israel's leadership—surely a considerable motif in the very structure of the book of Deuteronomy itself, beginning and end in particular. The reader may well wonder how we may treat as a distinctive authorship a group of writers who simply go over ground familiar in the received literature. In some important ways the authorship of Sifre to Deuteronomy makes a statement that is very much its own. That fact becomes clear when we consider the document's rhetorical, logical, and topical characteristics.

Four principal topics encompass the document's propositions, of which the first three correspond to the three relationships into which Israel entered: with heaven, on earth, and within. These yield systematic statements that concern the relationships between Israel and God, with special reference to the covenant, the Torah, and the land; Israel and the nations, with interest in Israel's history, past, present, and future, and how that cyclic is to be known; Israel on its own terms, with focus upon Israel's distinctive leadership. The fourth rubric encompasses not specific *ad hoc* propositions, that form aggregates of proofs of large truths, but rather, prevailing modes of thought, demonstrating the inner structure of intellect, in our document yielding the formation, out of the cases of Scripture, of encompassing rules.

Israel and God: The Implications of the Covenant

The basic proposition, spelled out in detail, is that Israel stands in a special relationship with God, and that relationship is defined by the contract, or covenant, that God made with Israel. The covenant comes to particular expression, in our document, in two matters, first, the land, second, the Torah. Each marks Israel as different from all other nations, on the one side, and as selected by God, on the other. In these propositions, sages situate Israel in the realm of heaven, finding on earth the stigmata of covenanted election and concomitant requirement of loyalty and obedience to the covenant.

First comes the definition of those traits of God that our authorship finds pertinent. God sits in judgment upon the world, and his judgment is true and righteous. God punishes faithlessness. But God's fundamental and definitive trait is mercy. The way of God is to be merciful and gracious. The basic relationship of Israel to God is one of God's grace for Israel. God's loyalty to Israel endures, even when Israel sins. When Israel forgets God, God is pained. Israel's leaders, whatever their excellence, plead with God only for grace, not for their own merit. Correct attitudes in prayer derive from the need for grace, Israel having slight merit on its own account. Israel should follow only God, carrying out religious deeds as the covenant requires, in accord with the instructions of prophets. Israel should show mercy to others, in the model of God's merciful character.

Second, the contract, or covenant, produces the result that God has acquired Israel, which God created. The reason is that only Israel accepted the Torah, among all the nations, and that is why God made the covenant with Israel in particular. Why is the covenant made only with Israel? The gentiles did not accept the Torah, Israel did, and that has made all the difference. Israel recognized God forthwith; the very peace of the world and of nature depends upon God's giving the Torah to Israel. That is why Israel is the sole nation worthy of dwelling in the palace of God and that is the basis for the covenant too. The covenant secures for Israel an enduring relationship of grace with God. The covenant cannot be revoked and endures forever. The covenant, terms of which are specified in the Torah, has duplicate terms: if you do well, you will bear a blessing, and if not, you will bear a curse.

That is the singular mark of the covenant between God and Israel. A mark of the covenant is the liberation from Egypt, and that sufficed to impose upon Israel God's claim for their obedience. An important sign of the covenant is the possession of the land. Part of the covenant is the recognition of merit of the ancestors. In judging the descendants of the patriarchs and matriarchs, God promised, in making the covenant, recognition of the meritorious deeds of the ancestors. The conquest of the land and inheriting it are marks of the covenant, which Israel will find easy because of God's favor. The inheritance of the land is a mark of merit, inherited from the ancestors. The land is higher than all others and more choice. All religious duties are important, those that seem trivial as much as those held to be weightier.

God always loves Israel. That is why Israel

should carry out the religious duties of the Torah with full assent. All religious duties are equally precious. Israel must be wholehearted in its relationship with God. If it is, then its share is with God, and if not, then not. But Israel may hate God. The right attitude toward God is love, and Israel should love God with a whole heart. The reason that Israel rebels against God is prosperity. Then people become arrogant and believe that their prosperity derives from their own efforts. But that is not so, and God punishes people who rebel to show them that they depend upon God. When Israel practices idolatry, God punishes them, e.g., through exile, through famine, through drought, and the like. Whether or not Israel knows or likes the fact, it is the fact that Israel therefore has no choice but to accept God's will and fulfill the covenant.

The heaven and the earth respond to the condition of Israel and therefore carry out the stipulations of the covenant. If Israel does not carry out religious duties concerning heaven, then heaven bears witness against them. That centers on the land of Israel in particular. Possession of the land is conditional, not absolute. It begins with grace, not merit. It is defined by the stipulation that Israel observe the covenant, in which case Israel will retain the land. If Israel violates the covenant, Israel will lose the land. When Israel inherits the land, in obedience to the covenant and as an act of grace bestowed by God, it will build the Temple, where Israel's sins will find atonement. The conquest of the land itself is subject to stipulations, just as possession of the land, as an act of God's grace, is marked by religious obligations. If Israel rebels or rejects the Torah, it will lose the land, just as the Canaanites did for their idolatry.

The land is not the only, or the most important, mark of the covenant. It is the fact that Israel has the Torah which shows that Israel stands in a special relationship to God. The Torah is the source of life for Israel. It belongs to everyone, not only the aristocracy. Children should start studying the Torah at the earliest age possible. The study of the Torah is part of the fulfillment of the covenant. Even the most arid details of the Torah contain lessons, and if one studies the Torah, the reward comes both in this world and in the world to come.

The possession of the Torah imposes a particular requirement, involving an action. The most important task of every male Israelite is to study the Torah, which involves memorizing, and not forgetting, each lesson. This must go on every day and all the time. Study of the Torah should be one's main obligation, prior to all others. The correct motive is not for the sake of gain, but for the love of God and the desire for knowledge of God's will. People must direct heart, eyes, ears, to teachings of the Torah. Study of the Torah transforms human relationships, so that strangers become the children of the master of the Torah whom they serve as disciples. However unimportant the teaching or the teacher, all is as if on the authority of Moses at Sinai. When a person departs from the Torah, that person becomes an idolater. Study of the Torah prevents idolatry.

Israel and the Nations: The Meaning of History

The covenant, through the Torah of Sinai, governs not only the ongoing life of Israel but also the state of human affairs universally. The history of Israel forms a single, continuous, cycle, in that what happened in the beginning prefigures what will happen at the end of time. Events of Genesis are reenacted both in middle-history, between the beginning and the end, and also at the end of times. So the traits of the tribal founders dictated the history of their families to both the here and now and also the eschatological age. Moses was shown the whole of Israel's history, past, present, future. The times of the patriarchs are reenacted in the messianic day. That shows how Israel's history runs in cycles, so that events of ancient times prefigure events now. The prophets, beginning with Moses, describe those cycles. What happens bears close ties to what is going to happen. The prophetic promises too were realized in Temple times, and will be realized at the end of time.

The periods in the history of Israel, marked by the exodus and wandering, the inheritance of the land and the building of the Temple, the destruction, are all part of a divine plan. In this age Rome rules, but in the age to come, marked by the study of the Torah and the offering of sacrifices in the Temple cult, Israel will be in charge. That is the fundamental pattern and meaning of history. The Holy Spirit makes possible actions that bear consequences only much later in time. The prefiguring of history forms the dominant motif in Israel's contemporary life, and the reenacting of what has already been forms a constant. Israel therefore should believe, if not in what is coming, then in what has already been. The very names of places in the land attest to the continuity of Israel's history, which follows rules that do not change. The main point is that while Israel will be punished in the worst possible way, Israel will not be wiped out.

But the cyclical character of Israel's history should not mislead. Events follow a pattern, but knowledge of that pattern, which is provided by the Torah, permits Israel both to understand and also to affect its own destiny. Specifically, Israel controls its own destiny through its conduct with God. Israel's history is the working out of the effects of Israel's conduct, moderated by the merit of the ancestors. Abraham effected a change in God's relationship to the world. But merit, which makes history, is attained by one's own deeds as well. The effect of merit, in the nation's standing among the other nations, is simple. When Israel enjoys merit, it gives testimony against itself, but when not, then the most despised nation testifies against it.

But God is with Israel in time of trouble. When Israel sins, it suffers. When it repents and is forgiven, it is redeemed. For example, Israel's wandering in the wilderness took place because of the failure of Israel to attain merit. Sin is what causes the wandering in the wilderness. People rebel because they are prosperous. The merit of the ancestors works in history to Israel's benefit. What Israel does not merit on its own, at a given time, the merit of the ancestors may secure in any event. The best way to deal with Israel's powerlessness is through Torah-study; the vigor of engagement with Torah-study compensates for weakness.

It goes without saying that Israel's history follows a set time, e.g., at the fulfillment of a set period of time, an awaited event will take place. The prophets prophesy concerning the coming of the day of the Lord. Accordingly, nothing is haphazard, and all things happen in accord with a plan. That plan encompasses this world, the time of the messiah, and the world to come, in that order. God will personally exact vengeance at the end of time. God also will raise the dead. Israel has overcome difficult times and can continue to do so. The task ahead is easier than the tasks already accomplished. Israel's punishment is only once, while the punishment coming upon the nations is unremitting. Peace is worthwhile and everyone needs it. Israel's history ends in the world to come or in the days of the messiah. The righteous inherit the Garden of Eden. The righteous in the age to come will be joyful.

God acts in history and does so publicly, in full light of day. That is to show the nations who is in charge. The Torah is what distinguishes Israel from the nations. All the nations had every opportunity to understand and accept the Torah, and all declined it; that is why Israel was selected. And that demonstrates the importance of both covenant and the Torah, the medium of the covenant. The nations even had a prophet, comparable to Moses, who was Balaam. The nations have no important role in history, except as God assigns them a role in relationship to Israel's conduct. The nations are estranged from God by idolatry. That is what prevents goodness from coming into the world. The name of God rests upon Israel in greatest measure. Idolators do not control heaven. The greatest sin an Israelite can commit is idolatry, and those who entice Israel to idolatry are deprived of the ordinary protections of the law. God is violently angry at the nations because of idolatry. As to the nations' relationships with Israel, they are guided by Israel's condition. When Israel is weak, the nations take advantage, when strong, they are sycophantic. God did not apportion love to the nations of the world as he did to Israel.

Israel at Home: The Community and Its Governance

A mark of God's favor is that Israel has (or, has had and will have) a government of its own. Part of the covenantal relationship requires Israel to follow leaders whom God has chosen and instructed, such as Moses and the prophets. Accordingly, Israel is to establish a government and follow sound public policy. Its leaders are chosen by God. Israel's leaders, e.g., prophets, are God's servants, and that is a mark of the praise that is owing to them. They are to be in the model of Moses, humble, choice, select, well-known. Moses was the right one to bestow a blessing, Israel were the right ones to receive the blessing.

Yet all leaders are mortal, even Moses died. The saints are leaders ready to give their lives for Israel. The greatest of them enjoy exceptionally long life. But the sins of the people are blamed on their leaders. The leaders depend on the people to keep the Torah, and Moses thanked them in advance for keeping the Torah after he died. The leaders were to be patient, honest, give a full hearing to all sides, make just decisions, in a broad range of matters. To stand before the judge is to stand before God. God makes sure that Israel does not lack for leadership. The basic task of the leader is both to rebuke and also to console the people.

The rulers of Israel are servants of God. The prophets exemplify these leaders, in the model of Moses, and Israel's rulers act only on the instruction of prophets. Their authority rests solely on God's favor and grace. At the instance of God, the leaders of Israel speak, in particular, words of admonition. These are delivered before death, when the whole picture is clear, so that people can draw the necessary conclusions. These words, when Moses spoke them, covered the entire history of the community of Israel. The leaders of Israel address admonition to the entire community at once. No one is excepted. But the Israelites can deal with the admonition. They draw the correct conclusions. Repentance overcomes sin, as at the sin of the golden calf. The Israelites were contentious, nitpickers, litigious, and, in general, gave Moses a difficult time. Their descendants should learn not to do so. Israel should remain united and obedient to its leaders. The task of the community is to remain united. When the Israelites are of one opinion below, God's name is glorified above.

The Laws and Law. The Structure of Intellect

The explicit propositional program of our document is joined by a set of implicit ones. These comprise repeated demonstration of a point never fully stated. The implicit propositions have to do with the modes of correct analysis and inquiry that pertain to the Torah. There are two implicit propositions that predominate. The first, familiar from other compilations, is that pure reason does not suffice to produce reliable results. Only through linking our conclusions to verses of Scripture may we come to final and fixed conclusions. The implicit proposition, demonstrated many times, may therefore be stated very simply. The Torah (written) is the sole source of reliable information. Reason undisciplined by the Torah yields unreliable results. These items may occur, also, within the rubrics of the specific propositions that they contain. Some of them moreover overlap with the later catalogue, but, if so, are not listed twice.

The second of the two recurrent modes of thought is the more important. Indeed, we shall presently note that it constitutes the one substantial, distinctive statement made by our authorship. It is the demonstration that many things conform to a single structure and pattern. We can show this uniformity of the law by addressing the same questions to disparate cases and, in so doing, composing general laws that transcend cases and form a cogent system. What is striking, then, is the power of a single set of questions to reshape and reorganize diverse data into a single cogent set of questions and answers, all things fitting together into a single, remarkably well-composed structure. Not only so, but when we review the numerous passages at which we find what, in the logical repertoire I called methodical-analytical logic, we find a single program. It is an effort to ask whether a case of Scripture imposes a rule that limits or imparts a rule that augments the application of the law at hand.

A systematic reading of Scripture permits us to restrict or to extend the applicability of the detail of a case into a rule that governs many cases. A standard repertoire of questions may be addressed to a variety of topics, to yield the picture of how a great many things make essentially a single statement. This seems to me the single most common topical inquiry in our document. It covers most of the laws of Deut. 12–26. I have not catalogued the laws of history, which generalize from a case and tell us how things always must be; the list of explicit statements of the proposition that the case at hand is subject to either restriction or augmentation, that the law prevailing throughout is limited to the facts at hand or exemplified by those facts, would considerably add to this list. The size, the repetitious quality, the obsessive interest in augmentation and restriction, generalization and limitation—these traits of logic and their concomitant propositional results form the centerpiece of the whole.

In a few units of thought I discern no distinctive message, one that correlates with others to form a proposition of broad implications. Perhaps others can see points that transcend the cases at hand. These items would correspond to ones we should expect from an authorship that remained wholly within Scripture's range of discourse, proposing only to expand and clarify what it found within Scripture. Were our document to comprise only a commentary, then the messages of Scripture, delivered within the documentary limits of Scripture—that is, verse by verse, in a sustained statement solely of what Scripture says restated in paraphrase—would constitute the whole of the catalogue. We now see that that is far from the fact. Relative to the size of the document as a whole, these items do not seem to me to comprise an important component of the whole. They show that had our authorship wished only to amplify and restate the given, without presenting their own thought through the medium of Scripture (as through other media), they had every occasion and means of doing so. But they did so only in a limited measure. Here is a sample passage.

> SIFRE TO DEUTERONOMY PISQA I:I
> 1.A. "These are the words that Moses spoke to all Israel in Transjordan, in the wilderness, that is to say in the Arabah, opposite Suph, between Paran on the one side and

Tophel, Laban, Hazeroth, and Dizahab, on the other" (Deut. 1:1):
B. ["These are the words that Moses spoke" (Deut. 1:1):] Did Moses prophesy only these alone? Did he not write the entire Torah?
C. For it is said, "And Moses wrote this Torah" (Deut. 31:9).
D. Why then does Scripture say, "These are the words that Moses spoke" (Deut. 1:1)?
E. It teaches that [when Scripture speaks of the words that one spoke, it refers in particular to] the words of admonition.
F. So it is said [by Moses], "But Jeshurun waxed fat and kicked" (Deut. 32:15).

2.A. So too you may point to the following:
B. "The words of Amos, who was among the herdsman of Tekoa, which he saw concerning Israel in the days of Uzziah, king of Judah, and in the days of Jeroboam, son of Joash, king of Israel, two years before the earthquake" (Amos 1:1):
C. Did Amos prophesy only concerning these [kings] alone? Did he not prophesy concerning a greater number [of kings[ ] than any other?
D. Why then does Scripture say, "These are the words of Amos, [who was among the herdsman of Tekoa, which he saw concerning Israel in the days of Uzziah, king of Judah, and in the days of Jeroboam, son of Joash, king of Israel, two years before the earthquake]" (Amos 1:1)
E. It teaches that [when Scripture speaks of the words that one spoke, it refers in particular to] the words of admonition.
F. And how do we know that they were words of admonition?
G. As it is said, "Hear this word, you cows of Bashan, who are in the mountain of Samaria, who oppress the poor, crush the needy, and say to their husbands, 'Bring, that we may feast'" (Amos 4:1).
H. ["And say to their husbands, 'Bring, that we may feast'"] speaks of their courts [of justice].

3.A. So too you may point to the following:
B. "And these are the words that the Lord spoke concerning Israel and Judah" (Jer. 30:4).
C. Did Jeremiah prophesy only these words of prophecy alone? Did he not write two [complete] scrolls?
D. For it is said, "Thus far are the words of Jeremiah" (Jer. 51:64)
E. Why then does Scripture say, "And these are the words [that the Lord spoke concerning Israel and Judah]" (Jer. 30:4)?
F. It teaches that [when the verse says, "And these are the words that the Lord spoke concerning Israel and Judah" (Jer. 30:4)], it speaks in particular of the words of admonition.
G. And how do we know that they were words of admonition?
H. In accord with this verse: "For thus says the Lord, 'We have heard a voice of trembling, of fear and not of peace. Ask you now and see whether a man does labor with a child? Why do I see every man with his hands on his loins, as a woman in labor? and all faces turn pale? Alas, for the day is great, there is none like it, and it is a time of trouble for Jacob, but out of it he shall be saved" (Jer. 30:5–7).

4.A. So too you may point to the following:
B. "And these are the last words of David" (2 Sam. 23:1).
C. And did David prophesy only these alone? And has it furthermore not been said, "The spirit of the Lord spoke through me, and his word was on my tongue" (2 Sam. 23:2)?

D. Why then does it say, "And these are the last words of David" (2 Sam. 23:1)?

E. It teaches that, [when the verse says, "And these are the last words of David" (2 Sam. 23:1)], it refers to words of admonition.

F. And how do we know that they were words of admonition?

G. In accord with this verse: "But the ungodly are as thorns thrust away, all of them, for they cannot be taken with the hand" (2 Sam. 23:6).

5.A. So too you may point to the following:

B. "The words of Qohelet, son of David, king in Jerusalem" (Qoh. 1:1).

C. Now did Solomon prophesy only these words? Did he not write three and a half scrolls of his wisdom in proverbs?

D. Why then does it say, "The words of Qohelet, son of David, king in Jerusalem" (Qoh. 1:1)?

E. It teaches that [when the verse says, "The words of Qohelet, son of David, king in Jerusalem" (Qoh. 1:1)], it refers to words of admonition.

F. And how do we know that they were words of admonition?

G. In accord with this verse: "The sun also rises, and the sun goes down ... the wind goes toward the south and turns around to the north, it turns round continually in its circuit, and the wind returns again—that is, east and west [to its circuits. All the rivers run into the sea]" (Qoh. 1:5–7).

H. [Solomon] calls sun, moon, and sea "the wicked" for [the wicked] have no reward [coming back to them].

The focus is upon the exegesis of the opening word of Deuteronomy, "words...." The problem is carefully stated. And yet, without the arrangement within what is going to be a commentary on Deuteronomy, we should have no reason to regard the composition as exegetical at all. In fact, it is a syllogism, aiming at proving a particular proposition concerning word-usages. Standing by itself, what we have is simply a very carefully formalized syllogism that makes a philological point, which is that the word "words of ...," bears the sense of "admonition" or "rebuke." Five proofs are offered. We know that we reach the end of the exposition when, at 5.H, there is a minor gloss, breaking the perfect form. That is a common mode of signaling the conclusion of discourse on a given point.

SIFRE TO DEUTERONOMY PISQA I:II

1.A. "... to all Israel:"

B. [Moses spoke to the entire community all at once, for] had he admonished only part of them, those who were out at the market would have said, "Is this what you heard from the son of Amram? And did you not give him such-and-such an answer? If we had been there, we should have answered him four or five times for every word he said!"

2.A. Another matter concerning "... to all Israel]:"

B. This teaches that Moses collected all of them together, from the greatest to the least of them, and he said to them, "Lo, I shall admonish you. Whoever has an answer—let him come and say it."

We proceed to the next word in the base verse, but now our comment is particular to the verse. The explanation of why Moses spoke to everyone is then clear. On the one hand, it was to make certain that there was no one left out, so No. 1. On the other, it was to make certain that everyone had a say, so No. 2. These two points then complement one another.

SIFRE TO DEUTERONOMY PISQA I:III
1. A. Another matter concerning "... to all Israel:"
   B. This teaches that all of them were subject to admonition but quite able to deal with the admonition.
2. A. Said R. Tarfon, "By the Temple service! [I do not believe] that there is anyone in this generation who can administer an admonition."
   B. Said R. Eleazar ben Azariah, ""By the Temple service! [I do not believe] that there is anyone in this generation who can accept admonition."
   C. Said R. Aqiba, ""By the Temple service! [I do not believe] that there is anyone in this generation who knows how to give an admonition."
   D. Said R. Yohanan ben Nuri, "I call to give testimony against me heaven and earth [if it is not the case that] more than five times was R. Aqiba criticized before Rabban Gamaliel in Yabneh, for I would lay complaints against him, and [Gamaliel therefore] criticized him. Nonetheless, I know that [each such criticism] added to [Aqiba's] love for me.
   E. "This carries out the verse, 'Do not criticize a scorner, lest he hate you, but reprove a wise person, and he will love you' (Prov. 9:8)."

Nos. 1 and 2 are quite separate units of thought, each making its own point. Shall we say that all we have, at I:I-III, is a sequence of three quite disparate propositions? In that case, the authorship before us has presented nothing more than a scrapbook of relevant comments on discrete clauses. I think otherwise. It seems to me that in I:I-III as the distinct and complete units of thought unfold we have a proposition, fully exposed, composed by the setting forth of two distinct facts, which serve as established propositions to yield the syllogism of No. 3. But the syllogism is not made explicitly, rather it is placed on display by the (mere) juxtaposition of fact 1 and fact 2 and then the final proposition, I:III.1, followed by a story making the same point as the proposition. The exegesis now joins the (established) facts [1] that Moses rebuked Israel and [2] that all Israel was involved. The point is [3] that Israel was able to deal with the admonition and did not reject it. No. 2 then contains a story that makes explicit and underlines the virtue spun out of the verse. Aqiba embodies that virtue, the capacity—the wisdom—to accept rebuke. The upshot, then, is that the authorship wished to make a single point in assembling into a single carefully ordered sequence I:I-III, and it did so by presenting two distinct propositions, at I:I, I:II, and then, at I:III, recast the whole by making a point drawing upon the two original, autonomous proofs. Joining I:I, and I:II, then led directly to the proposition at which the authorship was aiming. We have much more than an assembly of information on diverse traits or points of verses, read word by word. It is, rather, a purposeful composition, made up of what clearly are already-available materials.

SIFRE TO DEUTERONOMY PISQA I:IV
1. A. "On the other side of the Jordan" (Deut. 1:1):
   B. This teaches that he admonished them concerning things that they had done on the other side of the Jordan.

SIFRE TO DEUTERONOMY PISQA I:V
1. A. "In the wilderness" (Deut. 1:1):
   B. This teaches that he admonished them concerning things that they had done in the wilderness.
2. A. Another matter concerning "In the wilderness" (Deut. 1:1):
   B. This teaches that they would take their little sons and daughters and

toss them into Moses's bosom and say to him, "Son of Amram, 'what ration have you prepared for these? What living have you prepared for these?"

C. R. Judah says, "Lo, Scripture says [to make this same point], 'And the children of Israel said to them, "Would that we had died by the hand of the Lord in the land of Egypt [when we sat by the fleshpots, when we ate bread . . . for you have brought us forth to this wilderness to kill the whole assembly with hunger]" (Exod. 16:3).'"

3.A. Another matter concerning "In the wilderness" (Deut. 1:1):
B. This encompasses everything that they had done in the wilderness.

SIFRE TO DEUTERONOMY PISQA I:VI
1.A. "In the Plain" (Deut. 1:1):
B. This teaches that he admonished them concerning things that they had done in the Plains of Moab.
C. So Scripture says, "And Israel dwelt in Shittim [and the people began to commit harlotry with the daughters of Moab" (Num. 25:1).

SIFRE TO DEUTERONOMY PISQA I:VII
1.A. "Over against Suph [the sea]" (Deut. 1:1):
B. This teaches that he admonished them concerning things that they had done at the sea.
C. For they rebelled at the sea and turned their back on Moses days.
2.A. R. Judah says, "They rebelled at the sea, and they rebelled within the sea.
B. "And so Scripture says, 'They rebelled at the sea, even in the sea itself' (Ps. 106:7)."
3.A. Is it possible to suppose that he admonished them only at the outset of a journey? How do we know that he did so between one journey and the next?
B. Scripture says, "Between Paran and Tophel" (Deut. 1:1).
4.A. "Between Paran and Tophel" (Deut. 1:1):
B. [The word Tophel bears the sense of] disparaging words with which they disparaged the manna.
C. And so does Scripture say, "And our soul loathed this light bread" (Num. 21:5).
D. [God] said to them, "Fools! Even royalty choose for themselves only light bread, so that none of them should suffer from vomiting or diarrhea. For your part, against that very act of kindness that I have done for you, you bring complaints before me.
E. "It is only that you continue to walk in the foolishness of your father, for I said, 'I will make a help meet for him' (Gen. 2:18), while he said, 'The woman whom you gave to be with me gave me of the tree and I ate' (Gen. 3:12)."

The words of admonition, now fully exposed, apply to a variety of actions of the people. That is the main point of I:IV–VII. The matter is stated in a simple way at I:IV, V.1 (with an illustration at I:V.2), I:V.3, I:VI, I:VII. After the five illustrations of the proposition that the admonition covered the entire past, we proceed to a secondary expansion, I:VII.2, 3, which itself is amplified at I:VII.4. The main structure is clear, and the proposition is continuous with the one with which we began: Moses admonished Israel, all Israel, which could take the criticism, and covered the entire list of areas where they had sinned, which then accounts for the specification of the various locations mentioned by Deut. 1:1. When we realize what is to come, we understand the full power of the proposition, which is syllogistic though in exegetical form. It is to indicate the character and encompassing program of the book of Deuteronomy—nothing less.

SIFRE TO DEUTERONOMY PISQA I:VIII
1.A. "And Hazeroth" (Deut. 1:1):
   B. [God] said to them, "Ought you not to have learned from what I did to Miriam in Hazeroth?
   C. "If to that righteous woman, Miriam, I did not show favor in judgment, all the more so to other people!"
2.A. Another matter: now if Miriam, who gossiped only against her brother, who was younger than herself, was punished in this way, one who gossips against someone greater than himself all the more so!"
3.A. Another matter: Now if Miriam, whom when she spoke, no person heard, but only the Omnipresent alone, in line with this verse, "And the Lord heard ...," (Num. 12:2), was punished, one who speaks ill of his fellow in public all the more so!"

The basic point is made at the outset and the case is then amplified. The sin concerning which Moses now admonished the people was that of gossiping, and the connection to Miriam is explicit. The argument that each place-name concerns a particular sin thus is carried forward. The entire discourse exhibits remarkable cogency.

SIFRE TO DEUTERONOMY PISQA I:IX
1.A. "And Dizahab (Deut. 1:1):
   B. [Since the place name means, "of gold," what he was] saying to them [was this:] "Lo, [following Finkelstein] everything you did is forgiven. But the deed concerning the [golden] calf is worst of them all." [Hammer: "I would have overlooked everything that you have done, but the incident of the golden calf is to me worse than all the rest put together."]
2.A. R. Judah would say, "There is a parable. To what may the case be compared? To one who made a lot of trouble for his fellow. In the end he added yet another. He said to him, 'Lo, everything you did is forgiven. But this is the worst of them all.'
   B. "So said the Omnipresent to Israel, 'Lo, everything you did is forgiven. But the deed concerning the [golden] calf is worst of them all.'"

The place-name calls to mind the sin of the golden calf. This is made explicit as a generalization at No. 1, and then, No. 2, Judah restates the matter as a story.

SIFRE TO DEUTERONOMY PISQA I:X
1.A. R. Simeon says, "There is a parable. To what may the case [of Israel's making the calf of gold] be compared? To one who extended hospitality to sages and their disciples, and everyone praised him.
   B. "Gentiles came, and he extended hospitality to them. Thieves came and he extended hospitality to them.
   C. "People said, 'That is so-and-so's nature—to extend hospitality [indiscriminately] to anyone at all.'
   D. "So did Moses say to Israel, '[Di zahab, meaning, enough gold, yields the sense] There is enough gold for the tabernacle, enough gold also for the calf!'
2.A. R. Benaiah says, "The Israelites have worshipped idolatry. Lo, they are liable to extermination. Let the gold of the tabernacle come and effect atonement for the gold of the calf."
3.A. R. Yose b. Haninah says, "'And you shall make an ark cover of pure gold' (Exod. 25:17).

B. "Let the gold of the ark cover come and effect atonement for the gold of the calf."
4.A. R. Judah says, "Lo, Scripture states, 'In the wilderness, in the plain.'
   B. "These are the ten trials that our fathers inflicted upon the Omnipresent in the wilderness.
   C. "And these are they: two at the sea, two involving water, two involving manna, two involving quails, one involving the calf, and one involving the spies in the wilderness."
   D. Said to him R. Yose b. Dormasqit, "Judah, my honored friend, why do you distort verses of Scripture for us? I call to testify against me heaven and earth that we have made the circuit of all of these places, and each of the places is called only on account of an event that took place there [and not, as you say, to call to mind Israel's sin].
   E. "And so Scripture says, And the herdsmen of Gerar strove with the herdsmen of Isaac, saying, 'The water is ours.' And he called the name of the well Esek, because they contended with him' (Gen. 26:29). 'And he called it Shibah' (Gen. 26:33)."

I:X.1–3 carries forward the matter of *DiZahab* and amplifies upon the theme, not the proposition at hand. No. 4 then presents a striking restatement of the basic proposition, which has been spelled out and restated in so many ways. It turns out that Judah takes the position implicit throughout and made explicit at I:X.4. There is then a contrary position, at D. We see, therefore, how the framers have drawn upon diverse materials to present a single, cogent syllogism, the one then stated in most succinct form by Judah. The contrary syllogism, that of Yose is not spelled out, since amplification is hardly possible. Once we maintain that each place has meaning only for what happened in that particular spot, the verse no longer bears the deeper meaning announced at the outset—admonition or rebuke, specifically for actions that took place in various settings and that are called to mind by the list of words (no longer place-names) of Deut. 1:1.

SIFRE TO DEUTERONOMY PISQA I:XI
1.A. Along these same lines [of dispute between Judah and Yosé:]
   B. R. Judah expounded, "'The burden of the word of the Lord. In the land of Hadrach, and in Damascus, shall be his resting-place, for the Lord's is the eye of man and all the tribes of Israel' (Zech. 9:1):
   C. "[Hadrach] refers to the Messiah, who is sharp [hard] toward the nations, but soft [rakh] toward Israel."
   D. Said to him R. Yose b. Dormasqit, "Judah, my honored friend, why do you distort verses of Scripture for us? I call to testify against me heaven and earth that I come from Damascus, and there is a place there that is called Hadrach."
   E. He said to him, "How do you interpret the clause, 'and in Damascus, shall be his resting-place'?"
   F. [Yose] said to him, "How do we know that Jerusalem is destined to touch the city-limits of Damascus? As it is said, 'and in Damascus, shall be his resting-place. And 'resting place' refers only to Jerusalem, as it is said, 'This is my resting place forever' (Ps. 132:14)."
   G. [Judah] said to him, "How then do you interpret the verse, And the city shall be built upon its own mound' (Jer. 30:18)?"
   H. [Yose] said to him, "That it is not destined to be moved from its place."
   I. [Yose continued,] saying to him, "How do I interpret the verse, 'And

the side chambers were broader as they wound about higher and higher; for the winding about of the house went higher and higher round about the house, therefore the breadth of the house continued upward' (Ez. 41:7)? It is that the Land of Israel is destined to expand outward on all sides like a fig tree that is narrow below and broad above. So the gates of Jerusalem are destined to reach Damascus.
J. "And so too Scripture says, 'Your nose is like the tower of Lebanon, which looks toward Damascus' (Song 7:5).
K. "And the exiles will come and encamp in it, as it is said, 'And in Damascus shall be his resting place' (Zech. 9:1).
L. "'And it shall come to pass in the end of days that the mountain of the Lord's house shall be established at the top of the mountains and shall be exalted above the hills, and all nations shall flow into it, and many peoples shall go and say . . .' (Is. 2:2-3)."

SIFRE TO DEUTERONOMY PISQA I:XII
1.A. Along these same lines [of dispute between Judah and Yosé:]
B. R. Judah expounded, "'And he made him to ride in the second chariot which he had, and they cried before him, "Abrech"' (Gen. 41:43):
C. "[Abrech] refers to Joseph, who is a father [*ab*] in wisdom, but soft [*rakh*] in years."
D. Said to him R. Yose b. Dormasqit, "Judah, my honored friend, why do you distort verses of Scripture for us? I call to testify against me heaven and earth that the meaning of Abrech pertains to knees and is simply, 'I shall cause them to bend their knees' [appealing to the causative applied to the root for knee].
E. "For everyone came and went under his authority, as Scripture says, 'And they set him over all of Egypt' (Gen. 41:43)."

I:XI–XII simply lay out further instances of the same hermeneutical dispute between Judah and Yose. All three items—I:X–XII—form a single cogent dispute on its own terms. Then the composite establishes a distinct statement, which concerns figurative, as against literal, interpretation. Once worked out, the whole found an appropriate place here, at I:X.4.

JACOB NEUSNER
Bard College

Sifre to Numbers, Theology of

Sifre to Numbers stands out in the Rabbinic Midrash-compilations for a remarkable fact. The document scarcely acknowledges the Rabbinic theological structure and system that animate the other midrash-compilations of the formative age. In theological compositions it contains such a negligible quantity, and of such marginal and episodic quality, that we cannot make any claims about the presence of a theological system that is realized there. That judgment rests not only on the character of what the document presents. The characterization of Sifre Numbers as not engaged by theological reading of Scripture also derives from a comparison of other documents' approach to passages of Numbers. Specifically, when we compare the reading of Numbers 5 in Sifre to Numbers with the reading of the same topic in Mishnah-Tosefta and the two

Talmuds, we see how the latter focus upon theological issues ignored by the former. The documents of halakhic exposition explicitly articulate the theology of Numbers 5, by contrast to the narrowly *ad hoc* exegetical exposition accorded the same matter in Sifre to Numbers. The contrast helps us to see in context the remarkably slight interest in theology on the part of the compilers of Sifre to Numbers. First we survey the theological propositions we do find in the document, then provide an epitome of the treatment of Numbers 5 in Sifre to Numbers, and finally, spell out the reading of the same matter in the Halakhic expositions of the Mishnah and the Tosefta.

The Theological Propositions of Sifre to Numbers

The category-formations are shared among Pesiqta deRab Kahana, Genesis Rabbah, Song of Songs Rabbah, Leviticus Rabbah, Lamentations Rabbati, Ruth Rabbah, Esther Rabbah I, Sifra, and Sifre to Numbers. To the extent that Sifre to Numbers contains theological statements at all, familiar category-formations accommodate those statements. But that is to claim very little.

God and Man, God and Israel

The main point in the other midrash-compilations is, God's relationships with humankind in general ("the nations") and God's relationships with Israel in particular are complementary. The nations rejected, Israel accepted, God's dominion, embodied in the Torah. And the rest follows. But this document contains remarkably little reflection on God's relationship with the gentiles, e.g., with humanity in general. Its focus throughout is on God's love for Israel. The framers then take for granted that the gentiles have marked themselves as God's enemies. In the next rubric, we see the consequence: the nations also mark themselves as Israel's enemies.

The main point is familiar: God loves and yearns for Israel. The correlation of God's love for Israel and God's enduring presence within Israel extends even to Israel's uncleanness and sinfulness. God so loves Israel that even though they contract uncleanness, his presence remains with them (I:X.1). And sin is the cause of that uncleanness (I:X.2–3). But, too, Israelites did as Moses instructed them (I:XI.1). Israel is so precious that God dwells among them even when they are unclean. God accompanies Israel into Exile, to Egypt, Babylonia, Elam, Edom; and God will return with them when they come back to the Land (CLXI:III.2). Why does God so love Israel? It is because Israel accepted the Torah and carry out God's will.

But Israel does the opposite as well. When the Israelites carry out the will of the Omnipresent, then, "... the Lord lift up his countenance upon you." But when the Israelites do not carry out the will of the Omnipresent, then, "... who will not lift up a face and show favoritism" (Deut. 10:17). So Israel's deeds make the difference (XLII:2). When Israel obeys the word of the Lord their God, then all the blessings promised in the Torah come upon them. These blessings include property and good health; the blessing keeps Israel from the evil impulse. It prevents others from ruling over Israel and keeps Israel from demons. God will keep the covenant he made with the fathers of Israel. Israel is subject to a foreordained end. God will keep the soul of the Israelite at the hour of death and guard him in the world to come (XI:I.1–10). A mark of God's grace is to make a person pleasing to other people (XLI:II.2). It is further by giving the Israelite knowledge, understanding, enlightenment, virtue and wisdom (XLI:II.4), and mastery of the Torah (XLI:II.4). Various cases prove that gentiles who bring themselves near to God are themselves brought closer by God, and all the more so an Israelite who carries out the Torah will be drawn nearer to God by God's own intervention (LXXVIII:I.1).

This exposition compares favorably with those of the other midrash-compilations devoted to the problem at hand: gentiles' relationship with God and with Israel. The next category-formation, showing the parallel relationships of the gentiles with God and with Israel, completes the one significant theological program that the document sets forth.

God and the Nations, Israel and the Nations

The logic of the first theological category-formation dictates its continuation: the correlation of relationships, the nation's with God, the nation's with Israel, Israel's with God, God's with both other parties. The nations who hate Israel hate God. Those who support Israel support God. Whoever hates Israel is as if he hates God, whoever rose up against Israel is as if he rose up against God, whoever lays hands on Israel is as if he lays hands on the apple of God's eye. So too, whoever helps Israel is as if he helps God. Israel's suffering is suffering for God too. Everywhere Israel went into exile, God went into exile with them. And when they come back, God's presence will return with them (LXXXIV:IV.1). But in Sifre to Numbers, the specific stories about the nations and Israel, e.g., Balaam's blessing!—do not yield data that sustain weighty propositions pertinent to these matters. And that failure in an important component of the exposition of Numbers matches the still more striking one we shall encounter in a moment.

Israel's Encounter with God through the Torah

Here is an example of a theological category-formation well instantiated in other documents and scarcely noted in the one at hand. An Israelite cannot pick and choose among the commandments but must accept and keep them all (CXII:IV.2). One who studies the Torah but does not repeat it for others despises the word of the Lord (CXII:IV.3). This is a trivial point, hardly comparable to assertions elsewhere that through Torah-study Israel meets God.

Divine Justice and Mercy

The issue of justice, which shapes the generative logic of the entire theological system and structure, surfaces only rarely. A single point registers, the priority of mercy over justice in God's ultimate dispensation. God's attribute of bestowing mercy outweighs his attribute of bestowing justice (VIII:VIII.1–2). A mark of divine justice is that the punishment begins with the limb that begins the transgression. Now does this not yield an argument *a fortiori*: If in the case of the attribution of punishment, which is the lesser, from the limb with which she began to commit the transgression—from there the punishment begins, in the case of the attribute of bestowing good, which is the greater, how much the more so! (XVIII:I.1). But well might we claim, the main point has been missed, when we realize, the document does not contain speculation, systematic or even episodic, on the justice of the disposition of the wife accused of infidelity. And, beyond that point, the entire issue of divine justice, raised by that matter, is not treated. That others read Numbers 5 differently will soon become clear.

God's Judgment, Israel's Repentance and Atonement; God's Remorse, Israel's Consolation

For all the stress on God's love for Israel, nothing pertains to this fundamental principle.

Restoration: God will Bring the End through the Royal Messiah at a Time of His Own Choosing, and His Hand Is Not to Be Forced

There is no sustained reflection on eschatological questions involving the Messiah and the end of days, except for one item, which follows.

The End of Days

At the end of days there will be an eschatological war of Gog and Magog, a war in which Israel is saved and after which there is no period of subjugation. At the end of time there will be troubles of blight, mildew, hard labor, loss of ships, every sort of misfortunate. If Israel sounds an alarm with the trumpets, it will be saved. The trumpet calls Israel to God's mind, and that is only for salvation (LXXVI:II.1–4).

Creation Contains within Itself Signals of What Would Happen in Future History

God showed Jacob the house of the sanctuary in all its beauty, with the offerings being presented, the priests serving, and the Presence of God rising up (CXIX:III.3).

The Merit that Accrues in One Generation to the Benefit of Another Generation

The matter does not figure.

The Righteous Receive Their Reward Later On

Death atones for most sins, and death with repentance for the rest (CXII:IV.5).

Commandments Are the Marks of Israel's Distinction before God

Perhaps this proposition is taken for granted, but it is not articulated.

Propositions Particular to Sifre to Numbers

Not a single theological statement in the document registers a fresh point or adumbrates the working of a category-formation not known in other documents.

The Statement of Sifre to Numbers in the Context of the Theology of Rabbinic Judaism

The bits and pieces fit together into components of a familiar system and structure. But apart from the exposition of the election of Israel (Nos. 1, 2, above), nothing qualifies as a theological statement of a systematic character. Nor do these bits and pieces require us to invoke the Rabbinic structure and system that animate and are realized in other midrash-compilations. If the only Rabbinic document in our hands were Sifre to Numbers, we should find exceedingly difficult the reconstruction of the Rabbinic theological system. All we should find plausible is, the Rabbinic exegetes drew as appropriate on the theological category-formations of Scripture. For it is Scripture that to begin with draws the monumental parallels between Adam and Israel, Adam's relationship with God and Israel's relationship with God, and it is in Scripture that the Rabbinic sages learn to see God's enemies as Israel's enemies, and Israel's as God's. In that context, the original judgment—Sifre to Numbers neither adumbrates nor is animated by a theological system—takes on weight and meaning.

What Does Sifre to Numbers Contribute?

Here is an abbreviated outline of the document's reading of Numbers 5. In it Sifre to Numbers emerges as a highly disciplined document, bearing only modest accretions of interpolations, glosses, and amplifications, and very few topical appendices and other secondary accretions. Bold face type signals a citation from the Mishnah or the Tosefta.

VIII:I.1. "... then the man shall bring his wife to the priest ...:" according to the law of the Torah, the husband must bring his wife to the priest, but sages have ruled that **two disciples of sages are sent along with him on the way, so that he should not have sexual relations with his wife [during the trip, and thereby nullify the effect of the rite] [M. Sot. 1:3].** Rabbi says, "Her husband is regarded as trustworthy in her regard, and that is on the basis of an argument *a fortiori*: now if in respect to a woman in her menstrual period, on account of having intercourse with whom one is liable to extirpation, the husband is regarded as trustworthy [and no provision is made to make sure that the couple does not engage in sexual relations during the wife's period], in respect to an accused wife, on account of having sexual relations with whom one does not incur the penalty of extirpation, is it not reasonable that her husband should be held reliable as well?" [T. Sot. 1:2].

VIII:II.1. "... and bring the offering required of her ...:" "He must bring every offering that is incumbent on her," the words of R. Judah. And sages say, "He must bring the offering that renders her fit for him [but does not owe any offering that may otherwise become incumbent upon her, rather bearing responsibility only for those that relate to him,] for example, the offering in the aftermath of her uncleanness by reason of flux or by reason of having given birth. In such cases he brings animals out of his property and has not got the right to deduct the cost from the marriage settlement. But as to an offering that does not validate her relationship to him, for example, if she took upon her head a series of oaths as a Nazirite [and so has to bring animal offerings as part of the rite of purification], or if she inadvertently violated the Sabbath [and owes a sin-offering,] lo, while he brings these out of his property he deducts the value from her ultimate marriage-settlement."

VIII:III.1. "... a tenth of an ephah of barley meal ...:" That is, one out of ten parts of an ephah.

VIII:IV.1. "... a tenth of an ephah of barley meal ...:" Why is this matter made explicit? Because one might have argued to the contrary:

VIII:V.1. "... barley ...:" Why is this matter made explicit? Because one might have argued to the contrary: Since the meal-offering brought by a sinner [accompanying a sin-offering] comes on account of a sin, and this one is brought on account of sin, if I draw an analogy to the meal-offering of a sinner, which is brought only as wheat, so this one also should bring only a meal-offering of wheat. Accordingly, Scripture makes explicit the contrary fact, that this meal-offering derives from barley [and not wheat].

VIII:VI.1. "... he shall pour no oil upon it and put no frankincense on it, [for it is a cereal offering of jealousy, a cereal offering of remembrance, bringing iniquity to remembrance]:" That statement indicates that if one has put oil on it, he violates a negative commandment.

VIII:VII.1. "... for it is a cereal offering of jealousy ...:" The plural indicates that jealousy is present in two dimensions. Just as the woman has caused jealousy for the husband, so has she done for the lover. Just as she has caused jealousy below, so she has brought about jealousy above.

VIII:VIII.1. "... a cereal offering of remembrance, bringing iniquity to remembrance ...:" May I maintain that what is brought to remembrance is both merit and liability? Scripture states, "bringing iniquity to remembrance." "All references to remembrance that are in the Torah are for the good, but this one refers to punishment," the words of R. Tarfon. R. Aqiba says, "This one also is for the good, for it is said, '... and if the wife has not been made unclean ...,' [she will bear children]."

2. [Arguing to the contrary of the foregoing:] I know only that [the meal-offering] serves as a remembrance of sin. How do I know that it serves as a remembrance of merit? Scripture says, "A meal-offering of remembrance"—covering all possibilities.

3. [Continuing the exposition of Aqiba's position:] What would be an instance in which both of the requirements are carried out so that the requirements of strict justice are not perverted [and both the woman's bad deed and also her merit are brought into play]?. "If the woman was unclean, punishment affects he

IX:I.1. immediately, and if she has some sort of merit, the merit will suspend the penalty for three months, until her pregnancy becomes visible," the words of Abba Yose b. Hanan.

IX:I.1. "And the priest shall bring her" (Num. 5:16–22):
On the basis of the cited phrase sages have ruled: The bitter water is not administered to two accused wife at the same time [T. Sot. 1:6].

IX:II.1. "... and set her before the Lord:" [The stress on setting her indicates] that one should not set up with her neither her bondmen nor her bond women, because her heart relies on them [and she will not feel ashamed] [M. Sot. 1:6].

IX:III.1. "... and set her before the Lord:" It is before Nicanor's gate.
On the basis of this verse sages have ruled: The head of the priestly watch of a given week sets unclean people at Nicanor's gate, for at that location they administer the bitter water to accused wives [M. Sot. 1:5, T. Sot. 1:4].

X:I.1. "[And the priest shall bring her near and set her before the Lord;] and the priest shall take holy water:" "... holy water:" water falls into the classification of holy only if it has been consecrated by being drawn in a utensil. And what sort of water is that?. It is water in a flask.

X:II.1–2. "... in an earthen vessel:" The specification at hand indicates that the law has not treated all sorts of utensils as equivalent to a clay utensil. For one might have argued to the contrary: Since dust and water effect sanctification in the case of the rite of burning the red cow for the preparation of purification-water [Num. 19] and dust and water serve to effect consecration in the case of the accused wife, is it not reasonable to suppose that in both cases we should treat all manner of utensils as equivalent to a clay utensil? Accordingly, Scripture states explicitly, "... in a clay utensil," indicating that the law has not treated all sorts of utensils as equivalent to a clay utensil. "In an earthen utensil:" "A new earthen utensil," the words of R. Ishmael.

X:III.1. "... and take some of the dust that is on the floor of the tabernacle and put it into the water:" The verse indicates that if there is no dirt there, one brings dirt from some other place and puts it in that location, since it is the location [in the courtyard of the Temple] that effects the sanctification of the dirt.

X:IV.1. "It is because the law states, 'For the unclean they shall take some ashes of the burnt sin offering[and running water shall be added in a vessel]' (Num. 19:17)." In the present case there is a reference to dirt, and in that other case there is a reference to dirt. Just as in the latter case, the dirt must be scattered on the surface of the water, so elsewhere the dirt must be scattered on the surface of the water. "And just as in that other case, if the dirt is placed in the utensil before the water is put in, one has carried out his obligation, so here, if one has put the dirt in before the water, he has carried out his obligation."

X:V.1. "... and the priest shall take some of the dust that is on the floor of the tabernacle and put it into the water:"
It should be sufficient dirt so that it can be discerned in the water [M. Sot 2:2G]. There are three cases in the Torah that require that same volume of dirt: the ashes of the red cow, the dirt used for the rite of the accused wife, and the spit of the

childless widow [Deut. 25:15]. R. Ishmael says, "Also the blood of the bird [used in the rite of purification of the leper, Lev. 14]" [T. Sot. 1:8].

XI:I.1. "And the priest shall set the woman before the Lord:"

XI:II.1. "... and unbind the hair of the woman's head:" "The priest turns to her back and undoes her hair, so as to carry out in her regard the religious duty of unbinding her hair," the words of R. Ishmael.

2. Another matter: "The verse teaches concerning Israelite women that they keep their heads covered. And while there is no clear proof for that proposition, there certainly is ample evidence in its favor: And Tamar put dirt on her head" (2 Sam. 13:19).

3. R. Judah says, "If the woman's kerchief was pretty, he did not reveal it, and if her hair was lovely, he did not undo it. If her hair was covered in white, he would cover it in black. If the hair was covered with lovely black [kerchiefs], he did not undo them. And they would cover her with ugly things." "If she was wearing golden earrings or bracelets or nose rings, they would remove them from her, so as to make her appear ugly" [M. Sot. 1:6A–B].

XI:III.1. "... and place in her hands:" **Abba Hanin says in the name of R. Eliezer, "It is so as to tire her out** [M. Sot. 2:1A], so that she will repent [and avoid the coming rite by confessing her sin]. "And if this is how the Omnipresent takes pity for those who violate his will, all the more so will he take pity for those who do his will."

XI:IV.1. "... And in his hand the priest shall have the water of bitterness that brings the curse:" This verse of Scripture [in referring to the water of bitterness in the hand of the priest] indicates that the water is not turned into bitter water except in the hand of the priest.

2. Another matter: the water is called bitter because of how it ends up, for it makes the body bitter and brings sin to the surface.

XII:I.1. "Then the priest shall make her take an oath:" The priest imposes the oath, and the woman does not take the oath on her own volition. For logic might have dictated otherwise: the word "oath" appears in the present context, and the word "oath" is used presently [in another connection entirely, namely, that of the Nazirite, an oath a woman takes on her own account]. Just as the oath stated elsewhere requires that the person take the oath on her own volition, so the oath subject to discussion here may be taken on the woman's own initiative. Accordingly, Scripture states, "Then the priest shall make her take an oath." The priest imposes the oath, and the woman does not take the oath on her own volition.

XII:II.1. "... saying to the woman:" "He makes the statement in any language that the woman understands," the words of R. Josiah. "For one might have reasoned in this way [producing the contrary, and wrong, conclusion:] if in the case of the formula to be recited in the rite of removing the shoe performed by the childless widow [Deut. 25:1–5], which is a matter of only minor weight, the required statement has to be said in the Holy Language, the formula in connection with the accused wife, which deals with an infraction of a major order,—is it not reasonable that we should certainly not treat all other languages as equivalent to the Hebrew language. "Accordingly, Scripture says, '... saying to the woman,' meaning in any language that the woman understands," the words of R. Josiah. R. Ishmael says, "Such a proof hardly is required in any event. For it is stated, 'And the woman shall say, 'Amen, Amen.' "Now if the woman does not understand what has been said, how is she going to say, 'Amen, Amen.' "But is it possible that the woman says 'Amen' only in respect to the execration? "When Scripture says, "the Lord make you an execration and an oath among your people,' lo, it is clear that subject to discussion is [not only the execration but also] the oath [which, therefore, the woman certainly has understood. Hence it is not necessary to invoke the cited verse to prove Josiah's proposition. How then does Ishmael interpret the verse?] "What then does Scripture mean when it says, '... saying to the woman'? That verse serves to instruct the priest on the correct manner of administering the oath."

XII:III.1. "If no man has lain with you [and if you have not turned aside to uncleanness, while you were under your husband's authority, be free from this water of bitterness that brings the curse]:" [The phrasing of the statement to the woman] teaches that the priest first of all speaks of mitigating circumstances, saying to her, "Wine causes much to happen, so too lightheadedness, and also childishness. These have gone and led you astray. Do not cause the great Name written in sanctity to be blotted out by the water. [Rather confess and give up your claim on your marriage-contract, but do not go through the rite.]"

XIII:I.1–3. "But if you have gone astray:" I know that that statement pertains only to ordinary sexual relations. How do I know that it covers sexual relations dog-patch style? Scripture says, "... and if you have defiled yourself." [That would encompass all modes of sexual activity.] "... and some man other than your husband has lain with you:" That statement encompasses a eunuch. "... other than your husband:" This encompasses the wife of a eunuch [who also is subject to the rite] [M. Sot. 4:4B]. The priest would extend the stipulation at hand to all possible conditions.

XIV:I.1. "... let the priest make the woman take the oath of the curse:" (Num. 5:16–22): You may draw an analogy on the basis of the formulation at hand to all other oaths that are listed in the Torah. Since various oaths are imposed by the law of the Torah, without further specification as to the manner of taking the oath, but the Torah has given you specific details in one of the cases, [namely this one,] indicating that the oath is taken only along with a curse, I impose that same detail on all oaths that are listed in the Torah, so that they should be taken only as the present one is: the oath of the curse. [So whenever an oath is imposed, a curse for violating it also is included in the formula.]

XIV:II.1–2. "... the Lord make you an execration and an oath among your people:" Why is this statement made? Because it is said, "If a person hears a execration to give evidence as a witness" (Lev. 5:1), I know only that the law applies to a execration. How do I know that the same rule applies to an oath?

XV:I.1. "... when the Lord makes your thigh fall away and your body swell; and may this water that brings the curse pass into your bowels and make your body swell and your thigh fall away." And the woman shall say, 'Amen, Amen.' (Num. 5:16–22). **R. Yose the Galilean says, "This refers to the belly and thigh of the lover.** "You say that this refers to the belly and thigh of the lover. But perhaps it refers only refers to the belly and thigh of the beloved [the accused woman]? "When the verse says, '... and her body will swell and her thigh will fall away,' this refers to the woman's thigh and body. When, therefore, Scripture goes on and says, 'To cause the body to swell and the thigh to fall away,' this refers only to the body and thigh of the lover. "Scripture thus informs you that just as the penalty is visited on her, so the penalty is visited on him** [M. Sot. 5:1A]. "And is it not an argument a fortiori : if the divine attribute of inflicting punishment, which is less, applies equally to one who causes his fellow to stumble [as well as to the one who actually sins], along these same lines, all the more so will be the result of the divine attribute to do good [which will amply reward one who causes his fellow to do good].

XV:II.1. A "And the woman shall say, 'Amen, Amen:'" "'Amen' that I have not been made unclean, 'Amen' that I shall never be made unclean," the words of R. Meir. But sages do not concur in his view. Rather [they held]: "'Amen that I have not been made unclean, and if I have been made unclean, may the curse come upon her [me], 'Amen' as to this man, and 'Amen' as to any other man. 'Amen' as to when I was merely betrothed, 'Amen' as to when I was married. 'Amen' as to when I was awaiting marriage to the levirate brother, 'Amen' as to what may have taken place after I entered into marriage with my levirate brother in law.'"

2. Since various oaths are imposed by the law of the Torah, without further specification as to the manner of taking the oath, while the Torah has given specific details in one of the cases, the result is that I impose that same detail on all oaths that are listed in the Torah, so that they should be taken only as the present one is: the oath of the curse. [Further:] since oaths in general are listed in the Torah without further specification, the Torah has given details in the case of one of them, indicating that it is taken only with the expression of the Holy Name of God beginning with Y H, so I impose that same detail on all oaths that are listed in the Torah, which are to be taken only with the expression of the Holy Name of God beginning with Y H. [Further:] since oaths in general are listed in the Torah without further specification, the Torah has given details in the case of one of them, indicating that it is taken only with the expression "Amen," so I impose that same detail on all oaths that are listed in the Torah, which are to be taken only with the expression, "Amen."

XVI:I.1. "Then the priest shall write these . . ." (Num. 5:23–28). Might I draw the conclusion that [the priest [writes all of the curses that are contained in the Torah? "Scripture states, . . . these curses" [in particular].

XVI:II.1. "Then the priest shall write these curses:" Why is it made explicit that the priest does it? For logic might have suggested otherwise, on this basis: Here "... and he shall write ..." is said, and elsewhere [in connection with the preparation of a writ of divorce, Deut. 24:1] the same language is used: "he shall write." Just as in that other context the writing is valid when done by a member of any caste [not merely a priest] so here too the writing would be valid when done by a person of any caste, not only the priestly caste. Accordingly, Scripture states, "Then the priest shall write these curses."

XVI:III.1. "... in a book and wash them off into the water of bitterness:" The writing is to be written in something that can be blotted out.
On the basis of the present specification they have ruled: **They do not write the words either on a tablet or on paper or on leather, but on a scroll, as it is said, "... in a book." And one does not write the words with gum or with coppera but only with ink, as it is said, "... wash them off into the water of bitterness"—writing that can be blotted out** [M. Sot. 2:4].

XVII:I.1. "... and he shall make the woman drink the water of bitterness that brings the curse, [and the water that brings the curse shall enter into her and cause bitter pain. And the priest shall take the cereal offering of jealousy out of the woman's hand, and shall wave the cereal offering before the Lord]" (Num. 5:23–28). Why does Scripture say, "and he shall make the woman drink the water," since it in any event is stated, "And when he has made her drink the water"? [Obviously, he is going to make her drink it.] It is for this reason: **if the scroll has already been blotted out, and then the woman says, "I shall not drink the water," "they harass her and force her to drink it against her will"** [M. Sot. 3:3D], the words of R. Aqiba.

2. **If her scroll was blotted out and then she said, "I am unclean," the water is poured out and her meal-offering is scattered on the ashes** [M. 3:3C]. **And her scroll is not valid for the water-ordeal of another accused wife** [M. Sot. 3:3B].

3. "And the priest shall take the cereal offering of jealousy out of the woman's hand:" And not out of the hand of her agent. And the priest shall take the cereal offering of jealousy out of the woman's hand:" So if she produced menstrual blood [which would make her unclean so that she could not handle the cereal offering], she would not undergo the rite of drinking the bitter water.

XVII:II.1. "[And the priest shall take the cereal offering of jealousy out of the woman's hand,]" and shall **wave the cereal offering [before the Lord and bring it to the altar; and the priest shall take a handful of the cereal offering, as its memorial portion, and burn it upon the altar and afterward shall make the woman drink the water:]** He waves the offering back and forth, up and down. How do we know that that is the case? As it is said, "... which is waved and which is raised up" (Exod. 29:26) [M. Men. 5:6K–L]. An analogy, therefore, is drawn between raising up and waving. Just as raising up involves bringing the sheaf back and forward, so raising it up involves the same. And just as raising up involves raising up and bringing down the sheaf, so waving the sheaf requires raising it and lowering it.

On the basis of this exegesis, they have stated: The religious duty of waving involves waving backward and forward, upward and downward—that is the requirement of waving.

XVII:III.1. **"[And the priest shall take the cereal offering of jealousy out of the woman's hand, and shall wave the cereal offering] before the Lord[and bring it to the altar; and the priest shall take a handful of the cereal offering, as its memorial portion, and burn it upon the altar and afterward shall make the woman drink the water:"]** That is, to the east [M. Men. 5:6M].

XVII:IV.1. **"[And the priest shall take the cereal offering of jealousy out of the woman's hand,] and shall wave the cereal offering before the Lord and bring it to the altar;[and the priest shall take a handful of the cereal offering, as its memorial portion, and burn it upon the altar and afterward shall make the woman drink the water:"]** The verse teaches with reference to the meal offering of the accused wife that it requires both waving and also drawing near [to the altar, two procedures] [M. Men. 5:6/O].

XVII:V.1. ["And the priest shall take the cereal offering of jealousy out of the woman's hand, and shall wave the cereal offering before the Lord and bring it to the altar;] and the priest shall take a handful of the cereal offering, as its memorial portion, and burn it upon the altar [and afterward shall make the woman drink the water:"] This refers to the burning up of the handful of the meal-offering, which act is referred to as the act of remembrance.

XVII:VI.1. "[And the priest shall take the cereal offering of jealousy out of the woman's hand, and shall wave the cereal offering before the Lord and bring it to the altar; and the priest shall take a handful of the cereal offering, as its memorial portion, and burn it upon the altar] and afterward shall make the woman drink the water:" This refers to the matter which we have already treated.

What follows is the sole entry that contributes to the theological repertoire, the stress that what commences transgression also first suffers punishment.

XVIII:I.1. "And when he has made her drink the water, [then, if she has defiled herself and has acted unfaithfully against her husband, the water that brings the curse shall enter into her and cause bitter pain,] and her body shall swell, and her thigh shall fall away, [and the woman shall become an execration among her people. But if the woman has not defiled herself and is clean, then she shall be free and shall conceive children]" (Num. 5:23-28). I know only that her body and thigh are affected. How do I know that that is the case for the rest of her limbs? Scripture states, "... the water that brings the curse shall enter into her." So I take account of the phrase, "... the water that brings the curse shall enter into her." Why [if all the limbs are affected equally] then does Scripture specify her body and her thigh in particular? As to her thigh, the limb with which she began to commit the transgression—from there the punishment begins.

Along these same lines: "And he blotted out everything that sprouted from the earth, from man to beast" (Gen. 7:23. From the one who began the transgression [namely Adam], the punishment begins. Along these same lines: "and the men who were at the gate of the house they smote with piles" (Gen. 19:11). From the one who began the transgression the punishment begins. Along these same lines: "... and I shall be honored through Pharaoh and through all of his force" (Exod. 14:4). Pharaoh began the transgression, so from him began the punishment. Along these same lines: "And you will most certainly smite at the edge of the sword the inhabitants of that city" (Deut. 13:15). From the one who began the transgression, the punishment begins. Along these same lines is the present case: the limb with which she began to commit the transgression— from there the punishment begins.

That is the only point at which the exposition of the same chapter of Numbers by Sifre to Numbers and by Mishnah-Tosefta intersects. This forms a mere component of the much larger construction we are going to survey presently. Let us now complete our picture of the systematic exegesis of Numbers 5 in Sifre to Numbers.

XVIII:II.1. "... and the woman shall become an execration among her people:" People will say,] "May what happened to her happen to you [if you are lying]." So in the case of an oath, people will take an oath by her, saying, "May what happened to her happen to you."

XIX:I.1. "But if the woman has not defiled herself and is clean, [then she shall be free and shall conceive children]" (Num. 5:28). R. Ishmael says, "Now was the woman unclean, that Scripture should declare her clean? Why then does Scripture state, 'But if the woman has not defiled herself and is clean'? "Scripture thereby indicates that, once the woman got a bad name for herself, she became forbidden to have sexual relations with her husband [but now she is permitted to do so]." **R. Simeon b. Yohai says, "Do not for one moment imagine that merit suspends the effects of the bitter water** [M. Sot. 3:5A]. Why then is it stated, 'But if the woman has not defiled herself and is clean'? "Since Scripture states, 'If a man commits adultery with the wife of his neighbor, both the adulterer and the adulteress shall be put to death' (Lev. 20:10), we know that that is the rule only when there are witnesses who have admonished the couple that their intended action is punishable by the death-penalty.

XIX:II.1. "But if the woman has not defiled herself and is clean, then she shall be free and shall conceive children..." (Num. 5:23–28): She is regarded as clean so far as her husband is concerned, so far as the alleged lover is concerned, and [should her husband be a priest] so far as her right to eat food in the status of priestly rations is concerned.

2. "[But if the woman has not defiled herself] and is clean:" also as to the execration and the oath.

XIX:III.1–3. "... [then she shall be free] and shall conceive children" (Num. 5:28). **"The sense is that if she had been barren, now she will be visited with children,"** the words of R. Aqiba. Said to him R. Ishmael, "If so, all barren women will go and get themselves into trouble so that they will be visited with children, while the one who sits in her home loses out. "Rather, what is the sense of the statement, '... then she shall be free and shall conceive children'? "If she used to give birth with pain, now she will give birth in comfort. If she used to produce females, now she will produce males. If she used to produce swarthy children, now she will produce fair ones, if she used to produce short children, now she will produce tall ones" [T. Sot. 2:3S]. "then she shall be free and shall conceive children:" This statement excludes from the rite women known to be barren, unable to produce children [who do not fall into the category of those who can be subjected to the rite]. "... then she shall be free and shall conceive children:" Since the woman had been part of the general classification but then had been singled out for special treatment, Scripture restores her to the classification of the generality of women.

XX:I.1. "This is the law in cases of jealousy, [when a wife, though under her husband's authority, goes astray and defiles herself, or when the spirit of jealousy comes upon a man and he is jealous of his wife; then he shall set the woman before the Lord, and the priest shall execute upon her all this law. The man shall be free from iniquity, but the woman shall bear her iniquity]" (Num. 5:29-31). I know only that the law applies for the moment [at which it was given]. How do I know that it applies for all generations? Scripture says, 'This is the law in [cases of jealousy],'" the words of R. Josiah.

XX:II.1. "... when a wife, though under her husband's authority, goes astray:" **The reference to her husband serves to encompass a husband who** is in the category of a deaf-mute and one who is in the category of derangement, in which case the court expresses jealousy in behalf of such men [M. Sot. 4:5B]. [If a court does so,] it is with the effect of invalidating the wife's right to a marriage-settlement [M. Sot. 4:C]. Or can a court so express jealousy as to subject the wife to the rite of the bitter water as well? Scripture states, "Then the man shall bring his wife to the priest" (Num. 5:14)—the man, not the court.

XX:III.1. "... when a wife, though under her husband's authority, goes astray:" "[The reference to the husband's authority] bears the implication that a woman at the stage of betrothal [prior to the full consummation of the marriage] is exempt from the rite." If the betrothed woman is exempt, should the same implication exclude the woman in a levirate marriage as well? "Scripture says, '... when a wife, though under her husband's authority, goes astray,' so serving to encompass the woman in a levirate marriage [who is, after all, subject to the husband's authority]," the words of R. Josiah. R. Jonathan says, "Since the Scripture says, 'If any man's wife....' (Num. 5:12), that formulation serves to exclude the woman in a levirate relationship. "If the woman in a levirate relationship is excluded, should the same implication exclude the betrothed woman as well? "Scripture says, '... when a wife, though under her husband's authority, goes astray,' so serving to encompass the woman who is betrothed."

XXI:I.1. "[This is the law in cases of jealousy, when a wife, though under her husband's authority, goes astray and defiles herself] or when the spirit of jealousy comes upon a man and he is jealous of his wife; [then he shall set the woman before the Lord, and the priest shall execute upon her all this law. The man shall be free from iniquity, but the woman shall bear her iniquity]" (Num. 5:29-31). Why is this clause stated [namely, "and he is jealous of his wife"]? Since it says, "when the spirit of jealousy comes upon a man and he is jealous of his wife; [then he shall set the woman before the Lord,]" might one maintain that, just as prior to his expressing jealousy, it is a matter of optional concern [whether or not he does so and imposes the rite], so even after he has expressed jealousy, it remains an optional matter [whether or not he imposes the rite]? Scripture states, "when the spirit of jealousy comes upon a man and he is jealous of his wife," as a matter not of an option but of an obligation. [Once he has commenced the rite, he cannot cancel it.]

XXI:II.1. "... then he shall set the woman before the Lord, and the priest shall execute upon her all this law. The man shall be free from iniquity, but the woman shall bear her iniquity]" (Num. 5:29-31). If he has carried out the rite, he is free of sin, but if he has not carried out the rite, he is not going to be free of sin.

XXI:III.1. "... The man shall be free from iniquity " (Num. 5:29-31): [The husband should not feel guilty if the wife dies, and he should not say,] "Woe is me, for I have put an Israelite woman to death. "Woe is me, for I have caused the humiliation of an Israelite woman. "Woe is me, for I used to have sexual relations with a woman who was in fact unclean." Therefore it is said, "... The man shall be free from iniquity."

Ben Azzai says, "Scripture speaks of a case in which the woman emerges as clean. Since she has brought herself into this affair, she too should not escape some sort of punishment. Therefore it is said, 'The man shall be free from iniquity, but the woman shall bear her iniquity.'" R. Aqiba says, "Scripture comes to teach you the lesson that the end of the matter is death: 'Her body shall swell and her thigh shall fall away' (Num. 5:27). "Why then is it said, 'The man shall be free from iniquity, but the woman shall bear her iniquity'? "The man is free of sin, but that woman will bear her sin. "It is then not in accord with the statement, 'I shall not visit your daughters when they turn into prostitutes, nor your daughters-in-law when they commit adultery, for men themselves go aside with harlots and sacrifice with cult prostitutes, and a people without understanding shall come to ruin' (Hos. 4:14). "He said to them, 'Since you run after whores, the bitter water will not put your wives to the test.' "That is why it is said, 'The man shall be free from iniquity'—that is with reference to that sin [of which Hosea spoke. The husband is not guilty of having had sexual relations with a whore, though his wife is guilty, because he did not realize it, and, when he did, he took the correct action.]"

The important result may be stated succinctly: To the theological corpus of Rabbinic Judaism in the Midrash-compilations of the formative age, Sifre to Numbers contributes nothing.

The Contrast with Mishnah-Tosefta Sotah

Two documents of the same Rabbinic Judaism, generally regarded as synchronic, Sifre to Numbers and Mishnah-Tosefta being conventionally labeled "Tannaite," expound precisely the same topic of Scripture, Numbers 5, the halakhah of disposing of the wife accused of infidelity. But they do so in a systematic, theological framework, such as Sifre to Numbers does not construct.

So we contrast the reading of Numbers 5 by Sifre Numbers with the points of interest in that same topic expounded by the Mishnah and the Tosefta. Then we see the difference between Sifre to Numbers with its topical- and halakhic exegesis of a scriptural institution, and the Mishnah and the Tosefta, with their theological exegesis of the same matter.

As the halakhic sages in the Mishnah and the Tosefta re-present the ordeal imposed on the accused wife, they underscore the exact justice that the ordeal executes. The exposition of the topic in the Mishnah and the Tosefta, therefore also in the Talmuds, lays heavy emphasis upon how, measure for measure, the punishment fits the crime—but the reward matches the virtue as well. What the guilty wife has done, the law punishes appropriately; but, also, they point to cases in which acts of merit receive appropriate recognition and reward. In this way sages make the point that, within the walls of the household, rules of justice prevail, with reward for goodness and punishment for evil the standard in the household as much as in public life. Why sages have chosen the Halakhah of the accused wife as the venue for their systematic exposition of the divine law of justice is not difficult to explain. Here is the *locus classicus* in the Mishnah (given in bold face type) and the Tosefta (in regular type).

M. 1:7: **By that same measure by which a man metes out [to others], do they mete out to him: She primped herself for sin, the Omnipresent made her repulsive. She exposed herself for sin, the Omnipresent exposed her. With the thigh she began to sin, and afterward with the belly, therefore the thigh suffers the curse first, and afterward the belly. But the rest of the body does not escape [punishment].**

T. 3:2: And so you find that with regard to the accused wife: With the measure with which she measured out, with that measure do they mete out to her. She stood before him so as to be pretty before him, therefore a priest stands her up in front of everybody to display her shame, as it is said, And the priest will set the woman before the Lord (Num. 5:18).

T. 3:3: She wrapped a beautiful scarf for him, therefore a priest takes her cap from her head and puts it under foot. She braided her hair for him, therefore a priest loosens it. She painted her face for him, therefore her face is made to turn yellow. She put blue on her eyes for him, therefore her eyes bulge out.

T. 3:4: She signaled to him with her finger, therefore her fingernails fall out. She showed him her flesh, therefore a priest tears her cloak and shows her shame in public. She tied on a belt for him, therefore a priest brings a rope of twigs and ties it above her breasts, and whoever wants to stare comes and stares at her [M. Sot. 1:6C-D]. She pushed her thigh at him, therefore her thigh falls. She took him on her belly, therefore her belly swells. She fed him goodies, therefore her meal-offering is fit for a cow. She gave him the best wines to drink in elegant goblets, therefore the priest gives her the bitter water to drink in a clay pot.

T. 4:1: I know only with regard to the measure of retribution that by that same measure by which a man metes out, they mete out to him [M. Sot.

1:7A]. How do I know that the same is so with the measure of goodness [M. Sot. 1:9A]? Thus do you say:' The measure of goodness is five hundred times greater than the measure of retribution. With regard to the measure of retribution it is written, Visiting the sin of the fathers on the sons and on the grandsons to the third and fourth generation (Ex. 20:5). And with regard to the measure of goodness it is written, And doing mercy for thousands (Ex. 20:6). You must therefore conclude that the measure of goodness is five hundred times greater than the measure of retribution.

M. 1:8: **Samson followed his eyes [where they led him], therefore the Philistines put out his eyes, since it is said, And the Philistines laid hold on him and put out his eyes (Judges 16:21). Absalom was proud of his hair, therefore he was hung by his hair [II Sam. 14:25-26]. And since he had sexual relations with ten concubines of his father, therefore they thrust ten spear heads into his body, since it is said, "And ten young men that carried Jacob's armor surrounded and smote Absalom and killed him" (II Sam. 18:15). And since he stole three hearts—his father's, the court's, and the Israelite's—since it is said, "And Absalom stole the heart of the men of Israel" (II Sam. 15:6)—therefore three darts were thrust into him, since it is said, "And he took three darts in his hand and thrust them through the heart of Absalom" (II Sam. 18:14).**

M. 1:9: **And so is it on the good side.**

The remainder is cited below. The law of the accused wife renders urgent the question of whether and how justice governs in the household. How has Scripture provoked this view of the matter? Scripture, as we note, imposes the ordeal not only upon the adulteress but on the faithful wife. A spirit of jealousy suffices, whether or not the wife warrants the husband's suspicion. Surely the entire procedure reeks of injustice, and the promise of future offspring hardly compensates for the public humiliation that the innocent wife has undergone. It is in that context that, in the very presentation of the halakhah, the Oral Torah systematically lays out the evidence that, here, especially here, justice prevails. And that means not only that the wicked woman is punished, but that the righteous one is rewarded. What for Scripture is tacked on as an afterthought in the Oral Torah becomes a principal focus of exposition.

If in the very same context, Num. 5, as expounded in the Mishnah and Tosefta, we turn from the halakhah to the aggadah, we find precisely the same focus on how God's perfect justice is embodied in the very rite of the accused wife. In sages' view, which animates every line in the Oral Torah, the will of the one, unique God, made manifest through the Torah, governs, and, further, God's will, for both private life and public activity, is rational. That is to say, within man's understanding of reason, God's will is just. And by "just," sages understood the commonsense meaning: fair, equitable, proportionate, commensurate. In place of fate or impersonal destiny, chance, or simply irrational, inexplicable chaos, God's plan and purpose everywhere come to realization. So the Oral Torah identifies God's will as the active and causative force in the lives of individuals and nations.

But the more urgent question is, how do sages know that God's will is realized in the moral order of justice, involving reward and punishment? Sages turned to Scripture for the pertinent facts; that is where God makes himself manifest. But of the various types of scriptural evidence—explicit commandments, stories, prophetic admonitions—that they had available to show how the moral order prevailed in all being, what type did the prefer? The one bearing the greatest probative weight derived from the exact match between sin and punishment. Here is their starting point; from here all else flows smoothly and in orderly fashion. World order is best embodied when sin is punished, merit rewarded—both; one without the other does not suffice.

That body of evidence, the facts, that Scripture supplied recorded human action and divine reaction, on the one side, and meritorious deed and divine response and reward, on the other. It was comprised by consequential cases, drawn from both private and public life, to underscore sages' insistence upon the match between the personal and the public, all things subject to the same simple rule. That demonstration of not only the principle but the precision of measure for measure, deriving from Scripture's own record of God's actions, takes priority of place in the examination of the rationality of sages' universe. That is because it permeates their system and frames its prevailing modes of explanation and argument. The principle that all being conforms to rules, and that these rules embody principles of justice through exact punishment of particular sin, precise reward of singular acts of virtue defined the starting point of all rational thought and the entire character of sages' theological structure and system. What we see in the topic at hand is of special interest: when sages wish to show the justice of God, they turn to the case before us.

When sages in the halakhic documents—but not in Sifre to Numbers—examined the facts of Scripture to establish that principle of rationality and order in conformity to the requirements of justice and equity, what impressed them was not the inevitability but the precision of justice. Scripture portrays the world order as fundamentally just and reasonable, and it does so in countless ways. But Scripture encompasses the complaint of Job and the reflection of Qoheleth. Sages for their part identified those cases that transcended generalities and established the facticity of proportionate justice, treating them as not only exemplary but probative. They set forth their proposition and amassed evidence in support of it. And, to underscore the point that sages demonstrate in the present halakhic category: when God judges and sentences, not only is the judgment fair but the penalty fits the crime with frightening precision. But so too, when God judges and awards a decision of merit, the reward proves equally exact. These two together, the match of sin and penalty, meritorious deed and reward, then are shown to explain the point and purpose of one detail after another, and, all together, they add up to the portrait of a world order that is fundamentally and essentially just—the starting point and foundation of all else.

Here is sages' account of God's justice, which is always commensurate, both for reward and punishment, in consequence of which the present permits us to peer into the future with certainty of what is going to happen, so M. Sot. 1:7ff. What we note is sages' identification of the precision of justice, the exact match of action and reaction, each step in the sin, each step in the response, and, above all, the immediacy of God's presence in the entire transaction. They draw general conclusions from the specifics of the law that Scripture sets forth, and that is where systematic thinking about takes over from exegetical learning about cases, or, in our own categories, philosophy from history, noted earlier:

M. Sot. 1:7
A. By that same measure by which a man metes out [to others], do they mete out to him:
B. She primped herself for sin, the Omnipresent made her repulsive.
C. She exposed herself for sin, the Omnipresent exposed her.

We begin with sages' own general observations based on the facts set forth in Scripture. The course of response of the woman accused of adultery to her drinking of the bitter water that is supposed to produce one result for the guilty, another for the innocent, is described in Scripture in this language: "If no man has lain with you ... be free from this water of bitterness that brings the curse. But if you have gone astray ... then the Lord make you an execration ... when the Lord makes your thigh fall away and your body swell; may this water ... pass into your bowels and make your body swell and your thigh fall away" (Num. 5:20-22). This is amplified and expanded, extended to the entire rite, where the woman is disheveled; then the order, thigh, belly, shows the perfect precision of the penalty. What Scripture treats as a case, sages transform into a generalization, so making Scripture yield governing rules. The same passage proceeds to further cases, which prove the same point: where the sin begins, there the punishment also commences; but also, where an act of virtue takes its point, there divine reward focuses as well. Merely listing the following names, without spelling out details, for the cognoscenti of Scripture will have made that point: Samson, Absalom, Miriam, Joseph, and Moses. Knowing how Samson and Absalom match, also Miriam, Joseph, and Moses, would then suffice to establish the paired and matched general principles.

Justice requires not only punishment of the sinner or the guilty but reward of the righteous and the good, and so sages find ample, systematic evidence in Scripture for both sides of the equation of justice:

M. Sot. 1:9

A. And so is it on the good side:
B. Miriam waited a while for Moses, since it is said, "And his sister stood afar off" (Exod. 2:4), therefore, Israel waited on her seven days in the wilderness, since it is said, "And the people did not travel on until Miriam was brought in again" (Num. 12:15).

M. Sot. 1:10

A. Joseph had the merit of burying his father, and none of his brothers was greater than he, since it is said, "And Joseph went up to bury his father ... and there went up with him both chariots and horsemen" (Gen. 50:7, 9).
B. We have none so great as Joseph, for only Moses took care of his [bones].
C. Moses had the merit of burying the bones of Joseph, and none in Israel was greater than he, since it is said, "And Moses took the bones of Joseph with him" (Exod. 13:19).
D. We have none so great as Moses, for only the Holy One blessed he Be took care of his [bones], since it is said, "And he buried him in the valley" (Deut. 34:6).
E. And not of Moses alone have they stated [this rule], but of all righteous people, since it is said, "And your righteousness shall go before you. The glory of the Lord shall gather you [in death]" (Is. 58:8).

Scripture provides the main probative evidence for the anticipation that when God judges, he will match the act of merit with an appropriate reward and the sin with an appropriate punishment. The proposition begins, however, with general observations as to how things are, M. 1:7, and not with specific allusions to proof-texts; the character of the law set forth in Scripture is reflected upon. The accumulated cases yield the generalization.

This carries us back to the one point of theological reflection that we identified in the reading of Num. 5 by Sifre to Numbers. As we recall, the document takes up the Mishnah's proposition concerning Num. 5:23ff., that, when God punishes, he starts with that with which the transgression commenced, which sages see as a mark of the precision of divine justice. I need not repeat the presentation of Sifre to Numbers XVIII:I, given above. The point registers, a detail of the much more systematic exposition of the Mishnah-Tosefta. It is simple. Punishment is rational in yet a more concrete way: it commences with the very thing that has sinned, or with the person who has sinned.

So the principles of reason and good order pervade the world. We know that fact because Scripture's account of all that matters has shown it. But the exposition of justice commences with the topic at hand.

The Tosefta contributes further cases illustrating the exact and appropriate character of both divine justice and divine reward. What is important here is what is not made explicit; it concerns a question that the Mishnah does not raise: what about the gentiles? Does the principle of world order of justice apply to them, or are they subject to chaos? The answer given through cases here is that the same rules of justice apply to gentiles, not only Israelites such as are listed in the Mishnah's primary statement of the principle. That point is made through the cases that are selected: Sennacherib, who besieged Jerusalem after destroying Israel comprised by the northern tribes, Nebuchadnezzar, who took and destroyed Jerusalem in the time of Jeremiah. Now the sin is the single most important one, arrogance or hubris, and the penalty is swift and appropriate, the humbling of the proud by an act of humiliation:

> **T. Sot. 3:18**
> A. Sennacherib took pride before the Omnipresent only through an agent, as it is said, "By your messengers you have mocked the Lord and you have said, "With my many chariots I have gone up the heights of the mountains . . . I dug wells and drank foreign waters, and I dried up with the sole of my foot all the streams of Egypt" (2 Kgs. 19:23–24).
> B. So the Omnipresent, blessed be He, exacted punishment from him only through an agent, as it is said, "And that night the messenger of the Lord went forth and slew a hundred and eighty-five thousand in the camp of the Assyrians" (2 Kings 19:35).
> C. And all of them were kings, with their crowns bound to their heads.

> **T. Sot. 3:19**
> A. Nebuchadnezzar said, "The denizens of this earth are not worthy for me to dwell among them. I shall make for myself a little cloud and dwell In it," as it is said, "I will ascend above the heights of the clouds, I will make myself like the Most High" (Is. 14:14).
> B. Said to him the Omnipresent, blessed be He, "You said in your heart, 'I will ascend to heaven, above the stars of God I will set my throne on high'—I shall bring you down to the depths of the pit" (Is. 14:13, 15).
> C. What does it say? "But you are brought down to Sheol, to the depths of the pit" (Is. 14:15).
> D. Were you the one who said, "The denizens of this earth are not worthy for me to dwell among them"?
> E. The king said, "Is not this great Babylon, which I have built by my mighty power as a royal residence and for the glory of my majesty? While the words were still in the king's mouth, there fell a voice from heaven, O King Nebuchadnezzar, to you it is spoken, The kingdom has departed from you, and you shall be driven from among men, and your dwelling shall be with the beasts of the field, and you shall be made to eat grass like an ox" (Dan. 4:29–32).
> F. All this came upon King Nebuchadnezzar at the end of twelve months (Dan. 4:28–29).

As in the Mishnah, so here, too, we wish to prove that justice governs not only to penalize sin but also to reward virtue. To this point we have shown the proportionate character of punishment to sin, the exact measure of justice. The first task in this other context is to establish the proportions, now of reward to punishment.

Is reward measured out with the same precision? Not at all, reward many times exceeds punishment. So if the measure of retribution is exactly proportionate to the sin, the measure of reward exceeds the contrary measure by a factor of five hundred. Later on we shall see explicit argument that justice without mercy is incomplete; to have justice, mercy is the required complement. Here we address another aspect of the same matter, that if the measure of punishment precisely matches the measure of sin, when it comes to reward for merit or virtue, matters are not that way:

T. Sot. 4:1
A. I know only with regard to the measure of retribution that by that same measure by which a man metes out, they mete out to him [M. Sot. 1:7A]. How do I know that the same is so with the measure of goodness [M. Sot. 1:9A]?
B. Thus do you say:'
C. The measure of goodness is five hundred times greater than the measure of retribution.
D. With regard to the measure of retribution it is written, "Visiting the sin of the fathers on the sons and on the grandsons to the third and fourth generation" (Exod. 20:5).
E. And with regard to the measure of goodness it is written, "And doing mercy for thousands" (Exod. 20:6).
F. You must therefore conclude that the measure of goodness is five hundred times greater than the measure of retribution.

Having made that point, we revert to the specifics of cases involving mortals, not God, and here, we wish to show the simple point that reward and punishment meet in the precision of justice.

Before proceeding to the Tosefta's extension of matters in a quite unanticipated direction, let us turn to further amplifications of the basic point concerning the exact character of the punishment for a given sin. The fact is, not only does the sinner lose what he or she wanted, but the sinner also is denied what formerly he or she had possessed, a still more mordant and exact penalty indeed. At T. Sot. 4:16, the statement of M. Sot. 5:1, "Just as she is prohibited to her husband, so she is prohibited to her lover," is transformed into a generalization, which is spelled out and then demonstrated by a list lacking all articulation; the items on the list serve to make the point. The illustrative case—the snake and Eve—is given at T. 4:17–18. The list then follows at T. 4:19.

T. Sot. 4:16
A. Just as she is prohibited to her husband, so she is prohibited to her lover:
B. You turn out to rule in the case of an accused wife who set her eyes on someone who was not available to her:
C. What she wanted is not given to her, and what she had in hand is taken away from her.

The poetry of justice is not lost: what the sinner wanted he does not get, and what he had he loses:

T. Sot. 4:17
A. And so you find in the case of the snake of olden times, who was smarter than all the cattle and wild beasts of the field, as it is said, 'Now the serpent was smarter than any other wild creature that the Lord God had made'" (Gen. 3:1).
B. He wanted to slay Adam and to marry Eve.
C. The Omnipresent said to him, "I said that you should be king over all beasts and wild animals. Now that you did not want things that way, 'You are more cursed than all the beasts and wild animals of the field' (Gen. 3:14).
D. "I said that you should walk straight-up like man. Now that you did not

want things that way, 'Upon your belly you shall go' (Gen. 3:14).

E. "I said that you should eat human food and drink human drink. Now: 'And dust you shall eat all the days of your life' (Gen. 3:14).

T. Sot. 4:18

A. "You wanted to kill Adam and marry Eve? 'And l will put enmity between you and the woman' (Gen. 3:15)."

B. You turn out to rule, What he wanted was not given to him, and what he had in hand was taken away from him.

Sages' mode of thought through classification and hierarchization to uncover patterns does not require the spelling out of the consequences of the pattern through endless cases. On the contrary, sages are perfectly happy to list the other examples of the same rule, knowing that we can reconstruct the details if we know the facts of Scripture that have been shown to follow a common paradigm:

T. Sot. 4:19

A. And so you find in the case of Cain, Korah, Balaam, Doeg, Ahitophel, Gahazi, Absalom, Adonijah, Uzziah, and Haman, all of whom set their eyes on what they did not have coming to them.

B. What they wanted was not given to them, and what they had in hand was taken away from them.

Were we given only T. 4:19A, a construction lacking all explanation, we should have been able to reach T. 4:19B! Here is a fine example of how a pattern signals its own details, and how knowing the native categories allows us to elaborate the pattern with little further data. But whether we should have identified as the generative message, What he wanted was not given to him, and what he had in hand was taken away from him, is not equivalently clear, and I am inclined to think that without the fully-exposed example, we could not have done what the compositor has instructed us to do: fill out the et cetera. What a passage of this kind underscores is sages' confidence that those who would study their writings saw the paradigm within the case and possessed minds capable of generalization and objective demonstration.

As to T. Sot. 4:1, which we considered above, sages both distinguish the realm of the Torah from the realm of idolatry, Israel from the gentiles, and also treat the two realms as subject to one and the same rule justice. But then what difference does the Torah make for holy Israel, the Torah's sector of humanity? As the Tosefta's passage that we first met just now proceeds, discussion shades over into a response to this very question. The point concerning reward and punishment is made not at random but through the close reading of Scripture's record concerning not only the line of Noah—the Generation of the Flood, the men of Sodom and Gomorrah, the Egyptians—but also the founder of God's line on earth, Abraham. Abraham here, often head of the line with Isaac and Jacob, is deemed the archetype for Israel, his extended family. What he did affects his heirs. His actions form models for the right conduct of his heirs. What happened to him will be recapitulated in the lives and fate of his heirs.

So from retributive justice and the gentiles, the discourse shifts to distributive reward, shared by the founder and his heirs later on. Reward also is governed by exact justice, the precision of the deed matched by the precision of the response:

T. Sot. 4:1

G. And so you find in the case of Abraham that by that same measure by which a man metes out, they mete out to him.

H. He ran before the ministering angels three times, as it is said, "When he saw them, he ran to meet them"

(Gen. 18:2), "And Abraham hastened to the tent" (Gen. 18:6), "And Abraham ran to the herd" (Gen. 18:7).

I. So did the Omnipresent, blessed be He, run before his children three times, as it is said, 'The Lord came from Sinai, and dawned from Seir upon us; he shone forth from Mount Paran" (Deut. 33:2).

Justice extends beyond the limits of a single life, when the life is Abraham's. Now justice requires that Abraham's heirs participate in the heritage of virtue that he has bequeathed. Point by point, God remembers Abraham's generous actions in favor of Abraham's children into the long future, an intimation of a doctrine involving a heritage of grace that will play a considerable role in the theological system, as we shall see in due course. Here, point by point, what Abraham does brings benefit to his heirs:

T. Sot. 4:2
A. Of Abraham it is said, "He bowed himself to the earth" (Gen. 18:2).
B. So will the Omnipresent, blessed be He, respond graciously to his children in time to come, "Kings will be your foster-fathers, and their queens your nursing mothers. With their faces to the ground they shall bow down to you and lick the dust of your feet" (Is. 49:23).
C. Of Abraham it is said, 'Let a little water be brought" (Gen. 18:4).
D. So did the Omnipresent, blessed be He, respond graciously and give to his children a well in the wilderness, which gushed through the whole camp of Israel, as it is said, "The well which the princes dug, which the nobles of the people delved (Num. 21:18) teaching that it went over the whole south and watered the entire desert, which looks down upon the desert" (Num. 21:20).

E. Of Abraham it is said, 'And rest yourselves under the tree" (Gen. 18:4).
F. So the Omnipresent gave his children seven glorious clouds in the wilderness, one on their right, one on their left, one before them, one behind them, one above their heads, and one as the Presence among them.

The same theme is expounded in a systematic way through the entire account; it is worth dealing with the complete statement:

T. Sot. 4:3
A. Of Abraham it is said, "While I fetch a morsel of bread that you may refresh yourselves" (Gen. 18:5).
B. So did the Omnipresent, blessed be He, give them manna in the wilderness, as it is said, "The people went about and gathered it . . . and made cakes of it, and the taste of it was like the taste of cakes baked with oil" (Num. 11:8).

T. Sot. 4:4
A. Of Abraham it is said, "And Abraham ran to the herd and took a calf, tender and good" (Gen. 18:7).
B. So the Omnipresent, blessed be he, rained down quail from the sea for his children, as it is said, "And there went forth a wind from the Lord, and it brought quails from the sea, and let them fall beside the camp" (Num. 11:31).

T. Sot. 4:5
A. Of Abraham what does it say? 'And Abraham stood over them" (Gen. I 8:8).
B. So the Omnipresent, blessed be He, watched over his children in Egypt, as it is said, "And the Lord passed over the door" (Ex. 12:23).

T. Sot. 4:6
A. Of Abraham what does it say? 'And Abraham went with them to set

them on their way" (Gen. 18:16).
B. So the Omnipresent, blessed be He, accompanied his children for forty years, as it is said, "These forty years the Lord your God has been with you" (Deut. 2:7).

The evidence is of the same character as that adduced in the Mishnah: cases of Scripture. But the power of the Tosefta's treatment of Abraham must be felt: finding an exact counterpart in Israel's later history to each gesture of the progenitor, Abraham, shows the match between the deeds of the patriarchs and the destiny of their family later on. Justice now is given dimensions we should not have anticipated, involving not only the individual but the individual's family, meaning, the entire community of holy Israel. Once more, we note, a systematic effort focuses upon details. Justice is not a generalized expectation but a very particular fact, bread/manna, calf/quail, and so on. There is where sages find the kind of detailed evidence that corresponds to the sort suitable in natural history.

The focus now shifts shift from how justice applies to the actions of named individuals—Samson, Absalom, Sennacherib and Nebuchadnezzar—to the future history of Israel, the entire sector of humanity formed by those whom God has chosen and to whom he will give eternal life. It is a jarring initiative. The kinds of instances of justice that are given until that point concern sin and punishment, or the reward of individuals for their own actions. And these cases surely conform to the context: justice as the principle that governs what happens to individuals in an orderly world. But now we find ample evidence of the fundamental position in sages' system, the generative character in their consideration of all issues that, as the first principle of world order, that justice governs.

For sages not only accept the burden of proving, against all experience, that goodness goes to the good and evil to the wicked. They have also alleged, and here propose to instantiate, that the holy people Israel itself, its history, its destiny, conform to the principle of justice. And if claim that justice governs in the lives and actions of private persons conflicts with experience, the condition of Israel, conquered and scattered, surely calls into question any allegation that Israel's story embodies that same orderly and reasonable principle. Before us sages take one step forward in their consideration of that very difficult question, how to explain the prosperity of the idolaters, the gentiles, and the humiliation of those who serve the one true God, Israel. That step consists only in matching what Abraham does with what happens to his family later on.

If sages had to state the logic that imposes order and proportion upon all relationships—the social counterpart to the laws of gravity—they would point to justice: what accords with justice is logical, and what does not is irrational. Ample evidence derives from Scripture's enormous corpus of facts to sustain in sages view that the moral order, based on justice, governs the affairs of men and nations. But justice begins in the adjudication of the affairs of men and women in the Israelite household and from there radiates outward, to the social order of Israel, and thence, the world order of the nations. It is from the Halakhah before us that sages commence their exposition of God's perfect justice, in rewarding the innocent and punishing the guilty, because only there could they state their deepest conviction concerning justice: all things start in the Israelite household, the smallest whole social unit of creation. The Mishnah, all the more so, the Tosefta, show us what a theological exposition of Numbers 5 can accomplish.

When we compare what we do not have in Sifre to Numbers with what we do have in Mishnah-Tosefta Sotah, which treats the very same passage of Scripture, the result is clear. Sifre to Numbers makes only one contribution to a theological commentary to the midrash. It highlights the importance of the theological data located in abundance elsewhere. Rabbinic exegesis of Scripture undertook a number of different tasks, each requiring an appropriate corpus of exegetical questions for its accomplishment. The theological reading set forth in other midrash-compilations represents a set of choices to undertake what the compilers of Sifre to Numbers clearly decided to neglect. The contrast with the other Tannaite halakhic midrash-compilations, Sifra and Sifre to Deuteronomy, is not to be missed.

JACOB NEUSNER
Bard College

Song of Songs in Song of Songs Rabbah

Song of Songs Rabbah is usually designated exegetical, although it is preferable to refer to it as a "school-midrash," in contrast with the homiletical "synagogue-midrash." This is because it follows the biblical book verse-by-verse and word-by-word, providing a commentary supported by aggadic materials. As a result, the text of Song of Songs is omnipresent in the midrash. While this is, thus, a commentary on the biblical book, we must not forget that, as a Rabbinic work, it is submitted to the rules and limits imposed by the rabbis. Its inclusion and transmission as a part of the canon of the Judaism of the Dual Torah compel us to ask about the authorship's thematic intention, about the structure of its reasoning, and about the (literary) forms that have been selected for it.

Song of Songs Rabbah traditionally is referred to as *Shir ha-Shirim Hazita* by virtue of the first verse cited in it, Prov 22:27. It is important not to confuse it with other midrashic treatments of Song of Songs (*Midrash Zuta on Song of Songs*, ed. S. Buber, Berlín 1895, rep.: Tel-Aviv, no date; *Aggadat Shir ha-Shirim*, ed. S. Schechter, Cambridge, 1896; *Midrash Shir ha-Shirim*, ed. A. Grünhut, Jerusalem 1897, rep.: S. Wertheimer, Jerusalem 1981), with which it coincides in some sections but whose tradition is easily differentiable.

That Song of Songs Rabbah offers an allegorical interpretation is made clear at its beginning, when it concludes its commentary on Song 1:1(I:vii 5 B.–D):

R. Yudan and R. Levi in the name of R. Yohanan (said): "In every passage in this scroll in which you find the words, 'King Solomon,' the referent is in fact King Solomon. But whenever the text says [simply], 'the king,' it means the Holy One, blessed be he." But rabbis say, "Wherever you find 'King Solomon,' the reference is to the King who is the master of peace [a play on the Hebrew word for Solomon]. When it speaks of 'the king,' it refers to the Community of Israel."[1]

In this midrash, a love story concerning Solomon and Shulamit thus is universalized and interpreted within the framework of the concept of liberation (God and Israel). It attempts to represent the progressive liberation of the people of Israel, concentrating it in three "historic-mythical" issues: The Exodus from Egypt, the return from Babylonia, and the final liberation from the oppressive power "of the present," Edom-Rome, that prefigures the transition between the present and future world.

Of those three moments, the Exodus from Egypt bears the heaviest weight. It is held as a saving reality and a catalyst that transforms what was a familiar community (*bene isra'el*) into a people (*'am bene isra'el*). This is not surprising when we consider the place the biblical Song of Songs has in the Jewish liturgical calendar, read on the Sabbath of

---

[1] Textual references are from J. Neusner, *Song of Songs Rabbah. An Analytical Translation* (Atlanta, 1989).

Passover. Thus each spring every Jew feels the special emotion expressed at Song 2:11–12: "For, lo, the winter is past, the rain is over and gone. The flowers appear on the earth, the time of singing has come, and the voice of the turtledove is heard in our land."

The relationship of Song of Songs Rabbah to Passover is so direct and intimate that its composition may be viewed as intended to clarify and complete the reading of the biblical book on that festival. References to the Exodus are continuous; the Exodus's main characters—Moses, Aaron, Miriam, the Assembly of Israel—are constant points of reference; and Egypt, the Red Sea, the giving of the Torah at Mount Sinai, and the building of the Sanctuary, with its final projection to the Temple, are repeated many times in the book. Numerous examples may be cited:

> "O that you would kiss me with the kisses of your mouth." In what connection was this statement made? R. Hinena b. R. Pappa said, "It was stated at the sea...." R. Judah b. R. Simon said, "It was stated at Sinai...." R. Meir says, "It was said in connection with the tent of meeting" ... Rabbis say, "It was said in connection with the house of the ages [the Temple itself]".... (II:i 1–6 to Song 1:2)
>
> "We will make you ornaments of gold:" this refers to the spoil at the Sea. "Studded with silver:" this refers to the spoil of Egypt.... Another interpretation of "We will make you ornaments of gold:" this refers to the Torah.... Another interpretation of "We will make you ornaments of gold:" this refers to the Tabernacle.... R. Berekhiah interpreted the verse to speak of the ark.... (XI:i 1–8 to Song 1:11)
>
> "I am a rose of Sharon:" Said the Community of Israel, "I am the one, and I am beloved. I am the one who was hidden in the shadow of Egypt" ... "I am the one who was hidden in the shadow of the sea" ... "I am the one who was hidden in the shadow of Mount Sinai" ... "I am the one who was hidden and downtrodden in the shadow of the kingdoms. But tomorrow, when the Holy One, blessed be He, redeems me from the shadow of the kingdoms, I shall blossom forth like a lily and say before him a new song...." (XVIII:i 4–7 to Song 2:1)
>
> "As a lily among brambles:" R. Eleazar interpreted the verse to speak of those who came forth from Egypt ... R Azariah in the name of R. Judah in the name of R. Simon [interpreted to speak of Israel before Mount Sinai].... R. Huna interpreted the verse to speak of the kingdoms.... R. Abihu interpreted the cited verse to speak of the coming redemption.... (XIX:i 2.5.8.9. to Song 2:2)
>
> "My beloved is like a gazelle:" Just as a gazelle leaps from mountain to mountain, hill to hill, tree to tree, thicket to thicket, fence to fence, so the Holy One, blessed be he, leapt from Egypt to the sea, from the sea to Sinai, from Sinai to the age to come. (XXVI:i 2.A.–C. to Song 2:9)
>
> "O my dove ...:" When the Israelites went forth from Egypt, to what were they to be compared? To a dove that fled from a hawk ... That is what the Israelites were like at the sea ... "Let me hear your voice ..." For I have already heard it in Egypt ... R Eleazar interpreted the verse to speak of Israel when it stood at the sea ... R. Aqiba interpreted the verse to speak of Israel when it stood at Mount Sinai ... R. Yose the Galilean interpreted the verse to speak of the [subjugation of Israel to the] kingdoms ... R. Huna and R. Aha ... interpreted the verse to speak of the tent of meeting.... Said R. Tanhuma: ... I will interpret it ... that it speaks of the eternal house [the temple].... R. Elijah interpreted the verse to speak of the pilgrims who come up to celebrate the festivals.

(XXXI:i 6.A-E. 9.E.-F. XXXI:ii 1.B. 2.A. 5.A. 8.A. 9.A. 13.A. to Song 2:14)

"Upon my bed by night." ... Said R. Levi, "Said the Community of Israel before the Holy One, blessed be He, 'Lord of the world, in the past, you would give light for me between one night and the next night, between the night of Egypt and the night of Babylonia, between the night of Babylonia and the night of Media, between the night of Media and the night of Greece, between the night of Greece and the night of Edom." (XXXV:i 2.A.-B. to Song 3:1)

"... On his wedding day:" this refers to the day of Sinai, when they were like bridegrooms. "On his day of joy:" this refers to the words of the Torah: "The precepts of the Lord are right, rejoicing the heart" (Ps. 19:9). Another interpretation: "On his wedding day" refers to the tent of meeting. "On his day of joy" refers to the building of the eternal house. (XLIV:ii 8.A.-9.C. to Song 3:11)

The exile to Babylonia, the liberation from it, and the return are referred to with three verses of Song of Songs:

"Upon my bed by night:" this refers to the night of Babylon. "I sought him whom my soul loves:" this refers to Daniel.... "I will seek him whom my soul loves:" this refers to Daniel. "The watchmen found me, as they went about the city:" these are the Chaldeans. "Have you seen him whom my soul loves:" this is Daniel.... Therefore the prophet spites [Babylon], saying: "Come down and sit in the dust, O virgin daughter of Babylon" (Is. 47:1). That is to say measure for measure. Elsewhere: "They sit on the ground and keep silence, the elders of the daughter of Zion" (Lam. 2:10), and here: "Come down and sit in the dust, O virgin daughter of Babylon." Said R. Hunia, "This is what Jerusalem said to the daughter of Babylon: "You old whore! What do you think about yourself? Is it that you are a virgin? You are an old woman...." Says R. Joshua b. Levi, "Said the Holy One, blessed be he, 'I am going to bring punishment upon the daughter of Babylon, and even if Daniel should pray for mercy for her... I shall not listen to him.'" (XXXVIII:ii 1.B.-O. 31.A-33.A. 43.B.-C. to Song 3:4)

"You are all fair, my love; there is no flaw in you:" ... Said Zechariah:..." I have seen, and behold a candlestick all of gold, with a bowl on top of it ... and two olive trees by it" (Zech. 4:2). Two Amoras: One said, "The word translated bowl are to be read to spell the word, exile." The other said, "The letters of the word translated bowl should be read redemption." The one who reads the letters to spell "exile" holds that they went to exile to Babylonia and the Presence of God went with them. The one who reads the letters to spell "redemption" holds that the sense is, the one who redeem her is the one who saves her.... Said the Holy One, blessed be he, "Since that is the case, then: 'You are all fair, my love; there is no flaw in you.'" (Li:i 10.A.-I. to Song 4:7)

"With me from the Lebanon, my bride:" Said the Holy One, blessed be he, to them, "When you went into exile in Babylonia, I was with you: 'For your sake I have been sent to Babylon' (Is. 43:14). And when you return to the chosen house in the near future, I shall be with you.'" (LII:i 7.A.-B. to Song 4:8)

There are plenty of references to the liberation from the tyranny of the present, which appears as the ultimate redemption:

"O daughters of Jerusalem:" Said R. Yohanan, "Jerusalem is destined to be made a metropolitan capital of all cities and draw people to her in streams to do her honor...." R. Berekhiah... said,

"The Israelites are compared to a woman. Just as an unmarried woman receives a tenth part of the property of her father ... so the Israelites inherited the land of the seven peoples, who form a tenth part of the seventy nations of the world.... But in the age to come they are destined to inherit like a man, who inherits all of the property of his father...." "Just as a woman takes up a burden and puts it down [that is becomes pregnant and gives birth], takes up a burden and puts it down, then takes up a burden and puts it down and then takes up no further burden, so the Israelites are subjugated and then redeemed, subjugated and then redeemed, but in the end are redeemed and will never again be subjugated...." "In this world, since their anguish is like the anguish of a woman in childbirth, they say the song before him using the feminine form of the word for song, but in the age to come, because their anguish will no longer be the anguish of a woman in childbirth, they will say their song using the masculine form of the word for song..." (V:iii 2.A.–B., 4.A.B.D., 5.B.–E. to Song 1:5)

"Depart from the peak of Amana...:" Said R. Huna in the name of R. Justus, "When the exiles [returning to Zion when the messiah brings them back] reach Taurus Munus, they are going to say a song. And the nations of the world are going to bring them like princess to the messiah." (LII:ii 1.A.–C. to Song 4:8)

And there is no lack of apocalyptic glints to announce the redemption that will be preceded by a catastrophe:

"My beloved speaks and says to me:" He "spoke" through Elijah, and "said to me" through the messiah. What did he say to me? "Arise, my love, my fair one, and come away, for lo, the winter is past." Said R. Azariah, "'... for lo, the winter is past:' this refers to the kingdom of the Cutheans [Samaritans],[2] which deceives the world and misleads it through its lies ... 'the rain is over and gone:' this refers to the subjugation. 'The flowers appear on the earth:' the conquerors appear on the earth. Who are they? ... Elijah, the royal messiah, the Melchizedek, and the military messiah. 'The time of singing has come:' The time for the Israelites to be redeemed has come, the time for the foreskin to be removed. The time for kingdom of the Cutheans to perish, the time for the kingdom of Heaven to be revealed ... 'and the voice of the turtledove is heard in our land:' What is this? It is the voice of the royal messiah ..." The messiah will come only in the conditions described in that which was said by R. Simeon b. Laqish: [M. Sot. 9:15], R. Judah says, "In the generation in which the son of David will come, the gathering place will be for prostitution, Galilee will be laid waste, Gablan will be made desolate, and the men of the frontier will go about from town to town, and none will take pity of them; and the wisdom of scribes will putrefy; and those who fear sin will be rejected; and the truth will be herded away...." (XXX:iv 1.A.–4.B. 4.E.–6.B.... 2.A.–B. to Song 2:13)

The redemption is expected and hoped for. But, if the beloved, Israel, expects it anxiously, the anxiety of the lover, God, who is ready to hasten the moment, is not less:

---

[2] Commentators suggest it could be a reference to Rome or Byzantium as a Christian empire.

"The voice of my beloved! Behold he comes [leaping upon the mountains, bounding over the hills]:" R. Judah and R. Nehemiah and Rabbis: R. Judah says, "This refers to Moses. When he came and said to the Israelites, 'In this month you will be redeemed,' they said to him, 'Our lord, Moses, how are we going to be redeemed? And did not the Holy One, blessed be he, say to Abraham, "And they shall work them and torment them for four hundred years" (Gen 15:13), and now we have in hand only two hundred and ten years!' He said to them, 'Since he wants to redeem you, he is not going to pay attention to these reckonings of yours.... But 'He leaps' over reckonings, calculations, and specified times".... R. Nehemiah says, "This refers to Moses. When he came and said to the Israelites, 'In this month you will be redeemed,' they said to him, 'Our lord, Moses, how are we going to be redeemed? We have no good deeds to our credit.' He said to them, 'Since he wants to redeem you, he is not going to pay attention to bad deeds'".... Rabbis say, "This refers to Moses. When he came and said to the Israelites, 'In this month you will be redeemed,' they said to him, 'Our lord, Moses, how are we going to be redeemed? And the whole of Egypt is made filthy by our own worship of idols!' He said to them, 'Since he wants to redeem you, he is not going to pay attention to your worship of idols....'" R. Yudan and R. Hunia... say, "This refers to the royal messiah. When he says to the Israelites, 'In this month you are to be redeemed,' they will say to him, 'How are we going to be redeemed? And has not the Holy One, blessed be he, taken an oath that he would subjugate us among the seventy nations.' Now he will reply to them in two ways. He will say to them, 'If one of you is taken into exile to Barbary and one to Sarmatia, it is as though all of you had gone into exile. And not only so, but this state [the Roman Empire] conscripts troops from all of the world and from every nation, so that if one Samaritan or one Barbarian comes and subjugates you, it is as though his entire nation had ruled over you and as if you were subjugated by all the seventy nations.'" (XXV:i 1.A.–4.G. to Song 2:13)

Even though the people can and must perform meritorious deeds, everything depends on God. That explains the request at the end of the book that converts the whole midrash on a prayer, quite appropriate when remembering at Passover the liberation from Egypt, and as an expression of the hope for definitive redemption.

"Make haste, my beloved, and be like a gazelle..." To four matters the redemption of Israel is comparable: harvest, vintaging, spices, and a woman in labor. To a harvest, for if a field is harvested not at its right season, it does not produce even decent straw, but if it is harvested in its right season, then the entire crop is first class.... To vintaging, for if the grapes of a vineyard are not harvested at the right time, they do not produce even god vinegar, but if it is harvested at the right time, then the vinegar is first rate.... To spices, for when spices are picked when they are soft and moist, their fragrance does not give a scent, but when they are picked dry, then their fragrance gives scent.... To woman in labor, for when a woman gives birth before term, the fetus cannot live, but when she gives birth at term, the fetus can live... R. Aha in the name of R. Joshua b. Levi said, "[It is written], 'I the Lord will hasten it in its time, (Is. 60:22): if you have not attained merit, then 'in its time.' But if you have attained merit, then 'I will hasten it.' So may it be his will speedily in our days, Amen." (CXV:ii 6.A.–7.D. to Song 8:14)

The metaphor of human love-affairs suits to explain such a predilection of God for Israel; but which are the merits that make Israel specially fair and kind? Which are the merits that move God to consider her beautiful and to hasten the expected liberation? This is detailed throughout the midrash but especially in the comments on Song 1:5 and 1:15 and its parallel (Song 4:1 and 7:7):

> "I am very dark but comely." R. Levi b. R. Haita gave three interpretations: "I am very dark" all the days of the week, "but comely" on the Sabbath. "I am very dark" all the days of the year, "but comely" on the Day of Atonement. "I am very dark" among the Ten Tribes, "but comely" in the tribe of Judah and Benjamin. "I am very dark" in this world, "but comely" in the world to come. (V:ii 5.A.–I. to Song 1:5)
>
> "Behold, you are beautiful, my love; behold, you are beautiful:" "Behold you are beautiful" in religious deeds, "Behold you are beautiful" in acts of grace, "Behold you are beautiful" in carrying out religious obligations of commission, "Behold you are beautiful" in carrying out religious obligations of omission, "Behold you are beautiful" in carrying out the religious duties of the home, in separating priestly rations and tithes, . . . in carrying out the religious duties of the field, gleanings, forgotten sheaves, the corner of the field, poor person's tithe, and declaring the field ownerless, . . . in observing the taboo against mixed species, . . . in providing a linen cloak with woolen showfringes, . . . in planting, . . . in keeping the taboo on uncircumcised produce, . . . in keeping the laws on produce in the fourth year after planting of an orchard, . . . "Behold you are beautiful" in circumcision, . . . in trimming the wound, . . . in reciting the Prayer, . . . in reciting the Shema, . . . in putting a mezuzah on the doorpost of your house, . . . in wearing phylacteries, . . . in building the tabernacle for the Festival of Tabernacles, . . . in taking the palm branch and etrog on the Festival of Tabernacles, . . . in repentance, . . . in good deeds, . . . in this world, . . . in the world to come. (XV:i 1.A–X. to Song 1:15 and parallels)

Besides the strict fulfillment of the prescribed practices, the vital attitudes are also a requirement and a demonstration of love. When God tries those whom he loves, he waits for the loving answer of his creatures. Thus the midrash interprets Song 2:16: "He pastures his flock among the lilies."

To highlight the different intentions that underlay the composition of distinct Rabbinic works, we examine the treatment of the same story in the Babylonian Talmud and in Song of Songs Rabbah. The passage concerns the reaction human beings should have when facing suffering in general and bodily disease in particular. At M. Ber 9:3 we find a general theory: "Over evil a blessing is said similar to that recited over good; and over good a blessing is recited similar to that said over evil." At B. Ber. 60b this is developed:

> What is meant by being bound to bless for the evil in the same way as for the good? Shall I say that, just as for good one says the benediction, "who is good and bestows good," so for evil one should say the benediction, "who is good and bestows good"? But [contrary to this] we have learned: For good tidings one says, "who is good and bestows good;" [while] for evil tidings one says, "blessed be the true judge." Raba said: "What it really means is that one must receive the evil with gladness. . . ."

Contrary to Raba's dictum, B. Ber. 5b reports stories of ill sages who do not react as they should. For instance: "R. Yohanan once fell ill, and R. Hanina went in to visit him. He said to him: "Are your sufferings welcome to you?" He replied: "Neither they nor their reward...." This same episode appears in Song of Songs Rabbah:

> R. Yohanan was punished with suffering from gallstones for three years and a half. R. Hanina came up to visit him. He said to him, "How are you doing?" He said to him, "I have more than I can bear." He said to him, "Don't say that. But say, 'The faithful God.'" When the pain got severe, he would say, "Faithful God," and when the pain became greater than he could bear, R. Hanina would come in to him and say something over him, and he restored his soul. (XXXIII:ii 1.B.–F. to Song 2:16)

Maybe the most apodictic expression of the whole text of Song of Songs is "for love is strong as death," and with the same strength it is going to be treated in the midrash:

> "For love is strong as death:" As strong as death is the love with which the Holy One, blessed be he, loves Israel.... "Jealousy is cruel as the grave:" That is when they make him jealous with their idolatry.... Another explanation of "for love is strong as death:" As strong as death is the love with which the generation that suffered the repression loved the Holy One, blessed be he.... "Jealousy is cruel as the grave:" The jealousy that the Holy One, blessed be he, will hold for Zion, that is a great zealousness. (CVIII:ii 1.A.–D. 6.A.–D. to Song 8:6)

From what we have seen so far, we can realize the thematic intention of this composition: To celebrate the liberation of Israel and its redemption, accomplished by God in the past and promised for the future.

Structure of the Work

As noted above, Song of Songs Rabbah is an exegetical midrash, among the real and most meticulous of the type. Only a few verses of Song of Songs have no comment, and these are all cases of verses whose text is an almost literal repetition of a former passage. Still, there are verses that repeated in two places of Song of Songs that, in Song of Songs Rabbah, bear in both places the same or a quite similar commentary, no matter its length. This happens, for example, with Song 1:15, "Behold, you are beautiful, my love; behold, you are beautiful; your eyes are doves," which is repeated when the verse recurs at Song 4:1. Here, some manuscripts omit the repetition and use the formula "all the thing as in . . ." or "as we saw before...." But precisely because in other cases this is not done, we must imagine that such summaries are not original and must have been introduced by the copyists, to avoid the work of rewriting the passage or to save materials. That is the way the modern publishers understood the text and a majority of translators follow them.

Song of Songs Rabbah is formally similar to other midrashim to the Five Megillot (viz., Esther Rabbah, Ruth Rabbah, and Lamentations Rabbah). It begins with a series of *petihtaot*, in this case presented to introduce the first verse of the biblical book. The extension of those cannot be compared to the proems of Lamentations Rabbah, and, possibly, they have not the same finality, since the first verse, "The Song of Songs, which is Solomon's," recites the title and author of the book, so that the first section is going to focus on upholding the book's authorship by Solomon, paying special attention to its character as an inspired book.

Scholars debate whether there are four or five *petihtaot*. S.T. Lachs devoted various studies to trying to demonstrate that they are four.[3] Recently J. Neusner, in his *Analytical Translation*, identifies five units. The first four have the form of an homiletical unit, but they are presented anonymously, using as intersecting verses texts of Proverbs (twice), Psalms, and Qohelet; the fifth, nevertheless, begins with the most typical homiletical form and quotes the author whom it is attributed to: "R. Pinhas b. Yair opened...," with an intersecting verse from Proverbs. The analysis of those units from the perspective of opposition and complementarity between exegesis and homiletics can doubtless project a new light on the history of the text's redaction.

The five homilies end more or less with the same statement, which is not exactly a repetition of the title-verse but a confirmation that Solomon was the author of Song of Songs under the inspiration of the Holy Spirit: "The Holy Spirit rested on him (Solomon) and he wrote the following three books: Proverbs, Qohelet, and the Song of Songs." In three of those occasions the sentence is attributed to R. Yudan, and in two of them the text is absolutely the same. From this we may conclude that in one way or another the author/compiler wanted to transform into five units with identical aim what at the beginning were only four.

Before the real commentary of the book starts, there are two more sections on the first verse. Rather than a homiletical structure, both have a scholastic one, based on a philological analysis. One of them includes a discussion that may permit us to identify a second aim of the composition. It bring us back in time to a polemic of the period in which Song of Songs was included in the biblical cannon. This is despite the fact that, when Song of Songs Rabbah was composed, this was no longer an issue:

R. Yose says, "Qohelet does not impart uncleanness to hands, but as to Song of Songs there is dispute".... Said R. Aqiba, "Heaven forbid! No Israelite man never disputed concerning Song of Songs that it imparts uncleanness to hands. For the entire age is not so worthy as the day on which the Song of Songs was given to Israel. For the scriptures are holy, but the Song of Songs is holiest of all. And if they disputed, they disputed only concerning Qohelet." (I:iv,20A.–B. to Song 1:1)

Such extraordinary valoration and veneration of the biblical book appears a few times in Song of Songs Rabbah:

"While the king was on his couch, [my nard gave forth its fragrance]:" R. Meir says, "'While the king,' the King of kings of kings, the Holy One, blessed be he, 'was on his couch,' in the firmament, ['my nard gave forth its fragrance'], the Israelites gave forth a bad odor, saying to the calf, 'These are your Gods, O Israel' (Exod. 32:4)." Said to him R. Judah, "Enough for you, Meir. The Song of Songs is to be interpreted not to the disadvantage but only to the glory [of Israel]. For the Song of Songs has been given only for the glory of Israel." (XII:i 1.A.–E. to Song 1:12)

"He brought me to the wine cellar...:" R. Meir says, "Said the Congregation of Israel, 'The impulse to do evil took hold of me through wine, and I said to the calf, "These are your Gods, O Israel" (Exod. 32:4).' When wine gets into someone, it mixes up his mind." Said to him R. Judah, "That's enough for you, Meir! People interpret the Song of Songs not in derogatory way but only in a praiseworthy way [for Israel], for the Song of Songs was given

---

[3] S.T. Lachs, "Prolegomena to Canticles Rabbah" and "The Proems of Canticles Rabbah," in *Jewish Quarterly Review* 55 and 56 (1964–1965).

only for Israel's praise." (XXI:i 1.A.–F. to Song 2:4)

The long proems and the commentary to the first chapter constitute the longest section of the midrash, approximately a third of the total. By tradition, this midrash was edited reproducing the division in chapters of the biblical text, and it has also been translated following this order, and so it is usually quoted; but it seems that the original midrashic text was not divided this way, and there is actually no manuscript that has this division, not even the first printed edition (Pesaro, 1519). The Vilna (Vilnius) edition (1878) was also made following the biblical chapter-division. On the other hand, after the commentary of Song 2:7 and before the beginning of Song 2:8, all manuscripts mark a division with the expression *sdr' tnyn'*, that is, "second *seder*." This reference has nothing to do with the biblical Song of Songs as known to us, since, in the form we have it, there is no division into *sedarim*.

Neusner's *Analytical Translation* is formally structured by chapters (parts, *parashiyyot*), but internally shows a continuous analytical order that produces 115 major units of commentary, which practically correspond to the number of verses of the biblical book (117), in spite of the fact that many of those units have subdivisions. In two cases (Song 3:7–8 and Song 8:9–10), Neusner includes in one unit two biblical verses, reflecting the midrash's treatment. In this continuous order, Neusner even numbers the few repetitious verses that, as mentioned before, have no commentary: 1) 3:5 (unit 39) and 8:4 (unit 106), practically identical to 2:7 (unit 24); 2) 6:3 (unit 79), merely a linguistic variant of 2:16 (unit 33); 3) 8:3 (unit 107), identical to 2:6 (unit 23); and 4) 7:3 (unit 92), which is identical to 4:5 (unit 49). The numbering of the last one corresponds to the numbering of the *Revised Standard Version*, which follows the *Vulgate* and not the Hebrew text, where it is 7:4.

Although Song of Songs Rabbah is not a homiletical midrash at all, we find in three places the typical structure of homilies: *R. X patah* ... followed by a biblical verse. In two cases the supposed intersecting verse is taken from Proverbs (I:v to Song 1:1: Prov 2:4–5 and VI:i to Song 1:6: Prov 30:10), and in the third it is taken from Psalms (IV:vi to Song 1:4: Ps 118:24). There are no parallels of these homilies in other midrashim, and consequently we are inclined to consider them basically literary units. We know, however, that the verses of Song of Songs were frequently used as intersecting verses in homilies to the Pentateuch, read in the synagogue liturgical cycle. Their presence in midrashim like Genesis Rabbah or Leviticus Rabbah testify to this. Some studies on this matter show that there is a great similarity between the liturgical homilies collected in some midrashim on books of the Pentateuch and their use in other school-contexts.[4]

The homily is introduced in one passage at the place that corresponds to the already mentioned formula, *R. X commenced* (discourse) by citing (the verse) ..., and its "school" use is introduced in another passage by the formula *R. X interpreted* the verse to speak of.... For example, in Genesis Rabbah 39:2 to Gen 12:1 ("Go out of thy land") we read:

> R. Berekhiah commenced [discourse by citing the following verse of Scripture]: "Your anointing oils are fragrant" (Song 1:3). R. Berekhiah said: "What was he (Abraham) like?—A flask of myrrh sealed...."

In Song of Songs Rabbah we found this treatment of the same material:

---

[4] Cf. L.F. Girón–C. Motos, "*Patar y Patah en Qohélet Rabbah*," in *'Ilu. Revista de ciencias de las religiones*, cuadernos 3, Madrid 2000, pp. 159–197.

"Your anointing oils are fragrant:" R. Yohanan interpreted (*patar*) the verse to speak of Abraham. When the Holy One, blessed be he, said to him, "Leave your land and your birth place" (Gen 12:1), what was he like? He was like a flask of myrrh sealed with a tight lid and lying in the corner. The fragrance of that vial does not waft upward. But when someone came and moved it from its place, then its fragrance spreads upward. So said the Holy One, blessed be he, "Abraham, many good deeds do you have to your credit, many religious duties do you have to your credit. Move yourself about from place to place, so that your name may be great in the world: 'Go out....'" (III:iv 1.A.–2.C. to Song 1:3)

We notice that in each midrash the interpretation is attributed to a different rabbi (Berekhiah, Yohanan), but, as all scholars already agree, this has little significance.

We find the same phenomenon in Genesis Rabbah 62:2 to Gen. 27:28 and Song of Songs CX:i to Song 8:8, "We have a little sister."

Both texts are attributed to R. Berekhiah.

If we pay attention to Leviticus Rabbah, we find a very similar case in 23:1 to Lev. 18:3 in close relation with Song of Songs Rabbah XIX:i to Song 2:2: "As a lily among brambles." The Margolies edition of Leviticus Rabbah is the only source with the formula *R. Isaac opened . . . + Song 2:2*, and in Song of Songs Rabbah we find: *R. Isaac interpreted* the verse. . . . The whole passage of Song of Songs Rabbah embodies the long homily taken from Leviticus Rabbah.

From this, we see that many passages of Song of Songs Rabbah are also found in other midrashim. The Rabbinic hermeneutic that holds that Scripture is unitary permits the establishing of relationships between verses from different places and books. It is essential to draw a biblical text out of its context (decontextualize) in order to give it a different sense. Then it may find a new context. As Rivka Kern-Ulmer says "this is similar to the term 'intertextuality,' which means that the interpreters utilize previous texts, adding material and editing the text and that they draw upon a store of pre-existing or 'traditional' ideas."

Author, Date and Place of Edition

Practically all midrashim, including those that attributed to specific persons, have an unknown author or, more accurately, compiler or editor. Thus we cannot properly talk of an author of Song of Songs Rabbah; nor have we any evidence regarding its compiler or final editor. Nevertheless, as we have seen before, it is a carefully edited work, with a concrete idea and planning.

Similarly, we are unable to establish a date of composition of Song of Songs Rabbah. It is generally accepted that neither names of the sages mentioned, which are frequently transmitted in a mixed and corrupted way, nor references to historical events are useful in this regard. Linguistic evidence is perhaps the best source of information. Although there are no definitive conclusions, studies by the Academy of Hebrew Language in Jerusalem confirm the traditional idea regarding date of composition, which places it around 600 C.E.[5]

Scholars agree that composition of the midrash took place in the land of Israel, where, through the years, circumstances became more and more difficult for rabbis, initially due to internal Roman politics and, after the fourth century, due to the Chris-

---

[5] Cf. *Sefer ha-meqorot lemin hatimat ha-miqra' we'ad motsa'e tequfat ha-ge'onim* (Jerusalem, 1970).

tianization of social life. In this setting, a new interest developed in aggadic issues, an interest reflected in Song of Songs Rabbah:

> "For I am sick with love:" It has been taught on Tannaitic authority: when a person is not ill, he eats whatever he finds. When he gets sick, he wants to eat all sorts of sweets. Said R. Isaac, "In the past, the Torah was worked out in encompassing principles, so people wanted to hear a teaching of the Mishnah or of the Talmud. Now that the Torah is not worked out in encompassing principles, people want to hear a teaching of Scripture or of lore." Said R. Levi, "In the past, when money was available, people wanted to hear a teaching of the Mishnah, or law, or Talmud. Now that money is scarce, so that people are sick on account of subjugation, people want to hear only words of blessing and consolation." (XXII:ii 1.A.–E. to Song 4:7)

Four additional types of evidence support the document's provenance in the land of Israel: 1) most of cited sages are Palestinian; 2) all sources cited are Palestinian; 3) the document evidences the Aramaic of the Talmud of the land of Israel (Yerushalmi); and 4) when a passage is found both in the Bavli and Yerushalmi, Song of Songs Rabbah usually follows the latter.[6]

Literary Aspects

It is evident that the main concern of midrashic editors or compilers was not literary. Stylistic concessions are limited in all these works. These are, rather, theological-religious writings, and they belong within their own distinctive literary genre, that of midrash. Their development is fundamentally based on plays of words—homonymy and homophony—that permit diverse interpretations of biblical texts through the application of the hermeneutic rules fixed by the sages. Notably, when midrashic interpretations were created, there was no system of references—chapter and verse, for example—for citing biblical texts. Accordingly, citation required a literal quoting of the intended passage, or, sometimes, of just the first few words. As a result, we frequently find that the apparently wrong text of Scripture appears in support of a midrashic idea. This is because the reference in fact should be to a different segment of the cited verse. The difficulty is even greater when the quoted verse corresponds to the beginning of a liturgical *seder* or biblical *parashah*, while the correct reference occurs in the middle or at the end of that section.

On occasion, sages proposed reading the biblical text in a way other than that in which it was normally read:

> "O daughters of Jerusalem:" Rabbis say: "Do not read the letters that spell out 'daughters of Jerusalem' as given, but rather as 'builders of Jerusalem' [since the same consonants can yield that other reading]...." (V:iii 1.A.–B.)

The text is interpreted this way, and commentators feel free to begin with a new chain of justifications. This hermeneutic building is firmly based on the stable and unmovable foundation of three convictions: 1) everything is found in the Scripture; 2) there is nothing superfluous in Scripture; 3) Scripture is explained through its own content. This is fundamentally the midrashic method that, as we have said, makes few stylistic or literary concessions. There are, however, two schemes or structures that

---

[6] Cf. Lachs, "Prolegomena," p. 245.

may be characterized as literary: the homily and the *mashal*, or example.

The homily is a rhetorical piece that possibly had a connection to real life as a prescribed part of the synagogue service and served either as an introduction to the reading of the text of the Torah or as an explanation after the reading. The complete structure of the homily was composed by: 1) an introductory verse taken from a biblical book, generally from *ketubim*, that is described as "proem" or "intersecting verse;" 2) the application of this verse to various realities of Israelite history (Egypt, Red Sea, Sinai), religious life (Torah, ark, Temple, Law, circumcision, phylacteries, mezuzah, etc.), or to representative individuals (Moses, Aaron, David, Solomon, Daniel, Assembly of Israel, kings of Israel, high priest, Messiah, etc.), with an ethical and exhortatory conclusions; and, finally, 3) quotation of the passage that ought to be read, showing the relationship with one or more of the applications presented in point (2).

In spite of this connection to real life, it is very possible that the homilies transmitted in midrashim, exegetical as well as homiletical, are a product of "school" work, with which the sages trained themselves for their future religious duty. Frequently, more than a real homily, there is a catalogue of possible themes that can be used in a homily. One of the clearest examples of this model is catalogued as first proem of Song of Songs Rabbah. Departing from the quotation of Prov. 22:29, "Do you see a man who is diligent in his business? He will stand before kings, he will not stand before mean men," the midrash reviews the verse's application to various individuals considered as "experts:" Joseph, Moses, Daniel, the righteous, R. Hanina b. Dosa, and, finally, Solomon. Every one of them corresponds to a "dark person:" Potiphar, Pharaoh/Jethro, Nebuchadnezzar, the wicked-ones,[7] and the thieves; and the homily finishes with the assertion: "Not only so, but the Holy Spirit rested on him (Solomon), and he said the following three books: Proverbs, the Song of Songs, and Qohelet" (I:i 17.E.).

This is the longest extant version of this homily, but there are shorter ones, for example, in Qohelet Rabbah 1:1 and Pesiqta Rabbati 6, or in Exodus Rabbah 11:1 where, logically, the application ended in Moses. We must therefore imagine that the version in Song of Songs Rabbah is a kind of catalogue of all the possibilities.

The *mashal* is the second of the structures we can call literary. It has a precise scheme,[8] although incomplete in many cases, and, due to its narrative character, it is one of the few places in which the author can allow himself stylistic whims or nuances. The basic scheme consists of: (1) a rhetorical introduction: "what can this fact or this situation be compared to?;" (2) an answer that develops the example. Sometimes this scheme appears in a simplified form, and the first element is suppressed. In other cases, whether the first element is present or absent, a kind of advice is introduced before the text by means of the word *mashal*.

This last phenomenon may come from what in reality would have to be the complete structure of the example, where the first element of this scheme was preceded by another element that worked both as announcer of the *mashal* and as articulator of it with the preceding text: *'emshol lakh mashal*; this way the complete scheme was: "I am going to give you an example! what can this fact be compared to? To...."

The *meshalim* in Song of Songs Rabbah are relatively abundant (76 in the whole midrash) compared with other midrashim,

---

[7] The application to R. Hanina has no second part.

[8] Cf. D. Stern, *Parables in Midrash. Narrative and Exegesis in Rabbinic Literature* (Cambridge, MA, 1994).

and some of them appear together to exemplify the same situation or action. That these compilations do not contribute to the interpretation of the passage at hand suggests that they were created for sages or preachers, as an index (or "repertoire") of *meshalim* that represent the true antecedent to the medieval collections of tales.

In Song of Songs Rabbah there is an old *mashal*, that also appears in Gen. Rabbah 12:1 and that precisely exemplifies the utility and importance of the *mashal* as a hermeneutic resource. On the other hand, as we shall see, this *mashal* has a clear precedent in the classical Greek myth of Ariadne and Theseus:

R. Nahman said: "[The matter may be compared] to the case of a huge palace that had many doors, so whoever came in would wander from the path to the entry. A smart fellow[9] came along and took a skein of string and hung the string on the way to the entry, so everybody came and went following the path laid out by the skein. So too, until Solomon came along, no person could comprehend the words of the Torah. But when Solomon came along, everyone began to make sense of the Torah." (I:iv 3.B.–D. to Songs 1:1)

The Language Song of Songs Rabbah

The midrash is composed in a pure and paradigmatic Rabbinic Hebrew, constituting a clear example of the so called "language of the sages." Kutscher's assertions regarding its periods and places of origin are well known. Following his theory, Song of Songs Rabbah was a creation of *amoraim* in the land of Israel. In orthographic, morphological, and syntactic aspects, it is similar to the language of the earlier period, that is to say, Mishnaic Hebrew.

It is generally accepted that the use of Rabbinic Hebrew was restricted more and more at the beginning of the third century and that was increasingly used only in the treatment of specific themes, such as biblical commentaries even as it disappeared in others themes, such as halakhah. This being the case, it is assumed that a process of linguistic stagnation would occur and that biblical literary forms increasingly would displace Rabbinic colloquial. What attracts our attention concerning the language of Song of Songs Rabbah is that this return to biblical literary forms occurs only slightly, so that it is of no significance, while, on the other hand, there is a certain liveliness of expression, probably due to heated discussion. This calls to mind a spoken language that was more alive than is generally assumed.

Song of Songs Rabbah uses much less Aramaic than that found, for example, in Genesis Rabbah. Applying the parameters of the *Historical Dictionary of the Hebrew Language*, Genesis Rabbah is 25% in Aramaic while Song of Songs Rabbah is just a 16%. Unfortunately, the implications of this fact are unclear. The difference can be understood to reflect an increased artificiality of the language of Song of Songs Rabbah, which step-by-step became separated from the bilingualism that characterized earlier times. But the difference might also be a sign of the opposite, that is, of earlier composition or of composition using old materials. We cannot forget that even the Mishnah contains phrases and expressions in Aramaic. It is possibly that, especially in the cultured layers of society, what was said in Hebrew was written in Hebrew, and what was said in Aramaic was written in Aramaic; in this setting it was not deemed necessary

---

[9] Gen. Rabbah 12:1 adds: 'What did a certain smart fellow?' He came along...

to translate what was perfectly understandable to the people for whom it was written. In all, we must suppose that some parts of Song of Songs Rabbah are older than the rest, and the analysis of the language of those passages confirms this hypothesis.

There are also passages that are clearly composed later than others, and they are certainly not useful in dating the final compilation, as they might have been added at a later date. Thus we find the influence of Arabic in Vi:i 9.A, where the word *mdynt'* is clearly used to define a "town," on reference to Caesarea, and not to defining a "province," as it used to be in Aramaic and Hebrew; (see also VI:ii 5.I. and XC:ii 2A). But this sharply contrasts the use of this word in the other twenty-four passages in which it is doubtlessly signified "province" or "region," for example, IV:v 3.A.

Apart from the already mentioned Aramaic, an important component of the vocabulary of the Rabbinic Hebrew has its origin in Greek and Latin. Most frequently, these are legal terms or names of social or political institutions. Song of Songs Rabbah contains a large number of them, although some are only conjectural, because the medieval copyists did not understand them and transliterated them in diverse ways.

Editions and Manuscripts Sources

The first known printed edition of Song of Songs Rabbah appeared in a joint volume together with midrashim to the other four Scrolls in Pesaro (Italy) in 1519 (rep.: Berlin, 1926). Immediately afterwards or practically at the same time another edition was published, in Constantinople, in 1520. M.B. Lerner, in his edition of Ruth Rabbah,[10] tries to demonstrate that the latter was really a reprinting of an earlier edition, dated *circa* 1514, which would have been the real first edition; but we have no documentary evidence for that. A joint edition of midrashim to the Five Scrolls and midrashim to the five books of the Pentateuch was first printed in Venice, 1545, and entitled for the first time Midrash Rabbah. This edition was frequently reproduced more or less unaltered until 1878, when the famous Romm Publishing House at Vilna, known already at that time as "The Press of the Widow and Romm Brothers," put forward a new edition of the text accompanied by commentaries from the thirteenth to eighteenth centuries. This has been reproduced again and again until our day.

The most recent edition, by S. Dunsky (Tel Aviv, 1980), reproduces a mixed text. He chooses from the Pesaro and the Vilna editions, sometimes even copying both texts, one of them in square brackets, with numerous corrections in accordance with old commentaries and with a very useful body of notes. There are four complete manuscripts, two anthologies of selective type, and twelve fragments of different extension, ten of them coming from the *genizah* of the Old Synagogue in Cairo.

Among translations to European languages, the classical one is the English translation of M. Simon in the first half of the twentieth century.[11] Wünsche's German translation derives from the nineteenth century.[12] In the last twenty years, there have appeared the *Annalytical Translation* by J. Neusner[13] and mine in Spanish.[14]

LUIS F. GIRÓN BLANC
Universidad Complutense

---

[10] *The Book of Ruth in Aggadic Literature and Midrash Ruth Rabbah* (Doctoral Thesis) (Jerusalem, 1971) (Heb.).

[11] M. Simon, *Song of Songs*, in H. Freedman and M. Simon, eds., *Midrash Rabbah*. Vol. IX, London: Soncino Press, 1939.

[12] A. Wünsche, *Bibliotheca Rabbinica. Eine Sammlung alter Midraschim zum ersten Male ins Deutsche übertragen*, Leipzig 1880–1885.

[13] Above, n. 1.

[14] L.F. Girón-Blanc, *Midrás Cantar de los Cantares Rabbá* (Estella, 1991).

Song of Songs Rabbah, Theology of

Without resorting for cogency to a ready-made theological structure, are we able inductively to form the theological pieces of Song of Songs Rabbah into a self-contained whole? The criterion for cogency deriving from the traits of the data themselves is readily set forth: do the "theological things"—the events, persons, activities, objects, gestures, acts of omission or commission, and ideas the document sets forth as evidence of God's activity—coalesce into some few large formations of a theological character? And that means, do they tell a single, continuous story so as, on their own, to form a set of native category-formations? At issue are the traits of "theological things" viewed on their own and not in an accommodating structure.

To answer the inductive question, we categorize the "theological things" in topical groups. We inquire into the proposition that emerges from those groups and whether each component of a given class of "theological things" adheres to that proposition. What is required is classifying the "theological things" and showing how each item falls into the category-formation—the theological topic and its proposition—found for it. So the inductive labor involves making connections between and among the "theological things." The inductive approach requires the pieces of the puzzle to fit together on their own, bit by bit. The deductive approach to the theological systematization of the materials of Song of Songs Rabbah then asks the nurturing context to sustain order among the theological contents, the bits and pieces of the document.

The Theological Propositions of the Eight Parashiyyot of Song of Songs Rabbah

How shall we know on the basis of the evidence itself whether two or more theological statements cohere into a cogent proposition? The answer is derived from the answer to the question, do two or more facts coalesce to form a generalization? That whole, larger than the sum of the parts, accommodates more theological statements of particularity and allows for articulation, amplification, and extension of the principle at hand. There is a second way of formulating the same question. It is, Are we able to identify the main lines of narrative, the story that free-standing components of a theological character assist in telling? And can we find a place in that large story for each of the details? Here we have to survey the entire corpus of "theological things." The "theological things" of Song of Songs Rabbah cohere on their own, not only through the medium of a prevailing theological structure and system.

To spell this out more clearly: in the category of God's love are a variety of facts, e.g., things God has done for Israel, things that Israel does in response to God's love. And none of the "theological things" that are classified as evidences of God's love contradicts any other, e.g., God's conduct at the Sea and at Sinai is uniformly portrayed as motivated only by yearning for Israel. Israel's realization of the religious duties imposed by the Torah is always adduced as evidence of Israel's love for God and as traits of Israel—things Israel does—that God cherishes. Then the parts, the specific theological things are shown in the rubric at hand inductively to exhibit the marks of a self-contained whole. The facts jointly cohere, and the point that each makes proves congruent with the point that all others severally register. What follow are the rubrics that serve inductively to classify the theological data of Song of Songs Rabbah.

1. God and Man, God and Israel

The general principle of this rubric is, God enters into an intense relationship of love with Israel, and Israel with God. God's love for Israel responds to Israel's acceptance of the Torah at Sinai and continuing obedience to its commandments. God's relationship to mankind in general does not define the category-formation, God and man. Rather, it is defined by God's relationship to Israel and through Israel to the rest of humanity. The latter—God and the nations, Israel and the nations—is dealt with at No. 2, below. The fundamental theological principle is, Israel alone knows God as God has made himself known, which is in the Torah. God wishes to be exalted only by Israel. Israel alone produces martyrs to sanctify his name (XCVII:i.1,4, XCVIII:i.1). Just as in the foregoing, the point is: God embraces Israel for its loyalty to him, extending even to martyrdom. Israel alone accepted the Torah and God's dominion thereby (XCVIII:i.2).

How do God and Israel relate? Song of Songs Rabbah leaves no doubt: it is a relationship of lovers. God yearns for Israel. Israel yearns for God. Israel and God are reciprocally responsive and dependent, with Israel God's beloved. God's relationship to Israel and Israel's to God is captured in these pairs: God/nation; father/son; shepherd/flock; guard/vineyard; for me against my enemies, for him against those that spite him; song/song; praise/praise. Therefore Israel can ask what it needs, and God can ask what he needs, which is embodied in the sanctuary (XXXIII: i.1–8). How does Israel elicit God's love? It is through carrying out the religious duties. In reciting the Shema, studying the Torah in synagogues and houses of study and schools, Israel provokes the response of God's love (CI:i.1). Israel's sexual purity emits a fragrance pleasing to God (akin to the fragrance of the offerings). Israel saves up for God and God for Israel, religious duties and good deeds matched by what awaits those that take refuge in God (CII:i.1–2, 6–7).

God's original home was with mankind in the lower realm, the Temple. The offerings are marks of love, gifts of Israel's love to God. That God accepts them is an act of grace on his part (LXI:i.1, 4, 6–8). The house of the sanctuary represents God's and Israel's meeting place. Before it was built, God's presence was cramped, afterward, not. Before it was built, God's presence had no resting place, afterward, it did. Before it was built, Israel moved about, afterward, not. Before it was built, Israel was few in numbers, afterward, they multiplied (XVI:i.4–8). Israel's condition directly responds to the condition of the Temple and God's relationship to the Temple. But that is not the only place of meeting God. When God descends to the world, it is to Israel, specifically to the synagogues and school houses, where he collects the righteous that are in Israel (LXXVIII:i.1).

God so loves Israel as to call her his daughter, his sister, and his mother (XLIV:ii.1). God bestows marks of affection upon Israel, when, as at the Sea, Israel relies on God's salvation and consequently sings God's praises, or accepts the Torah, or makes offerings in the tabernacle or in the Temple. All these represent occasions at which God and Israel come together in their love: when Israel relies on God as at the Sea, accepts God's dominion as at Sinai, and accords to God atonement represented by burnt-offerings and peace-offerings (II:I.1–7). Israel is beautiful in making the offerings, comely in the Holy Things. Righteous Israelite women of the generation of the wilderness did not contribute their jewelry to the golden calf (LXXX:i.1–2).

Israel greatly yearns for union with God (II:iii.–v). Israel's love for God is intense; Israel extols God's love more than the Torah and its laws, e.g., of Passover, Pentecost, and Tabernacles; more than the Patriarchs (IV:vii, viii). Israel sees itself as dark in its deeds, but comely in the deeds of the forefathers. That contrast, between one condition and the other, is then worked out in other terms altogether. V:i.3–12 establishes the point, which is then extended. Israel was both rebellious and faithful in Egypt; rebellious and trusting at the Sea; rebellious and trusting at Marah, and so throughout. The review establishes the paradigm of an Israel that is both sinful and meritorious. The point then is, however much Israel may sin, Israel also exhibits contrasting virtue, and, all things together in the balance, should enjoy God's favor.

God and Israel relate through the covenant and the oaths that realize it. God is held captive by his oath to bring his Presence to dwell in Israel, an oath to Jacob and to Moses (XCIV:i.4–7). Through various media of sanctification, God has imposed his will on Israel to carry out his will in the world. God imposed an oath on Israel by the patriarchs and matriarchs who accomplished his will, by the tribal progenitors, by circumcision, by the martyrs in general or those of the generation of repression, by those who carried out God's will in the world and through whom he carried out his will, who poured out blood for the sanctification of God's name (XXIV:i.1–4). All of these represent those bound by the covenant.

"Israel" means those that love and are loved by God: those that will rise from the grave for eternal life. To express this idea, the Israel of Scripture serves as a metaphor, and "the maidens," who are the beloved, are the metaphor for that metaphor. So too the entire world was created only on account of the Torah. For twenty-six generations God looked down upon his world and saw it full of thorns and brambles, for example, the Generation of Enosh, the generation of the Flood, and the Sodomites. He planned to render the world useless and to destroy it: "The Lord sat enthroned at the flood" (Ps. 29:10). But he found in the world a single red rose, Israel, that was destined to stand before Mt. Sinai and to say before the Holy One, blessed be he, "Whatever the Lord has said we shall do and we shall obey" (Exod. 24:7) Said the Holy One, blessed be he, "Israel is worthy that the entire world be saved on its account.'" [Song: "for the sake of the Torah and those who study it...."] (XIX:i.5).

At III:V.1–12, the metaphor of God as the lover, the maidens as Israel, invokes a number of specific metaphors for making the relationship concrete. Israel loves God because God accords Israel victory over its enemies, No. 1; those who repent are the maidens who love god, No. 4; they are those who withstand refining, No. 5; they are the proselytes, No. 6; they are those who accept martyrdom, No. 7; they are those whom God loves, No. 8; they are those who persist in their love even not knowing the coming reward, No. 2, 9; they are those who are destined to rise from the grave for eternal life, No. 12. The formulation of the metaphor, "Israel," for those that God loves and that love God, then is made equally concrete. Israel's present condition among the nations is brief. In the age to come Israel will blossom forth in a brief moment and will praise God. Thus God loves Israel more than the seventy nations; Israel made for him the ark and sang the Song at the Sea in praise of him (XVIII:i.1–3). Israel was shadowed for a brief moment but blossomed forth in good deeds and praised God. Israel was hidden in the shadow of Sinai but blossomed forth in good deeds and praised God. And Israel is now hidden in the shadow of the kingdoms but will blossom forth in the age to come (XVIII:i.4–7).

Abraham, Isaac, and Jacob represent the flawless beloved of God. So too do Leah and Joseph. The flawless beloved, queens and concubines, are further represented by the Torah and the Mishnah and the book of Leviticus and the Supplements. They further are represented by the tree of life and the Garden of Eden, the fellowships of the righteous who study Torah in Eden. They further are represented by those that escaped from Egypt, the various groups of Israelites. And, finally, they are represented by the community of Israel (LXXXV:i.1–3, 6–7, 11). So the Patriarchs, the Torah, written and Oral, Israelites in the Garden of

Eden, those redeemed from Egypt, and the entire community of Israel all represent embodiments of God's love.

Israel at the Sea, singing the Song, or Israel at Sinai, declaring its obedience to God, Israel when subjugated to the kingdoms, singing its study of Torah, Israel at the tent of meeting, proclaiming song, and the pilgrim festivals, reciting the Hallel-psalms—these represent the interchangeable realizations of moments of God's love for Israel and vice versa (XXXI:ii). Israel yearns for God the way a woman yearns for her husband or the Evil Impulse yearns for wicked people. Even though Israel is faint, it continues to hope for God's salvation and continues to declare his unity (XCIX:i.1, 2).

Israel is God's bride, and God puts on nuptial robes. The nations are punished when Israel is prevented from keeping the Ten Commandments (LIV:i.1). If Israel through repentance opens the door however minutely, God will widen it vastly. Israel became God's beloved through the blood of the Passover and the blood of circumcision; at the sea in praising him; at Marah in accepting the commandments, acts of righteousness, and good deeds; at Sinai by accepting the Torah. When Israel hurts, God is pained (LXII:i.3–14). A mark of Israel's virtue is its rising in the night of Pentecost to receive the Torah (LXIV:i.3–4).

What, then, of Israel in relationship to God, and, concomitantly, how is Israel defined? Israel are those that know God, gentiles are those that reject him and worship idols. Israel is marked by religious duties and good deeds; the righteous are Israel's redemption; Israel will endure both in this world and the world to come; it is easy to tell Israelites from the nations; Israel is made ready for the coming redemption (XIX:i.11). Signals of Israel's coming redemption are Moses and Aaron, circumcision, the entry into the Land, the end of idolatry, the intervention at the Sea, the Song—interchangeably and in no special order (XXIX:i.1–2). The first, and as we now see, the generative native category-formation is the definition and character of God's and Israel's relationship. It is established by the Torah, God's self-manifestation, and the acceptance of the Torah's commandments by Israel at Sinai. The Torah is how Israel knows God, and those that do not accept the Torah cannot know God as God wishes to be known. The relationship then is defined as covenantal and marked by mutual love and reciprocal acts of dedication.

The upshot is simply stated. God's love for Israel is as strong as death, the jealousy over their idolatry is cruel as the grave. The same contrast is drawn between Isaac's love for Esau and Esau's hatred of Jacob; Jacob's love for Joseph and his brother's hatred of Joseph; Jonathan's love for David and Saul's hatred of David; a man's love for his wife and the jealousy she provokes in him by speaking with another man; the love of the generation that suffered the repression for God's sake, and the jealousy that God holds for Zion, that is his zeal for Zion (CVIII:ii.1–6). Now to the relationship of God to the gentiles, comparable to the relationship of Israel to the gentiles, and for the same reason.

2. God and the Nations, Israel and the Nations

The theological proposition of this rubric is, God rejects the nations, by reason of their idolatry, and Israel separates itself from the nations for the same reason. The nations respond by enticing Israel to idolatry and by hating Israel for its rejection of their idolatry and adherence to the Torah of Sinai.

All other category-formations subordinate themselves to the first: God and Man, yielding the key-relationship, God and Israel. The starting point is, God makes himself known to Man through the Torah, and the nations reject the Torah and therefore do not know God. That is why they worship idols. Only Israel knows and loves and worships God, as we have just seen. And that brings us to the parallel relationships that form the second principal category-formation, God/the nations, God/Israel. God's relationship with the nations is not comparable to God's relationship with Israel, and the nations' relationship with Israel serves merely as an instrument to carry out God's purpose in regard to Israel. The nations do not concede that the God of Israel is the one and only, the true God; they maintain he is no different from any other god (LXIX:i.1).

What difference distinguishes Israel from the nations? It is "Sinai," which stands for God's giving, and Israel's accepting, the Torah. That is the memorial monument, a witness to the nations of the world. Israel and the nations are there differentiated. The nations are differentiated from Israel by the Torah. The nations of the world fled from God's shade on the day on which the Torah was given, but Israel delighted in his shadow. Israel at Sinai displayed its loyalty to God, by agreeing to carry out the Torah even before knowing what was required by it. Israel is praised solely for its adherence to the Torah and ripened only at Pentecost, when the Torah was given (XX:i.1). At Sinai Israel was cleansed of its sins. The angels crowned each Israelite. There were no bereaved, no injured, among them. Moses then extolled the Israelites for being filled with Torah-teachings, for their modesty and self-restraint (XLVIII:ii, v). As a consequence of Sinai, Israel is further differentiated by the priestly watches and the offerings, then the Sanhedrin, associated with the Temple and priesthood. There follows the Day of Atonement, likewise a medium of atonement for Israel (XLVIII:vi, vii, viii, ix).

What of the nations in this context? Israel fights a war against the nations by reason of maintaining the Sabbath and circumcision, but they obey God without guile. So too they resist the nations and do not accept their idolatry (XXXI:I). Israel finds the Torah sweet, the nations find it bitter (XX:ii.1). At Sinai God placed the banners of the Torah over Israel, which are religious duties and good deeds (XXI:i.1). The character of the Torah, as sacred writing, registers. Through the Torah Israel has both a language and writing. Israelites know who are those that have a language but no writing or vice versa, and those that have neither writing nor a language of their own. There are those who know their mothers but not their fathers or vice versa or neither (LXXXIV:i.1)—so much for the gentiles, the idolaters.

Israel's encounter with the nations figures in its relationship with God. God punishes Israel through the gentiles, e.g., the four kingdoms. Even though Israel is enslaved among the nations of the world by arbitrary, discriminatory taxes, nonetheless their heart points upward toward their father in heaven (XIX:i.8). God will ultimately burn away the nations to save Israel (XIX:i.9). The nations cannot stifle the love of God for Israel. All their money cannot purchase a single item of the Torah. Nor can their money atone for the martyrdom of Aqiba and his fellows (CIX:I.1–3). The nations taunt Israel, saying that her God has gone away. But Israel remains steadfast, saying, once she had cleaved to him, she cannot depart from him, and vice versa (LXXVII:I.1). The foxes that spoil the vineyard that is Israel are Esau and his generals, that is to say, Rome. The vineyard hedge is restored by Noah or Daniel or Job (XXXII:ii.1,4–6). In Babylonian exile, Israel wallowed in idolatry, losing the priesthood and the throne. God nonetheless loved Israel even then (LXIII:i.1–2). Israel, not the nations, arises to God in repentance for its act of idolatry with the golden calf, and God forgave Israel, but that generation was not to enter the Land of Israel (LXV:i.1, 3, 4, 10).

Israel has fallen into the dominion of four kingdoms and emerged whole from each. Israel is the nation for whom peace is made. It complements this world and the world to come. Because of Israel's merit good things happen. Had Israel not accepted the Torah, God would have returned the world to formlessness and void. The nations taunt Israel for their condition of subjugation; Israel does good things for God and gets bad things in return. If Israel joins the nations, they will be made governors and generals. But Israel rejects gentile idolatry, and maintains that the nations cannot dance for Israel as did the angels, or as God will for the righteous in the age to come (LXXXIX:i.1–11).

God is radiant to Israel, ruddy to her enemies; radiant to Israel in the land of Egypt, ruddy to the Egyptians; so too at the sea; so too in the world to come; so too in the contrast between the Sabbath and the weekdays; the New Year and the rest of the year; this world and the world to come (LXX: i.1–2). Israel is comparable to moon and sun, but does not have the negatives of either. It gives pellucid light like the sun but is not oppressive like the sun; the moon is sometimes defective, but Israel, never. But while the sun and the moon do not cause fear, Israel does (LXXXVI:i.2).

3. Israel's Encounter with God through the Torah

The general principle of this rubric is Israel is Israel by reason of the Torah, and gentiles are gentiles by reason of rejecting the Torah. The Rabbinic sages find a great many occasions and ways of making that statement.

What, precisely, does the Torah offer? The sages should not be confused with philosophers or intellectuals, seeking mere knowledge of first principles, a meeting in mind. They are religious figures who want to know God. So to the question, what does the Torah offer, the answer yielded in so many words by Song of Songs Rabbah is, a direct encounter with God: opportunity and occasion. Accepting the Torah qualified Israel; that act afforded knowledge of not only God but what God wanted of man. That is expressed in the proposition that Israel's encounter with God matures. They originally saw God publicly, in Egypt, at the Sea, at Sinai face to face. Once the Torah was revealed, Israel had become a nation complete in all ways. So God spoke within the Tabernacle, representing the Temple, a more dignified locus for the encounter (XLII:i.1-2+3). At Sinai, by accepting the Torah Israel gave forth a good odor before God on high (XII:i.1, 2).

The Torah is Israel's ornament, comparable to the spoil at the Sea and the spoil of Egypt. The ornaments of the Torah are the letters and the words, the ruled lines. The tabernacle is Israel's ornament, so too the ark, the pillars before the ark. The Torah, the prophets, the Writings, and the Song of Songs all represent Israel's ornament. So God beautifies Israel through the Torah (XI:i.1–8). God's Presence takes up residence in the ark. The merit accruing to the Torah and those that study it forms an analogue to the ark. The palanquin is, further, the house of the sanctuary; the world is God's palanquin. The throne of glory also registers. The main point comes at the end. The Temple is God's place on earth, corresponding to his house in heaven (XLIII:i–v).

But the Torah is not the only mark of the covenant of love between God and Israel. The jewels around Israel's neck are the Torahs of Scripture (X:i.1–2). The members of the Sanhedrin, the teachers of Scripture and Mishnah, the children who study the Torah, the rabbis, the disciples and their intellectual accomplishments all represent the jewels that adorn Israel's neck (X:ii,1–4). It is an ornament when Israel declaims the Torah in public (X:iii.1–2). God meets Israel in synagogue and school house and bestows a blessing through the priests (XXVI:ii). Nonetheless, if the Torah is not the only "theological thing," it is the main one. Study of the Torah serves to bring the Holy Spirit upon the disciple. Teaching Torah in public is rewarded by the advent of the Holy Spirit, so that one may produce writings inspired by Heaven (I:IV.8; l I:V.1, 9).

When Israel received the Torah directly from God, the Israelites learned and did not forgot; when they asked Moses to serve as intermediary, they forgot their learning; but in the age to come their learning will be restored (II:ii.1, 13). Israel has no intrinsic merit. It enjoys God's love by reason of the merit of the Torah, and of the religious duties that they would perform: the mezuzah, the recitation of the Shema and the Prayer Said Standing (IX:i.10).

Israel at Sinai was perfect and sinless. God instructed Israel in commandments and good deeds. The Torah and Talmud form a gift that expresses God's love for Israel, and so do the priestly garments (CIV:I.1-4). God held Mount Sinai over the heads of Israel and said, "If you accept the authority of my Torah, well and good, but if not, I shall dump this mountain on you." There Israel gave priority to doing over hearing the Torah, an act of supreme loyalty. Israel was reborn at Sinai. But she sinned forthwith, with the golden calf (CVII:i.3-9).

God is embodied in the Torah. The teachings of the Torah, the ruled lines of the scroll, the letters—all are encompassed. Even the simplest matters contain meaning. Disciples of the sages likewise represent him. Even teachings of the Torah that deal with matters not to be recited in public are pleasant (LXXI:i.1-8, 21-22). The Sanhedrin leads Israel. Israel is strengthened by the water of the Torah, cleansed by the laws (LXXII:i.1,3). The Torah embodies God. The tablets of the covenant represent the arms, the words of Torah his ornaments; the details of the Torah the jewels, e.g., the Talmud; the book of Leviticus the body. Study of the Torah drains the strength of the people (LXXIV:i.1-9, see also LXXV:i.1).

When Israel supports Torah-study, it gets a reward in this world and the world to come. Unlettered people support those who study the Torah (LXXVII:i.1, 4).

This same set of theological themes encompasses not only Sinai but the wilderness in general. The wilderness is the source of Israel's ascent, decline and death. It also is the source of the Torah, the tabernacle, the Sanhedrin, the priesthood, the Levites, the monarchy—everything good that God gave to Israel (XL:i.1-2).

4. Divine Justice and Mercy

The general principle of this rubric is, God is both just and merciful. What happens to Israel is a mark of his justice and mercy. The gentiles subjugate Israel because that is how God has chosen to punish Israel for its sins, but the gentiles cause Israel to repent their sins, and God forgives them when they do—a mark of his mercy.

When the Court decrees fasts or when individuals afflict themselves, this suffering disturbs God, who is merciful (LXXXI:i.1-3). God's justice is revealed in the suffering of Israel under the gentiles, punishment for Israel's rebellion. His mercy is revealed when Israel is redeemed from the nations and when the nations receive recompense for what they did to Israel. In his mercy God sustains Israel in the age of gentile oppression, in the night of the Egyptians. When God comes to judge Israel, he transforms the attribute of justice into the attribute of mercy and so hastens the redemption of Israel. This is on account of the merit attained by Abraham. The kingdoms then will be punished for oppressing Israel (XXXIV:i.1-7). God rewards the pilgrims with the rain and the sun that the country needs for its crops; God rewards the act of circumcision with every kind of blessing (XC:ii.1,3, XC:iii.2, 3, 4, 6-7).

5. God's Judgment, Israel's Repentance and Atonement; God's Remorse, Israel's Consolation

The general principle of this rubric is the same as the foregoing, expressed in more concrete and specific terms. God brings about Israel's repentance. Israel atones for its sins, God forgives them and consoles Israel.

God sustains Israel with law and lore, with Torah in writing and Torah in memory, with the persons and activities and events represented by fire. Though Israel is sick, it is punishment and brings Israel closer to God; though sick, Israel is loved by God. The entire complex at XXII:i.1-8, diverse though it is, holds together within the notion that God loves Israel, therefore punishes Israel for its sins, bringing about a restoration in Israel's relationship with God (XXII:i.1-8). By smiting the children God punishes Israel for failing to keep the Torah (IV:ii.1). Israel makes haste to follow God to the Land, where God's presence dwells, in the sanctuary; when God removes his presence from the Land, Israel mourns, because they wanted to live in God's presence (IV:ii.1,2,5).

Israel is thus responsible for its own condition. Israel's fate is settled from within, through its own actions. Thus Jeroboam assigned the task of guarding the two golden calves, but Israel did not keep the watch of the priests and Levites. Ahab angered God and made Israel provide for God's enemies, not the true prophet. Jezebel did the same. Zedekiah did the same, thus Elijah and Jeremiah, respectively. Then the lesson is drawn in so many words at VI:iii.7: Israel did not keep the easy law pertaining to the Land of Israel, so it keeps the more onerous law assigned to the Exile.

There is an antidote to sin. The Torah overcomes the impulse to do evil (LXXXVII:i.9). Sin is a mark of neglect of the Torah. When Israel neglects the Torah and commandments, it lives in a perpetual night. When Israel suffers in the night of the nations' rule (here: Egypt), it then seeks succor through God's messengers (here: Moses) (XXXV:I.3-4, XXXVI:I, XXXVII:i). At XXXVIII:ii,1, the night is Babylon, and Daniel succeeds Moses. When Israel was redeemed the first time, from Egypt, Israelite sinners perished, those who repented were redeemed (XXX:i.1). Repentance is the key to all else. The person who overcomes his inclination to do evil, such as Moses, David, and Ezra, saves his entire generation (XLVIII:i.8).

But when Israel does sin, God punishes sin. Then, when Israel sins, it is disfigured by ailments. When Israel accepted the Torah, it was sinless—a point important earlier—so that, at that moment there were not found among them persons afflicted with flux, persons afflicted with *sara'at*, lame, blind, dumb, deaf, lunatics, imbeciles, fools, or hangers-on. But once they had sinned, in only a little while there were found among them persons afflicted with flux, persons afflicted with *sara'at*, lame, blind, dumb, deaf, lunatics, imbeciles, fools, and hangers-on (LI:i.2). Atonement comes about not only through repentance but through the Day of Atonement. Israel is cleansed by the Day of Atonement, which covers over their sins (LXXXVII:i.4).

Israel may sin, but it also performs acts of devotion. Israel contrasts its failures with its acts of devotion. Israel sleeps as to offerings but is awake as to reciting the Shema and saying the Prayer. The same contrast encompasses the house of the sanctuary as against synagogues and study houses; the end of days as to redemption; "I slept as to redemption but the heart of the Holy One is awake to redeem me" (LXII:i.1).

Israel is punished in this world because of transgression, but in the world to come they will be rewarded (LXXXVII:i.7). God punishes Israel for going after other gods. Nebuchadnezzar administered God's punishment CXII:i-iii. In the exile, Israel learned to obey God after all (XCIII:i.1): when sin had brought it about that the house of the sanctuary should be destroyed and Israel was sent into exile to Babylonia, Nebuchadnezzar said to them, "Do not listen to the Torah of your father in heaven, but, rather, fall down and worship the image that I have made" (Dan. 3:15). The Israelites said to him, "You big fool! The very reason that the Holy One, blessed be he, has handed us over to you is because we were bowing down to an idol—'She saw ... the images of the Chaldeans portrayed with vermilion' (Ezek. 23:14)—and yet you say to us, 'fall down and worship the image that I have made' (Dan. 3:15). Woe to you!" It is at that moment that the Holy One, blessed be He, said, "My vineyard, my very own, is for myself."

God's speech is sweeter than candy, for it speaks of repentance and forgiveness (LXXVI:i.1). Israel is afraid of God, but God sweetens his words to them (LXXVI:i.8).

6. Consolation and Restoration

The general principle of this rubric is, when Israel repents, God forgives them and consoles them for their suffering. He will further restore their condition, meaning, bring them back to the Land. That is in line with the comparison of Adam and Israel, Eden and the Land, the fall and the exile. Then there is this difference: Adam did not know the power of repentance, but the Torah has taught Israel about that power.

The restoration will return Israel to its condition of perfection. The Temple allowed Israel to raise its head among the nations, and now that it is in ruins, Israel is bowed down. God made it a ruin but will beautiful it in the world to come (XLVIII:ix.6–10). When Israel is restored to the Land, it will never be moved, and in the age to come when the restoration takes place, that will mark the end of history (V:iv.1, 3). Israel is presently plunged into a valley of troubles, into the depths. But when God draws Israel out of the valley or the depths, Israel will blossom in good deeds and sing a Song of praise (XVIII:iii.1–3).

Israel already knows how redemption takes place, for there was the first redemption, that from Egypt, to signal the model. The second followed the pattern, and the third and final redemption, at the end of days, is therefore known in advance. From Egyptian bondage, the Israelites were freed and redeemed and made prefects over the entire world, which surprised both the nations and Israel There are other such cases: Joseph, David, Mordecai, and finally the community of Israel. Even though its present situation is dark, God will bring light (LXXXVIII:i.1–5). God will restore his beloved, though soiled in sins, through the purification of prayer, to the Garden of Eden. God should not respond to the nations of the world, with their blaspheming and cursing of God, by destroying the world. He should take note of Israel, who bless and praise God, and preserve the world (CXV:i.1–5, CXV:ii.1–3).

7. The End of Days

The general principle of this rubric is, the restoration of Israel to the Land marks the beginning of the end of days and the advent of the age to come. The pattern of the endtime has been set by the first redemption and replicated in the second.

The yearning for redemption is as the yearning of a sick person for healing, as in the case of the generation in Egypt, a model for the generations that await the end of days (LXVIII:i.1). That matches the view that Israel was sinless at Sinai, also flawless, but with sin came illness. The ultimate salvation is adumbrated in the salvation from Egypt. God takes the initiative and acts in his own good time to save Israel. God came to Israel in Egypt, at the Sea, at Sinai, and will come to Israel at the occasion of the world to come, presenting himself to Israel as the Lord their God, so XXVI:i. The model of redemption from Egypt is taken over at the end, XXVI:iii. The first redeemer came but then disappeared and reappeared; the Temple, correspondingly, was built but destroyed, and will be restored (XXVI:iii).

This world already evinces in its contrasts the character of the end of days. In reference to the world to come, the contrast is drawn: weekdays and Sabbath, the rest of the year and the Day of Atonement, the Ten Tribes vs. Judah and Benjamin, and this world and the world to come. Just as are the contrasts in this age, so is the contrast between this age and the age to come (V:ii.5). Then even now, the Sabbath, the Day of Atonement, Judah and Benjamin— all embody a foretaste of the end of days and the world to come.

The pattern of Israel's redemption, the kind of salvific figures and activities involved in the procedure, and the outcome follows a single pattern for the redemption from Egypt, the restoration of Zion, and the advent of the royal Messiah at the end of days. The first set involves Moses and Aaron, the forty years in the wilderness, the advent of the princes, the removal of the Canaanites, the division of the Land, the figure of Joshua, and the firstfruits; the second, Daniel and Ezra, the Babylonian exile, Mordecai and Ezra, the removal of the foreskin, the destruction of the Babylonians and the rebuilding of the Temple, and the figure of Cyrus, with the firstfruits; and the third, Elijah and the messiah, the Samaritans, the subjugation, then the conquerors: Elijah, the royal messiah, Melchizedek, and the military messiah; the removal of the foreskin, the end of the Cutheans (I would have anticipated, Edom), and the advent of the royal messiah. So the three climactic moments in Israel's existence, the redemption from Egypt and entry into the Land; the Babylonian exile and the recovery of the Land and the building of the Temple; and the recovery of sovereignty under the royal messiah, the figures of Elijah and the messiah matching Moses and Aaron, Daniel and Ezra. The message could not be clearer: the past moments of salvation define the pattern for the future salvation (XXX:II.1-8, XXX:iii.1-8, and XXX:iv.1-6).

When God redeemed Israel from Egypt, he gave Israel no time to prepare but redeemed Israel straightaway. When Israel went into exile to Babylonia, God was with them. When Israel returns to the chosen House, he will be with Israel (LII:i.1, 7-10).

8. Abraham Represents the Beginning of God's People on Earth. The Merit that Accrues in One Generation to the Benefit of Another Generation

The general principle of this rubric is, Abraham forms the paradigm and the realized embodiment of Israel. Abraham embodies Israel in exile and in the Land, but his principal beginnings, at which he showed his true loyalty to God even at the cost of martyrdom, took place in Babylonia. In the first reading, CX:i.2, Abraham joined humanity to the Holy One; even as a child he carried out religious obligations and supererogatory deeds, accepting martyrdom even then. He met the test that God imposed on him, CXI:i.1, and so God made him the foundation for his construction in humanity. In the second reading, CXI:ii.1, Sodom is contrasted with Israel. Sodom contrasts with Abraham, not nourished by religious duties and good deeds. Israel, by contrast, stood firm in their good deeds, so Israel is destined to raise up righteous men. If so, why the exile and destruction? Israel has gone to Babylonia to mark the occasion and location of its union with God through Abraham. The third reading involves Hananiah, Mishael, and Azariah—yet another martyrdom through the fiery furnace, like Abraham. The final reading involves those who came back to Zion from the exile (CXI:iii.1f.) So the entire composite works on the cogent theme of Abraham/Exile.

Abraham is head of all righteous persons (L:i.5). Abraham was the best of all the righteous persons, and his virtues were made known when he was thrown into the fiery furnace (XIII:I). The same is so of Isaac and Jacob (XIV:I). So the Patriarchs provide the paradigm of Israel's service to God through suffering. That suffering atones for the sins of Israel (XIV:iii).

Abraham stands also for the Patriarchs. The Patriarchs represent Israel's response to God's love (III:iv). They are Israel's authentic being, their prayers compare with Israel's prayers as the scent of oil to the actual oil, so III:i. And the next initiative turns to Israel. Torah has been compared to water, Israel is now given the metaphor of oil. Then, III:iii, Israel is compared with oil. Israel knows bitterness now, but sweetness in the end. Israel is improved by crushing, as oil is improved by crushing. Oil does not mix with other liquids, Israel does not mix with the nations of the world. Words of Torah are compared with oil, as the precious to the trivial, so words of Torah replace trivial things. Oil is a source of light to the world, so is Israel. Oil is quiet when poured, and Israel produces no resonance in this world but will in the world to come (III:ii–iii).

Abraham embodies the best of the righteous; he suffered at his own volition, so as to suffer for his sins. Isaac and Jacob were blameless as well (XL:i.4–5). Abraham declined the kind of love offered to him by the King of Sodom. Daniel did the same, declining the rewards coming from an unacceptable source (XCV:i.2–5).

9. *Words of Torah Form the Medium for Israel to Know God's Love*

The general principle of this rubric is, God's love for Israel is embodied in the Torah.

Words of Torah form a coherent whole. They are comparable to sustaining fluids, water, wine, oil, honey, milk, bringing life to the world from heaven, carrying God's voice to Israel. Water comes from heaven, restores the soul, purifies, and so do words of Torah. They cover over Israel's nakedness/transgression. They can be mastered, but that takes work. Words of Torah flow like water, to those that are humble and low and self-abnegating (II:vii–viii II:ix). There is nothing in this statement that could not fit readily into the rubric common to Pesiqta deRab Kahana, Genesis Rabbah, and Song of Songs Rabbah, entitled, "Israel's encounter with God through the Torah."

10. *The Commandments Are the Marks of Israel's Distinction before God*

The general principle of this rubric is, the specific religious duties carried out by Israel distinguish Israel from the nations. They derive from the Torah and realize its promise. Song of Songs Rabbah forms long lists of those religious duties, which beautify Israel in God's sight. Israel may suffer in order to carry them out, all the more so winning God's affection for their steadfast loyalty and love.

The panoply of religious deeds, religious obligations of commission, religious obligations of omission, religious duties of the home, in separating priestly ration and tithes, the religious duties of the field, gleanings, forgotten sheaves, the corner of the field, poor person's tithe, and declaring the field ownerless, the taboo against mixed species, providing a linen cloak with woolen show-fringes, the rules governing] planting, the taboo on uncircumcised produce, the laws on produce in the fourth year after the planting of an orchard, circumcision, trimming the wound, reciting the Prayer, reciting the Shema, putting a mezuzah on the doorposts of your house, wearing phylacteries, building the tabernacle for the Festival of Tabernacles, taking the palm branch and etrog on the Festival of Tabernacles—all mark Israel's beauty in God's sight. These cover the field, garments, food, circumcision, recitation of the Prayer and the Shema, the keeping of the festivals, and the like. Then we proceed to the moral beauty of penitent Israel and Israel practicing good deeds, and end with this world and the world to come. The composition invokes the life of piety and faith to characterize what makes Israel beautiful before God (XV:i.1 = XCV:i.1).

The religious duties beautify Israel, now with reference to not shaving, circumcision, and show-fringes. Israel suffers for God's sake. Israel atones for other nations. Israel is loyal to God. They keep the pilgrim festivals even though the Temple was destroyed. They renew the Torah month by month. They are the light of the world (XV:i.5–6). Carrying out the commandments involves simple, inexpensive things, but produces a rich reward (XX:i.6). The religious duties embody God's love for Israel: show-fringes, phylacteries, Shema, Prayer; then tabernacle, Presence in the world to come; mezuzah (XXIII:i.1–5).

Israel, "the daughters of Zion/distinction," is marked by circumcision and show-fringes. They behold God ("the king who created") in his fullness. He makes peace between his works and his creatures: fire and Abraham, the sword and Isaac, the angel and Jacob (XLIV:i.1–4). At XLV:i, once more, a repertoire of virtues, some involving actions, others, restraint, all embodying obedience, characterizes Israel in a portrait of a comprehensive character. Israel is beautified by good deeds and act of loving kindness, performing religious obligations, both positive and negative. These encompass the priestly tithes and agricultural taboos; the laws of circumcision; reciting the Prayer and the Shema; use of the holy objects; keeping the Festival; repentance, good deeds, in this world and in the world to come. Israel is innocent and beautiful when ascending for the pilgrim festivals, which it observes even without the Temple. Israel is distinguished by not shaving, by circumcising, by show-fringes. It is modest. Israel accepts martyrdom for God's sake. Israel atones for the sin of other nations. Israel is loyal to God. God is loyal to Israel and will restore Israel to its land. Israel brings light to the world. Israel at the Sea, through the Song, attained its full beauty; the least of Israelites is full of religious deeds (XLVII:i.1–3).

If we are logging acts of religious loyalty, we cannot differentiate keeping commandments from one-time episodes that embody that same loyalty. Keeping the commandment of the Passover offering or of circumcision is comparable to Joshua's and Caleb's defense of the Land from the malice of the ten other spies. The blood of the Passover-offering and the blood of circumcision, Israel's acceptance of the Torah at Sinai, setting up the tabernacle, Israelite women's restraint in refraining from sexual relations during their periods and in not giving their jewels to make the golden calf, Joshua and Caleb, and Phineas' zealotry, all represent occasions on which God loved Israel. In all instances Moses embodied Israel's loyalty to God, and all represent acts of supererogatory devotion to God (LIII:i.1–5).

Israel sets God as a seal upon her heart and arm through the recitation of the Shema and the donning of phylacteries (CVIII:i.3). Though the Israelites are imprisoned in the everyday grind, when on the Sabbath they assemble at the synagogue to recite the Shema and declaim the Torah and the prophetic lections, their voices are heard by God and the angels. Israel should not envy one another or engage in dissension, because the angels hear and report it in good when they are engaged by hatred, jealousy, enmity, and contentiousness. So too when the Israelites recite the Shema with proper deliberation and in unity, God and the angels here, but when they are not one in intention and in thought in reciting the Shema, the heavenly host departs (CXIV: i.1–2).

11. God Will Bring the End through the Royal Messiah at a Time of His Own Choosing, and His Hand Is Not to Be Forced

The general principle of this rubric is, redemption is an act of grace and cannot be coerced.

When God redeems Israel, it is at his time, not Israel's. He responds then to the righteous people among Israel and to the merit acquired by their deeds. God will further ignore the character of Israel, performing an act of pure grace. And this will be through the royal messiah (XXV:I.1–4). The nations (the kingdoms) are bound by an oath that they not oppress Israel excessively and so force God to intervene, bringing on the coming of the end of days before God's plan. So too Israel is subject to an oath not to rebel against the dominion of the kingdoms and force the end. Both parties must leave space for the advent of the royal messiah to perform his task (XXIV:ii.1, 4, and compare XXIV:iii.2). When the Israelite exiles return to Zion, the nations are going to bring them to the messiah. God did as much long ago. Israel will be presented to the royal Messiah as gifts (LII:ii.1, 5, 7).

The Inductive Category-Formations and Their Coherence

The results of the inductive survey of theological things of Song of Songs Rabbah yield a handful of large statements, greatly elaborated but essentially simple. These coalesce into few but capacious category-formations, all of them common to the Rabbinic midrash-documents already analyzed. If the Rabbinic sages met to formulate the principles of Judaism (as we should call the task of such a council) or to tell the authoritative story (as their medium of expression would designate the labor), what are the principles, what is the story, that would emerge? The native category-formations yielded by an inductive reading of Song of Songs Rabbah encompass [1] God in relationship to Israel through the Torah, [2] God and Israel in relationship to the nations defined by the nations' rejection of the Torah, to which Israel's sin of rebellion against the Torah is comparable, [3] God's mercy and justice, which bring about punishment for Israel's sin but which also respond with forgiveness to Israel's repentance and restore Israel's natural condition in the Land, comparable to Adam's natural condition in Eden.

So at their council the Rabbinic sages could formulate principles of the faith in the manner of philosophers, e.g., God is thus and so, God has done and will do thus and so, Israel is such and such, and the like. Or, more suited to their idiom, they could have told a story in the manner of Scripture. Then at the council they would have agreed on the main lines of the story that would convey the faith: God did, does, and will do, in response to Israel, which did, does, and will do—and here are the details of the relationship between the principal actors of creation. The category-formations of Song of Songs Rabbah defined inductively coalesce into these propositions or narrative elements and therein accommodate the whole of the theological corpus of the document. The specific theological propositions of the discrete compositions and composites turn out to fit together into a simple corpus of theological principles or an equally simple narrative, vastly elaborated and articulated. Now we turn to a deductive examination of the same collection of "theological things." We start from the outside, not the inside, and ask whether that collection fits into a ready-made construction: the structure and system of Rabbinic Judaism that have already been defined. The details of Song of Songs Rabbah coalesce within a few capacious category-formations of a theological character: abstract propositions subject to recapitulation in narrative form. The result of an inductive reading is to show how Song of Songs Rabbah orders and regularizes the facts of Scripture, history, and nature transforming them into a systematic account of, and explanation for, Israel's being.

The Theological Propositions of Song of Songs Rabbah: The Principal Parts Viewed Deductively

The survey of the eight Parashiyyot has shown a simple fact, which in detail is iterated here. It is that the theology of Rabbinic Judaism constructed deductively (as noted in Theology of Rabbinic Midrash, General Traits) is epitomized also by the statement of that theology in Song of Songs Rabbah. That theology, adduced deductively, accounts

(1) for Israel among the nations,
(2) for Israel's inner life, and
(3) or the relationship with God that is established by corporate (embodied, unitary) Israel and by Israelite individuals.

In Song of Songs Rabbah, the propositional structures of the nurturing Rabbinic theology are systematically adumbrated. Its system, the source of dynamics, is invoked. Specifically, two theological structures, the theologies of history and (concomitantly) of Israel, and the systemic component that accounts for the movement of Israel through change together comprise the Rabbinic theology and define its recapitulation here.

As to the two structures: the first, Israel among the nations, collects the data of the document to state with great elaboration the normative Rabbinic theology of history. At issue is accounting for the situation of Israel among—in relationship to—the nations. Many "theological things" make a single statement on that subject.

Second, another structure sets forth in vast detail the theology of Israel on its own. At stake is spelling out how God's love for Israel is expressed through the Torah and through the commandments, and how Israel's devotion to God is realized in the study of the one and the practice of the other.

Third comes the source of dynamism, what I call, the system that animates and motivates the two structures, endows them with the power of narrative. Specifically, these two structures are not inert but active, by reason of the system that works itself out in and through them. The structures work together to tell a story. That concerns the working of Israel's moral condition in relationship to God. It is encompassed within the Rabbinic theology of reconciliation of Israel to God through repentance and atonement—the beating heart of the matter.

These three principal parts—the two structural, the third systemic—comprise a single working theology. It sets forth the coherent facts of relationship:

(1) God and humanity,
(2) God and Israel,
(3) the motive force governing Israel and the nations, which is Israel's moral condition.

The theology tells the story of Israel past, present, and eternal, always in relationship with God. The structures and working system then accommodate the bits and pieces of theological expression, the "theological things" that we have surveyed.

Accordingly, a comprehensive logic, a rational explanation of Israel's condition everywhere animate the document's reading of Song of Songs. By the transitive verb, "animate," I mean to express a very particular claim. It is that every detail of every theological composition and composite fits together with all other details when placed into the encompassing structure and working system at hand. A governing logic, a theology that is realized in hermeneutics, accounts for much of the Rabbinic exegesis of Song of Songs and all of its intellectually active components.

A brief elaboration of the matter, now framed in more conventional language, is called for. Here is what I conceive to form the theological platform, plank by plank.

1. Israel and God—The Election of Israel, the Marks of God's Love: the theology of Israel, beloved of God by reason of its devotion to the Torah and the practice of the commandments, explains Israel's task and condition. The task is to master and realize God's teaching in the Torah, as set forth by the Rabbinic sages. Its calling, shaped by the practice of the commandments, is to express its love for God and elicit a response of love from God for its realization of God's will.

2. Israel's Exteriority—Israel and the Nations, the Marks of God's Intervention: the Rabbinic theology of history, recapitulated here, explains the rationality of Israel's condition as God's elect, yet subjugated people. The nations, enemies of God, rule over Israel because Israel has sinned and God employs the nations to punish them and bring them to repentance, and hence, reconciliation. Rome, in particular, is the fourth and final kingdom, to be followed by Israel's dominion, realized by the messiah at the end of days.

3. Israel's Interiority—Israelites' Inner Condition, the Indications of God's Yearning: the theology of reconciliation through repentance, atonement, and renewal accords hope to Israel and guidance on overcoming its present deplorable condition of subjugation to the idolaters. The humiliation of God's people is because Israel at present is estranged from God through sin, defined as rebellion against God's teaching. But in his mercy God has afforded means of overcoming sin and its effects. That is through repentance and atonement, to which God responds with forgiveness. Israel then may repair its flawed interior being and consequently revise its deplorable exterior condition And, it goes without saying, in one measure or another, in one component or another, they also animate every Midrash-compilation of the formative canon.

Everything of consequence that happens makes sense because it fits together with everything else of consequence. The "theological things" are not random and arbitrary. A single narrative encompasses all. On what basis do I allege the coherence of the data into these larger structures to form a working system of thought? The reason is that the working system that pervades the Midrash-compilations and imposes order on the aggadic data of the entire formative canon of Rabbinic Judaism has already been described.

The Statement of Song of Songs Rabbah in the Context of the Theology of Rabbinic Judaism

Now to ask how Song of Songs Rabbah fits into an encompassing theological structure and operates in tandem with a governing theological system. Rabbinic theology viewed whole and embodied in Song of Songs Rabbah as well corresponds with, reworks the main points of, the large conception of the nations, Israel, and God and Israel, that sages show animates Scripture's account of matters. The sages' category-formations for Song of Songs in Song of Songs Rabbah therefore impose upon the scriptural poem that large conception of Scripture's message as a whole that the sages have derived in dialogue with Scripture itself. What sages contribute in Song of Songs Rabbah, then, is their power of generalization and rational construction, their capacity to translate mythic monotheism and its narrative into a theory of Israel's social order, realized in the Halakhah of Rabbinic Judaism and accounted for in its aggadah, the whole forming a vast reworking of, a Midrash built upon the Pentateuch and the Prophets.

Read by sages in *its* larger Scriptural setting and within *their* encompassing theological reconstruction of Scripture's setting, the Song of Songs speaks—and can only speak—of God's love for Israel and Israel's for God. In the setting of Pentateuch and Prophets, no other relationship pertains. The Song can have no other meaning. That is why I claim that, for their part, in approaching Song of Songs the sages worked from the whole of Scripture forward to this part of it. Then they faithfully rendered Scripture's principal propositions concerning the whole of the matter when they form their judgment of this part of it.

On what basis? It is the same basis on which the sages construct their reading of matters: Scripture read whole. That is to say, reading the same Scriptures as a continuous story in the way that they did, we find ourselves constrained to tell the same story, devise the same category-formations. For if we translate into the narrative of Israel, from the beginning to the calamity of the destruction of the (first) Temple, what is set forth in both abstract and concrete ways in the Oral Torah, we turn out to state a reprise of the Authorized History laid out in Genesis through Kings and amplified by the principal prophets.

Consider the four components of the theology of the Aggadah cited just now. Here, beginning with the integrating basics, encompassing the entire expanse of creation and humanity, from first to last things, are the ideas that impart structure and order to, and sustain, the whole. Starting with the doctrine of world order that is just and concluding with eternal life, here is the simple logic that animates all the parts and makes them cohere. The generative categories prove not only imperative and irreducible but, in the context of my narrative, also logically sequential. Each of the four parts of this account of the theology of the Oral Torah:

(1) the perfectly just character of world order,

(2) indications of its perfection,

(3) sources of its imperfection,

(4) media for the restoration of world order and their results belongs in its place and set in any other sequence the components of the Rabbinic theology become incomprehensible. Further, each component in order, drawing upon its predecessor, pointing toward its successor, forms part of an unfolding story that can be told in only one direction and in the dictated order and in no other way. Shift the position of an element of the structure and place it before or after some other, and the entire flow of thought is disrupted. That is the mark of a well-crafted theology, a coherent structure, a compelling system—that of the Torah, read systematically. And, we now realize, Song of Songs Rabbah invokes these same category-formations to make its part of the comprehensive statement.

The theological statement of Song of Songs Rabbah, for all the novelty of its symbolic vocabulary, finds its proper setting only within the theology of Rabbinic Judaism. That is why we can speak of Rabbinic theology *in*, but not *of*, Song of Songs Rabbah. A prevailing theological structure makes its appearance here as well. We simply cannot claim to identify a distinctive theological system that belongs to Song of Songs Rabbah in particular. The document makes its unique contribution to the formation of a single, coherent, encompassing theological system. But Song of Songs Rabbah does make a statement of its own, which we discern when we ask how, in detail, its "theological things" cohere. The answer defines what is distinctive in the theological category-formations of the document.

Does Song of Songs Rabbah Form a Theological Statement on its Own?

Song of Songs Rabbah does not form a theological statement on its own, even though the theological statement that it makes can be read autonomously. That is, we can compose a cogent theological system entirely within the framework of our document. But, when we do, we find ourselves recapitulating an encompassing theological system, vastly transcending the limits of Song of Songs Rabbah, and that is the system of Scripture itself. I have now answered the generative questions that provoke an inductive and a deductive reading of Song of Songs Rabbah. Readers may now test my results against the data and my writing of them:

(1) May we truly characterize the Rabbinic Midrash as theological not in theme alone but also in intent and focus? The individual coalesce into a few encompassing theological propositions (stated abstractly) or narratives (stated concretely).

(2) And may we describe that theological component as cogent and coherent? The results of inductive inquiry sustain the affirmative answer to this question: the native category-formations hold together in a single continuous story, they form a single coherent set of propositions.

The category-formations within which the discrete data of the document find their place yield a coherent story, tracking that of Genesis through Kings as read by the Prophets. It is the story of God's yearning for Israel, within mankind, because of Israel's willingness, stated at Sinai, to know God in the Torah and freely to choose to accept God's dominion in the Torah. At Sinai too, Israel sinned and rebelled. God punished Israel but forgives repentant Israel when Israel atones. Israel's situation even now replicates the paradigm of sin and suffering, punishment, atonement, and forgiveness. And ultimately, God will redeem Israel from the nations where, by reason of sin, Israel has been scattered, just as God redeemed Israel from Egypt.

In the Context of the Theology of Rabbinic Judaism: What Does Song of Songs Rabbah Contribute?

But it is not the only point of consequence in examining the document's theological structure and system. For the fact is, Song of Songs Rabbah, like Genesis Rabbah and Pesiqta deRab Kahana, also makes a distinctive, and in some ways unique contribution to the larger statement of Rabbinic Judaism. What the Rabbinic sages can have said only in response to Song of Songs is, God's love for Israel, and Israel's love for God, is comparable to the love of woman and man, and God yearns for Israel as much as Israel yearns for God—if that characterization of theological relationships in affective symbols was their intent, as it manifestly was, then only Song of Songs can have served to make that point. What is implicit in other Midrash-compilations can have been made explicit only here. So the system as a whole is not only recapitulated. Its principal message attained particularization only here. And in order to say, each concrete detail of the practice of the Torah and the commandments embodies that yearning of God for Israel and Israel for God—in order to formulate and set into the context of relationship those "theological things," events, activities, attitudes alike—only Song of Songs can have served. What is episodic elsewhere is routine here, what is characteristic over all comes to acute expression here.

The unique contribution of Song of Songs Rabbah is best captured in the debate on the status of Song of Songs in Scripture. For here we see fully articulated the position of the sages who deemed the love poems to belong in the canon—their physical sanctification as sacred scrolls to be protected by the purity laws:

MISHNAH-TRACTATE YADAYIM 3:5

G. All sacred scriptures impart uncleanness to hands.

H. The Song of Songs and Qohelet impart uncleanness to hands.

I. R. Judah says, "The Song of Songs imparts uncleanness to hands, but as to Qohelet there is dispute."

J. R. Yose says, "Qohelet does not impart uncleanness to hands, but as to Song of Songs there is dispute."

K. Rabbi Simeon says, "Qohelet is among the lenient rulings of the House of Shammai and strict rulings of the House of Hillel."

L. Said R. Simeon b. Azzai, "I have a tradition from the testimony of the seventy-two elders,

M. "on the day on which they seated R. Eleazar b. Azariah in the session,

N. "that the Song of Songs and Qohelet do impart uncleanness to hands."

O. Said R. Aqiba, "Heaven forbid! No Israelite man ever disputed concerning Song of Songs that it imparts uncleanness to hands.

P. "For the entire age is not so worthy as the day on which the Song of Songs was given to Israel.

Q. "For all the scriptures are holy, but the Song of Songs is holiest of all.

R. "And if they disputed, they disputed only concerning Qohelet."

S. Said R. Yohanan b. Joshua the son of R. Aqiba's father-in-law, according to the words of Ben Azzai, "Indeed did they dispute, and indeed did they come to a decision."

Song of Songs Rabbah settled the question: without reading the Song of Songs as the Rabbinic sages do here, there would have been no resolving of the dispute as to the status of the Song of Songs. The sages judged that the meaning of the love poems was, and can only have been, precisely the sense they imputed to them. On what basis did they reach that conclusion and affirm it? The entirety of Scripture attested to that meaning. Read start to finish, Genesis through Kings in light of Prophecy told the story of God's search for man and election of Israel—and the consequence of God's love for Israel. Reading forward from Scripture, the sages found in Israel's everyday life the embodiments of the love of Israel for God. Devotion to the Torah, practice of the commandments—the whole corpus of sanctification of the material transactions of Israel sustained that reading. Reading the entirety of Scripture into Song of Songs, producing Song of Songs Rabbah—that deductive process of working from the whole to the parts permitted no other result. For placing this component of Scripture into the context of the whole of Scripture yielded the conclusion reached here. Song of Song Rabbah contributes the articulation of what is implicit in the canon of Scripture: the reason why Song of Songs belongs. It is, as Aqiba says, holiest of all.

The upshot is simple. The theology of midrash emerges when we read Scripture as sages did, the whole, then the parts, illuminating the parts in light of the whole. They drew conclusions, then identified the connections implicit in those conclusions. To conclude where we began, when Solomon says, "O that you would kiss me with the kisses of your mouth! For your love is better than wine," to what can he have made reference, if not to Israel at the Sea or at Sinai, where God embraced Israel? And where can that kiss have taken place, if not at the tent of meeting, or the Temple itself? Scripture read in perspective and seen whole yields no other conclusion, though it affords many other possibilities for conveying that one conclusion.

JACOB NEUSNER
Bard College

Targum Jonathan of the Prophets I

Within the Judaic tradition of biblical interpretation, what are widely referred to today as the historical books of the Old Testament—that is, from Joshua through 2 Kings—are known as the Former Prophets. Prophetic works more strictly speaking are called the Latter Prophets. The biblical text itself comports rather well with that overall typology. Zechariah looks back to what the "former prophets" said (and how they were ignored) and hopes he will be heard in an appeal to his hearers not to be like their "fathers" (Zech. 1:4-6). Zechariah did not have a literary scheme in mind, but by his reference to the "former prophets" he conveyed his keen sense that the prophetic address of which he was a part was of primal importance within Israel, and was in the line of the revelation of the Torah (see Zech. 7:4-12).

The designation "Former Prophets" more clearly conveys the substance of the books concerned than does the phrase "the historical works." After all, some of the most distinguished prophetic figures of Israel appear within Joshua-2 Kings, including Joshua himself, Samuel, Elijah and Elisha, and Isaiah. Moreover, although the Former Prophets refer to the past, they do so in order to warn Israel in the present that those who come after the prophets—the same collectors who gathered the stories of prophets and of kings in order to demonstrate that the Torah is the only foundation of Israel's prosperity—must be obeyed if Israel is to survive and prosper. The books do not recount history as such, but speak of the past as a confirmation of the prophetic demand for loyalty to the Torah.

Both the Former and the Latter Prophets are extant in Aramaic in a single collection, known as Targum Jonathan. The date and character of each Targum within the collection needs to be assessed individually. As we will see in this entry and the one that follows, there is a definite pattern that associates some of these Targumim with definable periods and schools of thought. So although Targum Jonathan is not simply a random anthology of unrelated works, neither is it the work of a single translator.

Because the Targumim are Rabbinic in origin and purpose, it is natural to suppose that Rabbinic tradition might be a reliable guide in describing the history of Targumic development. But when the Talmud does address that issue, it does so in a manifestly ahistorical way. The entire corpus, Targum Jonathan as it stands, is ascribed within Rabbinic tradition (B. Meg. 3a) to Jonathan ben Uzziel, a disciple of Hillel, the famous contemporary of Jesus. (Hillel's most famous affinity with Jesus is that he taught a version of the golden rule. He explained to a proselyte that he should not do to his neighbor what he himself hated. That was the whole Torah, he said, while the rest is commentary and should be learned as such. Such, in any case, is the story in B. Shab. 31a.) There are compelling reasons not to accept that attribution at face value, because rabbis tend to be named in Rabbinic tradition for ideological reasons. Naming an authority for an opinion might give it weight, or it might suggest that it was a purely individual judgment, which should be superseded by others. The principal point of an attribution was that an opinion should be considered, not that it should be accepted; the issue of what we would call historical accuracy was not in play.[1] Indeed, the passage in B. Meg. 3a (quoted below) intimates both that Jonathan rendered the Targum for noble reasons and that he exceeded his authority by what he said.

The attribution conveys a sense of the

---

[1] For a lucid discussion, see Jacob Neusner, "Evaluating the Attributions of Sayings to Named Sages in the Rabbinic Literature," in *Journal for the Study of Judaism* 26 (1995), pp. 93-111.

controversy that the formal production of such a collection could involve:

> R. Jeremiah—or some say R. Hiyya b. Abba—also said: The Targum of the Pentateuch was composed by Onqelos the proselyte under the guidance of R. Eleazar and R. Joshua. The Targum of the Prophets was composed by Jonathan b. Uzziel under the guidance of Haggai, Zechariah, and Malachi, and the land of Israel quaked over an area of four hundred parasangs,[2] and a *bat qol* came forth and cried: Who is this that has revealed my secrets to men? Jonathan b. Uzziel arose and said, "I have revealed your secrets to mankind. But it is known to you that I have not done this for my own honor or the honor of my father's house, but for your honor—that divisions might not increase in Israel." He also sought to reveal the Writings by a Targum, but a *bat qol* came forth and said: Enough! For this reason—that the end of the messiah is told in it.

The opening intimates that the memory even of who attributed the Targum to Jonathan was uncertain. And whether it was Jeremiah or Hiyya, the fact remains that it was only in the fourth century that it was "remembered" that Jonathan had composed the Targum in the first century.

But anachronism is something this haggadah concerning Jonathan delights in. The biblical prophets named cannot have been actual contemporaries of Jonathan, who lived centuries after them. Indeed, because Haggai, Zechariah, and Malachi are taken within Rabbinic discussion to have been active near the time of the restoration of the Temple (around 515 B.C.E.), the chronology of the statement is as outlandish in moving backward to those prophets as it is in moving forward to the time of Jeremiah and Hiyya. It is most unlikely that this tale was intended to be taken literally.

The same Jeremiah (or Hiyya) identifies the companions of Daniel in Dan. 10:7 as Haggai, Zechariah, and Malachi. While they were prophets, and Daniel was not, he had a vision, while they saw nothing. Haggai, Zechariah, and Malachi are transitional to other figures, to Daniel in one haggadah and to Jonathan in another. Both transitions involve the disclosure of mysteries, whether Daniel's visions or Jonathan's "secrets." That seems to have been an association which reference to Haggai, Zechariah, and Malachi was intended to occasion.

In the same Talmudic text, Jeremiah/Hiyya wonders why Daniel's companions—the three prophets named—fled if they saw no vision, which is what Dan. 10:7 says they did. The answer is that their "star," or spirit, saw, while physically they did not. By the time of Jeremiah/Hiyya, who are usually dated within the fourth century, there is a Rabbinic anthropology current, in which one's spiritual self and one's physical self are seen as distinct. This anthropology permits communication between the three last biblical prophets and Daniel, or between the same three and Jonathan b. Uzziel, whatever their chronologies might have been. Jonathan is therefore in a position, as this haggadah would have it, to reveal what is

---

[2] It has been suggested on the basis of a traditional calculation that the area was the total size of the land of Israel; see G. Zlotowitz and H. Goldwurm, *Tractate Megillah: Talmud Bavli, the Schottenstein Edition* (Brooklyn, 1994). The editors cite Rashi's comment on Num. 13:25 by way of precedent. But Herodotus gives the length of the Persian royal road from Sardis to Susa as 450 parasangs (see Histories 5.52–53), which would make the area described here larger than most estimates of territorial Israel. In any case, a parasang came to nearly 6 kilometers; see Michael C. Astour, "Overland Trade Routes in Ancient Western Asia," in Jack M. Sasson, ed., *Civilizations of the Ancient Near East* III (New York, 1995), pp. 1401–1420, 1417–1420.

not to be revealed until the appointed time. As it turns out, then, B. Meg. 3a is no bland assertion of authorship but an evaluation of the kind of supernatural knowledge Targum Jonathan is believed to convey.

In fact, the Isaiah Targum claims just such eschatological knowledge. The following translation (of Targum Isaiah 24:16), as has become conventional, follows my edition of the Targum, and indicates departures from the Masoretic text by the use of italics:[3]

> From the *sanctuary, whence joy is about to go forth to all the inhabitants of the earth*, we hear *a* song for the righteous. *The prophet said, "The mystery of the reward for the righteous is visible* to me, *the mystery of the retribution for the wicked is revealed* to me! *Woe to the robbers, who are robbed*, and to *the plunder of the plunderers, which is now plundered."*

The revelation to the prophet of the Targum corresponds to the definitive revelation of "the kingdom of the Lord of hosts" on Mount Zion (Targum Isaiah 24:23), when the messiah builds the Temple there (Targum Isaiah 53:5). Prophecy, the kingdom, and the messiah are interwoven themes through Targum Jonathan as a whole, and the tradition in B. Meg. 3a is better taken as an index of Targumic ideology than as a historical reference.

It seems as unwise to dismiss the Talmudic attribution completely as it is to accept it uncritically. The focus on the immediate rebuilding of the Temple is most sensibly dated in the years soon after the Roman destruction of 70 C.E., and there are several cases in which Jesus' citations of Scripture correspond better to Targum Jonathan than to any other ancient version.[4] Moreover, the stated object of Jonathan, the avoidance of divisions in Israel, is precisely what is held (in Y. Hag. 77d) to have increased after the time of Hillel and Shammai. So, too, the place of the *bat qol* here is pivotal; the claim attributed to a slightly later time (that of Eliezer b. Hyracanus) would make such phenomena less authoritative than the rule of a majority of the sages. In B. B.M. 59a–b (a famous haggadah in which the purity of a stove is disputed), Eliezer proves he is correct against a majority by miraculous signs, and he is supported by a *bat qol*, which disputes even the propriety of arguing with Eliezer. But the majority persists, and Elijah himself warrants that they are right to do so in God's eyes (who jokingly remarks, "My sons have overturned me").

Taken in aggregate, such considerations suggest that it would be ill advised to dismiss the possibility of Jonathan's involvement in the development of the Targum. The growing awareness among scholars that Rabbinic traditions are not on the whole reliable in historical terms has resulted in a tendency among some to ignore what such haggadot have to say. That is unfortunate, because sometimes—as in the present case—haggadot may be as ideological informative as they are historically unreliable.

We also know from other haggadot in the Talmud that Jonathan was not considered the sole author of the Targum. Passages of the Prophets' Targum accord precisely with renderings given in the name of Joseph bar Hiyya, a rabbi of the fourth century. In B. Pes. 68a, for example, Joseph renders Is. 5:17 as "and the righteous shall possess the possessions of the wicked." The wording attributed to him agrees exactly (and the precise forms almost exactly) with that of Targum Jonathan (cf. Isaiah Targum 5:17b), and the sense of both versions is quite different from the Masoretic text and the Septuagint, where the image is of animals

---

[3] See Bruce Chilton, *The Isaiah Targum, Introduction, Translation, Apparatus, and Notes* (Wilmington and Edinburgh, 1987).

[4] See Bruce Chilton, "Four Types of Comparison between the Targumim and the New Testament," in *Journal for the Aramaic Bible* 2 (2000), pp. 163–188.

grazing among ruins. Once the decision was made to spell out the significance of the metaphor, which is typical of Targum Jonathan, the particular application to the righteous and their ultimate wealth is not surprising. Still, there is nothing inevitable about that application, and it seems arbitrary to deny a connection between the Targum Jonathan and Joseph bar Hiyya.

The Isaiah Targum has been subjected to more study than any of the other Targumim to the Prophets (both Former and Latter); it shows signs of a nationalistic eschatology that was current just after the destruction of the Temple in 70 C.E., and of the more settled perspective of the rabbis in Babylon some three centuries later. That finding of critical exegesis comports well with periods of the two rabbis identified in Talmud, the Tanna Jonathan b. Uzziel and the Amora Joseph bar Hiyya.

It appears that Targum Jonathan as a whole is the result of these two major periods of collecting and editing Rabbinic traditions of rendering the Prophets, the first period being Tannaitic, and the second Amoraic. Long after Targum Jonathan was composed, probably near the time the Fragments Targum to the Pentateuch was assembled, targumic addenda were appended in certain of its manuscripts; they are represented in the Codex Reuchlinianus from the twelfth century and in a manuscript from the Bibliothèque Nationale (numbered 75 in the current catalog) from the fourteenth century. The topic of the Targumic addenda will not immediately occupy us here, because they assume the existence of an established Targumic tradition, to which the medieval additions amount to creative extensions. But they are witnesses of the continuing consciousness that the production of Targumim was not simply a matter of translating but of conveying the sense of Scripture in its theological fullness. Although Reuchlinianus and Bibliothèque Nationale 75 do not represent the development of Targum Jonathan in its formative period, they do reflect the kind of interpretative enterprise which went into the development of the Targumim, and some of their distinct readings are well worth considering.

The Prophets' Targum, both to the Former and the Latter Prophets, has received renewed attention as the best source for the explication of Scripture in synagogues during periods of early Judaism and Rabbinic Judaism. The current phase of discussion is predicated upon the fundamental work of Pinkhos Churgin, who located Targum Jonathan in the intersection between worship in synagogues and Rabbinic discussion.[5] Today, it may seem obvious that the principal Targumim are the result of the dynamics between synagogues and schools,[6] but there have been times when an almost entirely folk origin has been proposed.[7] Churgin held that Targum Jonathan emerged during the formative period of Rabbinic influence, between the second century B.C.E. and the seventh century C.E. Linguistic discussion, primarily the work of A. Tal, E.Y. Kutscher, and M. Goshen-Gottstein,[8] focused attention particularly on the second century C.E., that is, just subsequent to the

---

[5] Cf. *Targum Jonathan to the Prophets* (New Haven, 1927).

[6] Cf. A.D. York, "The Dating of Targumic Literature," in *Journal for the Study of Judaism* 5 (1974), pp. 49-62; "The Targum in the Synagogue and the School," in *Journal for the Study of Judaism* 10 (1979), pp. 74-86; Chilton, *The Isaiah Targum*, pp. xxv-xxviii.

[7] Cf. R. Le Déaut, *Introduction à la littérature targumique* (Rome, 1966); J. Bowker, *The Targums and Rabbinic Literature. An Introduction to Jewish Interpretation of Scripture* (Cambridge, 1969); Martin McNamara, *Targum and Testament. Aramaic Paraphrases of the Hebrew Bible: A Light on the New Testament* (Shannon, 1972).

[8] Cf. Tal, *The Language of the Targum of the Former Prophets and its Position within the Aramaic Dialects* (Tel Aviv, 1975) (Hebrew); Kutscher, "Das zur Zeit Jesu gesprochene Aramäische," in *Zeitschrift für die neutestamentliche*

Aramaic of Qumran, and transitional to the language of the Amoraim, as the likely period of formation. But one of the features noted has been the stable, one might say standard, quality of the Aramaic employed in Targum Jonathan, which makes an assessment of date predicated upon linguistic considerations alone appear inadequate.[9]

Twenty-five years ago, the present writer took up a method of comparative analysis designed to substantiate or to qualify the work of linguists.[10] The exegeses incorporated in the Isaiah Targum were compared systematically with departures from the Hebrew text evidenced in the Septuagint, the Apocrypha and Pseudepigrapha, the scrolls of Qumran, the New Testament, the Mishnah, the two Mekiltas, Sifra, Sifre, the two Talmuds, Midrash Rabbah, the two Pesiqtas, the Pirqe de R. Eliezer, and the Yalkut Shimoni. The conclusion was that targumic traditions were incorporated within an exegetical framework, a version— perhaps incomplete—of Isaiah in Aramaic composed by a meturgeman (identified in Talmud as Jonathan b. Uzziel) who flourished between 70 and 135 C.E.[11] That work was completed by another meturgeman, identified in Talmud as Joseph bar Hiyya of Pumbeditha, who died in 333.[12] Throughout the process, the communal nature of the interpretative work of the meturgeman was acknowledged; insofar as individuals were involved, they spoke with the voice of synagogues and of schools. The production of the Isaiah Targum through the stages of two exegetical frameworks, one Tannaitic and one Amoraic, has been widely accepted, and applied to the understanding of Targum Jonathan as a whole.

Given the current state of our knowledge of the Targum Jonathan and of how our knowledge has developed, we will use the Isaiah Targum as a focus of our consideration. Once we have more clearly understood that document, we can use the results (continuing in the next entry) to understand the other documents within Targum Jonathan. The targumic themes of prophecy, messiah, and Shekhinah will prove especially informative of the purpose and origin of each of the documents.

Prophecy in the Isaiah Targum

The theme of a characteristically prophetic message of repentance is represented in both frameworks, and there is tragic recognition that the departure of the Shekhinah

---

Wissenschaft 51 (1960), pp. 46–54; *Studies in Galilean Aramaic* (Ramat Gan, 1976); M. Goshen-Gottstein, "The Language of Targum Onqelos and the Model of Literary Diglossia in Aramaic," in *Journal of Near Eastern Studies* 37 (1978), pp. 169–179. Although the discussion cannot now detain us, mention should also be made here of two articles that appeared in 1973, M. Delcor, "Le Targum de Job et l'araméen du temps de Jésus," in J.-E. Ménard, ed., *Exégèse biblique et judaïsme* (Strasbourg, 1973), pp. 78–107; S. Kaufman, "The Job Targum from Qumran," in *Journal of the American Oriental Society* 93 (1973), pp. 317–327.

[9] Cf. Bruce Chilton, *The Glory of Israel*, pp. xi. Since the time I wrote those pages, discussion of the development of the Aramaic language has tended to offer further support of the position I developed on an exegetical basis, as remarks below will indicate; cf. Chilton, *The Isaiah Targum*, p. xxi.

[10] Cf. Chilton, *The Glory of Israel*.

[11] Within that early framework, materials were incorporated that appear to reflect the interpretations of earlier periods, including the period of Jesus. Cf. Bruce Chilton, *A Galilean Rabbi and His Bible. Jesus' Use of the Interpreted Scripture of His Time* (Wilmington, 1986; also published with the subtitle, *Jesus' own interpretation of Isaiah*; London, 1984).

[12] Chilton, *The Glory of Israel*, pp. 2, 3; idem., *The Isaiah Targum*, p. xxi; for the sections of the Targum most representative of each meturgeman, cf. p. xxiv.

spells the end of prophecy (cf. 5:5, 6; 8:16, 17).[13] Within both frameworks, the elucidation, "The prophet said ...," is frequently added. It has been suggested[14] that the innovation is merely a liturgical help, as in many modern Christian lectionaries. In them, "Jesus" replaces "he" at the beginning of many readings. But it is difficult to imagine that an actual meturgeman, delivering a rendering orally, would need written warrant from a Targum to replace "he" with "the prophet said;" as compared to other changes instanced in Targum Jonathan, such conservative adjustments do not represent substantive transformations.

The suggestion is an example of how modern scholarship has not adequately allowed for the difference between ancient and modern usage of Scripture. By its very nature, performing an interpretation orally, and in a different language, involves the acknowledgment that one is not tied down to the text that is at the base of the performance. As envisioned in the Mishnah and Talmud (see M. Meg. 4:4 and B. Meg. 21b), the meturgeman would provide his rendering after some verses of Scripture had been read out in Hebrew. Because even someone who did not know Hebrew would realize that the Targumic interpretation was frequently much longer than the biblical text, there was a built-in recognition that a creative activity was involved. What the suggestion particularly ignores is the most obvious and crucial factor: within both exegetical frameworks, meturgemanin preface some of their most innovative renderings with the introduction.[15] In aggregate, the Aramaic interpreters implicitly claim to speak with quasi-prophetic authority, in the wake of the departed Shekhinah. Two such cases in the Isaiah Targum permit us to see the work of the meturgemanin of the two frameworks, virtually side by side, in chapters 21 and 22.

Chapter 21 is redolent of the military power of the Sassanids and the nascent threat of Arabians[16] and indulges in proleptic glee at "Babylon's" demise. As the meturgeman states in 21:9, "Fallen, *and also about to fall*, is Babylon."[17] The Amoraic setting of the meturgeman is also reflected in

---

[13] Cf. Chilton, *The Glory of Israel*, pp. 54–5. For the latter theologoumenon, cf. (for Is. 5:5, 6) Ecc. Rabbah 11:3, and (for 8:16, 17) Gen. Rabbah 43.3.2. The first statement is attributed to Aquila, and second is anonymous. Cf. Peter Schäfer, *Die Vorstellung vom heiligen Geist in der rabbinischer Literatur* (Munich, 1972), pp. 75, 135, 136, 139, 140, 143; Chilton, *The Glory of Israel*, pp. 48–52; L. Smolar and M. Aberbach, *Studies in Targum Jonathan to the Prophets* (New York, 1983), p. 11; K.J. Cathcart and R.P. Gordon, *The Targum of the Minor Prophets* (Wilmington, 1989), p. 199, n. 5, with its citation of B. B.B. 12a.

[14] By Kevin J. Cathcart and Robert P. Gordon, *The Targum of the Minor Prophets*: The Aramaic Bible 11 (Wilmington, 1989), p. 150. More recently, see Robert P. Gordon, "An Incipit Formula in Tg Prophets," in *Studies in the Targum to the Twelve Prophets, from Nahum to Malachi* (Leiden, 1994), pp. 74–82.

[15] Chilton, *The Glory of Israel*, pp. 52–53, 55; idem., *The Isaiah Targum*, pp. xiii, xiv. The observation is confirmed in respect of Targum Jonathan more generally in R. Hayward, *The Targum of Jeremiah* (Wilmington and Edinburgh, 1987), p. 32. Cathcart and Gordon, op. cit., translate an instance in which the Targumic *incipit* prefaces an expansive rendering at Hab. 2:1f.

[16] Chilton, *The Isaiah Targum*, pp. 40–43. In his recent monograph, Gordon has made additional arguments in the same direction, pp. 142–146.

[17] The significance of this interpretation was brilliantly explained by Churgin, pp. 28–29, and further pursued in Chilton, *The Isaiah Targum*, pp. 41–43 (see also idem, *The Glory of Israel*, pp. 5, 3, 45, 121). Gordon has tried to dispute the finding, on the grounds that the phrase "and is about to fall" is—in his words—"as much an exegetical matter as an expression of a particular historical perspective" (p. 140). That, of course, may be said of any targumic rendering. But even exegetes say things when they decide to employ "exegetical matter," and in the present case a meturgeman is speaking of the future demise of

a particularly revealing theological statement (21:12):

> The prophet said, "*There is reward for the righteous* and *retribution for the wicked*. If you *are penitent, repent while you are able to repent* . . ."

The meturgeman here addresses those individuals who are prepared to listen (cf. 33:13; 57:19), while the usual assumption of this Targum is that Israel is obdurate.[18]

A more typical complaint within the earlier framework (28:10a) takes up a theme also expressed within the close of the biblical canon (cf. Mal. 2:10–11):

> *They were commanded to perform the law, and what they were commanded they did not wish to do. The prophets prophesied concerning them, that if they repented . . . and they did not listen to the sayings of the prophets.*

In theological terms, a shift from the claim that repentance has been globally rejected to one in which individuals might be found who are penitent is considerable. Just that shift is involved as one moves from the Tannaitic framework to the Amoraic framework.

Repentance in 21:12 is also associated more with the eschatological judgment of individuals than with the restoration of the Temple and the people Israel's intended end in the earlier framework. The usage of the phrase "The prophet said" here is Amoraic, as it is at 21:8, 9, where reference is innovatively made to the imminent fall of Babylon, the ruling force with which the Amoraim in Babylon needed to reckon. Perhaps the closest approximation to the reading is to be found in Num. Rabbah 16.23, which cites Is. 21:12 and observes (with particular reference to the term "morning" in the Hebrew), "when the time of the world to come arrives, which is called morning, we shall know in whom he delights."[19]

The emphasis is quite different in chapter 22 of the Isaiah Targum, which focuses on the depredations of Jerusalem, the victories of the Romans, and the fate of the sanctuary,[20] characteristic interests of the Tannaitic meturgeman. A particular threat is directed against those who feast in a time when the prophet calls for fasting (22:12, 13), and the threat, articulated at 22:14, is couched in language also found in the Revelation of John:

> *The prophet said*, With my ears *I was hearing when this was decreed before* the Lord God of hosts: "Surely this *sin* will not be forgiven until you *die the second death*," says the Lord God of hosts."

The fact that the same theologoumenon appears in Rev. 2:11; 20:6, 14; 21:8 does not alone settle the questions of the chronology and meaning of the phrase. Charles Perrot and Pierre-Maurice Bogaert cite the usage in various Targumim and in Pirqe de R. Eliezer (34).[21] But at Is. 22:14 in particular, the rabbis from the second century

---

Babylon. Gordon himself concludes than he can offer no "decisive argument against Churgin's Sassanid explanation," although he also cautions that it is not "demanded by the evidence."

[18] Chilton, *The Glory of Israel*, pp. 37–46.

[19] The passage also connects Mal. 3:18 with Is. 21:12, which is reminiscent of the Isaian passage in Targum Jonathan. For a further discussion, including references to other analogies, cf. Chilton, *The Glory of Israel*, pp. 43, 44.

[20] Cf. Chilton, *The Isaiah Targum*, pp. 42–45, and *idem*, "Shebna, Eliakim, and the Promise to Peter," in J. Neusner, P. Borgen, E.S. Frerichs, R. Horsley, eds., *The Social World of Formative Christianity and Judaism* (Philadelphia, 1989), pp. 311–326, also available in *Targumic Approaches to the Gospels. Essays in the Mutual Definition of Judaism and Christianity*: Studies in Judaism (Lanham and London, 1986), pp. 63–80.

[21] *Les Antiquités bibliques II*: Sources Chrétiennes 230 (Paris, 1976), p. 56, n. 3.

onward regularly refer to death in the straightforward sense (cf. Mekilta *Bahodesh* 7.24–25; cf. B. Yom. 86a),[22] so that the communal eschatology of the Tannaitic meturgeman appears to be reflected here.

The Issue of Prophecy and the Phasal Development of Targum Jonathan

The idea of a phasal development within Targum Jonathan, resulting in two exegetical frameworks, the one developed prior to 135 C.E., and the other of Amoraic provenience, has been generalized from the Isaiah Targum to other documents within Jonathan in a way which could only be intimated twenty-five years ago.[23] In his commentary on the Jeremiah Targum, Robert Hayward advances an argument based upon the treatment of prophecy to suggest that an earlier, Tannaitic framework was especially influential in the text as it can be read today. He observes that the "translation of 'prophet' in certain cases as 'scribe' produces the association of priests with scribes" in the Jeremiah Targum, an association also made in Josephus and the New Testament.[24]

Scribes, on this reading, are "*a powerful and influential group*" during the time of the Targum's composition.[25] Care should be taken, however, not to apply Hayward's suggestion globally. There are instances in which the association is not operative in the Jeremiah Targum,[26] and the "prophets" of the Masoretic text often become "prophets of falsehood" as well as "scribes" in the Targum.[27] Meturgemanin of Jeremiah, as those of Isaiah,[28] evidently wished to insulate the unqualified usage of "prophet" as such from any charge of deception. That results in referring to prophets who lie[29] and in the grouping of other classes of leaders in criticisms from which prophets are protected. That is quite a different matter from the presentation of the Gospels, in which priestly and scribal leaders are particularly in view as a result of their alleged responsibility in the execution of Jesus.[30]

Hayward's comparison of the Jeremiah

---

[22] Cf. Chilton, *The Glory of Israel*, p. 56.

[23] Ibid., p. 117. The same paradigm is applied in Daniel J. Harrington and Anthony J. Saldarini, *Targum Jonathan of the Former Prophets* (Wilmington and Edinburgh, 1987), p. 3; Robert (or C.T.R.) Hayward, *The Targum of Jeremiah* (Wilmington Edinburgh, 1987), p. 38; Samson H. Levey, *The Targum of Ezekiel* (Wilmington and Edinburgh, 1987), pp. 3, 4; Kevin J. Cathcart and Robert P. Gordon, *The Targum of the Minor Prophets* (Wilmington and Edinburgh, 1989), pp. 12–14. Levey's acceptance of the paradigm is especially noteworthy in that he had earlier argued that Targum Jonathan (especially Isaiah) should be placed within the period of the ascendancy of Islam; cf. "The Date of Targum Jonathan to the Prophets," in *Vetus Testamentum* 21 (1971), pp. 186–196. Although the model has been applied, the editions cited do not, in fact, test it by consistent comparative reference to Rabbinica and early Christian literature, which is the method recommended in Chilton, *The Glory of Israel*.

[24] Hayward, op. cit., pp. 36, 37. He cites the Jeremiah Targum 8:10; 14:18; 23:11, 33, 34; 26:7, 8, 11, 16; 29:11 and *Antiquities* 12.3.3 §142; Mark 11:27; Matt. 2:4; 16:21: 20:18; Acts 4:5, 6.

[25] Hayward, op. cit., p. 33. His argument was earlier developed in "Some Notes on Scribes and Priests in *the Targum of the Prophets*," in *Journal of Jewish Studies* 36 (1985), pp. 210–221.

[26] Cf. 6:13; 18:18, from Hayward's own lists (pp. 32, 36, 37).

[27] Hayward, op. cit., p. 32; as he notes, and as is the case elsewhere in the Targum Jonathan, "teacher" is a possible surrogate for "prophet" in the Masoretic Text.

[28] Cf. Chilton, *The Glory of Israel*, p. 54, citing 9:14; 28:7.

[29] Hayward, op. cit., p. 33, helpfully corrects the surmise of Churgin that idolatrous prophets are particularly in view when the phrase "prophets of falsehood" appears.

[30] Cf. Michael J. Cook, *Mark's Treatment of the Jewish Leaders* (Leiden, 1978).

Targum with the Gospels illustrates a difficulty in the assessment of the Targumim in respect of more ancient documents. Words and phrases are more easily shared than are meanings, especially among speakers who commonly—and independently—refer to an authoritative collection of scriptures. The meturgemanin of Jeremiah sometimes referred to "scribes" in order to protect "prophets" from criticism; the Gospels' framers attack "scribes" in order to discredit an alternative view of religion. Unless the sense of references is evaluated, observations of brute similarities of usage are pointless, and may prove misleading.[31]

Hayward also notes a tendency to introduce the term "prophet" in the Targum Jeremiah, as at 35:4 (in reference to Hanan, the son of Yigdaliah). He does not observe, however, that the usage cited is part of a pattern within Jonathan generally, in which prophecy is associated with the Temple (cf. also the Isaiah Targum 8:2, in respect of Uriah the priest); that positive assessment of a priestly charism emerges only sporadically, and likely rests upon an ancient claim, much in the manner of Josephus.[32] Generally speaking, the whole of Jonathan represents a tendency to portray "prophecy as a unified phenomenon that is understood as true contact with God involving revelatory significance" and to introduce characterizations designed to protect the perceived integrity of prophecy.[33] That is the conclusion of Harrington and Saldarini in respect of the Targum of the Former Prophets, and it is sufficiently unexceptionable to be applied to the corpus as a whole.

From the second century, the rabbis taught that prophecy was a phenomenon proper to the land promised by God to his people (cf. Mekilta *Pisha* 1.42-44). Such an understanding was at apparent odds with the experience of Ezekiel, which is explicitly set in Babylon (see Ezek. 1:1-3), and was a problem that needed to be confronted in the Aramaic rendering of the book. As Samson H. Levey points out, the meturgemanin resolved the difficulty by having Ezekiel's revelation in 1:3 begin in Jerusalem and then renewed in the land of the Chaldeans.[34]

Cathcart and Gordon similarly associate the presentation of the prophets within the Targum of the Minor Prophets with the theology of the Amoraim. Unlike Hayward, they locate the usage of "scribe" in that latter phase of the Targum's development, on the theological grounds that the rabbis held that prophecy had passed from the prophets to the sages.[35] Obviously, that analysis falls to take account of the negative sense that sometimes accompanies use of the term "scribe" in Jonathan; if they are more correct than Hayward in their chronology, they are equally approximate in their exegesis. Moreover, they do not call attention to the connection of priesthood and prophecy at Hos. 4:4,[36] nor to the repeated theme of Israel's rejection of the prophetic message (cf. Hos. 6:5; 9:7; Zeph. 3:2); both of those features are important links to the Tannaitic phase of Targum Jonathan. Finally, they do

---

[31] Cf. the method of exegetical comparison recommended in *Targumic Approaches to the Gospels*, cited above.

[32] Cf. Joseph Blenkinsopp, "Prophecy and Priesthood in Josephus," in *Journal of Jewish Studies* 25 (1974), pp. 239-262.

[33] So Harrington and Saldarini, op. cit., pp. 11, 12. Cf. also Saldarini, "'Is Saul Also among the Scribes?' Scribes and Prophets in Targum Jonathan," in *Essays on Aggadah and Judaica for Rabbi William G. Braude* (New York, 1986).

[34] Levey, op. cit., p. 13.

[35] Cathcart and Gordon, op. cit., pp. 3, 199, n. 5, citing B. B.B. 12a. Cf. also Gordon, "Targum as Midrash: Contemporizing in the Targum to the Prophets," in M. Goshen-Gottstein, ed., *Proceedings of the Ninth World Congress of Jewish Studies* (Jerusalem, 1988), pp. 61-73.

[36] A reference to priesthood at the close of the verse in the Masoretic text occasions the statement, "*For they say, 'The scribe shall not teach, and the prophet shall not admonish.' So your people argue with their teachers.*" See also the link between false prophets and priests in Zeph. 3:4.

not observe the vital link between their Targum and the rest of Jonathan in its received form: the tendency to present the message of all the prophets as consonant. That is particularly accomplished by identifying the biblical prophets as such, despite the impression of redundancy which sometimes results (cf. Nah. 1:1; Hab. 1:1; Hag. 2:1; Zech. 1:1). Their distinction from the false prophets, cf. Hos. 4:5; Mic. 3:5; Zeph. 3:4; Zech. 13:2, 4 is another link to the normal pattern of Jonathan.

The theory of the formation of the Isaiah Targum in two principal phases was published in 1982. Prior to the revolt of Simeon bar Kosiba (bar Kokhba) in 132, the first exegetical framework of the Isaiah Targum was produced. It organized then current translations of the Hebrew text into a powerful vehicle of opposition to the Romans and propaganda for the restoration of the Temple. During the fourth century, the second exegetical framework of the Isaiah Targum was completed. With its completion, the whole of the Hebrew text was rendered, and the perspective of the translation as a whole was coordinated with the concerns of the Babylonian academies (especially Pumbeditha's, where the work was encouraged under Joseph bar Hiyya).

After the theory of two exegetical frameworks was developed for the Isaiah Targum, it was applied (as we have seen) to the Targum of the Former Prophets, the Targums of Jeremiah and Ezekiel, and the Targum of the Minor Prophets. Today, then, the phasal development of Targum Jonathan as a whole appears to be a matter of consensus. Even claims to offer radical departures from the consensus wind up confirming it. For example, it has recently been asserted that the Targum Jonathan was not intended for popular usage in synagogues, but for academic reflection.[37] In fact, the original theory of two frameworks called attention to the disparity between the Rabbinic experts who produced the Targumim and the synagogues which were the targets of the operation. Moreover, the difference between the interpretation of the first framework and the interpretation of the second framework is manifest. Propaganda for revolt and homilies for settled accommodation to the Sassanids are obviously not the same thing.

The consensus, then, is faring well in its third decade, although continuing historical work will no doubt be welcomed. The challenge which most pressingly remains to be faced, however, is of a different order. While the differences in the interpretative strategies of the distinct frameworks within Targum Jonathan have been widely recognized, little analysis of the particular characteristics of the frameworks as readings of Isaiah has been offered.

To some extent, no doubt, that has been a consequence of the conventional attitudes among Targumists. For much of the time since 1949, interest in the Targumim has been greatest among those concerned with the New Testament and Christian origins. Such scholars will be concerned with issues of dating and historical development first of all. But even Targumists who claim that no such application is in their minds often display the traits of historicists of the old style. They proceed as if questions of the purpose and theme and character of a Targum will take care of themselves, if only the Targumist will focus exclusively with how individual passages are to be dated.[38] Since historical allusions must always involve a strong element of inference, the circularity of the old historicism of some Targumists is evident.

To some extent, the analysis of exegetical frameworks was intended as a defense against circularity. The focus was not merely on this or that particular passage (which

---

[37] See Willem F. Smelik, *The Targum of Judges* (Leiden, 1995).

[38] Gordon concludes his monograph with a statement of that program, p. 153.

might be older or younger than the substantial interpretation which produced a Targum), but on characteristic terms and phrases which link a framework within a coherent, interpretative project. Characteristic interpretations within the framework were then compared with those presented within Rabbinic literature. The resolution of my analysis into two frameworks, one Tannaitic and one Amoraic, emerged out of that extended work of comparison. Obviously, inference remains a vital part of such an approach, but the inference proceeds on the basis of elements within each framework which are shown to be central, not on the problematic supposition that references to events from the past directly tell us the date of the Targum.

While the theory of two frameworks has done its work within the study of the literary history of Targum Jonathan, in another respect analysis has not been pursued. Globally, the differences of interpretative strategy from exegetical framework to exegetical framework are evident to Targumists, which is why the theory of frameworks has been well accepted in the first place. The next step, engaging the deeper literary issue, addresses the question, "What is the purpose and procedure of interpretation, such that a distinctive reading of the book of Isaiah (or of whatever book is at issue) results?"

Modern targumists are well aware that Targums are translations, but they sometimes do not reflect that every translation involves, together with a text to be rendered, the purpose and theory of the translator. That is now the object of our inquiry: the purpose and theory of the meturgeman of the Tannaitic framework and of the meturgeman of the Amoraic framework.[39] The Aramaic term meturgeman ("interpreter" or "translator") is here used collectively, of all those who were involved in the interpretative process of producing a given exegetical framework. The fact that we have access to two such frameworks, each evolved in association with the same base text (Isaiah in Hebrew), is a great help, since comparative characterization will become possible.

The Messiah in the Tannaitic Framework

The messianic perspective of the Tannaitic meturgeman comes to expression early in the Isaiah Targum (4:2-3):

> In that *time the messiah* of the Lord shall be for *joy* and for glory, and *those who perform the law* for pride and for praise to the survivors of Israel. And it shall come to pass that he who is left *will return* to Zion and he who *has performed the law will be established* in Jerusalem; he will be called holy, every one who has been recorded for *eternal* life *will see the consolations of Jerusalem*.

From the point of view of its content, the rendering is straightforward. The messiah is associated with the performance of the law (and therefore its correct interpretation), and those who actually do perform it anticipate eternal life in a consoled Jerusalem.

The likely social context of that anticipation, and its development, is not our particular concern here.[40] We wish rather to focus on how the meturgeman arrived at his rendering from the Hebrew text then available, in order to appreciate the interpretative method involved. The term

---

[39] In this regard, see Johannes C. de Moor, "Multiple renderings in the Targum of Isaiah," in *Journal for the Aramaic Bible* 31.1-2 (2001), pp. 161-180.

[40] That work is available in Chilton, *The Glory of Israel*, pp. 86-96.

"branch" in Hebrew has a richly messianic association within the biblical tradition (cf. Jer. 23:5; 33:15; Zech. 3:8; 6:12), and the meturgeman simply reads the association as the text. That is: what is there in Hebrew is replaced by what it is held to mean in Aramaic. Although that method is straightforward, it is also daring.

The dominance of the association is such that further transformations of the Hebrew text occur. "Fruit of the land" in 4:2b of the Masoretic text becomes "those who perform the law" in the Targum because the messiah is to be productive of that fruitful performance. That is what is to enable him to realize the promise of Israel in Israel's land. The eschatological perspective of this hope is articulated in the expressions "eternal life" and "consolations of Jerusalem," both of which recur in the Targum.

The idea of the messiah then, invoked by the term "branch" in Hebrew, is what the text conveys in the rendering of the meturgeman. That meaning occasions not only additions to the text, but also subtractions: "branch" and "fruit of the land" simply disappear, or at least seem to. We may contrast the technique involved with the interpretation by pesher at Qumran, where the Hebrew text is preserved in actual quotations (sometimes with variants),[41] and then interpreted. That permits of close fidelity to the Hebrew original (and certain variant readings), while also indulging some famously speculative developments of meaning.

The Tannaitic meturgeman takes the occasion of a principal trigger in the Hebrew text ("branch") to develop a messianic transformation of the whole by addition and subtraction. The transformation that is the agency of the interpretation, once it begins, affects the whole of the text. But because a verbal trigger is involved, the transformation is of a literal nature. "Branch" become messiah; "fruit" becomes the "law" performed; "life" becomes "eternal." Interpreting the text by literal transformation, the meturgeman underscores his rendering by what is omitted as well as by what is added. That is, the Targum is better understood if one knows that "branch" is now messiah and that "fruit" is now law. Those promises are still present, and vivified by the eschatological dimension of messianic meaning.

The literal transformation of the Tannaitic meturgeman may be compared and contrasted with the transformations typical of the Synoptic Gospels. There, transformation can occur on the basis not of text but of the supposed meaning of a passage. For example, the parable of the man, the seed, and the earth in Mark 4:26-29 does not appear in the Gospel according to Matthew, but Matthew does present a fuller parable of a man who planted seed, only to have his enemy introduce weeds (Mat. 13:24-30). The Matthean commitment to the fuller parable as the meaning of the image is represented by the detailed interpretation which is attributed to Jesus in Matthew (13:36-43).

Matthew actually instances two sorts of interpretation here. The easier sort is the careful explanation in 13:36-43. No transformation is involved, only a point by point explication (of what is already rather obvious). Even here, however, it is notable that the explanation proceeds more on the basis of the meaning of each image than with a view to literal interpretation. For that reason, there is no precise analogy to the technique of pesher. Rather, the approach better corresponds to the apocalyptic interpretation which influenced the Synoptic Gospels quite deeply. Within Matthew 13 itself, the interpretation of the parable of the sower presents another example of the same tech-

---

[41] See Chilton, "Commenting on the Old Testament (with particular reference to the pesharim, Philo, and the Mekhilta," in D.A. Carson and H.G.M. Williamson, eds., *It is Written: Scripture Citing Scripture, Essays in Honour of Barnabas Lindars* (Cambridge, 1988), pp. 122-140.

nique (see 13:18-23). Matthew's version is of a more explicitly apocalyptic cast than its Synoptic counterparts (see Mark 4:13-20 and Luke 8:11-15), but in each case the method of deciphering images in view of their meaning for the end of the world is evident. Ultimately derived from the sort of apocalyptic explanation which instanced in Daniel 7, although far less elaborate (and therefore probably not originally literary), Synoptic interpretations of this type present a consistent character. Matthew extends the technique somewhat in the present case.

The other type of Synoptic interpretation that Matthew instances here (that is, in 13:24-30) is of greater interest from the point of view of the Tannaitic meturgeman. The parable of the man who had to deal with his enemy's weeds is only distantly similar to the parable of the man, the seed, and the earth in Mark 4:26-29. Scholars have been divided over the issue of whether they are in fact related.[42] But whether Matthew represents a version of the Markan parable itself, or a cognate use of imagery, there is consensus that the Matthean form is Matthean, a characteristic development of an earlier usage. The transformation which Matthew's parable represents, then, is so dramatic that the issue of its antecedents is problematic.

Matthew's transformation here is conceptual, rather than verbal (as in the Targumic example we have considered). In describing the technique of the Tannaitic meturgeman of Isaiah as transformative, therefore, no implication of disregard for the Hebrew text should be taken to be implied. Indeed, the fact is that knowing what is not included from the Hebrew text actually enhances one's appreciation of the Targumic rendering. That suggests that, although targeted for usage in synagogues, the Targum was best enjoyed where it was produced: in academies. That insight will prove to be important for an assessment of the character of Targum Jonathan generally.

The technique of literal transformation is easily instanced in other examples of the messianic interpretation of the meturgeman. The theological problem posed by the Hebrew text of Is. 9:5 (9:6 in English versions) is neatly sorted out. How can the "son" who is referred to be called "wonderful, counselor, mighty God, everlasting father, prince of peace"? The meturgeman solves the difficulty by having the son called *"the messiah in whose days* peace *will increase upon us."* He is so named *"before the* wonderful counselor, *the* mighty God." An extra phrase and a preposition clarify the situation, and the assumption is that the "son" is the messiah, who is to be distinguished from God himself.

That assumption is explicitly flagged by the innovative introduction in the Targum, *"The prophet said to the house of David...."* With this preface, the meturgeman asserts that the true meaning of the prophet, whatever his words, was messianic, and messianic in a manner that did not compromise monotheism. Everything is dependent, then, on knowing whose "son" is at issue: David's progeny is the topic, specified so as to avoid the difficulty that the general imagery of the Masoretic text might occasion. Once the precise topic is established, the other changes already mentioned become explicable: the messiah is there so that "peace *will increase upon us,"* and he is named *"before the* wonderful counselor, *the* mighty God." Similarly, the "dominion" which rests on his shoulder in the Hebrew text becomes his agreement to accept and keep the law

---

[42] But see the bold analysis of Robert H. Gundry, *Matthew. A Commentary on His Handbook for a Mixed Church under Persecution* (Grand Rapids, 1994), pp. 261-265, which seems to me to resolve the issue in favor of Matthean reference to the Markan parable. Compare W.D. Davies and Dale C. Allison, *A Critical and Exegetical Commentary on the Gospel according to Saint Matthew* (Edinburgh, 1991), pp. 406-415, 426-432, for a more cautious assessment which nonetheless moves in the same direction.

in the Targum. Anyone who knew that would know that the secret of the Davidic Messiah's rule was fidelity to the law.

The messianic interpretation of Is. 11:1 comes as no surprise in the context of what we have already seen, and calls for little comment here. It simply pursues the interpretation of the "branch" referred to in the Masoretic text (*neser*, in the second half of the verse, where "*messiah*" appears in the Targum) in messianic terms:

> And a *king* shall come forth from the *sons* of Jesse, and *the Messiah* shall *be exalted* from *the sons of* his *sons*.

Just as "branch" in Hebrew occasions reference to the messiah in the second part of the verse, so the "stump" (*geza'*) of Jesse becomes the "*sons* of Jesse" in the first part of the verse. In contrast, the rendering involved in 14:29 is striking:

> Rejoice not, all you Philist*ines*, because *the ruler* who was *subjugating* you is broken, for *from the sons of the sons of Jesse the messiah* will come forth, and his *deeds* will be *among you* as a *wounding* serpent.

Because the imagery of the Hebrew text speaks of a viper coming from a snake, and of a flying serpent, the transformation of meaning involved here seems more extreme than what he have considered so far.

But the precise phrasing of the meturgeman's Hebrew text explains the innovative rendering: "from the root (*mishoresh*) of the snake the viper came forth...." The "root" is taken by the meturgeman to be akin to Jesse's "stump" in Is. 11:1, which is already (and straightforwardly) taken to be messianic. Once that has occurred, it is a simple and consistent transformation—again, along literal lines—to make the "rod" of Philistia into the ruler of the Philistines, set in antithesis to the victorious messiah.

The Messiah, then, is to supplant every ruler. So the "ruler of the earth" in the Hebrew of Is. 16:1 (set out here) must be the messiah:

> Send a lamb to the ruler of the earth, from Sela, by the wilderness, to the mount of the daughter of Zion.

That initial change is straightforward, but what follows demands some explanation:

> *They will offer tribute to the messiah of Israel, who prevailed over the one as* the wilderness, to the mount of the *congregation* of Zion.

The phrase "from Sela (*misela'*) by the wilderness" becomes a reference to the messiah "*who prevailed (detaqyph) over the one as* the wilderness." The verb *taqeyph* occurs frequently in the Targum, and is the preferred usage for the exertion of strength. It is occasioned here by taking *misela'* as if it were a participle, preformative *m* with *sela'*, taking the latter root in its etymological meaning of "split." (Because the messiah has displayed such strength, he is to receive "*tribute*," not just the "lamb" of the Masoretic text.) Once again, the meturgeman's playfulness involves a literal transformation, and one's enjoyment is enriched by recollecting the Hebrew counterpart of his rendering.

By comparison, the associations of messiah with the "throne" in Is. 16:5 and with the "crown" in 28:5 are quite easily explained along the lines of the literal transformation which is the model proposed here:

> Tg: *then the* throne *of the messiah of Israel* will be established...
> MT: and a throne will be established...
> Tg: In that *time the messiah of* the Lord will be a *diadem* of *joy* and a *crown* of praise...
> MT: In that day the Lord of hosts will be a crown of beauty and a diadem of praise...

Both those references have been identified as the work of the Tannaitic meturgeman, in view of their clear preoccupation with the theme of the imminent vindication of Israel over its enemies.

That motif, in turn, becomes the principle underlying the famous rendering of Is. 52:13–53:12. The issue that has consumed the secondary literature has been whether that interpretation is pre-Christian and whether it might have influenced the tradents of the New Testament. In view of the statement of 53:12, that the messiah "*handed over* his soul to death," it seems unlikely that this passage of the Targum was composed with a view to the challenges of Christian theology. On the other hand, the assumption that Jerusalem and the sanctuary have been desolated is evident throughout, so that a dating prior to 70 C.E. seems implausible. The rendering of 53:5 is telling:

> Tg: And he *will build the sanctuary which was profaned for our sins, handed over* for our iniquities; *and by his teaching his* peace *will increase* upon *us, and in that we attach ourselves to his words our sins will be forgiven us.*
> MT: And he was wounded for our transgressions, bruised for our iniquities; the chastisement that makes us whole was upon him, and by his wounds we are healed.

Attribution to the Tannaitic meturgeman(in) between 70 and 132 commends itself, because vindication is eagerly and pragmatically awaited. The messiah might well risk his life ("hand over his soul to death," 53:12), but the aim of that heroism is triumph on behalf of Israel.[43]

But if the dating of the passage is not all that complicated a matter, an innovation in the interpretative technique it manifests must be observed. The term "servant" is enough to invoke the messianic theme in 52:13, but in 53:10 the development of the theme is a little more complicated:

> MT: he will see his seed
> Tg: *they* will see *the kingdom of their messiah.*

"Seed," by the sort of literal transformation we have already observed, is rendered in terms of the seed of David, and in that vein the Messiah discovered.

But on what basis do "they" see, instead of the "he" of the Hebrew text? In addition to the principle of literal transformation, another transformation is at work here. It was first (although incompletely) identified by R.A. Aytoun. Over eighty years ago, he commented that "the exaltation of the Servant is applied to the messiah, but his sufferings fall in part upon Israel, in part upon the gentiles."[44] The present case shows that "exaltation" can fall to Israel, as well as to the messiah, because the passage continues in the Targum, "*they shall increase sons and daughters, they* shall prolong days; *those who perform the law* of the Lord shall prosper in his *pleasure.*" Their prosperity is all the more marked in that, as we have already seen, in the Targum the messiah, too, can become vulnerable to death. The

---

[43] For a full discussion, see Jostein Ådna, "Der Gottesknecht als triumphierender und interzessorischer Messias. Die Rezeption von Jes 53 im Targum Jonathan untersucht mit besonderer Berücksichtigung des Messiasbildes," in B. Janowski and Peter Stuhlmacher, eds., *Der leidende Gottesknecht. Jesaja 53 und seine Wirkungsgeschichte* (Tübingen, 1996), pp. 129–158.

[44] "The Servant of the Lord in the Targum," in *Journal of Theological Studies* 23 (1921–22), p. 178. He also observed "that though it seems to have departed far from the original Hebrew, yet actually the Targum has stuck remarkably close to the letter of the Hebrew." The present discussion will fill out his insight.

gentiles, Israel, and the messiah indeed constitute three distinct foci within the interpretation, but their relationship to one another is spelled out dynamically, within the eschatological vindication which is anticipated.

In the end, therefore, the literal transformation which is at the base of the meturgeman's technique within the Tannaitic framework is supplemented. Once the messianic rendering is achieved by literal means, there is a cumulative effect, so that the entire theme may be invoked by a single, verbal trigger within the Hebrew text. In addition, the theme of the messiah itself carries with it the distinction between those to whom messiah is a promise and those to whom messiah is a threat. And that conceptual transformation—applied to the messianic motif and whatever triggers it in the Hebrew text—is also a principle of interpretation which emerges in the Tannaitic framework. The limitation of that more global transformation to whatever occasions reference to the messiah makes the principle more predictable than the sorts of transformation which we find among the Synoptic Gospels. That limitation justifies the characterization of "literal transformation" overall as the hermeneutic of the Tannaitic framework. But that sort of transformation is pointing ahead to another kind, more clearly evidenced within the Amoraic framework.

Eternal Messiah, Eternal Shekhinah in the Amoraic Framework

The messiah is not absent from the Amoraic framework of the Isaiah Targum: the hope of messianic vindication continued to be a governing concern at that later stage. But the hope is expressed in a different key. The reference to "my servant" in the Hebrew text of Is. 43:10 is enough to occasion mention of "my messiah in whom I am well pleased" in the Targum:

> MT: "You are my witnesses," says the Lord, "and my servant whom I have chosen . . ."
> Tg: "You are witnesses *before me*," says the Lord, "and my servant *the messiah with* whom I *am pleased* . . ."

The point of that rendering in its present setting is that the messiah is an eternal witness before God, testifying to God's power in creation, his revelation to Abraham, his salvation at the Exodus, and his giving of the law at Sinai, all of which feature explicitly within the surrounding context in the Targum. As the Targum innovatively has God say within the same verse, "*I am he that was from the beginning, even the ages of the ages are mine . . .*:" God's eternity and the eternal witness of his Messiah go hand in hand. The situation addressed by that witnessing is one of exile:

> "For your *sins'* sake *you were exiled* to Babylon . . ." (Targum Isaiah 43:14).

The circumstances of the Babylonian Amoraim come to expression here, and the modulation of their theology, from the direct eschatology of the earlier period to an emphasis upon eternity and transcendence, becomes apparent. Part of that modulation is an interpretative matter. Literal transformation (from "servant" in Hebrew to "messiah" in Aramaic, as the example below will show) is still the occasion of the rendering, but it assumes that the reference to the servant of the Lord is alone enough to justify messianic reference. That is, the Amoraic meturgeman is more programmatic than the Tannaitic meturgeman.

The contrast becomes plain in a comparison of chapter 42 and chapter 43 in the Isaiah Targum. Chapter 42, where the concerns of the Tannaitic meturgeman are evident, refers simply to the "servant" (42:1) without explicitly messianic specification.

Nonetheless, immediate vindication is in view, when the purpose of that servant's commission is portrayed (42:7):

> Tg: to open the eyes of *the house of Israel who are as* blind *to the law*, to bring out *their exiles, who resemble* prisoners, *from among the gentiles*, to deliver *from the slavery of the kingdoms* those who are *jailed as* prisoners *of* darkness.
>
> MT: to open the eyes of the blind, to bring out the prisoner from the dungeon, from jail those who dwell in darkness.

The connection between the servant and the Messiah was not made within the Tannaitic framework until chapter 52, as we have already seen. Here, in chapter 42, the identification of the "servant" is different: the role of Israel as such is in view. In 42:8, God does not only say "my glory I will not give," but: "my glory—*that I am revealed upon you*—I will not give to another *people*." The "servant" in the Tannaitic framework may refer to Israel, as in 49:3 (which remains unchanged in the Targum): "You are my servant, Israel, in whom I will be glorified." But chapter 43—as we have already seen—assumes a global transformation of "servant" into "messiah," and on that basis the messiah becomes an eternal witness of divine power and vindication in 43:10.

A cognate shift in the key of hope is evident in the handling of the term "Shekinah," which refers to the presence of God in association with the cult. Within the Tannaitic framework, the association is quite direct. In response to his people's injustice, God removes his Shekinah from the priests when they pray (1:15), although its proper location is Mt. Zion (see 8:18; 17:11; 26:21), which is where it will soon return, when the messiah reestablishes the Temple (4:5):

> And then the Lord will create over the whole *sanctuary of* the Mount *of* Zion and *over the place of the house of the Shekhinah* a cloud *of glory*—it will be covering it by day, and *the dense cloud will be as* a flaming fire by night; for *it shall have* glory *greater than was promised he would bring upon it, the Shekhinah will be sheltering it as* a canopy.

The expectation of the Shekinah's return is physically conceived, as the cloud of the period of the exodus. Vindication and God's tangible presence in the sanctuary are inextricably linked. That is what drives the powerful conviction of the Tannaitic meturgeman that the book of Isaiah turns on the restoration of Israel, a restoration which makes Israel greater than it ever was before.

The realism of the eschatological hope of the Tannaitic meturgeman is different, in respect of reference to the Shekinah, from the conception common among the Amoraim. They held that the Shekinah had in some sense gone into exile with Israel, and was accessible within their academies in Babylonia. And there was a famous discussion of which synagogue (at what time) had the best claim to access to the Shekinah (B. Meg. 29a). In the same discussion, the statement in Ezekiel, "I have been to them as a little sanctuary" (11:16), is applied to synagogues and academies, which is just the application in the Targum Ezekiel (11:16):[45]

---

[45] In this case, I have departed from Levey's translation, in the interests of accuracy and in order to restore a lacuna in his rendering. It should also be mentioned that the principal manuscript, B.M. 2211, reads "you scattered." The Targumim, the Peshitta (so here also), and the Old Syriac Versions of the Gospels (see Luke 4:18) all occasionally engage in a play of changing pronouns in which divine discourse is internalized, as if God were speaking to or about himself.

Because I removed them far among the gentiles, and because I scattered them among the countries, therefore I have *given them synagogues, second to my* sanctuary, *because they are as* little in the countries to which they *have been exiled.*

The Amoraic conception of divine transcendence made the Shekhinah both more ambient and more focused on the individual whose halakhah was correct than was the case in the theology of the Tannaitic meturgeman.

So, B. Qid. 31a attributes to R. Isaac the opinion that anyone who transgresses secretly steps on the toes of the Shekhinah. (By the same logic, the passage goes on to relate Huna's habit of covering his head, since the Shekhinah was above him.) Once such a conception of the Shekhinah is applied to the book of Isaiah, it can only produce a contradiction of what the Targum, as framed by a Tannaitic meturgeman with a very different understanding, emphatically says. Is. 1:15 is said by Yohanan b. Nappaha and Eleazar to point at individual priests, not to the removal of the Shekhinah *grosso modo* (see B. Ber. 32b and B. Nid. 13b), which is the reference in the Targum as it stands (Targum Isaiah 1:15):

> And when *the priests* spread forth *their* hands *to pray for you,* I take up *the face of my Shekhinah* from you.

Just as the withdrawal of the Shekhinah communally could later be portrayed more individually, so the implication of an individually threatening removal of the Shekhinah is an individually efficacious return. That implication becomes explicit in Rabba's promise that Is. 4:5 means that "the Holy One, blessed be he, will make for everyone a canopy corresponding to his rank" (B. B.B. 75a). The communal canopy of the early framework of the Targum is here made into a series of tents.

Indeed, once the Amoraic theology of the Shekhinah is appreciated, the fact that the Tannaitic meturgeman's work was preserved becomes all the more impressive. Evidently, a measure of authority was accorded the work as representing the meaning of what Isaiah the prophet said. On the other hand, the Amoraic meturgeman who supplemented the earlier framework was confronted with the question of how to bridge the Tannaitic conception with his own. That challenge was met in a brilliant rendering of Isaiah's inaugural vision in chapter 6 (vv. 1–6):

> In the year that King Uzziah *was struck with it* [that is, leprosy], *the prophet said,* I saw *the glory of* the Lord *resting* upon a throne, high and lifted up *in the heavens of the height*; and the Temple *was* filled *by the brilliance of his glory. Holy attendants were in the height before* him; each had six wings; with two he covered his face, *that he might not see,* and with two he covered his *body, that he might not be seen*, and with two he *ministered.* And one *was* crying to another and saying: Holy *in the heavens of the height, his sanctuary,* holy *upon the earth, the work of his might,* holy *in the age of the ages* is the Lord of hosts; the whole earth is filled with the *brilliance* of his glory. And the posts of the *Temple* thresholds *quaked* from the sound of *the speech*, and the *sanctuary* was filled with *the dense cloud*. And I said: Woe is me! For *I have sinned*; for I am a man *liable to chastisement*, and I dwell in the midst of people *that are defiled with sins*; for my eyes have seen *the glory of the Shekhinah of* the *king of the ages*, the Lord of hosts! Then *there was given to* me one of the *attendants* and in his *mouth there was a speech* which he took *before him whose Shekhinah is upon the throne of glory in the heavens of the height*, above the altar.

The passages is interesting from several points of view, but its desire to avoid any disharmony with an Amoraic conception of

God is evident. The vision is dated to the time of Uzziah's diagnosis with "leprosy," not the time of his death. Isaiah sees God's "glory," not God himself, and the vision is not of seraphic angels, but of attendants whose wings are only for the purpose of discreet service.

Given all that restraint in the rendering of the vision, the bold new reference to the Shekhinah by the Amoraic meturgeman appears all the more striking. By tracing each reference through the passage, a cosmology of the Shekhinah, of the divine presence is relation to the world, emerges explicitly. The old, Tannaitic association between the sanctuary and the Shekhinah is preserved, but the location of that sanctuary is here changed. The first "holy" is glossed to refer to God "*in the heavens of the height*," which is identified as "*his sanctuary*." Mount Zion as such is not at issue, nor any place on earth. It is the second cry of "holy" which refers to the earth, as being "*the work of his might*" as a whole. Heaven is now the place of the sanctuary and therefore the place of the Shekhinah. Every place on earth attests God's might, but is not to be identified with the Shekhinah.

The essential duality of heaven and earth is underscored by the third cry of "holy." Here the issue is God's eternity, which is a particular emphasis of the Amoraic meturgeman (compare the wording of 43:10). That which always is, which can never be changed, is a vital aspect of divine transcendence, which is why (as we saw earlier) the messiah is an eternal witness to the efficacy of God. As the same verse which refers to the witness of the messiah innovatively says in the Targum (43:10 end), "*I am he that was from the beginning, even the ages of the ages are mine*, and there *is* no God *besides me.*" On such an understanding, of eternity as an irreducibly important dimension of God, only heaven can feature as a possible place of his Shekhinah.

What the prophet sees in the sanctuary on earth, therefore, is not the Shekhinah itself, but "*the glory of the Shekhinah of the eternal king*" (6:5). "Glory" is regularly used in the Targumim to speak of how God himself might be known, but here it serves to insist that even the Shekhinah may not be directly perceived on earth, not even in the sanctuary and not even by the prophet Isaiah. From the point of view of the interpretative strategy of the Amoraic meturgeman, a considerable advance over the sort of literal transformation we have seen at the Tannaitic level is involved. The term "king" is not merely identified as that which the meturgeman believes the text refers to; rather, a systematic understanding of how reference to God is possible at all is introduced. Isaiah can not see God, and can not even see God's glory. The glory he sees is of the Shekhinah of his eternity, which is in heaven.

The greater elaboration of the Amoraic meturgeman as compared to his Tannaitic predecessor is also event in the next verse. The localization of the Shekhinah is as precise as could be desired. The attendant takes the "*speech*" (the "burning coal" of the Hebrew Text) from "*before him whose Shekhinah is upon the throne of glory in the heavens of the height*" (6:6). What is implied by the rendering of the previous verse is spelled out in the present case: "Shekhinah" is that which is installed on the ultimate throne, in heaven. The phrase that closes the verse, "above the altar," simply represents the Hebrew text "from upon the altar" (*me'al hamizbeah*), but in suppressing the locational sense of "from"[46] and in its new language of "*the heavens of the height*," the Amoraic meturgeman specifies that the Shekhinah is enthroned far "above" the altar.

---

[46] The Aramaic reads *'eyl min*, so that the governing sense of the compound is "above," rather than "from upon." Here is another case in which conscious engagement with the text in Hebrew is evident, and part of the intended enjoyment of the translation.

The transformation which is the interpretative technique of the Amoraic meturgeman is systematic in two senses. First, the theology of transcendence which is involved is introduced, not only on the occasion of verbal triggers, but when and as the doctrinal need emerges to explain how God is related to the prophet's vision. Second, the theology of transcendence which is introduced is itself systematic, a way of thinking about God which is consistent with Amoraic theology but also relatable to the text of Isaiah in its traditionally Targumic form.

Tannaitic Eschatology, Amoraic Transcendence

The two renderings of Isaiah that we have considered by means of examples of the interpretations of the Tannaitic and Amoraic meturgemanin permit us insight into the development of distinct methods of transformation of meaning from the Hebrew text into the Aramaic Targum. In both cases, transformation is the appropriate category, because there is no question of simple translation. The Tannaitic meturgeman transforms the Hebrew of Isaiah literally into a messianic theology of the eschatological vindication of Israel. The Amoraic meturgeman transforms both the work of his predecessor and those parts of the Hebrew text which had not already been rendered into Aramaic by means of systematic indications of God's messianic transcendence.

The distinct idioms of transformation explain how the Tannaitic framework and the Amoraic framework can co-exist, without the latter simply swallowing up the former. The eschatology of messianic vindication can remain, because the Shekhinah whose presence is the pivot of all that the Tannaitic meturgeman says is understood by the Amoraic meturgeman to reside in the heavens of the height, eternal and unchanging. Just as the two frameworks are complementary in terms of interpretative technique, so they convey vivid and distinct perspectives of what the book of Isaiah means. What is for one level of interpretation a program of urgently anticipated messianic vindication is at the second level a hymn of eternal praise for an eternal, transcendent God who nonetheless desires to be revealed upon the earth, the work of his might. The traditional language Tannaitic eschatology is not swallowed up by the Amoraic meturgeman, but the emphasis upon transcendence in fact puts what is anticipated in a new place, ever secure in heaven.

BRUCE CHILTON
Bard College

Targum Jonathan to the Prophets II

The Former Prophets

In some ways, the Targum of the Former Prophets is the most mysterious within Targum Jonathan as a whole. As a translation, it stays programmatically close to the Hebrew text, in the manner of Onqelos. Linguistically, it is also the closest of the Targums to Onqelos. Both of them have been dated prior to 135 C.E., on the grounds that they are written in Middle Aramaic and show no influence of the Late Aramaic that emerged after 200 C.E.[1]

The innovative character of the Targum

---

[1] See Abraham Tal, *The Targum of the Former Prophets and Its Position within the Aramaic Dialects* (Tel Aviv, 1975); Daniel J. Harrington and Anthony J. Saldarini, *Targum Jonathan of the Former Prophets* (Wilmington, 1987), p. 3. Eveline van Staalduine-Sulman agrees with

of the Former Prophets becomes clear, however, when three expansive developments—involving substantial paraphrase rather than the usual program of correspondence to the Hebrew text—are considered. In aggregate, they develop a view of prophecy and the messiah that comports well with the Isaiah Targum. The first of these developments appears in Judges 5, within the song of Deborah.[2] The target of her prophecy, in a setting of hardship, is specified in the Targum (Jdgs. 5:9):

> *I was sent to give praise to the scribes of Israel who, when that affliction happened, did not cease from studying the Law; and who, whenever it was proper for them, were sitting in the synagogues at the head of the exiles and were teaching the people the words of the Law and blessing and giving thanks before God.*

Prophecy here is directed to the particular situation of Israel after the destruction of the *Second* Temple, when exile was a persistent condition, and rabbis were the principal authorities. Their role in the operation of synagogues, teaching and blessing and praising God, is Deborah's especial concern within the Targum, although the Masoretic text develops a different, military application.

Given the way in which prophecy is emphasized and articulated, it is not surprising that Deborah's own role as a prophet is underlined (see Jdgs. 5:3, 7).[3] But the exalted status of the prophetic vocation is also indicated by other means. Deborah herself is depicted as a woman of wealth (Jdgs. 4:5), so that no question of any financial motive for her prophetic activity could arise. And on several occasions, "prophet" takes the place of the word "angel" in the Masoretic text (Jdgs. 2:1, 4; 5:23): the ordinary communication of the heavenly realm is held to occur by prophetic means.

The term translated "angel" in English (*mal'akh*) actually means "messenger" in Hebrew, so that the shift to a prophetic reference is not in any sense arbitrary. Nonetheless, Judges attributes unusual powers and attributes to these figures, which then, in the Targum, are associated with the prophetic voice. Just that prophetic voice, in the case of Deborah, is commissioned in Jdgs. 5:9 (as we have seen) to praise the Rabbinic teachers who guide Israel in exile. The close connection between the heavenly court and the authority that stands behind the Targum Jonathan itself is intimated in the scene when the angel appears to Manoah, the father of Samson (Jdgs. 13). The angel in this case remains an angel (instead of being replaced by a prophet), but when Manoah asks his name, he calls himself "interpreter" in the Targum (13:18). In that this supernatural figure replies evasively in the Masoretic Text that his name is "my wonder," it is evident that the Targum elevates the functions of both prophecy and interpretation.

Just as the notion of prophecy is introduced on some occasions in order to stress the heavenly nature of the communication, so care is taken to differentiate the spirit of prophecy from other manifestations of spirit, when there is an obvious contradiction of God's commandments in the Torah. So Samson (from Jdgs. 13:25 and onward) is endowed with a spirit "*of power*," and no attribution of prophetic insight comes into question. "Power" is also attributed in this way to Jephthah (Jdgs. 11:29), and he is explicitly criticized for sacrificing his daughter. Had he only consulted Phinehas, that priest would simply have required redemption (the life of an animal in exchange for

---

this dating in her history of discussion and analysis; see *The Targum of Samuel* (Leiden, 2002), pp. 47, 711.

[2] Cf. Daniel J. Harrington, "The Prophecy of Deborah: Interpretative Homiletics in Targum Jonathan of Judges 5," in *Catholic Biblical Quarterly* 48 (1986), pp. 432–442.

[3] After all, even Othniel is associated specifically with the "spirit *of prophecy*" (Jdgs. 3:10).

the life of a human being), in a manner consistent with the Torah (Jdgs. 11:39).

The heroic stature of Phinehas is well attested within Rabbinic literature, in consequence of his killing the Israelite who took a Midianite wife in Numbers 25. The assumption that he ran great risk in doing so made him a favorite model of martyrdom; he was willing to "hand over his life to death," and in doing so purified Israel (see Sifre 131).[4] Whether or not his role as martyr is in the background of Judges Targum 11:39, it is plain that both priestly and prophetic authority is attributed to him.

The association of priesthood and prophecy is a feature of Josephus' theology,[5] and it is developed skillfully in Targum Jonathan to the Former Prophets. Hannah, the mother of Samuel, prays *"in a spirit of prophecy"* (1 Sam. 2:1), near the site of the sanctuary. Samuel himself is said to sleep in the court of the Levites (1 Sam. 3:3), since the meturgeman cannot imagine him doing so in the sanctuary itself.[6] In that safer haven, the *"glory"* of the Lord is revealed to him (3:10); it is the particular source of his word of prophecy (3:7).

Samuel is a good paradigm of the prophetic vocation. His prophecy against idolatry is accepted, and the people of Israel *"poured out their heart in repentance like water"* (1 Sam. 7:6). He succeeds in turning Israel back from their rebellion against *"the service of the Lord"* in the Temple (1 Sam. 7:2-3; compare Jdgs. 2:13; 1 Kgs. 14:8, 9), which is the particular sin which occasions exile in Targum Jonathan as a whole. The sanctuary is the precise place where *"the living God has chosen to make his Shekhinah reside"* (Josh. 3:10), and is for that reason the only appropriate repository of Israel's sacred wealth (so Josh. 6:19, concerning the spoil of Jericho). Prophecy and Temple are linked inextricably in Targum Jonathan of the Former Prophets, as they are in Targum Jonathan as a whole.

In view of the paradigmatic role of Samuel, the considerable expansion of the song of Hannah is all the more striking. Her prediction, within a recitation of the history of Israel's salvation, places the social context of the interpretation quite precisely (1 Sam. 2:5c):

> *So Jerusalem, which was like* a barren woman, *is to be filled with the people of her exiles. And Rome, which was filled with many peoples—her armies will cease to be; she will be desolate and destroyed.*

In language and imagery, as in its application to the difference in fortunes between Jerusalem and Rome, the passage builds upon the similar prediction of Is. 54:1 in the Isaiah Targum. Moreover, it makes the state of "exiles" the especial concern, in conformity with the song of Deborah in Jdgs. 5.

The songs of Deborah and of Hannah demonstrate a consuming interest in the prophetic vocation of insistence on Israel's devotion to the law and the sanctuary, and Israel's avoidance of the dangers of idolatry, which became especially severe in the period after the destruction of the Temple. The assumption of a continuing exile as the condition of Israel comports with the period after 135 C.E., when Jewish settlement in Jerusalem was prohibited by the Romans. Targum Jonathan of the Former Prophets responds to that situation by building a bridge between the heavenly communication of the classical prophets and what can be heard in synagogues from teachers who attend to the Torah.

Saul becomes a particular example of the

---

[4] The same expression appears in the Isaiah Targum 53:12; see Chilton, *The Isaiah Targum*, p. 105; idem, *The Glory of Israel*, p. 105.

[5] Cf. Joseph Blenkinsopp, "Prophecy and Priesthood in Josephus," in *Journal of Jewish Studies* 25 (1974), pp. 239-262.

[6] Eveline van Staalduine-Sulman explicates this point very well; see *The Targum of Samuel*, pp. 229-230.

necessity of faithfulness on the part of someone who is more a "teacher" than a "prophet." Although "the spirit *of prophecy*" may rest upon him (1 Sam. 10:10), it is essentially as a "scribe," rather than a prophet (so the Masoretic text), that he is referred to (10:5, 11–12). In that regard, Saul can function best as the negative example he undoubtedly is in 1 Sam. (15:23):

> *For like the sin of men who inquire of the diviner, so is the guilt of every man who rebels against the words of the Law; and like the sins of the people who go astray after idols, so is the sin of every man who takes away or adds to the words of the prophets.* Because you rejected the *service* of the Lord, *he has removed you* from being *the* king.

Saul has not yet visited the medium at Endor (cf. 1 Sam. 28), but the present passage makes it quite clear that all of Saul's sins, including that visit, amount to idolatry, rebellion against the words of the Torah, distortion of the teaching of the prophets, and a rejection of the service of the Lord in his Temple.

The figure of Saul is not simply tragic in the Targum; he is an example of how a teacher can go wrong, despite his proximity to authentic and direct prophecy (instanced by Samuel). David therefore becomes the counterpart model. David, Samuel, and Saul appear together in the scene at Ramah, a place of prophecy, in what explicitly becomes a house of study, a *beth 'ulphana'* (1 Sam. 19:18, 19, 22, 23). Because people may go there to learn, it is a place of "scribes" (19:20), not simply of prophets, and the final question of the passage is emblematic, "Is Saul among the *scribes*?" (19:24). The answer to that rhetorical question is obviously "yes," owing to Saul's proximity to Samuel (and the earlier appearance of the same rhetorical question in 1 Sam. 10:11–12). But scribes and teachers are liable to error; Targum Jonathan presents the rejection of idolatry, faithfulness to the law, and attentiveness to the prophets as the hallmarks of true teaching.

David has a particular place in the theology of Targum Jonathan, because he is the object of prophetic prediction. What is said by the prophet Nathan in 2 Sam. 7, commonly known as the Davidic covenant, is not simply a promise of enduring prosperity, but "*for the age that is coming*" (2 Sam. 7:19). Because the Davidic house is the object of that vision, David himself emerges as an instrument of prophecy (2 Sam. 22:1), and he announces the salvation of the house of Israel, despite their apparently poor fortunes "*in this world*" (22:28).

At the close of 2 Samuel, David expands the litany of salvation which Hannah already initiates, but with particular reference to the vindication which is to come (22:32):

> *Therefore on account of the sign and the redemption that you do for your Messiah and for the remnant of your people who are left, all the nations, peoples, and languages will give thanks and say, "There is no God except the Lord. . . ."*

Just as the Targumic Hannah invoked a characteristic element of the Isaiah Targum, in the comparison of barren Jerusalem and maternal Rome, so the Targumic David invokes an insistence dear to the Targum Jonathan, that there is no God but the Lord.[7] At the same time, the theme of the universal recognition of messianic vindication comes to open expression. David's "*words of prophecy*" are said to be "*for the end of the world, for the days of consolation that are to come*," days which will see "*the messiah to come who will arise and rule*" (1 Sam. 23:1, 3).

Targum Jonathan of the Former Prophets presents a full, well articulated hope of messianic vindication, involving the messiah in

---

[7] See Chilton, *The Glory of Israel*, pp. 6–7.

the destruction of Rome, renewed dedication to the service of the Lord in his Temple, and faithfulness to the Torah. Moreover, a theory of authority is intimated, in which true prophecy represents the claims of heaven upon the earth, and may in turn be represented away from Jerusalem, under conditions of exile, by the voice of faithful teachers and interpreters. Any number of handbooks and articles refer to this Targum as being a literal translation, and to some extent that reputation is justified. It is remarkably economical compared to the Targums to the Latter Prophets. But the innovative matter included, above all in the song of Deborah, Hannah, and David, make it clear beyond any reasonable contradiction that the Targum is a literary translation of the corpus as a whole,[8] targeted on the issue of messianic vindication as attested by the prophets and warranted by the authority of Rabbinic teachers in synagogues and schools.

The emphasis on the condition of exile (see the discussion of Judges 5:9 above) suggests that the framework of Targum Jonathan to the Former Prophets was essentially Amoraic. Unlike the Isaiah Targum, the immediate hope of a rebuilt Temple and a return from exile is not a programmatic feature. Even the messiah is present more as a symbol and seal of ultimate triumph than as an instrument of victory. These indications, together with the probable allusion to the tradition of the Isaiah Targum at 1 Sam. 2:5, suggest that Targum Jonathan to the Former Prophets emerged during the third century in Babylonia. It no doubt was composed on the basis of earlier materials, and the reference to prophets and teachers and scribes is comparable to both the Isaiah Targum and the Jeremiah Targum (both of which manifest a Tannaitic phase of development), but it is the economy of the Targum to the Former Prophets that is most striking.

That economy, however, only makes the expansions of the Targum all the more important as indices of its intent and setting. Deborah, Hannah, and David together attest—with the prophetic authority of God's own spirit—that the messiah is to come from the house of David as the seal of Israel's consolation. That rigorously developed theme makes little sense as a guiding principle prior to 135 C.E. within the school of Aqiba.[9] After all, the leader of the revolt of 132-135, Simeon bar Kosiba, could not claim Davidic descent. Instead, he had to rely on Balaam's oracle that a star would arise from Jacob to strike the enemies of Israel (Num. 24:17). Aqiba's apparent support for Simeon led to the rebuke in the Yerushalmi, "Aqiba, grass will grow from your jaw before the son of David comes" (so B. Ta. 4.8). That is, Aqiba is put in the wrong for the immediacy of his hope and for his identification of a non-David figure as the Messiah.

The Former Prophets Targum joins this Rabbinic critique of the Aqiban eschatology in a particularly telling manner. Aqiba has been widely reputed as the most careful of biblical exegetes: each particle of the Hebrew language was to be given its fully weight in interpretation.[10] This Targum normally represents its Hebrew text very faithfully and only departs in a systematic way to insist upon the Davidic identity of the messiah who is to come in God's own scheme of salvation, warranted by the prophets. So the methods of Aqiba, both scrupulous grammatical care and an inspired application of the biblical text to contemporary circumstances, are deployed in this Targum to refute the Aqiban eschatology.

The language of the Targum, finally, attests its purpose. It has long caused perplexity that, although Targum Jonathan as

---

[8] This is also the conclusion of Eveline van Staalduine-Sulman, pp. 701-717.

[9] So Leivy Smolar and Moses Aberbach, *Studies in Targum Jonathan to the Prophets* (New York and Baltimore, 1983).

[10] See Harry Freedman, "Akiva," in *Encyclopaedia Judaica* (Jerusalem, 1972), vol. 2, cols. 487-492.

a whole is composed in Middle Aramaic, a stage of the language which disappeared from current usage around 200 C.E., it is attested only in Babylonian sources from centuries later, when the contemporary dialect was Late Aramaic. Stephen A. Kaufman has rightly suggested that such phenomena would seem to indicate that a literary usage of interpretation was associated with Middle Aramaic,[11] and it is evident—although he does not make the observation—that the association continued until a much later period. He has not suggested why that might have been the case, but our analysis of the Former Prophets Targum now provides a reason. The very language of the period of the revolt of Simeon bar Kosiba, whose correspondence in Aramaic has been discovered, the interpretative language of support for the revolt, was now used to articulate the Rabbinic expectation of the continuing care of God for his people in exile, even as they awaited the Davidic messiah. The expression of open hostility to Rome underscores that this Targum is a Babylonian product, from the period of the third century, when a certain stability reigned in the academies there.

The Jeremiah Targum

The usage of Targum Jonathan during the Amoraic period is attested by an inscription discovered at Nippur.[12] The piece of pottery, dated between 350 and 500 C.E., presents readings from Jer. 2:1 and Ezek. 21:21-23 in a form consistent with the Targum we can read today. That confirmation of the usage of Targum Jonathan within the Amoraic period underlines the critical importance of the certain questions. What is the relationship between the Amoraic framework of that time and the earlier, Tannaitic framework? Why was the Aramaic dialect of the earlier time used long after its common usage had been eclipsed? How was the assertive theology of messianic vindication of the first framework understood, once it was incorporated within the second?

That there was such an incorporation is manifest not only in the fact that Targum Jonathan is passed on as a whole within Rabbinic tradition but also in the fact that the various renderings of Targum Jonathan, whatever the book rendered and whatever the framework concerned, share their school dialect of a revived Middle Aramaic. But now, the magic bowl from Nippur shows us that the Jeremiah Targum and the Ezekiel Targum could be applied in a context far from that school, in the quest of individuals for restoration. The bowl speaks of Jerusalem both positively (by means of Jeremiah) and negatively (by means of Ezekiel), in order to locate Israel within the spectrum between exile and restoration. So alongside the Rabbinic program of a limitation of the interpretative application of the text of the Prophets (to avoid such excesses as Aqiba's), we also have to reckon with a looser, non-programmatic—and yet persistent—association of that text with the experience of Israel in exile and the hope for vindication. The continuing conviction that the Targum attested Israel's return to glory helps to explain why the Tannaitic framework can have survived, complete with its realistic eschatology, even as the more conservative Amoraic framework emerged.

Following my analysis of the Isaiah Targum, Robert Hayward has suggested that

---

[11] See "The Job Targum from Qumran," in *Journal of the American Oriental Society* 93 (1973), pp. 317-327.

[12] See Stephen A. Kaufman, "A Unique Magic Bowl from Nippur," in *Journal of Near Eastern Studies* 32-33 (1973-1974), pp. 170-174.

the Jeremiah Targum evolved in two stages, principally during the first and the fourth centuries.[13] The messiah is characterized as "Messiah of righteous" in a way consistent with the Scrolls of Qumran;[14] such links confirm Hayward's finding that "The general tone of the messianic hope in this Targum is simple, straightforward, and uncomplicated; and there is the likelihood that it is of very ancient lineage."[15]

Hayward did not have access to Harrington and Saldarini's volume, which was published in the same year as Hayward's. So he was not in a position to see that the messiah in the Jeremiah Targum aligns himself more with the providential figure of the Former Prophets Targum than with the triumphant rebuilder of the Temple anticipated in the earliest stages of the Isaiah Targum. As son of David, he is keenly anticipated because his revelation among the people means their redemption, safety, and their recognition of the source of their vindication (23:5–6; 30:9, 21; 33:13, 15–17, 26), not because he triumphantly rebuilds the Temple. This messiah, as in the Amoraic phase (rather than the Tannaitic phase) of the Isaiah Targum, is a teacher in the manner of the rabbis: "the *people* shall yet *eagerly pursue the words of the messiah*" (Jeremiah Targum 33:13).

There is no question, however, of the messiah within the Jeremiah Targum simply reflecting the more settled expectation of the Amoraic period. He is also, as in the Isaiah Targum's early phase, associated quite closely with the priesthood (33:20–22), and with worship in the Temple (30:9, 21). The rebuilding of the sanctuary is in fact an object of faith in this Targum (31:12); it is just that the messianic means of its rebuilding is not articulated as it is in the Isaiah Targum. By comparison, then, a certain attenuation of a vigorous hope of restoration seems apparent.

It therefore comes as no surprise that, in Jeremiah Targum 2:21, the phrase "*as a plant of a choice vine*" is imported from Isaiah Targum 5:2 and applied to the people of Jerusalem. The point in the Isaiah Targum is to speak of Israel's identity as centered in the sanctuary,[16] but by the time of the Jeremiah Targum the phrase is more like a slogan and is applied in a less specific way. It speaks of Israel without specifying the need to rebuild the Temple. Likewise, in Jeremiah Targum 8:16 the theme of a rejection of the cult in the sanctuary is present, but entirely historicized:

> *Because they worshipped the calves which were in* Dan, *a king with his troops shall go up against them and shall take them into exile.* . . .

Where it is more typical of the Isaiah Targum to speak in terms of the contemporary defect of worship in the Temple, the Jeremiah Targum is inclined to speak of the punishment of idolatry by means of the destruction of the Temple as occurring in the distant past.

Still, the threat of idolatry is ever present, especially within the Sassanid regime in Babylon, which proffered an and astral aspect.[17] The worship of Venus was an espe-

---

[13] *The Targum of Jeremiah* (Wilmington and Edinburgh, 1987), p. 38. His observations of coherence with the biblical interpretation of Jerome (340–420 C.E.) are especially interesting (p. 35, as well as the index, p. 203).

[14] Cf. Jeremiah Targum 23:5 with 4QPatr 3–4; see also the reference to prophecy in Jeremiah Targum 1:2 with 11QPs DavComp 27.1; Hayward, p. 27.

[15] Hayward, p. 33.

[16] Hayward cites the *Liber Antiquitatum Biblicarum* 23:12; 28:4; 39:7 by way of comparison. But he follows a credulous school of British research in dating the *LAB* exclusively with the first century.

[17] See the imagery of the eagle in 18:1 and the discussion of both the eagle and the winged solar disk in Chilton, *The Isaiah Targum*, p. 37; Edith Porada, *Iran ancien. L'art à l'époque préislamique* (Paris, 1963), pp. 226 and 139–154.

cial concern. The planet is specifically mentioned in Jeremiah Targum 7:18 as "the star of heaven" in the context of idolatry, where the Masoretic text reads "the queen of heaven." A return from that Babylon, from a region that might eventually lead to a loss of Israel's identity, is therefore a paradigmatic concern, and Jeremiah is just the prophet to give occasion to emphasize that concern (see Jeremiah Targum 16:14, 15, and the Masoretic text). Yet although the concern for an end of exile is paradigmatic, it is not immediate. The meturgeman must look to the ministry of teachers to follow in the testimony of the prophets, much as in the Former Prophets Targum. But the Jeremiah Targum was an especially good occasion (given the themes of the biblical book) to dilate on the disastrous consequences of the failure to listen to such teachers (see 6:29):[18]

> *Behold, like* bellows *which blow what is burnt in the midst of the fire, so the voice of their prophets is silent, who prophesy to them: Return to the Law! But they have not returned. And like* lead *which is melted in the smelting pot, so the words of the prophets who prophesy to them are void in their eyes. Their teachers have taught them* without profit, *and they have not forsaken their evil deeds.*

In a condition of persistent exile, attention to the echo of the prophet voice under the authority of the rabbis becomes a matter of survival. But the fact that obedience is vital is no guarantee that it will be achieved.

As Robert Hayward remarks, the hermeneutic of prophecy and authoritative teaching requires a clear distinction between true prophecy, such as Jeremiah's (so 2:1, 2) and that of Haman the son of Yigdaliah (35:4), and the message of those described as "prophets of falsehood" (4:9, 10, 13; 5:13, 31; 7:8; 23:13-22; 28:1, 12, 15).[19] Hayward is inclined to hold that such figures deliberately "tell lies," where I have maintained that they simply says things that are wrong, intentionally or not.[20] In their error, they may also be described as "scribes" (6:13; 8:10; 14:18; 18:18; 23:11, 33, 34; 26:7, 8, 11, 16; 29:1) or "teachers" (29:15). But it would be hasty to conclude that "scribe" or "teacher" is inherently pejorative, although Hayward (p. 33) cites Jeremiah Targum 18:18 (with Hosea Targum 4:4) and 29:15 to this effect.[21] The overall pattern of usage associated prophets, scribes, and teachers (in their proper function, as well as in their failure), much as in the Former Prophets Targum.

Still, the usually negative characterization of the scribes is striking, and leads to the impression that in the mind of the meturgeman they are "*a powerful and influential group of his own day, who like the priests, have failed in their duties.*"[22] Passages such as Jeremiah Targum 2:12 (which refers innovatively to the destruction of the sanctuary) and especially 13:27—which refers to a *"respite"* of *"many days"* granted to Jerusalem—hold out the hope that repentance might yet permit Jerusalem to survive and

---

In Isaiah Targum 44:13, the innovative reference to a woman in a house fits the Sassanid period quite well; see Chilton, pp. 87-89, and Porada, p. 62.

[18] The passage is especially innovative in comparison to the Masoretic text. Hayward, p. 69, explains the logic of the rendering very well.

[19] Hayward, pp. 32-33.

[20] See Chilton, *The Glory of Israel*, p. 54. We both depart from the view of Pinkhos Churgin, who sees a constant connection with the issue of idolatry. He was obviously correct in maintaining that is a programmatic concern in the Jeremiah Targum, as in Targum Jonathan generally, but prophecy in the imagination of the meturgemanin may be false without being idolatrous.

[21] Hayward, p. 33.

[22] Hayward, p. 33, citing Jeremiah Targum 23:31-33. Other key passages include 8:10; 14:18; 18:18; 23:11, 33, 34; 26:7, 8, 11, 16; 29:1; see Hayward, pp. 36-37.

prosper. They most likely stem from the period prior to 135 C.E., when Hadrian prohibited Jewish settlement in the city.[23]

As in the case of the Isaiah Targum, but unlike the Former Prophets Targum, the Jeremiah Targum presents us with evidence of a Tannaitic framework, fashioned prior to the end of the second major revolt against Rome. Two, related questions emerge out of this observation. First: why should some Targumim represent such a framework, while others do not? Second: how should we characterize the first framework in its relationship to the second, Amoraic framework?

In answer to the first question, the Former Prophets Targum provides us, in its key innovations within the songs of Deborah, Hannah, and David, with a clear index of how the Amoraic meturgemanin of Targum Jonathan generally perceived the Scriptures. Right interpretation should continue the testimony of the prophets, promote repentance and keeping the Torah; its goal and seal is the messiah, son of David, who is to restore righteousness in Jerusalem. Earlier material (in the Tannaitic framework) associated with the rendering of the Latter Prophets which coordinated well with this theme—including the prophecy of Rome's demise and Jerusalem's prosperity, an attack on idolatry, criticism of priests, scribes, and teachers who were slack or in error, and the triumph of the messiah—might well be included.

Indeed, to the extent that the Tannaitic framework was already in use in some synagogues, inclusion of its interpretation would promote the acceptance of the Jeremiah Targum. As it was, those who framed Targum Jonathan already accepted that the appropriate language of the Targum was Middle Aramaic, an archaic form of the language by the Amoraic period. When, however, those responsible for Targum Jonathan at the stage of the Amoraic framework did not accept an earlier interpretation, they could simply employ the general policy of straightforward translation.

So, as Hayward points out, no reference to the Aqedah (the binding of Isaac, which had become the death of Isaac by the second century) is found in the Jeremiah Targum, although the rabbis had made such a connection by the Amoraic period.[24] In some perplexity, Hayward suggests that the Targum was composed before the connection had been made, although he himself is well aware of the influence of much later developments in the liturgical pattern of scriptural readings. It is much easier to suppose that in composing Targum Jonathan, as in Targum Onqelos, the meturgemanin were aware that the Aqedah was a recent innovation and did not represent it within their translations.[25]

That brings us to answering the second question posed above. Because the Amoraic meturgemanin were in a position to censor the work of their predecessors, the extent of the Tannaitic framework within any Targum must be a matter of conjecture. Still, the Isaiah Targum shows us how crucial a place the Temple played in that early framework, and the Jeremiah Targum confirms that the severe criticism of the priesthood in Jerusalem and of the scribes was involved in the Tannaitic framework. Fundamentally, the Tannaitic framework, which probably grew up out of the usage

---

[23] Hayward even suggests a date prior to 70, which leads to his hypothesis of a first century framework. But the reference to the imminent destruction of the Temple in 2:12 is better taken as a prediction after the event. For a brief but useful description of Roman policy under Hadrian, see A.R.C. Leaney, *The Jewish and Christian World 200 BC to AD 200* (Cambridge, 1984), pp. 122-125.

[24] Hayward, pp. 3-4.

[25] For further discussion of the issue, see Chilton, "Recent Discussion of the Aqedah," in *Targumic Approaches to the Gospels. Essays in the Mutual Definition of Judaism and Christianity* (Lanham, 1986), pp. 39-49.

of synagogues in sympathy with one another, focused on the messianic vindication of Israel, a vindication which was necessarily to include the defeat of Rome. Insofar as the Amoraic meturgemanin could use that tradition in their exilic attempt to maintain and enhance the identity of Israel during the indeterminate number of days prior to the messiah, they did so. In origin, however, the Targumic tradition of which Targum Jonathan was the final, literary outcome is a monument of the popular and the Rabbinic resistance to the presence of the Romans. The Jerusalem which was lost on the ground in 135 C.E. was preserved in the liturgy of synagogues, insofar as the usage of Targum Jonathan could be promulgated.

The Ezekiel Targum

In his treatment of the Ezekiel Targum, Samson H. Levey has argued for an even earlier date of the founding framework. He agrees that the product which can be read today is Amoraic, but he attempts to specify the foundation of the tradition with the school of Yohanan b. Zakkai, who survived after the siege which culminated in the burning of the city in 70 C.E.[26]

The book of Ezekiel itself presents the image of the Merkhabah, the chariot that serves as the throne of God (chap. 1), and involves the vision of God (Ezek. 1:26–28). That was the basis of a discipline of contemplation that evolved during the Rabbinic period, well into the Middle Ages and beyond.[27] But Yohanan himself taught that the Merkhabah was not to be repeated to the uninstructed (B. Hag. 13a), and Targum Jonathan is quite forthcoming in rendering the most sensitive passages.[28] An exception to that rule is the rendering of Ezek. 1:6, which assigns sixteen faces and sixty-four wings to each of the creatures; but that only provides a contrast to the usual, straightforward correspondence. Moreover, the probable reason for that multiplication of faces and hands is given in 1:8, where the Targum innovatively has the creatures perform the additional service of removing coals of fire from the firmament in order to destroy sinners. The Targum seems more eschatological than speculative in its innovations.

In that connection, it is worth recalling that R. Joseph in Pumbeditha also taught that the Merkhabah should be kept "under your tongue," as were the honey and milk in the Song of Songs (4:11; B. Hag. 13a). Indeed, Targum Ezekiel may be said to conform to the conventional reticence of the rabbis when it innovatively refers in 1:27 to a *"glory which the eye is unable to see...."* That is a far cry from the elaborate visionary descriptions often involved in contemplation of the Merkhabah.

Yet the Ezekiel Targum does represent a related sort of esoteric interpretation, which may be associated with the school of Yohanan. Although Yohanan was reported to be wary about whom he spoke to regarding

---

[26] See *The Targum of Ezekiel. Translated, with a Critical Introduction, Apparatus, and Notes* (Wilmington, 1987), pp. 2–5. He has backed away from (without actually abandoning) an earlier argument, that the Targum Jonathan was composed during the time of the Geonim (specifically, Saadia Gaon, during the early part of the tenth century); cf. "The Date of Targum Jonathan to the Prophets," in *Vetus Testamentum* 21 (1971), pp. 186–196.

[27] See M. Hag. 2:1; B. Shab. 80b; B. Men. 43b; B. Hag. 13a–14a; M. Meg. 4:10, and the still indispensable study of Gershom G. Scholem, *Major Trends in Jewish Mysticism* (New York, 1946).

[28] Levey's claim (p. 4) that Yohanan's program was one of "substituting Merkabah Mysticism for Messianic activism" can not be sustained on the basis of any statement attributable to Yohanan. For discussion, Levey cites Uri Herscher, *Yochanan ben Zakkai: Acrobatics at Yavneh* (Los Angeles, 1973).

the exegesis of Scripture, one of his most famous disciples admitted to a lapse in that regard. Eliezer b. Hyrcanus, the most celebrated traditionalist of his time, was once denounced as a rebel to a Roman judge. He was able to walk away from the tribunal, but he said he deserved being denounced, because he had once discussed the interpretation of Scripture with a heretic (probably a Christian) in Sepphoris (see B. A.Z. 16b-17a). Eliezer is said to have connected a key verse in the book of Zechariah, "In that day the Lord will be one and his name one" (14:9), with the eschatological expectation of the kingdom of God (see Mekhilta Amalek 2.155-159).[29]

The kingdom of God features in the Ezekiel Targum, as well as in the Isaiah Targum. The usage in the Ezekiel Targum (7:6-7a) makes the eschatological reference unmistakable:

> The end has come. The *retribution of the end which was to come upon you*, behold, it comes. *The kingdom has been revealed to you*, O inhabitant of the land!

Levey himself cites Targum Isaiah 28:5—and David Kimhi—by way of comparison, in that the term "diadem" in the Hebrew is also rendered eschatologically there, as here in Targum Ezekiel 7:7.[30] The "diadem" of Is. 28:5 refers to the crown of "the messiah" in the Isaiah Targum, while the "diadem" of Ezek. 7:7 becomes "the kingdom" in the Ezekiel Targum. That would suggest that we are dealing with the Tannaitic framework and a consistent theology of messianic and eschatological judgment.

Within the teaching of Jesus, the anticipation of the eschatological kingdom of God involved the claim that God could actually be perceived already to be at work within the world.[31] The Ezekiel Targum presents the context of such a vision as similar to the contemplation of the Merkhabah, and to that extent Levey's suggestion may be endorsed. On the other hand, his contention that the Ezekiel Targum is too early to show an interest in the messiah seems strained. From the Psalms of Solomon in the Pseudepigrapha to the Manual of Discipline that purported to regulate life at Qumran, a messianic aspect is evident within early Judaism. The absence of such reference within the Ezekiel Targum, even within passages which refer to David, is more likely the result of restraint on the part of the Amoraic meturgemanin.

In fact, the restraint of the meturgemanin of Ezekiel only extends to explicit use of the noun "messiah." The figure of the messiah is keenly anticipated (Ezekiel Targum 17:22-23):

> ... I myself will bring near *from the kingdom of the house of David which is likened to* the lofty cedar, *and I will establish him, a child among his sons' sons; I will anoint and establish him by my Memra* ... *and he shall gather together armies and build fortresses and become a mighty king; and all the righteous shall rely on him, and all the humble* shall dwell in the shade *of his kingdom*. ...

Given that the verb "anoint" is used here, and used innovatively in respect of the Hebrew text, it seems pedantic to deny that this is an explicitly messianic expectation. Similarly, "son of David" is not used word for word here; but to deny that the interpretation serves the Rabbinic expectation of such a figure would be silly. The Davidic messiah is to be king, and the righteous are therefore to be vindicated, just as in the Isaiah Targum 16.[32]

Once it has been appreciated that the

---

[29] For further discussion, see Chilton, "Regnum Dei Deus Est," in *Scottish Journal of Theology* 31 (1978), pp. 261-270; idem, *Targumic Approaches to the Gospels*, pp. 99-107.

[30] Levey, p. 33.

[31] See Chilton, *Pure Kingdom: Jesus Vision of God* (Grand Rapids, 1996).

[32] In an earlier work, Levey himself re-

Ezekiel Targum does in fact reflect the theology of messianic vindication that is more evident in the Isaiah Targum, its relative reserve is more easily explained as a result of a more recent date, nearer to the time of composition to the Targum of the Former Prophets than to the Tannaitic framework of the Isaiah Targum. Such an explanation would also correspond to a fact Levey's theory does not accommodate: the greater stringency of the translation in the Ezekiel Targum, which is comparable to the "literal" character of Targum Jonathan of the Former Prophets.

Finally, Levey himself points out that the interpretation of the Merkhabah in Ezekiel 1 was proscribed as a Haftarah (M. Meg. 4:10), and he cites the view that, "Were it not for Hananiah b. Hezekiah, the book of Ezekiel would have been withdrawn, because its words contradict the words of the Torah" (B. Hag. 13a).[33] Now the key point of the contradiction is Ezek. 1:26–27, the vision of the throne and the human form above it. How can that be reconciled with the insistence that "man shall not see me and live" (Exod. 33:20)? That problem is resolved in the Targum, because what appears is "*glory which the eye is unable to see.*" That resolution by recourse to the motif of "glory," of course, agrees with the rendering to Onqelos at Exod. 24:10, where there is a similar problem in the reference to a vision of God. At the same time, the reference to what the eye can not see alludes to Is. 64:3, which is taken of the eschatological reward of God's people in the Targum Isaiah, B. Shab. 63a, Exodus Rabbah 30.24, and 1 Cor. 2:9.

Such links with the book of Isaiah, even in Targumic form, permit us to return to the question of the number of the faces and wings of the creatures in Ezekiel Targum 1:6: altogether, 64 faces and 256 wings according to the Targum! At first sight, such speculation may seem baffling, and Levey suggests the gematria "they sang" (*ranu*).[34] In addition to that possibility, account needs to be taken of collation with the vision in Isaiah 6. In the interests of presenting a consistent view of the heavenly court, the "coals" of Isaiah 6 are mentioned in Targum Ezekiel 1:8, but associated with the cherubim and seraphim:

> Hands like the hands of a man were fashioned for them from beneath their wings on their four sides, *with which to take out burning coals of fire from among the cherubim underneath the firmament which was over their heads, giving them into the hands of the seraphim to sprinkle on the place of the wicked, the destroy the sinners who transgress his Memra.*

In this way, the seraphim in Targum Isaiah 6, who are called "*attendants*" in the Targum are associated with, but made distinct from, the creatures of Ezek. 1.

That opens the way for the creatures in "the likeness of a man" (Ezek. 1:5) to be treated in a way analogous to the treatment of the seraphim of Isaiah 6. There, the multiple wings of the "*attendants*" enable them to serve (rather than to fly). The creatures of the Targum Ezekiel appear with hands under their wings in v. 8, in order to hand coals over to the seraphim. Even the cubing of the number four (producing sixty-four) makes sense in the light of the Isaiah Targum 6:3, because the attendants cry out "holy" three times, and each usage refers

---

marked, "Everything points to a Targumic Messiah innuendo, but the Messiah's designation as such is absent;" see *The Messiah: An Aramaic Interpretation. The Messianic Exegesis of the Targum* (Cincinnati, 1974), p. 79. (Here, the alleged connection is to Hillel [cf. B. San 99a], rather than Yohanan.) The interpretation strikes me as quite straightforward and most unlike an "innuendo."

[33] Levey, p. 2.
[34] Levey, p. 21.

to a different dimension of sanctity (in heaven, on earth, in eternity). And, of course, once the faces are multiplied, the number of the wings must follow. The Ezekiel Targum therefore makes out the vision of the prophet to be consistent with the vision of Isaiah 6. That tendency seems to be stronger than any desire to reveal the secrets of the Merkhabah.

Ezekiel is emphatically identified as a *"prophet"* in the Targum (see 1:1 and 3:1-6, 14, 16, 22); his vision is of the *"Shekhinah"* (1:2) that has been removed (39:29), although it is from there (see 1:14) that the coals are to be poured out on the wicked in 1:8. The definitive return of the Shekhinah (see 48:35) corresponds to the punishment of the wicked, and *"the slain of Rome"* are to be flung into the valley of Gog (39:15-16). Those are themes we have seen connected in the Amoraic framework of the Isaiah Targum; in the Ezekiel Targum, they are explicitly connected to the promise that freedom from oppression follow if Israel will *"perform the Torah"* (2:10).

Just as that theme is more didactic in the Ezekiel Targum than it is in the Isaiah Targum, so the conception of prophetic inspiration is more mechanical (Ezekiel Targum 1:25):

> And at such time when it was his will to make the Dibbur *heard to his servants the prophets of Israel,* there was a voice which was heard from above the firmament. . . .

The usage of *Dibbur* (God's "utterance") makes its appearance rather late in the development of Rabbinic theology (perhaps during the third century) and is usually associated with the Temple and the giving of the law. That suits the present usage (after all, the vision of Isaiah 6 is explicitly situated in the Temple!) but it also suggests that the Ezekiel Targum was crafted well into the Amoraic period, say during the fourth and fifth centuries. Among the other Targumim, Pseudo-Jonathan represents the usage of *Dibbur* frequently, and that would tend to confirm the present dating.[35]

That setting explains why the meturgemanin, explicitly claiming to speak *"prophecy"* (11:14) have God say, "Because I removed them far among the gentiles, and because I scattered them among the countries, therefore I *have given them synagogues, second to my* sanctuary, *because they are as* little in the countries to which they *have been exiled"* (11:16). The theology of exile is a theology which makes sense of defeat in terms of punishment and redemption, and which appeals to God's faithfulness to his covenant as mediated by the prophets. Just that history of salvation is interwoven with the Hebrew text; as Levey remarks in reference to chap. 16 of the Ezekiel Targum (p. 51), it "is a remarkable exposition, interpolated into the Masoretic text, designed to counteract the prophetic denunciation of Israel as a worthless piece of brush by its very nature (Ezek. 15:5)."

The Targum's purpose at that particular point is related to the theme of the entire work, which can be positively expressed by means of the model of Israel in Egypt (so chap. 16). But because the pivot of redemption is obedience, the negative implication is also plainly articulated (20:25):

> Moreover, *since they had rebelled against my Memra, and did not wish to listen to my prophets, I removed them and delivered them into the hands of their foolish inclination; they went after and obeyed statutes which were* not *proper and ordinances by which they could not be established.*

---

[35] For further discussion of the usage and its absence from the Isaiah Targum, see Chilton, *The Glory of Israel*, p. 67.

But the positive expression is no less emphatic (29:21):

> At that *time I will raise up redemption* for the house of Israel, and to you I will give the opening of the mouth *in prophecy* among them.

Exile and redemption are the two poles of the definition of Israel's experience among the meturgemanin of Ezekiel.

True prophets therefore have painful things to say: "It is a *prophecy*, but it shall become a lamentation" (19:14). The imperative of the meturgemanin is not only to avoid those who "*have prophesied* falsehood," but those who "*have taught lies*" (13:8, see also vv. 14–16). It may ultimately be the case that it is the Lord who has misled such deceived deceivers (14:9), but the fact remains that (14:10):

> The guilt of *the one who comes to learn but does not learn*, shall be as the guilt of the *false* prophet.

The reference to scribes who kill and to priests who defile (22:25, 26) may well be aligned with the early lament that "*the prophets prophesied to them, but they did not repent*" (21:18).[36] But the assumption of the Ezekiel Targum is also that well instructed people are in Babylon (21:8, see also v. 9):

> I will *exile your righteous* from you, *in order to destroy your sinners.*

Ezekiel is commanded, "*Let your phylacteries be on your head*" (24:17), and the assumption of this Targum, substantially Amoraic with earlier elements, is that faithful learning, linked to liturgical practice in synagogues, will occasion the promise of salvation.

Haggai, Zechariah, and Malachi in Targum Jonathan

Haggai, Zechariah, and Malachi are grouped within the haggadah concerning the origin of Targum Jonathan, and it is claimed that Jonathan b. Uzziel composed the Targum on the basis of them ("from the mouth of Haggai, Zechariah, and Malachi;" B. Meg. 3a, discussed in the preceding entry). That assertion invites a consideration of the Targumim so named. Of the three, only Zechariah offers considerable expansions on the Hebrew text of the prophet. But that is not surprising: after all, Haggai—however translated—turns on the issue of the restoration of the Temple (which becomes the "sanctuary," as is usual in Targum Jonathan). For the concerns of the meturgemanin to be met, there is need only to underscore that what is said is stated as "a word of *prophecy*" (1:1, 3; 2:1, 10) for the purpose of restoring the "Shekhinah" to its proper place (1:8), and to insist that what was intended for the nation is also valid for the "congregation" (2:14) in exile.[37] Similarly, Malachi already speaks in Hebrew of the return of Elijah to restore appropriate worship in Jerusalem (3:23–24), and it is scarcely a liberty to speak of service in the "*sanctuary*" (1:10; 2:12; 3:7, 10) and the return of the "*Shekhinah*" in response to repentance (3:12), as the Targum does. So directly does Malachi address the concerns of the meturgemanin, the term "prophecy" is not even added to the introduction, unlike every other book of the Latter Prophets in Targum Jonathan.

---

[36] The failure to repent, despite more than ample warning, is a theme within the Isaiah Targum, see 5:25; 9:12, 17, 21; 10:4; 26:10; 50:2; 66:4, especially the last two passages.

[37] Cathcart and Gordon, p. 180, refer the usage to "the Judean community," but the usage of Targum Jonathan is clearly more inclusive than that. For discussion of the later usage of "congregation," rather than "house of Israel," see Chilton, *The Glory of Israel*, pp. 33–37.

Yet even as restoration is imagined in these tangible and cultic terms, the Malachi Targum attests the Amoraic conviction that prayer as such takes the place of sacrifice (1:11b):

> and at every time that you do my will I receive your prayer and my great name is sanctified because of you, and *your prayer is like a pure offering before me*; for my name is great among the nations, says the Lord of hosts.

Churgin correctly observed that the replacement of sacrifice, as distinct from the restoration of sacrifice, is typically an Amoraic theme within Targum Jonathan.[38] Moreover, the present rendering makes the worship purely Israel's, while an earlier expectation envisaged the inclusion of non-Jews (see below).

Similarly, the emphasis on a single covenant whose interpretation does not change (Malachi Targum 3:6) manifests the interests of those who insisted upon authoritative teaching in adherence to the prophets:

> For I the Lord have not *changed my covenant which is from of old*; but you, house of Israel, you think that whoever dies in this world, his judgment has ceased.

It has been argued that this statement must come from the period of the Sadducees, and that after that time "the doctrines of resurrection and accountability were no longer issues of dispute."[39] Neither assertion is fully convincing. The Sadducees' position is attributed to them only by unsympathetic observers—Josephus (War 2 § 165-166) and various Christians (Mark 12:18-27; Mat. 22:23-33; Luke 20:27-38; Acts 23:6-8). And Targumic texts as late as the Middle Ages continue to refer to the denial of resurrection within the dispute between Cain and Abel which is developed at Gen. 4:8.[40] As a whole, the Malachi Targum appears to reflect the Amoraic framework of meturgemanin.

The themes of both Tannaitic and Amoraic meturgemanin are more in evidence within the Zechariah Targum, which R. Joseph cited as an already extant source (see B. Meg. 3a; B. M.Q. 28b). At 3:8, the identification of the "branch" with the messiah is made explicit, as at Isaiah Targum 4:2, and the messiah is also portrayed as being "revealed," a locution reminiscent of 4 Ezra 7:28. Martin McNamara has argued that this usage is characteristic of the first century,[41] and it is repeated in 6:12-13 of the Zechariah Targum, where the messiah (for "branch" in the Masoretic text) is to build the Temple and be at peace with a *"high priest."*

Reference to the "kingdom of the Lord" at 14:9 in the Zechariah Targum may—as we have already discussed—reasonably be dated within the first century. Similarly, in 4:7-9, where the Hebrew text speaks of Zerubbabel building the Temple, in the Targum he merely starts to build it, and

---

[38] Cathcart and Gordon, p. 231, are equally correct when they point out that Philo and the Scrolls attest an "occasional spiritualizing of sacrifices." (They also cite "the existence of the synagogue long before A.D. 70," but that is beside the point: the history of the synagogue in Palestine is a fraught issue, and the notion that the synagogue replaces the Temple, as in the Ezekiel Targum, is a late notion. Cf. Dan Urman and Paul V.M. Flesher, eds., *Ancient Synagogues. Historical Analysis and Archaeological Discovery* [Leiden, 1995].) But those sources do not attest the motif of God's general acceptance of prayer in the place of sacrifice; that was Churgin's point (p. 28), and it still stands.

[39] See Cathcart and Gordon, p. 236.

[40] See Chilton, "A Comparative Study of Synoptic Development: The Dispute between Cain and Abel in the Palestinian Targums and the Beelzebul Controversy in the Gospels," in *Journal of Biblical Literature* 101 (1982), pp. 553-562, and idem, *Targumic Approaches to the Gospels*, pp. 137-149.

[41] *The New Testament and the Palestinian Targum to the Pentateuch* (Rome, 1966/1978), p. 249.

prepares the way for the *"messiah whose name is told from of old, and he shall rule over all kingdoms."* The relationship between Zerubbabel in the sixth century B.C.E. and the messiah at the end of time is not spelled out here, but the role of the messiah in restoring the Temple (as in the Isaiah Targum) is implicit. The status of the messiah—as superior to Zerubbabel or any other Davidic king—is even plainer in 10:4: *"messiah"* appears for "tent peg" in the Masoretic text, and is associated with *"king"* and *"strength in war."* These examples of realistic eschatology instance Tannaitic conceptions.

By comparison, the precise designation of the messiah as him whose *"name is told from of old"* seems to be an Amoraic motif (cf. Micah Targum 5:1; Psalms Targum 72:17; the Pirqe of R. Eliezer 3; B. Pes. 54a).[42] This hint of Amoraic interest is borne out by the typical themes of false prophecy (10:2; 13:4), paired with the teaching of lies (13:4). The form of the promise to Joshua in Zech. 3:7 coincides with the vision of Ezekiel, as well as with that of Isaiah, as discussed above:

> If you walk in ways *which are good before me*, and if you keep the charge *of my Memra*, then you shall judge *those who minister in my sanctuary* and you shall have charge of my courts, *and at the resurrection of the dead I will raise you to life* and will give you *feet to walk* among those *seraphim*.

The collation of the sanctuary and the heavenly court is assumed as in Isaiah 6, and the reference to attendants who *"minister"* agrees with the language of the Isaiah Targum. That occasions the introduction of the theme of resurrection here, which is a thematic interest in the Isaiah Targum (see 22:14; 65:6 15), but quite separate from the vision in the Temple. That new element marks a later development (as does the unveiled language of resurrection), along with the particular reference to the *"feet to walk among those seraphim,"* which is a contribution from Ezekiel Targum 1.

The exilic theology of the Amoraic meturgemanin is also evident in the rather full midrash of the two women in 5:9 as two *"provinces going into exile:"* the equation of women and states is also made in Isaiah Targum 32:9, and here the prophecy concerning Oholoah and Oholibah in Ezekiel 23—which the Ezekiel Targum also relates to "provinces" (23:2)—is being used to speak of the punishments of Israel and Judah. The extent of the midrash in the Zechariah Targum (5:5–11), suggests the importance of the theme to the meturgemanin. But a strong typology of the exodus is also introduced (10:11), to insist on the positive pole of the history of salvation, as well.

The Bad and the Good of Exile—Hosea, Amos, Nahum, Obadiah, Micah, and Zephaniah in Targum Jonathan

The full midrash on exile over a short run of material in Zechariah is pursued much more consistently in the Hosea Targum, owing to the nature of the material involved. The *"prophecy"* was designed to warn the *"inhabitants of the idolatrous city,"* that *"if they repent, it will be forgiven them; but if not, they will fall as the leaves of a fig-tree fall"* (Hosea Targum 1:1–3, see also 11:2). There are several such fulsome attacks on idolatry, a particularly worry in Sassanian Babylon, and the problem of wooden images is an especial concern (see 4:12; 8:6). The reference to the messiah can be as oblique

---

[42] So Cathcart and Gordon, pp. 122, 194, their citation of G.F. Moore's reading, and Chilton, *The Glory of Israel*, p. 114.

as in the Ezekiel Targum and with virtually the same wording, as when Judah and Israel "shall appoint themselves one head *from those of the house of David*" (2:2).

But "messiah" is used explicitly in 3:5, in association with the restoration of worship in the Temple by the Davidic king. This aspect of the Hosea Targum cannot be denied: to some extent, it is concerned with the cultic abuses of the Tannaitic period and even earlier, when "*they made the non-priest like the priest to desecrate my holy properties*" (Hosea Targum 4:9). Then, the problem was not the ambient idolatry of the Sassanids, but the predations of the priesthood, and the threat of the coming of the Romans, whose king would "*destroy their treasure-house and lay waste their royal city*" (13:15), was not only a vivid threat, but a matter of history. Such punishments pale in comparison of the judgment in Gehinnam that is to come, depicted in the final sentence of the Hosea Targum in a way that echoes the close of the Isaiah Targum.

Still, such glimpses of earlier interpretations are rather sporadic in the Hosea Targum. They are not easily arranged into the sort of exegetical frameworks evident in the Isaiah Targum and the Zechariah Targum. More typically, the Hosea Targum focuses on the history of salvation in its negative aspect, against those who would say, "*The scribe shall not teach, and the prophet shall not admonish*" (4:4). When the positive side comes to expression, it is in the wistful remembrance of when "*those of the house of Judah were fervent in worship until the people of God were exile from their land, and they who worshipped before me in the sanctuary were called the holy people*" (12:1). To imagine a restoration of such a condition involves anticipating "*the resurrection of the dead*" (6:2).

Idolatry is also an especial concern in the Amos Targum (2:8), as is the emphasis on prophecy (1:1; 3:8) and the rule of the "*kingdom of the house of David*" (9:11). There is also a signal interpretation, which represents the visionary language already discussed in connection with the Isaiah, Ezekiel, and Zechariah Targums (Amos Targum 9:1):

> *The prophet said, "I saw the glory of the Lord"*: it *ascended by the cherub and dwelled on* the altar, and he said, "*If my people Israel are not repentant to the law, overturn the lamp; king Josiah shall be slain, the house shall be laid waste, and the courts shall be broken up; and the vessels of the sanctuary shall go into captivity.*"

Here, vision and Temple are combined, as before, but in addition the negative side of the history of salvation is spelled out. Moreover, the language used had become traditional of omens of the destruction of the Temple (see B. Yom. 39b and B. Git. 56 a, b by way of comparison).[43]

The books of Obadiah and Nahum provided excellent opportunities to speak of the vindication of God's people. Esau was a well-established symbol for Rome (see B. B.B. 123b, for example), and is used as such in the rendering of Obadiah. The prediction is made that Jacob and Joseph will "*have dominion over them and slaughter them*" (Obadiah Targum 1:18); this arising, "to judge the *fortress* of Esau," was relished as the substance of "*the kingdom of the Lord*" (1:21). Nahum is also made to have "*prophesied*" (Nahum Targum 1:1), and the direction of he prophecy towards Nineveh is contrasted with Jonah's (1:1):

> *Beforehand Jonah, the son of Amitai, prophet from Gath Hephar, prophesied against her, and she repented from her sins. And when she proceeded to sin again, Nahum from Beth Koshi prophesied against her, as is written in this book.*

---

[43] Discussed in Chilton, *A Feast of Meanings. Eucharistic Theologies from Jesus through Johannine Circles* (Leiden, 1994), pp. 77–79.

By means of reference to Jonah in a sequence, Nahum's prophecy of doom is vindicated, and is presented as the last word against those who "*completely destroyed the sanctuary*" (1:8). Not only does that reference apply most naturally to the Romans, it applies most accurately to them after 135 C.E. Israel are described as already "*trusting in his Memra*" (1:7), as if repentance were accomplished, and not an unfulfilled condition. That sense that heaven has already turned in Israel's favor, that repentance has been offered and accepted, is typical of the Amoraic period.

The glories of return from exile from Babylon are anticipated in the Micah and Zephaniah Targums. The former remains concerned with the problem of false prophecy and bad teaching as the cause of exile (see Micah Targum 2:11), and the old theology of restoration remains in the interpretation of the mountain of chapter 4 in terms of the sanctuary, as in the Isaiah Targum (chap. 2). Moreover, this is associated with messianic rule (2:13):

> *The delivered shall go up as at the beginning, and a king shall go up, leading at their head, and he shall break the enemy who oppresses them, tread down strong fortresses; they shall inherit the cities of the gentiles and their king shall be at their head and the Memra of the Lord will be their help.*

The kingdom and messiah are associated in Micah Targum 4:7-8. But they are associated more closely than in the earlier Targumim, and the messiah is described as hidden because of Zion's sins, and as having a name from of old: all of those are probably Amoraic developments.[44]

Such references reach their climax in a prediction of return from Diaspora as then known (Micah Targum 7:):

> *At that time the exiles shall gather together from Assyria and the mighty cities, from Greater Armenia and the besieged cities, as far as the Euphrates and the Western Sea and the mountain ranges.*

Clearly, the social context implies more than rebuilding the Temple. God is to remember and return all of his people. He does so because he remembers the Aqedah, the binding of Isaac upon the altar and his sacrifice there, which is specifically mentioned (Micah Targum 7:20).[45] What was not mentioned earlier, even in the Jeremiah Targum at a point where its mention would have been natural, is now invoked without warrant from the Hebrew text. The Aqedah has become, by the fifth century, the surety of Israel's acceptance before God.

The Zephaniah Targum extends the range of the return further, "beyond the rivers of *India*" (3:10, for "Ethiopia" in the Masoretic text) and further emphasizes the threat of idolatry (1:4, 5, 8-9).[46] The issue of prophecy—whether true or false—and teaching remains strong (3:2, 4), but there are also some interesting new elements. A return to "*one chosen speech*" as a consequence of the return is specified (3:9), and the end of the exile also means the end of "all those who *enslave* you" (3:19). But also to be removed are "the *mighty ones of your celebrity*" (3:11), "*the judges of deceit*" (3:15) who need to be purged to make way for "a lowly people and *accepting mortification*" (3:12). This is a most skillful application of the theology of exile to the exiles themselves, and makes way for the next, and last, development in Targum Jonathan.

---

[44] See the discussion in George Foot Moore, *Judaism*, vol. II, pp. 343-345, 350-353; Chilton, *The Glory of Israel*, pp. 37, 79-81, 114.

[45] See Cathcart and Gordon, p. 128, citing Chilton, "Isaac and the Second Night: A Consideration," in *Biblica* 61 (1980), pp. 78-88.

[46] India also features innovatively in the Amoraic framework of the Isaiah Targum (see 18:1).

Joel, Jonah, and Habakkuk in Targum Jonathan—The Penitent Return

Although there is little new in the Joel Targum, what is there offers the possibility of repentance and forgiveness to the individual penitent in emphatic terms (Joel Targum 2:14):

> Whoever knows *that he has sins on his hands*, let him turn back *from them, and he will have compassion on him; and whoever repents, his sins shall be forgiven, and he will receive* blessings *and consolations, and his prayer will be like that of a man who presents* offerings and libations in the *sanctuary* of the Lord your God.

The startling thing here is not simply the individual focus of repentance and forgiveness, but the direct comparison between personal penitence and cultic sacrifice, a development which occurs near the end of the development of Targum Jonathan.

Such a comparison is all but assumed in the Jonah Targum, when the prophet (cf. 1:1) says that "I with the voice of *the praise* of thanksgiving will offer *my sacrifice before you*" (2:10). That statement is very close to the Masoretic text, in which Jonah says, "I with the voice of thanksgiving will sacrifice to you." But what is in the Masoretic text an accompanying action—singing while sacrificing—becomes understandable in the Targum as a replacement of sacrifice: the song reified as the offering. Moreover, there is recourse to the direct statement of the underlying theology in the Jonah Targum (3:9):

> *Whoever* knows *that there are sins on his hands, let him repent of them and he will have compassion on us.* . . .

The power of individual penitence is so great, it effects a change in the disposition of God toward the community. This confidence reaches its climax in the Habakkuk Targum (3:1):

> *The prayer which Habakkuk the prophet prayed when it was revealed to him concerning the extension of time which he gives to the wicked, that if they return to the law with a perfect heart it shall be forgiven them, and all their sins which they have sinned before him shall be as inadvertent error.*

Here is the theology of the later Amoraim, as Cathcart and Gordon observe (citing B. Yom. 86b),[47] which enables even those denounced as wicked to join the movement of repentance. The same Targum refers to the Roman practice of burning incense to standards in 1:16 (cf. 1QpHab 6:3-6; War 6 § 316),[48] so that the whole cannot be read as a simple statement of Amoraic theology, but the emphasis on repentance in an individual mode is plain.

Conclusion

Targum Jonathan to the Prophets grew up in stages that may be characterized by means of the types and styles of interpretation utilized. The earliest stage, associated with synagogal practice until the time of the revolt of Simeon bar Kosiba, is reflected in the incomplete exegetical frameworks of the Isaiah and Zechariah Targums. They center on the immediate restoration of worship in the Temple as the kingdom of God and the messiah are revealed. During the late third and fourth centuries these frameworks were filled out in the interests of a messianic theme of a return from exile within the entire history of the salvation of Israel. The result was the production of Targum Jonathan of the Former Prophets, as well as the Isaiah, Jeremiah, Ezekiel, and

---

[47] Cathcart and Gordon, p. 156.
[48] See Naphtali Wieder, "The Habakkuk Scroll and the Targum," in *Journal of Jewish Studies* 4 (1953), pp. 14-18.

Zechariah Targums. The fifth century saw the completion of the work, with Hosea, Amos, Nahum, Obadiah, Micah, and Zephaniah in Targum Jonathan representing a development of the exilic theology, and then Joel, Jonah, and Habakkuk in Targum Jonathan moving that theology in an individualistic direction.

Effectively, then, Targum Jonathan is a monument of Rabbinic activity, but of Rabbinic activity as it attempted to influence interpretation in synagogues. For that reason, at its earliest stages especially it represents traditional renderings not of its own making, even as it strives to present Scripture as the voice of the eternal Memra.

BRUCE CHILTON
Bard College

Targum, Conceptual Categories of

The literary genre targum originated in antiquity, when, following the destruction of the First Temple in 586 B.C.E. (and even more so after the destruction of the Second Temple in 70 C.E.), Jews became a bibliocentric community. Bereft of political sovereignty, juridical autonomy, and a functioning cultic hierarchy, the traumatized fragments of the Jewish nation adopted sacred scripture as their "constitution." The Bible itself records how Jewish polity in the post-exilic period was established by a convocation wherein the populace pledged allegiance to the sacred text, reaffirming the ancient covenant described in the Torah of Moses. Authorized "bookmen" (Heb.: sôperîm) interpreted the inherited text, trained disciples, and lectured to the community. And by the beginning of the Common Era, the public reading and exposition of Scripture was so established as to be regarded an ancient tradition.[1] All this established a "bibliocracy" wherein the Hebrew Bible provided historical identity, juridical legitimation, and a religious justification for communal existence.

Despite initial success, this entire enterprise, the culture it transmitted and the community it sustained, became increasingly endangered by both linguistic and conceptual challenges. First was the traumatic erosion of Hebrew as the language of Jewry. For not only was Hebrew regarded as the original language, the tongue used by God in his *creatio ex nihilo* and by all humanity when "the earth was of one language and one speech" (Gen. 11:1). More important, it was the sacred tongue in which God's Torah had been revealed. And just as it was forbidden to attempt to "translate" the deity from the invisible to the visible by physical representation, so it was wrong to translate sacred writ into another language. This antipathy is explicit in the hyperbole that when the Bible was translated into Greek "three days of darkness fell upon the world" and that what ensued when the Bible was translated "was as injurious to Israel as the day when the (golden) calf was made."[2] Indeed, modern linguistics confirms the ancient Rabbinic insight: as the "medium" of Jewish thought Hebrew

---

[1] See Ezra 7:25f., Neh. 8:1ff. Cf. Acts 15:21 and Josephus, *Contra Apionem* 2.17. The Palestinian lectionary was divided into 154 sections completed in a triennial cycle, while the Babylonian lectionary divided the Pentateuch into 48–54 sections, completed annually. Special readings from the Pentateuch, Prophets, and Hagiographa were assigned to the festivals, new moons, and special Sabbaths.

[2] See T. Meg. 8b, 9a, T. Shab. 116a, Soferim 1. Cf. M. Rubin, "The Language of Creation or the Primordial Language: A Case of Cultural Polemics in Antiquity," in *JSS* 49 (1998), pp. 306–633, U. Eco, *The Search for the Perfect*

not only conveys the "message" but actually constrains, shapes, and determines it. The language itself is a message, independent of whatever ideas the individual thinks he or she is conveying while using it.[3]

The Pharisaic-Rabbinic commitment to Hebrew reflected three realizations: a) Since any organic Jewish community must be on "speaking terms" with its ancestors, linguistic mutuality was a necessary component of an authentic inter-generational relationship. The historic language must be maintained for the benefit of all, the living and the dead, and any translation would be a fragmenting rupture, vertically as well as horizontally. b) The Hebrew language of the Bible serves as a barrier against distortions resulting from erroneous translations. Therefore the only religiously and intellectually honest attitude to translation must be one of contempt! c) An obviously emotive element is involved in a religious text,[4] and there is real power to the Jewish "linguistic unconscious," the system of assumptions and symbols that stands between these human beings and the world, out of which they actually build what they consider to be reality. For these reasons, despite the obvious difficulties involved, even when some use of translation became unavoidable, formal Jewish study, like formal Jewish worship, never ceased to be conducted in Hebrew.

The second challenge to the Jewish bibliocracy was that, like every living culture, it was ever-evolving: Judaism was not an event completed in the past, but a continuum. Once the Hebrew Bible was canonized it could not be altered, of course,[5] yet since "process" is the very basis of life, it would have to be *conceptually* translated. Torah would have to be constantly integrated into post-biblical culture, even if passages that contradicted basic Jewish belief, values, and law would require circumlocution, reinterpretation, and even contradiction in order to be "safely" conveyed in the school curriculum and the synagogue liturgy.

The birth of the targum represented a major change in Judaism, reflecting the tension between tradition and change: the attempt of a people to remain true to its ancient Book and yet live as an authentically evolving, self-aware community.[6] Targum

---

Language (Oxford, 1995), G. Lepschy, ed., *History of Linguistics*: Vol. I, *The Eastern Traditions of Linguistics* (New York, 1994), M. Idel, "*Reification of Language in Jewish Mysticism*," in S.T. Katz, *Mysticism and Language* (Oxford, 1992), pp. 42–79, A. Borst, *Der Turmbau von Babel* (Stuttgart, 1957).

[3] The very terms "medium" and "message" are multi-ordinal: their use in any specific case is dependent not on any permanent meaning but on the context. They do not have unchanging referents, but they actually define each other through their reciprocal relationship.

[4] Thus, the person who approaches it, even without data about the text, is already "involved," with an existential stance. Religious communication—textual or otherwise—is significantly subjective: religion is "humanistic" in the sense that its referent is human: feelings, commitments, aspirations, and imagination. The rabbis knew that the language of religious communication is crucial, that factual plausibility alone was inadequate. A statement would not be religiously true if it did not somehow move Jews to feel, think, or act. Judaism did attempt to present reality in coherent (or at least non-contradictory!) statements, but since any number of internally consistent theories may be equally plausible, it could not rely exclusively upon logical consistency as the criterion of its claim. The sacredness that it conveys had to be expressed in sacred symbols, verbal and otherwise; its linguistic "medium" and its "message" were inseparable.

[5] This also applied to completely problematic texts such as the erotic Song of Songs and the cynical Ecclesiastes, works whose canonicity had apparently been based on their presumed origin rather than upon their contents.

[6] If the entire matrix of a society that anthropologists call "culture" is the medium wherein its messages are conveyed, then a whole culture can also become the message when a new medium comes along. Thus, the message of any cultural epoch is the envi-

was intended to be a communication between the past, the present, and, in a sense, the future. This was a literally life-or-death issue, hence its self-justification, attributing its existence to divine injunction. Thus, where Scripture tells of God's instructing Moses, "And you shall write upon the stones all the words of this torah *very plainly* (Heb.: *be'er hetêb*)," the targums render it, "... read in one language and translated into seventy languages" (PT Deut. 27:8). And in the Talmud's report of the supposed translation of the Prophets into Aramaic by Jonathan b. Uzziel, the student of Hillel the Elder, this first century C.E. scholar is credited with having "declared the targum from the mouths of Haggai, Zachariah, and Malachi," thus affirming its antiquity, authenticity, and legitimacy, as well as the translation's being justified because it reconciled divergent exegesis. According to the legend,

> Palestine was shaken four hundred parsangs by four hundred parsangs. A heavenly echo came forth and demanded, "Who has revealed my secrets to mortal man?" Immediately Jonathan b. Uzziel rose to his feet and declared: "It is I who has revealed thy secrets.

But it is clearly known to you that I did this neither for my glory nor for the glory of my family. Rather, for thy glory have I done it, so that dissension might not increase in Israel."[7]

The translation of a *religious* text is never simply a technical endeavor, and the targum was expected to reconcile the functions of translation and interpretation, lest people be misled either by a strict *verbum e verbo* translation or mistaught by a free *sensus de sensu* paraphrase.[8] Some extant targum texts are painstakingly literal, occasionally constituting the only extant correct renderings, even preferable to the Hebrew Masoretic text itself.[9] Others are highly latitudinarian, for since Pentateuchal readings (supplemented by a Prophetic and Hagiographic reading chosen for its conceptual or semantic affinity) were often followed by a homily, the targum frequently includes or refers to materials from these sources. This methodological inconsistency reflects the Pharisaic-Rabbinic tradition that no translation, neither literal nor expansive, could be adequate, since "He who translates a verse verbatim is a liar! And he who alters it is a villain and a heretic" (B. Qid. 49a)!

The Major Targum Texts

Despite ideological opposition to the translation of Scripture, biblical texts were translated into Aramaic, as attested by both Mishnah references and Qumran finds. In fact, there is no evidence that the genre was originally oral or that it was composed

---

ronment of the preceding one. The Hebrew Bible had abstracted, classified, manipulated, and otherwise organized information in a distinctive manner. The Aramaic targum actually constituted a new way of dealing with old problems, of handling ideas, of stimulating intellectual discourse.

[7] T. Meg. 3a. Indeed, to translate (and to transcribe) is to make critical, decisive choices between alternatives, minimizing and not exploiting ambiguities, and thereby circumscribing intellectual possibilities. The goal of translation includes the impoverishment of imagination! Cf. Y. Meg. 4:5, Y. Ned. 5:6, T. B.B. 134a, T. Suk. 28a, T. Erub. 62a, Soferim 15. Similarly, "Aquilas the Proselyte translated the Torah under the supervision of (Heb. *lipnê*) Eliezer and Joshua, and he was praised" (M. Meg. 1:1).

[8] Hence the initial objection to the writing of targum and teaching it to the uninitiated, who might raise it to the level of dogma or revealed truth.

[9] Cf., e.g., Tg Exod. 30:35, Tg Deut. 22:5, Tg Ju. 5:24, Tg Is. 19:10.

to accompany the liturgical reading of Scripture in the synagogue. The earliest extant texts are essentially literal translations of the Hebrew, and targum was included in the curriculum of the Palestinian academies, placed between the Hebrew Bible and the Mishnah. Comprehension of a Scripture lection included the ability to translate the text into Aramaic.

Any convincing dating of a given targum involves both literary considerations and philological factors. The former depends on motifs and traditions that are clearly paralleled in early writings, and the latter is complicated by archaic linguistic forms that frequently persist, especially in juridical and historical orthography. Thus, any question of *terminus ante quem* or *terminus post quem* must provide either irrefutable parallels in antiquity or evidence of the targum's having been rewritten in later centuries deleting archaisms. The entire question of the conceptual influence of other literature on the targum (and the converse influence of the targum on other texts) is so complex that, despite the wealth of close parallels or clearly attested channels of transmission (judgments that themselves involve a theoretical posture!), the drawing of conclusions is largely arbitrary. The datable elements encompass at least eight centuries, from the first century B.C.E. through the rise of Islam in the seventh century C.E. Scholarly disagreements as to dating targum texts stem largely from the relative weight accorded to their earlier and later elements.[10]

In sum, dating techniques are of limited value, for no conclusive method exists for distinguishing between the tradition that may underlie a particular text and the particular version of that text found in the targum. And if extreme caution must be exercised with Rabbinic documents from late antiquity where traditions are attributed to particular sources, *a fortiori* this applies to targum, where sources are *never* identified. The basic issues of derivation or diffusion remain complex and difficult.[11]

Targum versions exist for all of Scripture (except for those texts written in Aramaic), with the best known being the so-called "Targum Onqelos" to the Pentateuch that is placed next to the Hebrew text in the *Biblia Rabbinica*. This targum exists in a unified scholastic redaction that, like the Hebrew Bible itself, has a *massorah* for purposes of textual control. It is the most literal of the Pentateuch targums, and, except for occasionally significant theological or juridical emendations, in both diction and grammatical structure it follows the Hebrew original. A substratum of Western Aramaic witnesses that this targum originated in Palestine, whence (along with the Mishnah and Tosefta) it was imported into Babylon where it was revised and redacted. By the third century C.E. it was considered the

---

[10] Some elements may be precisely dated, like the homily predicting that "the Romans will be destroyed and they will not exact tribute from Jerusalem" (Tg Hab. 3:17). It is indignant over the census tax imposed by the second Procurator Quirinius in 6 C.E. that was perceived as national servitude and that fomented widespread hostility until the revolt of 66 C.E. And it must surely have originated during that sixty-year period, for had the destruction of the Temple already occurred, the targum would have related to that far greater catastrophe. Again, the polemic regarding the Hasmonean High Priest Jonathan (PsJ Deut. 33:11) would not have been composed after the first century B.C.E. Yet this same targum has a reference to Mohammad's wife and daughter (PsJ Gen. 21:21) from, at the very least, seven centuries later!

[11] "The Aramaic Version of the Bible" cannot be addressed as a unitary corpus for it is a composite of accretions older than their final date of compilation. And the critical scholar must enter a plea of *non liquet* on some of the most intriguing questions: who the authors were, how materials were compiled, how textual transmission was maintained, and for what functional purposes were they intended.

authoritative Aramaic version of the Pentateuch, a status reflected by its being cited in the Talmud as a juridical source with the designation "our Targum." The other "official" targum is the so-called "Targum Jonathan to the Prophets" that bears a close affinity to Targum Onqelos. It too originated in Palestine and, after significant revision in linguistic conformity with Babylonian Aramaic diction and morphology, by the third century it was disseminated throughout the diaspora and subsequently regarded as ancient, reliable, and occasionally indispensable for correctly understanding obscure biblical passages.

These "official" targums are also known as "Babylonian targums" due to their a) locale of redaction, b) linguistic characteristics, c) use of supra-lineal punctuation in the earliest manuscripts. Their scanty historical allusions range from events as disparate as the reign of Yohanan Hyrcanus (135–105 B.C.E.) to the Sassanid regime in Babylon, with no Arabic linguistic characteristics or references to the fall of Babylon by the Arab conquest. With their largely *verbatim* renderings and terse paraphrases, they met the criteria for synagogue recitation as well as academic use. Nevertheless, the synagogue targum declamation was governed by procedures designed to preclude conveying the conception that the targum was equivalent in sanctity and authority to the Hebrew Bible. Thus, the "broadcaster"[12] could not use a written text nor could the Hebrew reader correct his rendition, lest this convey the impression that his lection was canonized.[13]

Unofficial targum exists in various forms. Palestinian targums to the Pentateuch are primarily found in the Pseudo-Jonathan (traditionally designated "Targum Jonathan b. Uzziel") and the Fragmentary Targum ("Targum Yerushalmi") printed in the *Biblia Rabbinica*, and the recently discovered Vat. Ms. *Neophyti* #1. These are written, largely, in Galilean Jewish Aramaic, and they incorporate a wealth of additions and emendations. Their "unofficial" status is clear, witness a) literary divergences within and between them, b) the absence of editorial control of paraphrase, grammar, and orthography, and c) the lack of consistent harmonization with normative Pharisaic-Rabbinic Judaism.

The targums to the Hagiographa, too, never enjoyed "official" status, though their wide currency is reflected by their inclusion in the *Biblica Rabbinica*. They incorporate lengthy addenda, including literary elements found only in texts of early Palestinian origin. Many of the extant texts are more commentary than translation. They manifest many Western Aramaic linguistic features, though these characteristics were progressively altered in conformity with the familiar Aramaic of the Babylonia Talmud. The free renderings in the Hagiographic targum texts are due to: a) their not being *essential* components of worship, b) their not being utilized for establishing juridical precedent, c) their being based upon biblical texts that had traditionally elicited homiletic expansion.

The various MSS. contain, by and large, the same basic text, yet they vary in degree of transition into Eastern Aramaic, extent of evolution from unvocalized to vocalized texts, and syntax and morphology. The targums reflect a variety of translation techniques, with significant differences in literary style, philological characteristics, and exegetical methodology between (and within) the various Hagiographic books. Historical allusions, loan words, and morphological characteristics indicate a long process of

---

[12] Note Aram. *meturgeman* or *turgeman* ex *rgm*, lit. "throw" or "broadcast" a speaker's words to an audience, either by amplification or translation.

[13] See the reluctance to commit even the "Oral Torah" to writing in Tanhuma, *Kî Tîssa* 34.

development, and many other diversities too preclude regarding the Hagiographa targums as a corpus.[14]

Nevertheless, for all its eclecticism and diversity, this potpourri targum genre preserved the Bible. In many respects it continued the earlier scribal tradition of glosses: *marginalia* incorporated into the biblical text itself that may be classified by function: to resolve textual difficulties by interpreting obscure words or simplifying syntax, to harmonize conflicting biblical texts, to reconcile the biblical text with accepted tradition, to incorporate theological, juridical and ritual elements of rabbinic Judaism, to provide specificity to historical, juridical or religious allusions, and to strengthen or mitigate the force of a passage. In sum, this Aramaic version of the Bible was an interpretive commentary incorporating the two categories of Jewish exegetical literature, halakhah and aggadah.

The Category of Halakhah

Halakhah, of course, is the institutionalization of those elements that in biblical Israel involved the three bureaucracies: the monarchy, the priesthood, and the judiciary. It is expressed in precise terminology, is based on objective criteria, and constitutes the grounding of the Jewish entity. The targum reflects the fundamental Rabbinic conviction that the written Torah is not the entirety of revelation. For, "The central conception distinguishing Rabbinic Judaism from all other conceptions of Judaism, past and present, is the belief in the myth of Moses as "our rabbi," and the conception that when God—also conceived in the model of the rabbi—revealed the Torah to Moses, he gave Torah in two parts, one in writing, the other as tradition handed on orally."[15] In fact, the targum refers the role and authority of the Rabbinical courts back to the biblical era itself, with allusions to their status and prerogatives ranging from the fixing of the Sabbatical year to the absolution from oaths, including practices that were no longer of practical consequence, such as those involving the Jerusalem Temple.[16]

---

[14] Thus, for example: 1) A first century targum to Job is mentioned by the Mishnah, and a fragment was discovered among the Dead Sea scrolls (11QtgJob), yet the extant Tg. Job is the product of ongoing development, containing both *verbum e verbo* translations differing from the Masoretic Hebrew text, as well as multiple readings and midrashic expansions. 2) The targum to Psalms intersperses addenda, including double-readings within literal translation. And like Tg. Job 4:10 it relates (Ps 108:10) to the fall of Constantinople in 476 C.E. 3) Tg Qohelet is paraphrastic in the extreme, attempting to reconcile the book's skepticism with the religious beliefs of post-biblical Judaism. 4) The targum to Chronicles is basically literal translation of the Hebrew. When citing synoptic passages from the Prophets it frequently follows Targum Jonathan, and when quoting the Pentateuch it occasionally utilizes Palestinian targum, with its onomastic suggesting a final composition in the eighth or ninth century C.E. 5) The targum to Proverbs bears Syriac linguistic characteristics, and where the Peshitta differs from the Masoretic Hebrew Bible it often corresponds to the former. 6) Extant targums to Esther widely differ in content and format despite this being the only hagiographic targum with regulations governing its recitation in the synagogue (Soferim 12:6).

[15] Jacob Neusner, "The Meaning of Torah Shebe'al Peh with Special Reference to Kelim and Ohalot," in *AJSreview* 1 (1976), p. 151. Further, "The Mishnah law is separate from, and autonomous of, Scripture, though in its unfolding it is made to interrelate, where it can, to Scripture" (p. 164). Rabbinic tradition lauds the ambiguity of Scripture, for "had the Torah been given in uncontroversial statements, there would be no room for the sage to exercise judgment in decision-making" (Y. San. 4:2).

[16] See PT Num. 30:3f., Deut. 15:2,17:8f., and cf. cultic practices in Num. 28:1ff., 29:1ff., 31, etc.

The targum is invariably declarative rather than argumentative: it never cites its textual sources and only rarely explains its exegetical logic. It shares an intellectual affinity with the Mishnah in that it presents itself as being *not* independent but explanatory of the Hebrew Bible. Although the Hebrew Scripture is clearly deemed the source of authority and legitimacy, the targums exercise the prerogative to determine which biblical verses should be translated literally and which should be expanded or explained. It also exercises the prerogative to choose from variant exegetical materials. By thus choosing *what* it hears within sacred Scripture and *how* it hears it, and by its selectivity in the Rabbinic law that it incorporates,[17] the targum becomes a statement *about* Scripture and not simply a translation *of* Scripture.

The targum almost invariably renders the biblical text according to the "Oral Law," harmonizing, explicating, specifying, and generalizing. For example, it amends the Bible's *lex talionis* in accordance with Rabbinic exegesis: "... *the monetary value of* an eye for an eye, *the monetary value of* a tooth for a tooth, *the monetary value of* a hand for a hand, *the monetary value of* a foot for a foot" (PsJ Deut. 19:21). And since biblical law permitted divorce, the targum renders the verse "But he hates divorce, says the Lord, God of Israel" (Mal. 2:16) by changing the subject, adding an object, and amending it in conformity with the majority Rabbinic opinion: "But *if you* hate *her*, divorce *her*, says the Lord, God of Israel."[18] Again, the divine edict to Hosea to "marry a woman of harlotry" and to beget children of harlotry from an adulteress (Hos. 1:2, 3:1) is a violation of Jewish law: an adulterous wife is forbidden both to her husband and to her paramour. The targum could neither translate this literally nor metaphorically, for, since adulterous marriages are necessarily dissolved, even if understood as a metaphor it would imply that the union of God and Israel was broken. Consequently, the targum presents the entire passage as an allegorical *usus loquendi*.

Jeremiah's describing the national catastrophe that God would bring upon Israel as "the fruit of their *thoughts*" implies that retribution may be exacted for mere intent. Since this contradicts Biblical-Rabbinic theology and law wherein only actual deeds create punishable liability, the targum amends "thoughts" to "deeds," with Israel to be punished for "the fruit of their *deeds*" (Tg Jer. 6:19). And regarding "the stubborn and rebellious son," the Bible had required due process, with the parents obliged to "seize him and bring him to the elders" (Deut. 21:19). So Zachariah's instruction that should a son prophesy falsely, "His father and mother who bore him shall pierce him through when he prophesies" (Zach. 13:3) constituted an apparent contradiction. Hence the targum paraphrases that his parents "shall *seize* him" when he prophesies, with his fate to be decided by judicial procedure (Tg Zach. 13:3).

The targum inserts a plethora of familiar Jewish regulations: the affixing of the *mezuzah* to doorposts and gates and the wearing of *tefillîn* (with even King Saul described as wearing phylacteries, and this during battle, no less!).[19] It specifies that on Yom Kippur, Jews are to abstain from eating, drinking, bathing, anointing, sandal wearing, and sexual intercourse, and it inserts dietary regulations such as refraining from eating live animals or severed limbs, proper slaughtering, removal of the

---

[17] For example, one brief section in Tg Qoh. includes diversities such as the intercalation of the lunar year (2:7), the rebellious son procedure (3:2), the prohibition against sexual intercourse during the mourning week (3:5), the rending of garments during mourning (3:7), and the purity of intent requirement for sacrificing (4:17)!

[18] So too Tg. Qoh. 7:26. Cf. Deut. 24:1ff., Is. 50:2, Jer. 3:1. Cf. contrary conclusion that, "He who divorces is hateful" (T. Git. 90b).

[19] PsJ Deut. 6:8, 11:18ff., T 2 Sam. 1:10.

sciatic nerve, and reciting Grace after eating.[20] Yet when surveying the targum's halakhah, neither its informing principle nor the criteria by which additions and alterations were made is at all clear, at least to this observer. For none of the apparent reasons was of sufficient force to produce consistency in any targum.

The Category of Aggadah

Targum texts are replete with aggadah, and the first determination regarding any passage is the category to which it belongs. For whereas halakhah strives for definitive conclusions, aggadah neither imposes authoritative belief nor precludes contradiction. It is not presented systematically or uniformly, nor does it conclusively prove its assertions. The genre constitutes values deriving either from an individual or from a segment of the community, whether of the masses or the learned academies. Thus, neither in the targum nor in cognate literature does it constitute necessarily universal Jewish, beliefs, attitudes, and norms. Further, since the sages utilized hyperbole rhetorically, distinguishing between the categories of halakhah and haggadah is absolutely essential for correctly ascertaining the intent of any dictum.[21]

The many internally-contradictory elements in any targum's aggadah attest to the eclectic use of sources and the variant purposes to which they were put, as well as to the non-dogmatic status of the genre itself.[22] This reflects the emphatic Rabbinic rejection of any exclusivist interpretation of Scripture. The many divergences within and among the targums necessitate (and presuppose!) inter-textual reading.

The sheer volume of aggadah in many targum texts reflects the fact that whereas juridical halakhah was the preserve of the educated elite, the homiletic aggadah was a genre to which the masses had ready access.[23] Further, targumic thought is characteristically presented "existentially," less in systematic abstraction and intellectual definition than in specific prescription and application. Thus, whereas there are no for-

---

[20] Cf. PT Gen. 9:4, 43:16, 45:4, 48:20, Num. 29:7, Deut. 8:10, 12:27.

[21] To read hyperbole literally is to misconstrue a text: "Whoever transgresses the words of the School of Hillel is subject to the death penalty" (Y. Ber. 1:4) is a *facon de parler* and not a juridical ruling!

[22] For example, PsJ to Genesis is replete with internal contradictions: in 2:7 Adam is created from the soil of the four corners of the earth, yet in 3:23 he is created from soil of the Holy Land. In 10:9 Nimrod is termed the arch-rebel against God, whereas in 10:11 he is eulogized as a righteous exemplar of his generation. In 16:3 Hagar is freed by Sarah before being given as a wife to Abraham, whereas in 21:14 she is still referred to as a slave. In 37:32 Zilpah's sons bring Joseph's tunic to Jacob, whereas in 38:25 it is Judah who brings it. There is direct contradiction between 43:14 and 45:27 as to whether Jacob retained his prophetic powers during Joseph's absence. In 45:12 Joseph identifies himself to his brethren by speaking Hebrew, whereas in 45:4 he uses the mark of his circumcision to identify himself as a Hebrew. In 49:21 the fleet Naphtali races to bring the tidings of Joseph's being alive and who later brings the ownership document for the family cave, whereas in 27:46 the messenger was Asher's daughter Serah.

[23] The Talmud homily compares the popular haggadah to tinsel goods to which all can have access and the scholarly halakhah to precious stones that are available only to the wealthy (T. Sot. 40a), yet they were deemed complementary, for, "Those who interpret the implications of Scripture declare: 'If you want to know the Creator of the World, study haggadah, for through it you will come to know God and cleave to his ways'" (Sifre Deut. 11:22).

mulations or abstract analyses of loyalty, righteousness, holiness, and mercy, there are both recurrent exhortations to, and specific legislation of, behavior predicated upon those "value concepts." Indeed, by incorporating both halakhah and aggadah, the targum conveys those human values that have a distinctive expression and consequence in the Jewish tradition and that may, therefore, be legitimately designated "Jewish values."

The most common conceptual categories of the targum are basal aspects of post-biblical Judaism: 1) the monotheistic idea, 2) the uniqueness of God, 3) names and circumlocutions of the divine (Memra, Shekînah, Yeqara, etc.), 4) the Torah as cosmic design, 5) creation and its aftermath, 6) astral influences on human destiny (mazal), 7) the angelic, the demonic and the occult, 8) divine revelations through word and wonder, 9) theodicy and the attribute of justice, 10) theodicy and the attribute of mercy, 11) the free will of mortal beings, 12) the evil urge in humanity, 13) the election of Israel, 14) the immutability of the divine covenant, 15) the concept of the Dual Torah, 16) the legitimacy of Rabbinic authority, laws, and institutions, 17) the divine judgment of mortals by their deeds, 18) the efficacy of repentance in averting punishment, 19) the divine receptivity to prayer, 20) rituals and their rationale, 21) the Torah study imperative, 22) the holiness imperative, 23) separation of the holy from the profane, 24) the category of individual merit (zekût), 25) the category of imputed merit, 26) the category of individual guilt, 27) the category of imputed guilt, 28) martyrdom and the sanctification of God's name (qiddûsh ha-shem), 29) human history and Jewish historiography, 30) the land of Israel in the past and the future, 31) the religious role of Jerusalem in the past and the future, 32) the theology of the exile, 33) the era of the messiah, 34) resurrection and the afterlife, 35) refutations of sectarian, Christian, Zoroastrian, and Moslem polemics.

The Targum on the Jewish Condition

The basic Jewish self-definition of being a people-in-exile pervades the entire targum, most succinctly in the targum to Lamentations. This commentary is marked by both exhortation and hope, describing catastrophes of the past and the eventual salvation for which Jews prayed. The targum emphasizes the religious aspect and relevance of the ancient and stylized Hebrew text, for unless historical events are invested with a "meta-historical" significance their very particularity makes them increasingly irrelevant as time progresses. Further, since the Jews were politically and militarily powerless, such emphasis would be ironically inappropriate, whereas religious enlightenment could find a receptive and responsible audience. The targum begins by asserting that there was meaning and justification for the national catastrophe. It was neither a function of historical "accident" nor of divine caprice, but the inevitable and deserved *quid pro quo* for acting against God's will (1:1–8 *et seq.*). This historiography theodicy necessarily magnified Israel's supposed transgressions, but it assimilated the disaster into a meaningful and hopeful theology.

The targum attributes the book of Lamentations to the prophet Jeremiah (1:1f., 18), yet whereas in 1:18 (as in Tg 2 Chr. 35:23) it reflects the tradition that the book mourns the death of righteous King Josiah, it telescopes history, so that the very same verse also deals with the destruction of the First Temple by Nebuchadnezzar and the razing of the Second Temple by the Romans (1:19)![24] The historical perspective of the targum extends from the days of Adam until

---

[24] It also refers to supposed events of the internecine Hasmonean wars (2:9) within a context including disparate events, such as that of Moses and the spies on one hand (2:17),

the days of the messiah, concentrating on Jewish polity from the conquest of the land of Israel through the extended exile that will continue until the restoration. The targum notes the irony of it all: the Hebrews had once wept over their entry into the land of Israel and now their descendants weep over having been banished from it (1:2 *et seq.*). This aspect of traditional Judaism is manifest throughout the targum: once they neglected the weal of the Temple, Jerusalem, and the Promised Land, and now they yearn for their restoration in the "end of days." For the Jews bear the burdens of a dispersed and despised people-in-exile living on the suffrage of its Christian or Moslem hosts who claim to represent the exclusively true faith.[25]

Judaism and Christianity related differently to Lamentations and to the destruction of the Second Temple, of course, and the targum contains elements basic to the Jewish-Christian disputation. These sometimes involve an actual point of contact or divergence between the Jewish interpretation of a given text and Christian treatment of it. Others involve elements of Jewish exegesis repudiating a concept or belief so prominently associated with Christianity that any Jew, with even slight contacts, could be expected to have heard about it in some form. For example, has Israel been abandoned or, as the Jews maintained, is Israel being punished? Is the destruction of the Temple and the exile of the People proof of the covenant's having been abrogated by God, or, as the Jews maintained, were these punishments proof that the covenant was still in force? It is hardly unreasonable to assume that "polemical" and "apologetic" concerns were among the targum's exegetical motivations.[26]

Thus, for example, whereas in Christian exegesis, "the breath of our nostrils, the anointed of the Lord, was taken in their pits . . ." refers to Jesus, whose self-sacrifice created the new dispensation from the burden of the Law, the targum identifies the subject as the Torah-following King Josiah and his killers as the Egyptians (cf. 3:27, 39, 41, 4:20, 5:5, etc). And the targum lauds the bearing of the "yoke of the command-

---

and the fall of Constantinople, capital of the Eastern Roman Empire on the other (4:21)! See Étan Levine, *The Aramaic Version of Lamentations* (New York, 1976), *ad loc.*

[25] Thus, where the maiden asks her lover, "For why should I be as a wanderer among the flocks of your companions," the targum has Moses question God, "For why should they be harassed among the herds of the Esauites and Ishmaelites who associate their idols with you as divine companions" (Tg Cant. 1:7)? And an exhortation after Islam's expansion and conquest of Palestine in 636–638 C.E. tells that if God's beloved Israel is willing to be strong among the nations and willing to pay out silver for gaining permission to declare the uniqueness of the name of the Master of the World, then the heavenly angels will be at the side of Israel's sages, and even if she be poor in merits derived from obeying the commandments, they will still seek divine mercy on her behalf (Tg Cant. 8:8). This refers to a special poll tax (*jizya*) paid to Moslem authorities for permission to practice Judaism. Only by this means would expanding Islam come to terms with the Jewish religious minority and absorb it politically as an *ahl al-kitab* exempted from the choice between Islam or the sword. The realities of Jewish life within the Moslem world are subsumed in the targum's interpretation of "Woe is me . . . that I dwell beside the tents of Kedar" as "Woe is me . . . that I dwell among the tents of the Arabs" (Tg Ps. 120:5).

[26] This applies wherever the targum injects a concept contrary to any well-known sectarian, Zoroastrian, Christian, or Moslem theological belief, idea, or symbol of its own that is incompatible with Judaism. Cf. R. Loewe, "Apologetic Motifs in the Targum to Song of Songs," in A. Altmann, ed., *Biblical Essays* (Cambridge, MA, 1966), pp. 159–196. See Jewish refutations of New Testament texts and exegesis in Étan Levine, *Un Judio Lee el Nuevo Testamento* (Madrid, 1980).

ments," affirming that acts bring salvation and that it is the enemies of Israel who create a burden of the Law by making the Torah scrolls into sandbags to burden the exiles! Recurrently the tragedy is blamed on false prophets and leaders who had influenced the people to violate the covenant, and, as had been foretold to Moses, this transgression eventuated in destruction and exile.[27] Nevertheless, Torah, repentance, and prayer yet remain, so, "Arise, O Congregation of Israel dwelling in exile. Busy yourselves with the Mishnah by night, for God's presence is among you, and with the words of the Torah at the beginning of the morning watch. Pour away your hearts' perversions like water, and turn in repentance. And pray in the synagogue in God's presence. Raise your hands to him in prayer..." (2:19).[28]

To counter any imputation that the Jews have been divinely rejected, where the Hebrew reads "she has *no comforter*," the targum has this refer to the *false gods* Israel had followed (1:2). God only appears to be "*as* an enemy" (2:4f., 5:5, etc.), and, understood literally, the Hebrew text states that Jerusalem is only "*like* a widow," i.e., only temporarily separated from her husband, like a woman *temporarily* unclean (1:1, 9, 17.) Similarly, to circumvent any antinomian implication that with the Temple's destruction the Sabbath and Festivals had been annulled, the targum paraphrases that the "*enjoyment* of Sabbaths and festivals has been annulled" (2:6).

The targum to Lamentations adheres to the traditional Jewish mourning practice of not allowing comforting and consolation to mute grief and legitimate pain. Yet while it specifies that the ninth of Ab was established as a fast day of lamentation, it also reassures that the exile is temporary: the messiah will arrive, there will be a great judgment day, and an ultimate reward awaits Jews who observe God's law, engage in repentance and prayer, and keep their faith in the national restoration.[29] It lauds the role of the suffering servant, including martyrdom for the sake of sanctifying God's name. For the suffering experienced in this world also constitutes the punishment for minor infractions, in order to assure an unalloyed reward in the world-to-come (3:28).

In sum, just as Jeremiah's lament over God's becoming to him "like a disappointing river, like waters that fail" was piously reversed by the targum into, "*Your word shall not disappoint me like a river whose waters fail*" (Tg Jer. 15:18), so was the somber book of Lamentations "translated" to convey the triumphal faith that, "*You will proclaim freedom to your people the House of Israel, through the Messiah King, as you did through Moses and Aaron on the day that you brought forth Israel from Egypt. And my youths will gather together from every place where they were scattered on the day of your fierce anger, O Lord, when there was no escapee or survivor among them . . .*" (Tg. Lam. 2:22).

---

[27] See 2:14, 17, 3:13, etc. And note the rendering of "For he has given you the early rain (*môreh*) in right measure (*lesedaqah*)..." as "For he has restored to you your *teachers* in *righteousness*..." (Tg Joel 2:23).

[28] This negates Pauline Christianity, which promulgated two premises about Judaism (apparently to unknowing gentiles): that Jewish righteousness required perfect conformity to the Law and that God in his righteousness cannot forgive penitent sinners *freely*, hence the necessity for the expiatory death of Jesus (Rom. 3:25, Gal. 3:10, 12). This shift of emphasis from forgiveness to "justification," was a theological posture totally rejected by all Pharisees.

[29] Cf. 1:9, 21f., 2:19, 3:24ff., 31, 39 ff., 4:22f., etc.

The Targum and Jewish Thought

One characteristic and succinct source of the genre's conceptual categories is the targum to Qohelet. This controversial biblical book had always been subjected to criticism, even by its own editor's pietistic epilogue (Qoh. 12:12ff.)! In fact, after Aqiba's time, the only conflict concerning the biblical canon involved Qohelet. And even when this most heterodox of all biblical works became the last to be added to the canon in the second century at the Yabneh academy, it clearly could not be transmitted without commentary.[30] Hence, the targum "translates" Qohelet into a handbook of Jewish pietism, with its techniques ranging from subtle changes of syntax, prepositional emendations, adjectival modifications, semantic alterations, and nuance shifts to blatant incorporations of explicating addenda. Nevertheless, the targum is presenting *peshat*! For its intent is to present what it considers to be the *primary* meaning of scripture, and "scripture never loses is *peshat*," no matter how many additional conclusions may be drawn from it.[31]

Just as the author (or redactor) of Qohelet had exploited Solomon's reputation for wisdom and wealth to legitimate his own empirical claims, so did the rabbis who attributed the book to Solomon gain its acceptance into the Bible and justify interpreting it according to the spirit of Pharisaic Judaism. And by adopting the tradition that "Solomon had prophesied concerning the distant future and the world-to-come of the messiah,"[32] the targum could render this cynical tract in the certainty that "All eating and drinking mentioned in this book refer to Torah and good deeds," and that luxurious garb and perfume refer to "good deeds and Torah study" that gain one's entry into the world-to-come, whereas "naked" meaning "bareness of merit."[33] And the targum's extensive literary allusions reflect the confident assumption that its readers (or listeners) were intimate both with the Bible and with its relevant Rabbinic commentaries.[34]

The targum avoids the manifest skepticism, determinism, and pessimism of the

---

[30] Qohelet challenges the very bases of religion, law, and ethics, denying divine justice, the afterlife, the meaningfulness of history, and the worth of human endeavor. He declares that all is cyclical, determined, wearying, and futile, that God is unknowable and frightening, and that divine justice in this world or in any imagined afterlife is an unverified self-delusion. Therefore, he espouses a golden mean of pragmatic amorality and the utilization of secular wisdom to most fully benefit from the relative pleasures that life affords. The Talmud records that the sages attempted to sequester the book because it was deemed internally contradictory (e.g. 2:4 vs. 7:4) and tended toward sectarianism. And some statements opposed the Pentateuch's dicta, such as Qoh. 11:9, which urges the youth to indulge in revelry that contradicts the injunction not to be led astray by desire (Num. 15:39). See M. Yad. 3:5, T. Shab. 30b and Qoh. Rabbah 1. Cf. Levine, *The Aramaic Version of Qohelet*.

[31] The concept *peshat* designates that aspect of a biblical text that, *to the person using the term*, conveys its *primary* meaning or significance; the term *derash* designates an *additional* facet of the biblical text, not a preferable alternative nor a substitute for the *peshat*.

[32] Tg Qoh. 1:1, Tg. 1 Kngs. 6:3, T. Sot. 48b.

[33] See 5:14, 8:15, 9:7ff. Cf. Qoh. Rabbah, *passem*, B. Shab. 30b, 153a.

[34] It opens with the "confession" of its supposed author, Solomon, who admits to having been estranged from God and deposed, accounting for the phrase, "I, Qohelet, *was* king..." (1:2, 12 *et seq.*). It also mentions Adam and Eve (7:29), Abraham and Sarah (4:13f., 7:28), Nimrod (4:13f.), Joseph (7:19), Moses (12:11), Elijah (10:20), Saul (2:15), the House of David (1:1f., 10:17), Solomon (1:1 *et seq.*), Jeraboam (1:2, 2:18, 3:11, 10:16), Rehaboam (1:2), Hezekiah (10:17), Manasseh (10:9), Rabshakeh (10:9) Sheba b. Bikri (3:11), and the Sanhedrin of Yavneh (2:4). It speaks of events in the Desert, in the land of Israel, and in Jerusalem, the division of the united monarchy, the cults

biblical Qohelet by reframing the opening question as to what benefits remain of life's labors. For the phrase "under the sun" itself suggests the recognition of another realm. Hence, "What remains after a man's death of all his labor which he labored under the sun *in this world, other than if he studied the word of God, to receive a good reward in the world-to-come before the Master of the Universe?*" (1:3).[35]

As the targum negates Qohelet's philosophy of life it also contradicts his concept of death. For mortality is *not* the ultimate injustice obliterating the distinction between the wise and the foolish, the righteous and the wicked. Rather, it is the logically necessary precondition for inaugurating the *poena talionis* and moral recompense. Speculation as to the day of one's death, the messianic age, the great judgment day and the world-to-come are indeed futile (and forbidden), yet this hardly makes these realities less certain. So one should prepare in this world for "*all* the days of life," accumulating merit for the eventual judgment of mortals *according to their deeds*.[36]

So whereas to Qohelet the ideal person is a Semiticized version of the "philosopher-king," the targum idealizes the saintly Torah sage (personified as a spiritualized Solomon), an exemplar of goodness (rather than ritual): bestowing charity, comforting mourners, serving scholars, and creating peace between all people. Since power and material wealth not used for charity undermine their owner's afterlife, Qohelet's adjuration about economic diversity ("cast your bread upon the waters") must refer to bestowing alms, and to "find it in the end of days" must signify ultimate reward in the Garden of Eden for the merit (*zekût*) of having supported the hungry poor in this world.[37] And where Qohelet rails against the injustice in the world—grinding oppression, cruelty,

---

erected in Dan and Bethel, and the Babylonian exile (1:2, 12, 16, 2:4f., 14, 18, 4:15, 5:28, 7:4, 10:6, 16f., 20, 12:11). It refers to institutions too: the monarchy, the priesthood, the judiciary, the circles of prophets and the assembly of sages (e.g., 1:8, 2:4, 12, 3:16, 4:17, 5:6, 8, 19, 7:1, 9:1, 10:6, 9, 20, 12:11).

[35] Again, whatever the length of a person's life, "After having served the Master of the Universe in this world, he will inherit in the world-to-come a reward for his labors" (5:11).

[36] Death may be a punishment, as in the case of unrepentant evildoers, yet it may also be a blessing, as in the case of the righteous who are granted respite and spared the necessity of experiencing trauma. For only the sinners truly die; having received on earth whatever rewards were due them, they die like beasts, whereas the righteous never actually die but are transported. Whoever has served God, observed the Law, performed good deeds, and shared his material assets is rewarded appropriately. And whoever labored in the Torah on earth is brought to the heavenly academy. An afterlife (*resurrectio carnis*, apparently) of deserved reward awaits the faithful. Cf. 1:4, 8, 18, 2:26, 3:19f., 4:2, 5:10f., 6:2, 6, 7:17, 24, 8:4, 15f., 9:4f., 19, 10:1, 11.

[37] 11:1. See 5:10 ff., 16, 9:7, 10:19. On meritorious deeds, cf. 2:8, 4:12, 5:6, 7:2, 16, 8:1, 9:16, etc., with the titles "Righteous" and "Sage" often combined. Performing meritorious deeds and studying Torah produces *zekût* or "accrued merit." This is conceived as an "interest-bearing" account that accrues to a person's benefit both in this world and in the world-to-come. Bearers of *zekût* avert evil decrees, alter nature, intercede for others through their prayers, and bring benefit upon all humankind, since the saintly and wicked elicit divine response upon their kinfolk as well as upon themselves (2:8; 4:9f., 12, 7:3, 9:16, 11:3). Indeed, unless one accumulates the merits of Torah and good deeds, a person is virtually dead while alive, for only these remain of all an individual's activity in this world (1:5, 6:6, 8, 7:15, 8:14, 9:5, 10, 11:7). A righteous person may often be unrecognized as such by other people and unrewarded by God in this world, but a future reward is assured. For the righteous person is saved from Gehinna and is brought to the Garden of Eden to sit among the saints to bask in the divine presence. Hence Qohelet's person who "sits in darkness" is any person who leaves this world "naked" of merit for the world-to-come (5:14f., 6:4, 7:1, 10:19, 11:3).

the absence of punishment, and the apparent similarity of fate awaiting both the saintly and the wicked, with God ruling indifferently, despotically and arbitrarily—the targum distinguishes between the fate of the wicked and that of the righteous. For when the righteous suffer and the wicked flourish, the injustice is more apparent than real: it is only so that in the world-to-come their respective rewards and punishments will be unalloyed.[38]

The condition of the Jewish people did require their having to reconcile obedience to God with allegiance to foreign rule. Hence the instruction, "I adjure you not to rebel against the government, even if its decrees against you should be severely repressive, for you must keep the commands of the king. But should you be ordered to deny God and forsake the Torah then do not obey" (Tg Qoh. 8:2). In this spirit, the patriarch Abraham is described as an exemplary Jewish martyr who, in the familiar midrashic motif reflecting an *auto de fe*, is willing to give up his life rather than worship the idols of Nimrod.[39]

The Jews were not living in complete cultural isolation. And since Christian exegesis exploited Qohelet to buttress its own theological posture just as the targum interpreted Qohelet in conformity with Rabbinic tradition, the question of whether polemics—specifically anti-Christian polemics—motivated the targum is surely legitimate. For example, while it interprets according to the Jewish principle that "All eating and drinking mentioned in this book refer to Torah and good deeds," in Christian exegesis the phrase refers to "the true bread and wine," i.e., Christ's body and blood.[40] And where the targum stresses the availability of divine forgiveness through bearing "the yoke of the law" and repentance, Pauline Christianity shifted the emphasis from forgiveness to "justification" based on two theological bases regarding Judaism that Jews themselves considered absurd.[41] Yet since the classifications "apologetic" and "polemical" are highly subjective,[42] all that can be demonstrated is that the targum emphasizes theological truths of an importance equivalent to that which Christianity attaches to its own concepts and symbols that are incompatible with Judaism.[43] And though parts of the Hebrew Scriptures (and post-biblical Jewish texts)

---

[38] Cf. 2:10, 16f., 3:9, 13, 5:7, 6:6, 7:15f., 20, 25, 8:6, 13f., 9:14, etc. Human suffering (individual and societal) is multi-factorial: for the wicked it is punitive while for the righteous it is purifying (1:1, 12, 2:15, 3:18, 7:3, 10:6). God is both transcendent and immanent: as a moral deity he relates to human beings and intervenes in history. And although divine wisdom is beyond human ken, he reveals his will through Scripture, his Holy Spirit and his prophets for he is accessible, responsive and loving (1:12, 5:7, 8:1, 7, 12, 9:9, 10:9, 11:3).

[39] Cf. 4:13f. Happily (and predictably) enough, the legend relates that God rescued him, Nimrod was deposed, and Abraham became king of Canaan. Again, never had there been anyone as righteous as Abraham, whose righteousness exceeded that of the thousand kings who built the Tower of Babel (7:28).

[40] See 2:24, 8:15. Cf. T. Shab. 30b, Qoh. Rabbah 8:15 and Jerome, *ad. loc.* And in 6:10 where it rendered "man" (Heb. *'adam*) as Adam, Christian exegesis understood it as signifying Jesus Christ in human form.

[41] These were that Jewish salvation required perfect conformity to the law of the covenant (Gal. 3:10), and that God in justice could not forgive penitent sinners *freely*, hence the necessity for the expiatory death of Jesus (Rom. 3:25).

[42] Thus, to validate the claim that the targum is polemically motivated must one demonstrate points of divergence between the targum and Christian exegesis of the identical biblical text? Or does it suffice to indicate how the targum explicitly or implicitly repudiates concepts known by Jews to be prominently associated with Christianity?

[43] In Christian exegesis, anything that in *interpretatio litteralis* opposes Church doctrine must be understood by the *interpretatio spiritualis*, not meaning "spiritual" in general, but specifically Christological.

may be opaque regarding things eschatological that Christianity stresses, others are explicit about the essential concept of resurrection, when "Many of those who sleep in the dust of the earth shall awaken, some to eternal life and some to eternal contempt" (Dan. 12:2), and when "The sages shall shine like the brightness of the heavens, and those who turn the populace to righteousness like the stars forever" (Dan. 12:3).

What the targum does indicate is that normative Jewish belief generally corresponded to what the authoritative scholars and expositors systematically presented as doctrine. The liturgy, law, and theology as represented in the targum were hardly matters of individual opinion. Deep within the systemic logic of Rabbinic Judaism (and recognized by others such as Paul in the New Testament and Josephus in Antiquities) was an eschatology involving the resurrection of the dead at the end of days. The targum expressed the essential Jewish beliefs that had existed long before Christianity came into existence: the resurrection, the last judgment and the restoration of the righteous to Eden, and the logical action consequences of this eschatology.[44]

The targum to Qohelet does contain elements of folk religion. Thus, on the one hand, it properly refers to God as the transcendent "Master of the Universe," "Heaven," and "Creator" who immanently intervenes in nature and human history through his "holy spirit" (*rûha de-qûdsha*), "presence" (*shekîntah*) or "word" (*memra', dibbûra*), dispensing reward and punishment.[45] Yet according to the old saying, "The almighty has many agents" (Num. Rabbah 18), and the targum also refers to angels and shades, named and unnamed, functioning in the world.[46] Furthermore, although the targum adjures against the study and practice of astrology (11:4), on fifteen different occasions it refers to *mazal*, a term variously signifying a heavenly body or constellation, often causative of immutable fate. And sometimes God acts indirectly through the intermediary agency of celestial powers that determine lifespan, wealth, and happiness.[47] This internally-contradictory posture is a problematic characteristic of Pharisaic-Rabbinic tradition, with indecision as to whether the influence of the planets on human life applies to the people of Israel, and the entire question of cosmic determinism vs. human free will. The *mazal* elements in the targum testify to the grip of astrology, extending even to cases where *mazal* triumphed over *zekût*, i.e., accrued merit! God determines *mazal* for reward and punishment, it is true, yet, due to its mechanistic and deterministic aspect, sometimes *mazal* is used to account for inexplicable events and apparent inequities. Thus, life itself—from the choice of a good wife to material weal—is dependent not only on merit but on *mazal*.[48]

Whereas the biblical Qohelet lauded pragmatic, secular sagacity,[49] the targum radically changes it all: "wisdom" becomes

---

[44] Thus, for the individual, "It is good to wait and be silent until God's salvation comes. It is good for a young man to train himself to bear the yoke of the commandments. Let him dwell alone and be silent, bearing the sufferings that come upon him for the sake of the unity of God's name, that are sent to punish him for the minor sin that he commits in this world, until he have mercy upon him and remove them from him, so that he may accept him perfected in the world-to-come" (Tg Lam. 3:26ff.).

[45] See 1:2, 12, 2:15, 24, 3:14, 4:4,7, 5:19, 6:6f., 10, 7:2f., 12, 14f., 8:6, 9:1f., 10:8, 11:3, 7, 12:13.

[46] Cf. 1:12, 5:5, 9: 9, 20, 10:9, 20, 12:5.

[47] See 3:9, 4:9, 5:17f., 6:2, 7, 7:15, 27, 9:2, 10:6. The term *mazal* may mean planetary influence *in distinction* to direct divine intervention, and it may sometimes represents unexplainable "luck" or "happenstance."

[48] 9:2, 9, 11f., 10:6, 11:4f. Cf. M. Abot 3:16, Y. Ta. 64b, B. Shab. 53b, 156a, B. Hul. 7b, B. M.Q. 28a, Tanhuma', *Shofetîm* 11a, Gen. Rabbah 1.

[49] Although the mortal search for ultimate truth is futile and frustrating, he repeatedly

"Torah," and the sage becomes the traditional *talmid hakam*, personifying virtue as well as wisdom, like the targum's exemplar Solomon who requests and is granted moral wisdom to distinguish good from evil (1:13). The targum echoes the Talmud's emphasis upon the *study* of Torah rather than the rote *practice* of its mandates. It contains no less than forty encomia of Torah study, and even the disparaging addendum of the biblical redactor is converted into a Torah exhortation (12:12ff.)! Although a person must be involved in mundane affairs, self-interest dictates that one's emphasis should be upon Torah wisdom, for it is more potent than the greatest secular power, since it benefits the individual and the community, both in this world and in the world-to-come.[50] Yet all this requires resisting the temptations of the omnipresent "Evil Inclination" that dwells in the human heart.[51]

The targum reflects the consensus of Rabbinic anti-esotericism: there are limitations to mortal wisdom. Torah is not a magical tool for obtaining bread in a time of famine nor for discovering the forbidden mysteries into which it is forbidden to delve: the day of one's death, the distant past, the messianic age, and the world-to-come. Yet God's will and the purpose and direction of human life are knowable, and although Torah is obtained through arduous human effort, God assists those who tread the path of righteousness. The sage who sits with the Torah scholars and identifies with Israel's pathos helps to avert the "evil decree" both by his sagacity and by his prayer for divine intercession. And he himself is assured the beatitudes of the world-to-come.[52] A person's Torah wisdom will remain with him eternally, for "just as he occupies himself with it in this world, and exerts himself by learning, so will it remain with him in the grave and not desert him, just as a wife does not desert her husband to sleep alone" (5:11).

By the same token, whereas the biblical Qohelet describes prayer as a futile petition to an unresponsive, unfathomable deity, the targum stresses the accessibility of God and the efficacy of prayer that may elicit divine forgiveness, alter human destiny, and free one from determined fate. Although there are especially favorable times for petition, one should never desist, since prayer averts many impending individual and societal disasters the very purposes of which may include motivating people to repentance and prayer.[53] Human destiny is not irrevocably sealed as long as one is alive. There is no automatic, magical efficacy to prayer, yet sincerity and the merit of the petitioner may assure its effectiveness. Righteous persons are those who repent during their lifetimes, thereby assuring their salvation in the afterlife, whereas the person who dies unrepentant "dies like an animal."[54]

---

praises the sage and the path of wisdom: a utilitarian guide through life's shoals, unrelieved by any sense of manifest destiny, social responsibility or involvement of the divine.

[50] See 2:10, 25, 3:12, 4:17, 5:6, 11, 17, 6:5f., 12, 7:5, 11, 13, 17f., 23, 8:15., 9:1, 4, 9ff., 10:4, 10, 11:7f., 12:10, 12. Torah is an antidote against one's "Evil Impulse," and desisting from this life-sustaining activity can even result in death (7:15, 10:4).

[51] See 3:11, 5:11, 19, 7:29, 9:14, 10:1, 4. The targum emphasizes interpersonal, rather than ritual, wrongdoing. Misdeeds include oppressing the poor, perverting justice, unworthy speech, not sharing one's food, engaging in witchcraft, carousing, informing to the secular authorities, not helping the oppressed to resist when evil is committed, and, in general, not distinguishing good from evil (2:2, 3:15f., 4:17, 5:5, 16, 6:6, 10:11, 11:4, 9, etc.) For religious sins of arrogance, idolatry and neglect, see 1:12, 3:12, 4:13, 5:17, 6:6, 7:9, 26, 8:1, 10:9f., etc.

[52] Cf. 1:8, 2:4, 14, 26, 3:11, 7:4f., 7, 24, 8:1, 9:11, 16f.

[53] See 2:14, 4:10, 17, 7:3f., 8:3, 5, 9, 10:12.

[54] Cf. 1:15, 3:18f., 4:17, 7:20, 9:5, 16, 12:13.

In sum, the targum overturns every heterodoxical stone in Qohelet's literary edifice and reconstructs a structure of Rabbinic concepts: a) It is not that "all is vanity," but it is the evil of the world that is vanity. b) It is not secular wisdom that is the *summum bonum* but Torah study and good deeds; the pious scholar brings blessings upon himself and all humanity. c) The suffering of the innocent purges them so they may receive unalloyed reward in the world-to-come. d) God is not frightening, arbitrary and unknowable; he is a merciful, responding ruler who welcomes the penitent and the prayerful. e) The results of human conduct are not unpredictable: appropriate divine reward and punishment are certainties. f) No amoral "golden mean" is the ideal, but unqualified commitment to God's law. g) Life should not be exploited for its transient, relative pleasures: it is, rather, an opportunity for earning eternal bliss. i) There is no uniform finality to life, for beyond the mystery of the grave there is the answer, the reckoning and the meaningfulness. j) Prayer and repentance are not exercises in futility; they affect the course of events in this world and in the world-to-come. k) Torah study creates an eternal reward.

Summary

The conceptual categories of the literary genre targum span the entire spectrum of Jewish thought throughout the first seven centuries C.E. In fact, later additions were incorporated into these texts even when Aramaic ceased to be a Jewish *lingua franca*. And the targum's continued influence after its final composition is attested by its having been retained in synagogue scriptural lections, studied co-extensively with the Hebrew readings of the liturgical calendar, cited in Bible commentaries and Rabbinic texts, and widely copied in manuscript form and later retained in the printed *Biblia Rabbinica*.

The library of Jewish books composed during the past two millennia contains vastly more detailed and sophisticated philosophy, theology, ethics, jurisprudence, linguistics, and exegesis than that found in the targum. Yet the targum remains the most concise overview of a long dialectical Jewish conversation with the Bible that united a widely diverse miscellany of people separated by time, place, and circumstances into a bibliocentric community. By relating the Hebrew Bible to the evolving aggregate of Jewish concepts, values, metaphors, symbols, experiences and behavioral norms the targum sustained historical integrity and intellectual coherence.

Despite its eventual decline in Jewish ritual and study, three factors have stimulated a modern surge of interest in targum: epigraphic discoveries in the Judean desert and elsewhere, heightened scholarly recognition of diversity within the Judaism of late antiquity, and the identification of a particularly valuable early targum manuscript.[55] Since the targum literature constitutes a repository of law and lore that includes unofficial, unedited texts, it can help correct the myopic tendency to attribute to the entire Jewish people only the ideas and values of its intellectual elite. Indeed, by critically transcending ahistoricistic,

---

[55] Vatican Library Ms. Neofiti #1 was identified as being a complete Palestinian Targum to the Pentateuch antedating the so-called Targum Jonathan ben Uzziel. The text with its copious marginalia was published with a scholarly commentary and polyglot translation. An index (compiled by the present author) providing literary sources and parallels where the targum differs from the Hebrew Bible. See A. Diez Macho, *Neophyti 1. Targum Palestinense Ms. de la Biblioteca Vaticana, I-V* (Madrid/Barcelona, 1968–1979).

harmonistic methodologies, a host of highly competent Judaica scholars are now contributing valuable insights into the targum itself and into that people of the Book who articulated their theology through the genre.

Bibliography

Faur, José, *Golden Doves with Silver Dots; Semiotics and Textuality in Rabbinic Tradition* (Bloomington, 1986).

Levine, Étan, *The Aramaic Version of the Bible; Contents and Context* (Berlin and New York, 1988).

ÉTAN LEVINE
University of Haifa

Theological Foundations of Rabbinic Exegesis

While there is a common misconception that Jewish theology is defined by the Hebrew Bible, Judaism in fact was established through the sages' interpretation of the Bible,[1] found in the midrashic literature of Rabbinic Judaism, which flourished in the first six centuries C.E. and continued into the Middle Ages. This article assumes that the application of the *middot*, the hermeneutic rules used in this Rabbinic, exegetical enterprise, referred to as "midrash," retains traces of the theological approach developed by the rabbis. The term "theological" in respect to midrashic literature characterizes the Rabbinic engagement with the divine.

The problematic nature of the midrashic texts, which do not communicate the circumstances that led to their creation, requires that the evidence for any theological categories be raised out of the interior logic of the data themselves that classify and define the system of the rabbis. The *middot* may represent the bridge between how the rabbis pursued their exegetical activities and how one can extract their theology. We assume the rabbis attempted to gain control over the material they approached. Controlling and limiting interpretation could have been a Rabbinic theological agenda, through which the sages created Judaism and distinguished it from other religious expressions.

The notion of midrash that religion and law are inseparable may be explained by the post-modern conception of the essence of religion. To the postmodern mind, religion is often a state of faith rather than action, spiritual rather than concrete. Midrash brings into the original revelation the continuing revelation of its readers. Judaism is a response to God's asking the Jewish people to live in a certain way. It is a realization that all of life is not only the sphere of interest of human beings alone but also God's. According to Judaism, God gave the Torah on Mount Sinai and then relinquished the right to interpret and change it. This responsibility was given to the sages of each generation, who are charged with interpreting the law according to the needs and problems of their own time. The resulting multiple readings of a particular scriptural lemma revolve around its essential meaning, which

---

[1] The author dedicates this essay to Professor Jacob Neusner, on the occasion of his seventieth birthday.

can never be adequately expressed in human language.

A word about Rabbinic reasoning as found in the midrashic texts: The sages' reasoning implies that there is a basic rationality to Scripture, that Scripture's code can be decoded by the *middot*, which can be applied again and again to different textual passages.[2] Every halakhic dispute contains a number of logical possibilities, which may be presented in a dialogical structure of midrash.[3] The question may be asked: What happens if contradictory rulings emerge or if neither side is able to persuade the other? Furthermore, this exegetical scheme does not explain why Rabbinic opinion may be more important than anyone else's. What is the particular claim of the rabbis to sole legal authority? The rabbis' answer is that their special education and their place in the chain of tradition gives them insight into the logic of the Torah that is unavailable to lay people. Rabbinic argument involves fluency in the already received corpus of Rabbinic law and argumentation. This insures that the evolving results of Rabbinic consideration and decision will combine with the received material to describe a single coherent whole. The sages' claim to the correct approach to Scripture may be summarized in the following three points: 1) the rabbis carry forward the revelation received at Sinai;[4] 2) they are trained in a particular mode of articulation; 3) their decisions give the tradition uniformity. This is the classical statement of the function of Jewish law. Furthermore, the rabbis used Jewish law, as they used Scriptural exegesis, to impress on their readership the validity and authority of their view of the world. The rabbis were fully convinced that their vision of Judaism was God's will for the world as expressed in the Torah.

Presentations of the principles and practice of midrash typically consist of listing the *middot*, describing how they work and illustrating them by means of examples taken from midrashic text. However, there are problems with the *middot*, since the brief theoretical definitions of the *middot* in midrash and related literature are too vague to account for their applicability. Additionally, the *middot* often overlap in their applications, and there is no clear distinction between similar rules. If well defined, or if systematically applied, the *middot* should provide procedures that, addressing the same text, any sage would obtain the same conclusions. Another inadequacy of the *middot* is that there is a near total absence of evaluative procedures. There are no reductions to standards of logical reasoning, because the *middot* are abstractions of intellectual behavior and of thought processes involving Scripture. All attempts to formalize the numerous explicit and tacit premises and conclusions of the *middot* are bound to fail, because there is another controlling force that cannot be formalized, the force of Rabbinic theology and its categories. There is some personal attachment to a certain solution in midrash, and not all exegetical problems are treated objectively. Therefore ontological and epistemological analyses are propagated.

Rabbinic Hermeneutics

The purpose of the *middot* is to infer new meanings from Scripture rather than to elucidate or harmonize the text itself. The creators of midrash conceived of Scripture as

---

[2] J. Neusner, *Symbol and Theology in Early Judaism* (Atlanta, 1999), p. xiii.

[3] R. Ulmer, "Discourse in Midrash: Textual Strategy and the Use of Personal Pronouns in Halakhic Midrash," in *Approaches to Ancient Judaism*, N.S. XIII (1998), pp. 51–70.

[4] J.-J. Petuchowski, *Ever Since Sinai* (Milwaukee, 1979), pp. 5ff.

a semiotic field that can be quarried for meanings. The rabbis of the midrash saw the graphic signs in this semiotic field, recognized them as linguistic signs, and interpreted the linguistic signs constructed from the semiotic field. Only through the signs' interpretation could God's message for Israel, which is hidden in Scripture, be construed. Rabbinic hermeneutics thus is the mediator between the Written Torah and its companion, the Oral Torah,[5] which is recreated in midrash.[6] Furthermore, Rabbinic hermeneutics and the hermeneutic rules that were applied by the sages function as a mediator between the Torah and the theological vision of the rabbis.

Generally, one may assume that a religion and its system specify how humans may gain access to divine revelation and justify the reasons for staying within its parameters.[7] The application of the *middot* retains some traces of the theology developed by the rabbis precisely because the *middot* are at the base of the Rabbinic negotiations with the revealed "Law." The desire to create theological authority through textuality modifies and re-imagines Scripture to fit the Rabbinic mode of thought. The underlying biblical text might be ambiguous, polysemic, and polyvalent, or, as expressed in more recent parlance, the text might be "indeterminate" (see below). Thus, the plentitude of meanings of Scripture is awaiting the exposition of the midrashist. By decontextualizing Scriptural texts, the creators of midrash are able to reconstitute them with a theological background that makes them relevant to new circumstances and new modes of expression; in the alternative, it enables them to reemphasize ever-present, traditional, presuppositions.[8] The sages almost subvert the texts of the Written Torah,[9] as if they were there to be endlessly expounded and reconstituted. Often an engaging theological issue emerges out of the centrality given to the indeterminacy of meanings of the text in the midrashic discourse, although indeterminacy is not necessarily the facilitator of multiple textual interpretations.[10] In addition, there is virtually no external support for the sages' interpretations. There are very few circumstances that admit a term from the outside to influence the rabbis' theological interpretations; one concrete example is the use of the secular concept of the evil eye, which was inserted into Scripture to explain certain events. Within the task of modifying and reimagining Scripture, the exegetical approach is defined by the her-

---

[5] W. Bacher, *Die älteste Terminologie der jüdischen Schriftauslegung* (Berlin, 1899), p. 89.

[6] J. Neusner, *The Comparative Hermeneutics of Rabbinic Judaism* (Binghamton, 2000), p. xiv, in a work that focuses on the Mishnah, Tosefta, Yerushalmi, and Bavli, writes: "How do I conceive hermeneutics to relate to the detailed work of exegesis? Common usage suffices: hermeneutics forms a governing process of interpreting data, mediating chaos into order, and exegesis takes up the consequent, episodic challenges to harmonious reason, coherence, cogency...." See also J. Neusner, "The Analogical-Contrastive Hermeneutics of the Halakhic Category-Formations," in *Approaches to Ancient Judaism, N.S.* XVI (1999), p. 114.

[7] J. Neusner, *From Literature to Theology in Formative Judaism. Three Preliminary Studies* (Atlanta, 1989), p. 45.

[8] This is similar to the term "intertextuality," which means that the interpreters utilize previous texts, adding material and editing the text and that they draw upon a store of pre-existing or "traditional" ideas.

[9] M. Hirshman asks the compelling question: "What principles legitimized the radical liberty with which the Rabbis investigated Scripture?" in *idem*, "Theology and Exegesis in Midrashic Literature," in Jon Whitman, ed., *Interpretation and Allegory. Antiquity to Modern Period* (Leiden, 2000), p. 113.

[10] D. Stern, *Midrash and Theory. Ancient Jewish Exegesis and Contemporary Literary Studies* (Evanston, 1996), p. 16 (Reprint of D. Stern, "Midrash and Indeterminacy," in *Critical Inquiry* 15, Autumn (1988) pp. 132–161.

meneutic framework that directs and arranges the often miniscule lemmata of the Written Torah that are found in the midrashic texts. The Torah is the intermediary between God and humanity; this is a transcendent God who manifests a radical "otherness." This otherness is communicated in the Written and Oral Torah. The hermeneutics of the rabbis facilitates an integration of the Torah and God into the text of the Rabbinic cultural sphere and its particular theology that is expressed in midrash and other Rabbinic genres of late antiquity.[11]

Theological Categories and Their Formation in Midrash

It has been argued that theological inferences can be gleaned from the recurring form and method of midrashic processes as well as from its substantive content.[12] One may observe that Rabbinic thought processes contain implicit generalizations and exclusive readings that are taken for granted. This web of generalizations has puzzled scholars for some time: Some theological statements are given in midrash; however, as explained above, the *middot* do not contain theological statements. We may assume that some of the theological statements of the Rabbinic textual corpus are part of the theological foundation of the *middot*. It is noteworthy that Jacob Neusner is the only scholar who has created and systematically applied "category-formation" and theology to midrash. Neusner asserts that a "formation of categories" occurs in the theological system of the midrash compilations.[13]

For Neusner, theological statements in Rabbinic exegesis account for the situation of Israel in relationship with God, with one another, and with others. Neusner further specifies the one consideration that seems to be always present in the mind of the Rabbinic sages when they engage in Scriptural interpretation: the theological question of the present situation of Israel as compared to the situation of the gentiles. What are the underlying reasons for this situation, will it change over time, and how will Israel be able to survive? Furthermore, what actions are to be taken? In my opinion, the answers to these theological questions posed by Neusner are provided by the results of the hermeneutically guided inquiries into the Torah. Neusner mentions one major proposition, namely that Israel knows God through the Torah, while the gentiles do not know God, because they rejected the Torah. In the presence of the midrash, and in the assumed historical setting of defining the theology of Judaism against competing biblical explanations, it is the gentiles who rule over Israel, although God rules as sovereign over all humankind.

Therefore, according to Neusner, the Oral Torah[14] poses and answers the following theological questions by the application of the *middot*: Why do the gentiles prosper? Why does Israel suffer? What is required of Israel to love their God, improve their situation, and establish justice? In my view,

---

[11] J. Neusner, *The Foundations of the Theology of Judaism* (Northvale, 1991).

[12] J. Neusner, *The Hermeneutics of the Rabbinic Category-Formations: An Introduction* (Lanham, 2001), p. xv. The first modern attempt to systematize Rabbinic theology in particular, and Jewish theology in general, was made by K. Kohler, *Grundriss einer systematischen Theologie des Judentums auf geschichtlicher Grundlage* (Leipzig, 1910. Repr. Hildesheim, 1979).

[13] J. Neusner, The *Theological Category-Formations of Rabbinic Midrash*; [1] God, Man, and Israel. I am grateful to Professor Neusner for providing me with an electronic "preprint" of his work.

[14] J. Neusner, *The Theology of the Oral Torah* (Montreal, 1999), p. 28.

the Rabbinic dogma of God, Israel, and the gentiles is relevant to the theological foundations of midrash and its inherent *middot*. Midrashic exegesis is based upon the theological statements about God and God's relationship to humans and God's place in the world. Simultaneously, midrashic exegesis creates the theological statements. In pursuing these theological objectives, the rabbis emphasize their own hermeneutics, which serves to delineate their theology. The text thus assumes a meaning in the immediate presence of the creators of the midrashim; unquestionably, meaning is extracted through the application of different methods of inquiry which is the means of creating a Rabbinic theology. The mere existence of the complex *middot* suggests a profound theology of the Rabbinic world-view.

Some Basic Theological Statements in Midrash

The theology pertaining to the *middot* does not only yield general propositions but it is implicit in some of the midrashic statements. Some eminent categories of these theological implications may be defined as aesthetical and ethical attitudes towards the Law. One example is the theology of "the joy in the Law" and of "beautifying the Law."[15] The antithesis between humans and God can only be resolved if humans glorify God by fulfilling the law in a particular manner; the fulfillment of the law requires human action and the additional element of utilizing aesthetically pleasing religious paraphernalia, as in the following text, which adds the term "beautiful:"

Mekhilta, Shirata 3[16]
And I will glorify Him (Exod. 15:2). R. Ishmael says: "And is it possible for flesh and blood to add glory to his Creator? It means: I shall be beautiful before him in observing the commandments. I shall prepare before him a beautiful Lulav, a beautiful Sukkah, beautiful fringes and beautiful Tefillin."

Another example of an ethical implication is "the zeal for the Law:" the pious will not insist upon the leeway of an applicable law (Gen. 22:33) or make the law more stringent in cases when a milder application is accepted; however, the pious will not apply the less stringent application to themselves (Meir). The leniency in Rabbinic interpretation might also involve giving up some endowed rights (e.g., the Prosbul; M. Sheb. 10:3). The result of Rabbinic interpretation might be viewed as a fluctuation between seemingly "new" laws and the reshaping of old ones. Even after the *middot* are applied, one finds halakhic statements that derive from the Torah, *mi-de-oraita*, and such that derive from the rabbis, *mi-de-rabbanan*. Moreover, a few Rabbinic decrees even object to biblical Law. Nevertheless, the rabbis of the early midrash rely upon theological statements that tradition derives from the same source as the Written Torah.[17] The partic-

---

[15] S. Schechter, *Some Aspects of Rabbinic Theology* (New York, 1909), pp. 160f.

[16] Based upon J.Z. Lauterbach, ed. and trans., *Mekilta de Rabbi Ishmael: A Critical Edition on the Basis of the MSS and Early Editions with an English Translation, Introduction and Notes* (Philadelphia, 1933–1935), vol. II, p. 25.

[17] J. Neusner, *What, Exactly, Did the Rabbinic Sages Mean by "the Oral Torah": An Inductive Answer to the Question of Rabbinic Judaism* (Atlanta, 1998), p. xii, points to the distinc-

tion between biblical and scribal law as follows: "In any event the distinction between a rule of the Torah and one of the scribes plays no role in the conception of the dual Torah as spelled out in Rabbinic classics. For it is self-evident that a law revealed by God to Moses at Sinai is explicitly labeled as 'Torah,' but orally-formulated and orally transmitted, and hence is not the same thing as a law promulgated by scribes or rabbis."

ular term *halakhah le-mosheh mi-sinai* refers to the halakhah[18] revealed to Moses on Sinai.[19] The dogma of the Sinaitic origin of Rabbinic hermeneutics is not primary, but the dogma of the Sinaitic origin of (Rabbinic) law is essential. All this means that an educated, reasoned, and emotional approach to revelation according to the application of the *middot* seems possible. The rabbis maneuver the principles of logic in any way they saw fit, as long as they arrived at the required legal and theological results that were shaped by the Rabbinic worldview. Controversies occurred only in respect to the necessity or efficacy of this or that manipulation of logic, but not in respect to the underlying epistemological assumptions.[20] Logic is therefore not always applicable in the explanation of the *middot*. However, it does not necessarily follow that the results of the exegesis are wrong, if logic is not applicable, for, as logic teaches, denial of the antecedent of some aspects of Rabbinic hermeneutics does not imply the denial of the consequent Rabbinic theological statement or law unless their relationship happens to be exclusive. A law may be correct, i.e., it is of divine origin, but it may be improperly derived from Scripture. In any case, logic itself cannot be made an issue of faith but the *middot* are a matter of faith.[21]

As mentioned above, there are laws that are not contained in the Bible and cannot be proved by simple Scriptural proof.[22] The proof, if any, lies in tradition and the fact that these laws had been practiced for a long time and are therefore similar to revealed laws. One may argue that there may not have been a Biblical justification for Rabbinic theology at all, especially, if the *al tikre* (do not read this, but rather ...) hermeneutic is considered,[23] which seems to consist of random substitutions of biblical lemmata with Rabbinic "lemmata." Rather, the justification for such a theology might have been based upon the theology inherent in the *middot*. This leads to the questions: Which are the true sources of Rabbinic theology? Did the rabbis develop their laws from looking inside the Torah or looking at the world? Is midrash study of the Bible or theological legend which surmises that one is to take seriously both the interpretive and theological dimension of the text?

Generally, midrash is a religious activity sustained by the theological interest in the exposition of the Bible. Reconnecting to the biblical religious precepts and the biblical world and time is the major aim of midrashic activity and the theological foundation of its propositions. Its aim and purpose are generally limited to human existence and ethical instruction. Theological and ethical foundations of behavioral norms are the basis of halakhah; however, this theology does not have many dogmas, as has been noticed often before.[24] By discovering the significance of singular biblical lemmata the hermeneutics of midrash assist in realizing and recognizing God's will and word. Reading just one lemma or letter or sign does not render meaning; there has to be a cohesive element that spells out a coherent statement and controls a system—in

---

[18] S. Safrai, "Halakhah le-Mosheh mi-Sinai," in Y. Sussman and D. Rosenthal, eds., *Mehkerei Talmud* (Jerusalem, 1990), p. 30.

[19] Neusner, *What, Exactly, Did the Rabbinic Sages Mean by "the Oral Torah,"* pp. xiff.

[20] Petuchowski, *Ever Since Sinai*, pp. 88f.

[21] D. Stern, *Midrash and Theory*, p. 25, in his brief discussion of Augustine, also refers to the matter of faith: "To be sure, one could argue that Rabbinic Judaism also possesses a 'rule of faith' under which all multiple interpretations are subsumed. The problem, however, is in stipulating in what this rule consists."

[22] Such laws are found in M. Pe. 2:6 and M. Yad. 4:3.

[23] M. Fishbane, *The Garments of Torah. Essays in Biblical Hermeneutics* (Bloomington, 1989), p. 26.

[24] S. Schechter, "The Dogmas in Judaism," in *Studies in Judaism* (Philadelphia, 1945), p. 147. See also L. Jacobs, *A Jewish Theology* (London, 1973), pp. 21ff.

short: midrash is not gibberish or a random collection of Rabbinic sayings.[25] I assume that the cohesive element in the case of midrash is theological. The *middot* focus upon certain lemmata and tell us what to do with these signs, thereby creating theological meaning. Additionally, the Rabbinic system of theological norms is controlled by certain sentences that provide the following presuppositions which are at the same time core beliefs: the uniqueness of God, the covenant with Abraham, the revelation of the Torah, the chosenness of Israel, the Exodus, the redemption of Israel, the existence of good and evil, and others.[26] Often the theology is transparent only through examples, such as the many narrative passages that talk about God or ethical behavior in human dimensions. Israel accepted the Torah and God loves Israel and the dual Torah defines Israel's life and determines Israel's future. The present situation of the rabbis is caused by Israel's sin, which God justly and reasonably punishes. Adherence to the commandments and repentance will bring about God's forgiveness.[27] Neusner defines four principles of the theology of the Oral Torah,[28] which may be summarized as follows: 1) creation was planned by God according to the Torah, and God rules justly; 2) the perfection of creation will follow the same rules of justice; 3) flaws in creation are marked by Israel's condition; 4) there will be a resurrection of the dead and justice will prevail. In respect to the application of the *middot* we may conclude: Since these matters are reasonable, humans can navigate their daily lives according to principles that can be raised from the biblical text by reasoned inquiry which is guided by the *middot*.

The Middot *Assist in (Re)creating the Oral Torah*

In a way the *middot* are utilized to recreate the Oral Torah; without the Oral Torah many laws and events in the Torah could not have been realized simply because the Torah often does not contain the application of the law.[29] The sages, according to Neusner, propose in some midrashic works, particularly in Genesis Rabbah, a reconstruction of human existence along the lines of the ancient design of Scripture as they read it.[30] Based upon Umberto Eco, I would conclude that the interpreters did not see *nova* (new things) but the manner of seeing is *nove* (a new way).[31] Additionally, it has been noted that the repeated expression or the rephrasing of a tradition leads to the existence of something new.[32] The Oral and the Written Torah are separate but complementary. The oral tradition is regained and projected into the future through the *mid-*

---

[25] J. Neusner, *The Theology of the Oral Torah*, p. xvi, states: "I claim that the Oral Torah builds all structures upon certain premises and propositions. A single logic infuses the whole." He further specifies some premises of the theology of the Oral Torah that cannot be completely contradicted, for example, viewing sin as rebellion.

[26] B.J. Bamberger, *The Search for Jewish Theology* (New York, 1978), pp. 51, 61.

[27] Neusner, *The Theology of the Oral Torah*, discusses many additional categories.

[28] Neusner, *The Theology of the Oral Torah*, pp. xiif.

[29] J. Neusner, *Incarnation of God: The Character of Divinity in Formative Judaism* (Binghamton, 2001), p. 125.

[30] Often reiterated by J. Neusner, for example in his teaching book *Invitation to Midrash: The Workings of Rabbinic Bible Interpretation* (Atlanta, 1992), pp. 102f.

[31] U. Eco, *Semiotics and the Philosophy of Language*, p. 152.

[32] S.D. Fraade, *From Tradition to Commentary: Torah and Its Interpretation in the Midrash Sifre to Deuteronomy* (Albany, 1991), p. 227, n. 211.

dot and the ensuing norms and explanations that make the Torah relevant and put forth a theology of the interpreters. Furthermore, some revelations became relevant only at a later point. In principle, the whole Torah was given at Sinai; nevertheless a lot had to be recovered by the application of the *middot*. Thus, midrash is a constant discovery of its sources, as is explained in the expositions found in the beginning of Genesis Rabbah which demonstrates a concentration of theological insights and numerous hermeneutic strategies.[33]

Genesis Rabbah 1:1[34]

In the beginning [bereshit] (Gen. 1:1). R. Oshaya commenced: Then *I was with Him as a nursling [amon], a source of delight every day, [rejoicing before Him at all times]* (Prov. 8:30).
Amon means "tutor" (pedagogue).
Amon means "covered."
Amon means "hidden."
And there are some who say, *Amon* means "great."
Amon means "tutor," as in the verse, *as an amon carries the suckling child* (Num. 11:12). *Amon* means "covered," as in the verse, *those who are covered in scarlet* (Lam 4:5). *Amon* means "hidden," as in the verse, *and he hid Hadassah* (Est. 2:7). *Amon* means "great," as it says, *are you better than No-Ammon* (Nah. 3:8)? This we translate: Are you better than Alexandria the Great, which is situated in the [Nile] delta? Another interpretation: *Amon* means "artisan [uman]." The Torah declares, I was the artisan's tool that the Holy One, blessed be He, used [when he practiced His craft]. It is customary, when a human king builds a palace, he does not build it out of his own head, but he employs an architect [*uman*]. Even the architect does not build it from his head, but he uses plans and blueprints in order to know how to plan the rooms and the doorways. So, too, the Holy One, blessed be He, looked into the Torah and created the world. Thus the Torah said, *By means of the beginning did God create* (Gen. 1:1). And the word for "beginning" refers only to the Torah, as it says: The *Lord acquired me at the beginning [reshit] of His course* (Prov. 8:22).

This midrash utilizes an encyclopedic method of interpretation, which is not part of the regular enumerations of the *middot*. Here it resembles a hierarchy of atomic properties that are ruled by relations of entailment from the lower to the upper node. The representation of the content of the lexical item *amon* utilizes some knowledge from other Scriptural verses, and it is not difficult to decide which properties are essential to the overall statement of the midrash. As usual, the midrash uses the method of focusing upon certain lemmata which are linked by the same root and its variant propositions. The words of the midrash have to be read accumulatively and from the bottom up. Every single mention of *amon* and its surprising new meaning have to be considered. Against the usual understanding of *amon* as "nursling" the midrash establishes the opposite meaning of *amon* as "tutor" from another Scriptural passage. The amazing result is that the Torah can fit both of these terms as well as the other meanings of *amon*. Every single meaning is applicable. Additionally, the many uses of the root AMN and the encyclopedic aspect of this midrash may finally culminate in the term "*amen*" which is the worshipers' response to the Torah. This aspect includes that the Torah is covered in garments, when

---

[33] This text shows how midrash may be viewed as an interposition between the signs of Scripture as the rabbis position themselves in relation to revelation.

[34] Y. Theodor and H. Albeck, eds., *Midrash Bereshit Rabba mit Kritischem Apparat und Kommentar*, 2nd ed. (Jerusalem, 1962).

it is carried like a small child during the Torah procession and that the Torah is not immediately visible; "hidden" and "covered" may mean that the Torah is stored in the ark and that it is covered by its garments. On the level of midrashic interpretation, the sense is that the linguistic signs of the Torah have to be uncovered. On a more metaphorical level, it is obvious that the Torah had to be revealed because it was hidden, it was taught and written from meager beginnings until great wisdom was pronounced by it.

A major theological concern of the rabbis was that the Torah had to be differentiated from anything similar, in particular from anything Egyptian; thus, the Torah is greater than No-Ammon. No-Ammon is actually ancient Thebes; by virtue of the hermeneutic strategy of "updating" the midrash changes the ancient temple complex at Karnak (Thebes) and the necropolis on the Western shore of the Nile to the Hellenistic Egyptian metropolis of Alexandria, situated in the Nile delta. This method of updating or translating brings into view a better-known or contemporary city, Alexandria, a center of wisdom and learning of the Hellenistic world. The hermeneutic strategy thus enables the formation of a theological statement: the Torah given to Israel is greater and contains more wisdom than the greatest source of wisdom of the nations.

The artisan part of the above midrash demonstrates that the Torah was the plan and the blueprint of the world that was to be created. This is the so-called dogma of "the pre-existence of the Torah," which is another major theological expression of rabbinc Judaism. Additionally, it means that God is bound by the plan in the Torah, and if God is bound by the plan of the Torah, so much more will the Torah bind humans. The implication of the *mashal* method is to show God's integrity and his plan for the world and for humanity. The essential, theological result of the hermeutic strategies and the resulting reading is that *bereshit* (Gen. 1:1) means the world was created "with *reshit*." This is the overall theological proposition of the midrashic unit; it could have been stated at the beginning of the unit, but, as is often the case in midrash, the midrash has to be read backwards to gain this conceptual understanding of a sequential order of things. The Rabbinic method—utilizing explicit or implicit *middot*—requires to go through steps of analyses and "different" readings of a polysemic term; all of which are all valid.[35]

The *middot* are also designed to negotiate the conceptual distance between God and human speech and culture. Rabbinic text expects that God's message is compatible with both an eternal encoding of the icon of distance in the text of the Torah and an abatement of it, precisely because the distance can never be overcome. In permitting the decoding and the explanation of the text of the Torah, the literally mysterious and incomprehensible God makes room for the deployment of normal human logical-linguistic convention. The transfer of divine categories into human categories is accomplished by the *middot* and their theological foundations. On a more practical level, one has to be absolutely certain that objects, animals, plants, procedures and classifications mentioned in the Bible refer to the correct objects and classifications, etc. This transfer of Scriptual signs into human language is one of the major issues in the approaches by two sages, Ishmael and Aqiba.

If the Bible is given in human language, as claimed by Ishmael, then it is the language of the recipient, Moses, the people of Israel, and their interpreters, the sages. This is not in complete contradiction to Aqiba, who saw the language of the Bible

---

[35] Concerning the polysemous nature of texts, see U. Eco, *Semiotics and the Philosophy of Language*, p. 149.

as the language of revelation, the language between God and humanity. For example, whereas the Hebrew particle "*et*" has a syntactic function in the Bible, the midrash must add lexemic information, if we follow Aqiba's injunction. However, A.J. Heschel's phenomenological approach associates the methods of Aqiba and Ishmael by referring to the duality of the Torah:[36] The Torah is from heaven (*torah min-ha-shamayim*), and the Torah is from Sinai (*torah mi-sinai*). This means that *torah min-ha-shamayim* expresses every single detail of the halakhah in divine terms, and *torah mi-sinai* embodies only the general principles of the *halakhah* in human speech. Aqiba's vision of the Torah embraces both, the form and the content of the Torah, which are divine and all-inclusive. The theology of the hermeneutics may establish itself in the differences between the interpretation of Aqiba and Ishmael.[37] In the hermeneutical approach of the rabbis, Scriptural interpretation becomes a sacred enterprise, because Scripture is written revelation and this revelation is a continuum of graphic signs which have referentiality. The content of the Torah is conceptualized in this process based on the literal analysis of midrash. This is accomplished by presenting inventories and categories of topics dealt with by rabbis (following the paradigm of theological topics established by Jacob Neusner).[38] If any theological foundations are inherent in the midrashic *middot*, theological inferences can be gleaned from the recurring forms and methods of midrashic exegesis as well as from its substantive content.[39]

Exegesis and Theory

The theological foundations of the *middot* could be explored to their fullest, if a theory of midrash would offer the possibility of integrating recent trends of literary criticism and textlinguistic as well as semiotic approaches.[40] The hermeneutics of "indeterminacy" ultimately explores the boundaries of the biblical text, the receptor and the subjectiveness of the Rabbinic interpretation. The subjectiveness of biblical exegesis is the entrance way through which the rabbis can interject their theological concerns, and the *middot* can sustain some of the limits of the endless possibilities of an indeterminate text. Within this context, I assume that the initial interpreter knows what is significant at the outset of the interpretive task. This pre-knowledge is limited to the sages, and it is to be utilized in order to control the environment of interpretation that becomes context-free and unconcerned with most timely and present-day constraints.[41] Nowhere in midrash does it say that the rabbis had to interpret a biblical lemma because a specific contemporary case or issue had to be dealt with. The *middot* merely assist in implementing a pre-existing theological issue as efficiently as possible.

What then is the theology of interpretation as exemplified by the *middot*? The meaning of interpreting the text through exegesis assumes that the interpretation is

---

[36] A.J. Heschel, *Torah Min Ha-Shamayim be-Aspeklaryah Shel Ha-Dorot (Theology of Ancient Judaism)*, Vol. 1 (London and New York, 1962), p. 23.

[37] M. Hirshman, "Theology and Exegesis in Midrashic Literature," p. 120, remarks in regard to the emergence of Rabbinic hermeneutics: "Perhaps the position of the school of R. Yishmael that the Torah was written in the language of people encouraged the attempt to specify the norms and codes of exegesis."

[38] Neusner, *The Theology of the Oral Torah*, passim.

[39] Petuchowski, *Ever Since Sinai*, p. 98.

[40] Eco, *The Limits of Interpretation*, p. 11.

[41] A useful definition of "context" in linguistic terms specifies that a context is a coded class of possible co-texts or textual environments.

legitimate by relying upon the concept of the unbroken chain of tradition. Additionally, the concept of the dual Torah assisted in laying claim to this chain of interpretation and to the interpretative construction of a divine will for the people of Israel. The *middot* lead the Rabbinic interpreters and create a dynamic between the Biblical text and the *middot* that expound it, since the words of the text are not explicated through fixed terms of references as in dream interpretation or in Philo's allegorical interpretation.[42] Choosing and creating sets of *middot*, thus trying to limit interpretation or at least superficially streamlining the approaches to the text, means that the sages tried to gain control over exegetical activities. The interpretation through extrinsic information is avoided in midrash; rather, the hermeneutic strategies produce meanings for a given Scriptural text without consideration of "scientific" data. In the extreme, Rabbinic exegesis often focused upon the connections between similar biblical meanings in such *middot* as *gezerah shavah* and *binyan av*. The meanings that the sages looked for were thus hidden but manifest meanings. This was a key element in their hermeneutical approach and in their theology: the belief that everything is in the Bible and that by linking lemmata theological truths are yielded. The sages gained control over the limitless interpretation by quantifying its scope and they were thus in a position to delimit and define Judaism.

Undoubtedly, in the reading of any text, understanding the terms utilized is essential. There are two main linguistic issues involved here: a qualitative and a quantitative linguistic aspect. The qualitative aspect presupposes that the human language involved is known and the quantitative aspect determines the scope of that language. Both of these issues are addressed in midrash. The qualitative aspect is administered within the *middot* whenever the denotative and connotative meanings of a Scriptural term are elucidated. This depends on the religious context and is often accomplished by analogy, inference and other context-based *middot*. The quantitative aspect is also accomplished within the *middot*; it involves issues of subsumption, for example, in the *middot* dealing with the general and the particular. These theological foundations of several *middot* will be explored in the following.[43]

The Middot in Theological Context

Gezerah Shavah: This hermeneutic rule consists of the fundamental epistemological operation of comparison and contrast which is very usable in teasing out theological statements. This is a basic technique of concept formation; when *gezerah shavah* is applied to the biblical corpus in Rabbinic textual analysis, a distinctive sameness is found. In the Scriptural discourse there are linguistic "labels"[44] which are analogous; these may have similar or different meanings in different contexts. On the other hand, there may be different labels in different contexts with apparently the same meaning intended. The intended meaning can be extrapolated if all the appearances of the label can be assumed to have the same meaning. In such a case the proposed single meaning in the midrash is the divinely intended meaning. The procedure in the

---

[42] I. Heinemann, *Darkhei Ha-Agadah* (Jerusalem, 1949), p. 152, describes the Rabbinic use of allegory: "[it] almost always followed established scriptural metaphors."

[43] For a detailed list of the *middot*, see HERMENEUTICS: TECHNIQUES OF RABBINIC EXEGESIS and HERMENEUTICS, CRITICAL APPROACHES.

[44] A "label" refers to identical words, similar phrases or a similar root in Scripture.

following text is similar, the lemmata "abominable" and "abomination" are the "labels" that accomplish the theological feat of an intended divine meaning.

Sifre Deuteronomy, Re'eh 99 (Finkelstein ed., pp. 159–160)[45]
You shall not eat anything abominable (Deut. 14:3). R. Eliezer says, "From where [do we learn] that someone who slits the ear of a first-born animal and eats of it, violates a negative commandment? From the verse, *You shall not eat anything abominable* (ibid.)." Others say that this applies only to consecrated animals that have become unfit, since Scripture says here *abominable things* and it says elsewhere *You shall not sacrifice unto the Lord your God an ox, a sheep, . . . for it is an abomination unto the Lord your God* (Deut. 17:1). Just as the *abominable thing* mentioned in the latter verse refers to consecrated animals that have become unfit, so does the *abominable thing* mentioned here [in the former verse] refer to consecrated animals that have become unfit.

The possibly predetermined result of the exegetical inquiry, consecrated animals that have become unfit are abominable in God's eyes, is advanced by the underlying theological principle of the *gezerah shavah*. The detection of divine intention is guided by Rabbinic theological intention that permits thematic comparisons. In another text, a more complicated case of the intended divine meaning, which is extrapolated by the application of *gezerah shavah*, finds meanings of a label that seem to vary in one context. But if this label is coherent in all other verses, the same meaning can be generated by *gezerah shavah*. Example:

Sifre Deuteronomy, Re'eh 100 (Finkelstein ed., p. 160)[46]
These are the animals that you may eat: the ox, the sheep, and the goat, the hart, and the gazelle, and the roebuck (Deut. 14:4f.). This teaches us that wild animals are included with domestic animals; from where [do we learn] that domestic animals are included with wild beasts? From the verse, *these are the beasts* (Lev. 11:2) which teaches that a *beast* is called an *animal* and an *animal* is called a *beast*, and that there are more unclean animals than clean ones, since every time Scripture itemizes the fewer kind; this is so because it says [in this instance], *These are the beasts that you may eat . . . the hart, and the gazelle, and the roebuck* [*and the wild goat, etc.*] (Deut. 14:4f.).

Obviously, if a label ("beast") appears often in the text its meaning is more certain. A problem arises if a word or phrase is only used once in Scripture; in this case its meaning becomes a subject of conjecture. In other cases a very general term might have to be limited by *gezerah shavah*. By applying this theologically determined *midah* that permits the exegete to narrow a term, Sarah's late conception is defined in a theologically significant manner, i.e., it has ramifications that go beyond her own family. The term "make" is defined by *gezerah shavah* in a Rabbinically desired theological sense; generally, "to make" is a verb with a wide range of applications which can only be determined through additional propositions in a verse.

Genesis Rabbah 58:8
Sarah said, God has made joy for me; everyone who hears will rejoice with me (Gen.

---

[45] L. Finkelstein, ed., *Sifre 'al Sefer Devarim* (Berlin, 1939; repr. New York, 1969). The translation is based upon R. Hammer, trans., *Sifre: A Tannaitic Commentary on the Book of Deuteronomy* (New Haven and London, 1986), p. 146.

[46] Based upon R. Hammer, trans., *Sifre*, pp. 146f.

21:6). R. Berekhiah, R. Judah b. Simon, R. Hanan in the name of Samuel b. R. Isaac: If Reuben is happy, what difference does it make to Simon? So too, if Sarah was remembered, what difference did it make to other people? When our matriarch Sarah was remembered, many barren women were remembered with her; many of the deaf had their ears opened; many of the blind had their eyes opened; many of the feeble minded had their minds opened. The term "make" is used here and also in the following verse: and *he made a release to the provinces* (Est. 2:18). Just as the term "make" used there indicates that a gift had been given to the entire world, so the term "make" used here indicates that a gift had been given to the entire world. R. Levi said, She added to the lights of heaven. The term "make" (Gen. 21:6) is used here and also in the following verse: *And God made the two lights* (Gen. 1:16).

It is clear that the type of reasoning as in the above mentioned text is somewhat dependent upon one's overall context of knowledge. In Rabbinic interpretation the overall context of knowledge is a theologically framed presupposition that may be gained from the perception of words and their possible relations. Since Scripture is a closed document, there would be little material to refer to other than Scripture itself.[47] In terms of linguistics this would mean that the Rabbinic conclusions are predetermined since the available data are finite.[48] It is possible that the rabbis also attempted to limit interpretations by limiting the *middot* in their search for finiteness. We could imagine a "fixed" text that is interpreted through the application of a "fixed" hermeneutics. The finiteness of the number of *middot* was partially accomplished in creating ever-changing "sets of rules," from 7 to 613. However, these attempts at limiting and restricting midrashic readings ultimately failed, and only a diffuse number of explanatory restrictions controlled the exegesis in later midrash.

Ribui u-mi'ut: The general followed by the particular subsumes everything, which is like the particular, and it invokes a limitation by systematically eliminating the proposed meanings. This method lends itself to theological implications by limiting and focusing based upon Rabbinic theological reasoning. Under the heading "one might think . . ." the following text proposes to eliminate certain applications, such as a partnership or brothers who inherit an estate. The result of this speculation is that the consecrated objects mentioned in one Scriptural passage are limited in respect to donorship.

Sifre Deuteronomy, Re'eh 77 (Finkelstein ed., pp. 142–143)[49]

Only your holy things that you have and your vows you shall take and go to the place [which the Lord shall choose] (Deut. 12:26). To what does this verse refer?. . . . R. Aqiba says, the verse speaks about substitution of consecrated objects. *You shall take and go to the place [which the Lord shall choose]* (ibid.). One might think that this applies also to the firstborn and the tithes, hence the verse says, *and your vows* (ibid.). One might think that the tithe of cattle applies also to partnerships, hence the verse says, *that you have* (ibid.). I might exclude brothers who had acquired it from the estate and have afterwards divided it, hence the verse says, *that*

---

[47] A closed document means that a text may possess the sum of its readings that were elicited over the course of its history; see H.-G. Gadamer, *Truth and Method* (Tübingen, 1973; New York, 1989), pp. 76f.

[48] The Torah is finite and a delimited scroll, see Neusner, *Torah: From Scroll to Symbol*.

[49] Based upon R. Hammer, trans., *Sifre*, pp. 131f.

you have (ibid.). Ben Azzai says, one might think that the tithe of the cattle applies also to an orphan, hence the verse says, *only* (ibid.).

The *middah* in the above text follows the theological implications of individual responsibility; the pronoun "you" has to be limited to the individual Israelite. Furthermore, no substitution of consecrated objects is possible. From the outset, the theology of this rule might imply that God's creation is expansive and limitless and created "objects," such as the heavenly lights, might be expanded to include the planets, etc., however, humans are limited and their expressions have to be curtailed to reflect exact requirements.

The General and the Particular—kelal u-ferat: In theological terms, this *middah* can refer to the interpretation involving a biological genus and a species[50] as in the interpretation of animals that are listed in the Torah. Under the rule *kelal u-ferat* a limiting effect is intended when only the species mentioned is signified, whereas under *perat u-khelal* an amplification of a term is intended. In midrash, in the *kelal u-ferat* application, the genus is mentioned as an approximation of the intended meaning and the species is added to specify that meaning. In the lemma *of the livestock [behemah], of the herd and of the flock* (Lev. 1:2) the general term could have several connotations and might include other types of animals; however, it is clarified by means of mentioning a more particular species. The question might be raised, why the species was not simply mentioned without the genus? We are told that unintended extensions might have been proposed. In the alternative, certain details suggested by the genus might have been missed. Mainly, the genus is in the text to inform us, that other, dissimilar, species of the same genus (such as asses) are not to be included. The rule *kelal u-ferat* thus has the theological implication of limiting the inclusion of animals which is ultimately determined by God. The logic of this procedure cannot be determined by the vagueness of natural language, which sorts animals into an overclass and several subclasses. The hermeneutic rule acts as a qualifier in this linguistic predicament and its application is governed by Rabbinic theology which is ultimately determined by the divine will.

On the other hand, in *perat u-khelal* some species are initially listed to indicate the divinely intended kind of subject. The genus is added later on in order to indicate that other subjects of the same kind are also included. In the biblical lemma *an ass or an ox or a sheep or any beast [behemah]* (Exod. 22:9), the species exemplifies the subjects prescribed by the divine text. The genus serves to extend the application of the law concerned with similar subjects. This also implies that the initial list is not complete or exhaustive and open to Rabbinic interpretation. The genus is not simply mentioned alone, but without the species the exceptions might have been proposed. Additionally, certain details suggested by the species might have been ignored. The theological difference between Ishmael and Aqiba in regard to logical amplification or limitation, either as *kelal u-ferat* or *ribui u-mi'ut*, is a matter of emphasizing certain aspects of the language of the Torah, as discussed above. In *kelal u-ferat* the mention of a species serves to define in a precise manner the initial genus, whereas in *ribui u-mi'ut* the explicit mention of the species emphasizes the exclusion of a number of dissimilar subjects which are not explicitly mentioned, but which nevertheless belong to the initial genus. In *perat u-khelal*, the final genus serves to more broadly define the full extent of the list of species. It adds more species, which are not explicitly listed, to those explicitly mentioned in the Scriptural text; this is a possibility for Rabbinic intervention and the expression of a particular theology.

---

[50] U. Eco, *The Limits of Interpretation*, p. 205.

Hekesh (Juxtaposition): This rule clearly permits the expression of a Rabbinic theological approach to interpretation. The elements or verses from Scripture that are juxtaposed under this rule may express a theological choice made by the interpreter. In Sifre Deuteronomy, Re'eh 106 (Finkelstein ed., p. 167),[51] the application of the hermeneutic rule of *Hekesh* shows that the same rule applies to the firstlings and second tithe; this is based on the lemma "in the place which he shall choose," which appears in two verses: *And you shall eat before the Lord your God in the place which he shall choose* (Deut. 14:23), and *You shall eat it before the Lord your God [year by year in the place which the Lord shall choose]* (Deut. 15:20). The conclusion of the midrashic passage, "Just as the second tithe of one year may be consumed in the next year, so may the firstling of one year be consumed in the next year," expresses the simple ruling that the permission to consume the designated objects may be postponed from one year to the next.

Kal va-homer: One *middah*, the *kal va-homer*, is very useful in extracting the underlying theology: it serves to create antithetical comparisons between God's behavior versus human behavior. God can see sin and humans cannot always fathom the extent of "sinning." In the alternative, this *middah* maximizes God's compassion that eclipses any righteous behavior of humans.[52] The interpretation focuses upon a lemma from Genesis that explains Joseph's behavior towards the "sinners," his brothers. Joseph greets his brothers in this world; how much more will God greet him in the world-to-come and remove the hatred of the brothers. The *kal va-homer* is the most deductive form of Rabbinic argument, although inductive and deductive stages of reasoning are not differentiated. In regard to the purely deductive aspects, no Rabbinic legislation and no sermonizing would be possible. Instead of a reductional hermeneutics, based upon a conviction that the Scriptural lemma has only one correct meaning, the *kal va-homer* opens up the possibility of an unfolding meaning of the lemma in terms of its symbolic potentials: Joseph's greeting even extended to the words of the Psalmist.

Tanhuma, Buber edition, Va-yeshev 7
And when his brothers saw that their father loved him more than all his brothers [they hated him and could not speak peaceably to him] (Gen. 37:1–4). This means that he came to inquire after their welfare and they did not answer. Why? Because it was his custom to inquire after their welfare. There you have a man who, before he became a ruler, asked about the welfare of his fellow men. But once he becomes a ruler, he becomes presumptuous and no longer cares to inquire after the welfare of the inhabitants of the town. But Joseph was not like this. Although he had become a ruler, it was his habit to ask after the welfare of his brothers, as it says *and he asked them about their welfare* (Gen. 43:27). The Holy One, blessed be he, spoke to him: "Joseph, you began to ask after the welfare of your brothers in this world but they hated you. But in the world to come I will give you peace and remove the hatred between you. Therefore David said: *Behold, how good and how pleasant it is for brothers to dwell together in unity* (Ps. 133:1)."

---

[51] Based upon R. Hammer, trans., *Sifre*, p. 153.

[52] The following example is from a "later midrash." Neusner observed that beginning in the fifth/sixth century C.E., a different mode of speech was developed in Rabbinic literature (and in art) that appealed to "symbolic modes of discourse" instead of the propositional ones; furthermore, a new mode of discourse commenced that was able to convey theological statements. See Neusner, *Symbol and Theology in Early Judaism*, p. xv.

A *kal va-homer* in Sifre Deuteronomy, Ekev 37 (Finkelstein ed., pp. 71–72),[53] serves as a proof for the initial proposition of the midrashic unit which claims that Israel is nicer than other lands. The lemmata *And it shall come to pass* (Deut. 7:12) and *for the land which you enter to possess [is not as the land of Egypt]* (Deut. 11:10) were said to pacify the people Israel, who were still yearning for Egypt. This theological concern for the beauty of the land of Israel and leaving behind Egypt is expressed by a series of *kal va-homer* applications that relate to the different names of Mt. Hermon (Sirion, Senir, Hermon) and the four kingdoms that fought over the mountains of Israel. The conclusion in respect to multiple names and fights is that the land of Israel is beautiful and a special gift of God to the people of Israel. The theological foundation of this *middah* relates to the chosenness of Israel and the promise of the land of Israel to the descendants of Abraham.

Rule Thirteen: This hermeneutic rule means literally "two writings [verses] that deny each other until a third comes that reconciles them." It refers to a situation in which two conflicting propositions[54] are present in Scripture, or, in which two propositions are determined to be in conflict. The *middah* recommends that a third proposition be located that somehow will resolve the disagreement. Such reconciliation may result in a modification of one or both initial propositions. This hermeneutic rule really opens up the biblical text and allows for injections of Rabbinic theology. On the other hand, from the point of logic, one might argue that the two propositions are not affected by the third and that the third proposition shows in fact that the presumed conflict does not occur at all. Exod. 19:20 says: *The Lord came down upon Mount Sinai*, and Deut. 4:36 says: *Out of heaven He made you hear his voice*. These verses implies that God was both "down," close to earth, *and* "up," in the heavens. The conflict is resolved by rule Thirteen in Sifra 1:7: "A third [passage comes and decides between them]. *For from heaven I spoke with you* (Exod. 20:22). This teaches [us] that the Holy One, blessed be he, bent the heavens of the highest heaven onto Mount Sinai and spoke with them. And thus David says in the Book of Psalms, *He bowed the heavens and came down; thick darkness was under His feet* (Ps. 18:10)." Additionally, this hermeneutic rule alleges with reference to Exod. 20:19 that "you yourselves have seen that I have talked with you from heaven." This means that God brought the heavens down to earth and spoke. Typically, this *middah* works by showing that one or both of the initial propositions are are conditional, or contingent, rather than general. Num. 7:89 says, *Moses went into the tent of meeting* to speak with God, while Exod. 40:35 says that Moses *was not able to enter* into it *because the cloud dwelt upon it*. The latter clause was needed to resolve the contradiction between the first two statements, making them both conditional. Thus, Moses came in and spoke with God when the cloud departed, and he stayed out when it was there.

In comparison to the other *middot*, there is a distinct theological approach in this rule: whole propositions are involved rather than specified forms (as in *kelal u-ferat*). The Rabbinic interpreters searched the biblical text for a premise, which was not formally pre-defined. Additionally, sometimes there was no third verse that could resolve the conflict; in this case the text was opened for massive Rabbinic intervention. Also, rule Thirteen is applied when the antecedents of the conflicting propositions are one and the same.

Further *middot* (8–11) from the list of Ishmael resolve apparent redundancies and discrepancies in Scripture. Since these discrepancies are based upon tensions or inconsistencies between propositions, the only

---

[53] R. Hammer, trans., *Sifre*, pp. 71f.

[54] Such propositions are called "p-terms;" see U. Eco, *The Limits of Interpretation*, p. 237.

way to resolve them is by Rabbinic theological interjection. Thus, the hermeneutic rule *Kol davar she-hayah bi-khelal ve-yatza* (anything that was part of a general term and came out) provides the major and minor premises in Scripture. Once the premises of the Scriptural lemmata have been determined in a "correct" manner, Rabbinic interpretation may ensue.

The Nature of the Biblical Text

The biblical text may be viewed as an "aesthetic subject," which allows us to describe the interrelationship between the text and the Rabbinic interpreters and to proceed from the productive encounter between both. Umberto Eco established three intentions of interpretation: the *intentio operis* that, in terms of midrashic hermeneutics, refers to descriptive text theories, the *intentio lectoris* responsible for arranging the aesthetics of reception, which in midrash enables the recognition of the graphic character of Scriptural signs, and the *intentio auctoris*, which represents the viewpoint of a traditional historical-critical exegesis of the biblical text and which assigns the task of correcting the biblical text to the rabbis. This is most important for the theological foundations of Rabbinic interpretation because it addresses the entrance way of the interpretation. Rabbinic exegesis concentrates to a large extent on the graphic sign, which is an aesthetic "object." The meaning of this *sign* is essential, which means that midrash is almost without exception metalinguistic, since it interprets the linguistic signs construed from Scripture.[55] Midrash is a discourse on the meaning of linguistic signs; it expresses what God wants to say. Rabbinic interpretation seldom deals with the empirical world that is also contained in Scripture; rather, it makes the linguistic world of Scripture its world of experience. From a series of events to a theological paradigm, everything within the realm of the Rabbinic experience was a repetition of Scripture. Things were not new but already known.

Creativity in respect to Scripture, which is the major vehicle of interjecting theological propositions, is made possible by the Rabbinic use of some purely deductive processes, such as a hermeneutics based upon opposition, conditional syllogism and apodosis. Any restriction of exegesis in such areas would be close to antinomy, which would have to be excluded. Rabbinic "theological" interference, possibly transmitted through the oral tradition and thus given at Sinai, can only be applied to inductive processes. These include hermeneutic situations that allow for more than one possible answer to a question, however, it is conceivable that there is a divine decision as to which answer is correct.

The Time Cycle

It has often been noted that the sages were not interested in astrology, the key discipline for interpreting time. A similar disregard for time is found in Rabbinic exegesis, in which the biblical text loses any time reference. The biblical narrative serves as a basis for the religious praxis of the rabbis and the exegete understands Scripture's

---

[55] See A. Goldberg, "Die funktionale Form Midrasch." In *Rabbinische Texte als Gegenstand der Auslegung. Gesammelte Studien II* (Tübingen, 1999), p. 216.

meaning in his own time. Thus, the present, at any given moment, forms the context of Scripture.[56] Midrashic interpretation is hermeneutical,[57] because there are no boundaries between the time of the rabbis and the time of Scripture. All signs in Scripture and the rabbis are in one semiotic field, and the signs in Scripture are indeterminate from the perspective of time. The aspect of time that we view as the "past," the utilization of an "earlier" and available textual medium, forms a constant present of the rabbis. The sages interject themselves into this past that becomes their present in the process of interpretation. Everything that is happening in their present has a model, which means that it occurs in Scripture. This is a total absence and negation of newness. Under this premise, the midrashic enterprise has an almost perfect coherence with the past, and merely seems to organize this past. For the Torah narrative, any sequence moves at least as instantly from future to past as in midrash. In Rabbinic theology, the movement of historical time forms a seamless web with no distinctive chronological divisions.[58] This can only be accomplished by textual interpretation and the vistas created by it. Future interpretations retroactively fill in the content of the original teaching.

The Truth of the Message and Nature of Scripture

The midrashic view of the Hebrew Bible further rejects the possibility that there is an external source of knowledge such as philosophy, medicine or astrology, any historical source or any work by an ancient author, which are as dependable and authoritative as Scripture.[59] There is almost no external corroboration of the theological implications of Scripture or any "facts" gathered from the text itself. This constructed a self-referentiality which developed into another essential feature of midrashic hermeneutics.[60] Scripture is the utmost authority because it is a communication of God to Israel, and as such divorced from the events reported in it. The interpreter of Scripture perceives that what is being said is that some events took place, but he also comprehends that there is no immediate access to that event. The exegete has only access to a linguistic communication. Nevertheless, the hermeneutic rules bring into the event of the "original" revelation the contention that a continuation of this revelation is possible by exegesis. Later revelations as such require exegesis which confirms the notion that the Oral Torah is the companion and as such co-existent with the Written Torah.

---

[56] Heinemann, "The Nature of the Aggadah," in G. Hartmann and S. Budick, eds., *Midrash and Literature* (New Haven, 1986), pp. 48f., refers to the aspect of time in aggadic midrash: "the creators of aggadah looked back into Scripture... they looked forward into the present and the future... the aggadists do not mean so much to clarify difficult passages in the biblical texts as to take stand on the burning questions of the day, to guide the people and to strengthen their faith."

[57] G.L. Bruns, "The Hermeneutics of Midrash," in R.M. Schwartz, ed., *The Book and the Text* (Cambridge, 1990), p. 210, n. 5, mentions that midrash is not eisegesis, but "hermeneutical practice that tells us a good deal about what it is to understand a text."

[58] Heschel, *Torah Min Ha-Shamayim*, vol. 1, p. 199.

[59] This seems to be a major point where the unfolding Christian exegesis differed. Christian exegesis at the time of Augustine at least purported that the exegete know the sciences in order to understand Scriptures because an allegorical interpretation often needed to be allocated to scientific facts.

[60] The development of Rabbinic literature into a self-referential literature took several centuries; thus, Rabbinic literature may be differentiated into separate documents.

If the participants in the interpretative effort begin to question the above assumptions of the divine origin and the nature of Scripture by examining the methods of interpretation and their own motivations, or otherwise depart from the theological plan of interpretation, the midrashic enterprise spins out of control; we may assume that such enterprises were not included in the resulting oral or written texts or were pursued by outsiders who were not accepted into the Rabbinic circles that practiced midrashic exegesis. One of the drawbacks of the rule-controlled interpretation is that it fails to discover anything drastically new in respect to theology. Pursuant to this theory, the matrix of theology was inherent in the Torah,[61] and the sages merely extracted its theological details. In terms of control over theological issues, one might observe that different religious groups declined to subordinate their theological readings of Scripture to Rabbinic rule-governed theology. It is possible that the Sages had a notion that the Hebrew Bible was in a position of saying everything. There existed some superfluidity of every meaning in this notion. However, Rabbinic theology had to invent or to continue some method of controlling "the free interpretation" of Scripture.[62] One of the crucial attempts in this realm was the unsuccessful systematization of the hermeneutic approach which was "squeezed into a corset" of rules.

Beyond these attempts, any part of Scripture can be linked with any other part, any sign related to any other sign. Since the signs are independent of any context, interpretation becomes inter-textual: Scripture is interpreted from Scripture, not from the world. In semiotics this enables the interpreters to relate signs to each other even after they have been isolated from their original contexts. In Rabbinic interpretation, this resulted in the phenomenon of an atomistic approach to Scripture, which allows the interpretation to concentrate on a single sign of varying length. One lemma in midrash may consist of one single graphic sign, a letter, a trope, a sentence or a verse, but rarely beyond that, usually without regard to the surrounding text and thus without taking notice of the overall sense. The record of divine speech and action was taken for granted, the legitimacy of Scripture is not contested and the only disputes that developed concerned exegetical meaning and not the status of Scripture as holy writing. Since the divine in Scripture is recorded in what superficially appears to be human language,[63] it can be comprehended by the application of hermeneutics, which in this case extends the divinity of the text into its interpretation.[64] The text can be reopened even though it is closed as a canon. The emergence of Rabbinic hermeneutics permitted to enter theology into Scripture. Hermeneutic rules extended the holiness of the text; however, there must have been a "good" (true) interpretation of the text and a "bad" one that had to be rejected. In order to eliminate the "bad" interpretation the explicit and implicit rules for acceptable interpretation were provided by the "gatekeepers" of the Rabbinic approach.

A reading of the text of Scripture discloses its overall meaning: Genesis is a creation story and a tale about the patriarchs and matriarchs. However, although Genesis Rabbah as a whole recapitulates this framework, the exegesis of the rabbis does not stop at this aspect.[65] Rabbinic midrash goes on to interpret and to correlate the text to

---

[61] Neusner, *Torah: From Scroll to Symbol*, p. 37.

[62] Eco, *Semiotics and the Philosophy of Language*, p. 150.

[63] Heschel, *Torah Min Ha-Shamayim*, vol. I, p. 189.

[64] Within this context it is important to emphasize that Rabbinic exegesis does not utilize allegory; Philo utilized allegorical interpretation when he derived concepts from the text of Scripture. In contrast, Rabbinic exegesis is propositional.

[65] For example, Genesis Rabbah 1:26.

its theology. It does so, however, not by taking the text in its unity, in which case the result would be a rewritten Bible,[66] which refers to the intention of rewriting the Bible or biblical books for a specific, Hellenistic or sectarian, audience. Instead, the rabbis applied the *middot* by focusing on the individual signs in isolation.

The *middot* were necessary to interpret the Written Torah, to extract the theology from the revealed and available word of God, which makes the language of the Bible different from the communication between humans. This unique status of biblical signs of being a combination of superficially human language and Divine revelatory medium is unique and cannot readily be compared to the exegesis of works of fiction or corpora of legal texts. Rabbinic Judaism was text centered and its literature is different than the Gospels, since it does not deal with the records of single rabbis;[67] rather, the distinctive modes of thinking are dependent upon the linguistic character of the revelation which is explained in words. Rabbinic exegesis is propositional, not allegorical; Rabbinic exegesis continually determines, "this Scriptural lemma means the following." Since all lemmata are part of divine Scripture, their meanings are true if the hermeneutic rules have been correctly applied. The validity of the scriptural interpretation gained from this applied exegesis was dependent upon its acceptance by the rabbis and their circles, the religious elite.[68] Validity and truth do not mean in any way that there is only one correct meaning for the text; in spite of everything, the interpretation may convey many different meanings or insights depending upon the interpreter. Midrash is therefore hermeneutic discourse at its best and not any other genre of literature, although it may comprise bits and pieces of other literary genres.[69] However, truth, that is the correctness of any interpretation, is not something that is established by authoritarian imposition, rather, it is dependent upon the underlying theological assumptions that are already expressed in the Bible and were fully utilized by the Sages. Midrash seems to be a collective effort by a group—"the rabbis"—who utilized the generative theological power of the *middot* to create the medium of midrash.

Therefore, the often-perceived "coherence of Rabbinic Judaism" in its formative texts is partially due to the constraints utilized in the discourse of the interpretations; these constraints become visible in the *a priori* religious principles of the midrashic interpretations. In order to obtain the right answers, suitable to all theological inquiries, variables of interpretation must be controlled and limited. It is part of that larger program of Rabbinic theology and midrashic hermeneutics that can only be spelled out on the basis of internal evidence.

Conclusion

In the application of the *middot*, we find a certain density of theological categories[70] that provide us with the notion of sense. Midrash must decode past events and graphic

---

[66] Such as the as the Greek Esther or the Esther story in Josephus, *Bell.*, VI.

[67] J. Neusner, *The Four Stages of Rabbinic Judaism* (London and New York, 1999), p. x.

[68] Eco, *Semiotics and the Philosophy of Language*, p. 152, remarks that "The power consists in possessing the key for the right interpretation or (which is the same) in being acknowledged by the community as the one who possesses the key."

[69] A general weakening of the midrashic form and its theology transpired over the centuries; see J. Elbaum, "From Sermon to Story; the Transformation of the Akedah," in *Prooftexts* 6, no. 2 (1986), pp. 97–116.

[70] Neusner, *From Literature to Theology in*

signs from the past in a religious manner. This means that something that has already been determined has to be decontextualized. Subsequently, this has to be presented as something that belongs to the system of Rabbinic Judaism and is practical in the world.[71] The Rabbinic interpreters utilizing the *middot* assume that their interpretation yields the correct theological approach to the text; thus the rules can only be applied with the applicable theological presuppositions. This coincides with the performative function of midrash as an activity of inquiry which serves as a matrix for future generations of interpreters. There are norms and order in the Torah which are uncovered by the "norms" of Rabbinic midrash through the application of its explicit and implicit hermeneutics.

Bibliography

Fishbane, Michael, *The Garments of Torah. Essays in Biblical Hermeneutics* (Bloomington, 1989).

Neusner, Jacob, *The Foundations of the Theology of Judaism* (Northvale, 1991).

———, *The Four Stages of Rabbinic Judaism* (London and New York, 1999).

———, *The Theology of the Oral Torah* (Montreal, 1999).

———, *The Hermeneutics of the Rabbinic Category-Formations: An Introduction* (Lanham, 2001).

———, *Incarnation of God: The Character of Divinity in Formative Judaism* (Binghamton, 2001).

Petuchowski, Jakob J., *Ever Since Sinai*. 3rd revised ed. (Milwaukee, 1979).

Stern, David, *Midrash and Theory. Ancient Jewish Exegesis and Contemporary Literary Studies* (Evanston, 1996).

Ulmer, Rivka, "Discourse in Midrash: Textual Strategy and the Use of Personal Pronouns in Halakhic Midrash," *Approaches to Ancient Judaism*, N.S. XIII (1998) pp. 51–70.

RIVKA KERN-ULMER
Bucknell University

Theology of Rabbinic Midrash

The Midrash compilations differ from one another in topic, logic, and rhetoric. But all of them share a structure of category-formations and participate in common in a single theological system. What, exactly, do I mean by "theology"? A suitable definition is given by Ingolf Dalferth:

> Theology rationally reflects on questions arising in pre-theological religious experience and the discourse of faith; and it is the rationality of its reflective labor in the process of faith seeking understanding which inseparably links it with philosophy. For philosophy is essentially concerned with argument and the attempt to solve conceptual problems, and conceptual problems face theology in all areas of its reflective labors.[1]

Formative Judaism, p. 45, indicates that there are several components in a "well-crafted and cogent system," among these are a "repeated message" and the question "of how to get in."

[71] Eco, *The Limits of Interpretation*, p. 215.
[1] Ingolf U. Dalferth, *Theology and Philosophy* (Oxford, 1988), p. vii.

In general terms, *theology thinks philosophically about religion.* Religion supplies the data, theology orders the data into propositions that can be generalized, tested against further data, and shown harmonious and cogent throughout. In Rabbinic Judaism, the Torah supplies the data, the facts of God's presence and activity among men. The sages adduce from those data generalizations, rules that may apply to other data. They form a coherent system of such generalizations about God and his self-manifestation in the Torah. Theology is a generalizing science.

Each midrashic document shares with all the others a corpus of theological ideas that cohere. When the Rabbinic sages read any passage of Scripture, they bring to bear a body of cogent theological narratives and of coherent ideas, organized in governing category-formations. That is shown by a simple fact. The Rabbinic Midrash compilations prove purposeful. They do not express chaotic, inchoate religious attitudes, incoherent notions about this and that. Rather, the Rabbinic Midrash translates into a principle of reading Scripture—hermeneutics—a particular theological conception. That hermeneutics repeatedly comes to concrete expression in details of the reading of passage after passage of Scripture. The upshot is readily stated: (1) A theology realized in (2) hermeneutics generates (3) exegesis, thus provoking (4) that particular and determinate reading that produces a Midrash exegesis.

The Midrashic Exercise of Generalization and Systematization

Scripture gives the particular fact, Midrash in its theological formation then embodies the fact as a case that yields a general rule. One example of Midrash exegesis as the transformation of a datum into a case to yield a rule is simply stated. God saved Israel at the Sea by doing certain things; when God saves Israel at the end of days, he will do those same things. The initial fact or *act* of salvation then is generalized into the exemplification, the *procedure* of salvation. Precisely what God did at the Sea he will do in the end of days. That yields the theological model of salvation, indicating what is to be looked for and expected. In the Rabbinic Midrash, then, the Rabbinic sages transform cases into rules; as in the Mishnah and the Talmuds they turn laws into jurisprudence, jurisprudence into social policy. Here, then, the religious information established by Scripture is translated into theological knowledge bearing broad implications for all eternity.

The upshot is simple. The Rabbinic Midrash shows the way in which the Rabbinic sages turned Scripture's theological facts—things that God said or did—into generalizations that further bring into being and encompass new theological facts. For, in this context, Scripture represents the counterpart, for the domain of holy Israel, of the facts of nature. Nature's facts generate propositions, syllogisms that are capable of yielding theories governing a broad range of further facts. For the Rabbinic sages, Scripture's facts work in a comparable way, and the Midrash embodies that working. So, to summarize, the Rabbinic Midrash turns the facts of Scripture into rules capable of encompassing further facts, forming data into a capacious structure, a working system—theology.

Theology Deriving from the Realization of the Encounter with God in Scripture

Rabbinic Midrash takes place in the encounter, in the Torah, between God and Israel. It also spells out, on the foundations of the revealed record of the Torah (encompassing Prophets and Writings), the character and implications of that encounter.

The categorical structure of every document of the Rabbinic Midrash encompasses the components, God and man; the Torah; Israel and the nations. The working-system of the Torah finds its dynamic in the struggle between God's plan for creation—to create a perfect world of justice—and man's will. That dialectics embodies in a single paradigm the events contained in the sequences, rebellion, sin, punishment, repentance, and atonement; exile and return; or the disruption of world order and the restoration of world order.

Let me set forth a somewhat more elaborate synopsis of this point, defining the four principles of the theology that animate the Rabbinic Midrash compilations, process, and exegeses:

> 1. God formed creation in accord with a plan, which the Torah reveals. Those who possess the Torah—Israel—know God and those who do not—the gentiles—reject him in favor of idols. What happens to each of the two sectors of humanity, respectively, responds to their relationship with God. Israel in the present age is subordinate to the nations, because God has designated the gentiles as the medium for penalizing Israel's rebellion, meaning through Israel's subordination and exile to provoke Israel to repent.
> 2. The perfection of creation, realized in the rule of exact justice, is signified by the timelessness of the world of human affairs, their conformity to a few enduring paradigms that transcend change. No present, past, or future marks time, but only the recapitulation of those patterns.

The third proposition is what imparts energy to the Midrash process in particular:

> 3. Israel's condition, public and personal, marks flaws in creation. What disrupts perfection is the sole power capable of standing on its own against God's power, and that is man's will. What man controls and God cannot coerce is man's capacity to form intention and therefore choose either arrogantly to defy, or humbly to love, God. Because man defies God, the sin that results from man's rebellion flaws creation and disrupts world order. The paradigm of the rebellion of Adam in Eden governs, the act of arrogant rebellion leading to exile from Eden thus accounting for the condition of humanity. But, as in the original transaction of alienation and consequent exile, God retains the power to encourage repentance through punishing man's arrogance. In mercy, moreover, God exercises the power to respond to repentance with forgiveness, that is, a change of attitude evoking a counterpart change. Since, commanding his own will, man also has the power to initiate the process of reconciliation with God, through repentance, an act of humility, man may restore the perfection of that order that through arrogance he has marred.
> 4. God ultimately will restore that perfection that embodied his plan for creation. In the work of restoration death that comes about by reason of sin will die, the dead will be raised and judged for their deeds in this life, and most of them, having been justified, will go on to eternal life in the world to come. The paradigm of man restored to Eden is realized in Israel's return to the land of Israel. In that world or age to come, however, that sector of humanity that through the Torah knows God will encompass all of humanity.

The universalizing method of paradigmatic thinking about matters of Scriptural narrative yields a universalistic message concerning the destiny of humanity.

The message that Scripture yields through Rabbinic Midrash exegesis involves the comparison of Adam and Israel, each having possessed paradise—the Garden of Eden, the land of Israel, respectively—and each having lost it. The last things are to be known from the first. In the just plan of creation humanity was meant to live in Eden, and Israel in the land of Israel in time without end. Humanity sinned and lost Eden. Israel sinned and lost the Land. So the sages state, had Israel not sinned, Scripture would have closed with the book of Joshua: the people settled in the Land. Then, at the other end of time, the eschatological restoration of humanity to Eden, Israel to the Land, will bring about that long and tragically-postponed perfection of the world order, sealing the demonstration of the justice of God's plan for creation. Risen from the dead, having atoned through death, humanity will be judged in accord with his deeds. Israel for its part, when it repents and conforms its will to God's, recovers its Eden. So the consequences of rebellion and sin having been overcome, the struggle of humanity's will and God's word having been resolved, God's original plan will be realized at the last. The simple, global logic of the system, with its focus on the world order of justice established by God but disrupted by humanity, leads inexorably to this eschatology of restoration, the restoration of balance, order, proportion—eternity for all who worship the one true God.

Components of that system surface hither and yon, and to see how the Midrash compilations participate in the system, we do well to consider how that is the case. To do so, I take six propositions central to the theological system and structure just now sketched and show how various Midrash compilations set forth those propositions. That exposition of fundamental points of a single theological system and structure comes to expression without regard to its documentary venue. When we differentiate one document from another, or from all others, we cannot point to a theological emphasis or preference that distinguishes one from another or from all others. A single system surfaces hither and yon, indifferent to documentary lines. My study of the twelve documents of the Rabbinic Midrash has repeatedly pointed to that fact. Now I wish in a more general exercise to instantiate it, doing so six times. My simple point is, the theological expositions we are about to consider can have appeared in any document; they fit into any compilation, whatever its particular topical program or even its distinctive doctrinal position, e.g., Sifra on the Mishnah's category-formations. I readily concede that six other propositions can have served with the same effect: to illustrate the theological cogency of the Rabbinic Midrash. To disprove the proposition at hand, I should have to identify six other presentations in a systematic manner of propositions that contradict the system and structure outlined above. That I cannot do.

I claim there is none in the whole of the Rabbinic Midrash. That is to say, my six propositions yield six contrary ones. In the Rabbinic Midrash, can I find at any point equivalently systematic constructions that argue for the contrary view? No, I cannot. If I were to frame a null hypothesis, it would look something like this. Rabbinic Midrash does not rest upon a coherent theological foundation. That is shown by the fact that in the Rabbinic Midrash compilations, I can adduce evidence of equal probative value for the proposition that, e.g., the dead are raised by the messiah in preparation for judgment, and the dead are not raised (by anybody) and are not judged. Now we shall test that null hypothesis. I do it by presenting a denial of the six propositions we are about to survey in the Midrash compilations. Were I to find in the dozen documents counterpart demonstrations of the opposite of these propositions, it would disprove my claim that these propositions animate the Midrash compilations uniformly: [1] God will resurrect the dead and judge all for eternal life; [2] God will undertake the restoration of humanity to Eden in the form of Israel to Zion; [3] Scripture yields exile and return as the paramount motif of the Scriptural narrative; [4] the redemption from Egypt adumbrates the redemption for the world to come; [5] Israel is destined for life in the world to come; [6] gentiles/idolaters denied the world to come. Now I state as fact: none of these propositions contrary to those I shall now present is entertained in a comparably systematic manner, or in any way at all, in any Midrash compilation. That proves that the system now instantiated in affirmative terms prevails and characterizes the entirety of the Rabbinic Midrash compilations.

The Resurrection of the Dead and Judgment unto Life Eternal

Paradigmatic thinking in monotheism necessarily generates the conviction of resurrection. This is stated in so many words. The certainty of resurrection derives from a simple fact of restorationist theology: God has already shown that he can do it, so Genesis Rabbah LXXVII:I.1: "You find that everything that the Holy One, blessed be he, is destined to do in the age to come he has already gone ahead and done through the righteous in this world. The Holy One, blessed be he, will raise the dead, and Elijah raised the dead." Sages deem urgent the task of reading outward and forward from Scripture, and at the critical conclusion of their theological system the Oral Torah focuses upon Scripture's evidence, the regularization of Scripture's facts.

Among the components of that doctrine, that resurrection of the dead is a doctrine set forth by the written Torah and demonstrable within the framework of the Torah occupies a principal place in the Oral Torah's exposition of the topic. That proposition is demonstrated over and over again. Evidence from the Torah concerning the resurrection of the dead is ubiquitous:

SIFRÉ TO DEUTERONOMY CCCVI:XXVIII.3:
A. And so did R. Simai say, "There is no passage [in the Torah] that does not contain [clear evidence concerning] the resurrection of the dead, but we have not got the power of exegesis [sufficient to find the pertinent indication].
B. "For it is said, 'He will call to the heaven above and to the earth, that he may judge his people' (Ps. 50:4).
C. "'He will call to the heaven above': this refers to the soul.
D. "'and to the earth': this refers to the body.
E. "'that he may judge his people': who judges with him?
F. "And how on the basis of Scripture do we know that Scripture speaks only of the resurrection of the dead?
G. "As it is said, 'Come from the four winds, O breath, and breathe upon these slain, that they may live' (Ez. 37:9)."

Further proofs of the same proposition are abundant, with the following instances representative of the larger corpus. First, we note the recurrent formula, "how on the basis of the Torah do we know...?" Then we are given a sequence of cases, each one of them, as noted earlier, deriving from an individual, none of them appealing to the eternity of the collectivity of Israel.

Standing under God's Judgment

How to stand in judgment, meaning, go through the process of divine review of one's life and actions and emerge in the world to come, restored to the Land that is Eden? Proper conduct and study of Torah lead to standing in judgment and consequent the life of the world to come, and not keeping the one and studying the other deny entry into that life. What is striking is the appeal to Eden for just this message about reentry into the Land.

> LEVITICUS RABBAH XXXV:VI:1F.:
> 1. A. Said R. Abba b. Eliashib, "[The reference at Lev. 26:3 to statutes is to] statutes that bring a person into the life of the world to come.
>   B. "That is in line with the following verse of Scripture: 'And he who is left in Zion and remains in Jerusalem will be called holy, everyone who has been recorded for life in Jerusalem' [Is. 4:3]—for he is devoted to [study of] Torah, which is called the tree of life."

Now comes the reference to Eden:

> 2.A. It has been taught in the name of R. Eliezer, "A sword and a scroll wrapped together were handed down from heaven, as if to say to them, 'If you keep what is written in this [scroll], you will be saved from the sword,
>   B. "'and if not, in the end [the sword] will kill you.'"
>   C. "Whence is that proposition to be inferred? 'He drove out the man, and at the east of the Garden of Eden he placed the cherubim, and a flaming sword which turned every way, to guard the way to the tree of life' [Gen. 3:4].
>   D. "The [first] reference to 'the way' refers to the rules of proper conduct, and the second reference, '[the way to] the tree of life' refers to the Torah."

The same message is given in a different framework:

> 3.A. It was taught in the name of R. Simeon b. Yohai, "A loaf and a rod wrapped together were given from heaven.
>   B. "It was as if to say to them, 'If you keep the Torah, lo, here is bread to eat, and if not, lo, here is a staff with which to be smitten.'
>   C. "Whence is that proposition to be inferred? 'If you are willing and obedient, you shall eat the good of the land; but if you refuse and rebel, you shall be devoured by the sword' (Is. 15:19–20)."

The world to come, involving resurrection and judgment, will be attained through the Torah, which teaches proper conduct. That simple doctrine yields the proposition here.

The Restoration of Humanity to Eden

How, exactly, do the sages envisage restoration? Predictably, because they think paradigmatically and not in historical (let alone cyclical) sequences, the sages find models of the end in beginnings. That is why in this context they cluster, and systematically review, the two principal ones, liberation, restoration. First is the account of Israel's liberation from Egypt, the initial act of redemption, which will be recapitulated in the end. Second, comes the story of Adam and Eden for their picture of the world to come, the return of Adam to Eden, now in the form of Israel to Zion.

Whatever model serves out of Scripture, the restorationist eschatology is stated in so many words in the following, which appeals to the rhetoric of return, restoration and renewal:

> LAMENTATIONS RABBATI CXLIII:I.1FF.
> A. "Restore us to yourself, O Lord, that we may be restored!:"
> B. Said the Community of Israel before

the Holy One, blessed be He, "Lord of the world, it all depends on you: 'Restore us to yourself, O Lord.'"

C. Said to them the Holy One, blessed be He, "It all depends on you: 'Return to me and I will return to you, says the Lord of hosts' (Mal. 3:7)."

D. Said the Community of Israel before the Holy One, blessed be He, "Lord of the world, it all depends on you: 'Restore us, O God of our salvation' (Ps. 85:5)."

E. Thus it says, "Restore us to yourself, O Lord, that we may be restored!"

Israel insists that restoration depends on God, but God repays the compliment, and the exchange then is equal: God restores Israel when Israel returns to God, just as we learned when we examined the category of repentance and atonement.

Now we see a sequence of models of redemption. First, as anticipated, comes the explicit comparison of Adam's Eden with the coming restoration, part of a sequence of recapitulated paradigms:

2.A. "Renew our days as of old:"

B. As in the days of the first Adam: "So he drove out the man and he placed at the east of the garden of Eden the cherubim" (Gen. 3:24). [The word for "east" and the word for "of old" using the same letters, the sense, is this: "Renew our days like those of him in connection with whom *kedem* is stated." After being driven out, Adam repented of his sin.]

The restoration involves the Temple offerings as well, which later on are defined in particular; this is here too "as in the days of old:"

3.A. Another interpretation of the phrase, "Renew our days as of old:"

B. That is in line with this verse: "Then shall the offering of Judah and Jerusalem be pleasant to the Lord as in the days of old and as in ancient years" (Mal. 3:4).

But the restoration is multi-dimensional, since it involves, also, the figures of Moses and Solomon:

C. "as in the days of old:" this refers to Moses: "Then his people remembered the days of old, the days of Moses" (Is. 63:11).

D. "and as in ancient years:" this refers to the time of Solomon.

Noah and Abel, for reasons that are specified, now are introduced; they are necessary for the reason given at the end:

4.A. [Another interpretation of the phrase, "Renew our days as of old:"]

B. Rabbi says, "'as in the days of old' refers to the time of Noah: 'For this is as the waters of Noah unto me' (Is. 54:9).

C. "'and as in ancient years' refers to the time of Abel, prior to whose time there was no idolatry in the world."

Noah represents the moment at which God made his peace with humanity, even in humanity's flawed condition. Of intense interest for my analysis, within the restorationist pattern, Abel stands for the time before idolatry, so explicitly excluding idolaters from the world to come. While Noah, representing all of humanity, and Abel, standing even for antediluvian humanity, make their appearance, the upshot remains exclusionary. The restoration to perfection involves the exclusion of imperfection, and so idolaters cannot enter the new Eden. But, later on, we shall see other, inclusionary dimensions that logically complete the doctrine of the gentiles in the world to come.

Exile and Return

The pattern that is adumbrated in these statements encompasses not only restoration, but the recapitulation of the paradigm of oppression, repentance, and reconciliation. For restoration cannot stand by itself but must be placed into that context in which the restoration takes on heavy weight. So not only Adam and Eden, but the entire past of suffering but finally of salvation, is reviewed in the same context. Many salvations, not only one, are recorded for Israel, all of them conforming to a single pattern, which imparts its definition upon the final act of salvation as well, the one that comes with personal resurrection and all-Israel's entry into the world to come. So the paradigm of trouble but salvation for Israel works itself out, and it gives reassurance that God will redeem Israel in the future, as he did in the past; a pattern governs throughout. Indeed, the surest evidence of the coming redemption is the oppression that now takes place.

This point is stated in a variety of ways, taking an important place in the set of doctrines set forth around the theme of the world to come. Here is the simplest statement of why suffering and oppression present cause for renewed hope:

LAMENTATIONS RABBATI CXXII:I.1
1.A. "The punishment of your iniquity, O daughter of Zion, is accomplished, he will keep you in exile no longer"

Now comes the point that the very condition of Israel, its life in exile, serves as guarantee of the redemption that God is going to bring about. That relationship of complementarity—oppression, redemption—is why the act of oppression, now realized, validates the hope for the Messiah to signal the advent of the redemption fulfilled in the world to come. The theology not only accommodates the dissonant fact of Israel's subjugation but finds reassurance in it, as is stated in so many words:

B. R. Helbo in the name of R. Yohanan said, "Better was the removing of the ring by Pharaoh [for the sealing of decrees to oppress the Israelites] than the forty years during which Moses prophesied concerning them, because it was through this [oppression] that the redemption came about, while through that [prophesying] the redemption did not come about."

C. R. Simeon b. Laqish said, "Better was the removing of the ring by Ahasueros decreeing persecution of Israel in Media than the sixty myriads of prophets who prophesied in the days of Elijah, because it was through this [oppression] that the redemption came about, while through that [prophesying] the redemption did not come about."

D. Rabbis said, "Better was the Book of Lamentations than the forty years in which Jeremiah prophesied over them, because in it the Israelites received full settlement of their iniquities on the day the temple was destroyed.

E. "That is in line with the following verse: 'The punishment of your iniquity, O daughter of Zion, is accomplished.'"

In narrative form the statement sets forth the proposition that Israel's future is already clear from its present. Here the prophets provide the key to interpreting the one and anticipating the other. Just as the prophetic prediction of the ruin of Jerusalem has been realized, so the same prophets' promises of ultimate salvation will also come about. That yields a certainty about what is going to happen. The whole then forms a coherent pattern, one that reveals what will happen through what has happened.

If we deal with "last things," for the Oral Torah, "last" does not define a temporal category, or even an ordinal one in the exact sense. By "last things," the sages' theology means, the model of things that applies at the last, from now on, for eternity. By that, in the sages' case, they mean to say, the last, the final realization or recapitulation of the ever-present and enduring paradigm(s), creation and Exodus, for instance, as we just noticed. That is, I cannot sufficiently stress, a paradigm organizes and classifies relationships, treats concrete events as merely exemplary. So the actualities of this one's conduct with, and attitude toward, that One are restated in generalizations, laws or rules. "Love God" defines a relationship, and actions and attitudes that express that relationship then may be exemplified by incidents that show what happens when Israel loves God, or what happens when Israel does not love God. These further may be captured, many cases by a single pattern.

Redemption from Egypt, Redemption for the World to Come

In concrete terms that means intense interest will focus on the way in which the redemption of Israel from Egypt compares with the advent of the world to come. This point is made explicitly. The fall of the oppressor at the start of Israel's history and the fall of the nations at the end, character of the redemption of that time sand of the coming time, will be matched by the fall of the other at the end and the traits of the redemption that is coming. To see how this is made concrete is to enter into the theological workshop of the sages. No passage more clearly exposes the character of their thought—both its method and its message—than the one that requires them to select paradigmatic moments out of the detritus of history:

> PESIQTA DERAB KAHANA VII:XI.3
> 2.A. R. Levi, son-in-law of R. Zechariah, in the name of R. Berekhiah said, "As at the news concerning Egypt, so they shall be startled at the fall of the adversary (Is. 23:5)."
> B. Said R. Eliezer, "Whenever the name of Tyre is written in Scripture, if it is written out [with all of the letters], then it refers to the province of Tyre. Where it is written without all of its letters [and so appears identical to the word for enemy], the reference of Scripture is to Rome. [So the sense of the verse is that Rome will receive its appropriate reward.]"

Now the fall of Egypt is matched by the fall of Rome, which, we surely should anticipate, is a precondition for the advent of the world to come, at which point, at a minimum, the subjugation of Israel to the pagan empire ceases:

> 3.A. R. Levi in the name of R. Hama bar Hanina: "He who exacted vengeance from the former [oppressor] will exact vengeance from the latter.

Now the first redemption, from Egypt, is shown to match point by point the final redemption, from Edom/Rome. Each detail finds its counterpart in an amazing selection of consequential facts, properly aligned—ten in all:

> B. "Just as, in Egypt, it was with blood, so with Edom [= Rome] it will be the same: 'I will show won-

ders in the heavens and in the earth, blood, and fire, and pillars of smoke' (Job 3:3).

C. "Just as, in Egypt, it was with frogs, so with Edom it will be the same: 'The sound of an uproar from the city, an uproar because of the palace, an uproar of the Lord who renders recompense to his enemies' (Is. 66:6).

D. "Just as, in Egypt, it was with lice, so with Edom it will be the same: 'The streams of Bosrah will be turned into pitch, and the dust thereof into brimstone, and the land thereof shall become burning pitch (Is. 34:9). Smite the dust of the earth that it may become lice' (Exod. 8:12).

E. "Just as, in Egypt, it was with swarms of wild beasts, so with Edom it will be the same: 'The pelican and the bittern shall possess it' (Is. 34:11).

F. "Just as, in Egypt, it was with pestilence, so with Edom it will be the same: 'I will plead against Gog with pestilence and with blood' (Ez. 38:22).

G. "Just as, in Egypt, it was with boils, so with Edom it will be the same: 'This shall be the plague wherewith the Lord will smite all the peoples that have warred against Jerusalem: their flesh shall consume away while they stand upon their feet' (Zech. 14:12).

H. "Just as, in Egypt, it was with great stones, so with Edom it will be the same: 'I will cause to rain upon Gog . . . an overflowing shower and great hailstones' (Ez. 38:22).

I. "Just as, in Egypt, it was with locusts, so with Edom it will be the same: 'And you, son of man, thus says the Lord God: Speak to birds of every sort . . . the flesh of the mighty shall you eat . . . blood shall you drink . . . you shall eat fat until you are full and drink blood until you are drunk' (Ez. 39:17-19).

J. "Just as, in Egypt, it was with darkness, so with Edom it will be the same: 'He shall stretch over Edom the line of chaos and the plummet of emptiness' (Is. 34:11).

K. "Just as, in Egypt, he took out their greatest figure and killed him, so with Edom it will be the same: 'A great slaughter in the land of Edom, among them to come down shall be the wild oxen' (Is. 34:6-7)."

Merely juxtaposing "Egypt" and "Edom" suffices to establish that we shall compare the one and the other, and the paradigm of redemption emerges. The known, Egypt, bears the distinguishing trait of marking Israel's initial redemption; then the unknown can be illuminated. Therefore, say "Edom" (= Rome) and no one can miss the point: The stakes are sufficiently identified through the combination of the native categories, and all the rest spells out what is clear at the very outset. I do not think the method of paradigmatic thinking finds more lucid expression than in this articulate statement that the redemption that is coming replicates the redemption that is past in a world that conforms to enduring paradigms. And that must encompass, also, the return to Eden that we have many times considered.

Life in the World to Come

This brings us to the actualities of the world to come, what people are supposed to be doing then. What is going to happen in the age to come? Israel will eat and drink, sing and dance, and enjoy God, who will be lord of the dance. What about the restored Temple? The war of Gog and Magog having concluded, the dead having been returned to the Land and raised, the next stage in the restoration of world order requires the reconstruction of the Temple, where, as we recall, God and humanity, Heaven and earth, meet.

GENESIS RABBAH XCVIII:II.7
A. "Then Jacob called his sons and said, 'Gather yourselves together, that I may tell you what shall befall you in days to come:"
B. R. Simon said, "He showed them the fall of Gog, in line with this usage: 'It shall be in the end of days . . . when I shall be sanctified through you, O Gog' (Ez. 38:165). 'Behold, it shall come upon Edom' (Is. 34:5)."
C. R. Judah said, "He showed them the building of the house of the sanctuary: 'And it shall come to pass in the end of days that the mountain of the Lord's house shall be established' (Is. 2:2)."
D. Rabbis say, "He came to reveal the time of the end to them, but it was hidden from him."

So in the now-familiar sequence of restoration, [1] final war, [2] advent of the Messiah and the resurrection and judgment, and [3] the age to come, next in sequence must be [4] the restoration of Israel to the Land, and [5] rebuilding the Temple, destroyed by reason of Israel's sin.

But what purpose would now be fulfilled by the restoration of the Temple cult—the priesthood to the altar, the Levites to the platform, and all Israel to their courtyards, men's and women's respectively? Since the bulk of offerings in the Temple set forth by Moses in the written Torah had focused upon atonement for sin and guilt, what purpose would the Temple, and its surrogate, the synagogue, now serve? There is only a single one. In the age to come, responding to redemption, all offerings but the thanksgiving offering, appropriately, will cease, all prayers but thanksgiving prayers will cease. So it stands to reason:

LEVITICUS RABBAH IX:VII.1
A. R. Phineas and R. Levi and R. Yohanan in the name of R. Menahem of Gallia: "In time to come all offerings will come to an end, but the thanksgiving offering will not come to an end.
B. "All forms of prayer will come to an end, but the thanksgiving prayer will not come to an end.
C. "That is in line with that which is written, 'The voice of joy and the voice of gladness, the voice of the bridegroom and the voice of the bride,
D. "'the voice of them that say, "Give thanks to the Lord of hosts"' [Jer. 33:11]. This refers to the thanksgiving prayer.
E. "'Who bring a thanksgiving offering to the house of the Lord' [Jer. 33:11]. This refers to the offering of thanksgiving sacrifice.
F. "And so did David say, 'Your vows are incumbent upon me, O God [I will render thanksgivings to you]' [Ps. 56:13].
G. "'I shall render thanksgiving to you' is not written here, but rather, 'I shall render thanksgivings [plural] to you' [Ps. 56:13].
H. "The reference [of the plural usage], then, is to both the thanksgiving prayer and the thanksgiving offering."

Predicting the character of the Temple offerings in the future presents no difficulty when we recall that at that time, judgment will have taken place, sin removed, and atonement completed. So much of the work of the cult will have been accomplished, leaving only the one thing that remains: to give thanks. And it is not to be missed that the offering that will go forward is the offering that gentiles as much as Israelites may present, yet another mark of the eschatological universalism that characterizes the Judaic monotheism.

Idolaters, meaning, Gentiles and the World to Come

So much for individuals and the community, for Israelites and for all Israel. What of gentiles, meaning, idolaters? As we realize full well, gentiles with their idolatry simply will cease to exist; some will perish, just as Israelites will perish, just as the Generation of the Flood, the Generation of the Dispersion, the Men of Sodom, and certain Israelites will perish. But some—a great many—will give up idolatry and thereby become part of Israel. The gentiles as such are not subject to redemption; they have no choice at the advent of the world to come but to accept God or become extinct. But that is not the precise formulation that the system as I see it will set forth. Rather, the correct language is not, the gentiles will cease to exist, but rather, the category, "gentiles with their idolatry," will cease to function. Idolatry having come to an end, God having been recognized by all mankind, everyone will enter the category, "Israel."

Predictably, the sages seek analogies and patterns to work out in concrete terms the result of their compelling logic. In the present matter, the future of gentiles is worked out by analogy to Holy Things—the opposite, and the match in context, of gentiles. Some can be redeemed, some not.

MEKHILTA ATTRIBUTED TO R. ISHMAEL LXVII: I.31:
B. As to Holy Things, there are those that are subject to redemption and there are those that are not subject to redemption;
C. as to things that may not be eaten, there are those that are subject to redemption and there are those that are not subject to redemption;
D. as to things that may not be used for any sort of benefit, there are those that are subject to redemption and there are those that are not subject to redemption;
E. as to fields and vineyards, there are those that are subject to redemption and there are those that are not subject to redemption;
F. as to bondmen and bondwomen, there are those that are subject to redemption and there are those that are not subject to redemption;
G. as to those subject to the death penalty by a court, there are those that are subject to redemption and there are those that are not subject to redemption;

Now, the paradigm having established the possibilities, we come to the critical point.

H. so in the age to come, there are those that are subject to redemption and there are those that are not subject to redemption.

The nations cannot be redeemed. That is by definition: their idolatry in the end does them in:

I. The nations of the world are not subject to redemption: "No man can by any means redeem his brother nor give to God a ransom for him, for too costly is the redemption of their soul" (Ps. 49:8-9).
J. Precious are the Israelites, for the ransom of whose lives the Holy One, blessed be he, has given the nations of the world:
K. "I have given Egypt as your ransom" (Is. 43:4).
L. Why so?

M. "Since you are precious in my sight and honorable, and I have loved you, therefore I will give men for you and peoples for your life" (Is. 43:3-4).

Once more the past forms a presence in the immediate age, as much as the present participates in the past. Here the future of the gentiles realizes their present. They are idolaters—that is why to begin with they are classified as gentiles—and therefore they will not be redeemed, meaning, they will not stand in judgment or enjoy the eternal life of the world to come.

What of gentiles in general, apart from those self-selected by their conduct toward Israel for eternal Gehenna? In the age to come gentiles will renounce idolatry and accept the one God. There simply will be no more gentiles, everyone will serve God and come under the wings of his Presence, within Israel.

MEKHILTA ATTRIBUTED TO R. ISHMAEL XXXIII: I.1

A. "Who is like you, O Lord, among gods? [Who is like you, majestic in holiness, terrible in glorious deeds, doing wonders?]:"

B. When the Israelites saw that Pharaoh and his host had perished at the Red Sea, the dominion of the Egyptians was over, and judgments were executed on their idolatry, they all opened their mouths and said, "Who is like you, O Lord, among gods? [Who is like you, majestic in holiness, terrible in glorious deeds, doing wonders?]"

Now the nations participate in praising the one, true God of all creation:

C. And not the Israelites alone said the song, but also the nations of the world said the song.

D. When the nations of the world saw that Pharaoh and his host had perished at the Red Sea, the dominion of the Egyptians was over, and judgments were executed on their idolatry, they all renounced their idolatry and opened their mouths and confessed their faith in the Lord and said, "Who is like you, O Lord, among gods? [Who is like you, majestic in holiness, terrible in glorious deeds, doing wonders?]"

Once more the selected paradigm finds the future in the past, the pattern that governs in the quality of the relationship:

E. So too you find that the age to come the nations of the world will renounce their idolatry: "O Lord, my strength and my stronghold and my refuge, in the day of affliction to you the nations shall come ... shall a man make himself gods" (Jer. 16:19-20); "In that day a man shall cast away his idols of silver ... to go into the clefts of the rocks" (Is. 2:20-21). "And the idols shall utterly perish" (Is. 20:18).

The final step in the unfolding of creation according to plan will be the redemption of the nations of the world, their renunciation if idolatry and acceptance of God's rule. That will bring to perfect closure the drama that began with Adam. The nations' response to Israel's Exodus and redemption from Egypt prefigures what is to come about at the end.

The gentiles' rejection of the Torah as portrayed in Rabbinic Midrash chooses as its setting not the last judgment but the first encounter, that is, the giving of the Torah itself. In the timeless world constructed by the Oral Torah, what happens at the outset exemplifies how things always happen, and what happens at the end embodies what has always taken place. The basic thesis is identical—the gentiles cannot accept the Torah because to do so they would have to deny their very character.

But the exposition retains its interest because it takes its own course.

Of special interest, the Torah is embodied in some of the ten commandments—not to murder, not to commit adultery, not to steal; then the gentiles are rejected for not keeping the seven commandments assigned to the children of Noah. The upshot is that the reason that the gentiles rejected the Torah is that the Torah prohibits deeds that the gentiles do by their very nature. Israel ultimately is changed by the Torah, so that Israel exhibits traits imparted by their encounter with the Torah. So too with the gentiles, by their nature they are what they are; the Torah has not changed their nature. Once more a single standard applies to both components of humanity, but with opposite effect:

> SIFRÉ TO DEUTERONOMY CCCXLIII:IV.1FF.:
> 1.A. Another teaching concerning the phrase, "He said, 'The Lord came from Sinai'":
>   B. When the Omnipresent appeared to give the Torah to Israel, it was not to Israel alone that he revealed himself but to every nation.
>   C. First of all he came to the children of Esau. He said to them, "Will you accept the Torah?"
>   D. They said to him, "What is written in it?"
>   E. He said to them, "'You shall not murder' (Ex. 20:13)."
>   F. They said to him, "The very being of 'those men' [namely, us] and of their father is to murder, for it is said, 'But the hands are the hands of Esau'" (Gen. 27:22). 'By your sword you shall live' (Gen. 27:40)."

At this point we cover new ground: other classes of gentiles that reject the Torah; now the Torah's own narrative takes over, replacing the known facts of world politics, such as the earlier account sets forth, and instead supplying evidence out of Scripture as to the character of the gentile group under discussion:

>   G. So he went to the children of Ammon and Moab and said to them, "Will you accept the Torah?"
>   H. They said to him, "What is written in it?"
>   I. He said to them, "'You shall not commit adultery' (Exod. 20:13)."
>   J. They said to him, "The very essence of fornication belongs to them [us], for it is said, 'Thus were both the daughters of Lot with child by their fathers' (Gen. 19:36)."
>   K. So he went to the children of Ishmael and said to them, "Will you accept the Torah?"
>   L. They said to him, "What is written in it?"
>   M. He said to them, "'You shall not steal' (Exod. 20:13)."
>   N. They said to him, "The very essence of their [our] father is thievery, as it is said, 'And he shall be a wild ass of a man' (Gen. 16:12)."
>   O. And so it went. He went to every nation, asking them, "Will you accept the Torah?"
>   P. For so it is said, "All the kings of the earth shall give you thanks, O Lord, for they have heard the words of your mouth" (Ps. 138:4).
>   Q. Might one suppose that they listened and accepted the Torah?
>   R. Scripture says, "And I will execute vengeance in anger and fury upon the nations, because they did not listen" (Mic. 5:14).

At this point we turn back to the obligations that God has imposed upon the gentiles; these obligations have no bearing upon the acceptance of the Torah; they form part of the ground of being, the condition of existence, of the gentiles. Yet even here, the gentiles do not accept God's authority in matters of natural law:

S. And it is not enough for them that they did not listen, but even the seven religious duties that the children of Noah indeed accepted upon themselves they could not uphold before breaking them.

T. When the Holy One, blessed be He, saw that that is how things were, he gave them to Israel.

Now comes another parable, involving not a king but a common person:

2.A. The matter may be compared to the case of a person who sent his ass and dog to the threshing floor and loaded up a *letekh* of grain on his ass and three *seahs* of grain on his dog. The ass went along, while the dog panted.

B. He took a seah of grain off the dog and put it on the ass, so with the second, so with the third.

C. Thus was Israel: they accepted the Torah, complete with all its secondary amplifications and minor details, even the seven religious duties that the children of Noah could not uphold without breaking them did the Israelites come along and accept.

D. That is why it is said, "The Lord came from Sinai; he shone upon them from Seir."

In the conclusion at hand we see how the Judaic version of monotheism forms a complete system, making provision for all humanity within the framework of the revealed Torah.

Theology, Hermeneutics, and Exegesis

The theology of the Rabbinic Midrash tells a simple, sublime story.

[1] God created a perfect, just world and in it made man in his image, equal to God in the power of will.

[2] Man in his arrogance sinned and was expelled from the perfect world and given over to death. God gave man the Torah to purify his heart of sin.

[3] Man educated by the Torah in humility can repent, accepting God's will of his own free will. When he does, man will be restored to Eden and eternal life.

In our terms, we should call it a story with a beginning, middle, and end. In sages' framework, we realize, the story embodies an enduring and timeless paradigm of humanity in the encounter with God: man's powerful will, God's powerful word, in conflict, and the resolution thereof.

The Rabbinic sages claimed in their Midrash exegesis fully to spell out the message of the written Torah, as they do explicitly in nearly every document and on nearly every page of the Midrash compilations, so too did others outside of their circles. The sages' reading of Scripture recovers, in proportion and accurate stress and balance, the main lines of Scripture's principal story, the one about creation, the fall of man and God's salvation of man through Israel and the Torah, when the Torah succeeds in teaching Israel to repent. If, as Brevard Childs states, "The evangelists read from the New [Testament] backward to the Old,"[2] we may say very simply, *the sages through Midrash exegesis read from the written Torah forward to the oral one.*

JACOB NEUSNER
Bard College

---

[2] *Biblical Theology of the Old and New Testaments*, p. 720.

Women, Midrashic Constructions of

Women figure in the midrash in a variety of ways. This essay addresses the following themes: the construction of women as "other;" revisions of human creation; enumerations and justifications of female disadvantages; perspectives on women's ritual obligations; portrayals of women as wives; personifications of Israel in female terms; and renderings of some representative biblical women and two women from Rabbinic times.

Women as Other

Rabbinic views about women vary but all rest on the conviction of women's essential alterity from men. The talmudic statement that "Women are a separate people" (B. Shab. 62a) asserts that females are human entities created by God with physical characteristics, innate capacities, and social functions inherently dissimilar from those of males.[1] Women's bodies exempted them from the ritual of circumcision, the fleshly symbol of the special alliance between God and Jewish males, stressing the midrashic conviction that men were connected with the divine image in ways inaccessible to women. It is not surprising that the second sex occupied a subordinate place in Rabbinic Judaism's idealized world view, in which females were perceived to be other in ways that were not only ineradicable but problematic for males.

The aggadic passage at B. Nid. 31b points out several of the corporeal and spiritual areas where the Rabbinic sages perceived women as profoundly different from men. These include the perceptions that males are welcomed at birth because of their physical potential for generativity and because they enter the covenant through circumcision.[2] Females, on the other hand, are empty wombs requiring male insemination,[3] their birth delays their parents' resumption of sexual relations by an additional week, and their menstruation can require them to be separated from their husbands for almost half of each month:[4]

---

[1] For more detailed discussion of this talmudic passage and female alterity in Rabbinic literature in general, see Judith R. Baskin, *Midrashic Women: Formations of the Feminine in Rabbinic Literature* (Hanover, 2002), pp. 13-43.

[2] On the numerous dilemmas inherent in ancient and Rabbinic Judaism's perception of God as masculine and the corollary that human masculinity was expressed through procreation, see Howard Eilberg-Schwartz, *God's Phallus and Other Problems for Men and Monotheism* (Boston, 1994); Jacob Neusner, *Androgynous Judaism: Masculine and Feminine in the Dual Torah* (Macon, 1993); and Shaye J.D. Cohen, "Why Aren't Jewish Women Circumcised?" in Maria Wykes, ed., *Gender and the Body in the Ancient Mediterranean* (Oxford, 1998), pp. 136-154.

[3] On late antique views of human conception, see Baskin, *Midrashic Women*, pp. 19-21; Jan Blayney, "Theories of Conception in the Ancient Roman World," in Beryl Rawson, ed., *The Family in Ancient Rome: New Perspectives* (London, 1986), pp. 230-39, and Helen King, "Reading the Female Body," in Wykes, *Gender and the Body*, pp. 199-203.

[4] On Rabbinic regulations regarding the *niddah*, the menstruating woman, see Baskin, *Midrashic Women*, pp. 22-29; and Shaye J.D. Cohen, "Menstruants and the Sacred in Judaism and Christianity," in Sarah B. Pomeroy, ed., *Women's History and Ancient History* (Chapel Hill, 1991), pp. 273-299; Charlotte Elisheva Fonrobert, *Menstrual Purity: Rabbinic and Christian Reconstructions of Biblical Gender* (Stanford, 2000); Judith Hauptman, *Rereading the Rabbis* (Boulder, 1998), pp. 147-176; and Tirzah Meacham, "An Abbreviated History of the Development of the Jewish Menstrual Laws," in Rahel S. Wasserfall, ed., *Women and Water: Menstruation in Jewish Life and Law* (Hanover, 1999), pp. 23-39.

R. Isaac citing R. Ammi further stated: "As soon as a male comes into the world peace comes into the world...."
R. Isaac citing R. Ammi further stated: "When a male comes into the world his provisions come with him, [the Hebrew for] 'male' (*zakhar*) [being composed of the consonants for the words for] 'this is provision' (*zeh khar*).... [Conversely,] a female has nothing with her, [the Hebrew for] 'female' (*n'kevah*) implying 'she comes with nothing' (*n'kiyyah ba'ah*). Unless she demands "her food, nothing is given to her...."
".... And why did the Torah ordain that in the case of giving birth to a male [a woman may resume sexual relations with her husband] after seven days, but in the case of a female [relations may not resume until] after fourteen days? [On the birth of] a male, with whom all rejoice, she regrets her oath [uttered during the pains of childbirth of never again engaging in sexual relations] after seven days, [but on the birth of] a female, about whom everybody is upset, she does not regret her oath [of abstaining from sexual relations] until after fourteen days. And why did the Torah ordain circumcision on the eighth day? In order that the guests should not enjoy themselves while his father and mother are not in the mood for it [since they must abstain from intercourse until the eighth day]."

It was taught: R. Meir used to say, "Why did the Torah ordain that the uncleanness of menstruation should continue for [an additional] seven days? Because being in constant contact with his wife [a husband might] develop a loathing towards her. The Torah, therefore, ordained: Let her be unclean for seven days in order that she shall be beloved by her husband as at the time of her first entry into the bridal chamber."[5]

The final segment of B. Nid. 31b goes on to attribute distinctions between man and woman to differences in their modes of creation, a topic discussed in more detail below. The passage suggests that the preferred position for sexual intercourse is that in which the man, on top, looks towards his origins in the earth (i.e., to the cosmic substance from which God created him) while the woman, facing upward, looks toward the man from whose body she was created. Moreover, the text continues, because woman was created from a bone, which can be used as a musical instrument, her voice is described as sweet. A woman's sweet voice can be as much of a sexual incitement as her physical beauty, and B. Nid. 31b concludes with a proof text from Song of Songs 2:14, "Let me hear your voice;/For your voice is sweet/And your face is comely," evoking the pleasant and the problematic aspects of women's sexual attractiveness to men, both of which play significant roles in Rabbinic constructions of female qualities.

Re-visioning Female Creation

For the rabbis, woman's otherness originated in her creation. While midrashic tradition understood the biblical accounts of human beginnings as one continuous story, assuming that the male and female of Genesis 1 were the Adam and Eve of Gen. 2:4-3, questions about the details of human creation remained. The sages wondered whether both man and woman could have been created simultaneously in the divine image, as

---

[5] For more detailed discussion of this topic and its ramifications, see Baskin, *Midrashic Women*, pp. 44-64.

Gen. 1:27 appeared to imply, or if woman was the later and essentially lesser creation of Gen. 2:22.

The issue of simultaneous creation is addressed by Genesis Rabbah 8:1, commenting on "And God said: Let us make humanity . . ." (Gen. 1:26):

> ". . . You have formed me before and behind" (Ps. 139:5). . . . R. Jeremiah b. Leazar said: "When the Holy One, blessed be he, created the first *'adam*, he created it with both male and female sexual organs, as it is written, 'Male and female he created them, and he called their name *'adam'* (Gen. 5:2)." R. Samuel bar Nahman said, "When the Holy One, blessed be he, created the first *'adam*, he created him with two faces, then split him and made him two backs—a back for each side. . . ."

This midrash explains the apparent contradictions in the biblical accounts of the origins of man and woman by imagining that the original human being was a single entity with both male and female sexual characteristics. However, even in this vision of a primal androgyne the first human is still constructed as male. Only afterwards, as Samuel bar Nahman elaborates, did God separate the female "side" from the male individual to create a new and independent being. In these interpretations, both biblical versions of human creation are accounted for and any possibility of imagining an autonomous female creation separate from the original man is obviated.

The assumption that the initial human creation was a solitary male from whose body a woman was subsequently built is the view that most commonly appears in the Rabbinic aggadah. This is definitively stated in B. Ket. 8a, in the context of a discussion of the appropriate number of benedictions to be recited at a wedding feast:

> . . . The whole world agrees that there was only one creation [and it was of man alone], [but they differ in this] one holds that we go according to the [divine] intention [which had been to simultaneously create two human beings, man and woman] and the other holds that we go according to the fact [only man was created and woman was later created out of him]. [This is the import] of that statement of Rab Judah, [who] asked: "It is written, 'And God created man in his own image' (Gen. 1:27), and it is written, 'Male and female he created them' (Gen. 5:2). How is this [to be understood]? [In this way]: In the beginning it was the intention [of God] to create two [human beings in the divine image], and in the end [only] one was created."

In an extended midrashic excursus on the second version of creation, Genesis Rabbah 18:2 meditates on women's inherent and inevitable weaknesses as a consequence of her secondary formation:

> R. Joshua of Siknin said in R. Levi's name: "*Vayyiven* ('And He built' [Gen. 2:22]) is written, signifying that he considered well (*hitbonnen*) from what part to create her. Said he: 'I will not create her from [Adam's] head, lest she be swelled-headed; nor from the eye, lest she be a coquette; nor from the ear, lest she be an eavesdropper; nor from the mouth, lest she be a gossip; nor from the heart, lest she be prone to jealousy; nor from the hand, lest she be light-fingered; nor from the foot, lest she be a gadabout; but from the modest part of man, for even when he stands naked, that part is covered.' And as he created each limb he ordered her, 'Be a modest woman.' Yet in spite of all this . . . she is swelled-headed . . . she is a coquette . . . she is an eavesdropper . . . she is prone to jealousy . . . she is light-fingered . . . she is a gadabout."

In this literal revision of the construction of the female body, God is described as attempting to build a woman who would personify what the framers of Rabbinic Judaism believed to be ideal female qualities of humility, sexual modesty, domesticity, discretion, and passivity. However, despite the best divine intentions, woman, once built, possessed a profusion of undesirable characteristics.

This is not to say that females are seen as lacking in positive qualities. Woman's nurturing attributes, as well as her physical characteristics, are seen as essential to her most important functions as mother and wife. Genesis Rabbah 18:3 explains, "And the Lord God built (*vayyiven*) the rib that he had taken from the man into a woman" (Gen. 2:22) as follows: "R. Hisda said: 'He built more chambers in her than in man, fashioning her broad below and narrow at the top, so that she could receive child.'" This aggadic comment concludes by honoring the wifely role: "And he brought her to the man" (Gen. 2:22). "R. Abin observed: 'Happy the citizen for whom the king is best man!'" Moreover, women are also credited with having desirable traits that are deficient in men. Genesis Rabbah 18:1 cites the view that "And the Lord God built (*vayyiven*) the rib" (Gen. 2:22) means that woman was created with more instinctual understanding and common sense (*binah*) than man, pointing out that a young woman is considered an adult at the age of twelve while a boy only reaches legal maturity at thirteen.

Accounting for Women's Disadvantages

Most voices within Rabbinic literature agreed that women did not belong in the realms of communal governance, worship, and learning. The men who formulated these strictures were well aware of the dichotomy they had established between male privilege and female disempowerment, and some felt compelled to explain the exclusion of women. Several extended aggadic narratives catalog and justify a series of female deficiencies as consequences of the nature of female creation and the first woman's deleterious moral choices. In a lengthy passage, Genesis Rabbah 17:8 expands on "So the Lord God cast a deep sleep upon the man; and, while he slept, he took one of his ribs and closed up the flesh at that spot" (Gen. 2:21) as follows:

> R. Joshua was asked: "Why does a man come forth [at birth] with his face downward, while a woman comes forth with her face turned upwards?" [He answered,] "The man looks towards the place of his creation [the earth], while the woman looks towards the place of her creation [the rib]." "And why must a woman use perfume, while a man does not need perfume?" "Man was created from earth," he answered, "and earth never putrefies, but Eve was created from a bone. For example: if you leave meat three days unsalted, it immediately goes putrid." ". . . And why does the man make [sexual] demands upon the woman, whereas the woman does not make demands upon the man?" "This may be compared to a man who loses something," he replied; "he seeks what he lost, but the lost article does not seek him." "And why does a man deposit sperm within a woman while a woman does not deposit sperm within a man?" "It is like a man who has an article in his hand and seeks a trustworthy person with whom he may deposit it." "Why does a man go out bareheaded while a woman goes out with her head covered?" "She is like one who has done wrong and is ashamed of people; therefore she goes out with her head cov-

ered." "Why do [women] walk in front of the corpse [at a funeral]?" "Because they brought death into the world, they therefore walk in front of the corpse.... And why was the precept of menstruation given to her?" "Because she shed the blood of Adam [by causing his death], therefore was the precept of menstruation given to her." "And why was the precept of dough (*hallah*) given to her?" "Because she corrupted Adam, who was the dough of the world, therefore was the precept of dough given to her." "And why was the precept of the Sabbath lights given to her?" "Because she extinguished the soul of Adam, therefore was the precept of the Sabbath lights given to her."

This passage reinforces the inferior nature of female creation and woman's subordination to man on the farfetched grounds that males are born looking down to the place of their origin, the earth, while females are born facing upwards towards the rib from which they were formed. Avot de-Rabbi Nathan B 9, a close parallel to this text, preserves the frequent aggadic statement that this is why the male takes the superior position in sexual intercourse. Genesis Rabbah 17:8 goes on to attribute several unpleasant characteristics to women in general, including shrillness; these are portrayed as consequences of female creation from a bone.

Women are also deemed less fortunate than men in Genesis Rabbah 17:8 because they are compelled to be sexually passive while men may actively seek out women for sexual relations. The aggadah explains that this is because the man is seeking his lost rib; he is complete only when he is joined in sexual congress with the woman whose formation he made possible. The woman, objectified as the "missing rib," must wait to be found since "lost articles" do not seek their owners. While female sexual passivity was seen as absolutely essential for the smooth functioning of Rabbinic society, the rabbis perceived the requirement of female loyalty to one sexual partner at a time as an inconvenience from which men, who could enjoy sexual contacts with more than one woman, were exempt. Since a woman who bore a man's children had sexual contact only with him, women were constructed as trustworthy vessels for the deposit of his seed. The assertion that women were disadvantaged in comparison to men because men had the possibility of additional spouses or at least permitted sexual access to more than one woman at a time, is also found in another enumeration of female disabilities at B. Erub. 100b.

Genesis Rabbah 17:8 also cites veiling as a female burden and connects having to cover one's face in public with guilt and shame. Avot de-Rabbi Nathan B 9 adds the comment: "In the same way Eve disgraced herself and caused her daughters to cover their heads." M. Sot. 3:8 raised this disadvantage in answering the question "How does man differ from a woman? He may go with hair unbound and with garment rent, but she may not go with hair unbound and garments rent." B. Git. 90a-b declared that a woman who went out with her hair unfastened and spun in the street with her armpits uncovered must be divorced for her immodesty, while in B. Ket. 65a a widow who let her veil slip during a court proceeding was perceived by other women as making sexual advances to their husbands and was driven out of town.[6]

---

[6] On veiling of women in the ancient world, see Molly Myerowitz Levine, "The Gendered Grammar of Ancient Mediterranean Hair," in Howard Eilberg-Schwartz and Wendy Doniger, eds., *Off with Her Head! The Denial of Women's Identity in Myth, Religion, and Culture* (Berkeley, 1995), pp. 76–130.

Genesis Rabbah 17:8 connects the social institution of women's wearing veils with their guilt and shame over Eve's role in bringing death into the world. This theme is also found in B. Erub 100b, where women's curses are said to include being "wrapped up like a mourner." Women are additionally linked with death in Genesis Rabbah 17:8 because of their roles at funeral processions, where they walked in front of the deceased. Avot de-Rabbi Nathan B 9 comments at this point: "Why do women march first in front of the bier? What is it they say? [They say] 'We caused all the inhabitants of the world to come to this.'"[7] Indeed, women's connection with keening and chanting dirges is an ancient one in the Middle East. Composition of funeral dirges was apparently the one area of Rabbinic literary culture in which women could publicly display their creativity; the collection of eight elegies in B. M.Q. 28b attributed to the women of Shoken-Zeb in Babylonia is probably the most extensive quotation of women's words in the Talmud.[8]

Women and Ritual in the Aggadah

Genesis Rabbah 17:8 connects women's supposed role in bringing death into the world with the three religious obligations that Rabbinic Judaism considered specific to women: the observance of limitations on marital contact between the onset of menstruation and the wife's ritual immersion (*niddah*); the separation and burning in the oven of a piece of the dough used in making Sabbath bread, a reminder of Temple sacrifice (*hallah*); and kindling of Sabbath lights (*hadlaqah*). In fact, men could fulfill either of the last two commandments if no woman was present and her observance of the first was purely for the benefit of her husband to preserve him from ritual impurity. Doubtless, performing these observances provided many women with satisfying spiritual avenues for sanctification of aspects of daily life. Yet, at least some strands of Rabbinic tradition, including also Tanhuma Noah 1, constructed these rituals as eternal punishments or atonements to remind women of Eve's responsibility in the death of Adam, and therefore in all human mortality. A portion of Avot de-Rabbi Nathan B 9 goes even farther:

> Why were the commandments of menstrual purity given to woman and not to man? Because Adam was the blood of the Holy One, blessed be he; Eve came and spilled it. Consequently, the commandments of menstrual purity were given to her so that the blood which she spilled might be atoned for.

According to M. Shab. 2:6, disregard of these three commandments brings dire consequences: "For these transgressions do women die in childbirth: for heedlessness of the laws concerning their menstruation, the dough offering, and the lighting of the Sabbath lamp."

What lies behind this formulation connecting women's commandments with Eve's supposed responsibility for death? It is repeated often enough to merit description

---

[7] The linkage of women with death constitutes a distinctive strand in the Rabbinic discourse about women and the dangers they represent. See Baskin, *Midrashic Women*, pp. 68–71; and Mordechai A. Freidman, "Tamar, a Symbol of Life: The 'Killer Wife' Superstition in the Bible and Jewish Tradition," in *Association for Jewish Studies Review* 15:1 (Spring, 1990), pp. 23–61.

[8] On women and mourning rituals, see Meir Bar Ilan, "The Keening Women," in idem, *Some Jewish Women in Antiquity* (Atlanta, 1998), pp. 52–77; and Galit Hasan-Rokem, *Web of Life: Folklore and Midrash in Rabbinic Literature* (Stanford, 2000), p. 111.

as a mainstream Rabbinic view. Ross S. Kraemer has suggested that the severity of these statements may reveal a Rabbinic effort to remove external non-Jewish associations from female rituals that had parallels in the "religious observances of women in the various forms of paganism with which Jewish women were likely to come into contact."[9] A complementary explanation may be that such dire pronouncements are part of a Rabbinic polemic against widespread non-compliance with these precepts, perhaps particularly in regard to non-observance of *niddah* regulations.

In B. Ber. 31b, these three female commandments are linked with women's obligation to pray, based on an extended exegesis of Hannah's prayer in 1 Samuel 1:

> "If you will look upon the affliction of your maidservant and will remember me and not forget your maidservant, and if you will grant your maidservant a male child . . ." (1 Sam. 1:11). R. Yose b. R. Hanina said: "Why these three [repetitions of] 'maidservant'? Hannah said before the Holy One, blessed be he: 'Sovereign of the Universe, you have created in woman three criteria of death [some say armor joints of death], namely, *niddah*, *hallah*, and the kindling of the light on Sabbath. Have I transgressed in any of them?'"

According to B. Ber. 31a, "many of the most important laws [relating to prayer] can be learned from these verses relating to Hannah." For later Jewish tradition, Hannah's candid prayer from the heart became the model for women's prayers, which were to be recited individually, did not follow any fixed liturgical pattern, and could be voiced in any language.[10]

While Rabbinic halakhah generally exempts women from participation in many ritual aspects of Jewish life, especially those that take place at specified times in the public domain, women are obligated in domestic observances such as rejoicing during the Sabbath and the festivals (B. Pes. 109a); participation in *qiddush* (sanctification of wine) on the Sabbath (B. Ber. 20b); eating *matzah* (unleavened bread) and drinking four cups of wine at the ritual meal on the first evening of Passover (B. Pes. 43b and 108a). They are also responsible for lighting the Hanukkah lamp (B. Shab. 23a) and listening to the reading of the *megillah* (scroll of Esther) on Purim (B. Meg. 4a, Y. Meg. 2:5). The reason given in each case is that women, too, were involved in the miracles of redemption these festivals celebrate. An aggadic passage in B. Sot. 11b is one of several that ascribe Israel's exodus from Egypt to female virtues:

> R. Aqiba explained: "It is in the merit of the righteous Jewish women of that generation that Israel was redeemed from Egypt. At the time that they would go to draw water, the Holy One would arrange for there to be small fish in their pails—they would draw half a pail of water and half a pail of fish. They would then take two pails to their husbands in the fields, one

---

[9] Ross Shepard Kraemer, *Her Share of the Blessings: Women's Religions among Pagans, Jews, and Christians in the Greco-Roman World* (New York, 1992), p. 100.

[10] For women and prayer, see Baskin, *Midrashic Women*, pp. 79–83; and Meir Bar Ilan, "Prayers by Women," in idem, *Some Jewish Women in Antiquity*, pp. 78–113. On Hannah's prayer, see also Dvora Weisberg, "Men Imagining Women Imagining God: Gender Issues in Classic Midrash," in Marc Lee Raphael, ed., *Agendas for the Study of Midrash in the Twenty-First Century* (Williamsburg, 1999), pp. 63–83. On the permissibility of prayer in the vernacular, a necessity for women since few learned Hebrew, see B. Sot. 32a–33a, and Ruth Langer, *To Worship God Properly: Tensions between Liturgical Custom and Halakhah in Judaism* (Cincinnati, 1998), pp. 22–23.

with warm water and the other with fish. They would wash and feed them, and when their husbands would desire them they would go between the banks of the fields together, as it is written, 'When you lie between the banks...' (Ps. 68:14)... And the women would conceive and when the time came to give birth they would go to the field and give birth under the apple tree, as it is written, 'I woke you under the apple tree' (Song 8:5)."

Similarly, midrashic traditions teach that the monthly observance of the new moon, the festival of Rosh Hodesh, was given to women as a reward for not having participated in the sin of the golden calf (Pirkei d'Rabbi Eliezer 45; Y. Pes. 4:1; Y. Ta. 1:6):

> The women were unwilling to give their golden earrings to their husbands. They said to them: "You desire to make a graven image and a molten image without any power." The Holy One, blessed be he, gave the women their reward in this world and in the world to come. What reward did he give them in this world? That they should observe the New Moons more stringently than the men. And what reward did he give them in the world to come? That women are destined to be renewed like the new moons.

Women as Wives

Rabbinic Judaism considered marriage as foreordained and essential for all adults. Within the confines of marriage, procreation, a legal obligation for men, could take place and the lineage of children, a significant concern in Rabbinic culture, could be assured. Marriage also served as a licit channel for sexual energies for both women and men, as a source of mutual companionship, and it provided the social mortar and division of labor on which Rabbinic society depended. In Rabbinic Judaism's vision of the ideal ordering of human life, however, marriage could not be a partnership between equals. According to B. San. 22b, Samuel b. Unya is said to have taught: "Before marriage a woman is a shapeless lump. It is her husband who transforms her into a useful vessel." In fact, the parallel is drawn that just as God formed the character of the people of Israel, so does a husband shape the personality of his wife. "For he who made you will espouse you—his name is the Lord of Hosts" (Is. 54:5).

A significant body of aggadic homiletical material is devoted to the theme of marriage as the prerequisite for achieving fully human status for both males and females. The connection of marriage with creation is a major theme in this discourse. Parallel comments in Genesis Rabbah 8:9 and 22:2 maintain the precedence of man in God's creation of humanity while stressing the crucial role of marriage and procreation in human life: "In the past, Adam was created from the ground, and Eve from Adam; but henceforth [with the birth of offspring to the first couple] it shall be, 'In our image, after our likeness' (Gen. 1:26): Neither man without woman nor woman without man, nor both of them without the Shekhinah." This invocation of the Shekhinah, the indwelling nurturing aspect of the divine designated by a feminine noun, indicates that the female does share in God's image in some way when she is linked to a male by bearing his child.

Similar comments are found in Genesis Rabbah 17:2 on Gen. 2:18, "It is not good for man to be alone." The final statement in this extended passage suggests that a man attains to the divine image only when joined in marriage to a woman with whom he will father children. Procreation is the overwhelming value to be achieved in marriage since what makes man like God is his ability to generate new life in the body of his wife. This is the nearest parallel to divine creativity that a male can achieve and it is of such importance that all men are legally obligated to procreate. Many of the biblical verses cited as proof texts in this passage refer to a man and his "house" or "household" (Hebrew: *bayit*). For the rabbis, a man's wife is his "house," a construction built from his body to bear his children and fulfill his sexual and domestic needs.

Rabbinic folklore underscores the personal and societal value of matrimony in its vision of marriages as foreordained; so crucial is this conviction that several midrashic traditions describe matchmaking as God's principle occupation since the completion of creation (e.g. Leviticus Rabbah 8:1). According to B. Sot. 2a, Rabbah b. Bar Hanah is said to have related in the name of R. Johanan: "It is as difficult [for God] to pair [a woman with a man] as was the division of the Red Sea." Similarly, the Talmud relates (B. Sot. 2a and B. San. 22a) that forty days before the embryo is formed, a heavenly voice goes forth and ordains: "The daughter of so and so for so and so."

Rabbinic endorsements of marriage are unabashedly androcentric: they detail why marriage is a good thing for men and advise how men might best comport themselves within a marital relationship. The advantages of marriage for women are generally assumed rather than voiced. Certainly in a patriarchal society in which unprotected women were at risk, where childless women faced a perilous future, and where there may have been a shortage of males, it is not surprising that marriage was seen as crucial for a woman's well being. As B. Yeb. 113a puts it, "More than the man desires to marry does the woman desire to be taken in marriage." B. Ket. 75a declares that "A woman is satisfied with any sort [of husband]."

An ongoing Rabbinic discourse considers traits that distinguish good and bad wives; not surprisingly, negative qualities in husbands are not much considered. Thus, Hiyya was said to maintain, "A wife should be taken mainly for the sake of her beauty; and mainly for the sake of children" (B. Ket. 59b). The implication appears to be that a wife must not be treated as a bondwoman doing heavy work like grinding, which would impair her attractiveness or adversely affect her pregnancies; rather, she should work in wool in return for the maintenance her husband allows her. Elsewhere, Hiyya is credited with the view that "It is sufficient for us that they rear up our children and deliver us from sin [by bearing children and providing a sexual outlet]" (B. Yeb. 63a). The most desirable qualities in a wife are delineated in a passage in B. Shab. 25a, in response to the query, "Who is rich?" In Meir's view, it is he who takes pleasure in his wealth. Tarfon said: "He who possesses a hundred vineyards, a hundred fields and a hundred slaves working in them." But Aqiba is cited as responding, "He who has a wife comely in deeds." In this statement, referring back to the description of the ideal wife of Prov. 31:31 ("And let her deeds praise her in the gates"), the Rabbinic vision of the wife whose domestic undertakings enable her husband's activities for the sake of Heaven is incarnated.

Indeed, the classic "good wife" story in Rabbinic literature is that of Aqiba's wife, who becomes a paradigm of female loyalty and devotion. This story, versions of which appear in six different places in Rabbinic writings, encapsulated what many strands of Rabbinic tradition must have seen as the virtues of the model wife. Born into a wealthy household, Rachel, as she is named in only one of the narratives about her, is said to have forfeited a rich dowry from her father in order to marry Aqiba when he was a destitute and illiterate shepherd. According to the account in B. Ned. 50a, Aqiba's wife, unnamed in this source, sent her uneducated husband away to study for twelve years and then another twelve, despite great personal suffering. When he returned with thousands of students, he lauded her before them, declaring that all his learning rightly belonged to his wife.[11] In Rabbinic terms Aqiba's wife is exemplary because of her willingness to erase herself from her husband's daily life; she serves as a paradigm of what is expected of the wife of the scholar whose studies may take him far away for long periods of time. Such a wife garners cultural esteem through enabling the men of her family to pursue their studies, even though this may mean enduring economic deprivation and a husband's absence for long periods of time. According to sources including B. Ber. 17a and B. Sot. 21a, this is precisely how wives earn merit: "By sending their sons to learn [Torah] in the synagogue, and their husbands to study in the schools of the rabbis, and by waiting for their husbands until they return from the schools of the rabbis."

The story of Aqiba's wife illuminates the degree to which Rabbinic leaders were torn between devotion to Torah study and the legal obligations to procreate and attend to one's wife. Although the option of an ascetic and celibate life entirely devoted to the divine was always deemed impermissible, certain threads within Rabbinic literature preserve a deep-seated ambivalence about the benefits of marriage, particularly for scholars who might prefer to devote all their energies to study of the divine word, despite the legal imperative to procreate. Many of these issues are raised in a lengthy discussion of the boons and woes of matrimony in B. Yeb. 61b–64a, prompted by the mishnaic ruling that a man may not abstain from the duty of procreation (M. Yeb. 6:6).

In the Babylonian Rabbinic community, cultural imperatives insisted that young men be married as early as possible. This produced the untenable situation of husbands abandoning wives and families for extended sojourns at far distant places of study, resulting in the creation of a class of "married monks."[12] A long passage in B. Ket. 62b-63a preserves a number of anecdotes about men who studied away from home. These appear in the context of an adumbration of M. Ket. 5:6, which ordains the frequency with which men should perform their conjugal duty depending on their profession. B. Ket. 62b rules that the scholar is to perform his marital obligation once a week, ideally on Sabbath eve. However, B. Ket. 62b also preserves the determination, attributed to "the sages," that "Students may go away to study Torah without the permission [of their wives even for] two or three years." The ambivalence the rabbis felt over these two contradictory approaches to marital responsibility is reflected in the statement of Raba, the leading Babylonian Rabbinic authority of the fourth century, to the effect that the rabbis accepted the ruling that students might leave their wives for long periods of time even though they put their lives at risk by doing so. Two anecdotes are then recounted in which rabbis neglected to return home when expected because they were distracted by their studies. In one instance, disappointed anticipation caused a waiting wife such grief that she began to weep. At that exact moment, the roof on which her husband was sitting collapsed, and he was killed. The rabbi in the second story also met an untimely end, because he put study before his duty to his wife. These warnings

---

[11] For a more detailed discussion of these narratives, see Tal Ilan, *Mine and Yours are Hers: Retrieving Women's History from Rabbinic Literature* (Leiden, 1997).

[12] Daniel Boyarin, *Carnal Israel: Reading Sex in Talmudic Culture* (Berkeley, 1993), pp. 165–66. He notes, p. 136, that the conflict between the demands of marriage and the imperative to total devotion to study remained unresolved in Rabbinic culture. See also David Biale, *Eros and the Jews: From Biblical Israel to Contemporary America* (New York, 1992), p. 55; and Michael L. Satlow, *Tasting the Dish: Rabbinic Rhetorics of Sexuality*, (Atlanta, 1995), p. 278, who finds a general "redactorial drift" elsewhere in the Babylonian Talmud, as well, towards lessening female conjugal rights when they interfered with male prerogatives.

that death could be the penalty for the husband who neglects his obligations to nurture his family provides a strong counterweight to the wholesale permission to abandon home for immersion in Torah.

The final aggadah in this passage is indicative of the irredeemable conflict the Babylonian rabbis perceived over the values of family responsibility and devotion to the explication of the divine word:

> R. Joseph the son of Raba [was] sent [by] his father to the academy under R. Joseph, and they arranged for him [to stay there for] six years. Having been there three years and the eve of the Day of Atonement approaching, he said, "I would go and see my family." When his father heard [of his premature arrival] he took up a weapon and went out to meet him [declaring], "You have remembered your harlot (*zontekha*)." Another version: He said to him, "You have remembered your dove (*yontekha*)." They got involved in a quarrel and neither ate the final meal before the fast.

The father in this disturbing aggadic tradition is Raba, the Rabbinic leader who was quoted earlier in this passage (B. Ket. 62b) as endorsing the practice of study away from home despite the known risks. By terming his daughter-in-law a "whore," the father is really directing his wrath at his son's lack of sexual control. This distressing narrative is the final word in a lengthy talmudic passage, B. Ket. 62b–63a, that began with concern over a wife's right to sexual attention but ends by seemingly endorsing male abstinence and devotion to Torah.[13] No happy ending to reconcile the dilemma is offered; at some unresolvable level both men are right. Meanwhile wives remain the passive partners in most of these accounts; when they are depicted as acting, it is always in support of enabling their husband's selection of study over family.

Rabbinic literature also contains several stories detailing unacceptable wifely conduct. The arenas in which a wife could rebel against her husband's authority or insult his dignity were exceedingly limited, and it is not surprising that most of these stories involve either food preparation or sexual behavior; indeed, references to food and food preparation are often euphemistic metaphors for sexual practices.[14]

Genesis Rabbah 17:3 (parallels at Lev. Rabbah 34:14 and Y. Ket. 11:3, 34b) comments on "I will make a fitting helper for him" (Gen. 2:18) with an account of wifely rebellion and its punishment:

> If he is fortunate, she is a help; if not, she is against him. R. Joshua b. Nehemiah said: If a man is fortunate, she is like the wife of Hananiah b. Hakinai [who patiently awaited her husband's return from years of study]; if not, she is like the wife of R. Yose the Galilean. R. Yose the Galilean had a bad wife; she was his sister's daughter and used to put him to shame. His disciples said to him: "Master, divorce this woman, for she does not act as befits your honor." "Her dowry is too great for me, and I cannot afford to divorce her," was his reply. Now it happened once that he and R. Eleazar b. Azariah were sitting and studying, and when they finished, the latter asked him, "Sir, will you kindly permit that we go to your home together?" "Yes," replied he. As they entered, she cast down her gaze [in anger at the unexpected visitors] and was making her way out when [her husband] looked at a pot standing on the pot-range and asked her, "Is there anything in the pot?" "There's a hash

---

[13] On this passage, see also Boyarin, *Carnal Israel*, p. 156 n. 37; and Satlow, *Tasting the Dish*, p. 278.

[14] On Rabbinic associations of food and sexual behavior, see Baskin, *Midrashic Women*, pp. 106–107, 113.

in it," she answered [perhaps to discourage the guests]. He went and uncovered it, and found some chickens. R. Eleazar b. Azariah heard what had passed and as they ate together he observed, "Sir, did she not say it was hash, yet we have found chickens" "A miracle has happened," replied he. When they finished [Eleazar b. Azariah] said to him: "Master, abandon this woman, for she does not treat you with proper respect." "Sir," he replied, "Her dowry is too great for me and I cannot divorce her." "We [your students]," said the other, "will apportion her dowry among ourselves so you can divorce her." And they did so for him; they apportioned her dowry and had her divorced from him, and made him marry another and better wife.

The passage continues with the suffering that then befell the discarded wife as a consequence of "her sins." These included being married to a brutal husband who beat her in public; in her moment of deepest humiliation she was forced to accept the charity of her former husband, perhaps the cruelest punishment of all.

"Bad wives" were at a grave disadvantage, and their rebellions are indicative of their limited arenas of influence. In fact, these "bad wife" stories are intended to be didactic. They delineate for men the boundaries of female freedom, and they demonstrate to women potential penalties for their attempts to exceed them, particularly the risk of divorce that remained a ready expedient for men in unhappy marriages. It is, nevertheless, important to point out that while divorce was legally easy to obtain (if sometimes financially painful), a number of sages harbored ethical qualms about the severing of marriage bonds. Genesis Rabbah 18:5 comments on "Hence a man leaves his father and mother and clings to his wife, so that they become one flesh" (Gen. 2:24):

> Said R. Aha in the name of R. Hanina b. Papa: "Throughout the book of Malachi, 'The Lord of Hosts' is used [in reference to God], whereas here [in reference to divorce] we have 'The God of Israel,' as it says, 'For I detest divorce—said the Lord, the God of Israel' (Mal. 2:16). It is as though one might say, 'His name has no bearing on divorce save in the case of Israel alone.'" R. Hanan said: "When Nehemiah came up [to the land of Israel] from the land of Exile [he found that] the women's faces had been blackened by the sun, so that [their husbands] had gone and married strange wives, while these [rejected wives] would go around the altar weeping. Thus Malachi says, 'And this you do a second time, you actually repeat [the sin committed] at Shittim! [Num. 25:1-2].' You cover the altar of the Lord with tears, weeping, and moaning, so that he refuses to regard the oblation any more and to accept what you offer" (Mal. 2:13). The Holy One, blessed be he, said: 'Who will accept weeping and sighing from them [the treacherous husbands]? Having robbed her, and deprived her of her beauty, you cast her away!'"

This passage makes clear that marriage is a good that must be cherished and preserved. Although the halakhah allows a man to divorce his wife, a higher ethical standard demands a sense of concern and responsibility towards a dependent human being.

Marriage as Metaphor

In a system of theological imagery envisioning human marriage as the closest approximation of the intimacy that could exist between human and divine, the relationship between wives and husbands also assumed sacred significance.[15] Both in the Bible and throughout later Jewish literature, the relationship between a man and a woman is often understood metaphorically as signifying the intimate bonds between God and human beings. Traditional Rabbinic interpretation of the Song of Songs, for example, always assumed that the biblical book's love poetry between a man and a woman was an allegory detailing the passion between God and the people of Israel. Ironically, a consequence of this formulation was that women were erased from the equation. Thus, Song of Songs Rabbah 7.11 §1 explicated "I am my beloved's, and his desire is for me" (Song 7:11), as follows:

> There are three yearnings: The yearning of the community of Israel is only for their father who is in heaven, as it is said, "I am my beloved's, and his desire is for me." The yearning of a woman is only for her husband: "And your desire shall be for your husband" (Gen. 3:16). The yearning of the Evil Impulse is only for Cain and his ilk: "To you is its desire" (Gen. 4:7).

In this passage, the male community of Israel is constructed as the female beloved; in the relationship between God, who is characterized as masculine, and the male community of Israel, characterized as feminine, there is no place for woman. At best, women direct their yearnings towards their husbands, and share by reflected glory in their husbands' communion with the divine.

Jacob Neusner has observed about this feminization of Israel in Song of Songs Rabbah, that just as a wife must submit faithfully to her husband and follow him wherever he leads with perfect faith in his wisdom and judgment, so the male Israel must direct full devotion and faith to God and wait patiently for God's redemption. "Implicit in this representation of the right relationship, of course, is the promise that the feminine Israel will evoke from the masculine God the response of commitment and intervention: God will intervene to save Israel, when Israel makes herself into the perfect wife of God."[16]

Israel is also personified in female terms as one of the childless women of the Hebrew Bible whose prayers for offspring are ultimately fulfilled. These women are said to include Sarah, Rebecca, Leah, Rachel, the wife of Manoah (Samson's mother), and Hannah. The seventh is not an individual who lived in the past but is the personified Israel of some future time, based on Second Isaiah's characterization of Zion as a barren woman: "Shout, O barren one,/You who bore no child!/Shout aloud for joy,/You who did not travail!/For the children of the wife forlorn/Shall outnumber those of the espoused/—said the Lord" (Is. 54:1).[17]

A typical example appears in the homiletical midrash collection Pesikta de-Rab Kahana 20.1; the final reference is to the future of Zion:

> Finally, the words, "He sets the childless woman among her household" apply to Zion [of whom it is said]:

---

[15] On human marriage as symbolic of the relationship between God and the Jewish people, see Arthur Green, "Bride, Spouse, Daughter: Images of the Feminine in Classical Jewish Sources," in Susannah Heschel, ed., *On Being a Jewish Feminist: A Reader* (New York, 1983), pp. 248–260; Moshe Idel, "Sexual Metaphors and Praxis in the Kabbalah," in David Kraemer, ed., *The Jewish Family: Metaphor and Memory* (Oxford, 1989), pp. 197–224; Jacob Neusner, "Judaism," in Jacob Neusner, ed., *Women and Families* (Cleveland, 1999), pp. 50–82, pp. 53–68.

[16] On Rabbinic constructions of marriage, see Baskin, *Midrashic Women*, pp. 88–118; Hauptman, *Rereading the Rabbis*, pp. 60–76; and Michael L. Satlow, *Jewish Marriage in Antiquity* (Princeton, 2001).

[17] On this theme, see Mary Callaway, *Sing, O Barren One: A Study in Comparative Midrash* (Atlanta, 1986), pp. 59–65.

"Shout, O barren one,/You who bore no child!" (Is. 54:1); so [too] do the words "As a happy mother of children," [as it says] "And you will say to yourself,/'Who bore me these for me/ When I was bereaved and barren,/ Exiled and disdained'" (Is. 49:21).

In this and similar homilies, the repeated fulfillment of the prayers of the childless wife become prophetic consolation texts, pointing to the ultimate restoration and flowering of the nation and land of Israel. Conversely, Israel is represented throughout *Lamentations Rabbah* as a widow, mourning her husband and children.

Representations of Women and Their World in the Midrash

The Rabbinic sages believed that Jewish society functioned best when its female members remained in the domestic domain under the aegis of male authority. Unaccompanied women who ventured beyond the home risked accusations of immodesty and sexual license. Rabbinic writings expressed particular uneasiness about women in groups, both in the public sphere, where such women were accused of licentiousness and sorcery, and in the domestic world of women to which men had limited access. A statement in M. Avot 2:7, attributed to the first century C.E. sage Hillel, constructs the Rabbinic social world view as follows:

> The more flesh, the more worms, the more possessions, the more anxiety; the more wives, the more witchcraft; and the more bondwomen the more lewdness; the more bondmen the more thieving; the more study of the Law the more life; the more schooling the more wisdom; the more counsel the more understanding; the more righteousness the more peace. If a man has gained a good name he has gained [something] for himself; if he has gained for himself words of the Law he has gained for himself life in the world to come.

In this succinct summary of human possibilities, women both free and enslaved, are suspected of involvement in sorcery and sexual license, while male slaves are assumed to be dishonest. Only free Jewish men are allowed the potential to achieve meaningful lives, both in this world and the world to come, through their options to choose to function in the communal worlds of worship, study, and leadership. Women, like slaves, had limited alternatives and undesirable choices.

These views permeate aggadic exegeses of biblical women. The negative portrayal of the founding mothers of the Jewish people in Genesis Rabbah 18:2, cited above, is typical of Rabbinic critiques of other admirable biblical women. B. Meg. 14b criticizes the judge Deborah and the prophet Huldah for arrogance in their dealings with men: "R. Nahman said: 'Haughtiness does not befit women. There were two haughty women, and their names are hateful, one being called a hornet [a literal meaning of Deborah, usually translated as "bee"], the other a weasel [the literal meaning of Huldah].'" B. Meg. 15a preserves the remark that "Rahab inspired lust by her name; Yael by her voice; Abigail by her memory; and Michal, daughter of Saul, by her appearance." Here, as elsewhere in aggadic midrash, biblical women of courage and action are objectifed and reduced to their imagined sexual impact on men, whether by reputation, voice, nostalgia, or outer beauty. Generally, midrashic constructions of scriptural women are based on their interactions with the central male figures in the narratives in which they appear: beloved wives like Sarah and Rachel are generally praised, even when the textual evidence is against them; more ambiguous characters, like Miriam, who challenged her brother Moses, and Leah and her daughter Dinah, discussed in more detail below, come in for heavy criticism.

Foreign women, who are usually understood to exemplify unrestrained sexuality and ill will towards Israel are represented with particular hostility in aggadic sources. This is the case with the Egyptian Hagar of Gen. 16 and 21 and the Midianite Cozbi of Num. 25. Rahab, the noble harlot of Josh. 2 and 5:25, who is said to have sheltered two Israelite spies in Jericho because she recognized the overwhelming power of Israel's God, and who was later saved with her family when Joshua destroyed her city, is, together with Ruth, the Moabite ancestress of King David, among the few women from outside the Israelite community who are praised in the aggadah. According to various midrashic traditions found particularly in Sifre Numbers 78, Rahab married Joshua, became the ancestress of prophets, and was not, in fact, a prostitute at all but variously an innkeeper, perfume maker, and maker of fine linen.[18] The metamorphosis of this fallen woman into a mother in Israel confirmed the Rabbinic message that neither gender, foreign origins, nor a dubious previous history were barriers to those who sincerely wished to join the Jewish people. Transformed to a pious proselyte and devoted wife of Joshua, Rahab's otherness was vitiated, her dangerous sexuality defused, and her disturbing independence undercut. In the very terms of her rehabilitation, Rabbinic Judaism's complex construction of women and their conflicting propensities for both disruption and amelioration is fully revealed.

The connection of polygyny to witchcraft in M. Avot 2:7, cited above, is part of a larger biblical and Rabbinic discourse that describes polygynous marriages as contentious and unpleasant for all involved. The most extended biblical example of the co-wife motif is found in the matriarchal narratives about Leah and Rachel, the two sisters the patriarch Jacob married in Haran (Gen. 29-30). Leah, the unloved and unattractive wife, was fertile, while Rachel, her beautiful and beloved sister, was apparently barren. Genesis Rabbah 71 highlights this aspect of the rivalry by citing several traditions to the effect that it is children who secure a woman's position in her home.[19]

A frequently repeated midrash, however, portrays the usually antagonistic sisters as colluding against the central men in their lives in one particular episode. Rachel was said to have been aware that her father, Laban, intended to deceive Jacob by substituting Leah for herself on the wedding night, and she warned Jacob in advance. Thus, Jacob gave Rachel certain tokens so that he would be sure of her identity, even in a dark tent. Nonetheless, B. Meg. 13b and B. B.B. 123a relate:

> When night came, she said to herself, Now my sister will be put to shame. So she handed over the tokens to her. So it is written, "When morning came, there was Leah!" (Gen. 29:2). Are we to infer from this that up to now she was not Leah? What it means is that on account of the tokens that Rachel gave up to Leah he did not know until then.

This description of Rachel's sisterly consideration for Leah arises out of the textual difficulty of explaining why Jacob did not realize the identity of his new wife until the morning.

While one might ask whether this midrash depicting Rachel's generosity in preserving her sister from humiliation is a

---

[18] See Baskin, *Midrashic Women*, pp. 154–160, for a more detailed discussion of Rahab in midrashic sources.

[19] See Baskin, *Midrashic Women*, pp. 145–150, for a more detailed discussion of Rachel and Leah in the aggadah; on the dilemma of female infertility, see *Midrashic Women*, pp. 119–140.

paeon to the possibilities of admirable behavior and self-sacrifice between females or a warning to men about the ultimate unreliability of women, there is no ambiguity in other Rabbinic traditions praising Rachel for her kindness to her sister. These appear in interpretations of "Now God remembered Rachel" (Gen. 30:22), the preamble to the birth of Joseph (Genesis Rabbah 73:4), and most strikingly in the final segment of Lamentations Rabbah, Proem 24, where Rachel describes herself as hiding beneath the bed on which Jacob lay with her sister in order to respond to Jacob so that he would not recognize Leah's voice and humiliate her. In this homiletical text built on Jeremiah's prophecies of ultimate redemption, Rachel's merits are said to succeed in achieving divine intercession for Israel when the pleas of the patriarchs and Moses have failed:

> Forthwith the mercy of the Holy One, blessed be he, was stirred and he said, "For thy sake, Rachel, I will restore Israel to their place." And so it is written, "Thus said the Lord: A cry is heard in Ramah—wailing, bitter weeping—Rachel weeping for her children. She refuses to be comforted for her children, who are gone. Thus said the Lord: Restrain your voice from weeping, your eyes from shedding tears; for there is a reward for your labor declares the Lord. They shall return from the enemy's land" (Jer. 33:15–16).

As these traditions indicate, Rabbinic midrash maintains a strongly positive view of Rachel, despite the biblical evidence that she was bitterly jealous of her fecund sister. Even this is turned in Rachel's favor in Genesis Rabbah 71:6, where we learn that Rachel envied only the extent of Leah's good deeds, reasoning, "Were she not righteous, would she have borne children?"

Leah does not fare so well in the aggadah. Genesis Rabbah 70:19 presents her as complicit and unrepentant in the deception of Jacob:

> In the evening they came to lead her [into the bridal chamber] and extinguished the light. "What is the meaning of this?" he demanded, and they replied: "Do you think we are shameless, like you?" The whole of that night he called her "Rachel," and she answered him. In the morning, however, "Behold it was Leah "(Gen. 29:25). He said to her: "What, you are a deceiver and the daughter of a deceiver!" She responded, "Is there a teacher without pupils, and didn't your father call you 'Esau,' and you answered him! So too did you call me [by someone else's name], and I answered you!"

The rabbis were also distressed by the mandrake episode in which Rachel traded away her husband's attentions to Leah in the hope of enhancing her own fertility. While Genesis Rabbah 72:3 castigated Rachel for treating Jacob's devotion so slightingly, and explained that it was for this reason that Rachel was not buried with her husband, the midrashic tradition is even harder on Leah. According to Genesis Rabbah 80:1, Leah acted like a harlot when she went to meet Jacob on his return from the fields and baldly declared, "You are to sleep with me, for I have hired you with my son's mandrakes" (Gen. 30:16). Some statements suggest that Dinah's questionable behavior in going out to visit the daughters of Canaan in Gen. 34, which resulted in her ruin, was predictable from the behavior of her mother. Commenting on the proverb, "As the mother, so the daughter," Genesis Rabbah 80:1 preserves the following interpretation:

> "A cow does not gore unless her calf kicks; a woman is not immoral until her daughter is immoral" [said Kahana].... "If so," said [Resh Lakish] "then our mother Leah was a harlot!" [since we find her daughter Dinah acting immorally]. "Even so," he replied;

"because it says, 'Leah went out to meet him' (Gen. 30:16), which means that she went out to meet him adorned like a harlot; therefore [we find] 'And Dinah, the daughter whom Leah had borne to Jacob, went out'" (Gen. 34:1).

The disquiet expressed here about the brazenness of both Leah and Dinah is a recurrent theme in Rabbinic discourses on women.

However, the rabbis did not deprecate all female solidarity. A striking counterexample to the assumption that female togetherness constitutes danger, is found in the very positive portrayals of the daughters of Zelophehad, the biblical sisters of Num. 27:1, who successfully argue that they should inherit from their father who died without male heirs. According to Sifre Numbers 133:

> When the daughters of Zelophehad heard that the land of Israel was being apportioned among the males of the tribes but not the females, they consulted together as to how to make their claim. They said: The compassion of God is not like human compassion. Human rulers favor males over females but the one who spoke and brought the world into being is not like that. Rather, God shows mercy to every living thing.

In this midrash, the daughters of Zelophehad are represented as canny and competent women who trusted that divine mercy would transcend the mutable norms of a human society in which women were subordinate beings. According to the Rabbinic sages, these admirable sisters epitomized the females of the wilderness generation who are said to have consistently outshone their male contemporaries in their faith in God and their personal courage.

Many of the Rabbinic sages were also aware of intelligent and acute women they encountered in their daily lives and some must have wondered why such apparently able minds should be discouraged from undertaking serious study or assuming communal leadership roles.[20] The most illustrative indications of Rabbinic anxiety when confronted with intellectually able females are the traditions associated with Meir's learned wife Beruriah and the wealthy and politically prominent Yalta.

In a number of aggadic passages, a woman named Beruriah is portrayed as demonstrating a profound knowledge of Rabbinic biblical exegesis, a clever ability to handle traditional texts, and a quick wit. Yet praises of Beruriah's halakhic skills are somewhat illusory, since no actual legal rulings are ever attributed to her beyond one early reference in the Tosefta. Moreover, even Beruriah's reputed scholarly expertise became a problem for Rabbinic Judaism. In a medieval reference that may reflect earlier sources, she is shown to reap the tragic consequences of the "light mindedness" inherent in women: the eleventh century French commentator Rashi relates a tradition in his commentary on B. A.Z. 18b that Beruriah was seduced by one of her husband's students and subsequently committed suicide.[21]

---

[20] On the general exclusion of women from study in Rabbinic Judaism, see Boyarin, *Carnal Israel*, pp. 167-196; see also Mayer Gruber, "The Status of Women in Ancient Judaism," in Jacob Neusner and Alan J. Avery-Peck, eds., *Where We Stand: Issues and Debates in Ancient Judaism* (Leiden, 1999), vol. 2, pp. 151-176, who demonstrates the variety of ways in which the rabbis of the Talmud deliberately disempowered women in the communal domains of prayer and study.

[21] For more detailed discussions of Beruriah and Yalta, see Baskin, *Midrashic Women*, pp. 79-87. Examples of Beruriah's astuteness appear in B. Pes. 62b, B. Ber. 10a, and B. Erub. 53b-54a. On the lack of historicity in references to Beruriah in the Babylonian Talmud, see Tal Ilan, "The Historical Beruriah, Rachel,

Recent scholarship has shown that the Beruriah who appears in the Babylonian Talmud is a literary construct with little historical reality. Nor can any credence be given to Rashi's account of her ignominious downfall. The Beruriah traditions in the Babylonian Talmud, built around the faint historical memory of an actual woman capable of making subtle legal distinctions, articulate the rabbis' astonishment at such an anomalous woman and may also attest to the existence of minority strands within Rabbinic Judaism that recognize and approve of female intellectual activity. Certainly, they constitute additional evidence of a degree of Rabbinic doubt about the justice of women's enforced role of intellectual passivity.

A Rabbinic determination to undercut traditions of female autonomy is also visible in texts about Yalta, an aristocratic Jewish woman of considerable learning who is represented as exercising significant communal authority in the Jewish community in Babylonia. Yalta, among the few named women in Rabbinic literature, figures in seven aggadic narratives in the Babylonian Talmud. While virtually no historicity can be applied to any of the details of these stories, they reflect a Rabbinic awareness of women whose strong personalities, control of significant financial resources, and/or impressive lineage afforded them far more public influence than ordinary women could imagine. While several of the seven extant stories about Yalta report her ability to act independently against Jewish Rabbinic and political authority when necessary, two Yalta stories, B. Qid. 70a-b and B. Ber. 51b, demonstrate a Rabbinic desire to curtail such instances of female pretension.[22]

The narrative in B. Ber. 51b appears in a discussion of the extent to which women should be included in the rituals that conclude a meal:

> Ulla was once at the house of R. Nahman. They had a meal, and he said grace and handed the cup of benediction to R. Nahman. R. Nahman said to him: "Please send the cup of benediction to Yalta."[23] [Ulla refused to do so and] said to him: "R. Yohanan said: 'The fruit of a woman's body is blessed only from the fruit of a man's body, since it says, "He will also bless the fruit of your body" (Deut. 7:13). It does not say the fruit of *her* body, but the fruit of *your* [masculine singular] body....'" Meanwhile Yalta heard and furiously went to the wine cellar and broke four hundred jars of wine. R. Nahman said to him: "Let the master send her another cup." [Ulla] sent it

---

and Imma Shalom," in *Association for Jewish Studies Review* 22:1 (1997), pp. 1–17, particularly, pp. 1–8; and idem, *Integrating Women into Second Temple History* (Tübingen, 1999), pp. 176–179. See also the analyses of Boyarin, *Carnal Israel*, pp. 178–183; and Rachel Adler, "The Virgin in the Brothel and other Anomalies: Character and Context in the Legend of Beruriah," in *Tikkun* 3, no. 6 (1988), pp. 28–32, 102–105.

[22] On Yalta, see also Tal Ilan, *Integrating Women into Second Temple History*, pp. 171–174; Rachel Adler, "Feminist Folktales of Justice: Robert Cover as a Resource for the Renewal of Halakhah," in *Conservative Judaism* 45/3 (1988), pp. 40–56; and Charlotte Elisheva Fonrobert, "Yalta's Ruse: Resistance against Rabbinic Menstrual Authority in Talmudic Literature," in Wasserstein, *Women and Water*, pp. 60–81.

[23] There are indications elsewhere in the Talmud that this was often done as a courtesy to the women of the household; see for example B. B.M. 87a, where various suggestions are put forward as to why the angels who visited Abraham in Gen. 18 asked after Sarah: "R. Yose b. R. Hanina said: 'In order to send her the wine-cup of benediction.'" The issue is whether women are obligated to partake of the cup or whether it is simply sent to them as a courtesy. Ulla makes quite clear that women are not obligated and should not be encouraged to think they are.

to her with a message: "All that wine can be counted as a benediction." She returned answer: "Gossip comes from peddlers and vermin from rags."

Ulla, a sage from land of Israel who frequently visited Babylon to report on the work of Palestinian Rabbinic leaders, is connected with strict interpretations of halakhah. It is also worth noting that it is Ulla who is credited with the statement, "Women are a separate people" (B. Shab. 62b). He refuses to show customary respect to Yalta by passing her the cup over which the *qiddush* (sanctification) had been recited on the grounds that women are already blessed through male participation in fulfilling this commandment. Moreover, he justified his refusal to honor Yalta on the grounds that *qiddush* celebrates fertility, a male obligation in which women simply serve as passive vessels. Yalta, infuriated by Ulla's rudeness in excluding her, demonstrated both her wrath and her wealth by smashing the wine jars. However, neither Yalta's high social position nor her asperity alter the outcome. Ulla still excluded her from full participation in the *kiddush* because of her gender.

Conclusion

Suspended between halakhah, with its determinations of the minimum legal requirements governing daily life, and aggadah, which aspired to a higher ethical standard in human relationships, the Rabbinic vision of women is complicated and unresolved, as in any area in which ideal norms collide with experienced reality. Rabbinic Judaism attempted to confine female activities to the domestic sphere of family and family-based economic activities where women could facilitate the more culturally valued religious, intellectual, and communal endeavors of their male relatives. While the sages did not hesitate to express their compassion, appreciation, and need for those significant women in their lives who fulfilled the expectations of their culture and gracefully yielded to male dominance, a hermeneutics of suspicion informs most midrashic ruminations on the second sex: Rabbinic convictions of the essential alterity and inferior moral qualities of women were never forgotten.

JUDITH R. BASKIN
University of Oregon

INDEX OF ANCIENT SOURCES

HEBREW BIBLE/OLD TESTAMENT

Genesis

1:1	115, 298, 356, 360, 385, 780–781, 951–952	3:24	112, 174, 226, 970
		4:1	226
		4:2	318
		4:2–4	226
1:2	776	4:4	306
1–2	335	4:7	991
1:4	136, 356	4:8	765, 922
1–4	232	4:8–15	226
1:5	317	4:13	318
1:6–8	318	4:14	318
1:8	356	4:16–26	226
1–8	232	4:17	319
1:11–12	335	4:19–22	342
1:16	956	4:22	319
1:26	24, 981, 986	4:23	25
1:26–27	782–783	4:25–26:11	227
1:27	337, 782, 981	4:26	78, 227
1:31	114	5:1b–2a	782
2:2	472, 785–786	5:2	783, 981
2:3	786	5:32	26, 31
2–3	226	6:1–2	342
2:4	980	6:1–4	226
2:4–28:9	226, 298	6:1–6	563
2:6	85	6:3	379
2:8	335	6:4–12	226
2:8–15	363	6:9	26
2:15	112, 174, 360	6:10	31
2:16	112, 174	6–14	219
2:18	336–337, 830, 986, 989	7:11	85
		7:12	85
2:18–20	336	7:13	31
2:19	337	7:23	845
2:20	337–338	8:8	855
2:21	982	8:21	651
2:22	981–982	9:18	31
2:23	337	9:20–27	226
2:24	990	9:22	31
3:1	853	9:24	31
3:4	969	9:25	31
3:8	651	10	336, 344
3:9	112, 174, 176, 764	10:1	31
3:11	112, 174	10:7	743
3:12	830	10:9	71
3:14	853–854	11:1	786–787, 927
3:14–15	318	11:1–9	226
3:15	854	11:4	85
3:16	327	11:5	767, 782
3:17b	244	11:7	786–787
3:19	454, 714	11:8	85, 336
3:23	112, 174	11:19	365

11:29	319	19:31	321
11:31	338	19:33	86
12	364–365	19:36	977
12:1	865–866	20	365
12:1–6	226	20:6	489
12:2	5	20:7	770
12:3	347	20:12	319
12:4	792	20:13	364, 369
12:6	765	20:16	369
12:10	137, 144	21	475, 993
12:10–13	47	21:5	792
13:10	86	21:6	956
13:16	113	21:8	717
14:1	93, 109	21:9	321
14:9	107	21:10	321
14:14	287, 303, 309	21:11	321
14:15	309, 489	21:16–17	336
14:18	53, 765	21:26	792
14:20	320, 713	22	472, 689
15	718, 792	22:2	765
15:2	38, 303, 340	22:5	713, 718
15:2–18	226	22:8	385
15:5	713	22:10	322, 717
15:9ff.	116	22:12	37
15:12	714	22:13	719
15:13	791–792	22:20	275
15:13–14	714	22:20–23	336
15:14	329	22:33	948
15:16	791	24	238, 570
16	993	24:1	427, 713
16:1–6	226	24:2–3	37
16:2	320, 368	24:3	342
16:3	792	24:10	103
16:6–12	227	24:15	336
16:12	977	24:47	336
16:16	792	25:1–18	367
17:1–5	227	25:19	366
17:9–14	320	25:20	336
17:15–22	227	25:22	37, 695
17:16	230	25:22–23	734
17:19	558	25:23	107, 734
17:24	792	26:2–5	347
17:27	212	26:29	832
18	249, 996	26:33	832
18:2	227, 321, 855	26:35–36	342
18:3	119, 321	27:1–2	347
18:4	119, 715, 855	27:5	322
18:5	715, 855	27:22	977
18:6	855	27:23	713
18:6–7	370	27:28	866
18:7	716, 855	27:34	720
18:8	321, 716	27:40	977
18:9–15	212, 558	27:46–28:2	342
18:11	427	28:3–4	347, 348
18:12	787–788	28:11–15	227
18:13	367, 787–788	28:11–17ff.	570
18:16	856	28:15	96
19:11	845	28:20	94
19:17	551	28:20–22	94, 97, 345

28:22	346	37:24	324
29	570	37:27	324
29:1	98	37:34	722
29:2	993	37–50	227
29:5	336	38	307, 324, 686
29:6-7	102	38:14	230
29:10-11	322	38:18	230
29:10-12	103	38:24	230
29:17	323	38:26	230
29:22	104	39:1	355
29:24-25	104	39:9	96
29:25	994	39:10-13	721
29:25-27	104	40:1-3	49
29-30	993	40:5ff.	227
29:35	211	41:1ff.	227
29:40	101	41.15	325
30:2	368-369	41:42	721-722
30:6	323	41:43	30, 722, 833
30:15	103	41:45	240, 287
30:16	994-995	41:50	240
30:22	369, 994	41.56	325
30:42	421	41:57	49
31	227	42:2	792
31:1	96	42:8	325
31:7	366	42:18	118, 724
31:11-17	345	42:21	367
31:19	323	42:27	335
31:20	370	42:35	335
31:24	489	42:36	367
32:1	345	43:7	367
32:15	24	43:21	335
32:21	370	43:27	958
32:26	216	46:1-4	341
32:26-30	489	46:20	240
32:28-32	240	47:9	792
32:29	323	47:28-31	345
33:4	290, 323	48	345
33:11	713	48:1-20	346
33:35	720	48:22	338
34	788, 994	49	788
34:1	323, 995	49:3	485
34:12	211	49:4	43
34:27	371, 789	49:5-7	345, 788
35:3	782	49:6	788-790
35:5-7	345	49:6a	789
35:6-7	344-345	49:6b	789
35:7	782	49:9	106, 118, 723
35:22	43, 307, 323	49:10	681
36:24	291	49:11-13	115
36:27	736	49:28	346
36:31-32	736	49:28-29	346
36:36	736	49:31	819
36:43	71	50:1	346
37:1-4	958	50:4-5	556
37:3	324	50:5	776
37:5-11	49	50:7	851
37:5ff.	227	50:9	851
37:13	324, 337-338	50:24	346
37:19	789-790	50:24-5	345

50:25	346	11:4	139, 146–147
82:14	291	11:5	146
92:7	401	11:5–6	145
		11:6	146
Exodus		11:7	145
1	533	12	198, 226, 533, 792
1:1	356	12:1	45
1:7	347	12:1–2	647, 767
1–9	227	12:1–13	184
1–11	644	12:1–13:16	74
1–13	239	12:1–18	644
1:19	327	12:1–23:19	74
2	570	12:1–24:10	505
2:1–2	367	12:1–28	184, 186, 504
2:2	116	12:2	500–503
2:3	607	12:3	486
2:4	851	12:5	285
2:6	328, 688	12:10	555
2:10	328	12:12	145, 653
2:11	80	12:13	145
2:11–12	28	12–14	211
2:12	80, 283	12:14–20	184
2:13–17	80	12–17	227
2:14a	565	12:19–50	644
2:17	102	12:21	503, 505
3:1–4:17	328, 494	12:21–28	184, 285
3:2	505	12:22	135–138, 141–142, 418
3:7	505		
3:8	505	12:23	135, 145, 487, 855
3:10–12	558	12:29	485–486, 489, 491
3:16	345	12:29–32	647
3:20	539	12:30	146, 487, 491
4:6–7	538	12:35–36	329
4:14	622	12:37	498–500
4:20b	790	12:40	791–793
4:22	84, 487, 657	12:42	488
4:26	78	13:1–16	644
4:27	103	13:2	280, 486, 513–514
4:27–28	537	13:10	503
4:31	718	13:12	280, 486
5:14	581	13:17	329
6:2	505	13–17	74
6:6–7	115	13:17–18	647
6–7	145	13:17–22	644
6:26	71	13:18	249
6:27	71	13:19	851
7:1	770	13:21	716
7:17–25	329	14:4	845
7:19	146	14:7	86
8:12	973	14:13	67
8:15	146	14:19	84
8:19	540	14:20	379
9:7	146	14–20	644
9:8–9	498–499	14:21	329
9:22	146	14:24–25	143
9:24	655, 657	14:31	653
9:29	658	14:–31	74
11:2–3	329	15:1	78, 742

15:1–21	74	21:1	271, 354
15:2	11–12, 482, 738, 740, 948	21:1–22:23	74
		21:2–6	211
15:3	249	21:16	284
15:8	658	21:19	211
15:11	15	21:22	487
15:12	15	21:23	518
15:18	728	21–23	644
15:22–17:7	74	21:26	277
15:22–26	602	21:27	277
16	227	21:35	518
16:1ff.	119	22	136
16:3	830	22:3	518
16:9ff.	475	22:4	128–129, 518
16:25	286	22:5	126–129
16:27–30	608	22:7	275
16:45	716	22:9	279, 957
17	211	22:10	275
17:8–16	330	22:12	494
17:8–18:27	74	22:21–28:32	226
18:1–5	539	22:24–23:19	74
18:1–27	330	22:27	744
18:5	330	23:2	403, 471
18:6	539	23:10–11	608
18:7	539	23:11b	608
18:13	237	23:14	297
18:13–18	539	23:16	502
18:21–22	539	23:20a	536
19:1	330	24	339, 546, 644, 800
19:1–20:26	74	24:1	718
19:1ff.	475, 647	24:1ff.	796
19:3	658, 713, 721	24:5	796, 797
19:5	240	24:7	516, 743, 873
19:5–6	609	24:9–10	796
19:14	658, 721	24:10	919
19:17	721	24:11	796–797
19:20	285, 721	24:12	546
19–20	474–475	25:9	16
20	211, 227	25:17	831
20:1	354	25:22	653
20:2	385	25:31	18
20:2–17	685	25–31	644
20:3	740	25:40	16, 18, 656
20:5	849, 853	26:1	19
20:6	849, 853	26:6	660
20:8	472, 814	26:11	660
20:8–11	608	26:15	653, 656
20:10	275	26:29	653
20:11	418, 785	26:30	16
20:13	284, 977	26:31	653
20:14	765	27:10	653
20:19	101, 354, 959	27:20	112, 175
20:20	14	28:3	211
20:21	766	29:26	843
20:22	285, 959	29:38	298
20:24	720	29:45	145
20:25	226	30:12	647
21	211	30:17	579

30:20–21	505	2:4–5	186
30:26	505	4	198
30:32	505	4:1	354
31:1–6	16	4:1–5	177
31:2	16	4:13–21	177
31:3	16	4:22–26	177
31:6	16	4:23	178
31:12	505	4:28	178
31:12–13	74	4:32	178
31:12–17	74	5:1	841
31:15	505	5:1–5	177
31:18	354, 405	5:1–6	187
32	547	5–6	187, 198
32:1–34:9	644	5:8	275
32:4	864	5:11	811
32:7	79	5:20–26	289
32:16	354	6:1–6	505
32:19	354	6:1–7	187
33:5	727	6:2	820
33:6	380	6:7–9	186
33:20	919	6:12	354
34:4	354, 582	6:27	820
34:5–7	470	7:1	820
34:6	82, 470	7:11	820
34:6–7	470–471	7:13	186
34:10	471	7:20	281
34:10–40:38	644	7:37	281
34:12	505	8:1–10:7	430
34:14	505	8–10	438
34:18–24	505	9:24	579
34:19	486, 514	10:1	579
34:21	608	10:2	579
34:22	502	10:4	579
34:26	505	11	732
34:27	354	11:2	955
34:27–28	354	11:4	731
34:28	79, 418	11:4–8	730, 732
34:29	546–547	11:5	731
35:1–3	74, 608	11:6	796, 798
35:2	505	11:7	731
35:3	749	11:33	296
35:12ff.	246	11:36	296
35:30	16	11:41	526
35:30–36	16	12:2–5	338
35:31	16	13	450
36:1	19	13:1–8	180
36:33	1	13:1–17	282
37:1	16	13:4	282
39–40	17	13:5	282
39:43	17	13:9–17	180
40:34	579	13:10	183, 282
40:35	959	13–14	183, 198
		13–15	190
Leviticus		13:18	281
1:1	354	13:18–21	282
1:2	278, 727, 957	13:18–28	180
1:3–17	505	13:21	177
1:15	275–276	13:24	281
1–16	644	13:24–28	282

13:29	282	22:28	387
13:29–37	180, 282	23:11	647
13:30	282	23:15–16	340
13:33–53	180	23:17	186, 580
13:40	283	23:23ff.	475
13:40–44	180	23:30	423, 428
13:42	284	23:33–43	192
13:45–46	180	23:39	419
13:47	181	23:39–40	417
13:47–59	180–181	23:39–43	648
14	182, 840	23:40	418, 421, 423–424, 426–428
14:1–32	180		
14:13	283	23:40ff.	425
14:14	283	23:42	715
14:34	284	24:2	112
14:45	284	25:3–7	608
16	198	25:8	343
16:1–34	195	25:45	63, 68
16:1ff.	648	26	471
16:3	196	26:3	969
16:9	196	26:3–13	813
16:11	196	26:40	818
16:12	196	26:45	472
16:12–15	41	27:32	517
16:13b	296	27:34	407
16:14	196	29:6–7	102
16:15	196	29:7–8	102
16:16	196	29:9	102
16:18	196		
16:18–21	41	*Numbers*	
16:20	41, 196	1–4	644
16:23	196	1:46	499
16:24	196	2:3	329
16:30	197, 480	3:12	486
16:31	196	5	192, 198
17:11	432	5:1–31	190
17–27	644	5:5–8	289
18:3	866	5:5–10	288
18:5	562	5–6	644
18:6–23	431	5:12	766, 846
18:8	433	5:14	846
18:20f.	211	5:15	811
19:2	448	5:16–22	839, 842
19:3	176, 283	5:18	848
19:10	442–443	5:20–22	851
19:11	284	5:23–28	842, 844–845
19:17	45, 46	5:23ff.	851
19:18	45, 562	5:27	847
19:27	654	5:28	845
19:32	427–428	5:29–31	846–847
20:9–21	431	6:1–21	242
21:1	432	6:23	713
21:2	433	6:24	481, 659
21:5–6	609	7	644
21:11	289	7:1	647, 651–652, 654, 656, 658, 660
21:19–20	441		
22:12–13	434	7:1–6	578, 581–582
22:14–16	608–609	7:1ff.	578
22:26	177, 647	7:2	660–661

7:3	661	19	579
7:5	662	19:1	820
7:9	582	19:1–20	186
7:10–17	584	19:1ff.	647
7:12	579	19:17	119, 294, 839
7:45	661	19:19	119
7:89	653–654, 959	20	128
8:1–9:14	644	20–25	227
8:4	16	20–27	644
9:2	254, 272, 294	21:2	95
9:3	255–256	21:5	830
9:12	555	21:7	119, 715
9:13	254	21:17	78, 98
9:15–14:45	644	21:18	855
10:1	354	21:20	855
10:35–36	480	22:5	332
11:6	331	22:6	332
11:8	855	22:14–17	635
11:12	951	22:20–30	636
11:16–17	571	22:30	638
11:24–25	571	23:21	636–637
11:24–30	548	24:1	637
11:26	689	24:5	476
11:27	716	24:6	639
11:29	689	24:14	637
11:31	855	24:15	638
12	548	24:17	912
12:1	328	24:25	332
12:2	831	25	993
12:3	64, 470, 548	25:1–2	990
12:11	183	25:1–5	332
12:12	183	26:9	71
12:14	274	26:59	367
12:15	851	27:1	995
13	766	28:1	354
13:2	331	28:1–4	647
13–14	227	28:2	254–256, 272, 294, 727
13:25	890		
14:15	274	28:3	297
15	227, 644	28:10	256
15:22–26	177	28–30	644
15:22–29	177	29:1	45
15:27	178	29:1–6	45
15:29	483	29:12–38	192
15:32–36	608	29:15	297
15:37–41	473, 681	29:18	297
15:38	295	29:21	297
15:39	938	29:24	297
16	227, 548	29:27	297
16:2	331	29:30	297
16:3	331	29:31	297
16:10	793	29:33	297
16:15	793	29:35–39	648
16:17	794	29:37	297
16–17	227, 644	30:15	46
16:32	331	31	771
16:35	331	31:16	332
18:15	486	31–32	227
18–19	644	31–34	644

32:1	716	8:3	537
34	771	8:4–20	563
35	644	8:7	715
35:6–15	5	8:8	716
36	644	8:11–14	563
		9:1–10:11	563
Deuteronomy		9:7	814
1	766	9:9	79, 418
1:1	827, 829–831	9:10	354, 405
1:1–30	54	9:18	354
1–11	644	9:29	79
1:17	80, 82	10:1–6	354
1:20ff.	766	10:12–11:32	564
1:22–23	331	10:14	82
1:23	540	10:17	82, 482, 834
1:25	561	10:18	97
2–3:22	562	11:10	959
2:5	562	11:10–26:15	54
2:7	856	11:13–21	473
2:23–24	562	11:18	564
3:23–4:1	54	11:19	473
3:23–4:40	562	11:29	276
4:2	210, 235, 307	11:29–30	765
4:3	562	12:1–14	564
4:4	662	12:1–16	564
4:5	64	12:13–34	564
4:6	562	12:15–16	564
4:7	782	12:16	564
4:9	562	12:17–31	565
4:11	721	12:17–32	564
4:19	794–795	12:23	139
4:29–30	610	12:26	279, 956
4:31	82	12–26	629, 644
4:34	562	12:32	307
4:36	285, 562	13:1–11	565
5:4	653	13:2	551
5:6–6:9	607	13:9–11	565
5:6–21	685	13:12–18	565
5:12	472, 814	14:1–2	609
5:12–15	608	14:1–31	565
5:18	765	14:3	955
5:19	354	14:4f.	955
5:28–29	766	14:7	730–732
5:29	814	14:8	731, 735
5:30–31	766	14:22	647
6:4	482–483	14:22–27	565
6:4–9	54, 473	14:26	279
6:5–9	469	14:28	565
6:7	312, 473	15:1–3	300
6:13	537	15:1–18	566
6:16	537	15:17	566
7	562	15:19	280, 513
7:2	562	15:21	44
7:6	609	16:1	503
7:8	816	16:1–8	184, 186, 502
7:9	83, 782	16:1–17:7	566
7:12	959	16:2	285
7:13	996	16:9	660–661
8:1–3	563	16:9ff.	475

16:13–15	192	27:9–27	768
16:14	566	27–34	644
16:18	80	28	227
16:18–20	566	28:10	11
17:1	44, 955	28:49	68
17:2	277	28:66–68	66
17:3	794–795	28:69	68
17:6	277	29:1	68
17:8–18	566	30	227
17:16	67, 660	30:4	551
17:17	660	30:9	717
17:18	800–801	31:2	332
17:18–19	599	31:9	354, 358, 360, 827
18:15	547, 770	31:14	54
18:18	770	31:18	770
18:18–22	766	31:24–26	354
20	566–567	31:24–30	78
21:1–14	567	31:30ff.	768
21:10	286	32	769
21:11	286	32:1–34:12	54
21:15–21	567	32:4	83
21:15–22:4	567	32:15	827
21:17	485	32:21	512–513
21:19	933	32:24	140–141, 379
22:1–4	568	32:25	137–140, 142
22:5–23:14	568	32:27	797
22:9–11	608	32:41	512
22:12	295, 385	32:43	480
23:4	742	32:47	408, 781
23:15–24:4	568	33	789
24:1	296, 843	33:2	420, 855
24:1–4	211	33:3	83, 125
24:1ff.	933	33:11	723
24:6	569	33:17	5, 118, 724, 790
24:6–25:3	568	33:21	80
24:8–9	569	33–34	227, 374
24:9	814	34:5	516
24:14	569	34:6	851
24:16	817	34:12	360
24:17–18	569	34:28	516
24:19	298	134:15	845
24:21	442		
25:1–3	569	*Joshua*	
25:1–5	840	1:7–8	599
25:4–19	569	2	993
25:15	840	5:25	993
25:17	814	6:27	5
25:17–19	647	7:5	499–500
25:18	118, 724	7:6	722
25:19	814	8:31	358
26	471, 569	9:2a–f	212
26:12–15	569	10:12	78
27	763	10:18	556
27:2–7	765	10:21	147
27:4	765	10:22	556
27:5	765	10:26–27	556
27:6	765	18:13	608
27:7	765	23:6	354

Judges

3:9	682
3:11	682
4:2	489
4:13	86
4:14	147
5:1	79
5:4	515–516
5:4–5	514
5:20	86, 489
5:26	487
6:1	691
7	572
7:9	489
7:12	142
7:13ff.	489
7:25	572
13:2–5	558
13:7	557
13–14	241
14:3	86
14:4	243
14:18	242
16:1	692
16:4	692
16:21	849
16:32	86
18:1–8	563
21:25	683

Ruth

1:4	103
1:16	757
2	570
3:3	529

1 Samuel

1:1	727
1–2	475
1:6	368–369
1:11	985
1:19	718
1:80	558
2:2	15
2:6	657
2:25	540
2:26	558
2:40	558
2:52	558
6:3	583
9	549, 570
9:3	549
9:6	549
9:11	549
9:13	549
9:18	549
9:19	549
10:1	103
10:1–27	542
10:10	542
10:11	542
10:12	542
10:16	65
11:2	549
11:4	549
11:6	549
11:26	727
12:3	793
14:13	549
14:14	549
14:16	549
15	694
15:21	552
15:28	64
16:12	742
16:18	740
17:14	71
17:26	727
18:6	81
18:7	81
20:41–42	693
31:4	694

2 Samuel

1:10	694
5:24	146–147
6:7	583
6:8	583
7	607
7:23	482, 782
13:19	840
14:25–26	849
14:30b	212
15:6	849
15:7	87
15–16	553
15:25–26	87
17:23	552
18:9	87
18:14	849
18:15	849
20:7–10	553
22:1	79
23:1	827–828
23:2	827
23:6	828

1 Kings

1:13–15	561
2:8	658
2:11	569
2:12	569
2:15	569
3:4	750
5:1	73
5:4	72
5:16–26	217
6:14	79

8:12	78	2:6	552
8:63	662	2:9	549, 569
8:66	99	2:10	549
9:9	212	2:11	657
10:18	7	2:16–18	570
10:18–20	7	4	538, 542, 547–548
10:19	661	4:1	560
12:16	79	4:1–7	560
12:24a–z	213	4:8–11	560
13:1–7ff.	539	4:8–37	560
13:4	539	4:10	550
14:26	17	4:27	560
17	570	4:29a	543
17:1	559, 658	4:29b	543
17:5	559	4:31	547
17:6	559	4:32–35	547
17:8–16	538, 546	4:42–44	544
17:9	550	5:1–14	572
17:10	548, 550	5:5	572
17:10a	559	5:22	543
17:10c–13	559	6:30	722
17:17a	560	7:3	143
17:17b	560	7:4	137, 141–142
17:18	538, 570–571	7:5	143
17:19	550	7:6–7	143
17:19–20	560	7:7	143
17:22	560	7:8	143
17:23	658	7:9	143
17:24	560	7:9–11	143
18:10	73	7:12	143
18:30	545	7:16	144
18:38	129	7:35	143
19:5–7	537	8:1	144
19:19–21	537, 561	8:7–15	546
20:1	73	12:30	143
20:1–21:21	571	12:31	143
20:4	572	14:6	354
20:15	73	14:14	73
20:17–18	572	18:24	87
20:27–29	572	19:4	490
21:1–21	572	19:21–22	87
21:27	722	19:23–24	87, 852
22:24	554	19:25	87
		19:35	490, 852
2 Kings		23:25	354
1:1–2:1	560	24:13	17
1:1–12	561	25:16	17
1:2	540		
1:2–5	560	*1 Chronicles*	
1:2–17a	538	1:27	71
1:3	540	1:29	170
1:9–10	561	2:55	172
1:10	563	4:18	173
1:12	563	5:12	172
1:16	657	5:29	367
2	537	6:13	17
2:1	560	7:7	17
2:2	552	8:33	173
2:4	552	10:1	170

11:2	172	20:21	80
11:15	170	23:14	172
11:25	172	24:27	604, 695
12:9	17	25:7	172
12:33	172, 662	25:8	170–171
13:4	171	28:3	172
14:15	146	30:9	171
14:17	5, 73	32:5	380
15:2	78	32:12	71
15:11–15	583	32:19	171
16:25	171	32:21	170
16:27	380	32:32	172
17:3	172	33:13	422
17:5–6	171		
17:21	171, 482–483	*Ezra*	
18:8	17	1:1ff.	475
18:9	170	1:2	73, 731
21:2	170	1:3	73
21:29	17	3:12	468, 608
23:17	173	4:1	512
24:4–6	582	4:21	71
24:6	172	6:2	71
24:19	583	6:3	70, 73
28:2	170	6:14	71
28:6	171	7:9	71
29:9–10	95	7:25f.	927
29:11	82	8:27	794
		16:9	715
2 Chronicles		16:40	486
1:3	17	18:4	82
1:27	71	20:33	818
2:1–15	217	21:14	731
3:1	238	21:31	747–748
3:4	73	23:20	486
5:1	17	23:45	729
6:15	171	29:14	488
7:19	170	30:13	487
7:22	170	30:14	488
8:14	172	30:16	487
9:17–19	7	30:24	486–487
9:18	7	36:20	79
11:2	172	37:9	968
11:16	171	38:15	723
12:7	171	38:22	973
13:8	170	38:165	974
13:22	604, 695	39:17–19	973
14:1	171	41:7	833
15:2–7	609–610		
15:3	610	*Nehemiah*	
15:4	610	8:1ff.	927
15:5	610	9:32	482
15:6	551		
16:7	172	*Esther*	
16:10	172	1:1	65, 69
18:9	172	2:7	951
18:10	172	2:18	717, 956
18:12	172	3:1	490, 714
18:18	743	3:4	721
20:1	170	3:7	608

3:9	64	*Psalms*	
3:12ff.	490	1:1	605
3:14	67	1:8–9	168
4:1	5, 720, 722	2:6	765
5:3	543	2:7	536
5:9ff.	490	5:8	476
6:1ff.	490	5:16	480
6:9	722	8:2	83
6:11	722	8:3	83
7:4	69	9:13	481
8:2	721	9:17	158
8:12	240	10:14	64
8:15	5, 722	10:15	486
8:17	72	11:6	115
9:4	4–5	16:5	115
9:15	10	16:8	420
9:30	64	16:11	419–421
10:3	64	17:14	162
		18:10	285, 959
Job		19:8	79, 564
1:14	745	20:10	479
1:15	745	22:4	483, 485, 489
1:16	746	22:7	555
1:17	745	22:8	555
1:19	745	22:16b	555
2:8	746	22:18	555
3:3	973	23:5	115
3:16	83	24:8	82
3:19	747	24:12	82
5:5	287	26:6–7	424
12:5	86	26:8	476
12:6	86	28:2	159
12:10	657	29	474
12:13	82	29:9	159
12:16	474	29:10	873
15:34	729	30:1	79
17–37	42	33:1	480
20:20	794	34:8	102
21:5	42	34:19–20	555
21:7	42	35:10	480
21:10–12	85	36:8	741
21:14–15	85	37:32	51
25:2	654	37:33	51
26:8	657	37:35–36	550
27:3	783	39:5–7	749
28:4	85	39:12	794
28:5–8	85	40:8	742
30:3	487–488	41	552
31:10	788	41:9	552
31:34	746	42:5	381
32:16	743	45:2	162
34:20	486, 491	45:11	655
37–42	42	47:29	651
38:8	42	49:8–9	975
39:7	379	49:16	162
40:29	740	50:4	968
42:17b	163	50:7	743
		52:3	729
		56:13	974

58:4	734	103:20	729
60:9	212	104:1	427
60:14	476	104:1–2	477
61:7–9	162	104:2–3	654
66:13–14	94	105:7	71
67:19	313	105:33	746
68:5	427, 480	105:36	485, 746
68:14	986	105:39	715
68:27	83	106:7	830
68:30	72	106:20	738
68:33	159	106:23	64
69:13	377	107:4	541
69:14	476	107:6	541
69:34	159	107:10	541
72:11	72, 421	107:14	541
72:19	72	107:23–29	540
73:25	732	107:23–30	545
74:2	765	110:6–7	481
74:11	487	111:9	483
75:4	744	111:10	698
75:9	115, 486	113–118	424
76:9	516	114:1	424, 453
78:38	479	115:1	424, 453
78:48	746	116:1	312, 424, 453
78:51	485	116:10–15	553
79:10	480	116:13	115
80:1	420	116:15	246
80:4	426	118:10	453
80:9	115	118:20	751
80:14	731	118:22–23	551
81:9	158	118:24	865
81:13–14	813	118:25	424, 550
82:1	83, 716	118:26–27	550
82:6	744	118:28	453
82:16	716	119:62	741
84:8	160	119:105	564
85:5	970	126:2	78
85:8–10	659	129:3–4	816
86:8	83	129:31	512
89:7–8	83	132:1–6	79
89:9	83	132:2	95
89:20–38	607	132:14	718, 832
90:3	162	133:1	958
90:5	161	135:8	487
91:10	659	136:7	480
92	469–470	136:10	486, 491
92:1	161	136:13	31
92:13	427	137:1	386
95:5	82	138:4	977
95:6	476, 718	139:5	981
96:12	423	144:12	817
96:12–13	423	144:14	139
96:13	423	145:9	82
96:14	423	146:10	480, 489
99:9	718	147:8	731
102:1	421	147:12	765
102:17	421–423	149:1	81
102:18	422–423	151	198
103:1	480		

Proverbs

1:12	729
2:4–5	865
2:6	82
2:20–21	356
3:17	477
3:18	419, 477
3:19	82
4:4	419
5:13	606
6:13	606
6:16–19	452
6:20–35	607
6:23	419
8	228
8:10	417, 419
8:22	780, 951
8:22–30	477
8:25	236
8:30	951
9:5	97, 417
9:10	248
10:25	81
10:27	419
14:13	98
18:9	70
20:21	736
22:27	857
22:29	868
23:23	64
25:19	168
25:25	275
26:4–5	168
28:10	729
30:10	865
30:20	96
31:31	987

Qohelet

1:1	828
1:5–7	828
1:15	750
2:4	938
2:18–21	565
3:16	456
4:5	751
6:2	565
7:4	938
9:4	748–749
11:9	938
12:12ff.	938

Song of Songs

1:1	857, 864–865, 869
1:1.17E	868
1:2	858
1:3	865–866
1:4	287, 865
1:5	860, 862
1:6	865
1:11	858
1:12	864
1:15	862–863
2:1	858
2:2	702, 858, 866
2:6	865
2:7	865
2:9	858
2:10	487
2:11–12	858
2:13	860–861
2:14	859, 980
2:16	862–863
3:1	859
3:1–4	556
3:4	859
3:5	865
3:6	418
3:7–8	865
3:9	654
3:9ff.	654
3:11	654–656, 859
4:1	862–863
4:4	5
4:5	865
4:7	859, 867
4:8	859–860
4:11	917
4:16	651
5:1	651–652, 655
5:10–15	83
6:3	865
6:10	420
7:2	1, 17
7:3	865
7:4	865
7:5	833
7:7	862
7:11	991
8:3	865
8:4	865
8:5	986
8:6	863
8:7	418
8:8	866
8:9–10	865
8:14	862

Isaiah

1:15	906
1:16	715
2:2	723
2:2–3	833
2:3	765
2:12–18	84
2:20–21	976
3:10	356
3:26	399

4:2b	900	34:6–7	973
4:3	969	34:7	488
4:4	715	34:9	973
4:6	715	34:11	973
5:1–7	551	35:5	78, 114
5:5	894	35:5–6	546
5:17	891	35:6	78
6:2	656, 743	40:1–2	389, 396, 648
6:3	468, 480, 483	40:2	389, 396
6:11	487	40:3	536
7:14	24, 36	40:5	480
7:21	98, 117, 716	40:26	698
8:16	894	42:1	536
8:17	894	42:7	905
9:5	901	42:10	81
10:32	87, 490	42.13	249
11:1	902	42:13	82
11:4	741	43:3–4	976
11:11	98, 117, 488	43:4	975
13:1	551	43:10	115, 904–905
14:11	750	43:18	614, 618
14:13	852	43:19	614, 618
14:13–14	87	44:22	480
14:14	852	45:7	471
14:15	852	45:17	81
15:19–20	969	48:13	487
16:1	902	48:18	814
16:5	902	49:3	905
19:1ff.	488	49:14–16	648
19:2	486, 488, 551	49:21	992
19:3	487	49:23	855
19:4	487	49:24	540
19:13	487	50:2	933
19:22	487	50:7	554
20:18	976	51:4	655
21:9	714	51:12–15	648
21:11	488, 490	52:8	480
21:11–12	491	52:9–10	557
21:12	488, 490, 895	52:13	903
22:1–14	378	52:13–53:12	903
23:1	212	53:5	741, 903
23:5	488	53:7	554
23:13	746	53:10	903
26:11–12	134	53:12	903
26:20	137–138	54:1	991–992
26:21	139	54:1ff.	648
27:3	87	54:5	986
27:13	98, 117, 718	54:9	970
28:5	902	54:11–14	648
29:10	608	54:13	303, 468
30:3	379	54:16	147
30:29	78, 84	54:17	147
31:1	67	55:1	310
31:3	67	55:2	417, 419
32:11–13	381	56:7	550
32:25	480	57:1	135
33:8	383	57:15	483
34:4	551	58:8	78, 851
34:5	723, 974	58:13	46

58:13–14	46	17:8	620
60:1–3	648	17:13	197
60:5	78	17:21–22	608
60:21	729	17:22	608
60:22	861	23:5	900
61:10–11	648	25:11	487
62:6	490	25:15	115
63:3	116	25:26	303
63:3–4	490	25:31	487
63:11	970	26:8	551
64:3	919	29	200
65:8–9	27	30:4	827
65:24	480	30:5–7	827
65:25	9	30:6	81
66:6	973	30:18	832
66:9	369	30:19	148
66:20	581	30:20	417
66:24	548	31:3	379
		31:9	212
Jeremiah		31:11	480
1:1–3	647	31:12	78
1:4–8	558	31:15–16	102
1:5	734	31:15–17	388
1:11f.	303	33:11	974
2:2	610	33:15	900
2:3	609	33:15–16	994
2:4–6	647	42:16	67
2:7	112, 175	44:1	487–488
2:16	487	44:15	488
3:1	933	46:14	487
5:6	723	46:19	487
7:11	550	49:12	714
9:2	96	49:20	724
9:5	140–141	51:7	115
9:6	140	51:39	748
9:7	140	51:41	303
9:9	140	51:64	827
9:12	140–141		
9:13	140	*Lamentations*	
9:15	141	1:1	112, 175
9:19–21	375	1:1–2	648
9:20	83, 139	1:8	395
9:23	141	1:10	742
10	200	1:17	449
10:6	82	2:3	382, 488
10:7	82	2:10	400
10:10	477	3:5	73
10:14b–15	15	4:4	83
10:15	15	4:5	951
10:16	15	4:11	126, 136
11:15	384	5:18	381
13:11	727		
13:17	382	*Ezekiel*	
14	142	1:1–3	897
14:10	142	1:3	897
14:19	384	7	142
15:1	112, 175	8:14	556
16:19–20	976	8:16	500
17:6	619	11:16	905

16:3	606	*Hosea*	
16:6	606	1:2	933
16:7:8	606	2:17	610
16:9	119	2:21	706
16:11	788	3:1	933
16:27–29	606	3:4	610
16:48–50	86	3:4–5	610
16:49	320	3:5	610
21:3	136	4:4	897
21:8	135	4:5	898
21:36	136	4:14	847
21:37	136	5:15	382
23:14	879	6:5	897
26:3	87	6:7	112, 174
27:3	87	9:7	897
28:2	88	9:15	112, 175
28:10	88	11:1	535, 557, 653
28:14	27	12:5	489
28:16	27	12:12	662
36:25	197	14:1–3	648
		14:2	119
Daniel			
2:1	325	*Joel*	
2:19	490	2:16	83
2:21	82	4:18	86, 98, 117
2:24ff.	490	4:21	480
2:28	551		
2:38	73	*Amos*	
3:15	879	1:1	827
3:22	558	2:16	553
4:2ff.	490	3:7	106, 723
4:28–29	852	3:12	494
4:29–32	852	3:17	610
6:6–15	543	4:1	827
6:17ff.	490	8:9	555
6:26	73	8:14	96
7:1ff.	490	9:1	721
7:4	106, 118, 723	9:6	428
7:5	118, 723	9:13	745
7:7	714		
7:9b	558	*Obadiah*	
7:13	551	1:8	729
7:13–14	554	1:21	732, 736
7:16	743		
7:20	118, 488, 724	*Jonah*	
7:24	488	1:4–6	540
8:13	483	1:8	244
9:9	82	1:11	244
9:11	112, 175, 384	1:12	244
9:27	235, 551	1:15b–16a	540
10:6	558, 654	3:4	243
10:7	890		
10:11	490	*Micah*	
11:38	794	2:13	716
12:1	551, 743	3:5	898
12:2	941	3:12	381
12:3	420, 699, 941	5:2	557
12:4a	547	5:14	977
12:11	551	7:6	551, 565
		7:19	480

INDEX OF ANCIENT SOURCES

Nahum
- 1:1 — 898
- 1:2 — 45
- 1:15a — 537
- 2:5 — 420
- 3:8 — 951

Habakkuk
- 1:1 — 898
- 2:2 — 49–50

Zephaniah
- 3:2 — 897
- 3:4 — 897–898

Haggai
- 2:1 — 898
- 2:8 — 82

Zechariah
- 1:1 — 898
- 1:4–6 — 889
- 1:8 — 427
- 1:9 — 718
- 2:9 — 126, 134
- 2:10 — 551
- 3:1–5 — 555
- 3:8 — 900
- 4:2 — 420
- 6:12 — 900
- 7:4–12 — 889
- 8:4 — 148
- 8:5 — 148
- 9:1 — 832–833
- 9:9 — 550
- 9:14 — 719
- 9:14–15 — 719
- 11:11b — 552
- 12:10 — 554
- 12:11 — 556
- 13:2 — 898
- 13:3 — 933
- 13:4 — 898
- 13:7 — 552
- 14:1–10 — 32
- 14:2 — 741
- 14:7 — 489–490
- 14:8 — 117, 715
- 14:9 — 482, 918
- 14:12 — 973
- 14:18 — 98
- 14:21b — 550

Malachi
- 1:3 — 107
- 2:10–11 — 895
- 2:13 — 990
- 2:16 — 933, 990
- 3:1–3 — 550
- 3:1a — 536
- 3:4 — 970
- 3:7 — 970
- 3:18 — 895
- 3:22 — 79, 354, 358
- 3:23 — 147–148

NEW TESTAMENT

Matthew
- 2:1–18 — 327
- 2:4 — 896
- 2:22–23 — 557
- 4:1–11 — 537
- 4:1–13 — 537
- 5–7 — 561
- 6:17 — 558
- 6:22–23 — 564
- 7:7–11 — 563
- 7:12 — 688
- 8:513 — 559
- 9:37–38 — 561
- 10 — 561–562
- 10:5 — 563
- 10:26–35 — 564
- 10:34–36 — 565
- 11:24 — 546
- 11:25–27 — 562
- 12:11 — 566
- 12:39–42 — 564
- 12:40 — 557
- 13 — 561
- 13:18–23 — 901
- 13:24–30 — 900–901
- 13:36–43 — 900
- 16:21 — 896
- 17:1–8 — 561
- 18:6–7 — 569
- 18:10–14 — 568
- 18–19 — 561
- 20:18 — 896
- 22:1–10 — 566
- 22:23–33 — 922
- 23:4–7 — 564
- 23:23–36 — 564
- 23–26 — 561
- 23:35 — 564
- 27:24b — 557
- 27:43 — 555
- 27:62–28:20 — 557
- 28:16 — 558

Mark
- 1:1–3 — 536
- 1:2 — 550

INDEX OF ANCIENT SOURCES

1:9–11	536	9:33–37	548
1:11	536	9:38	548
1:12–13	537	9:38–50	548
1:14–15	537	9:41	548
1:15–18	550	9:43–48	548
1:16–20	537, 561	10:13–16	548
1:21–28	537	10:27	548
1:29–31	538	10:32–45	549
1:36	541	10:35	549
1:40	541	10:37	549
1:40–45	538	10:46–52	546, 549
2:1–12	538	10:48	549
2:14	537, 561	11:1	549
3:1–6	539, 566	11:1–6	549
3:5	539	11:2	549
3:6	539	11:7–11	550
3:13–35	539	11:12–14	550
3:14	539	11:20	550
3:21	539	11:27	896
3:22	538	12:1–12	551
3:31–32	539	12:10–11	551
3:31–35	564	12:18–27	922
3:33–35	539	12:28–34	562
4:13–20	901	13:1–37	551
4:26–29	900–901	13:7	551
4:35–41	540	13:8	551
5:1–20	541	13:12	551
5:21–23	542	13:14	551
5:21–24	542	13:19	551
5:23	542	13:24	551
5:24a	542	13:25	551
5:24b–34	542	13:26	551
5:35–43	542	13:27	551
5:42	542	13:34–37	565
6:1–6	542	13:37	565
6:7–13	543	14:3–9	551, 560
6:8	543	14:12–16	549
6:14–29	543	14:16	550
6:30–44	544	14:17–31	552
6:45–52	545	14:26	552
6:52	545	14:27	552
7:1–5	564	14:32–52	553
7:1–23	545	14:44–45	553
7:24–30	546	14:53–72	554
7:31–37	546	14:55	554
7:31–38	546	14:60–61	554
7:37	546	14:65	554
8	546	14:71	553
8:1–10	544	15:1–15	554
8:14–21	545	15:4–5	554
8:22–26	546	15:20	555
9:1–13	546	15:21–41	555
9:2	546	15:24	555
9:3	547, 550	15:34	555
9:7	547	15:38	555
9:9	547	15:40	555
9:13	546, 547	15:42–47	556
9:14–29	547	16:1–8	556
9:16	547	24:8	552

Luke

1:1–2:52	558
1:18	558
1:32–33	559
1:34	558
1:35	559
1:46–52	558
3:20–21	568
4:18	905
6:31	688
7:1–17	559
7:2–3	559
7:7b	559
7:8	559
7:10	559
7:12b	560
7:13	560
7:15	560
7:15b	560
7:16–17	560
7:21	560
7:36	560
7:36–50	560
7:37	560
7:38	560
7:40–42	560
7:44–50	560
8:11–15	901
9:28–36	561
9:51–56	560
9:51a	560
9:54	560, 563
9:59–62	561
10:1	540, 562
10:1–3	561
10:1–18:14	561
10:2	561
10:4–16	562
10:4b	543
10:17–30	561
10:21	562
10:21–24	562
10:22	562
10:23–24	562
10:29–37	562
10:33	563
10:38–42	568
11:1–3	563
11:9–13	563
11:14–26	563
11:19–20	540
11:27–36	564
11:29–32	564
11:34–36	564
11:37–12:12	564
11:37–38	564
11:39–52	564
11:50	564
12:2–9	564
12:14	565
12:16–21	565
12:35–53	565
12:41ff.	565
12:54–13:5	565
13:6–9	565
13:10–21	566
13:22–35	566
14:1–6	566
14:1–14	566
14:5	566
14:15–35	566
15:3–7	568
15:8–10	568
16:1–18	568
16:19–18:8	568
17:1–2	569
17:1–9	563
18:9–14	569
20:27–38	922
21:8	565
22:19	700
22:43	553
22:44	157
24:3	570
24:13ff.	572
24:49	569
24:49–53	569
24:50–53	569
24:51	569
51–53	565

John

1:43–51	570
2:1–11	570
2:4	570
2:6–7	570
2:11	570
2:24	570
4:1–42	563
4:1–44	570
4:19	770
4:25	770
4:39	571
4:46–54	559
6:9	544
7:27–28	543
12:1–8	551
19:36	555
20:1	571
20:11–18	571
20:14	571
20:17	571
20:17a	571
20:17b	571

Acts

1:1	569
1:9–11	570

1:18	553	*1 Corinthians*	
2:1–4ff.	571	2:9	919
2:3	571	2:13	33
2:4	570	10:20a	547
2:15a	571	11:18–22	566
4:5	896		
4:6	896	*Galatians*	
5:1–11	571	3:10	940
5:3b–4	572	3:17	215
5:5a	572	4:22	11
5:6	572	4:29	321
5:9b	572		
5:10a	572	*1 Timothy*	
5:10b	572	5:3–16	563
5:39	239		
6:8–15	571	*Hebrews*	
7:15	326	5:5–10	53
7:16	236	7:1–7	53
7:20	328	7:1–10	597
8:5–17ff.	563		
8:26–40	572	*James*	
8:27c	572	5:17	543
8:36	572		
9:1–21	573	*1 Peter*	
9:16	573	2:4ff.	240
10:9–16	573	2:9	240
10:11	574		
10:13	574	*Jude*	
10:14	574	14	603
13:18	215		
15:21	927	*Revelation*	
23:6–8	922	2:11	895
		20:6	895
Romans		20:14	895
3:25	940	21:8	895
4:25	552		
10:19	513		

APOCRYPHA OR SEPTUAGINT

Genesis LXX		*Numbers LXX*	
1:1	780	16:15	793
1:26–27	782		
2:2	785	*Deuteronomy LXX*	
5:1b–2a	782	4:19	794
11:7	786	5:6–21 LXX	203
18:12	787	17:3	794
22:12	536		
25:22	559	*2 Samuel LXX*	
49:6	788	15:27	553
		20:10	553
Exodus LXX			
3:14	227	*1 Kings LXX*	
24:11	796	13:6	539
		17:8–24	570
Leviticus LXX		19:7–8	553
11:6	796, 798		

2 Kings LXX
4:31	542
13:20–21	542

Psalms LXX
148	550

Isaiah LXX
7:14	557
29:13	545
35:5a	549
35:6a	549
35:8a	549

Ezekiel LXX
1:1	574
2:9	574
4:14	574

Daniel LXX
6:4	554
7:14	558
12:3	213
13:46	558

Zephaniah LXX
3:8a	547

Add. Dan.
Bel
v. 15	490

Susanna
46	558

EpArist.
4ff.	206
47–50	213
128–171	248
310	210

1 Maccabees
1:62f.	246
8:17	216

2 Maccabees
2:28–32	246
3:4	573
3:5	573
3:25–26	573
3:35	573
4:11	216
6:18–7:42	245–246
7:9	239
7:28	781
7:36	246

3 Maccabees
6:10	246
6:38	245
7:17	245

4 Maccabees
16:20	322

Sir
11–12	15
24:8–12	477
44:22–45:1	328
49:10	611
50:25	513

Tobit
5:5	571
12:19	571
12:20	571

Wisdom of Solomon
2:12–20	555
7:22–30	228
11:17	781
11–19	597
14:15f.	200
16:20–1	34
19:13–14	320

OLD TESTAMENT PSEUDEPIGRAPHA

ApocMos
24.2	244

1 Enoch
1:9	603
6:2	343
6:6	343
7–8	691
8:1	343
15:7	343

Epistle of Barnabas
7	554

4 Esr.
7:28	922
14	800
14:44–47	206

Genesis Apocyphon
22.17	320

Jos. Asen.
1–21	240
8.5	240
9	240
10.10–13	207
12.2	240, 247

12.5	240	22:1–5	341
15.5	240	22:4	341
15.12	244	22:10–24	346
16.6	240	22:13	342
19.5	240	22:20	343
21.13f.	240	23:5	346
21.21	240	23:8	343
22–29	240	25:1–10	343
		26:18	348
Jubilees		26:24	348
1:7–25	339	30	343
1:27–29	339	32:2–3	345
2:14	337	32:24–26	341
2:16	785	34:1–10	338
2:19	340	39:6	341
3:3	337	42:12	336
3:3–4, 6a	337	42:25	326
3:4	337	44:3	341
3:6	337	44:4	341
3:8	337, 340	44:5–6	341
3:8–13	340	44:5a	341
4:15	342	45:5–6	347
4:17	341	45:14	346–347
4:17–18	338	45:16	345
5:1	343	46:1	347
6:17–19	340, 475	46:9	236, 326
6:18	340	46:16	341
6:23–31	338	49:23	338
7:20–25	343	50:2–4	343
7:21	343		
7:38–39	341	*Liber antiquitatum biblicarum* (Pseudo-Philo)	
7b	342	1.1	687
8:6–7a	342	1.1–4	687
8:8–9	342	1.2	687
8:11–9:13	336	1.3–4	687
8:17	344	3.10	680, 686
8:19	340, 344	3.11	683
9:4	344	4.11	680
9:14	336	6	680
9:15	344	6.4	680
10:13	341	6.9	680
10:18	336	6.11–18	319
10:25	336	6.17	680
10:29–34	344	8.3	683
12:15	338	9.3	792
12.16–17	320	9.4	681
12:27	341	9.5	686
13.25–27	320	9.7	681
14:20	340	9.8	683
15:1–4	340	9.10	559, 681
16:13	340	9.13	688
17:10	336	9.15	688
19:10	336	9.16	28
20:1–11	346	10.1–6	681
20:3–6	343	11.5	683
21:1–25	346	11.6–9	688
21:10	341	11.10–13	688
22	348	12.4	685
22:1	343	12.7	683

12.8	690	34.4	692
13.10	684	34.5	692
15.5	688	35.3	687
15.6	684	36.3	685
16.1	681	36.4	687
16.5	681	37.1	682
18.3	681	37.4	682
18.5	688–689	38.1	682
18.10–11	690	38.4	685
18.13–14	686	39.6	685
19.2	685	39.7	690, 914
19.3	681	39.10	682
19.7	679, 685–686	40.2	689
19.10	685	41.1–2	683
19.12–13	686	41.3	683
19.15	686	42.3	683
20.1	684	43.5	692
20.2	681	44.6	685
20.5	681, 689	44.7	686
20.8	330	44.10	687
21.1	686	45.3	683, 685–686, 693
21.4	681	46	683
21.9	684	47.4–5	692–693
21.10	684	47.7–8	692–693
22.3	684	47.8	683, 685
22.5	681	48.4	683
22.9	685	53.2	683
23.10	684	54.2	685
23.11	684	55.2	685
23.11–12	690	55.8	685
23.12	914	56.2	683
23.13	686	56.3	683
24.3	682	57.4	683
24.4	684	58.4	694
24.6	682	59.1	683
25.1–2	682	59.4	683, 688
25.3–13	682	60	683
25.7	687	61	683
25.13	684	62	683
27.10	682	62.3	685
27.12	682	62.9	687
27.14	682	62.11	685, 693
28.4	684, 690, 914	64.9	687
28.5	684, 689	65.3	694
29.1	682	65.4	693
30.1	686, 690	65.5	679, 683, 694
30.2	682, 684, 690		
30.4	690	*Syballine Oracles*	
30.7	684	3:97–98	787
31.2	684	8:294–301	554
31.7	682		
32.2–4	689	*T. 12 Patr.*	326
33.2	687		
33.3	684, 687	*T. Abr.*	
33.6	682	10	689
34.1	682, 684, 691		
34.1–5	691	*T. Jos.*	
34.2–3	691	2–9	240

DEAD SEA SCROLLS

Pesher Habakkuk (1QpHab)
2.2	309
4.17ff.	309
6:3–6	926
7:1–5	50
9:8–12	50
11:5–8	50

Rule of the Community (1QS)
2:1–4	481
5:1	605
5.20ff.	309
6.9f.	309
6:24	604
8.11f.	309
8:14–16	604
8:15	605
8:26	604
10:10	473

Damascus Document (CD)
1.18	310
6.3–9	309
7.9ff.	309
7.13b–8.1a	308
9:2–8	45
10:20–21	46
20:6	604

Temple Scroll (11QT)
14:0–13	44
52:3–5	44

1Q14	52
1QGenApoc	
19:14–20	47
4Q128–4Q157	41
4Q158–4Q186	50
4Q161	52
4Q162	52
4Q163	52
4Q164	52
4Q166–167	52
4Q174	53
1 14	605
4Q177	53

4Q242	200
4Q246	559
4Q249	605
4Q252	42–43
1 II 7–8	43
1 IV 5–6	43
II 6–7	43
4Q370	48
4Q371–372	513
4Q373	48
4Q374	48
4Q423, frg. 3	245
4Q464	48
4Q464a	48
4Q464b	48
4Q470	48
4Q491	604
4Q550	603
4QCatena	53
4QDa	
18 5:18–20	605
4QFlorilegium	53
4QMidrEschata	53
4QMidrEschatb	53
4QMMT	603
4QpaleoExodm	603
4QPatr	914
4QpIsac	
23.2.10	310
4QpIsae	
1–2.2f.	309

4QpNah		4QtgJob	163
1–2.2.7	310		
3–4.1.2,7	310	5Q543–547	350
3–4.2.2,4	310		
3–4.3.3,7	310	5Q550A–E	603
4QPNNah	51	7Q2	200
4QpPsa		11Q2–18	41
1–10 III 15–16	50		
1–10 IV 8–9	51	11Q13	53
4QPsa		11Q20–31	41
1–10.3.14ff.	309		
		11QMelch	603
4Qsamc	212		
		11QPs	914
4QSb			
5 1:1	605	11QPsa	
		27.11	309
4QSd			
1 1:1	605	11QtgJob	41, 163, 932

CLASSICAL WORKS AND AUTHORS

Aphrahat		Demetrius	
Dem.		frg. 5	249
4.9	26		
5:7–8	27	Dio of Prusa	
13.5	26	*Orations*	
23.13–14	27	57	241
Aristobulus		Ephrem	
frg. 2	221	*Comm. in Gen.*	
		6:9	27
Aristotle		11.2	37
On the Heavens		16:8–13	27
2, 2	699	23.1	37
		34.3	38
Augustine			
Contr. adv. leg.		Eupolemus	
2.2	21	*On the Kings in Judea*	
		frg. 1	216
Basil the Great		frg. 2	217
Ep.			
190	34	Euripides	
		Iphegenia in Aulis	
Clement of Alexandria		1524–25	322
Strom.			
7.33	249	Eusebius	
		Comm. in Is.	
Corpus Hermeticum		1:21–2	33
1.4–19	232	29:13–14	33
11:5–8	232	*Comm. in Ps.*	
		77:13	31
Cyril of Alexandria		*Praep. ev.*	
Comm. in Os.		8.8.56–7	33
4.73	31	9.8.1	327
45.114	31	9.17.3	319

9.18.1	320	Jerome	
9.20	238	*Adv. Ruf.*	
9.20.1–4	219	1.13	2, 28
9.20.3	219	*Comm. in Am.*	
9.22.4	323	1:1	32
9.23	238	*Comm. in Eccl.*	
9.27-7–10	328	1:14	35
9.29.2	327	*Comm. in Is.*	
9.37	238	7:14	36
9.38	33	*Comm. in Malachi*	
10.18–19	33	2:10–12	31
11.5.1–3	34	*Comm. in Zach.*	
11.5.3	21	6:9–15	28
12	34	14:5	32
12.1.4	21, 33	prolog.	30, 39
12.4.2	33	*Ep.*	
Proof of the Gospel		18(B).20	21
6.18.32–42	32	37.3	35
		Qu. Hebr. in Gen.	
Ezekiel		22:2	35
Exagoge		41:43	30
168–169	338	*Stromateis*	
210	249	1.11.2	28
		1.153	28
Firmicus Maternus			
Mathesis		Josephus	
4.17.2	320	*Ant.*	
Prooemium		1.5	316
5	320	1–11	233
		1–11.296	232
Herodotus		1.17	235, 236, 307, 316–317
Histories			
5.52–53	890	1.22	237
		1.24	306, 307
Hilary of Poitiers		1.25	307, 317
Commentary on the Psalms		1.29	317
2.2	28, 34	1.30	318
		1.35	318
Homer		1.37	317
Iliad		1.50	318
1.260–74	241	1.53	318
24:332	545	1.54	306
24:340–341	545	1.58	318
24:345–346	545	1.59	318
24:351–352	545	1.61	318
Odyssey		1.62	319
3:34–38	544	1.64	319
3:63–68	544	1.108	333
3:254–308	543	1.114	319
4:30	544	1:118	787
4:36	544	1.121	219
4:51	544	1.151	319
4:53–58	544	1.157	237, 319
4:65–68	544	1.161	319
4:512–547	543	1.166–168	237
9:101–565	541	1.167	319
10:1–69	541	1.187	320
11:404–434	543	1.192	317, 320
		1.194	320

1.197	321	2.305	329
1.198	321	2.314	329
1.200	321	2.318	792
1.205	321	2.321	249
1.214	317	2.322	329
1.215	321	2.334	329
1.216	321	2.348	333
1.226	321	3.104–106	16
1.232	322	3.3	330
1.233	322	3.11	330
1.239–41	236	3.31	330
1.239–241	219	3.40	330
1.240	219	3.40–60	330
1.244	322	3.62	330
1.246	322	3.63	330
1.249	322	3.73f.	237
1.288	322, 324	3.81	333
1.291	323	3.90	330
1.301	323	3.94	317
1.311	323	3.96	330
1.333	323	3.123	306, 330
1.335	323	3.143	317
1.336	323	3.146	330
1.337	325	3.179–187	306
1.344	323	3.190	330
2.9	324	3.205	317
2.15–17	324	3.209	331
2.19	324	3.230	317
2.31	324	3.257	317
2.34	324	3.259	317
2.45	325	3.264	317
2.75	325	3.268	333
2.94	325	3.296	331
2.95	325	3.302	331
2.97	325	3.322	333
2.98	326	4.8	517
2.101	325	4.14	331
2.125	326	4.16	331
2.161	326	4.22	331
2.199	236, 326	4.27	330
2.201–349	237	4.33	331
2.204	326, 792	4.48	517
2.205	326	4.51–53	332
2.207	327	4.54–56	332
2.218	327	4.78	332
2.226	327	4.104	332
2.229	327	4.107	332
2.230	328	4.126	332
2.231	328	4.126–30	332
2.233	328	4.158	333
2.234–35	328	4.197	307
2.238–53	328	4.198	317
2.243	208	4:212–213	473
2.243–253	237	4.226	306
2.246f.	208	4.228	306
2.264	328	4.326	237
2.265	328	4.327	332
2.275	329	5.1.48	569
2.294–95	329	5.277–82	236

5.289	325	1:73–2.150	207
6.14	319	1.109	233
7.333–34	321	1.112	233
8, 194–195	10	1.116–120	233
8.50–60	233	1.218	217, 238
8.56	307	1.384	236
8.143	233	2.17	927
8.144–146	233	2.91–96	322
8.262	333	2.135f.	202
9.224–5	32	2.192	236
10	201	4.319	236
10.79	307	12.21	236
10.108	235	182f.	202

Vita

208f.	307
361	233
418	233
429	333

10.181	235		
10.186–281	235		
10.195	325		
10.210	235		
10.218	235, 307		
10.267	235		
10.276	235		
10.281	333		

Justin
Dialog.

11.33–58	213	36.2	24
11.151	237	40	554
12	201	43.8	24
12.3.3§142	896	62.2–3	24–25
12.6–118	217	68.7	24
12.108	202	70.5	24
12.109	316	71.1	24
12.160–222	307	73.6	24
15	13	112.4	24
15, 23–30	16	131.6	25

Historiae Philippicae 36

2.12–13	329

Is.

33.18	24

18.16	314		
18:16–17	521		
18.85–89	769		
19, 357	16		
19–36	237		

Letter of Aristaeus to Philocrates

20.260	316	§46	222
20.261	316	§128–141	222
20.267	233	§142–148	222
20.268	317	§142–171	222
42:13	338	§295	222
Pref. 1.14	306	§310	222

Bellum Judaicum

1.108	236

Lucretius

5.982–87	318

2.165–166	922		
2.166	314		
3.351–4	307		
3.353	307		

Origen
Ad Gen.

41.43	30

C. Celsum

1.57	770

4.622–9	307		
5, 184–227	13		
5.217f.	306		
5.218	306		
5.406	236		
6.316	926		

Comm. in Cant.

prol.	21

Comm. in Canticum

prolog.	29

C.Ap.

Comm. in Psalms

1:35ff.	797	intro.	33
1.38–40	233	prolog.	29
1.42	316		
1.51f.	233		

Hom. Gen.

2	30
2.1–2	30
3	30

Hom. in Ex.

5.5	31

Philocalia

2.3	33

Philo

Abr.

26.134	320
217	304
232–244	309

Agr.

51	228, 232

Cher.

27	227, 305
48	305

Conf.

168–175	25
181	787
187	787
190	304–305

Contempl.

78	304

Decal.

5.18	330
175	305

Deo

4	227
9–12	232

Ebr.

144	305

Flacc.

121	236

Fug.

68–70	25
179	305

Gig.

24	305

Her.

45.221	330
197	306
265	305

Ios.

39.232	326
180–181	338

Migr.

35	305
89–93	305

Mos.

1.2.7	327
1.2.9	328
1.4.15	328
1.5.18	327
1.5.18–24	327
1.15.18	328
1.26.144	329
1.36.198	330
1.40.221	331
2.21.103	330
2.88	306
2.187–292	305
2.292	216
102f.	306
117–123	306

Mut.

65	304
125–128	305
131	230
134	230
137	230
138	304
140	304

Opif.

9.35	318
24	236
24f.	228
76	784
77	304
129	338
134	784

Plant.

32ff.	305

Post.

34.116–17	319

QE

2.2	225
2.62	228
2.73	330
2.75	330
2.85	330

QG

1:28	338
1.74	318
1.82–85	230
2.5	30
2.7	30
2.82	319
4.51	305
4.243	304

Sacr.

1.2	318

Somn.

1.39	305
1.94	305
1.164	304
2.252	305

Spec.

1.8	304
1.12.66	330
1.214	305
3.1–6	227
3.178	304
4.49	305

Plato
  Symposium
   189–190a   784

Pliny
  Natural History
   5, 70   13

Polyhistor
  frg. 1   218

Sextus Empiricus
  Adv. math.
   1.252   31
   1.278   30

Tacitus
  Histories
   5.5.2   320

Tertullian
  Ag. Marc.
   3:7   554

Theodoret
  Commentary on the Psalms
   135:13   39
  Interpret. in 1 Tim.
   1:3–4   21
  Qu. in Ex.
   26   39
  Qu. in Gen.
   45   39

Yannai
  Qedushtot
   1   485
   3   488
   7   489

Zenodotus
  Comp. Iliad I
   260   271

RABBINIC WORKS

Bavli
  Arak.
   26b   300
  A.Z.
   9a–10a   235
   16b–17a   918
   18b   995
   43a   14, 790
   53b   319
  B. Bat.
   4a   13
   12a   894, 897
   13a   300
   14b–15a   353–354
   15a   358
   16b   319
   75a   906
   115b–116a   299, 313
   116a   298
   123a   993
   123b   924
   124b   55
   134a   929
  B. Mes.
   39b   326
   57b   264
   59a–b   127, 891
   59b   403, 702
   70b   127
   86b   321
   87a   996

  B. Qam.
   38b   321
   54a   264
   54b   264
   60a   128
   60b   126
   62b   264
   63a   264
   63b–64a   518
   64a   264
   82a   310
   97b   4, 5
   107b   264
  Bek.
   6a   264
   37a   264
   44a   327
   51a   264
  Ber.
   5a   339
   5b   862
   6a   11, 482
   8a   476
   9a–b   329
   10a   995
   11b   464, 471
   11b–12a   473
   17a   468, 988
   18b   439
   19a   233
   20b   985

21b	275	60a	327
22a	259	62b	988–989
28b	474	62b–63a	988–989
29a	474	65a	983
31a	985	75a	987
31b	288, 296, 315, 985	Mak.	
32b	906	24a	330
47b	55	Meg.	
51b	996	1:8, 9a–b	789
57a	11	3a	148, 889, 891, 921–922
60b	862		
61a	338	4:10	917
64a	468	4a	985
Bes.		7b	259
16a	313	9a–b	779, 798, 800
Erub.		10a	14
13a	409	13b	332, 993
18a	338	14a	319–320
28a	264	14b	992
53a	319	15a	992
53b–54a	995	16b	11
86b	439	18a	801
100b	983–984	21b	894
Git.		25a	324, 464
40b–41b	300	25b	324
56a	924	28a	528
56b	924	28b	55, 468
57b	246, 270	29a	905
60a	404	31a	468, 475–476
60b	405	Men.	
90a	296	20a	264
90a–b	983	25b	264
Hag.		28b	14
2a	300	29b	24, 525
3b	482	32a–b	13
4a	297	35a–b	13
12a	259, 299	35b	11
13a	319, 917, 919	40a	312
13a–14a	917	43b	917
13b	410	55b	264
Hul.		65a	313
7b	941	65a–b	313
11a	471	65b	298
60b	354	78a	264
66a	55, 264	91a	264
66b	264	109a–110a	14
67a	264	Mes.	
88b	264, 294	1:13	12
89a	11, 319	M.Q.	
137b	400	28a	795, 941
Ker.		28b	922, 984
6b	264	Naz.	
21a	264	2b	12
Ket.		23b	321
8a	981	34b	264
25a	202	35a	264
27b	326	35b	264
30a	259	Ned.	
59b	987	3a	296, 315

32b	320	109a	320
37b	13	110a	331
50a	2	Shab.	
Nid.		15c	163
13b	906	17a	802
31b	979–980	22a	324
33a	264	25a	987
46b	235	25b	312
Pes.		28b	13
3b	147	30a	24
6b	264, 290	30b	168, 938
29a	259	31a	688, 889
43b	985	53b	941
50b	168	59a–b	2
59a	233	62a	13, 979
62b	995	62b	997
66a	270, 272, 274	63a	290, 919
66a–b	254, 294	79b	13
68a	891	85b	410
88a–b	300	86aff.	474
93a	498	103b	297
94b	319	104a	407
108a	985	108a	313
109a	985	115a	163, 801
119a	331	119b	477
Qid.		123b	125
21b	264	127a	467
24b	264	133b	12
31a	906	137a	439
33a	430	153a	938
38a	332	156a	795, 941
49b	55	Sheb.	
70a–b	996	4b	264
R.H.		20b	472
10b–11a	475	26a	259, 264
15a	800	37b	264
16b–17a	312	41b	55
17b	470	42b	264
24a–b	14	43a	264
27a	472	Sot.	
San.		2a	987
17a	268, 526	5a	320
21b–22a	801	12a	327
22a	987	12b	137, 327, 332
22b	986	15a	315
34a	125, 290, 406	16a	264, 294
38b	782	17b	11
45b–46a	279	21a	988
52a	331	36b	325
69b	319	36b–37a	329
86a	55, 439	37a	329
96b	270	46a	264
97a	469	46b	264
99b	354	49a	468
101a	314, 327	Suk.	
102a	168	51b	13
105b	476	Ta.	
106a	332	4.8	912
108b	30, 319	4a	38

8a	479	1:5	474
9a	330	2:2	474
25a	6	2:3	473
27b	467	9:1A–B	748
Tem.		9:2	275
14b	404	9:3	862
Yeb.		Bik.	
61b–62a	299	2:3	784
61b–64a	988	3:3	13
63a	987	3:8	13
82b	235	Ed.	
88a	326	1:13	300
113a	987	8:7	586
Yom.		Erub.	
24a	264	3:4	800
28b	319	Git.	
39b	924	4:2–5:9	300
69a	14	4:3	300
74a	55	4:5	300
75b	477	9:10	296
86a	896	Hag.	
86b	926	1.1	297
Zeb.		1:8	302, 525
4b	264	1:8A	176
5b	264	1:8B	176
41a–b	263	1:8D	176
41aff.	256	1:8D–E	176
50a–51a	271	1:9	176
50bff.	265	2:1	431, 917
102a	330	Hor.	
		1:5	178
Mishnah		2:1	178
Ab.		Kel.	
1:1A	586	1:17	797
2:7	992–993	11:8	2
3:14	409	28:4	12
3:16	941	Ket.	
3:17	619	5:6	988
4:20	620	Mak.	
5:1	697	1:6	313
6:7–8	168	3:16	468
A.Z.		Meg.	
3:2	6	1:1	929
B. Bat.		2:1	801
8:3	125	3:5	475
10:8	125	4:4	894
B. Qam.		4:8	12
8:7	177	4:10	324, 919
Bek.		Men.	
6:7	441	5:1	186
7:3C	441	5:5	810
7:6F–H	441	5:6/O	844
9:1	517	5:6K–L	843
9:5	517	5:6M	844
9:6	517	7:1	186
Ber.		13:10	14
1:3	474	Mid.	
1:4	473	1:4	14

2:3	14	Shab.		
2:6	14	2:6	984	
Ned.		23:5	750	
2:1	327	24:4	750	
Neg.		80b	917	
1:1–4	179	Sheb.		
1:5–6	179	1:6	588	
2:1–5	179	10:3	300, 948	
3:1–2	179	Sheq.		
3:3	180	1:4	302	
3:4	180	6:3	14	
3:5	180	Sot.		
3:6	180	1:3	837	
3:7	180	1:5	14, 839	
3:8	180	1:6	839	
4:1–3	180	1:6A–B	840	
4:1–8:10	180	1:6C–D	192, 848	
4:6	180	1:7	191, 848, 850	
6:8	180	1:7A	849, 853	
9:1–3	180	1:8	849	
10:1–9	180	1:9	849, 851	
10:10	180	1:9A	849, 853	
11:1–12	180	1:10	851	
12:1–7	180	2:1A	840	
13:1–12	180	2:2G	839	
13:7	182	2:4	843	
13:8	182	3:3B	843	
14:1–13	180	3:3C	843	
14:8	14	3:3D	843	
Nid.		3:5A	845	
2:5	615	3:8	983	
5:7	616	4:5B	846	
Oh.		4:5C	846	
1:8	477	5:1	853	
Pes.		5:1A	842	
1:1	467, 695	9:15	860	
2:5–6	586	Suk.		
2:6	949	2:9	615	
4:1E	443	3:1A–B	424	
4:1F–G	443	3:8	12	
4:2A	443	4:5	424, 588	
4:2B–C	443	4:9	588	
4:2D	443	Ta.		
5:1–9:11	186	2:1	476	
7:3–4	443	2:1–4	478	
7:7A–G	442	4:8	314	
7:7H–I	442	Tam.		
10:4	469	5:1	473	
R.H.		7:1	469	
1:1	502, 668	Yad.		
3:3–4	12	3:5	474, 888, 938	
4:4	475	4:3	586, 949	
4:5–6	478	4.6	300	
San.		4:6	303, 313	
10:1	468, 521	4.7	299	
10:3	320	4:7	313	
11:2	99	Yeb.		
74a–b	247	6.6	299	

6:6	988	Pes.	
7:5	435	3:8b	298
7:9	434	4:13	272
Yom.		Pis.	
3:6–7	196	4:13	254, 301
3:8	196	4:13f.	294
3:9	13, 196	Qid.	
3:9–10	13	5:17	319
3:10	13–14	R.H.	
4:1	196	2:4	12
4:2–3	196	2:10–14	478
5:1–2	196	San.	
5:3	196	4:7–8	801
5:4	196	7:11	252, 271–272, 301
5:5–6	196	12.10	314
6:2–6	196, 554	13:3	312
6:7–8	196	Shab.	
7:1	197	30b	938, 940
7:1–2	196	116a	927
7:3–4	196	Sheb.	
8:1–7	196	4:21	800
8:6–7	197	Sot.	
Zeb.		1:2	837
14:4	797	1:4	839
		1:6	839
Tosefta		1:8	840
Bek.		2:35	846
5:9A	442	3:2	192, 848
Ber.		3:3	192, 848
1:11	614, 618	3:4	192, 848
4:15	471	3:11	320
Bes.		3:12	320
2:12	471	3:18	852
Bik.		3:19	852
7:9	479	4:1	848, 853–854
Ed.		4:2	855
2:10	477	4:3	855
Er.		4:4	855
8:24	176	4:5	855
62a	929	4:6	855
Git.		4:16	853
90b	933	4:17	853
Hag.		4:18	854
1:9	176	4:19	854
2:1	431	6:2–3	82
3:35	313	40a	934
Kip.		48b	938
1:8	313	Suk.	
2:3–4	13	2:10	12
2:4	14	4:6	2, 8
Meg.		28a	929
2:3	528	Ta.	
3:5	475	1:10–12	478
3:6	475	Yad.	
3a	929	2:20	299
4:21	645	Yeb.	
8b	927	8.4	299
9a	927		

Yom.
  3:5–6   444
Zeb.
  8:29   445

Yerushalmi
  A.Z.
    3:1, 42b–c   5–6
    3:3, 42d   16
    40d   529
  B. Bat.
    8:1   299
  B. Qam.
    5b, 6:3   132
    61b   132
  Ber.
    1:4   934
    3:1   529
    4:1   529
    4:3, 8a   474
    7d   529
    9:1, 12d   783
  Erub.
    18b   264
    27b   264
  Git.
    4:5   300
    9:11   296
  Hag.
    1.1   297
    2, 77d   567, 569
    2.1   299
    2:1, 77b   125
    77d   891
  Hor.
    48c   529
  Ket.
    11:3, 34b   989
    32b   260
  Mak.
    1a   264
    2:5, 31d   5
  Meg.
    1.11   330
    1:11, 71c   801
    1:11, 71d   13, 779, 789
    2:5   985
    3:4   528
    3:7, 74b   475
    4:1   645
    4:1, 75c   13
    4:5   929
    11, 71c   801
    73b   528
  M.Q.
    3:1, 81d   471
  M.S.
    7a   264
    55d   528

Naz.
  7:2   529
  24b   262
  25a   264
  27b   264
Ned.
  5:6   929
  37d   472
Pe.
  1:1, 16a   788
  8:9,21b   2
  41b   528
Pes.
  4:1   986
  6.1   294
  6:1   254
  6:1, 33a   270, 272
  65a   264
Qid.
  11b   264
San.
  1, 52d   4
  1:1   529
  2:4, 20c   798, 800–801
  4:1, 22a   268
  4:2, 22a   471
  37b   264
Shab.
  1:4, 3c   802
  4c   528
  13c   528–529
  14d   528
  19:3, 17a   288
  44b   264
Sheb.
  15b   264
  32a   264
  35c   529
Sheq.
  2:7, 47a   1
  5:7, 49b   2
  6, 50a   6
Sot.
  1:4   529
  5:5   353
  15b   264
  31a   262
  42a   262, 264
  43a   264
Suk.
  50b   264
Ta.
  1:6   986
  2:2, 65c   474
  3b   528
  4:2, 68a   796
  64a   529
  64b   941
  67d   529

Ter.		5:5, 42c	445
55b	264	5:5, 42d	445
Yeb.		5:7, 43a	445
6.6	299	6:3, 43c–d	14
Yom.		8:1, 44d	445
3:6, 40d	445		

TARGUMIC TEXTS

Palestinian Targum
Genesis

9:4	934	27:46	934
15:4	934	37:13	338
43:16	934	37:32	934
48:20	934	38:25	934

Numbers

28:1ff.	932	42:5	326
29:1ff.	932	42:8	326
29:7	934	43:14	934
30:3	932	45:4	934
31	932	45:12	934

Deuteronomy

		45:27	934
		48:22	338
		49:21	934
8:10	934	Exodus	
12:27	934	1:15	327
15:2	932	16:2	329
17:8f.	932	18:6	640
27:8	929	18:27	640
		39:37	330

Numbers

Targum Neofiti
Genesis

		12:1	328
3:25	640	19:2	643
27:40	640	Deuteronomy	
29:22	640	6:8	933
31:22	640	11:18ff.	933

Numbers

		19:21	933
22:30	638	33:11	930
23:9a	639	Joshua	
23:21	637, 640	3:10	910
24:1	637, 640	6:19	910
24:6	639	Judges	
24:14	637	2:1	909
24:15	638	2:4	909

Deuteronomy

		2:13	910
2:6	640	4:5	909
32:10	640	5:3	909
32:14	640	5:7	909
33:29–30	640	5:9	909
		5:23	909
		11:29	909

Targum Pseudo-Jonathan
Genesis

		11:39	910
		13:18	909
2:7	934	13:25	909
2:20	338	1 Samuel	
3:23	934	2:1	910
10:9	934	2:5	912
10:11	934	2:5c	910
16:3	934	3:3	910
21:14	934	3:7	910
21:21	930	3:10	910

INDEX OF ANCIENT SOURCES

7:2–37:6	910	2:2	154
7:6	910	2:8–9	154
10:5	911	2:12	154
10:10	911	2:20	154
10:11–12	911	4:3	155–156
15:23	911	4:6	154
19:18	911	4:11	156
19:19	911	4:13	154
19:20	911	4:15	149
19:22	911	4:16	154
19:23	911	5:5	156
19:24	911	5:10	154
23:1	911	5:11	156
23:3	911	5:12	154
28	911	5:14	149, 151

2 Samuel
		5:16	154
7:19	911	6:1	156
22:1	911	6:2	156
22:28	911	6:3	154
22:32	911	6:4	154

1 Kings
		6:5	156
6:3	938	7:1	156
14:8	910	7:13	156
14:9	910	7:14	157

Tg 1 Chr.
		8:2	157
29:18	173	8:9	155
		8:14	156

Targums to Hagiographa

TgEsth I

Tg 1 Chr.
		1:7	155
2:6	171	3:1	155
2:55	172	3:7	156
14:15	172	7:7	155
17:2	170	8:16	156
17:8	170		

TgEsth II
23:16	172	1:1	151
25:2	171	4:16	156
28:2	171		

TgJob
32:23	171	1:1	165

Tg 2 Chr.
		1:1.5	165
6:37	171	1:6	165–166
6:38	171	1:7	165
12:14	172	1:8	165
15:4	172	1:9	165
18:27	172	1:15	166
20:3	172	1:16	165
20:4	172	1:21	166
20:20	172	2:1	166
24:16	172	2:3	165
32:1	171	2:7	165
32:21	172	2:9	165
33:13	172	2:11	165
35:23	172, 935	3:3	166

TgCant
		3:17	166
1:1	154	3:19	166
1:2	154	4:7	166
1:6.16	155	4:10	166, 932
1:10	156	4:11	166
1:14	156	5:4	166
1:15	154, 156	5:7	165–166

5:8	165–166	3:50	154
5:12	164	3:57	155
5:13	164	3:59	154
5:17	166	3:60	154
5:18	165	3:61	155
5:24	166	3:64	157
10:15	166	4:1	154
11:5	165	4:13	154
11:8	166	5:7	154
12:5	166	TgProv	
12:9	165	1:7	168
14:18	166	2:5	168
15:10	166	3:4	168
15:19	166	3:13	168
15:20	166	3:32	168
15:21	166	5:14	168
15:29	166	5:21	168
18:13	166	6:12	168
19–23	164	8:13	168
22:19	166	10:2	169
22:22	166	11:4	169
24:13	166	15:3	168
25:3	166	15:33	168
28:7	166	17:18	168
28:22	166	20:27	168
28:27	166	21:1	168
28:33	165	21:20	168
30:19	166	22:4	168
32:8	165	28:4	168
32–33	164	28:7	168
34:9	165	28:9	168
34:36	165	29:18	168
35:10	166	29:26	168
36:5	165	TgPs	
37:21	166	1:2	160
38:7	166	3:5	159
40:6	165	4:5	160–161
42:7	165	6:6	161
42:9	165	6:9	159
42:10	165	6:10	159
TgLam		7:12	158
1:1	154, 937	9:5	159
1:1–4	154	9:8	158–159
1:3	156	10:11	159
1:4	156	11:7	158
1:5	154	13:4	160
1:9	156, 937	14:2	160
1:16	155	17:2	159
1:17	154–155, 937	17:14	162
1:19	152, 935	18:9	158
1:20	154–156	18:10	159
1:22	156	18:11	159
2:1	154	18:16	159
2:9	154, 156, 935	18:28	161
2:17	156, 935, 937	18:29	161
2:19	154, 156, 937	18:31	160
3:4	154	19:14	159
3:28	154, 157, 937	21:2	162
3:40	156	21:10	162

22:17	158	72:1	162
22:25	159	76:9	158
25:18	159	77:3	160
25:19	159	78:13	161
27:7	159	78:59	159
27:13	162	79:1	160
28:2	159	79:7	160
29:11	160	80:11	160
30:6	162	81:1	159
33:13	159	81:9	159
34:5	160	82:1	159
34:11	160	84:7	162
34:18	159	84:10	159
37:13	158–159	87:2	161
37:20	161–162	88:7	161
37:31	160	89:49	160–161
41:13	162	89:53	162
43:3	160	90:1	161
44:4	159	90:4	161
45:1	161	91:5	160
45:10	161	91:6	160
45:80	161	94:10	161
48:12	161	97:8	161
49:10	162	101:8	162
49:15	162	103:1	160
49:16	160–161	103:4	162
50:3	161	106:48	162
50:5	159	107:32	161
50:21	162	116:10	161
51:13	159	118:29	161
51:14	160	119:153	159
51:17	160	119:159	159
53:3	160	120:4	162
53:7	161	126:4	161
54:4	159	137:8	160
57:6	160	140:11	161–162
60:9	160	140:12	160
62:12	161	143:1	159
63:4	162	TgQoh	
63:6	160	1:3	157, 939
64:2	159	1:4	156, 939
65:3	159	1:12	154–155, 939–942
68:7	162	1:15	157, 942
68:14	160–161	1:15.18	156
68:15	162	2:5	155
68:16	160	2:10	156, 940, 942
68:16.17	159	2:11	156
68:17	160	2:15	154, 938, 940–941
68:19	160	2:24	154, 940–941
68:33	160	3:11	156–157, 938, 942
69:1	161	4:4	154, 941
69:7	160	4:17	156, 939, 942
69:15	161	5:5	155, 941–942
69:16	162	5:6	156, 939, 942
69:28	161	5:10	157
69:32	159, 161	5:10.16	156
69:33	160	5:11	156, 939, 942
69:34	159	5:17	155, 942
70:5	160	5:18	155

6:2	155, 939	Tg I	
6:5	156	1:10	154
6:6	157, 939–940, 942	3:7	154
6:8	156, 939	4:12	155
6:9	156	4:13	155
6:10	157, 940–941	4:14	155
7:2	156, 939	7:8	155
7:3	154, 156, 939–940	Tg II	
7:7	154, 156, 942	1:1	154
7:9	154, 942	1:2	154, 157
7:13	154, 942	3:3	154–155
7:20	156, 940, 942	4:13	154
7:24	157, 939, 942	4:14	154
8:5	156, 942	4:16	154
8:12	154, 940	5:1	155
8:13	154–155	6:1	154, 157
8:24	154	TgAmos	
9:2	155, 941	1:1	924
9:7	157, 939	2:8	924
9:10	156, 939	3:8	924
9:11	155, 942	9:1	924
9:14	157, 940, 942	9:11	924
9:16	155–156, 939, 942	TgCant	
10:1	157, 939, 942	1:7	936
10:4	157, 942	8:8	936
10:6	155, 939–940	TgDeut	
10:8	154, 941	22:5	929
10:9	155, 938–941	TgExod	
10:11	157, 939, 942	30:35	929
10:20	155, 938–939, 941	TgEzek	
11:1	157, 939	1:1	920
11:4	155, 941–942	1:2	920
11:7	154, 939, 941	1:5	919
11:13	154	1:6	917
12:13	156, 941–942	1:8	917, 919–920
TgRuth		1:14	920
1:1	153, 156	1:25	920
1:5	155	1:26–27	919
1:6	155–156	1:26–28	917
1:13	153	1:27	917
1:16	156	2:2	924
1:17	153	2:10	920
1:22	153	3:1–6	920
2:4	153–154	3:14	920
2:7	153	3:16	920
2:12	155–157	3:22	920
2:13	155	7:6–7a	918
3:7	156	11:14	920
4:5	153	11:16	905, 920
4:6	153	13:8	921
4:7	153	13:14–16	921
4:21	156	14:9	921
Tg 2 Chr.		14:10	921
3:1	321	15:5	920
7:10	173	17:22–23	918
Tg *aher*		19:14	921
49:10	162	20:25	920
125:5	162	21:8	921

INDEX OF ANCIENT SOURCES

21:9	921	21:10	895
21:18	921	21:12	895
21:21–23	913	22:12	895
22:25	921	22:13	895
22:26	921	22:14	895, 923
23:2	923	24:16	891
24:17	921	24:23	891
29:21	921	26:10	921
39:15–16	920	26:21	905
39:29	920	28:5	902, 918
48:35	920	28:7	896
TgHab		28:10a	895
1:16	926	32:9	923
3:1	926	33:13	895
3:17	930	42:1	904
TgHos		42:7	905
1:1–3	923	43:10	904–905, 907
3:5	924	43:14	904
4:4	915, 924	50:2	921
4:9	924	52:13	903
4:12	923	52:13–53:12	903
6:2	924	53:5	891, 903
8:6	923	53:10	903
11:2	923	53:12	903, 910
12:1	924	54:1	910
13:15	924	57:19	895
TgIsa		65:6	923
1:15	905–906	65:15	923
4:2	922	66:4	921
4:2–3	899	TgJdgs	
4:5	905	5:24	929
5:5	894	TgJer	
5:6	894	2:1	913, 915
5:17b	891	2:2	915
5:21	914	2:12	915
5:25	921	2:21	914
6	919	4:9	915
6:1–6	906	4:10	915
6:3	919	4:13	915
6:5	907	5:13	915
6:6	907	5:31	915
8:2	897	6:13	896, 915
8:16	894	6:19	933
8:17	894	6:29	915
8:18	905	7:8	915
9:12	921	7:18	915
9:14	896	8:10	896, 915
9:17	921	8:16	914
9:21	921	13:27	915
10:4	921	14:18	896, 915
11:1	902	15:18	937
14:29	902	16:14	915
16	918	16:15	915
16:1	902	18:1	914
16:5	902	18:18	896, 915
17:11	905	23:5	914
19:10	929	23:5–6	914
21:8	895	23:11	896, 915
21:9	894–895	23:13–22	915

23:31–33	915	3:12	921
23:33	896, 915	3:23–24	921
23:34	896, 915	TgMic	
26:7	896, 915	2:11	925
26:8	896, 915	2:13	925
26:11	896, 915	4:7–8	925
26:16	896, 915	5:1	923
28:1	915	7:20	925
28:12	915	TgNah	
28:15	915	1:1	924
29:1	915	1:7	925
29:11	896	1:8	925
29:15	915	1:18	924
30:9	914	TgObad	
30:21	914	1:18	924
31:12	914	TgPs	
33:13	914	72:17	923
33:15–17	914	108:10	932
33:20–22	914	120:5	936
33:26	914	TgQoh	
35:4	897, 915	1:1	938, 940
TgJoel		1:1 et seq.	938
2:14	926	1:1f.	938
2:23	937	1:2	938–939, 941
TgJon		1:5	939
1:1	926	1:8	939, 942
2:10	926	1:12 et seq.	938
3:9	926	1:13	942
TgLam		1:16	939
1:1–8 et seq.	935	1:18	939
1:1f.	935	2:2	942
1:2	937	2:4	938–939, 942
1:2 et seq.	936	2:4f.	939
1:18	935	2:7	933
2:4f.	937	2:8	939
2:6	937	2:12	939
2:14	937	2:14	939, 942
3:13	937	2:16f.	940
3:24ff.	937	2:18	938–939
3:26ff.	941	2:25	942
3:27	936	2:26	939, 942
3:31	937	3:2	933
3:39	936	3:5	933
3:39ff.	937	3:7	933
3:41	936	3:9	940
4:20	936	3:12	942
4:21	936	3:13	940
4:22f.	937	3:14	941
5:5	936	3:15f.	942
5:5.	937	3:16	939
21f.	937	3:18	940
TgMal		3:18f.	942
1:10	921	3:19f.	939
1:11b	922	4:2	939
2:12	921	4:7	941
3:6	922	4:9f.	939
3:7	921	4:10	942
3:10	921	4:12	939

4:13	942	9:5	939, 942
4:13f.	938, 940	9:7ff.	938
4:15	939	9:9	940–941
5:7	940	9:9ff.	942
5:8	939	9:11f.	941
5:9	941	9:16f.	942
5:10f.	939	9:19	939
5:10ff.	939	10:9f.	942
5:14	938	10:10	942
5:14f.	939	10:12	942
5:16	939, 942	10:16	938
5:19	939, 941–942	10:16f.	939
5:20	941	10:17	938
5:28	939	10:19	939
6:4	939	11:3	939–941
6:5f.	942	11:7f.	942
6:6f.	941	11:9	942
6:12	942	12:5	941
7:1	939	12:10	942
7:2f.	941	12:11	938–939
7:3f.	942	12:12	942
7:4	939	12:12ff.	942
7:4f.	942	TgZech	
7:5	942	1:1	921
7:11	942	1:3	921
7:12	941	2:1	921
7:14f.	941	2:10	921
7:15	939, 942	2:14	921
7:15f.	940	3:7	923
7:16	939	3:8	922
7:17	939	4:7–9	922
7:17f.	942	5:5–11	923
7:19	938	5:9	923
7:23	942	6:12–13	922
7:25	940	10:2	923
7:26	933, 942	10:4	923
7:29	938, 942	10:11	923
8:1	939–940, 942	13:4	923
8:2	940	13:13	933
8:3	942	14:9	922
8:4	939	TgZeph	
8:6	940–941	1:4	925
8:7	940	1:5	925
8:9	942	1:8–9	925
8:13f.	940	3:2	925
8:14	939	3:4	925
8:15	938, 940, 942	3:9	925
8:15f.	939	3:10	925
9:1	939, 942	3:11	925
9:1f.	941	3:12	925
9:4	942	3:15	925
9:4f.	939	3:19	925

MIDRASH AND OTHER RABBINIC WORKS

Avot DeRabbi Natan A		37:7	252
9	984	37:55	271
31	410	46	796
37	793		

Avot DeRabbi Natan B

9	983
37	780, 800

Damascus Document

4:12–19	597

De Dea Syria

34	794

De Iona

5	244
8	244
13	244
29–32	244
32f.	241
69–98	243
92	243
101	243
103–107	243
111–140	243
115	242
153–156	243
183–219	243
192–194	243
203	241

De Sampsone

7	243
11	243
14	243
15–16	244
16	244
18	242
19	243
21f.	242
23f.	243
24	242–243
24f.	243
26	242
38f.	243
41	242–243

Deuteronomy Rabbah

3.8	329
4.5	321
5.10	318
8.1	318
11.10	328

Dibrei Hayamim shel Moshe Rabbenu

2.6–7	328

Divre Malkhe Isra'el

50b	791, 794

Eccl. Rabbah

3.14	321
3.15	319
5.12	331
9.9	270
9.14	270
9.15	319
11.3	894

Eikhah Rabbah

1.16	246
5	354

Esther Rabbah I

1.1	65
1.1.4–11	63
2.1.1	63
2.1.4–11	63
3.1.1–5	63
4.1	63
6.1	63
7.1	62–63
7.4	331
7.11	332
8.1	63
9.1	63
10.1	69
10.1.15	63
11.1	63
12.10	4
17.1	63
18.1	63–64
18.2	64
18.3	63
18.4	64
23.1	64
23.2	64
28.1	64
34.1	64
38.1.9	65
51.1	65
54.1	65

Exodus Rabbah

1.18	327
1.20	327
1.25	327
1.26	328
1.27	327
1.28–29	772
1.29	28
1.30	28, 327
2.5	329
2.14	329
5.5	779
6	354
9.13	488
11.1	868
11.4	516
12.3	329
17.5	487
18.2	486, 489

18.4	486	12.15	114
18.5	24, 489	14.1	114
20.11	329	14.6	116
30.24	919	15.3	115
31.3	331	15.4	116
31.17	318	16.4	116, 319
35.3	19	16.6	111
41.5	405	17.2	986
51.8	329	17.3	989
		17.4	318, 338
Genesis Rabbah		17.8	982–984
1	941	18.1	264, 982
1.1	299, 409, 951	18.2	981, 992
1.1.2	115	18.3	982
1.2	112	18.4	338
1.4	473	18.5	990
1.6	114	18.6	111
1.7	115	19.4	111
1.11	407	19.6	111
1.12	781	19.7	112, 327
1.14	259, 288, 408, 780	19.9	112
2.1	114	19.9.2	174
2.2	113	20.1	112
2.3	116	20.5	114
2.4	116	20.7	113
2.5	116	20.12	315
3	477	21.2	112
3.2	115	21.7	111
3.6	470	22.2	259, 408, 986
3.9	111, 317	22.6	118
4.1	115	22.7	318
4.2	145	22.8	319
4.6	116	22.12	318
4.7	318	23.3	319
5.1	113	23.7	319
5.4–5	116	24.1	111
6.1–2	116	24.2	114
6.5	113	24.5	111
7	115	24.7	111
7–11	114	24.9	111
8.1	784	25.3	142
8.2	113	26.2	111
8.3	115	27.1	111
8.6	111	27.2	111
8.9	782, 986	27.6	111
8.11	779, 783	28.3	529
9.2	115	28.4	410
9.3	115	28.5	119
9.4	114	28.8	119
9.12	111	29.3	119
10.9	115, 472, 779	30.7	319
10.10–11	786	30.10	118
11.2	470	31.1ff.	119
11.10	114	31.8	409
12.1	115, 869	31.10–11	30
12.2	116	32.3	114
12.6	111, 470	32.7	114
12.9	111	32.8	319
12.14	299	33.1	114

33.3	114	51.8	321
34.2	111	51.8–10	321
34.3	111	51.9	321
34.4	111	51.11	113
34.10	111	52.11	112
34.13	112	53.9	112
36.1	111	53.10	717
36.6	119	53.14	113, 338
38.3	114	53.15	259, 408
38.6	114	54.4	119
38.7	779, 787	54.5	119
38.9	114	54.20	117
38.13	319	55	765
39.1	113	55.1	113–114
39.2	865	55.9	321
39.3	113	56	322
39.5	113	56.1	120
39.9	113	56.2	120, 718
39.11	4	56.7	120
39.14	319	56.9	117, 718
40.1	112	56.10	117
40.6	119	58.8	955
40.8	119	59.11	322
41.9	113	61.7	488
42.2	107, 119	62.2	866
42.3	470, 486	63.3	779, 793
42.3.1–6	756	63.6	734
42.4	319	63.7	37, 107, 734
42.4.1	93, 109	63.8	38
42.13	489	64.4	118
43	320	65.1	731, 735
43.2	120	65.9	114
43.3	119	65.13	117
43.3.2	894	65.16	322
43.6	113	65.23	117
43.8	713	66.3	117
44.1	113	67.4	720
44.5	118	68.9	119
44.15	116	68.12	720
44.17	116, 714	68.12–13	117
44.18	116, 714	69.4	119
44.19	116	70.1	94
44.21	117	70.2	95
45.2	320	70.3	95
46.9	119	70.4	96
48.6	114	70.5	97
48.10	119, 715	70.6	97, 117
48.12	119	70.8	98, 106
48.14	321	70.8–9	117
48.17	779, 787	70.9	101
49.5	113	70.10	101
49.7	113, 271	70.11	102
49.9	111, 114	70.12	102
49.11	119	70.13	323
50.2	321	70.16	489
50.4	321	70..16	323
50.11	331	70.19	104, 994
51.5	113	71	993

71.6	994	2:6	488
72.3	994	3:1	374
73.4	994	3:1.1	391
73.30	475	4:1	375
74.5	323	4:1.1	395
75.4	113	5:1.10–12	395
75.9	113	6:1	375
76.5	120	6:1.1–2	393
76.7	24	7:1	375, 399
77.1	117	8:1	375
77.1.1	968	8:1.1–9	393
78.9	290	9:1	377
78.12	114	9:1.1–4	393
78.13	117	10:1	375
78.14	117	10:1.1	391
79.6	118	10:1.4–5	391
80.1	994	11:1	375
82.14	291	11:1.1	394
83.1	736	12:1.1–3	394
84.5	120	12:9:1.1–2	398
84.6	120	13:1	375
84.8	324	13:1.1–3	394
84.12	324	14:1.3–5	394
84.19	119	15:1	375
84.20	722	16:1	375
85.2	325	16:1.1	394
87.6	721	17:1	377
87.7	325	17:1.1	391
88.5	115	18:1	378
90.3	30	19:1	375
90.6	325	19:1.1	394
91.2	792	20:1	375, 378
91.5	325–326	20:1.1–2	392
91.6	326	21:1.2–3	395
91.7	326	22:1	375
92.7	273, 303	22:1.2–3	394
95.1	115	22:1.5	394
96.6	779	22:1.8–9	394
97.8	17	24:1	388
98.2	117, 722	24:1.1	378, 388
98.2.7	974	24:1.1–21	388
98.3	117	24:2	375, 381, 388
98.6	789	24:2.1	388, 392
98.8	118	24:2.2	392
99.2	106, 118, 723	24:2.3	388, 392
100.11	326	25:1	375
475.4	735	27:1	375
		29:1.1	392
Jerahmeel		30:1	375
45	328	31:1	375
		31:2.1	391
Lamentations Rabbati		31:2.5	392
1:1.1–7	374, 391	35:2	375
1:2	489	35:3	375
2:1	374	35:3.1–2	394
2:1.1–12	393	35:4	375
2:2	374	35:4.1	391
2:2.1–4	391	35:6	375

35:7	375	66:1.2	398
35:8.1–2	394	69:1	376
36:2	375	69:1.4	391
36:2.1	395	69:1.7	390
36:3.2	395	73:1	376
36:3.6	395	73:1.1–2	390
36:4	375	75:1	376
36:5	375	75:1.2	394
36:5.1–4	394	79:2	376
36:8.1	397	79:2.1	391
37:1	377	83:1	377
37:1.3–8	394	83:1.2	391
37:2	378	85:1.1	394
39:3	375	85:1.3	392
40:1	377–378	85:1.4	393
40:1.2–4	391	86:1	376
40:2	375	86:1.1	395
40:2.3	392	86:1.5	395
40:2.4	392	87:1	376
41:1	376	87:1.1–6	390
41:1.1	393	88:1	376
41:1.4	393	88:1.1	391
41:1.6–7	394	89:1	376
42:1	376	89:1.1–2	395
42:1.1–3	390	89:1.3	392
43:3.1	395	89:3.2	395
43:3.4	395	91:1.1–5	393
44:1	377	92:1.3–4	393
46:1.1	391	93:1.1	395
48:1	376	95:1	376
48:1.2–4	394	100:1.1–2	392
48:1.6	394	100:1.9	392
48:1.7	395	100:1.15	392
49:1	377	100:1.15–16	392
49:1.1	392	101:1.3	393
49:1.2	392	111:1.1	395
50:1	376	115:1.3	393
50:1.12	395	122:1	376
50:2.1	395	122:1.1	396, 971
51:1.2	397	123:1	376
53:1	376	123:1.2	392
53:1.4–5	394	123:1.4	392
54:1.2–3	395	125:1.1	396
55:1.1–2	392	127:1.3	393
55:1.2–14	395	129:1	376
56:1	376	130:1	376
56:1.14	389	130:1.3	391
57:1.1–3	395	131:1	377
57:2	376	137:1	378
59:1.1	397	140:1	377
59:2	376	140:1.1	396
59:2.1	397	141:1	377
59:3	378	141:1.1	396
59:3.1	397	142:1	377
60:1	376	143:1	377
61:1	376	143:1.1–4	396
62:1.1–2	395	143:1.1ff.	969
64:1	376	144:1	377
65:1.2	391	Proem 24	994

Leqah Tov
Exod. 4:20, 12b	779
Gen. 1:1	802
Gen. 1:1, 1b	779

Leviticus Rabbah
2:1–3	448
2:3.2.B	727
2:3.5	448
2:4	727
2:4.1–2	448
3:1.1–4	456
3:1.6	456
3:3.3	456
4:1.1–5	456
5:1.1	450
5:1.6	450
5:2	450
5.3	331
5:3	450
5:7.1	449
5:8	728
7:1.1	449
7:1.2	449
7:3	429
7:6.1	449
8:1	987
9:1.3	453
9:3.3	448
9:7.1	974
9:8.1	448
9:8.2	448
9:9	788
10.5	318
10:6.1	456
11:1.1	454
11:5.1	452
11.6	330
11:7	756
12:3.1	455
12:6.1–3	448
13:1.1	449
13:1.3	449
13:2.1	449
13:2.4	449
13:5	730
13:5.1ff.	450
14:1	784
14:1.1	454
14:7.1	455
15:4.1	452
15:9.1	450
15:9.2	453
16:1.1–13	452
16:2.1–3	452
16:6.1–2	452
16:7.1	452
16:8.1–2	452
17:1.1	452
17:2.1–2	452
17:3.1ff.	452
17:4.1–4	745
17:4.3	746
17:7.1	453
18:1.1	455
18:1.11	455
18:1.14	455
18:2.1–6	452
18:4.1–2	448
19:4.1–4	453
19:6	6
20:2.1	455
20:2.3–6	455
20:13.1	453
20:13.2	453
21:1–21:4.1	450
21:6.1	451
21:11.1	451
21:11.3	451
22:1–3	453
22:10.1–3	451
23:1	866
23:1–6	449
23:7.1	455
23:9.1–5	454
24:2.6	452
24:4.1	456
24:5	448
24:6	448
25:3.1	454
25:4.1	454
25:5.1	454
26:8.5	453
27:1.1	455
27:2.2	455
27:3.1–2	454
27:4.1	453–454
27:4.2	454
27.5	319
27:5.1	448
27:6.2	448
27:8.1	448
27:9.1	454
27:12.1	453
28:3.1–2	456
28:4.1–6	450
28:6.1–4	451
29:2.1–2	450
29:3.1	452
29:5.2	450
29:7.4–5	454
29:11.1–2	454
29:13.3	448
30:1	417
30:2.8	448
30:4	423
30:5	424
30:6	424

30:7	425	Ki Tissa 1	469
30:8	426	Mishpatim 13	479
30:9	427	Msekhta *dePaskha* 11	137
30:9.1	453	*Nezikin* 9	277
30:10	427	*Nezikin* 14	129, 131
30:10–12.1	453	Pisha 1	283
30:11	428	Pisha 1.42–44	897
30:12	428	Pisha 4	285
30:13.1	453	Pisha 13	486
30:16.1	451	Pisha 14	488, 779, 792
31:1.1	455	Pisha 16	529
31:1.6	455	Pisha 17	487
31:11.1	451	Shirata 3	482, 948
32:1.1	455	Sim. 149.15–21	312
34	354	Sim. 218.28–29	297
34:1.3	455		
34:6.1	453	Mekhilta deRabbi Shimon bar Yohai	
34:14	989	14	326
35:1.1–4	451	14:13	142
35:2.2	451	15:11	15
35:3.1	452	19:16	474
35:4.1	451	81	330
35:5.1	451	Bo 12	488, 491
35:6.1	451	Bo 12:40	792
35:6.1f.	969	Mishpatim 22:5	132
35:7.1	451		
36.1	299	*Memar Marqa*	
36:2.1	453	2:11	792
36:3.1	455		
36:4	772	Midr. Tann.	
36:4.1	454	138f.	312
36:5.1	454		
36:5.4	454	Midrash Exodus	
36:6.1	454	14:9	793
37:4	38		
39:4.1–2	452	Midrash HaGadol Deuteronomy	
		4:19	779
Meg. Taan.		17:3	779
331	313	733	512
334	299		
338	298, 313	Midrash HaGadol Exodus	
		4:20	779
Mekhilta attributed to R. Ishmael			
1	314	Midrash HaGadol Genesis	
5	329	49:16	789
22.20	225		
26:1.1	78	Midrash Psalms	
27:1.1	84	8.2	321
33:1.1	976	9.7	37
67:1.31	975		
Amalek 2.155–159	918	Midrash Teh.	
Amelek 1	330	1.2	29
Bahodesh 1	479	19	482
Bahodesh 4	330	27:1	477
Bahodesh 7	472	75	488
Bahodesh 7:24–25	896	78:5	479
Bo 15	263	104:4	477
Intro on Exod. 13:17	329	136:6	486, 491

Midrash Tehillim
　92:5　　　　　　　470

Numbers Rabbah
　1.8　　　　　　　329
　3　　　　　　　　354
　4.20　　　　　　332
　8.9　　　　　　　489
　10.1　　　　　　320
　10.3　　　　　　331
　12.13　　　　　　330
　13.6　　　　　　317
　14　　　　　　　482
　15.7　　　　　　330
　15.10　　　　　18
　15.20　　　　　326
　16.8　　　　　　331
　16.23　　　　　895
　18.1　　　　　　331
　18.4　　　　　　331
　18.10　　　　　793
　18.13　　　　　331
　18.21　　　　　430
　20.9　　　　　　332
　20.11　　　　　332
　20.23　　　　　321
　22.7　　　　　　331

Pesiqta deRab Kahana
　1:1　　　　　　　651
　1:1.4　　　　　　670
　1:2　　　　　　　652
　1:3　　　　　　　654
　1:4　　　　　　　657
　1:5　　　　　　　658
　1:6　　　　　　　660
　1:7　　　　　　　660
　1:8　　　　　　　661
　2:1.1　　　　　　670
　2:1.1ff.　　　　670
　2:3　　　　　　　670
　2–12　　　　　　646
　4:1　　　　　　　676
　4:1ff.　　　　　676
　4:9–10　　　　　673
　5:12　　　　　　676
　5:14　　　　　　673
　5:18　　　　　　673
　6　　　　　　　　646
　6:1ff.　　　　　672
　6:3　　　　　　　672
　6:4　　　　　　　672
　6.61b　　　　　　298
　7:1　　　　　　　486, 673
　7:2　　　　　　　673
　7:4　　　　　　　676
　7:5　　　　　　　486, 489
　7:6　　　　　　　486
　7:7　　　　　　　486

　7:11　　　　　　488, 676
　7:11.3　　　　　972
　7:12　　　　　　676
　8　　　　　　　　287
　8:1　　　　　　　671
　8:1.9　　　　　　671
　8:2　　　　　　　672
　8:4.1　　　　　　671
　9:1　　　　　　　673
　9:1ff.　　　　　673
　9:2　　　　　　　673
　9:4.2　　　　　　676
　9:4.3　　　　　　676
　9:9.1　　　　　　673
　11:1　　　　　　674
　11:1ff.　　　　　674
　11:21　　　　　　25
　12:1　　　　　　671
　12:2　　　　　　671
　12:10　　　　　671
　12:12　　　　　674
　12:19　　　　　674
　12:20　　　　　672
　12:21　　　　　674
　12:24　　　　　673
　13:3　　　　　　671
　13:9　　　　　　671
　13–22　　　　　647
　14:4　　　　　　671
　14:5　　　　　　671
　15:1　　　　　　671
　15:3　　　　　　674
　15:5　　　　　　671
　16:1　　　　　　674–675
　16:3　　　　　　671
　16:5　　　　　　674
　16:6　　　　　　674
　16:7　　　　　　674
　16:8　　　　　　675
　16:9　　　　　　675
　16:10　　　　　675
　16:11　　　　　674
　17:1　　　　　　489–490, 675
　17:2　　　　　　675
　17:3　　　　　　675
　17:4　　　　　　675
　17:7　　　　　　675
　18:1　　　　　　675
　18:3　　　　　　675
　19:1　　　　　　675
　19:2　　　　　　675
　19:3　　　　　　675
　19:4　　　　　　675
　19:6　　　　　　670, 675
　20:1　　　　　　675
　20:2　　　　　　675
　20:5　　　　　　676
　20:6　　　　　　676
　21:1　　　　　　676

21:3	676	48	792
21:5	676	48.21	328
21:6	676		

Prologus in Pentateuchum, Patrologia Latina

22:1	676	28:112	781
22:3	676		
23:1	670, 676		
23:2	676	Qohelet Rabbah	
23:4	670	1	938
23:6	670	1:1	868
23:7	676	8:15	940
23:8	676		
23:9	676	Ruth Rabbah	
23:10	327	1:1	738–739
23:11	676	1:1.1	742
23–28	647	1:1.2–3	756
24:1	674	1:1.5	756
24:2	674	1:1.8	755
24:5	674	1:2.6	757
24:6	674	1:4	137
24:7	674	1:6	139
24:8	674	2:1	739
24:10	674	2:1.2	757
24:11	674	2:1.3	757
25:1	674	2:1.7	757
25:4	674	3:1	738
26:12	674	3:1.2–3	755
27:1	672	3:1.4	755
27:2	675	3:2	738
27:7	675	3:2.1	755
27:9	675	3:3	739
28	287	4:1	739
28:1	672	4:2	740
28:5	672	4:2.2	756
28:7	672	5:1	739
28:8	672	5:3	739
38:1	672	5:12	529
208:9	672	5.14	321
		8:1.3	740
Pesiqta Rabbati		9:1.1	745
5	330, 802	9:1.1–2	756
6	330	10:1	738
6.2	325	11:1.1C	739
7.4	317	16:1.2B	740
16, 84a	298	18:1.1–3	740
17.4	486	19:1	740
17.5	486	20:1	740
43	246	20:1.3–4	756–757
46	470	21:1.1	747
48	298	21:1.1–3	740, 756
Add. 2:4	486	21:1.4	756
		22:1	740
Pirqe de-Rabbi Eliezer		22:1.1	760
29	147	25:1	740
30	321	25:1.5	759
34	895	26:4	740
38	324	27:1.2–4	758
40	329	31:1.2–3	758
44	479	34:1	740
45	986	34:1.1	756

35:1.1–5	741	1:7	272, 285, 959
35:2	741	1a–b	271
38:1.1	741	3:6.2	621
38:1.2	760	3a	252
40:1.1–5	758	7:5.1	808
40:1.1ff.	741	12:12	517
41:1.4	758	22:1.1	810
46:1.1	758	98:6.1	621
48:1.1	758	240:1	813
52:1.1	760	263:1	815
53:1	741	269:1	817
55:1.1B	741	269:2	817
56:1	741	Aharé Parasha	
57:1	741	4:2–3	444
59:1.5	741	Aharé Pereq	
68:1	741, 754	6:3.6	445
74:1	738	7:1–4	445
79:1	742	Emor Parashah	
80:1	742	1:1–4	432
81:1	742	1:4–7	433
85:1	742	3:7–10	441
89:1	742	Emor Pereq	
		5:3–5	435
Samaritan Book of Asatir		Hobah Pereq	
9.13	327	10:4–6	444
		intro.	279
Seder Eliahu Rabbah		intro. 3	274
13	321	intro. 5	276
29	489	intro. 7	278
		intro. 9	280
Seder Eliahu Zutta		Qedoshim Pereq	
23	482	3:1–5	442
		Tsaw Parashah	
Seder Olam Rabbah		4:4	445
3	792	Tzav 11	288
5	338		
9	332	Sifra Em. Per.	
14	17	15:5	296
26	235		
		Sifre	
Sefer Hayashar		65	323
13	323	131	910
14	324, 326		
251ff.	328	Sifre to Deuteronomy	
		1:1	820, 826
Sefer Torah		1:2	828
1:6	780	1:3	829
1–6	799	1:4	829
		1:5	829
Sekhel Tov		1:6	830
Exod. 4:20	791	1:7	830
		1:8	831
Sifra		1:9	831
1:1	281	1:10	831
1:2	281	1:11	832
1:3	282	1–30	56
1:4	282	11:22	934
1:5	283	26	56
1:6	284	27	228

31	473	15:2.1	842
31–54	56	16:1.1	842
33, piska 343	515	16:2.1	842
43	88	16:3.1	843
55–103	56	17:1.1	843
77	279	17:2.1	843
143	297	17:3.1	844
148	277, 795	17:4.1	844
160	797	17:5.1	844
161	406	17:6.1	844
211	286	18:1	851
269	296	18:1.1	835, 844
301	469	18:2.1	845
304–357	56	19:1.1	845
306:28.3	968	19:2.1	845
321:5	142	19:3.1–3	845
343	474	20:1.1	846
343:4.1ff.	977	20:2.1	846
356	796–797	20:3.1	846
Ekev 37	959	21:1.1	846
Re'eh 77	956	21:2.1	847
Re'eh 99	955	21:3.1	847
Re'eh 100	955	40	481
		40:2.4	835
Sifre to Numbers		41:2.2	834
1	262	41:2.4	835
1:10.1	834	42	788
1:10.2–3	834	42:2	834
1:11.1	834	44:1.1	578
2	288–289	44:2.1	580
8:1.1	837	44:2.2	580
8:2.1	837	44:2.3	580
8:3.1	838	45:1.1	581
8:4.1	838	45:1.2	579, 581
8:5.1	838	45:2.1	581
8:6.1	838	45:2.2	581
8:7.1	838	45:2.3	581
8:8.1	838	45:2.4	582
8:8.1–2	835	46:1.1	582
9:1.1	839	46:1.2	582
9:2.1	839	46:2.1	582
9:3.1	839	46:2.2	583
10:1.1	839	47:1.1	583
10:2.1–2	839	47:1.2	584
10:3.1	839	64	287
10:4.1	839	68	271
10:5.1	839	76:2.1–4	836
11:1.1	840	78	993
11:1.1–10	834	78:1.1	835
11:2.1	840	84	270
11:3.1	840	84:4.1	835
11:4.1	840	112	288
12:1.1	840	112:4.2	835
12:2.1	840	112:4.3	835
12:3.1	841	112:4.5	836
13:1.1–3	841	119:3.3	836
14:1.1	841	133	995
14:2.1–2	841	161:3.2	834
15:1.1	842		

Soferim	
1	927
1:7	24, 779, 793, 798
1:8	12
4:4	312
6:4	796
8:6	148, 150
12:6	932
14:18	476
15	929
18:2	469
Soferim (B)	
1:8	780
Song of Songs Rabbah	
1.1.1	325
1.2	330
1:2.1	476
1:4.3B–D	869
1:4.8	876
1:4.20A–B	864
1:5	865
1:5.1	876
1:5.9	876
1:7.5B–D	857
1:9.4–6	476
1:11.1	476
1:12.3	476
2:1 1–6	858
2:1.1	476
2:1.1–7	872
2:1.16	482
2:2.1	877
2:2.2	476
2:2.13	877
2:3–5	872
2:7–8	881
2:9	881
2:9.5	487
2:11.1	487
2:12.1	487
3:1	881
3:2–3	881
3:3	881
3:4	881
3:5.1–12	873
4:2.1	878
4:2.2	878
4:2.5	878
4:3	469
4:6	865
5.1	327
5:1.3–12	873
5:2.5	880
5:2.5A–I	862
5:3.1A–B	867
5:3.2A–B	859
5:3.4A.B.D.	860
5:3.5B–E	860
5:4.1	879
6:1	865
6:1.9A	870
6:2.5I	870
7.11.1	991
9:1.10	877
10:1.1–2	876
10:2.1–4	876
10:3.1–2	876
11:1.1–8	858, 876
12:1.1	876
12:1.1A–E	864
12:1.2	876
13:1	881
14:1	881
14:3	881
15:1.1	882
15:1.1A–X	862
15:1.5–6	882
16:1.4–8	872
18:1.1–3	873
18:1.4–7	858, 873
18:3.1–3	879
19:1	866
19:1.2.5.8.9	858
19:1.5	873
19:1.8	875
19:1.9	875
19:1.11	874
20:1.1	875
20:1.6	882
20:2.1	875
21:1.1	875
21:1.1A–F	865
22:1.1–8	878
22:2.1A–E	867
23:1.1–5	882
24:1.1–4	873
24:2.1	883
24:2.4	883
24:3.2	883
25:1.1–4	883
25:1.1A–4G	861
26:1	880
26:1.2A–C	858
26:2	876
26:3	880
29:1.1–2	874
30:1.1	878
30:2.1–8	880
30:3.1–8	880
30:4.1–6	880
30:4.1A–4B	860
30:4.2A–B	860
30:4.4E–6B	860
31:1	875
31:1.6A–E	859
31:1.9E–F	859

31:2	874	68:1.1	879
31:2.1B	859	69:1.1	875
31:2.2A	859	70:1.1–2	876
31:2.5A	859	71:1.1–8	877
31:2.8A	859	71:1.21–22	877
31:2.9A	859	72:1.1	877
31:2.13A	859	72:1.3	877
32:2.1	875	74:1.1–9	877
32:2.4–6	875	75:1.1	877
33:1.1–8	872	76:1.1	879
33:2.1B–F	863	76:1.8	879
34:1.1–7	877	77:1.1	875, 877
35:1.2A–B	859	77:1.4	877
35:1.3–4	878	78:1.1	872
36:1	878	80:1.1–2	872
37:1	878	84:1.1	875
38:2.1	878	85:1.1–3	873
38:2.1B–O	859	85:1.6–7	873
38:2.31A–33A	859	85:1.11	873
38:2.43B–C	859	86:1.2	876
40:1.1–2	877	87:1.4	878
40:1.4–5	881	87:1.7	878
42:1.1–2+3	876	87:1.9	878
43:1–5	876	88:1.1–5	879
44:1.1–4	882	89:1.1–11	876
44:2.1	872	90:2.1	877
44:2.8A–9C	859	90:2.2A	870
45:1	882	90:3.2	877
47:1.1–3	882	90:3.3	877
48:1.8	878	90:3.4	877
48:2.5	875	90:3.6–7	877
48:6	875	93:1.1	878
48:7	875	94:1.4–7	873
48:8	875	95:1.1	882
48:9	875	95:1.1–5	879
48:9.6–10	879	95:1.2–5	881
50:1.5.	881	95:2.1–3	879
51:1.2	878	97:1.1	872
51:1.10A–I	859	97:1.4	872
52:1.1	880	98:1.1	872
52:1.7–10	880	98:1.2	872
52:1.7A–B	859	99:1.1	874
52:2.1	883	99:1.2	874
52:2.1A–C	860	101:1.1	872
52:2.5	883	102.1.1–2	872
52:2.7	883	102.1.6–7	872
53:1.1–5	882	104:1.1–4	877
54:1.1	874	107:1.3–9	877
61:1.1	872	108:1.3	882
61:1.4	872	108:2.1–6	874
61:1.6–8	872	108:2.1A–D	863
62:1.1	878	108:2.6A–D	863
62:1.3–14	874	109:1.1–3	875
63:1.1–2	875	110:1	866
64:1.3–4	874	111:1.1	880
65:1.1	875	111:2.1	880
65:1.3	875	111:3.1f.	881
65:1.4	875	114:1.1–2	883
65:1.10	875	115:2.6A–7D	862

Tadshe
2	330

Tanhuma
5	324
6	331
13	330
17	475
25	470
Balak 8	489
Bo 17	486
Bo 18	486, 491
Lekh Lekha 9	486
Va'era 13	488
Va'yeshev 7	958

Tanhuma Exod.
19	779
22	779

Tanhuma Genesis
4	781

Tanhuma Korah
2	331

Tanhuma Noah
1	984

Tanhuma Num
8	328
8.9	328
14–15	329

Tanhuma Pequdei
2	330

Tanhuma Piqukei
1	331

Tanhuma Qorah
7	793

Tanhuma Shemot
8	328

Tannaim Deuteronomy
34:5	516

Testament of Joseph
7.1–2	325
18.4	324

Yalqut
165	328

Yalqut Gen.
3	779

INDEX OF SUBJECTS

Aaron 330–331
Abdon 683
Abigail 992
Abimelech 682
Abisha ba'al Hamemerim 762, 772
Abot, *mashal* in 619–620
Abraham
  in *Ant.* 321–322
  ikhtisar and voyage to Canaan 365
  in Jub. 340–342
  in *LAB* 680–681
  in Lev. Rab. 454
  likeness on coins 4–5
  man created on account of his merit 116–120
  in Philo 229
  and return of God to world 111
  in Song Rab. 880–881
  and Torah 92, 118–119
Abram, in *Ant.* 319–320
Abu Sa'id b. Abu'l-Hasan b. Abi Sa'id 766–767
Acts of the Apostles, as midrash 571–574
Adam
  in *Ant.* 317
  Israel equated with 110–112, 174–176
  in Jubilees 336–337
  in Philo 229
  in Tg Psalms 161
adultery, in *m*. Sot. 190–192
a fortiori (hermeneutic method) 263, 270
Against Rufinus (Jerome) 28
Aggadot
  in Church Fathers 249–250
  development of 593–594
  genre analysis 123–128, 130–148
  hermeneutics of 302
  in Philo 224–226
  in Targumim 934–935
  time, in 961n56
  women and ritual in 983–986
Ahasveros 6–7
Aheliab 16
Akhenaten 209
Albeck, Hanoch 509
Alexander, Philip 600–601
Alexander the Great 11, 207
Alexandrian and Palestinian Fathers 28–36
Alexandrian community 206–209, 269–270
'Al hakol yitgadal 480
Allegorical Commentary on Genesis (Philo) 226–227

allegory
  as hermeneutic method 29–30, 38, 133, 220–223
  in Josephus 306
  in Philo 228–230, 270n16, 303–305, 697
  and Yohanan b. Zakkai 314–315
al tiqre (hermeneutic method) 290–291, 297–298
Amalek 64
"Amen" 477
'Amidah 479, 480, 480n70, 481–483
Ammonites 377
Amorites 338
Amos Targum 924
Amram 111
Analytical Translation (Neusner) 865
anastrophe 270
androgyny 783–784, 981
angelology, in Targumim 155, 160, 166, 171–172
aniconism 2
animals, artistic depictions of 8–9
anthropomorphism
  and Samaritans 767
  in Targumim 154–155, 159, 165, 171, 786
Antiochene Fathers 36–39
Antiquities (Josephus) 232–234, 317–332
Aod 682, 691–692
Aphrahat 26–27, 726
Apocalypse of Moses (Eupolemus) 204, 244–245, 247
Apostolic Fathers 23–25
Aqedah 471–472, 688–689, 717, 765, 916
Aqiba 24
  exegesis rules of 259, 265n49, 287–291, 302, 314–315
  exegetical practice of 408–409
  school of, in tannaitic midrash 507–508, 511
  and Sifre 56–57
  wife of 987–988
Arabic, Torah-commentaries in 776
Aramaic Levi Document 345
Aristaes 219
Aristarchus 33
Aristobulus 200, 221, 305
Aristotle 699
Artapanus 208–209
art, in midrash 1–20
  anti-idolic approaches to 2–3
  artifacts used in ritual contexts 11–15

artisans in midrashic sources   15–20
　currency in midrash   3–6
　depictions of animals   8–9
　design and building of Tabernacle   16–19
　etymology of related concepts   1–2
　human figures in   9
　road markers   6
　Temple beauty   13–15
　wreaths, in imagery   9–10
　zodiac in synagogue mosaics   10
artisans, in midrashic sources   15–20
astrology   941
astronomy   794–795
atonement. *See also* Day of Atonement; sin and atonement
　in Esth. Rab. I   61
　in Lev. Rab.   456
　in *m.* Hor.   177–179
authorship. *See also* mudawwin
　of Bible, and Rabbinic tradition   353–355
　Mek. R. Ish.   75
　and midrash   200
　Moses and   220–221
　of Sifra   435–437
'Av harahamim   481
Avot DeRabbi Natan A
　Hillel's exegetical rules in   252–256
　as on *m.* Avot   403n8
Avtalion   270

Baal Shem Tov   467
Baba Rabba   763–764
Babel   336
Babylonia   120
Babylonian Talmud. *See* Bavli
Babylonian Targums   930–931
Babylonia, return from   859
Balaam   825
Bar Kokhba   4
3 Baruch   204, 247
Basil the Great   34
Bat Qol   702
Bavli
　evidence of Rabbinic preaching   528
　lack of exegetical material in   531
　references to *sipre*   55
Benjamin   118
Ben Qatin   13
Beruriah   995–996
Beth Alpha synagogue   6, 9, 19
Beth Shean synagogue   19–20
Beth Shearim catacombs   8
Bethyra   252, 254
Bezalel   16–19
Bialik, Chaim Nahman   1
Bible
　authorship, and Rabbinic tradition   353–355

　rewritten Bible   232–234, 316–317, 333n1, 634–635, 679
Biblical Antiquities. See Liber antiquitatum biblicarum (Pseudo-Philo)
Binah   698
Binyan av.   276–278
Birkat hapesuqim   479
Bloch, Renée   595–597, 606
Boaz
　in Ruth Rab.   740–742, 754, 761
　in Tg. Ruth   154
Boethusians   313
Book of Enlightenment (Hillukh)   773–775
Book of Jubilees, The: A Critical Text (VanderKam)   349
Book of the Prayer of Aseneth   239–240
Book of the Zohar   696–698, 704–705
Boyarin, Daniel   601–602
Byzantine hymns   491n145

Cain
　in *Ant.*   317–318
　missing dialogue   765–766
Cairo Geniza fragments   630, 641
Canaan   31, 229
"canon"   701
Canticles, Targum. *See* Targum Canticles
Chicatella, Joseph   697, 700
Chorazin synagogue   9–10
Christianity
　and Israel's identity   724–726
　and midrashic literature as response to   110, 709–710
　Philo's impact on   232
　and Qohelet   940–941
　and Septuagint's changed verses   786
Chronicles, Targum. *See* Targum Chronicles
Church Fathers, and Rabbinic midrash   20–40
　Alexandrian and Palestinian Fathers   28–36
　Antiochene Fathers   36–39
　Apostolic Fathers   23–25
　contact with Rabbis   22
　and narrative aggadic material   32–33, 39
　preaching activities of   530
　research summary   21–22
　role of   22–23
　Syriac Fathers   25–27
　validity of allegorical exegesis   29–30, 38
　western Fathers before Origen   23–25
circumcision   320, 979
city of refuge   6
Clement   28
Cleodemus/Malchus (Malchas)   218–219
Codex Assemani   66, 431
coins/currency   3–6, 11
commandments, in Song Rab.   881–883
Commentary of the Octateuch (Eusebius of Emesa)   37

Commentary on Exodus (Ephrem)   27
Commentary on Genesis (Ephrem)   27
Commentary on Isaiah (Eusebius)   33
Commentary on the Psalms (Origen)   29
Commentary on the Song of Songs (Origen)   29, 33
Commentary on the Twelve Prophets (Cyril of Alexandria)   31
Constantine   709-710
context (hermeneutic method)   296, 312
Contra Apionem (Josephus)   202-203, 233
contradiction   294-295
converts   740
corpse-uncleanness   182
covenant
    in *LAB*   683-685
    in Lam. Rab.   374-378, 388-390
    in Qabbalah   706
    in Sifre Deut.   822-823
craftsmanship   1-2, 15-20
Creation
    in *Ant.*   317
    dates calculated from   343-344
    of Eve   336-337, 980-982
    future history accounted for in   116-118, 397-398, 454
    hierarchy of, in Septuagint   781
    Israel and Adam, equated   110-112, 174-176
    in Jubilees   335-336
    purity in   339-340
    and Septuagint   780-786
Cyril of Alexandria
    Commentary on the Twelve Prophets   31
    and Rabbinic midrash   31

Damages, restitution for   518
Damascus Document   49
Daniel   26
Daniel LXX   201, 213-214
David   683, 685, 693, 740, 742, 911
Day of Atonement   195-198
De Abrahamo (Philo)   226
Dead Sea Scrolls, biblical interpretation in   40-54
    halakhik exegesis   45-47
    harmonizing interpretation   43-45
    hermeneutics and theology of   307-309
    pesher texts   48-53, 307-308, 410
    plain sense commentary   42-43
    retelling the Bible   47-53
    Targumim   41-42
death   939n36, 984
Deborah   992
    in *LAB*   682, 684, 686-687
    in Tg. Ps.-J.   909
Decalogue   688
Defter   770

De Iona   241-244
De Iosepho (Philo)   226
Demetrius   215-216
Demonstrations (Aphrahat)   26-27
derash   302
De Sampson   241-244
destiny   155
Deuteronomy   54-59
Deuteronomy LXX   794-796
deuterosis   20-21
De vita Mosis (Philo)   226
Dialog with Trypho (Justin Martyr)   24-25
diaresis   270, 303
diaspora
    Alexandrian community   206-209
    institutions and writing conditions   201-202
Didache   23
Dinah   323
Diodore of Tarsus   37
Dissertation on Balaam (Ghazal ad Doweik)   776
divine names. *See* God—name of
Dorse Hamuroth   293, 310
Dorshe Reshumot   293, 310
drama   239
drash   125n29
Dura Europos synagogue   2-3, 6, 9

Ecclesiastes, nature of   523, 938-943
Eden   229. *See also* Creation
Egypt
    Alexandrian community in   206-209
    in Philo   229
Eldad   689
Eliezar b. Hyrcanus   891, 918
Eliezar b. Yose the Galilean's 32 rules   285-287
Elohim   154, 165
Elon   683
end of days. *See* Israel—restoration of, at end of days
endogamy   342
Ennion   2
Enoch   229
En Samasam syanagogue   9
Ephraim   727
Ephrem
    Commentary on Exodus   27
    Commentary on Genesis   27
    Gen. Apocryphon   27, 47-48
    Hymns   27
    Liber antiquitatum biblicarum   27
    and Rabbinic midrash   27, 37-38
Ephrem (Syrian hymnist)   491n145
epistemology   124n20
Epistle of Aristaeus   200, 207
Epistle of Barnabas   23
Epstein, Jacob Nahum   496-497, 509

Esau 322, 720, 733–737
eschatology 686–687, 973–975. *See also* Israel—restoration of, at end of days
1 Esdras LXX 214
esotericism 699
Esther 62, 154
Esther, book of 5, 201
Esther LXX 213–214
Esther Rabbah I 59–74
   gender focus of 62
   sample passage 65–74
   survey of 63–65
   theme of 59
   theological propositions 59–61
Esther Targum. *See* Targum Esther
etrog 194
euergetism 14
Euhemeros 218
Eupolemus 216–218
   Apocalypse of Moses 204, 244–245, 247
   bilingualism 203–204
   On the Kings of Judaea 216, 218
Eusebius
   Commentary on Isaiah 33
   Proof of the Gospel 32
   and Rabbinic midrash 32–34
   on rise of Christianity 710–711
Eusebius of Emesa
   Commentary of the Octateuch 37
   and Rabbinic midrash 37–38
Eve
   creation of 336–337, 980–982
   in Philo 229
evil 705
Exagoge (Ezekiel) 239
exclusion (hermeneutic method) 302
exegesis. *See* hermeneutics, Rabbinic
exegesis, Vermes's theory of 599
exile
   Israel in, after rejecting God 374–375, 390–392
   as paradigmatic motif of Scripture 967–968, 971–972
   in Tg. Psalms 161
Exodus
   Commentary on Exodus (Ephrem) 27
   Ezekiel's drama on Exodus 239
   mediated by Mek. R. Ish. 74–88
   Moses's parentage 367
Exodus LXX 790–793, 796
exogamy 342
Exposition of the Law (Philo) 227
Ezekiel 239
Ezekiel Targum 917–921
1 Ezra 201, 213
Ezra literature 206

Family, Israel as 712–713, 733–737
Finkelstein, Louis 438
Firkovich manuscript collection 496n11
firstfruits 340
Fishbane, Michael 526, 607–610
In Flaccum (Philo) 223
Flavius Josephus. *See* Josephus
Florilegium (4Q174) 52
folk religion 941
folk-tales 762
Former Prophets 889
Fragment Targums 630, 641, 931
Friedmann, Meir 494

Galen 33
Gehenna 162
gematria (hermeneutic method) 270, 290, 301–302, 406
genealogy 214–215, 342
   in configuring Israel 720
   expanded, in *LAB* 687
general statement-specific statement (hermeneutic method) 261–265, 278–282, 957
Genesis
   changed verses in Septuagint 780–790
   mediated by Gen. Rab. 88–90, 92
   re-telling in Jub. 333–350
   in *Zohar* 696–698
Genesis Apocryphon 597, 634
Genesis Apocryphon (Ephrem) 27, 47–48
Genesis Commentary 42–43
Genesis LXX 780–790
Genesis Rabbah 88–121, 709–724
   approaches to exegesis (of Scripture) 98–101, 103
   chapters and subdivisions 90–91
   classification of 89–90
   on exegetical scope of Torah 408–409
   Israel and Rome 93–94, 110, 112–113, 120, 711, 714–715, 720, 729–737
   Israel's history and future salvation in 90, 92, 104–105, 108–109, 397–398, 710–724
   language in 869
   logic of coherent discourse in 91–93
   paradigmatic approaches to history in 105–108, 712–713
   propositions of 88–89
   sample passage 94–105
   theology of 110–121
genre theory, and midrash 121–148
   defining 121–123
   generic analysis 128–148
   Hellenstic Jewish writers and 200
   and Rabbinic literature 122–128
   rewritten Bible 333n1
   textual content 124n23, 126
gentiles. *See* nations, and Israel
Gerizim, Mt., sanctity of 14, 764–765
Gevurah 698

gezerah shavah (hermeneutic method)
    254–256, 259, 261, 265, 271n31, 273–276, 294,
    311, 401, 478–480, 482, 954–956
Ghazal ad Doweik 776
Ghazal b. Abi as-Sarur 776
Gideon 682, 686–687
Gnosticism 232, 703, 784
God
    grace 822
    will of, subject to reason 575
God—covenant with
    in *LAB* 683–685
    in Lam. Rab. 374–378, 388–390
    in Qabbalah 706
    in Sifre Deut. 822–823
God—justice and mercy of
    in Esth. Rab. 61
    in Gen. Rab. 113–114
    in Lam. Rab. 393–395
    in Lev. Rab. 451–455
    in Pes. Rab. Kah. 674
    in Ruth Rab. 756
    in Sifre Num. 835–836, 850–856
    in Song Rab. 877
God—name of
    Philo's exegesis of 227–228
    in Qabbalah 700, 707
    in Targumim 154, 165, 168, 170
government, erroneous decisions of 177–179
Greece 120
guilt-offerings 187–188

Habakkuk Targum 926
Haggadah. *See* Aggadot
Haggai 921–923
Haggai Targum 921–923
Hagia Sophia 10
Hagiographa, Targum to 148–173, 931–932
Halakhah
    category formations and midrash 173–177,
        198–199
    development of 593–594
    halakhik exegesis in Dead Sea Scrolls
        45–47
    hermeneutic foundations of 302
    in Horayot 177–179
    and *mashal* 612–615
    in Negaim 179–183
    in Pesahim 184–187
    in Shebuot 187–189
    in Sotah 190–192
    in Sukkah 192–195
    in Targumim 932–934
    in Yoma 195–198
Halakhot, genre analysis 123–128, 131–148
Hallel-Psalms 185
Ham 31
Haman 59–62, 64
Hanina 19

HaRabban, Joseph 772
Havdalah 479
Hebrew language
    erosion of 927–928
    in Scripture, and contemporary to rabbis
        400
    as tool for creation of world 409
Hecataeus of Abdera 207, 218
hekhre'a 270
Helene of Adaibene, Queen 13
Hellenistic Jewish midrash
    Alexandrian community 206–209
    allegorical interpretive method in 220–223
    Apocalypse of Moses 244–245
    Aristaes 219
    characteristics and features of 247–250
    Cleodemus/Malchus (Malchas) 218–219
    defined 199–201
    Demetrius 215–216
    diaspora institutions and 201–203
    Eupolemus 216–218
    Ezekiel's drama on Exodus 239
    Hebrew-Greek bilingualism 203–204
    hermeneutic methods in 301, 401
    Josephus 232–238
    Lives of the Prophets 245
    4 Maccabees 245–247
    non-allegorical hermeneutics 242–244
    onomastica 204
    oral *vs.* written tradition 203
    overview 205–206
    Philo 223–231
    poetry 238
    Pseudo-Eupolemus 219–220
    romances 239–240
    Septuagint 209–215
    sermons 241–242
Hellenistic rhetorical schools 269–271, 527
heqqesh (hermeneutic method) 255, 259, 262,
    276, 294, 311, 958
hermeneutics, Rabbinic
    analogies in 251
    approaches to, in Gen. Rab. 98–101, 103
    atomistic approach in 962
    examples of principles 272–285
    Hellenistic and Roman models 269–271,
        527
    hidden meanings 301–302
    in Houses debates 311–313
    limited by Scripture 826
    in liturgy 477–483
    in Mek. R. Simeon 498–505
    methods defined and examined 250–251,
        294–301
    philosophy of language in 400–411
    principles in practice 263–265
hermeneutics, Rabbinic—methods
    al tiqre 290–291, 297–298
    context 296, 312

exclusion 302
a fortiori 263, 270
gematria 270, 290, 301–302, 406
general statement-specific statement 261–265, 278–282, 957
gezerah shavah 254–256, 259, 261, 265, 271n31, 273–276, 294, 311, 401, 478–480, 482, 954–956
heqqesh 255, 259, 262, 276, 294, 311, 958
inclusion 302
logical inconsistency 299–300
ma'aseh 299, 612–613, 615, 629
mashal 298–299, 612–630
no redundancy 296–297
order 295–296
pragmatism 300
precedent 299, 612–613, 615
prooftexting 480–481
qal vahomer 254, 256, 259, 261, 271n31, 273, 299, 303, 311, 401, 958–959
reductio ad absurdum 299, 303
ribbui 401
ribui u-mi'ut 956–957
unusual form 297, 304
wordplay 297, 312
hermeneutics, Rabbinic—rules
  Aqiba's exegesis rules 259, 265n49, 287–291
  Eliezar's rules 285–287
  Hillel's exegetical rules 252–256, 301
  Ishmael's thirteen principles 257–260, 266–267, 272–285, 289, 467–468
  as means of controlling "free interpretation" of Scripture 962
  principles summarized 265–268, 954–960
  process and purpose 703–704, 707–709
  in Qumran documents 307–309
  Rabbinic use of Hillel's and Ishmael's methods 260–263
  in Sadducee-Pharisee debates 302, 313–314
  schematicization of Tannaitic midrashim via 507–509
  scholars having studied 268–269, 507–509
  in Sifre Deut. 826
  in Song Rab. 867–869
  theological justification for 945–947, 953–954
  tradition of the *middot* 271–272
heroes, biblical 8–9, 460
Hesed 698
hiddur mitzvah 11
hierarchization, in Sifra and Mishnah 803–804, 807–808, 810
Hilary of Poitiers 34
Hillel, House of 311–313
Hillel's exegetical rules 252–256, 258–260, 266, 270, 272–285, 301, 527
Hillukh 773–775

Hippolytus 25
history, paradigmatic nature of 90, 92, 104–105, 108–109, 397–398, 411–413, 665–669, 711
Hiyya 890, 987
Hod 698
Hoffmann, David Tsvi 56, 494–496, 506, 511, 533
Hokhmah 698
Homer
  Iliad 545
  Odyssey 541, 544
Homeric poetry 32, 220
  exegesis of 269n15, 270, 303
Homilies on Genesis 2 (Origen) 30
Horayot 177–179
Hosea Targum Hosea 923–924
household
  Passover ritual in 183–187
  Sukkot ritual in 192–195
Houses debates 302, 311–313
houses, uncleanness of 182–183
Hymns (Ephrem) 27

Ibn abi-Usaybya 776
Ibn Daud, Abraham 780
Ibrahim Ibn al-Ayyah 776
icons 2
idolatry
  aniconism 2
  artisans and their craft 15–16
  ceases to exist, in end days 975–978
  greatest sin 825
  and Qabbalah 703
'ikhtisar 363–368
Iliad (Homer) 545
inclusion (hermeneutic method) 302
infidelity, in *m. Sot.* 190–192
intentionality, and atonement of sin 198
interpretation, intentions of 960
Isaac
  in *Ant.* 322
  binding of 471–472, 688–689, 717, 765, 916
  in Jubilees 347–348
  in Philo 229
  and return of God to world 117
  and Torah 118–119
Isaiah Targum. *See* Targum Isaiah
Ishmael ar Rumaihi 772
Ishmael b. Elisha
  exegetical practice of 507–508, 527
  school of, in tannaitic midrash 507–508, 511, 533
  and Sifre 56
  thirteen principles 257–260, 266–267, 272–285, 289, 467–468
Islam, and Israel 936n25

Israel
- and Adam, equated 110–112, 174–176
- "congregation of Israel," in Targumim 155–156, 161
- heroes of 93
- merit accrues, to benefit generations (*zekhut*) 116–120, 398, 451, 454, 716, 759, 855, 939n37
- in Pes. Rab. Kah. 667–674
- in Philo 229
- return from Babylonia 859
- social condition of 106, 416, 461–462

Israel—and God
- covenant, in *LAB* 683–685
- covenant, in Lam. Rab. 374–378, 388–390
- covenant, in Qabbalah 706
- covenant, in Sifre Deut. 822–823
- encounter in Torah 956–968
- God's special love for 448–449, 462
- and leadership 680–683, 739, 825
- in Ruth Rab. 738, 752–753
- in Sifre Num. 834–835
- in Song Rab. 872–874, 884–885

Israel—and nations
- in Esth. Rab. I 59–65
- in Gen. Rab. 93–94, 110, 112–113, 120, 711, 714–715, 720, 729–737
- in Lam. Rab. 391–392
- in Lev. Rab. 414–416, 448–450, 457–458, 726–733
- in Pes. Rab. Kah. 672–673
- in Ruth Rab. 754–755
- in Sifre Deut. 823–825
- in Song Rab. 874–876

Israel—history and salvation of, paradigmatically 90, 92, 104–105, 108–109, 397–398, 411–413, 710–724
expand this

Israel—identity of
- Christianity and 724–726
- as family 712–713, 733–737
- as God's wife 154, 990–992
- in Lev. Rab. 726–733
- in Targumim 935–937
- Torah-acceptance as primary 737–738, 752–756

Israel—restoration of, at end of days
- in Esth. Rab. I 61
- in Gen. Rab. 114–115, 716–717, 720, 735–737
- in Lam. Rab. 396–397
- in Lev. Rab. 416, 453–455
- in Pes. Rab. Kah. 675–676
- in Ruth Rab. 756–758
- sanctification, and salvation of 459–463
- in Sifre Num. 836
- in Song Rab. 879–880
- in Targumim 156–157, 161–162, 166–169

as theological proposition of midrash 969–971
Issachar 229

Jacob
- in *Ant.* 322–324
- in Jubilees 338, 340–341, 344–348
- merit of 120
- in Philo 229
- and return of God to world 111, 117–118
- and Torah 118–119
- vows taken by 94–95

Jacob b. Aaron 773–774
Jair 682, 685
Jephthah 682
Jeremiah 890
Jeremiah Targum 896–897, 913–917
Jerome
- and Rabbinic midrash 28, 31, 35–36, 38
- *Against Rufinus* 28
- *Stromateis* 28

Jerusalem
- beauty of 13

Jesus Christ 725
Jésus et Israël (Isaac) 22
Joel Targum 926
John, Gospel of, as midrash 570–571
Jonah Targum 926
Jonathan 685, 687, 693
Jonathan ben Uzziel 889, 921
Joseph
- in *Ant.* 324–326
- Israel compared to 721–722
- in Jubilees 347
- in Philo 229, 326

Joseph and Aseneth 204, 239–240, 247
Joseph bar Hiyya 891–892
Josephus
- *Ant.* as re-written Bible 232–234, 316–317, 634
- chronology in 234–235
- Cleodemus and Polyhistor in 219
- *Contra Apionem* 202–203, 233
- critique of myth in 236–238
- Hebrew-Greek bilingualism 203
- hermeneutics of 306–307
- *Judaic War* 233–234
- midrash in paraphrase of Pentateuch 317–332
- "moralizing" of 306
- reliance on *deuterosis* 34
- and Sadducees 314
- sources 235–236
- *Vita* 202, 217n75

Joshua
- in *LAB* 681–682, 684, 686, 689
- likeness on coins 6
- *Samaritan Arabic Book of Joshu* 773

Joshua, book of   764
Jubilees   333-350, 634
   dual-functioning midrash in   334-335, 344-348
   historical and textual studies of   348-350
   midrash in   333-335
   polemic-informed midrash in   334, 338-344
   as "rewritten Bible"   333, 339-340
   text-weighted midrash in   334-338
Judah   229
Judah bar Ilai   439
Judaic War (Josephus)   233-234
Judith   200
Julian   710
Julian of Eclanum   32-33
Julius Africanus   217n72
Justinian   10-11
Justin Martyr   24-25

Kabbalah. *See* Qabbalah/Qabbalism
Kahana, Menahem   505, 509
kal va-homer. See qal vahomer.
Karaites/Karaism   350-374. *See also mudawwin*
   beliefs and theology of   350-352, 404n13
   Firkovich manuscripts   496n11
   liturgy   464n5
Kenaz, in *LAB*   682, 684, 686-687, 689
Keter   698
Khirbet Susiya synagogue   6
kingdom of God   918, 922
Kitab al-Kafi (Yusuf ibn Salama)   775-776
Kitab al-Khilaf (Munajjah ibn Sedaqa)   776
Kitab al-Mirat (Abu Ibrahim ibn Faraj ibn Maruth)   776
Kitab al-riyad wal-hada'iq (Qirisani)   357-359
Kitab al Tarikh (Abu'l Fath)   763, 773
Kitab at-Tabbakh (Abu'l Hassan al-Suri)   769, 775-776
kitvei haqodesh   701
Kohath   111
Korah   331
Kugel, James   601

Lamentations Rabbati
   covenental theology of   374-378, 388-390
   divine justice and mercy   393-395
   doctrines neglected in   396-399
   God and Israel in   390-391
   Israel and the nations in   391-392
   Israel and the Torah   392-393
   mashal in   625n3, 626
   repentance and judgment in   395-396
   sample passage   378-388
Lamentations Targum   935-937
Land, Holy (Land of Israel)   685-686, 823
language, and midrash   400-411, 869-870, 927-928
languages, origins of   786-787
Latter Prophets   889

law, aesthetic and ethical attitudes towards   948-950
law, in Targumim   160-161, 165-166, 172
leadership   680-683, 739, 825
Leah   323, 993-994
Le Déaut, Roger   598
Legatio ad Gaium (Philo)   223
Lekha Dodi (hymn)   472
leprosy   452
Letter of Aristaeus to Philocrates   222-223
Letter of Jeremiah   200
Letter of Mordechai to Alexander   200, 218
Levey, Samson H.   917-919
Levi
   in Jubilees   344-346
   and return of God to world   111
   in Septuagint   788-790
Leviticus
   amplified by *m. Neg.*   179-183
   in Lev. Rab.   411-428
   sanctification in   412
   in Sifra   429-447
Leviticus LXX   798
Leviticus Rabbah   411-428, 447-463
   example passages   417-428
   and Israel's identity   726-733
   paradigmatic approaches to history in   411-413
   sanctification and salvation in   459-463
   topical program and propositions, developed   413-417, 447-458
Leviticus Targum   41
Levy, Israel   494-495
Liber antiquitatum biblicarum (Pseudo-Philo)   27, 597, 600, 634, 679-694
   sample texts from   687-694
   themes of   680-687
liberation, in Song Rab.   857-863
lists, exegetical propositions by   103
literary theory, and midrash   601-602
liturgy
   alphabet and language   801
   community variances in   466-467
   liturgical calendar and Pes. Rab. Kah.   646-649
   medieval rites   466n10, 468n24
liturgy, midrash in   463-492
   piyyutim hymns   484-491
   prayer as Scripture-based   464-465
   in prayer-texts   469-477
   public reading of Scripture in worship service   465
   in Rabbinic study-texts for ritual performance   467-469
   use of midrashic hermeneutic techniques in   477-483
Lives of the Prophets   245
logical inconsistency (hermeneutic method)   299-300

Logos, in Philo 227–228
Lot 321
Lucretius 318
Luke, Gospel of, as midrash 558–570
lulab 194

Ma'aseh (hermeneutic method) 299, 612–613, 615, 629
1 Maccabees 245
3 Maccabees 200, 207
4 Maccabees 212, 245–246
mahzor 463n1
Maimonides 526, 699
Malachi 921–923
Malachi Targum 921–923
Malkhut 698, 705–706
Manns, Frederic 600–601, 604
Marianos 19
Mark, Gospel of, as midrash 536–556
marriage
    endogamy 342
    intermarriage and impurity 342–343
    unfaithfulness in 190–192
    and women 986–992
martyrdom 246n59
mashal (hermeneutic method) 612–630
    in Abot 619–620
    characteristics of 298–299, 612–615, 621–622, 626–630
    exegetical parable 621–622
    halkhic parable 621
    in Lam. Rab. 625n3, 626
    and *Ma'aseh* 612–613, 615
    in Mishnah 615–617
    and *Nimshal* 614–615, 627
    in Sifra 620–622
    in Sifre to Deuteronomy 624–625
    in Sifre to Numbers 623–624
    in Song Rab. 625–626, 868–869
    in Tosefta 617–619
Maskilim 699–700
Matthew, Gospel of, as midrash 556–558, 900–901
mazal 941
Medad 689
Media 60, 118, 120
Megillot, Targums to. *See* Targum Megillot
Mekhilta Attributed to R. Ishmael 74–88
    authorship 75
    classifications of main points of 76–77
    history and influence of 74–76
    and Mek. R. Simeon 494–495
    Neziqin 76
    sample passages 78–88
Mekhilta de R. Simeon b. Yohai 493–510
    about 493
    exegetical characteristics of, with textual examples 497–505
    manuscript evidence of 505–506
    scholarship on 506–510
    transmission and reconstruction of 493–497
Mekhilta of the Consecration 430–431
Mekhilta to Deuteronomy 57. *See also* Midrash Tannaim
Melamed, Ezra Zion 496–497, 509
Melchizedek (11Q13) 53
Memar Marqah. *See Tibât Marqe*
Memra 154, 158, 160, 165, 170–171
menstruation 979
Merkhabah 917, 919–920
Meroth synagogue 9, 10n64
messiah-theme
    in Lam. Rab. 397
    in Ruth Rab. 757–758
    in Song Rab. 883
    in Tg. Ezekiel 917–921
    in Tg. Isaiah 899–908
mezal 155
mezuzah 473n42
Micah 683, 685, 692–693
Micah Targum 925
Michal 992
middot 271–272, 400–401, 945
Midianites 691–692
Midrasch Tannaim zum Deuteronomium (Hoffmann) 508n26
midrash
    Alexander on 600–601
    authoritative texts of 602–605
    as connecting Oral and Written Torah 523, 525–526, 576
    development of relationship to Oral Torah 585–594
    as edited collections 532
    evolving definitions of 595–601
    forms of exegesis in 532–534
    historical development of 402–406, 520–522, 526–531, 596, 599
    and literary theory 601–602
    and Mishnah 524–525
    origins of, in Hebrew Bible 605–611
    as post-70 activity 600
    proto-midrashic practices 410
    and Rabbinic sermons 527–531
    as response to Christianity 110, 709–710, 726
    schools classification system 507–508, 511, 533
    Scriptural basis of 522–523
    theological category formations of 947–948
"midrash" (term) 604–605, 695–696
Midrash Haggadol 57, 495–497, 505, 511
Midrash Halakhah. *See* Midrash Tannaim
Midrash of Thirty-Two Hermeneutic Rules 401, 403n7
Midrash Philon 200

Midrash Tannaim 510–520
  aggadic material in 512–513
  documentary origins 510–511
  halkhic material in 513–514
  hermeneutics in 516–517
  relationship to Mishnah 517–518
  relationship to Sifre 514–516
  relationship to Talmud 518–519
  study of 519–520
miktsoa 125
milluim 430
Miriam 993
Mishnah
  as canonical 701–702
  characteristics of 522
  connection to Scripture 524
  mashal in 615–617
  parallels with Sifra 440–445
  and Sifra 803–804, 807–808, 812
mishnah 21
Mishnah of Rabbi Eliezer 401
Moabites 377
mode, of Rabbinic literature 124n22
Monobases, King 13–14
morals/morality
  characteristics of, in Mek. R. Ish. 76
  in Lev. Rab. 461–462
Mordecai 10. *See also* Esther; Esther Rabbah I
  in Esth. Rab. I 59–60, 62, 64
  in Gen. Rab. 722
  likeness on coins 4
Moriah, Mt. 765
mosaics, in synagogues 2–3, 6, 10
Moses
  Artapanus on 208
  as author 220–221
  and the building of the Tabernacle 16–19
  effects on human history 209
  Josephus on 307, 327–331
  in *LAB* 681, 683–684, 686, 688
  most favored by God 455–456
  parentage omission in Exodus 367
  in Philo 229
  as "recorder" of Torah 358–362
  and return of God to world 111–112
  in Samaritan midrash 762, 767–772
Moses de Leon 704
mountains, in Targum Psalms 159
mudawwin
  concept of 355–357, 371–374
  delay of data in narrative span 363–368
  as "narrator" of Scripture 362–363
  as "recorder" of Scripture 357–362
  relation to Rabbinic tradition 353–355
  semantics and etymology 352–353
  voice of narrator and characters 368–371
Muslim/Meshalma ibn Murjan 776
mystical movements 466
myth, rejected by Josephus 236–238

Nabratein Torah Shrine 9
nafshot 289
Nahor 338
Nahum Gamzo 259, 288
Nahum Targum 924–925
Naomi 740, 742
narrative, conjectural additions to 32–33
narrator, Biblical. *See mudawwin*
nations, and Israel
  in Esth. Rab. I 59–62, 63–65
  in Gen. Rab. 93, 112–113, 119–120, 714–715, 720
  in Lam. Rab. 376–378, 391–392
  in Lev. Rab. 414–416, 448–450, 457–458
  in Pes. Rab. Kah. 672–673
  in Ruth Rab. 754–755
  in Sifre Deut. 823–825
  in Sifre Num. 835
Negaim 179–183
Nehunia b. Haqanah 259
Neofiti, Targum to 630–631, 635–639, 641–642
neqevah 783
"nested quotations" 689–690
Netsach 698
Neusner, Jacob
  and category-formations in midrash 947
  on midrash 600
  on Mishnah and midrash 522, 524
  on Sifra 435–437
  on Song Rab. 865
New Testament, midrashic nature of 534–574
  Acts of the Apostles 571–574
  Gospel of John 570–571
  Gospel of Luke 558–570
  Gospel of Mark 536–556
  Gospel of Matthew 556–558
  scholarship and introduction 534–536
New Year 44–45, 448
Nicanor of Alexandria 14
Nimrod, in *Ant.* 319
Nimshal 614–615, 627
nimusa 160
Ninth of Ab 646
Nishmat kol hai 480n70
Noah
  in *Ant.* 319
  in Jubilees 341
  nakedness of 31, 43
  in Philo 229
  virginity of 26
  weakness of 119
nomological hermeneutics 311–316
Nomos (Moses' Law) 203, 209
no redundancy (hermeneutic method) 296–297
notarikon 270, 290, 301–302, 477
Numbers, ch. 5 examined 848–856

INDEX OF SUBJECTS

Numbers LXX 793–794
"*nusah sepharad*" 467

Oath of testimony 187, 189
oaths, in *m. Sheb.* 187–189
Ode 14, 200
Odyssey (Homer) 541, 544
offerings, daily whole 195–198
Old Palestinian Targum 640–641
Old Testament 733
Old Testament Pseudepigrapha 200–201
omanut 1
Onias, temple of 14
On Jerusalem (Philo the Epic Poet) 238
On Jonah 201, 241
onomastica 204
Onqelos, Targum 153, 630, 640–644, 786, 908, 930–931
On Sampson 201, 241
On the Judeans (Alexander Polyhistor) 203–204
On the Kings of Judaea (Demetrius) 216
On the Kings of Judaea (Eupolemus) 216, 218
oral exegetical tradition, in Rabbinic midrash 34
Oral Torah
    development of relationship to midrash 585–594
    differentiated from Written 406–410
    as exegetical 121–122
    and hierarchical categorization in Sifra 807–808, 810, 812–813
    and intellect of God 813
    midrash as connecting to Written Torah 523, 525–526, 576
    as midrashic 121–122
    origins of 400–406, 521–522
    in Qabbalah 706
    theology of 950–953
oral *vs.* written tradition 203
'*orayta*' 168
order (hermeneutic method) 295–296
Origen
    Commentary on the Psalms 29
    Commentary on the Song of Songs 29, 33
    Homilies on Gen. 2 30
    and Rabbinic midrash 28–31, 33, 35
Origen and the Jews (de Lange) 22
Orpah 740
Orthodox Judaism 402n5
'*ot* 473n42

Paganism 89, 202
Palestinian Talmud. *See* Yerushalmi
Palestinian Targum 630, 640, 643, 931
parable. *See mashal* (hermeneutic method)
pardes 301–302
Passover Haggadah 597
Passover ritual
    in Alexandrian community 207–208
    liturgy 476
    in *m.* Pes. 184–187
    in Pes. Rab. Kah. 646
    Seder meal 469
    and Song Rab. 858–859
past and present, in Gen. Rab. 105–106
patriarchs
    lives of 93, 120, 715
    merit of, benefiting generations 116–120, 398, 451, 454, 716
    in Targumim 166
peace-offerings 448
Pentateuch
    as divinely written text 405–406
    graphemes even exegeted 406–409
    midrash in Josephus's *Ant.* 317–332
    Samaritans's *Tibât Marqe* 762, 764, 767–770
    Yefet ben 'Eli's commentary 351–352
Pentecost 646
Persia 60
Pesahim 184–187
Pesharim 597, 600, 605
peshat 301–302
Pesher Genesis. See Genesis Commentary
Pesher Habakkuk 50–51
Pesher Habakuk 410
Pesher Hosea A and B (4Q166–167) 52
Pesher Isaiah 52
Pesher Micah (1Q14) 52
Pesher Nahum 51–52
Pesher Psalms 51
pesher texts, at Qumran 48–53, 307–308
Pesiqta deRab Kahana 663–679
    depictions of animals in 8
    lectionary cycle of 663–664, 677
    and Lev. Rab. 75
    and liturgical calendar 646–649, 664–665
    and midrash in liturgy 476n56
    natural-paradigmatic cycle in 665–669, 677–679
    repentance and judgment in 674–675
    rhetoric of 649
    sample passage 651–662
    theological propositions of 670–676
    theological statement of 677–679
    topical program of 649–651
Pesuqe dezimra' 479
Philistines 119
Philo 223–231
    Allegorical Commentary on Genesis 226–227
    allegory in 228–230, 270n16, 303–305, 697
    De Abrahamo 226
    De Iosepho 226
    De vita Mosis 226
    Exposition of the Law 227
    In Flaccum 223
    halakhik interpretation 224–226
    hermeneutics of 304–306, 315

impact of   231–232
Legatio ad Gaium   223
Logos of   227–228
Quaestiones   200, 202, 225–226, 305
and Rabbinic midrash   34, 200, 231
Philo the Epic Poet   238
Phinehas   910
phylacteries   11
pietistic movements   466
piyyutim hymns   484–491
Pleroma   706
Poemendres   784
poetry   485
Polybius   214
polygyny   993
Polyhistor   203–204, 218
polytheism   780
Porphyry   33
Porton, Gary   599–600
portraiture   16
pragmatism (hermeneutic method)   300
prayer
  grounded in Scripture   464
  in Qohelet   942
  Scripture and midrash in   469–483
  in Tg. Psalms   159–160
Prayer of Menasseh (Ode 12)   200
Prayer of Nabondius (4Q242)   200
precedent (hermeneutic method)   299, 612–613, 615
Priestly Benediction   481n72
priests, and targumic authorship   645–646
priests, consecration of   430–431
Procopius of Gaza   37
procreation   986–987
Proof of the Gospel (Eusebius)   32
prooftexting (hermeneutic method)   480–481
prophecy
  in Targumim   160, 172
  in Tg. Isa.   893–896
  in Tg. Ps.-J.   896–899, 908–911
Prophets   46
proselytes   737, 740–741
Proto-Palestinian Targum   641–644
prototype   253, 262
Proverbs Targum. *See* Targum Proverbs
Psalm   151, 200
Psalms Targum. *See* Targum Psalms
Pseudo-Aristaeus   210
Pseudo-Eupolemus   219–220
Pseudo-Philo. *See Liber antiquitatum biblicarum* (Pseudo-Philo)
pshat   125n29
Ptolemy   800–801
punishment   452, 853. *See also* God—justice and mercy of
purity
  in Creation   339–340

intermarriage and impurity   342–343
in *m. Neg.*   179–183

Qabbalah/Qabbalism   695–709
  Book of the Zohar   696–698, 704–705
  and liturgy   466–467, 470n32, 472, 477
  Maskilim and *sekhel*   699–700
  as midrash   700–709
  motifs in   706–707
  origins   695
  Sefirot   697–698, 700, 705–706
Qabbalat Shabbat   474
qal vahomer (hermeneutic method)   254, 256, 259, 261, 271n31, 273, 299, 303, 311, 401, 958–959
Qaraites. *See* Karaites/Karaism
Qasrin   9
Qedushah deSidra'   468n24, 480n70
Qedushat hayom   480, 482
Qedushot (Yannai)   485
Qeriat Shema   479
Qirqisani   355, 358–360
Qohelet   523, 938–943
Qohelet Targum. *See* Targum Qohelet
Quaestiones (Aristobulus)   221
Quaestiones (Philo)   200, 202, 225–226, 305
Qumran. *See also* Dead Sea Scrolls, biblical interpretation in
  authoritative texts of   603–604
  Jubilees fragments   349–350
  liturgy at   473n42, 481n72
  "midrash" used   604–605

Raba   989
rabbis/sages
  academies and functions   530, 532–533
  and authorship of targums   645–646
  literature, characterized   122–125
  origins and preservation of rabbinism   402–406
  purpose and activities of   945
  synagogal and other activities   527–531
  training of   531, 702
Rachel   992–994
Rahab   992–993
rash oath   187, 189
reason   575–576, 826
Rebecca   322
Rebekah   336
redemption   376–378
reductio ad absurdum (hermeneutic method)   299, 303
Reichman, Ronen   440–441
remez   301–302
repentance
  in Esth. Rab. I   61
  judgment and, in Lam. Rab.   395–396
  judgment and, in Pes. Rab. Kah.   674–675

judgment and, in Song Rab. 878–879
in Lev. Rab. 453
in *m.* Yom. 197–198
in Ruth Rab. 756–757
resumptive repetition 363n31
Reticius of Autun 34
Reuben 229, 323–324
Reuther, Rosemary 521
rewritten Bible 232–234, 316–317, 333n1, 634–635, 679
Rhineland Pietists 466, 477
ribbui (hermeneutic method) 401
ribui u-mi'ut (hermeneutic method) 956–957
ritual
   artifacts used in 11–15
   midrashic features of 700
   and women, in Aggadah 983–986
Robert, André 605–606
Romanos the Melode (Syrian hymnist) 491n145
Rome/Romans 120
   coins and currency 3–6, 11
   imperial iconography 8
   Israel and, in Gen. Rab. 93–94, 110, 112–113, 120, 711, 714–715, 720, 729–737
   rule over Israel 450, 458, 714
Rosh Hoshanah, liturgy of 475, 478
Rule Thirteen (hermeneutic rule) 959
Ruth 740–742, 758
Ruth Rabbah 737–761
   gender in 62, 737
   propositions of 754–759, 760
   rabbinization of 760–761
   sample passage 742–752
   theology of 752–754, 761
   topical program of 738–742
Ruth Targum. *See* Targum Ruth

Sabbath
   liturgy 468, 474
   and Septuagint 785
Sadducee-Pharisee debates 302, 313–314
sages. *See* rabbis/sages
Samaritan canon 603
Samaritan midrash 762–777
   aggadic midrash 773
   Asatir 762, 770–772
   halakhic and polemical writings 775–776
   Hillukh 773–775
   Kitab al Tarikh 763, 773
   Malef 773
   Molad Moshe 770–772
   Samaritan Arabic Book of Joshu 773
   Samaritan Pentateuch 764–766
   Samaritan Targum 766–767
   Tibåt Marqe 762–764, 767–770
Samson 683, 692
Samuel 683, 685, 910

Samuel bar Nahman 388
sanctification, in Lev. 412, 448, 459, 462–463
Sanhedrin, Hillel's exegetical rules in 252–256
Sanhedrin, thrones of 8
Sarah 787–788, 992
Sarai 319–320
Saul 683, 693–694, 910–911
scribes, in Targumim 896–897, 915
Scripture
   approaches to, in Gen. Rab. 98–101
   assumptions about, among midrashists 601
   authorship (*See* authorship; *mudawwin*)
   characteristics of, in Mek. R. Ish. 76
   exegetical practices within 410
   and genre 123n13
   and Halakhik category-formations 198–199
   and Hebrew "bibliocracy" 927
   midrash as connecting Oral Torah to 523, 525–526, 576
   nature of, and rabbinic exegesis of 960–963
   nomological approach to hermeneutics of 311–316
   origins of midrash in 605–611
   perfect and infallible 296, 300
   public reading in worship service 465
   and Rabbinic prayer 464
   semantics, in Qabbalah 701
   in Sifre to Numbers 574–576
   subject to human logic 300
scrolls 12
Sedaqa al-Hakhim 776
Seder meal 469
Seder 'Olam Rabbah 217, 235
seder tefillah 463n1
Sefer ha-Razim 794
Sefer Ha-Yashar 634
Sefer Torah 800–801
Sefer Yetsirah 707
Sefirot 697–698, 700, 705–706
sekhel 699–700
Selihot 470
semantics, in midrash 400–411
semukhim 275–276
Septuagint 777–802
   additions 212–214
   "aggadic" embellishment in 212
   alternative stories 214
   canonical approach 210–211
   changed verses as parenthetic reference 779–796
   Deut. 4:19 794–796
   Deut. 17:3 794–796
   Exod. 4:20b 790–791
   Exod. 12:40 791–793
   Exod. 24:11 796
   Gen. 1:1 780–781

Gen. 1:26-27   782-784
Gen. 2:2   785-786
Gen. 5:1b-2a   782-784
Gen. 11:7   786-787
Gen. 18:12   787-788
Gen. 49:6   788-790
genealogy and chronology   214-215
"halakhik" exegesis in   211
as interpretation   209-210
Lev. 11:6   798
Num. 16:15   793-794
number of translators   800
origins of   222, 799-802
Rabbinic criticism of   24
Rabbinic knowledge of Septuagint tradition   796-802
seres   270
sermons, Rabbinic   201, 241, 527-531
sexual intercourse   980, 983
sexual restraint and passivity   455, 983
Sha'arei Orah (Gates of Light)   697, 700
Shalom, Meir Ish   511
Shammai, House of   311-313
Shavuot   475, 476
Shebuot   187-189
Shebuot   340
Shekhinah   904-907, 920
Shekina   154, 158, 171
Shema   469, 473-474, 477
Shemaya   270
Shem, tents of   43
Shir ha-Shirim Hazita. See Song of Songs Rabbah
shofar   12, 471
Siddur Ha'Ari   467
Sifra   429-447, 803-820
  commentary as earliest stratum of   437-439
  hierarchical classification in   807-808, 810
  Hillel's exegetical rules in   252-256
  Ishmael's thirteen principles   257-260
  as joining two Torahs   807
  literary program of   432-435
  mashal in   620-622
  not a propositional document transcending Leviticus   806
  origins of   429, 437, 439, 446
  parallels with Mishnah   440-444
  purpose of   803-805
  structure and manuscripts of   429-432
  syllogistic stratum of   439-440
  synchronistic analysis of   435-437
  three forms of rhetoric in   805
  topical traits of   806
Sifre to Deuteronomy   820-833
  Deuteronomy in   54-59
  documentary origins   507-508
  mashal in   624-625
  and Midrash Tannaim   512-516
  nature of   820-821
  sample passage   826-833
Sifre to Numbers   833-857
  contrast to tractate Sotah in   848-856
  exegetical forms and syllogisms   577
  God and Israel in   834-835
  intrinsic exegetical forms   577-578
  mashal in   623-624
  outline of Num. 5 in   837-847
  propositions of   574-576, 834-837
  sample passage   578-585
Sifre Zuta to Deuteronomy   57, 514
Simeon
  in Philo   229
  in Septuagint   788-790
simile. See *Mashal* (hermeneutic method)
Simlai   782-783
sin and atonement
  collective, in *m. Hor.*   177-179
  in *m. Yom.*   197-198
Sirach LXX   213
Sitra Achra   705
Sitz im Leben   484n80
Sodom/Sodomites   320-321
Solomon
  as author   864
  in Tg. Qohelet   154
  throne of   6-9
Song of Songs
  and Hippolytus   25
  nature of   523
  recited on eve of Sabbath   474-475
Song of Songs Rabbah
  authorship and dating   866-867
  category-formations   883-884
  in context of Rabbinic Judaism   885-888
  editions and manuscripts   870
  homily in   865-866, 868
  language in   869-870
  literary aspects   867-869
  mashal in   625-626, 868-869
  structure of   863-866
  themes of   857-863
  theological propositions of   871-885
Songs in Praise of Moses b. Amram, the Prophet   772
Sotades   238
Sotah   190-192
star worship   794-796
Stoicism   220
Stromateis (Jerome)   28
suffering   452
Sukkah   192-195
Sukkot, festival of   192-195
synagogues
  bas-relief imagery   8-9
  diasporan   202
  liturgy and Pes. Rab. Kah.   646-649

mosaics in   2-3, 6
piyyutim   484n80, 491n145
Rabbinic activity in   527-528
replace Temple   922
Samaritan   763
sermons   201, 241
targums in   645-646
wreaths in decoration of   9-10
zodiac represented in   10
Synoptic Gospels, interpretation in   900-901
synthesis   270
Syriac Fathers   25-27

Tabernacle, design and building of   16-19
Tabernacles, festival of
 in Lev. Rab.   416-417
 in *m*. Suk.   192-195
Talmud, as genre   123
Talmud of the Land of Israel. *See* Yerushalmi
Talmud Torah. *See* Torah-study
TaNaKh   523
tannaitic midrashim   429
 schools of   56, 507
 textual research into   508-509, 511-512
Targumim   630-646
 Aggadot in   934-935
 angelology   155, 160, 166, 171-172
 anthropomorphism   154-155, 159, 165, 171, 786
 audience and authors   645-646, 892, 901
 as collections   532
 compared to Rabbinic midrash   632-634
 compared to Rewritten Bible   634-635
 conceptual categories of   935
 content of hidden midrash in   642-644
 dating techniques   930
 Eusebius of Emesa and   37
 to Hagiographa   148-173
 Halakhah in   932-934
 hidden interpretation in   636-640
 Jewish identity in   935-937
 Jewish thought in   938-944
 literary character of   635-640
 messiah in tannaitic framework   899-904
 against midrash   152
 origins of   927-929
 from Qumran   41-42
 sources of   640-642
 three types   630
 translation in   635-636, 929
Targum Amos   924
Targum, Babylonian   930-931
Targum Canticles
 doctrine   153-157
 manuscripts and composition   149
 Rabbinic parallels   153
Targum Chronicles   932n14
 doctrine   170-173

exegetical method   170
manuscripts and composition   169
Targum Esther
 doctrine   153-157
 hermeneutics   152
 manuscripts and composition   148, 150-151, 932n14
 Rabbinic parallels of   153
 throne of Solomon in   6-9
Targum Ezekiel   917-921
Targum, Fragment   630, 641, 931
Targum Habakkuk   926
Targum Haggai   921-923
Targum Hosea   923-924
Targum Isaiah
 prophecy in   893-896
 tannaitic and amoraic frameworks of   899-908, 923
Targum Jeremiah   896-897, 913-917
Targum Job   41-42
 doctrine   165-167
 language and interpretation   164-165
 manuscripts and composition   163-164
Targum Joel   926
Targum Jonah   926
Targum Jonathan of the Former Prophets (Targum Pseudo-Jonathan)   630, 641-644
 authorship   889-892
 language   912-913
 messianic vindication in   911-913
 phasal development of   896-899
 prophecy in   908-911
 tannaitic and amoraic frameworks of   916-926
Targum Lamentations   935-937
 doctrine   153-157
 hermeneutics   152
 manuscripts and composition   149, 150
 Rabbinic parallels   153
Targum Leviticus   41
Targum Malachi   921-923
Targum Megillot
 doctrine of   153-157
 hermeneutic methods of   152
 language of   151
 manuscripts and composition   149-151
 Rabbinic parallels of   152-153
Targum Micah   925
Targum Nahum   924-925
Targum Neofiti   630-631, 635-639, 641-642
Targum, Old Palestinian   640-641
Targum Onqelos   153, 630, 640-644, 786, 908, 930-931
Targum, Palestinian   630, 640, 643, 931
Targum Proto-Onqelos   642-643
Targum, Proto-Palestinian   641-644
Targum Proverbs   932n14
 doctrine   168-169

language 167–168
manuscripts and composition 167
Targum Psalms
  doctrine 158–162
  manuscripts and composition 157–158
  methodology of 158
Targum Pseudo-Jonathan. *See* Targum Jonathan of the Former Prophets (Targum Pseudo-Jonathan)
Targum Qohelet
  conceptual categories in 938–943
  doctrine 153–157
  manuscripts and composition 149–150
  paraphrastic 932n14
  Rabbinic parallels 153
Targum Ruth
  doctrine 153–157
  hermeneutics 152
  manuscripts and composition 149–150
  Rabbinic parallels 153
Targum, to Hagiographa 148–173, 931–932
Targum Yerushalmi 630, 641, 931
Targum Zechariah 921–923
Targum Zephaniah 925
Tashlikh ritual 479–480
taxonomy, in Sifra and Mishnah 803–804, 807–808, 810
Teacher of Righteousness 309
Tefillah 479
tefillin 11–13, 473n42
tekhne 1–2
tekhnitai 2
Temple
  beauty of 13–15
  destruction of 374–375, 935–936
  location of 321–322
  and Passover ritual 186–187
  and Sukkot ritual 192–195
Ten Commandments 688
Tertullian 25
Theodore of Mopsuestia 38
Theodoret 39
Theodotus 238
theology, of Rabbinic Judaism
  basic statements of, in midrash 948–950
  defined 964–965
  in encounter in Torah, of God and Israel 956–968
  in Esth. Rab. I 59–61
  in Gen. Rab. 110–121
  of Karaites/Karaism 350–352, 404n13
  in Lam. Rab. 374–378, 388–390
  in Mek. R. Ish. 76–77
  in Pes. Rab. Kah. 670–679
  of Qumran 307–309
  in Ruth Rab. 752–754, 761
  six propositions of, in midrash 968–978
  in Song Rab. 871–885

theological category formations in midrash 947–948
Theophrastus 32
thrones, projections of 6–9
Tibåt Marqe 762–764, 767–770
Tiberius Julius Alexander 223n12
Tiferet 698, 705
tikuney soferim 270
time, nature of 665–669, 960–961. *See also* history, paradigmatic nature of
Tiqqunei Zohar 705
Tishré 1–22 646
Tobit 200
Torah
  development of relationship to midrash 585–594
  in Esth. Rab. I 60–61
  and Qabbalah 696, 706
  and theology of midrash 950–953
Torah—and Israel
  in Gen. Rab. 113, 115–116
  in Lam. Rab. 392–393
  in Lev. Rab. 449–451
  in Pes. Rab Kah. 673–674
  in Song Rab. 876–877, 881
  in Tgs. of Megillot 155–156
  Torah-acceptance as defining Israel 737–738, 752–756
Torah scrolls
  in liturgy 480
  preparation of 12
  sanctity of 524–525
  "three scrolls of Torah found in Temple court" 796–798
Torah-study 463n2, 464, 695–696, 823, 942
Torat Kohanim 429
Tosefta
  mashal in 617–619
  parallels with Sifra 444
totafot 473n42
tropologia 30n40
Two Mekhiltot on the Amalek Portion, The (Kahana) 509
tzofim 407–408

Ulla 997
umanut 1–2
uncleanness
  in *m. Neg.* 179–183
  in *m. Sheb.* 187–189
unfaithfulness 190–192, 848–851
Universal History (Polybius) 214
unusual form (hermeneutic method) 297, 304

Ve-anvehu 12–13
veiling 983–984
Venus 914–915
Vermes, Geza 333n1, 598–599

Verus Israel (Simon)   22
Vita (Josephus)   202, 217n75
vows, taking   94–95

Watchers   343n14
Wisdom of Solomon   200, 212
women   979–997
   creation of Eve   336–337, 980–982
   disadvantages of   982–983
   Esther, in Esth. Rab. I   62
   marriage   990–992
   in midrash   992–997
   as other   979–980
   ps.-Philo's feminism   690–691
   and ritual, in Aggadah   983–986
   unfaithfulness, in *m.* Sot.   190–192, 848–851
   as wives   986–990
wordplay (hermeneutic method)   297, 312
wreaths, in imagery   9–11
Wright, Addison G.   597–598
Writings   46, 149–157
Written Torah. *See* Scripture

Yannai   19, 485–491
Yefet ben 'Eli   351–352, 355–357, 360–363. *See also mudawwin*
Yehuda, Eliezar Ben   1

Yeqara   158, 171
Yerushalmi
   parallels with Sifra   444–445
   Rabbinic activity in synagogues   528–529
Yerushalmi Targum   630, 641, 931
Yesod   698, 705
Yohanan   258, 917–918
Yohanan b. Bag Bag   260n27
Yohanan b. Zakkai   293n2, 314–315
Yoma   195–198
Yom Kippur   13–14, 470, 476
Yoser benediction   480n70, 481
Yusuf b. Salama al-'Askari   776
YYY   165

Zadokite Fragments (Damascus Document)   49
Zechariah   921–923
Zechariah Targum   921–923
Zekhut   451, 759, 939n37
Zelophehad   995
Zephaniah Targum   925
zodiac   10
Zohar, Book of the   696–698, 704–705
Zohar Hadash   704
Zur Einleitung in die halachischen Midraschim (Hoffmann)   506